MW01057140

A CONSTRUCTIVE CHRISTIA
FOR THE PLURALISTIC WORLD

VOLUME 1

Christ and Reconciliation

VOLUME 2

Trinity and Revelation

VOLUME 3

Creation and Humanity

CREATION AND HUMANITY

Veli-Matti Kärkkäinen

WILLIAM B. EERDMANS PUBLISHING COMPANY

GRAND RAPIDS, MICHIGAN / CAMBRIDGE, U.K.

Published 2015 by
Wm. B. Eerdmans Publishing Co.
2140 Oak Industrial Drive N.E., Grand Rapids, Michigan 49505 /
P.O. Box 163, Cambridge CB3 9PU U.K.

Printed in the United States of America

20 19 18 17 16 15   7 6 5 4 3 2 1

Library of Congress Cataloging-in-Publication Data

Kärkkäinen, Veli-Matti.
    Creation and humanity / Veli-Matti Kärkkäinen.
        pages   cm.   — (A constructive Christian theology for the pluralistic world; v. 3)
    Includes bibliographical references and index.
    ISBN 978-0-8028-6855-8 (pbk.: alk. paper)
    1. Creation.   2. Creationism.   3. Theological anthropology — Christianity.   I. Title.

BT695.K37   2015
231.7'65 — dc23

                                                                    2014040147

www.eerdmans.com

Contents

Abbreviations

ANF   *The Ante-Nicene Fathers: Translations of the Writings of the Fathers down to* A.D. *325.* Edited by Alexander Roberts and James Donaldson et al. 9 vols. Edinburgh, 1885-1897. Public domain; available at www.ccel.org

AOA   *Animals on the Agenda: Questions about Animals for Theology and Ethics.* Edited by Andrew Linzey and Dorothy Yamamoto. Urbana and Chicago: University of Illinois Press, 1998

Aquinas, *ST*   *The Summa Theologica of St. Thomas Aquinas.* 2nd rev. ed. 1920. Literally translated by Fathers of the English Dominican Province. Online Edition Copyright © 2008 by Kevin Knight; http://www.newadvent.org/summa/

BB   *Belief and Bloodshed: Religion and Violence across Time and Tradition.* Edited by James K. Wellman Jr. Lanham, Md.: Rowman and Littlefield, 2007

B&E   *Buddhism and Ecology: The Interconnection of Dharma and Deeds.* Edited by Mary Evelyn Tucker and Duncan Ryūken Williams. Cambridge: Harvard University Press, 1997

Boisvert, *RPS*   Kate Gayson Boisvert. *Religion and the Physical Sciences.* London and Westport, Conn.: Greenwood, 2008

B&S   *Buddhism and Science: Breaking New Ground.* Edited by B. Alan Wallace. New York: Columbia University Press, 2003

Calvin, *Institutes* John Calvin. *Institutes of the Christian Religion.* Translated
by Henry Beveridge. Available at www.ccel.org

C&C *Chaos and Complexity: Scientific Perspectives on Divine
Action.* Edited by Robert John Russell, Nancey Murphy,
and Arthur R. Peacocke. Vatican City and Berkeley, Calif.:
Vatican Observatory and Center for Theology and the
Natural Sciences, 1995

CD Karl Barth. *Church Dogmatics.* Edited by Geoffrey William Bromiley and Thomas Forsyth Torrance. Translated
by G. W. Bromiley. 14 vols. Edinburgh: T. & T. Clark,
1956-1975. Online edition by Alexander Street Press, 1975

CGA *Creation and the God of Abraham.* Edited by David B.
Burrell, Carlo Cogliati, Janet M. Soskice, and William R.
Stoeger. Cambridge: Cambridge University Press, 2011

E&E *Evolution and Emergence: Systems, Organisms, Persons.*
Edited by Nancey Murphy and William R. Stoeger. Oxford: Oxford University Press, 2007

EMB *Evolutionary and Molecular Biology: Scientific Perspectives
on Divine Action.* Edited by Robert John Russell, William R. Stoeger, S.J., and Francisco J. Ayala. Vatican City
and Berkeley, Calif.: Vatican Observatory and Center for
Theology and the Natural Sciences, 1998

GDT *Global Dictionary of Theology.* Edited by Veli-Matti Kärkkäinen and William Dyrness. Assistant editors, Simon
Chan and Juan Martinez. Downers Grove, Ill.: InterVarsity, 2008

GHD *God and Human Dignity.* Edited by R. K. Soulen and
L. Woodhead. Grand Rapids: Eerdmans, 2006

GLC *God, Life, and the Cosmos: Christian and Islamic Perspectives.* Edited by Ted Peters, Muzaffar Iqbal, and Syed
Nomanul Haq. Surrey, U.K.: Ashgate, 2002

HE *Hinduism and Ecology: The Intersection of Earth, Sky, and
Water.* Edited by Christopher Key Chapple and Mary
Evelyn Tucker. Religions of the World and Ecology. Cam-
bridge: Harvard University Press, 2000

I&E *Islam and Ecology: A Bestowed Trust.* Edited by Richard C. Foltz, Frederick M. Denny, and Azizan Baharuddin. Cambridge: Harvard University Press, 2003

ISHCP *Islam and Science: Historic and Contemporary Perspec-*

	tives. Edited by Muzaffar Iqbal. 3 vols. Surrey, U.K.: Ashgate, 2012

ISCHP 1: Studies in the Islam and Science Nexus
ISCHP 2: Contemporary Issues in Islam and Science
ISCHP 3: New Perspectives on the History of Islamic Science

J&E   *Judaism and Ecology: Created World and Revealed Word.* Edited by Hava Tirosh-Samuelson. Cambridge: Harvard University Press, 2002

LW   *Luther's Works.* American ed. (Libronix Digital Library). Edited by Jaroslav Pelikan and Helmut T. Lehman. 55 vols. Minneapolis: Fortress, 2002

McGrath, *ScT*   Alister E. McGrath. *A Scientific Theology.* Vol. 1, *Nature.* Vol. 2, *Reality.* Vol. 3, *Theory.* Grand Rapids: Eerdmans, 2001, 2002, 2006 [2003]

Murphy and Brown, *DMN*   Nancey Murphy and Warren S. Brown. *Did My Neurons Make Me Do It? Philosophical and Neurobiological Perspectives on Moral Responsibility and Free Will.* Oxford: Oxford University Press, 2007

NP   *Neuroscience and the Person: Scientific Perspectives on Divine Action.* Edited by Robert John Russell, Nancey Murphy, Theo C. Meyering, and Michael A. Arbib. Vatican City and Berkeley, Calif.: Vatican Observatory and Center for Theology and the Natural Sciences, 1999

NPNF[1]   *A Select Library of the Nicene and Post-Nicene Fathers of the Christian Church.* Edited by Philip Schaff. 1st ser. 14 vols. Edinburgh, 1886. Public domain; available at www.ccel.org

NPNF[2]   *A Select Library of the Nicene and Post-Nicene Fathers of the Christian Church.* Edited by Philip Schaff and Henry Wace. 2nd ser. 14 vols. Edinburgh, 1890. Public domain; available at www.ccel.org

OHFW   *The Oxford Handbook of Free Will.* Edited by Herbert Kane. 2nd ed. Oxford: Oxford University Press, 2011

OHRS   *The Oxford Handbook of Religion and Science.* Edited by Philip Clayton. Associate editor, Zachary Simpson. Oxford: Oxford University Press, 2006

Pannenberg, *ST*   Wolfhart Pannenberg. *Systematic Theology.* Translated by Geoffrey W. Bromiley. 3 vols. Grand Rapids: Eerdmans, 1991, 1994, 1998

Pannenberg, *TA*   Wolfhart Pannenberg. *Anthropology in Theological Perspective.* Translated by Matthew J. O'Connell. Philadelphia: Westminster, 1985

PC   *Physics and Cosmology: Scientific Perspectives on the Problem of Natural Evil.* Edited by Nancey Murphy, Robert John Russell, William R. Stoeger, S.J. Vol. 1. Vatican City and Berkeley, Calif.: Vatican Observatory and Center for Theology and the Natural Sciences, 2007

PE   *The Problem of Evil.* Edited by Marilyn McCord Adams and Robert Merrihew Adams. Oxford: Oxford University Press, 1990

Peacocke, *ATI*   Arthur Peacocke. *All That Is: A Naturalistic Faith for the Twenty-First Century.* Edited by Philip Clayton. Minneapolis: Fortress, 2007

PITP   *Personal Identity in Theological Perspective.* Edited by Richard Lints, Michael S. Horton, and Mark R. Talbot. Grand Rapids: Eerdmans, 2006

PL   Patrologia Latina [= Patrologiae cursus completus: Series latina]. Edited by J.-P. Migne. 217 vols. Paris, 1844-1864

PPT   *Physics, Philosophy, and Theology: A Common Quest for Understanding.* Edited by Robert J. Russell, William R. Stoeger, and George V. Coyne. Vatican City: Vatican Observatory, 1988

QCLN   *Quantum Cosmology and the Laws of Nature: Scientific Perspectives on Divine Action.* Edited by Robert J. Russell, Nancey Murphy, and C. J. Isham. Vatican City and Berkeley, Calif.: Vatican Observatory and Center for Theology and the Natural Sciences, 1993

QM   *Quantum Mechanics: Scientific Perspectives on Divine Action.* Edited by Robert J. Russell, Philip Clayton, Kirk Wegter-McNelly, and John Polkinghorne. Vatican City and Berkeley, Calif.: Vatican Observatory and Center for Theology and the Natural Sciences, 2001

RB   *Religion and the Body.* Edited by Sarah Coakley. Cambridge: Cambridge University Press, 1997

SBE   *Sacred Books of the East.* Translated by Max Müller. 50 vols. Oxford: Oxford University Press, 1879-1910. Also available at www.sacred-texts.com

SPDA   *Scientific Perspectives on Divine Action: Twenty Years of*

	Challenge and Progress. Edited by Robert John Russell, Nancey Murphy, and William R. Stoeger, S.J. Vatican City and Berkeley, Calif.: Vatican Observatory and Center for Theology and the Natural Sciences, 2008
SRPW	*Science and Religion in a Post-colonial World: Interfaith Perspectives*. Edited by Zainal Abidin Bagir. Adelaide, Australia: ATF Press, 2005
Tillich, *ST*	Paul Tillich. *Systematic Theology*. Vol. 1. Chicago: University Press of Chicago, 1951
TRV	*Teaching Religion and Violence*. Edited by Brian K. Pennington. Oxford: Oxford University Press, 2012
WA	Weimarer Ausgabe (the Weimar edition of Luther's works)
WHS	*Whatever Happened to the Soul? Scientific and Theological Portraits of Human Nature*. Edited by Warren S. Brown, Nancey C. Murphy, and H. Newton Malony. Theology and the Sciences. Minneapolis: Fortress, 1998

Unless otherwise indicated, all citations from patristic writers come from the standard series listed above.

Josephus's writings are from the Sacred Texts Web site: http://www.sacred-texts.com/jud/josephus/index.htm.

Unless otherwise indicated, contemporary Roman Catholic documents, documents of Vatican II, papal encyclicals, and similar works are quoted from the official Vatican Web site: www.vatican.va.

Contemporary World Council of Churches documents are quoted from their official Web site: http://www.oikoumene.org/, unless otherwise indicated.

Bible references, unless otherwise indicated, are from the Revised Standard Version of the Bible, copyright 1952 (2nd ed. 1971) by the Division of Christian Education of the National Council of the Churches of Christ in the United States of America. Used by permission. All rights reserved.

The Qur'anic references, unless otherwise indicated, are from The Holy Qur'ān: A New English Translation of Its Meanings © 2008 Royal Aal al-Bayt Institute for Islamic Thought, Amman, Jordan. This version of the Qur'ān is also available online at http://altafsir.com.

Hadith texts are from the Hadith Collection Web site: http://www.hadithcollection.com/ (2009-).

Buddhist texts, unless otherwise indicated, are from "Tipitaka: The Pali

Canon." Edited by John T. Bullitt. *Access to Insight,* May 10, 2011 (http://www
.accesstoinsight.org/tipitaka/index.html).

Hindu texts, unless otherwise indicated, are from the Sacred Texts Web
site: http://www.sacred-texts.com/hin/index.htm.

Preface

This book is one of the five volumes in the series titled A CONSTRUCTIVE CHRISTIAN THEOLOGY FOR THE PLURALISTIC WORLD. The goal of this series is to present a dynamic constructive Christian theology for the pluralistic world shaped by cultural, ethnic, sociopolitical, economic, and religious diversity, as well as the unprecedented influence of the sciences. While robustly Christian in its convictions, building on the deep and wide tradition of biblical, historical, philosophical, and contemporary systematic traditions, this project seeks to engage our present cultural and religious diversity in a way Christian theology has not done in the past. Although part of a larger series, each volume can still stand on its own feet, so to speak, and can be read as an individual work.

The current book is third in the series after *Christ and Reconciliation* (2013) and *Trinity and Revelation* (2014). The remaining two volumes are *Spirit and Salvation* and *Community and Hope*. Along with traditional topics, constructive theological argumentation in this series also engages a number of topics, perspectives, and issues that systematic theologies are missing, such as race, environment, ethnicity, inclusivity, violence, and colonialism. A consistent engagement with religious and interfaith studies is a distinctive feature of this series. The current volume, like the last one, majors also in a deep and wide dialogue with natural sciences from cosmology and physics to neurosciences and brain study.

The introductory chapter gives a brief orientation to overall methodology (more extensively discussed in the lengthy introduction to volume 1). In the beginning of each major topic, the honing and clarification of methodological issues continue. The project is funded by the conviction that the material presentation of theological themes itself helps to shape and clarify the method — and of course, vice versa. I fully agree with the observation of the American Reformed theologian David Kelsey that in the real sense of the word, the clarification of methodology is "largely retrospective," if not for other reasons, then because "the intellectual and imaginative challenges peculiar to different theological topics are so diverse that any set of methodological rules purporting to cover them all would have to be so general as to be useless."[1] Although I hesitate to go as far as Moltmann, who confessed that the methodological "road emerged only as I walked it,"[2] neither am I following Pannenberg, who devoted decades to a most detailed clarification of all kinds of methodological issues before venturing into a tightly presented *summa*.

In any case, I have to admit that there is "a good deal of unfinished business in these pages. I have presupposed the truth of certain philosophical positions, the defense of which requires extended argument, and I have done no more than a gesture in that direction."[3] This is particularly true because "ours is an age of specialization. Knowledge in the various fields of science philosophy, and even religious studies has reached such a level of depth and intricacy that today one can in general only master a single discipline and can, at best, stay conversant with just a few others."[4] While every scholar writing in an interdisciplinary mode in our times can only be deeply grateful for the amazing array of resources available, the sheer magnitude and diversity of (re-)sources also overwhelm even the brightest minds.

If there is any lasting value to my continuing interdisciplinary and interfaith explorations in Christian constructive theology, it may be best expressed in terms of having "the merit of a challenge,"[5] to borrow from the famed American Lutheran theologian Philip Hefner, himself a leading expert in religion-science dialogue. Attempting a constructive theological program for the sake of our pluralistic world may have some intrinsic value even when the end result is far from satisfactory. After all, our "post"-world prefers humble explanations rather than world-embracing *summae*. I find it reassuring that in the preface to his mature, widely acclaimed work Hefner lamented that in his earlier writings he had "mixed different types of thinking . . . without justifying the mixture or clarifying how the recipe would work," and that "age has

---

1. D. Kelsey, *Eccentric Existence*, 1:12.

2. Moltmann, *Experiences in Theology*, p. xv, emphasis in original.

3. MacIntyre, *Dependent Rational Animals*, p. xii.

4. Clayton, *In Quest of Freedom*, p. 11.

5. Hefner, *The Human Factor*, p. xv, citing Gustafson, "Theology Confronts Technology," p. 391.

simply intensified what were once distracting youthful tendencies."[6] I fear that in my case this "mixing" is even worse because not only do I lack the breadth and width of the knowledge of the masters, but my project is, if possible, even more hybrid and ambitious in its goal. Certainly do I share the sentiment of the theological giant of the last century, Karl Barth, who penned in his preface to the doctrine of creation: "In taking up the doctrine of creation I have entered a sphere in which I feel much less confident and sure. If I were not obliged to do so in the course of my general exposition of Church dogmatics, I should probably not have given myself so soon to a detailed treatment of this particular material. I know many others to whom, in view of their greater gifts and interest and qualifications, I would willingly have entrusted this part of the task if only I could have had more confidence in their presuppositions."[7]

Most of the writing of the current volume took place during my yearlong research leave in 2012-2013. It was made possible by the regular quarter-long sabbatical from Fuller Theological Seminary and a six-month Lilly Theological Fellowship (facilitated by the American Theological School Association). I am deeply grateful for these institutions. In the fall of 2012 I was also a Research Fellow in the interdisciplinary "Neuroscience and Soul" research program organized by the Center for Christian Thought of Biola University, La Mirada, California, and funded by the John Templeton Foundation. Intensive weekly interaction in the group of neuroscientists, psychologists, philosophers, and theologians inspired greatly my thinking and writing process. My thanks go to this extraordinary group of scholars who heard me present portions from part 2 on theological anthropology and who, even when disagreeing with me, always embodied hospitality and friendship: Emily Esch, Doug Huggman, Keith Edwards, J. P. Moreland, Jason Runyan, Sharon Sann, and Kirk Winslow. Similarly, a big thanks goes to visiting scholars for their seminars and contributions: Mark Baker, John W. Cooper, Tim O'Connor, Jeffrey M. Schwartz, and Richard Swinburne. Without the enthusiastic and witty leadership team of three young philosophers, the Center would not be what it is: Gregg Ten Elshof, Thomas M. Crisp, and Steve L. Porter.

Few writers have been assisted — as well as corrected and challenged — by such a group of leading international scholars as I have been on this project. The following scholars read parts or all of the manuscript and provided feedback: Prof. Alister E. McGrath (Oxford University); Prof. Emeritus Richard Carlson (University of California, Riverside); Prof. Justin L. Barrett and Prof.

---

6. Hefner, *The Human Factor,* p. xiii.
7. Barth, *CD* III/1, preface.

Warren S. Brown (Graduate School of Psychology, Fuller Seminary); Prof. Joel B. Green (School of Theology, Fuller Seminary); Prof. Amos Yong (Regent University, Virginia Beach); Dr. Olli-Pekka Vainio (University of Helsinki). Discussions and communication with a number of other colleagues have encouraged and inspired me greatly: Prof. Robert John Russell (Center for Natural Sciences and Theology, Berkeley, Calif.); Prof. Graham Buxton (Tabor College, Adelaide, Australia); Dr. Mark Worthing (Australian Lutheran College, Adelaide, Australia); Dr. Aku Vainio (University of Notre Dame; University of Helsinki); and a number of my Fuller colleagues, particularly Prof. Oliver Crisp, Prof. Pamela King, and my former student Dr. William Whitney, among others. Perhaps the most formative figure in my continuing immersion into the science-religion conversation has been my famous philosopher colleague, Prof. Nancey Murphy, the "Lady Wisdom." Not only has she guided me into the literature and discussions of philosophical and theological ramifications of natural sciences and theological anthropology, but she also graciously allows me to coteach with her interdisciplinary doctoral seminars in science-religion topics. A number of my colleagues at the University of Helsinki, in addition to those already mentioned, have supported me with this project over the years, particularly Prof. Risto Saarinen and Prof. Miikka Ruokanen.

My location at Fuller Theological Seminary, currently one of the largest — and by any standards, the most diverse — divinity schools in the world, provides extraordinary opportunities for continuing creative work. Remarkable library and information technology services, unusually generous sabbatical policy, and interdisciplinary and international collegiality with experts from various theological, intercultural, and behavioral scientific fields facilitate, enrich, and challenge my scholarly work. More than a decade of high-level editorial assistance from the seminary's editor Susan Carlson Wood has meant more to my publishing career than I am able to express in words. Finally, I could not survive without the competent and dedicated research assistants, doctoral students funded by the Center for Advanced Theological Studies, who collaborate in all aspects of the research process. For this volume, Dan Brockway and Christopher O'Brian worked for innumerable hours checking all references; Dan also worked hard in finding sources, particularly those related to global diversity. Joshua Muthalali compiled the index.

I dedicate this volume to my closest community — indeed, a communion of love: my wife, Anne, and my two daughters, Maiju and Nelli. For the past thirty-four happy years they have shaped my life, inspired my thinking, and shown me love beyond measure.

Introduction: In Search of a New Methodological Vision for Constructive Theology

Desiderata of a "Transversal" Constructive Theology

As orientation to the current volume, this introduction briefly outlines the methodological vision of this project, presented and defended in earlier volumes.[1] The vision for doing constructive theology in a religiously pluralistic and culturally diverse "post-world" — postmodern, postfoundationalist, poststructuralist, postcolonial, postmetaphysical, postpropositional, postliberal, postconservative, postsecular, post-Christian — can be sketched like this:

> Systematic/constructive theology is an integrative discipline that continuously searches for a coherent, balanced understanding of Christian truth and faith in light of Christian tradition (biblical and historical) and in the context of historical and contemporary thought, cultures, and living faiths. It aims at a coherent, inclusive, dialogical, and hospitable vision.

The nomenclature "systematic" is most unfortunate since the ultimate goal of constructive theology is not a "system"! Rather, constructive theology seeks a coherent and balanced understanding. In terms of the theory of truth, it follows coherence theory. One current way of speaking of coherence compares it to a web or a net(work) that underwrites postfoundationalist rather than foundationalist epistemology. That metaphor is fitting as it speaks of the

---

1. Since detailed bibliographic references are contained in the discussion in vol. 1, *Christ and Reconciliation,* they are not repeated here, except for direct citations.

attempt to relate every statement to other relevant statements and ultimately to the "whole." The way the current project conceives coherence has not only to do with inner-textual coherence but also with the "fit" of theological statements with "reality." Hence, Christian theology whose "object" is God and everything else stemming from the creative work of God (Aquinas) operates with the widest possible notion of coherence.

Pannenberg has famously argued for the nature of systematic theology as the "science of God,"[2] which presupposes the existence of truth apart from human beings and human beings' social construction thereof.[3] At the same time, Pannenberg importantly contends that humans never have direct, uncontested access to the infinitely incomprehensible God.[4] Rather, human grasp of truth is only provisional,[5] as the biblical conception of truth — unlike the Hellenistic view, which posits a fixed "truth" just to be discovered — is historical and thus evolving.[6] Rather than on firm "foundations," theological argumentation builds on a *post*foundationalist epistemology because of *"the contested nature of theological truth claims."*[7] A postfoundationalist approach, unlike nonfoundationalist[8] epistemology, seeks "to engage in interdisciplinary dialogue within our postmodern culture while *both* maintaining a commitment to intersubjective, transcommunal theological argumentation for the truth of Christian faith, *and* recognizing the provisionality of our historically embedded understandings and culturally conditioned explanations of the Christian tradition and religious experience."[9] While everyone in contemporary theology may be not be happy to use the nomenclature "science of God," Pannenberg's vision — when robustly and intentionally skewed toward the postfoundationalist, fallibilist, and perspectival direction — still makes the important point that constructive theology's end is correspondence, however partial and proleptic, with the "truth" of God.

Constructive theology's nature as an "integrative" discipline points to its most distinctive feature in the current theological curriculum. It means that to

2. Aquinas, *ST* 1a.1.7.

3. Pannenberg, *ST* 1:50.

4. Pannenberg, *ST* 1:4-6; for a full discussion, see his *Theology and the Philosophy of Science,* pp. 297-326 particularly.

5. See further Vainio, *Beyond Fideism,* p. 132.

6. See Pannenberg, "What Is Truth?" pp. 1-27.

7. Clayton, *Adventures in the Spirit,* p. 28, emphasis in original (in commenting on Pannenberg's theology).

8. See Hauerwas, Murphy, and Nation, eds., *Theology without Foundations.*

9. Shults, *The Post Foundationalist Task of Theology,* p. 18, emphasis in original.

practice constructive theology well, one has to utilize the results, insights, and materials of all other theological disciplines, that is, biblical studies, church history and historical theology, philosophical theology, as well as ministerial studies. Closely related fields of religious studies, ethics, and missiology also belong to the texture of systematic work. That alone is a tall order. But as the rest of the working definition implies, to do constructive theology well one has to engage also nontheological and nonreligious fields such as natural sciences, cultural studies, and, as will be evident in this project, the study of living faiths (most importantly, Judaism, Islam, Buddhism, and Hinduism). The use of materials and insights, at times even methods (such as exegesis or historiography), however, is guided by the principle according to which the systematician must listen carefully to related disciplines but also go beyond their inputs, domains, and questions.

The nomenclature "coherence," however, may mean more than one thing. When applied to the theological task, one can think only of inner coherence: the relation of theological statements to the rest of Christian tradition. This is of course the program of the cultural-linguistic method. That, however, is not necessarily the case. Rightly the philosopher Nancey Murphy, who operates with Quine's web metaphor, is fully alert to the potential charges of relativism and combats them quite successfully.[10] To extend the web metaphor: granted there are no foundations, but there are "hooks" from which the foundation hangs! This project builds on the important conviction that coherence theory, when applied to theology, must check the "correspondence" of its statements with both inner and external statements.[11]

A methodological approach that "celebrates diversity, pluralism, and contextuality, while at the same time pursuing shared resources of human rationality and interdisciplinary conversation,"[12] is particularly appropriate in an investigation undertaken in the matrix of theology, religious studies, and sciences. This kind of interdisciplinary discourse, "a complex, multileveled transversal process,"[13] breaks through the limitations of any specific discipline with standard borders. It seeks mutual learning, interaction, and engagement in its quest for a coherent vision. The term "transversal" — borrowed from mathematics and employed by some leading interdisciplinary theologians — indicates "a sense of extending over, lying across, and intersecting with one

---

10. Murphy, *Beyond Liberalism and Fundamentalism,* pp. 98-108.
11. See Pannenberg, *ST* 1:21-22; see also pp. 18-19.
12. Van Huyssteen, *Alone in the World?* p. 5.
13. Van Huyssteen, *Alone in the World?* p. 9.

another."[14] While the idea of transversality as a stated goal has only appeared on the theological radar screen recently, as an idea it is hardly new. Just think of Aquinas, who regularly consulted all known sciences, in addition to philosophy (and in some cases whatever little he knew of other religions), to formulate a Christian view; indeed, even earlier, we can see an "interdisciplinary" approach in the Chinese classic *I Ching* (*The Book of Change,* ca. twelfth century B.C.E.) and Confucius's comments thereon several hundred years later.[15] Hence, one cannot embrace the idea of "nonoverlapping magisteria" in relation to religion and science.[16]

The principle of transversality does not float freely in the air, as it were; it is not a smorgasbord where one can pick and choose as one wishes, to use another metaphor. A useful and meaningful transversal interdisciplinary investigation acknowledges not only the theory-laden nature of each inquiry but also the rootedness of such an inquiry in a particular tradition. For the theologian, the guiding tradition is the biblical-historical and contemporary theological wisdom, the deposit of faith. That tradition, however, is neither a straitjacket that limits creative pursuit of knowledge nor a basis for mere repetition and defense. Rather, remaining "tied to specific communities of faith without being trapped by these communities,"[17] the investigation honors contextuality (and seeks to avoid abstract generalizations)[18] and builds on a shared identity of the wider community of faith. Appreciation and critique of tradition are part of the task.[19] The epistemology of modernity, of course, denies the existence and value of tradition in its naive search for an interest-free and "neutral" knowledge.[20] The premodern mentality, with its foundationalist epistemology, takes the tradition as the unquestionable foundation. The postfoundationalist epistemology differs from both, however, and locates itself in the dynamic and challenging place of being committed to a tradition but not imprisoned within its strictures.[21] The particular community and its tradition, hence, play an important role in the transversal inquiry: "There is no rationality except a socially embod-

---

14. Van Huyssteen, *Alone in the World?* p. 20. See further, Schrag, "Transversal Rationality."

15. I was inspired by Gay, "Neuroscience and Religion," p. 10.

16. Gould, "Nonoverlapping Magisteria," pp. 16-22.

17. Van Huyssteen, *Alone in the World?* p. 12.

18. See van Huyssteen, *Alone in the World?* p. 36 and passim.

19. See further, van Huyssteen, *Alone in the World?* p. 46 and passim.

20. See Zimmermann, *Incarnational Humanism,* pp. 35-36.

21. Newbigin, *Proper Confidence,* p. 50.

ied rationality."[22] Traditions are public; they "are patterns of thought and practice that are handed on . . . from one person to another in community, from one generation to the next."[23] "As socially established, they are not privately devised."[24] As such, traditions are "enormously complex tangles of concepts, beliefs, and practices of all kinds that make up communities' cultures."[25] Although there is continuity, there are also "cracks and seams, contradictions and stark breaks."[26]

Following Alasdair MacIntyre, it can be said that "the idea that there can be a kind of reason that is supra-cultural and that would enable us to view all the culturally conditioned traditions of rationality from a standpoint above them all is one of the illusions of our contemporary culture. All rationality is socially embodied, developed in human tradition and using some human language."[27] In this regard — with all their legitimate and marked differences — there is a certain kind of correspondence between the Christian and scientific community as built on both "tradition" and "authority." Even new investigations happen on the basis of and in critical dialogue with accumulated tradition, represented by scholars who are regarded as authoritative. For the Christian church this tradition is the narrative, the story of the gospel confessed by all Christians:

> The Christian community, the universal Church, embracing more and more fully all the cultural traditions of humankind, is called to be that community in which a tradition of rational discourse is developed which leads to a true understanding of reality, because it takes as its starting point and as its permanent criterion of truth the self-revelation of God in Jesus Christ. It is necessarily a particular community among all the human communities. . . . But it has a universal mission, for it is the community chosen and sent by God for this purpose. This particularity, however scandalous it may seem to a certain kind of cosmopolitan mind, is inescapable.[28]

---

22. Newbigin, *Gospel in a Pluralist Society,* p. 87.

23. D. Kelsey, *Eccentric Existence,* 1:3.

24. D. Kelsey, *Eccentric Existence,* 1:17.

25. D. Kelsey, *Eccentric Existence,* 1:17.

26. D. Kelsey, *Eccentric Existence,* 1:4.

27. As paraphrased by Newbigin, "Religious Pluralism," p. 50; so also p. 52; the reference is to MacIntyre, *Whose Justice? Which Rationality?*

28. Newbigin, *Gospel in a Pluralist Society,* pp. 87-88.

If this methodology is successful, then "Christian theology should be able to claim a public or 'democratic' presence in interdisciplinary dialogue," as Wentzel J. van Huyssteen aptly puts it.[29]

Particularly with regard to the comparative theology facet of this investigation — namely, engaging Jewish, Islamic, Hindu, and Buddhist beliefs of "creation" — one has to be careful in following the transversality principle. The reasons are many and obvious. First of all, systematic theologians are not experts in religions — and even if we were, it would take a lifetime to learn even one tradition in any deeper way. Therefore, we must do everything to avoid making "the systematic theologian into an amateur collector of religious curiosities."[30] The systematician should let the authoritative and representative voices of each tradition formulate their respective views.

Second, granted the systematician knows enough to be able to dialogue meaningfully, integrating the contributions of religions in an already wide menu substantially complicates the task. Understandable is the temptation by modernistically driven theologians to give up the distinctive testimonies and "ground beliefs" of each tradition, and in the name of the common core of religions try to make them speak about (or at least mean) the same thing. That "first-generation theological pluralism,"[31] however, is neither interesting nor useful. It also deviates from the principle of hospitality as it denies the right of the other to be *other*. As I have argued with some detail in the methodological orientation to this five-volume project (in the introduction to *Christ and Reconciliation*), not only is theology confessional (rightly understood), but so also is comparative theology. It is not confessional in terms of violence and oppression but rather in a way that makes room for distinctive identities, differing testimonies — and passionate search for a common understanding even in the midst of our deepest and most deeply held differences. Confessionalism is neither a denial of the pluralistic nature of theology as a discipline. Here pluralism does not mean a theologian's lack of personal beliefs and convictions, but rather that, as in any academic discipline, "people of differing beliefs can cooperate, discuss, argue, and converse."[32]

The beginning of both part 1 and part 2 will provide a detailed orientation to the topics and flow of argumentation in the following chapters.

29. Van Huyssteen, *Alone in the World?* p. 41.
30. K. Ward, *Religion and Revelation*, p. 37.
31. See further, *Trinity and Revelation*, chap. 14.
32. K. Ward, *Religion and Revelation*, pp. 45-49, here p. 45.

I. CREATION

1. A New Vision for the Christian Theology of Creation

The Doctrine of Creation in Transition

A contemporary constructive theology of creation has the twofold task of critically retrieving the best of theological tradition and tapping into new opportunities and resources in the beginning of the new millennium. Let us highlight briefly the most important ones.

First, the rich biblical and historical tradition of creation theology should be carefully reexamined. Unlike the holistic and embodied biblical (particularly OT) perspectives, theological tradition often holds dualistic explanations that contrast nature and the human, soul and spirit, secular and sacred, and so forth. The severing of "person" from "nature" was made a leading theological theme in classical liberalism. A related lacuna in Christian theology was forgetting the cosmic dimensions. Whereas in the biblical and patristic traditions "cosmic" Christologies and pneumatologies are present, particularly in modern theology, semisecular, largely immanentist "religion of the heart" explanations were dominant. Part of the retrieval of tradition involves forging again a dynamic link with the Jewish tradition. This is important for the sake of both interfaith hospitality and improving Christianity's self-understanding.[1]

Second, Christian theology of creation is a statement not only of creation but, first and foremost, of the Creator. As long as we fail to clarify what kind of God we are talking about, our account of God as Creator is left in the

1. Moltmann, *God in Creation*, p. 4.

air. All theology must be a trinitarian theology. A trinitarian doctrine leads to a relational, communal view of creation, "as an intricate relationship of community — many-layered, many-faceted and at many levels."[2] "Classical panentheism," the distinctive approach of this project (*Trinity and Revelation,* chap. 10), supports such a trinitarian, relational, and dynamic view of the Creator.

Third, not only because of the impending natural catastrophes due to human exploitation but also for the sake of honoring God's creative act as divine handiwork, creation theology must be an "ecological theology."[3] Such a theology is directed toward the flourishing of creation. While not escapist, such a theology "sees creation together with its future."[4] In other words, the doctrine of creation must be both earth-centered and oriented toward the future liberation of the cosmos (Rom. 8:19-23).

Fourth, the unprecedented influence of natural sciences should be acknowledged in a new way. "The natural sciences today offer to Christian theology . . . precisely the role that Platonism offered our patristic, and Aristotelianism our medieval forebears."[5] Rightly the British physicist-priest John Polkinghorne calls the religion-science dialogue a new form of "contextual" theology.[6] In this outlook, any attempt by theologians to intentionally avoid integral dialogue with natural sciences must be rejected, be it the classical liberal tradition's separation between "person" and "nature," or Barth's making the doctrine of creation merely an "article of faith" without the need for engagement with sciences, or Radical Orthodoxy's outright rejection of any dialogue with nontheological disciplines.[7] Dialogue with sciences must be had not only because dialogue advances bridge building and fosters hospitality, but first and foremost because it *"is demanded by the Christian understanding of the nature of reality itself."*[8] What we are seeking in this project is *"a community* of scientific and theological insights."[9] This engagement happens under a radically different worldview from that of the past: ours is dynamic, interrelated,

---

2. Moltmann, *God in Creation,* p. 2.

3. A key theme in Moltmann, *God in Creation.*

4. Moltmann, *God in Creation,* p. 5.

5. McGrath, *ScT* 1:7.

6. See Polkinghorne, *Theology in the Context of Science,* chap. 1.

7. Cf. the Radical Orthodox thinker Conor Cunningham's *Darwin's Pious Idea.* I am grateful for Dr. Olli-Pekka Vainio for reminding me of this work.

8. McGrath, *ScT* 1:21, emphasis in original. See also Torrance, *Theological Science,* p. 10.

9. Moltmann, *God in Creation,* p. 13, emphasis in original.

evolving, in-the-making. It relies on subtle and humble explanations, seeks to discern relationality and mutual conditioning, and envisions holistic ways of understanding.[10]

Fifth, the task of constructing a new theology of creation should be conceived as an ecumenical task — the term "ecumenical" understood in its widest sense, namely, referring to the whole inhabited world, in this case the global Christian family.[11] Along with that, there is a dire need for the theological academy to collaborate across genders, races, and classes, as well as across geographical boundaries. Predominantly white, male theologians' tradition of creation theology has to be balanced, corrected, and redirected by rich insights of female theologians of various persuasions as well as by male and female theologians from different contexts.

Sixth, the fact that "all cultures have their myths or theories of creation"[12] both necessitates a most careful consideration of theological implications and, at the same time, offers a platform for mutual conversation.[13] The presence of "creation" myths among other living faiths is an invitation — and an obligation — for Christian theology to engage them in mutual dialogue.

All the various aims and desiderata outlined above mean that a fruitful constructive theology of creation must be dialogical and seek a robust, dynamic engagement with various fields of knowledge, agendas, and perspectives. This does not, however, mean making theology bow down under every secular "flag." It is not true what Tillich claimed — that philosophy/culture asks the questions and theology answers. Rather, theology asks questions as much as it seeks to respond to them. Hence, "theological questions to scientists"[14] are as important as the questions of scientists. In this respect, the British Radical Orthodox theologian John Milbank is right that "if theology no longer seeks to position, qualify or criticize other discourses, then it is inevitable that these discourses will position theology."[15]

Yet another challenge and opportunity for a constructive theology of creation relates to the perennial question of how to speak of creation — and the Creator. Let us take a focused look at the topic.

10. See Clayton, *Adventures in the Spirit*, pp. 22-37 particularly.
11. Lønning, ed., *Creation — an Ecumenical Challenge*.
12. Gunton, *The Triune Creator*, p. 1.
13. See Schmid, "Creation, Righteousness, and Salvation," pp. 102-17.
14. Pannenberg, *Toward a Theology of Nature*, chap. 1 (pp. 15-28).
15. Milbank, *Theology and Social Theory*, p. 1.

Metaphors and Participation: The Nature of the Knowledge of the Created Reality

According to Moltmann, the current ecological doctrine of creation "must try to get away from analytical thinking, with its distinctions between subject and object. . . . This means that it will have to revert to the pre-modern concept of reason as the organ of perception and participation (methexis)."[16] While Moltmann's statement makes a valid point in urging that theological method resist reductionist, overly intellectual and analytic accounts of created reality, it also has to be qualified in two respects. First, a return to a communicative and participatory knowledge does not have to mean a return to a premodern concept of reason. How could we return, living as we do on this side of the Enlightenment? That would mean blocking the dialogue with contemporary conversation partners. Second, participatory knowledge does not have to be antagonistic to analytical thinking; a quick look at the leading theologians in tradition leaves no doubt about sophisticated intellectual and analytic capacities in the service of a "premodern" doctrinal formation.

What about theology-science engagement? Are metaphors fitting in speaking of issues scientific? Against common assumptions, the use of metaphors is rampant in sciences,[17] not only in the past — recall the metaphor of a machine used of a living being in the seventeenth century — but also nowadays. Just think of big bang, big bounce, big crunch, and other metaphors used of the universe's "beginning" and "end."[18]

Honoring the nature of created reality as a divine gift[19] helps theology avoid the kind of technocratic, possessive knowledge of God so prevalent in modern and contemporary cultures, which can only lead to exploitation. Participation does not possess; it gratefully *participates*.[20] Participatory knowledge honors the relational, mutually dependent, and symbiotic nature of all created processes, including humanity as part of it.[21]

Although participatory knowledge, as said, does not have to be exclusive of the analytic and rational, it honors the metaphorical and symbolic nature of human language and knowing. The clue to the power of metaphor — which

16. Moltmann, *God in Creation*, p. 2.
17. See Soskice, *Metaphor and Religious Language*, p. 99.
18. See Happel, "Metaphors and Time Asymmetry," pp. 103-34.
19. For important comments on creation as gift, see Tanner, *Economy of Grace*, p. 63.
20. Moltmann, *God in Creation*, pp. 2-3.
21. For important comments, see Moltmann, *God in Creation*, pp. 2-4.

technically is nothing other than "misnaming"[22] — is that "a good metaphor implies an intuitive perception of the similarity of the dissimilars."[23] Whereas *concepts* have to be unequivocal and hence mean the same at all times, metaphors, by their very nature, are equivocal. Whereas concepts "limit and demarcate, . . . [metaphors] *de*-restrict and can throw open the realm of possibilities." In that sense, metaphors may assume the form of play.[24] This is to say that metaphors attempt to say "more" as they seek to express something that transcends the limits of human concepts. The reason traditional theology and contemporary fundamentalism have not been keen on symbols and metaphors is their alleged dismissal of cognitive content. That is not necessarily the case. That symbols evoke imagination and can play with several meanings does not have to make them meaningless in the sense of the content of communication; indeed, the polysemy (or multivalence) may help convey dimensions and features that would otherwise be inaccessible. "If our world is richer than statistics and bloodless abstractions, we need a language with power of suggestion."[25]

Having briefly clarified some distinctive features and emphases of the current approach to the theology of creation, we are ready to sketch the outline of the discussion in part 1. (The beginning of part 2 contains a similar orientation.)

Orientation to Part 1: Creation

The next chapter (chap. 2) seeks to clarify the relationship between religions and sciences with a view toward constructive theological work. Not only Christian but also Jewish, Islamic, Buddhist, and Hindu attitudes toward contemporary (natural) sciences are compared and contrasted. At the end of that discussion, the major alternative to religious explanations, namely, naturalism, is investigated. Because there are different types of naturalisms, a tentative typology for the sake of comparison is first constructed.

The purpose of chapter 3 is to construct a distinctively *Christian* vision of nature, that is, nature as *creation*. Take seriously the term "construct." It reminds us that there are differing approaches to assessing the nature, value, and ontology of "nature." A theistic vision, common to all Abrahamic tra-

---

22. See Polanyi and Prosch, *Meaning*, p. 75.
23. Aristotle, *Poetics* 22.
24. Moltmann, *Experiences in Theology*, p. 162.
25. Dulles, *Models of Revelation*, p. 142.

dition, represents one such construction in contrast not only to the Asiatic faiths but also to both modern and postmodern philosophies. This is not to put theology and sciences at odds, but rather to clarify the theological point of view in the study of creation. Building on that conversation, chapter 4 seeks to lay out in some detail a robust trinitarian theology of creation, which also helps clarify crucial issues such as the possibility and condition of creation independently from the Creator, the meaning of creation "out of nothing," and the value of creation. Although in constructive theology it is useful — perhaps even necessary — to construct first the theological account of nature, in this case from a distinctively Christian perspective, before engaging sciences, in science-religion dialogue one could also begin from the sciences' side and then engage religion/theology.

Before continuing the construction of a trinitarian theology of creation in detailed dialogue with contemporary scientific cosmologies, a careful look at the visions of origins and cosmologies in four other living faiths is in order (chap. 5). Although that presentation goes beyond description, including tentative engagement from the Christian theological perspective, that dialogical task can only be finished during the course of the subsequent topics in part 1, particularly those related to the sciences.

Chapters 6 and 7 delve into many complicated questions about how to best find consonance and difference between most recent knowledge in the natural sciences concerning the origins and evolution of the universe and life on our planet in relation to theological and religious convictions. The former chapter emphasizes the "beginnings," which topic in itself may mean many things. Along with cosmological theories of the origins of the universe, the questions of the emergence, evolvement, and diversification of life-forms will be studied from a theological perspective. Understandably, we take a careful philosophical-theological look at the current state of neo-Darwinist versus religious/theological understanding. The latter chapter shifts the focus to continuing creation, named the doctrine of providence in traditional theology. An essential contemporary problem and challenge in the conversation has to do with how to best understand God's continuing presence and action in the world. A new way of envisioning divine action — in a trinitarian-pneumatological framework — will be attempted.

The last chapter in part 1 will take up a most urgent and complex issue, namely, suffering, evil, and decay in nature. Rather than attempting any kind of full-scale theodicy, we will approach the question of nature's suffering from two perspectives. On the one hand, the "natural evil" proper — suffering, decay, and death unrelated to human action — will be correlated with scientific knowledge of entropy and other relevant issues and put to a theological assessment. On the other hand, nature's suffering at the hands of humanity, that is, "pollution" of nature, will be investigated both from Christian and from interfaith perspectives.

Two standard topics will be omitted in this context: theodicy (to be discussed under eschatology, in *Community and Hope,* part 2) and the theme of (spiritual) "powers," whether good (angels) or evil (demons, evil angels, Satan). Spiritual powers are best discussed under pneumatology (part 1 of *Spirit and Salvation*).

2. Theology of Creation in the Matrix of Sciences, Religions, and Naturalisms

The Significance of Science for Religions and Theology

The simple reason why constructive theology should be deeply interested in science is that science is a universal phenomenon and, as such, of great interest to all religions.[1] The "triumphal march" and "sheer magnitude of its reach" simply make science a phenomenon not to be ignored.[2] Indeed, one of the most exciting developments in recent years has been the rise of "religion[/theology] and science" as a "fully differentiated arena of thought and scholarship with its own independent set of methodological principles."[3]

There is also the theological reason for dialogue: when "Christians confess God as the Creator of the world, it is inevitably the same world that is the object of scientific descriptions." As a result, theologians have the task of relating their statements to those of scientists.[4] While some see every scientific advancement as a step away from religion and faith, it can also be argued that "science has actually advanced to the point where what were formerly religious questions can be seriously tackled."[5]

We will begin with relating sciences to Abrahamic faiths and, thereafter,

---

1. Rashed, "The End Matters," p. 37. For a current massive discussion, see McNamara and Wildman, eds., *Science and the World's Religions*, vol. 1, *Origins and Destinies;* vol. 2, *Persons and Groups;* vol. 3, *Religions and Controversies.*

2. See Muzaffar Iqbal, "Islam and Modern Science," p. 3.

3. Haq, introduction to *GLC*, p. xvii.

4. Pannenberg, "Contributions from Systematic Theology," p. 359.

5. P. Davies, *God and the New Physics*, p. ix.

to Asiatic faiths. The bulk of the chapter is then devoted to considering Christian theology's ways of relating to science. The last part of the chapter engages forms of naturalism, including scientism, from the perspective of the religions.

Science and Abrahamic Faiths

The Embrace of Science in Jewish Tradition

No other ethnicity can boast so many leading scientists throughout history and in the contemporary world than the Jewish — from Galileo and Newton to Einstein and Heisenberg. Of all Nobel Prizes in physics, Jews have gathered almost a third![6] And yet, the Jews entered the scientific field relatively late, at the beginning of the twentieth century.[7] However, a number of leading scientists did not do their work distinctively as Jews; most of them were both secular and fairly assimilated.[8]

Until modernity rabbis were sages who were looked upon also as intellectuals in science. In the contemporary world, that role has changed radically. Indeed, many conservative rabbis are currently leaning toward a literalist interpretation of Scripture and hence the American Christian Right type of creationism.[9] This separation between the domains of religion and science, however, is a new development. For the defining medieval philosophers such as Maimonides, nothing could have been more strange. Until Baruch Spinoza, the semi-atheist Jewish philosopher, an integral relation between religion and science persisted. After modernity it was severed.[10]

The OT, unlike the Qur'an and, say, the Vedas, does not discuss cosmology as a separate topic; the little it offers is partially borrowed from the environment. Nor is there much attention to nature itself (unlike the Qur'an), although some of the sages, particularly Solomon, are depicted as masters of the knowledge of nature (1 Kings 5:10-14).[11] In the "prophetic" tradition of the OT, the emphasis is on the covenant rather than speculations into the

---

6. For details, see Efron, *Judaism and Science*, pp. 1-11.

7. Efron, *Judaism and Science*, part 3, offers a detailed account.

8. Cantor and Swetlitz, eds., introduction to *Jewish Tradition*, pp. 15-16.

9. Samuelson, "Judaism and Science," p. 45.

10. A delightful exception is the high-level engagement of contemporary science by the American rabbi David W. Nelson, *Judaism, Physics, and God*.

11. There is the persisting, widely known legend of Abraham teaching mathematics and sciences, including "natural sciences," to the Egyptians. Josephus, *Antiquities of the Jews* 1.8.2.

mysteries of the world.[12] Rather than being mystical and speculative, for the most part the OT's depiction of nature is that of an orderly cosmos brought about and controlled by Yahweh. This "disenchantment process" helped pave the way for the rise of scientific explorations.[13]

Unlike the Muslims (and some Hindus), the Jews have never entertained the idea of a "Jewish science."[14] Therefore, the sorts of science-religion clashes experienced among Christians (and much later in Muslim contexts) are by and large unknown[15] (except for the more recent Orthodox rabbis' reservations mentioned above). As in mainline Christian tradition, evolutionary theory is embraced.

The Islamic Struggle with Modern Science

The relationship between Islam and science is currently under scholarly debate, particularly concerning its history and relation to the rise of modern science in the West.[16] The standard opinion is that after the glorious rise of Islamic science, its "golden age" lasted until the eleventh century (C.E.), and featured such luminaries as Ibn-Rushd (Averroes) and Ibn Sina (Avicenna), finally giving way to the "age of decline."[17] However one judges the history of Islamic science, the current Western scientific and philosophical academia should mind its debt to the Islamic influence on the rise of sciences.[18]

Modern science came to Islamic lands only in the nineteenth century, and currently the Islamic world at large is in the process of catching up; leading Muslim scholars lament the status of scientific education at large in most Muslim lands.[19] As the Pakistani-Canadian chemist-priest Muzaffar Iqbal

12. See K. Ward, *Religion and Creation*, chap. 1.

13. Famously argued in Cox, *Secular City*, pp. 18-21.

14. Efron, *Judaism and Science*, p. 255.

15. Therefore, Efron (*Judaism and Science*, p. 257) by and large dismisses as irrelevant Barbour's fourfold typology for the Jewish context.

16. For up-to-date information and resources, see the Web site of the Center for Islam and Science, http://www.cis-ca.org/. For a useful discussion and survey, see also Stenberg, *The Islamization of Science*.

17. Abdalla, "Ibn Khaldūn," pp. 29-30; Muzaffar Iqbal, *Islam and Science*, chaps. 1, 3, and 5. According to the well-known thesis of Max Weber, the decline was due to lesser intellectual capacities of the Arabs; see Hoodbhoy, *Islam and Science*, p. 2. For Averroes's work and influence, see Guessoum, *Islam's Quantum Question*, pp. xiii-xxiii.

18. See Kamali, "Islam, Rationality and Science," pp. 17-18.

19. A detailed, deeply self-critical, up-to-date account is given in Guessoum, *Islam's Quantum Question*, chap. 1.

notes, none of the main producers of modern science is a Muslim. Unlike the West, in Islamic contexts the link between religion and science is far tighter. According to the Algerian astrophysicist Nidhal Guessoum, "most if not all the books on cosmology that have been written by Arab authors in recent years present cosmology not as a branch of astronomy but practically as a branch of Qur'anic exegesis."[20] The Iranian physics professor Mehdi Golshani's book *The Holy Quran and the Sciences of Nature* is a representative example. Insightfully, Iqbal reminds us that while science-religion discourse in the West is constructed in terms of "science-*theology*" dialogue, in Muslim contexts it is "*Qur'an*-science" engagement.[21] That said, unlike the Christian tradition (and more recently, Jewish tradition), religion-science dialogue is still a marginal phenomenon among Muslims.[22] Indeed, many Muslims sincerely believed that the alleged conflict between religion and science only related to Christianity but not to their own tradition.[23]

Not unlike in many other religious traditions, Islamic scholars and scientists offer a fairly obvious typology of responses to modern science:

1. Rejection of science because of its alleged opposition to revelation
2. An uncritical embrace of the technocratic practical results of Western science in pursuit of power- and competence-equality with (as they are perceived) more developed Western nations
3. An effort to build a distinctively "Islamic science" based on the authority of the Holy Qur'an and Hadith
4. An attempt to negotiate between the legitimacy and necessity of contemporary scientific principles and methods while at the same time critiquing the metaphysical, ethical, and religious implications of the scientific paradigm[24]

Ironically, the advocates of the first category are rapidly becoming a marginal phenomenon in Islamic lands, neither because Muslims by and large would endorse any of the seeming atheistic ethos advanced by modern sci-

---

20. Guessoum, *Islam's Quantum Question*, p. 180; see also Guessoum, "The Qur'an, Science, and the (Related) Contemporary Muslim Discourse."

21. Muzaffar Iqbal, *Islam and Science*, p. xxi.

22. Muzaffar Iqbal, "Islam and Modern Science," pp. 11, 15.

23. Mir, "Christian Perspectives," p. 99.

24. My typology here differs somewhat from that of Golshani, "Does Science Offer Evidence?" pp. 96-97; yet another kind is suggested by Ibrahim Kalin, "Three Views of Science," chap. 2. Materially, though, there are not significant differences.

entific culture nor because they would not oppose the hegemony, as they see it, of contemporary Western cultures because of the scientific superiority, but simply because of the uncritical embrace of the instrumental use of science in pursuit of technological,[25] particularly military, competence (category 2).[26] Because of the alleged neutrality and value-free nature of modern science, its practical fruits are being enjoyed unabashedly without much or any concern for the serious philosophical-ethical-religious challenges to core Islamic values. Some are going so far as to let their religious views be changed to accommodate the demands of science.[27] No wonder the best Islamic theologians are deeply worried.[28]

Deeply critical of and disappointed with the antagonism of the secular scientific paradigm, some Muslim intellectuals have been envisioning the possibility and necessity of an Islamic science.[29] The main complaints against modern science and its "blind" use by Muslims include "the refusal to even study Western science critically, often as a result of a kind of intellectual inferiority complex that simply equates Western science with the continuation of Islamic science" without any serious consideration of the dramatic difference of paradigms; the assumption of science's value-free, neutral nature; the failure to acknowledge that modern science "has helped to destroy all other perspectives on nature, including the religious"; its disastrous ethical implications; and so forth.[30] What would an Islamic science look like? According to Nasr, it would include "stop[ping] the worship-like attitude towards modern science and technology," returning to an in-depth study of authoritative Islamic sources, studying carefully pure sciences (including at the best institutions in the West) instead of focusing merely on applied fields, and rediscovering and reviving those fields of sciences in which Islam first achieved great competency, namely, medicine, agriculture, architecture, and astronomy. Above all, it would mean

25. According to Muzaffar Iqbal (*Islam and Science*, p. xv), "science and technology" are most often used "in one breath, without a pause."

26. Nasr, "Islam and Science," p. 72. For a full-length critique and analysis, see Nasr, *Traditional Islam in the Modern World*; see also the important work by Osman Bakar, *Tawhid and Science*.

27. From the writings of leading Muslim philosophers and theologians one can easily find deeply critical judgments of this development. See, e.g., Nasr, "Islam and Science," pp. 76-78; Özdemir, "Towards an Understanding," pp. 5-6.

28. Nasr, "Islam and Science," p. 72. At the end of the sentence, he quotes Q 18:81: "the truth has come and falsehood has vanished away; verily falsehood is bound to perish."

29. Golshani, "Islam and the Sciences of Nature," pp. 77-78; see also his "How to Make Sense of 'Islamic Science.'"

30. Nasr, "Islam and Science," pp. 72-76 (quotations from pp. 73 and 74).

adopting the Qur'an, Hadith, and *Sunna* as authoritative controls over scientific work.[31] Not only scientists at large find this kind of "sacred science" deeply flawed and suspect, but also some leading Muslim scientists have expressed grave concerns.[32] It has even been dubbed a "mystical quest."[33]

As an alternative to Islamic science, some leading scientists argue that there should not be in principle a contradiction between whatever science *qua science* discovers and Islamic faith. They strongly reject the whole idea of Islamic science and argue for the universal nature of the scientific pursuit and therefore its compatibility with Islam — or any other faith system — as long as (in this case) Islamic scientists are aware of philosophical and metaphysical presuppositions of the scientific work.[34] These "mainline scientists" (category 4 above) are also critical of secular philosophers and scientists with Muslim backgrounds who have left Islamic faith behind or at least do not allow it to guide their work as intellectuals, such as the Pakistani nuclear physicist Pervez Amirali Hoodbhoy, who later in his life has come to support scientific naturalism.[35]

It seems to me the fourth category in my typology comes materially close to the mutual critical engagement model followed in this project. Both approaches consider the scientific enterprise as "universal" in the sense that no faith or ideological tradition can own it, but on the other hand, each faith tradition has to assess its presuppositions from its own tradition's point of view, in hospitable dialogue with others.

As in the Christian tradition, a vibrant Muslim creationist movement exercises wide influence among laypeople in various global locations.[36] Another, similar kind of science-appealing development, materially similar to some

31. Briefly in Nasr, "Islam and Science," pp. 78-83; more widely in Nasr, *Need for a Sacred Science.* A widely known, accessible presentation is his lecture to MIT students in November 1991 titled "Islam and Modern Science"; http://www.muslimphilosophy.com/ip/nasr1.htm (6/3/20130).

32. Guessoum, *Islam's Quantum Question,* chap. 4, is the most up-to-date exposition of the pursuit by S. H. Nasr and a number of other Muslim scholars of Islamic science and its critique from a Muslim and scientific point of view. For another careful discussion, see Howard, *Being Human in Islam,* chap. 4.

33. Sardar, "Islamic Science," p. 180; see also Sardar, *Explorations in Islamic Science,* pp. 62-67; see also Guessoum, *Islam's Quantum Question,* pp. 125-29.

34. For a detailed discussion of Salam, see Guessoum, *Islam's Quantum Question,* pp. 129-35.

35. See Guessoum, *Islam's Quantum Question,* pp. 132-35.

36. A leading Muslim creationist, now with a ministry also in the United States, is the Turkish thinker Harun Yahya (http://www.harunyahyausa.com).

traditionalist/fundamentalist Hindu or Buddhist or Christian enterprises, the *I'jaz*, "miraculous scientific facts in the Qur'an,"[37] likewise builds apologetics with appeal to alleged correspondence between science and scriptural teaching.[38]

Modern Science and Asiatic Faith Traditions

Science in Hindu Outlook

In contrast to the post-Enlightenment Western ideals of total objectivity, externalization of nature, and desacralization of nature, from of old the Hindu vision saw science and its pursuit not as "a pure objective enterprise but as part of ritualistic experience."[39] Spirituality and what Westerners call science are intimately related.[40] Consider this: "India is the one and only country in the world that simultaneously launches satellites to explore the space *and* teaches astrology as a Vedic science in its colleges and universities." In fact, since 2001, astrology has been taught as a scientific subject in Indian colleges and universities.[41] Not surprisingly, Indian traditions hardly know the separation between natural and human sciences.[42] In keeping with that, Hindus have made significant contributions to fields such as astronomy, mathematics, chemistry, and, say, metallurgy, as well as pursuing the study of love, compassion, and spiritual unity.[43]

The question of science's relation to Hinduism is complicated historically in somewhat the same manner as that in Islam. What is undisputed is that beginning in the mid–nineteenth century, a vast and wide intellectual renaissance started in India resulting in its current great scientific pursuit. Disputed historical questions include these: whether that was a new beginning or rather

37. For details, see chap. 5 in Guessoum, *Islam's Quantum Question*.

38. See, e.g., the book by the French medical doctor Maurice Bucaille, *The Bible, the Qu'ran, and Science*.

39. Menon, "Hinduism and Science," p. 10.

40. See Witsz, "Vedānta, Nature, and Science," pp. 30-39.

41. Nanda, "Vedic Science," p. 30, emphasis in original; Raman, "Traditional Hinduism and Modern Science."

42. Gosling, *Science and the Indian Tradition*, p. 7; see chap. 7 for an empirical study of opinions about science in a university setting.

43. See Menon, "Hinduism and Science," p. 12; see also Gosling, *Science and the Indian Tradition*, pp. 1-2.

a continuation of an ancient pattern; what its relation to the British colonial influence is, including the introduction of the Western educational system; and what, if any, is the relation of the current rise of science to Hindu traditions.[44] Bhikhu Parekh has famously classified Indian responses to Western (secularizing) influences under three categories: the "critical traditionalists," who believe Indian foundations can be redeemed even if some important aspects of the West are incorporated; the "modernists," who wish to adapt to the European lifestyle; and the "critical modernists," who envision a creative synthesis.[45] The important Hindu reformer Keshub Chunder Sen represents the middle category in his seemingly uncritical embrace of science (even if it led to revision of religious beliefs).[46] Swami Vivekananda belongs to the first group: while not dismissing modern science, he demanded that Hindu philosophy be adopted as the basis and control, because ultimately, "the metaphysical and the physical universe are one, and the name of this One is Brahman."[47] While critical of the secular and "external" approach to science, Vivekananda was not opposed to science in principle. For example, he embraced evolutionary theory. But he also critiqued it for making the struggle for survival the driving force.[48] Spiritual and divine realities should not be excluded from evolutionary theory, he argued strongly, similarly to Aurobindo Ghose and others.[49]

Not unlike some Muslims, a group Hindu scientists have attempted to develop a credible "Hindu science" (also called "Vedic science") paradigm.[50] Among them, the most legendary is Acharya Jagadish Chandra Bose (d. 1937), a polymath, physicist, biologist, and archaeologist. His most well-known claim relates to the alleged capacity of inorganic matter to give a response to electrical stimuli similar to that of living beings.[51] Understandably, he was critiqued both by the scientific community and by some Hindu thinkers.[52]

44. See Paranjape, "Science, Spirituality and Modernity," pp. 3-14.

45. Parekh, *Colonialism, Tradition, and Reform.* In this section I am indebted to Gosling, *Science and the Indian Tradition,* chap. 2.

46. Sen, *Epistle to Indian Brethren,* p. 15.

47. Vivekananda, "The East and the West: VII. Progress of Civilization."

48. Vivekananda, "Questions and Answers." The citation is an approving reference to the idea of a Samkhya philosopher Patanjali. (Samkhya is one of the Vedanta schools, of which more below.)

49. As paraphrased by Gosling, *Science and the Indian Tradition,* pp. 23-24; see pp. 23-25 for details and sources.

50. For a critical assessment, see Nanda, "Vedic Science."

51. For a detailed discussion with sources, see Chatterjee, "Acharya Jagadish Chandra Bose."

52. For details, see Raju, "Sri Aurobindo and Krishnachandra Bhattacharya," chap. 5.

Buddhist Appraisals of Science

Modern Buddhism's relation to Western science is not totally different from that of Hinduism.[53] Its claims about science emerged in a polemical manner as Buddhists worked hard to convince Westerners, including Christians, that their understanding is not superstition but rather a rational, sound account of reality.[54] The Buddhologist José Ignacio Cabezón suggests a typology not different from ones devised by Christian theologians. The first model, "Conflict/Ambivalence," represents only a small minority of Buddhists. Cabezón mentions pre-Chinese-takeover Tibet as a place where science, along with other Western influences, was greeted with deep suspicion. (In that light, it is significant that the exiled leader, the XIV Dalai Lama, has invested extraordinary energy and skill in promoting science.)[55] Generally speaking, a negative attitude toward science among Buddhists in the contemporary world may have more to do with Western science's general hostility toward religion. By and large, however, rather than conflictual, the Buddhist attitude is named "Compatibility/Identity." It can manifest itself either in terms of similarity between Buddhism and science or in the idea that "Buddhism is science" and therefore it and science are more or less identical.[56] As in all other faith traditions, there is a growing body of contemporary (mostly popular) literature written by Buddhists around the world concerning the astonishing compatibility between, say, quantum mechanics and compassion or emptiness and relativity theory.[57]

The final category is "Complementarity," which as a middle position seeks to negotiate both similarities (unlike the first option) and differences (unlike the second option). Whereas both Buddhism and science focus on "empirical" investigation of reality, Buddhism complements the reductionist materialism with the inclusion of mental/spiritual/"inner." Whereas sciences rely only on rational, conceptual, and analytic method, Buddhism also utilizes intuition, meditation, and "inner" resources. And so forth.[58]

---

53. See Payne, "Buddhism and the Sciences," chap. 9.

54. Lopez, *Buddhism and Science*, p. xi. For an informed up-to-date discussion, see also Yong, *The Cosmic Breath*, chap. 5.

55. See further, Jinpa, "Science as an Ally?"

56. Olcott, *The Buddhist Catechism*, pp. 95-109 (available at www.sacredtexts.com); similarly Bhikshu, *A Buddhist Catechism*, p. 43 n. 85, available at http://www.bps.lk/olib/wh/wh152.pdf (5/29/2013).

57. For a listing and critical analysis of these and many others, see Lopez, *Buddhism and Science*, pp. 2-4 particularly. See also the widely quoted essay by Verhoeven, "Buddhism and Science."

58. Cabezón, "Buddhism and Science," pp. 41-56; see Ames, "Emptiness and Quantum

Although undoubtedly the Buddhist notion of complementarity is different from the Christian concept, *methodologically,* I suppose, the two approaches to science share many features.[59] I wish to add the obvious observation that — perhaps against the assumption of Buddhists — it can be argued that Christian tradition has been a major catalyst in facilitating the empirical study of nature with its idea of the orderliness and rationality of the created order. This takes us to the distinctively Christian engagement of science.

Science and Religion in Mutual Critical Dialogue: A Christian Theological Assessment

Differing Ways of Relating Science and Theology

The following typology helps us structure Christian approaches to science:[60]

- Theology in Continuity with Science
- Science in Continuity with Theology
- Theology and Science as Separate Realms
- Mutual Interaction of Theology and Science

For the first category, classical liberalism is a grand example. With its categorical separation between "nature" and "history," it made the former the realm of natural sciences and the latter that of "human sciences." Hence, no conflict arises. While Schleiermacher serves as an example of the third category (separation), he provides a template for the first because, for him, the doctrine of creation was merely about the world's dependence on God rather than about its beginnings.[61] Process theism, having rejected *creatio ex nihilo*[62]

Theory." An important current project on the forefront of Buddhist-science engagement is His Holiness, the Dalai Lama XIV's Mind & Life Institute. For activities, programs, and publications, see http://www.mindandlife.org/. See also Dalai Lama, *The Universe in a Single Atom.*

59. B. A. Wallace, "Buddhism and Science," p. 24.

60. A. M. Clifford, "Creation," pp. 225-40; the classic typology is that of Barbour, *Religion in the Age of Science,* pp. 3-30.

61. A. M. Clifford, "Creation," p. 226.

62. For key statements, see, e.g., Whitehead, *Process and Reality,* pp. 405, 410; for an insightful critique of Whitehead's concept of "creativity," which is not about God creating the world in the beginning but rather about the way of understanding the basic nature of reality, see Gilkey, *Naming the Whirlwind,* pp. 110-14.

and making God the One who provides the lure for evolutionary emergence, can hardly imagine facing a threatening challenge from natural sciences.[63] The critical point about this category is of course the timidity of theology to engage natural sciences *critically.* Instead of a genuine mutual dialogue, there is emphasis on accommodation.

The category of "Science in Continuity with Religion" has deep roots in the pre-Enlightenment theology and worldview in which theology was seen as the queen of sciences.[64] As long as the Scripture principle stayed intact, the authority of Scripture surpassed that of the sciences and philosophy. On the contemporary scene, the fundamentalist and antimodernist movement known as creationism, with its advocacy of an antievolutionary scientific paradigm as an alternative to mainline natural sciences, represents this category. It is based on literal interpretation of the biblical message, including matters of science and a search for archaeological/paleontological "evidence" in support of a young earth theory.[65] The obvious problem with this approach is that it lacks scientific credibility and hence even at its best remains a purely religious affair. Furthermore, its evidentialist epistemology, ironically, is naively modernist even if it seeks to combat Enlightenment views.

The third category, "Theology and Science as Separate Realms," is most notoriously represented by Barth and neo-orthodoxy. It is a result of several interrelated convictions and orientations: the fideistic elevation of divine revelation as the judge of all matters of knowledge; the rejection of natural theology and discontinuous linking of God and world; and — most ironically — the acceptance of classical liberalism's categorical separation between nature and history. Along with Radical Orthodoxy,[66] neo-orthodoxy rejects dialogue with sciences.[67] The main fallacy of the attempt to separate theology and science is not totally different from that of the first two categories, namely, the fail-

63. While not a process theologian, Teilhard de Chardin held a somewhat similar attitude (*Phenomenon of Man,* pp. 283-85); I am indebted to A. M. Clifford, "Creation," p. 228 n. 85.

64. Zakai, "The Rise of Modern Science," pp. 125-51.

65. For a succinct, up-to-date description, see Schwarz, *Creation,* pp. 163-65. Creationism's most well-known earlier advocate was Henry M. Morris, with a number of best-selling books, including *Beginning of the World* (Denver: Accent Books, 1977); *Scientific Creationism* (San Diego: Creation-Life Publishers, 1974). For the Institute for Creation Research he founded and a number of resources, see http://www.icr.org/. For the (in)famous court trials over teaching science in the schools beginning in the 1920s, see Edward Larson, *Trial and Error: The American Controversy over Creation and Evolution* (New York: Oxford University Press, 1985).

66. Milbank, "Radical Orthodoxy," pp. 33-45.

67. For stated reasons, see Barth's short preface to *CD* III/1. See Nebelsick, "Karl Barth's Understanding of Science," pp. 165-214; see also Gilkey, *Maker of Heaven and Earth,* pp. 26, 149.

ure of theology to have a public voice and also to make its own contribution to sciences. Although I fully endorse Milbank's decrial of theology's "false humility"[68] before the secular academy, blocking the way for dialogue is an unacceptable attitude. In terms of a ray of hope — regarding neo-orthodoxy particularly — we should be mindful of the late Scottish theologian T. F. Torrance's robust way of redeeming key aspects of Barth's theology in the service of "scientific theology."[69]

The orientation adopted in this project is best embodied in the "Mutual Interaction of Theology and Science" template. It "reject[s] the idea that the domain of religious faith and the domain of scientific thought are exemplified by rival and opposing notions of rationality."[70] Positively, it seeks a mutual critical dialogue and engagement.

"Critical Mutual Interaction"

The Roman Catholic Church's Vatican II — unlike the antimodernist, authoritarian position of the pre-Council era[71] — stated that "earthly matters and the concerns of faith derive from the same God," and hence in principle cannot violate each other.[72] In the work of the leading twentieth-century Catholic dogmatician Karl Rahner, the principle of mutual interaction became a leading theme in the dialogue.[73] Strongly advocating evolutionary theory,[74] he also wanted to make sure that the distinction, if not separation, between natural sciences and theology be maintained.[75] Among Protestant theologians, no one has labored

---

68. Milbank, *Theology and Social Theory*, p. 1.

69. For a careful account, see McGrath, *Thomas F. Torrance*, pp. 195-235.

70. Van Huyssteen, *Alone in the World?* p. xv; Gould, *Rock of Ages*, pp. 4-5.

71. Even the highly influential encyclical *Humani Generis* by Pius XII that advocated the use of natural sciences still unequivocally rejected any scientific insights that might "transgress the limits . . . established for the protection of the truth of Catholic Faith and doctrine" (#43); for developments in Catholic theology, see Coyne, "Evolution and the Human Person," pp. 11-17.

72. *Gaudium et Spes*, #36. The late Pope John Paul II urged actively and facilitated high-level interactive projects in science and theology in his highly acclaimed encyclical *Fides et Ratio* (1998) and other publications such as "Message of His Holiness Pope John Paul II," pp. 15-16.

73. For a programmatic essay, see Rahner, "Natural Science and Reasonable Faith," pp. 16-55.

74. See the influential essay by Rahner, "Christology within an Evolutionary View," pp. 157-92.

75. Rahner, "Natural Science and Reasonable Faith," pp. 17-22.

in pursuing critical mutual dialogue more than Pannenberg. He argues that a "failure to claim that the world that the sciences describe is God's world is a conceptual failure to confess the deity of the God of the Bible."[76] While theology must be mindful of the differences in method between itself and natural sciences — without undermining some general philosophical and epistemological assumptions such as the orderliness of the world[77] — it should also remember that "the truth claim of creation is strengthened by the fact that in principle theology can integrate scientific statements into its coherent description of the world as the creation of God."[78] The Lutheran Pannenberg's Reformed counterpart Moltmann similarly pursues mutual critical dialogue under the telling rubric "companions in tribulations."[79] Generally speaking, two kinds of scholars engage this fourth category: scientists with training in theology, and theologians, as well as Christian philosophers, with wide learning in the sciences.

Leading contemporary American scientist-theologian Robert John Russell's "creative mutual interaction" model looks at the dialogue in terms of both "coherence" and "dissonance." Theology should not merely serve as science's religious interpreter; rather, "theology can indeed offer creative suggestions in the form of questions, topics, or conceptions of nature which scientists might find helpful in their research and as judged by their own professional criteria."[80] In this project, Russell's nomenclature shifts into "*critical* mutual dialogue" to highlight the mutuality of the relationship.

The epistemology most often invoked in such an enterprise is "critical realism." Critical realism seeks to negotiate between the naivete of Enlightenment rationality with its dream of an indubitable certainty, on the one hand, and on the other hand, the dismantling of the whole rational and scientific work by some extreme postmodern approaches. Importantly, critical realism has been connected with epistemic holism, also known as epistemic emergence or epistemic antireductionism, by Peacocke. All these terms highlight the key values of this idea: it resists reductionism, affirms emergence, and puts top-down and bottom-up explanations in a mutually conditioned relationship. Critical realism does not in any way undermine metaphors and models as a way of explanation, but rather utilizes them.[81] Pushing aside com-

76. Pannenberg, *ST* 2:59-60, here p. 60.

77. For differences and similarities, see Stoeger, "Reductionism and Emergence," pp. 231-32; Polkinghorne, *Quantum Physics and Theology*, chap. 1.

78. Pannenberg, *ST* 2:71; see also p. 70.

79. For a detailed account, see Moltmann, *God in Creation*, pp. 33-36 (quotation p. 34).

80. R. Russell, *Cosmology*, pp. 4-24 (quotation p. 21).

81. See further, Soskice, "Knowledge and Experience," pp. 173-84.

peting views such as antifoundationalism (Richard Rorty), "truth-as-social-convention" (Michel Foucault), and related deconstructive postmodern approaches, as well as the foundationalisms of modernity,[82] McGrath argues for (what I call) a postfoundational epistemology that operates with a "web metaphor."[83] Instead of a foundation, the "web or tapestry metaphor eliminates the 'base-superstructure' distinction, and proposes in its place an interconnected network of beliefs, each of which depends upon others for its plausibility."[84] Unlike postliberalism, this approach builds not only on internal coherence but also on external coherence (see introduction to *Christ and Reconciliation*).[85] In sum, this approach (which also guides the current project) "attempts to offer a view of the world, including God, which is both internally consistent and grounded in the structures of the real world. It aims to achieve extra-systemic correspondence with intra-systemic coherence, regarding both these criteria as of fundamental importance."[86] Polkinghorne summarizes well these key ideas:

> Without abandoning ourselves to epistemological despair, we can be postmodern enough to recognize that, in the aftermath of the demise of Cartesian confidence in clear and self-evident ideas, we find ourselves in a situation in which the enterprise of rationality calls for a certain attitude of bold commitment, going farther than what could be justified beyond any possibility of logical scruple. At the same time, one can see that science, with its intertwining of interpretation and experience, involves the epistemic circularity of believing in order to understand while at the same time having to understand in order to believe. The fruitfulness of human rational enquiry strongly encourages the belief that this circularity is benign and not vicious.[87]

Science and the "Secular Believer"

Not all theologians, however, are convinced that the approach outlined above is to be followed. Recently Philip Clayton, a leading expert on science-religion dialogue, has come to critique the approach of Pannenberg, Russell,

82. McGrath, *ScT,* vol. 2, chap. 7 (pp. 3-54).
83. For a detailed discussion, see *Christ and Reconciliation,* pp. 5-15 particularly.
84. McGrath, *ScT* 2:36.
85. McGrath, *ScT* 2:39-54. Cf. Vainio, *Beyond Fideism,* pp. 73-76.
86. McGrath, *ScT* 2:56.
87. Polkinghorne, "Anthropology in an Evolutionary Context," pp. 90-91.

and others outlined in this section. Under the nomenclature "critical faith," this theologian claims that "faith of this sort exists in, with, and through the world's ambiguities and uncertainties. It is troubled by the problem of evil, though not completely destroyed by it; it is humbled before other religious traditions, though not ready therefore to proclaim the equivalence of all faiths; it is respectful of the power of scientific predictions and explanations, though not prepared to reduce the spiritual dimension to what science can grasp of it."[88]

This kind of believer can be named a "secular believer" to whom doubt is not external to beliefs but rather "can instead be internal to the dynamic of belief."[89] Rather than defending the conservative effort to maintain certainty or liberals' willingness to continue believing notwithstanding radical new scientific findings, Clayton dares *"to acknowledge the possibility of the impossibility of religious belief."* In this scheme, the existence of God is ultimately left open, made a problem rather than a matter of certainty.[90]

Notwithstanding critique, Clayton also feels much in common with Pannenberg's well-known project of not presupposing the truth of Christian doctrine but rather making it a matter of rational argumentation, whose truth will be manifested in the eschaton. Where their ways part is that whereas for Pannenberg "history waits only for the final manifestation of" the truth of God as proleptically present in Christ's resurrection,[91] Clayton wishes to leave open — without any "proleptic evidence" such as the historicity of Christ's resurrection — the question of the final verdict of truth and hence the question of Christianity's superiority among other faiths. Clayton follows the American philosopher Charles Sanders Peirce's famous principle: "truth is the character which . . . we may *justifiably hope* will be enjoyed by beliefs that survive however long or far inquiry is pursued or prolonged."[92] In sum, Clayton's critical faith of the secular believer looks something like this:

> On this view theologians can engage in research and reflection without presupposing in advance that their research will finally confirm what they

88. Clayton, *Adventures in the Spirit*, p. 24; see L. Dupré, *The Other Dimension*, among many of his works.

89. Clayton, *Explanation from Physics*, p. 138. Clayton couldn't disagree more with the claim that doubt is sin, as in Gutting, *Religious Belief and Religious Skepticism*.

90. Clayton, *Adventures in the Spirit*, pp. 25-26 (quotation p. 25, emphasis in original).

91. Clayton, *Adventures in the Spirit*, p. 29; see also pp. 26-29.

92. Wiggins, "Reflections on Inquiry and Truth," p. 114, cited in Clayton, *Adventures in the Spirit*, p. 30, emphasis in original.

hope to be true. For example, one might engage in dialogue with other religious traditions without knowing in advance that the comparisons will favor the superiority of one's own tradition over the others. Similarly, one can engage closely with scientific results, and with the spirit of naturalism, without at present knowing that the best arguments will in the end favor the theistic position.[93]

While I find much in Clayton's view to commend, I also think that in theology one cannot do any meaningful investigation without some deep, underlying commitments and beliefs. Those beliefs do not have to be dogmatic, nor immutable — but they must be there. Hence, I find Pannenberg's approach (to use him as a type) closer to the way most theologians, even "secular believers," actually function. Rather than pushing aside any "expectations," I consider basic theological claims as "hypotheses" hopefully (!) to be confirmed in the course of investigation.

The notion of "secular believer" points to a very important phenomenon in contemporary philosophy and worldviews in the Global North: naturalism, to which our discussion now turns.

Naturalism in Religious and Theological Assessment

A Typology of Naturalisms

As is routinely noted, the definition of "naturalism" is far from settled.[94] A rough working definition that may be able to embrace various versions of naturalism is something like this: "the philosophy that everything that exists is a part of nature and that there is no reality beyond or outside of nature."[95] The following tentative typology is meant to assist in discussion, and has only heuristic value:[96]

93. Clayton, *Adventures in the Spirit*, p. 31.

94. Owen Flanagan's analysis ("Varieties of Naturalism," pp. 430-52) identifies no fewer than fifteen varieties, and he claims many more could be added. Regarding how "unnatural" philosophical/scientific naturalism is to folk psychology, see P. M. Churchland, *Engine of Reason*, p. 322.

95. Goetz and Taliaferro, *Naturalism,* p. 6; a similar definition is that of Clayton, *Mind and Emergence*, p. 164.

96. See also Clayton's typology ("On Divine and Human Agency," pp. 164-66). A full-scale discussion of forms of religious naturalism is Stone, *Religious Naturalism Today.*

1. "Antisupernaturalist" or Antitheistic Naturalism (or Scientism)
2. "Religion-friendly" [Non]Theistic Naturalism
3. Theistic Naturalism
4. Agnostic Naturalism

Examples of antitheistic forms of naturalism (#1) abound among current scientists and philosophers of science.[97] At least for the past century, it has been almost the default position among philosophers and scientists.[98] Named also scientism,[99] it "denies that there are any spiritual or supernatural realities. . . . It is the view that anything that exists is ultimately composed of physical components."[100] Consequently, "all knowledge of the universe falls within the pale of scientific investigation."[101]

The second category, which I call (for lack of a better term) "religion-friendly" [non]theistic naturalism (#2), is a "spiritually evocative naturalist interpretation of human life."[102] Unlike secular naturalism (#1), this category does not reject religion,[103] but at the same time (unlike #3), it declines to accept any kind of transcendent ("supernatural") deity or metaphysical being.[104] It can be called "religious naturalism," which speaks of religion merely in terms of an ultimate creative mystery as well as "personal wholeness and social coherence."[105] Religion scholar Karl Peters's identification of "god" with the process of creation itself (rather than conceiving God as

97. For details, see Barr, *Modern Physics and Ancient Faith*, chaps. 1–3.

98. Stroud, "The Charm of Naturalism," p. 23.

99. J. Kim, *Physicalism, or Something Near Enough*, p. 149; similarly E. O. Wilson, *On Human Nature*, p. 201; see also Fodor, "Is Science Biologically Possible?" p. 30. For the classic, oft-quoted statement, see Bertrand Russell, *Why I Am Not a Christian*, p. 44.

100. Nielsen, "Naturalistic Explanations of Theistic Belief," p. 402, cited in Goetz and Taliaferro, *Naturalism*, p. 9. For a penetrating analysis of "naturalist ontology," see chap. 1 in Moreland, *Consciousness and the Existence of God*.

101. "Naturalism," in *Encyclopædia Britannica Online*. The original manifesto of naturalism was Woodbridge, *An Essay on Nature*.

102. Wildman, *Science and Religious Anthropology*.

103. Haught (*Is Nature Enough?* pp. 7-8) names "soft naturalism" (as opposed to "hard") those naturalisms that are open to religious explanations but do no in the final analysis presuppose anything transcendent. The distinction between soft and hard was proposed by Rolston, *Science and Religion*, pp. 247-58.

104. If I have correctly understood, a parallel program is that of Hardwick, *Events of Grace*; for a summary statement of main points, see pp. 5-6.

105. Goodenough, *The Sacred Depths of Nature*; the designations in citations are from Peacocke, "Prologue," p. 7.

Creator)[106] serves as an example. In fairness to its most noted current advocate, Wesley J. Wildman, I have tried to maintain in the nomenclature the self-designation "theistic naturalism," although, respectfully, I think that to speak of "theism" in the absence of *theos* (deity) only adds to the confusion. Instead, it should be called "religion-friendly" or "religious" naturalism. Then it could also embrace forms of nontheistic religions (Theravada Buddhism and forms of Hinduism, among others). It seems to me that rejecting metaphysics (as problematic as that term may be)[107] is self-contradictory on two accounts: First, because "naturalism" in itself is a stated opinion about the "meaning" of human life, it represents a "metaphysics" of sorts, just differently. Second, any nonmetaphysical explanation of religion simply is meaningless. A mere naturalistic account of religion leads into such an immanentist reduction that no living faith tradition, not even Buddhism, could take it without radically changing the tradition's identity.

What really can be called *theistic* naturalism (#3) was advocated by the late British biochemist-priest Arthur Peacocke. Like his scientist fellows, Peacocke was "seeking as *naturalistic* a formulation of the content of Christian faith as is achievable" while, in contrast to their antitheistic prejudices, he was "still doing justice to the data on which that theology rests." In other words, he sought to honor the "completeness and reality of the natural world of the sciences" without rejecting the referential meaning of "God." He believed there really is an ultimate reality named God in theistic faiths.[108] Peacocke's theology, unlike the previous category (#2), "affirms that the natural, including the human, world owes its existence to another entity, a Creator God, who is real and 'personal.'" Where Peacocke differs from the more traditional theists (in all Abrahamic traditions) is that although God has purposes for this world, "God does not implement these purposes through 'miracles' that intervene in or abrogate the world's natural regularities, which continue to be explicated and investigated by the natural sciences."[109] This nondualist view of the world (and God-world relation) is based on *emergent monism;* that is, everything

---

106. K. Peters, *Dancing with the Sacred,* p. 1. If I correctly understand, it seems to me a parallel project is that of Wieman, *The Source of Human Good.*

107. For a detailed discussion of the kind of metaphysics adopted in this project, see chap. 9 in *Trinity and Revelation.*

108. Peacocke's preface to *ATI,* pp. 3-4 nn. 2-3 (p. 3), contains his own listing of the most relevant earlier essays on which the mature position is based.

109. Peacocke, "Prologue," p. 9. Unfortunately, Peacocke mistakenly claims to find support for this antimiraculous noninterventionist view in Eastern Orthodox theology by taking out of context a statement from Lossky (*Mystical Theology of the Eastern Church,* p. 70).

evolves "as a consequence of relationships in complex systems," and new layers, having emerged, cannot be reduced to (although they are dependent on) lower levels.[110]

My response to Peacocke is mainly affirmative in that his proposal can be reconciled with not only the classical panentheism of this project (see chap. 10 in *Trinity and Revelation* and chap. 3 below) but also Abrahamic faith's doctrine of God and creation. But I have two reservations. The first has to do with what Peacocke calls "miracles," which I will discuss in chapter 7. The second one is wider and has to do with the wisdom of adopting the term "naturalism" for a project that so radically differs from the current usages of the term in science and philosophy (of science). As soon as the *theistic* naturalist introduces God, all affirmations about "naturalism" seem incredible to nontheists.[111] Furthermore, unlike the priest-scientist Peacocke's sensibilities, most people of the world, among all religions — plus many who do not consider themselves religious in the traditional sense of the word — do not find it "natural" at all to believe that there is a merely "natural" explanation for the mysteries of the world.

The final category (#4), agnostic naturalism, somewhat ambiguously refers to the growing number of "recovering" hard-core (scientific) materialists/naturalists who are becoming more and more skeptical about naturalism's truthfulness and meaningfulness. Just think of recent publications such as *The Waning of Materialism* (2010), in which over twenty philosophers critique and find alternatives for materialism (and strict naturalism).[112] The formerly leading American strict naturalist-materialist philosopher Thomas Nagel's 2012 title *Mind and Cosmos: Why the Materialist Neo-Darwinian Conception of Nature Is Almost Certainly False* not only issues a devastating critique of the self-sufficiency of scientism but also sets forth the bold claim that there is a necessary connection between the cosmos and human consciousness. He also refutes the (neo-Darwinian) "reductionist explanation of the origin of life."

Whereas in the past the exclusion of mind/consciousness from the scientific paradigm led to great advances, Nagel argues that it is time to get them connected again because mind is not an afterthought but rather an integral

110. Peacocke, "Prologue," p. 9; see also his "Emergent Monism," chap. 2.

111. Importantly Flanagan ("Varieties of Naturalism," p. 435) claims that the defining feature that characterizes all main forms of naturalism stemming from the time of the Enlightenment is antisupernaturalism; hence, he does not consider it consistent to use the term "naturalism" for theistic views.

112. Koons and Bealer, eds., *The Waning of Materialism*.

aspect of reality. But that would of course mean going beyond the naturalist paradigm, though not necessarily to a religious one.[113] Although Nagel himself continues as a staunch atheist, he challenges scientific academia to take the "Designer" arguments seriously rather than as a matter of indifference and scorn. He even claims that an "[a]theistic account has the advantage over a reductive naturalistic one in that it admits the reality of more of what is so evidently the case, and tries to explain it all."[114] Interestingly, Nagel is willing to label himself an "objective idealist" because he considers intelligibility (mind and consciousness) to be behind and related to the order of nature.[115] Although the worldview of another staunch naturalist-materialist, Jaegwon Kim, is not only atheist but also physicalist, even he is willing to admit that, by speaking of "physicalism," we can really have only "something near enough."[116] The theologian's response to the signs of an eradication of strict naturalist-materialist edifices is a cautiously hopeful "let us wait and see" regarding the implications for the perception of religion and its relation to science.

A Theological Critique of Antitheistic, Scientific Naturalism

The basic dilemma of naturalism — similarly to positivism — is that its main postulate, namely, that all that there is, is that which we are able to "see" (investigate), cannot of course be verified within its own logic of reasoning.[117] The verification of this claim grows particularly difficult because the natural sciences now believe that while finite with regard to "beginning," the cosmos may be infinite in size. Even if the cosmos appeared to be finite, we know enough of the vastness of the universe(s) to know that what can be investigated via any imaginable human means is just a small fraction of reality.[118] Hence, the rejection of that which is "beyond" cannot be naturalistically proven.[119] There are also well-known deep and wide problems in how to define "empirical" investigation and what we are justified to conclude on that basis.[120]

---

113. Nagel, *Mind and Cosmos*, pp. 3-10 (pp. 3, 6, respectively).

114. Nagel, *Mind and Cosmos*, p. 24.

115. Nagel, *Mind and Cosmos*, pp. 15-17.

116. See J. Kim, *Physicalism, or Something Near Enough*, p. 1.

117. See Haught, *Is Nature Enough?* p. 2.

118. See Haught, *Is Nature Enough?*

119. For a more detailed critique of naturalism, see Schilbrack, "Problems for a Complete Naturalism," pp. 269-91, and more briefly, McGrath, *ScT* 1:129-32.

120. Classic works are Anscombe, "Causality and Determination"; Cartwright, *How the*

There are other weighty challenges to scientific naturalism. To the perennial question of why there is something rather than nothing and who produced it, naturalism cannot of course give an answer (unless it goes beyond its own limits). The grounding of ethics — the "ought" — seems to many to be irreconcilable with merely immanentist resources. Others point to experiences that seem to prove naturalism false; if individuals' experiences do not count much, the cumulative evidence of the history of religions certainly does — and add to that the equally long history of metaphysical reflection. And so forth.[121] It is hard to oppose the conclusion of Alvin Plantinga, a persistent critic of metaphysical naturalism: "Naturalism is presumably not a religion. In one very important respect, however, it resembles religion: it can be said to perform the cognitive function of a religion. There is that range of deep human questions to which a religion typically provides an answer." Hence, it can be named a "quasi religion."[122] It is only to the embarrassment of science that a number of its leading spokespersons seem to be totally ignorant of the "dogma" and "the religious nature of scientific materialism," as the Buddhologist Alan Wallace calls it.[123] With this in mind, R. C. Lewontin rightly ridicules the tendency in some current "scientific" accounts to attribute agency to inert chemicals and discerns a "theological" motif embedded therein.[124]

Some theologians and religionists have recently been enthused by the provocative work of the philosopher Robert N. McCauley, *Why Religion Is Natural and Science Is Not* (2011). Is that a major support for religion and theology? Probably not. Why? First of all, the book is not about a typical science-religion comparison along the metaphysical and epistemological lines but rather more like a cognitive science of religion paradigm (see below, chap. 10) in which the nature of human cognition (in relation to religious and scientific claims) is the focus. Second, his thesis is that whereas science's many theories and methods are highly counterintuitive to human cognition (just think of quantum theory), *popular* religion's assumptions, including the maker of the universe and the meaningfulness of the world, stick naturally with human intuitions. Focusing on popular religion, his corollary conclusion is that *theological* claims are no more "natural" than scientific ones, but rather "[t]heological incorrectness

---

Laws of Physics Lie; Cartwright, *The Dappled World*; J. Dupré, *Disorder of Things*, esp. part 3; J. Dupré, *Human Nature*, pp. 163-70.

121. For a short discussion, see Clayton, *Mind and Emergence*, pp. 172-79.

122. A. Plantinga, "Religion and Science."

123. B. A. Wallace, "Introduction," pp. 10-20.

124. Lewontin, *The Doctrine of DNA*, pp. 108-9, cited in Gunton, *The Triune Creator*, pp. 186-87 n. 14.

is inevitable."[125] In theological estimation, then, McCauley's book is not necessarily very interesting because theology's task — as defined in this project — is to inquire into the epistemological and metaphysical truthfulness of claims about God and the world. Whether they are "natural" or counterintuitive has very little do with their value in that regard.

Much more relevant to the theological work is the Christian philosopher Alvin Plantinga's recent argument that "there is superficial conflict but deep concord between science and theistic religion, but superficial concord and deep conflict between science and naturalism."[126] Abrahamic faiths' belief in humanity having been created in the image of God (to be discussed in detail in part 2) implies that therefore there is a correspondence between the rationality/intelligence implanted in human nature by God and the rational nature of reality.[127] Hence, for a theist the intelligibility, meaningfulness, and order of nature seem "natural." In contrast, "strict naturalism cannot successfully describe, accommodate, or undermine either the reality of purposeful explanation, or libertarian free choices, or experiences of pleasure and pain, or the existence of persons."[128] How "natural" is the claim of the materialist D. C. Dennett that "[a]n impersonal, unreflective, robotic, mindless little scrap of molecular machinery is the ultimate basis of all the agency, and hence meaning, and hence consciousness, in the universe"?[129] (Here one is reminded of McCauley's thesis of the counterintuitive nature of basic scientific claims!)

Christian theological engagement of science in its attempt to offer a contemporary account of the doctrine of creation takes up the metaphysical challenge presupposed in any meaningful scientific work and argues boldly for the possibility and necessity of a religious interpretation of nature as creation. This is not unwarranted for several interrelated reasons. First, "Theism does not have the same difficulty as naturalism on the problem of emergence of consciousness and values, partly because theism does not hold that these emerged from nonconscious, value-less sources. Goodness has always existed in the divine nature, and the goodness in the cosmos is itself part and parcel of a created reality by an all-good God."[130] Of course, theists cannot prove their ultimate convictions (any more than can scientific naturalists), but at least they

125. McCauley, *Why Religion Is Natural and Science Is Not,* citation on p. 9.

126. A. Plantinga, *Where the Conflict Really Lies,* p. ix.

127. Already Aquinas posited this connection: *ST* 1.93.4, 6; A. Plantinga, *Where the Conflict Really Lies,* pp. 3-4.

128. Goetz and Taliaferro, *Naturalism,* p. 7; also p. 13.

129. Dennett, *Darwin's Dangerous Idea,* p. 203.

130. Goetz and Taliaferro, *Naturalism,* p. 92.

can point to a reasonable, "natural" explanation entertained by humanity for millennia. Here, what John Henry Newman called "informal inference" might be of some help. In this scheme, an accumulation of viewpoints, probabilities, and intuitions begins to convince the thinker of the validity of the position even when no infallible or uncontested "foundational" claims or proofs can be presented.[131] Second, it is a historical fact that the distinctively Christian view of nature as creation, against the prejudices to the contrary among current natural scientists, played a critical role in the evolution of natural sciences, particularly when compared with Greek cosmologies and philosophies.[132] Third, Christian theology claims that the orderliness and rationality of nature are inherently built in by the Creator, as will be discussed in chapter 3.

What about other faith traditions with regard to naturalism?

Religions and Naturalism

By and large, religions categorically oppose scientific naturalism if it means making the world totally void of any divine or "supernatural" ("spiritual") Being/Ultimate Reality. The Iranian Muslim scholar Hamid Parsania's comment is illustrative: "Islam's perspective on man and the world is not mundane or materialistic. In the mundane outlook, physical nature and the life of this world hereunder constitute all of reality. Islam's outlook on the world is religious, and in a religious outlook the physical world is but a part of reality — the other part being beyond the physical realm, or, precisely, metaphysical."[133] Similarly, the leading twentieth-century Vedanta theologian Sri Aurobindo's claim of "the manifestation of God in Matter" and that the reason evolution can happen is that "Life is already involved in Matter and Mind in Life because in essence Matter is a form of veiled Life, Life a form of veiled Consciousness,"[134] defeats scientific naturalism's refusal to consider "nonnatural" factors.[135]

What about nontheistic religions? Buddhism, at least in its original form, does not posit a creator of any sort (of which more below). Even the more

131. For details and sources, see Connolly, *John Henry Newman,* chap. 3.
132. A classic essay is Foster's three-part article in *Mind,* "The Christian Doctrine of Creation and the Rise of Modern Natural Science" (1934-1936).
133. Parsania, "Unseen and Visible," p. 158. As is well known, S. H. Nasr is a relentless Muslim critic of scientific naturalism (and at times even many scientific theories of origins of creation); see, e.g., his "Question of Cosmogenesis," pp. 181-84.
134. Aurobindo (Ghose), *The Life Divine,* book 1 (quotations from pp. 4, 5, respectively).
135. As exposited by K. Ward, *Religion and Creation,* p. 94.

theistically oriented cluster of Mahayana traditions usually refuses to take God as the ultimate explanation. Something similar applies to the nontheistic Vaisesika Hindu tradition. Its proponents do not need — at least in principle — God as an intellectual principle as they go about empirical and scientific study of the world.[136] Yet another, in many ways similar, tradition is the Nyāya tradition with its focus on logic and reasoning (which, however, leans more toward theism). That said, nearly all Hindu traditions, while opposed to all notions of *creatio ex nihilo,* provide theistic explanations of the emergence of the cosmos. And it is clear without saying that God is the ultimate origin, sustainer, and goal of all Abrahamic theologies. To that list could be added many more religions, such as Shintoism. Even more importantly, all religious traditions, including forms of nontheist Buddhism and Hinduism, differ radically from the current scientific naturalism in their belief about the spirit(ual) constituting the origin of everything rather than the physical. In that sense, calling Theravada Buddhism, for example, atheistic is highly problematic. It's refusal to introduce God into world-explanation does not lead it to embrace physical as the primary "stuff."

We begin, first, with constructive work toward a trinitarian Christian theology of creation, to be engaged later with views from other faith traditions and contemporary scientific cosmologies. The next chapter will attempt a theological construction of nature as creation. A distinctively trinitarian account of creation, in chapter 4, will then build on that basis.

136. See further, Clooney, *Hindu God, Christian God,* pp. 26-27.

3. Nature as Creation: A Theological Interpretation

Nature in Modernity

Alienation and Disengagement

It was of course in the seventeenth century that the radical reinterpretation of nature happened due to the Enlightenment and scientific revolution. The reworked concept of nature is characterized by several interrelated features: quantification, mechanization, seeing nature as "other," and secularization.[1] The image of a machine rather than a living organism became dominant.[2] The autonomy of nature pushed to the margins the idea of God as the first cause.[3] Understandably, this "secular"[4] interpretation of nature did not please all, even outside theological circles. New types of vitalistic conceptions were put forth,[5] but these attempts were hardly able to turn the tide.

1. Westfall, "Scientific Revolution," pp. 86-87 particularly.
2. For nature as machine, see McGrath, *ScT* 1:107-10.
3. Ironically, modernity's project of the domination of nature and utilitarianism was prepared in part by the Italian Renaissance humanists (Pico della Mirandola, Giannozzo Manetti, Marsilio Ficino, etc.), who one-sidedly emphasized the difference of humanity from (or supremacy over) the rest of creation (Trinkaus, *In Our Image*). Among the Enlightenment advocates, none surpasses Francis Bacon (Bauckham, *Living with Other Creatures*, pp. 47-58); see also Moltmann, *God for a Secular Society*, pp. 98-99.
4. *Trinity and Revelation* (chap. 9) analyzes the complex issue of secularism and its implications.
5. For details and sources, see McGrath, *ScT* 1:101-2.

The late British theologian Colin Gunton's *Enlightenment and Alienation* argues strongly that deficient accounts of the doctrine of creation have resulted in alienation as well as "disengagement" and "displacement." As a result of the "tearing apart of belief and knowledge," alienation entered in modernity.[6] Disengagement followed, that is, "standing apart from each other and the world and treating the other as external, as mere object."[7] Behind modernity's tendency to objectify lies its hidden dualism, which "attempts to split a complex reality into polar opposites, such as spirit and matter, value and fact, faith and reason, transcendent and immanent, usually favoring one over the other."[8] A tragic corollary of the distancing has to do with the environment due to human desire for autonomy.[9] Other people and nature are used instrumentally, as a tool of "technocratic attitude,"[10] rather than experienced relationally and in terms of mutual belonging. It also rips from nature any purpose.[11]

A related lacuna of modernity is its perverted vision of rationality. It is not that reason itself is perverted, but rather that its alleged autonomy as the human person becomes the "seat of rationality,"[12] pushing aside God, the Creator. When God as the unifying factor for creation is rejected,[13] the empty place is filled with the modernist category of the "universal."[14] Human reason and universals take the place of God. The most ironic implication of the modern denial of a personal Creator is what Gunton rightly names "modern pantheism," which simply means that "when the being of the world is no longer attributed to the personal agency of God it is itself made the bearer of divine or creative powers."[15]

Rather than human liberation and integration with nature, a new kind of "slavery" emerges[16] in the world left under the power of human reason alone, which ultimately "operates deceptively or oppressively."[17] In other words, when the true "one," God, is displaced, "false and alienating gods rush in to fill the

---

6. Gunton, *Enlightenment and Alienation,* p. 5; see also Havel, *Open Letters,* cited in Gunton, *The One, the Three, and the Many,* p. 71.

7. Gunton, *The One, the Three, and the Many,* p. 14.

8. Zimmermann, *Incarnational Humanism,* p. 11.

9. Gunton, *The One, the Three, and the Many,* pp. 19-20.

10. Gunton, *The One, the Three, and the Many,* p. 14.

11. Shakespeare, *Radical Orthodoxy,* Kindle #165 (hereafter K).

12. Gunton, *The One, the Three, and the Many,* p. 101.

13. Gunton, *The One, the Three, and the Many,* p. 28; see also p. 101.

14. Gunton, *The One, the Three, and the Many,* p. 34.

15. Gunton, *The Triune Creator,* p. 37; also pp. 37-39, 170-75.

16. Gunton, *The One, the Three, and the Many,* pp. 28-29.

17. Gunton, *The One, the Three, and the Many,* p. 31.

vacancy."[18] The oppression may express itself politically, socially, and in relation to nature. Rather than diversity and plurality, homogeneity and totalitarianism lie on the horizon for the world of modernity.[19]

"Secularism" and the Flattening of Ontology

Not all are convinced of the legitimacy of such absolutely irreversible breaks in intellectual history as Gunton and many others claim about modernity. Radical Orthodoxy maintains that modernity is rather a continuation of developments started in the late medieval period under the tutelage of Scotus and his school, which came to their zenith with Descartes and Kant.[20] Consequently, "late" modernity represents not a break in but rather an intensification of modernity.[21]

In the Radical Orthodox assessment, the Scotist view of univocity has rendered "all existence merely phenomenal and ephemeral, lacking altogether in depth, or any symbolic pointing beyond itself towards either eternal truth or abiding human values."[22] Catherine Pickstock lists the main complaints against Scotist philosophy in this way: "the shift towards a univocal ontology, knowledge as representation, and causality as primarily efficient, is philosophically questionable and has negative implications for the upholding of a Christian vision and for the synthesis of theology and philosophy."[23]

This development brought about "secularism," a radical shift from the time when "there was no 'secular.'"[24] What is deeply ironic, however, is that what modernity and postmodernity advocate as nonreligious secularism is at its core deeply religious and fundamentally theological. If the "'scientific' social theories are themselves theologies or anti-theologies in disguise,"[25] how much more does natural sciences' alleged "neutral" atheism have religious/

---

18. Gunton, *The One, the Three, and the Many*, p. 38.

19. See Gunton, *The One, the Three, and the Many*, pp. 28-40.

20. Pickstock, "Duns Scotus," p. 545.

21. As argued in detail in Pickstock, *After Writing*, chaps. 1; 2; 3; see also Milbank, *Theology and Social Theory*, chap. 10 and passim; G. Ward, *Cities of God*, p. 81 and passim.

22. Pickstock, "Duns Scotus," p. 545; see also Pickstock, *After Writing*, pp. 122-23 and passim.

23. Pickstock, "Duns Scotus," p. 544. Duns Scotus gives the classic definition in *Ordinatio* I, d. 3, part 1, q. 2, #26 (in *Philosophical Writings*, p. 20).

24. Milbank, *Theology and Social Theory*, p. 9.

25. Milbank, *Theology and Social Theory*, p. 3.

theological implications? In other words, for Radical Orthodoxy, there is no "neutral" secularism.[26] This is the positive insight of Radical Orthodoxy's view of secularism, notwithstanding whether or not the Scotus-driven "modernity" argument stands historical scrutiny.[27] It points to the dominant philosophical-theological orientations of modernity and its appraisal of nature. They are in direct opposition to Christian tradition's ontology of participation,[28] the idea that being is nothing in itself but is based on its relatedness and dependence on the Creator.[29]

Enter postmodern thinkers, particularly of the Continental tradition, and we note that the view of nature in modernity is challenged by massive forces of deconstruction. A brief engagement of that rhetoric tells me that there may have been a much more abrupt break between modernity and late-modernity/postmodernity than what Radical Orthodoxy is willing to admit.

The Postmodern Deconstruction of Nature

Continental postmodern philosophy is not only deconstructing the rationality and objectivity of concepts and values;[30] importantly to this discussion, it also maintains that "nature is not possessed of the epistemological finality and inevitability implied by the category of the *given;* it is created in the process of historical construction, and may be reconstructed as and when required."[31]

---

26. Milbank, *Theology and Social Theory,* p. 280.

27. I myself for one doubt if Scotus can be made the "first modernist"; similarly, several critics such as D. Ford, "Radical Orthodoxy and the Future of British Theology" and "A Response to Catherine Pickstock"; Cross, "Where Angels Fear to Tread." In defense of Scotus, see T. Williams, "The Doctrine of Univocity," pp. 579-80. Whereas for the British Radical Orthodox theologians Duns Scotus becomes the villain of history, for the British Reformed theologian Gunton, a significant precursor to modernity is rather William of Ockham, as his thoughts headed toward a mechanistic understanding of the relationship between God and world, making room for the rise of science. See particularly Gunton, "The Doctrine of Creation," p. 151.

28. For a short statement, see J. K. A. Smith, *Introducing Radical Orthodoxy,* pp. 74-75, 193-95.

29. Milbank, *The Word Made Strange,* p. 44; see further, Pickstock, *After Writing,* pp. 121-34. Milbank rightly underlines that matter needs transcendence to be "real" ("Materialism and Transcendence," pp. 393-426).

30. A highly useful and inspiring account is given in D. Harvey, *Condition of Postmodernity.* In this section I am indebted to McGrath, *ScT* 1:110-24.

31. McGrath, *ScT* 1:111.

Not surprisingly, traditional metaphysics is virtually thrown out and transcendence rejected.[32]

A corollary implication among many postmodernists is that even natural sciences are therefore but social constructions and "stories," no more reliable than, say, political opinions. They push the claim of the perspectival and relativistic nature of human knowing to its logical end. Where modernists see "purpose, design, hierarchy, centring, and selection," these postmodernists discern "play, chance, anarchy, dispersal, and combination."[33] The deconstruction of natural sciences' results and rationality was already present in the programmatic essay by Jean-François Lyotard, *The Postmodern Condition,* which believes the sciences are based on "paralogy," a form of faulty and contradictory reasoning, featuring inconsistencies and contradictions.[34]

This postmodern rebuttal of the rationality of the scientific enterprise is both misguided and deeply biased. Many of the claims of these postmodern "philosophers of science" — who are usually absent any needed training in natural sciences altogether — carry no philosophical or scientific value.[35] Just consider the enormous validity of mathematical explanation in all physical sciences.[36] Although not every physicist is ready to say exactly what the Oxford University mathematical physicist Roger Penrose claims — "mathematical truth is absolute, external, and eternal, and not based on man-made criteria; and . . . mathematical objects have a timeless existence of their own, not dependent on human society nor on particular physical objects"[37] — even a more moderate statement of the value of mathematics suffices to dismantle abstract postmodern philosophical rebuttals. While contemporary philosophy of science should not return to the idyllic, naive, and "precritical" ethos of modern science with its utopia of everlasting, smooth progress, neither are there any grounds for embracing the ill-informed and destructive criticism of sciences among deconstructive postmodernists. Critical realism's rejection of foundationalism — the cornerstone of modernist epistemology — does not have to mean a shift to nonfoundationalism if that means the equally naive idea that something reasonable can be said without any reference to the world "outside the text."

32. For commentary, see Zimmermann, *Incarnational Humanism,* pp. 175-89.

33. Hassan, *Dismemberment of Orpheus,* pp. 267-68; cited in McGrath, *ScT* 1:121-22.

34. Lyotard, *Postmodern Condition,* p. 60.

35. For a seasoned critique of postmodern deconstruction of natural science, consult Gross, Levitt, and Lewis, eds., *Flight from Science and Reason;* Koertge, *A House Built on Sand.*

36. McGrath, *ScT* 1:213.

37. Penrose, "Modern Physicist's View"; cited in McGrath, *ScT* 1:213.

Although the modernist construction of nature as autonomous and the postmodern deconstruction of its rational basis are both mistaken in theological assessment, both moves make a critical positive statement for the purposes of this discussion, namely, that nature is a socially constructed concept.

Nature as Creation: A Theological Account

Nature as a Socially Constructed Category

In its current usage, the term "nature" has three distinct meanings: the physical world as studied by the natural sciences, human nature (as distinct from, but not unrelated to, nonhuman creatures), and, when used "as a 'surface' concept, the term refers to ordinarily observable features of the world" and finds expression particularly in the contemporary distinction between nature and the urban (or the natural and the human-built) environment.[38] Outside philosophical-scientific interpretations, nature has been viewed variously in different cultural epochs and throughout Christian piety and thinking. In premodern cultures nature was often depicted in hostile and dangerous terms. It represented reality untamed and threatening. The further into the past one goes, the more dramatically this can be seen, culminating in mythical conceptions of nature "monsters." This differs dramatically from the modern and contemporary Western mind-set, which invests nature with particular innocence and nostalgia. The latter attitude was of course prepared by Romantic thinkers such as the Frenchman Rousseau and the German Goethe, not to ignore English Romanticism. In the settlement of the new continent, the idyllic wilderness mentality is yet another expression of that same orientation.[39] Christian tradition knows a number of images and impressions of nature, such as Calvin's "theater" and "book." But romanticization is not limited to Western cultures; it is also a current trend among some Indian and Hindu thinkers.[40]

As our discussion so far in this chapter clearly indicates, against commonsense intuitions, "nature" is neither a given nor an innocent concept.[41]

---

38. McGrath, *ScT* 1:81-82 (citation on p. 82), following the outline of Soper, *What Is Nature?* pp. 155-56.

39. See further, McGrath, *ScT* 1:82-85, 102-5.

40. Patton, "Nature Romanticism," pp. 39-58.

41. Still unsurpassed is the massive terminological study by C. S. Lewis, *Studies in Words*, pp. 24-74. This section is deeply indebted to the detailed investigation in McGrath, *ScT* 1, chap. 3, including its excellent and varied sources.

"Nature is already an interpreted category,"[42] in other words, a socially constructed category.[43] Even expressions such as "natural" are far from "natural"![44] Socially constructed and mediated, "nature" is "not an objective entity in its own right," and therefore nature's intellectual justification and merit pose a significant task for a contemporary constructive Christian theology.[45] Against common assumptions, even natural sciences are not free from the burden of interpretation: neither scientific observations nor their interpretations are interest-free enterprises.[46] As John Hick reminded us decades ago, our seeing of the world is *seeing-as.*[47] This is not to deconstruct the whole project of human perception of the world, any more than it is to debunk the rationality of the scientific enterprise. Rather, it is a rejecting of the foundationalism and "indubitable certainty" of modernity, on the one hand, and an acknowledgment of the positive importance of the humble and "perspectival" explanations of late modern epistemologies on the other. The acknowledgment of the interpreted nature of "nature" also opens up the possibility and legitimacy of a religious, theological reading of nature as creation.

Embracing the notion of the socially constructed and historical nature of "nature" does not have to mean that therefore the whole concept of nature is subsumed under social and historical categories. And of course, it is clear without saying — and it hardly takes a philosophical defense of critical realism to say it — that "nature" as the cosmos exists. The social construction argument is not denying the real existence of nature per se. What it is denying is an essential understanding of nature that assumes that there is only one way of seeing nature.

The Interpretive Nature of "Nature" as a Theological Asset

Although traditional Christian intuitions may be shaken by the claim that nature is a socially constructed concept, even more shaking should happen in the camp of naive naturalists who take for granted "the belief that there is

42. McGrath, *ScT* 1:113, emphasis in original.

43. See Evernden, *Social Creation of Nature.*

44. See Fish, *Doing What Comes Naturally.*

45. McGrath, *ScT* 1:87. For an important discussion, see Soulé, "Social Siege of Nature," pp. 137-70.

46. For a formative argumentation, see Hanson, *Patterns of Discovery,* chap. 1.

47. Hick, *An Interpretation of Religion,* pp. 140-42; Kellenberger, "'Seeing-as' in Religion," pp. 101-8.

some objective concept of 'nature' in the first place, which may be discovered by unbiased observation and reflection."[48] Modernity's account of nature as a self-sustaining entity, divorced from the Creator, discussed above, hardly can be said to be innocent, any more than the contemporary "scientific-naturalist" cum atheistic approaches. In one word: this project seeks to dismantle once and for all the older "essential" concept of nature for the sake of the socially constructed one.

The contested nature of "nature" should be welcomed by theologians as it gives new and unsurpassed resources in loading the concept with a robust trinitarian theological meaning. At the same time, theologians should be constantly reminded of the impossibility of speaking properly of "natural theology," "natural knowledge of God," or "natural law" unless nature's meaning is determined. It is too bad that even the most recent major theological accounts of the doctrine of creation are basically silent about this essential task.[49]

Against all a-theistic accounts, whether philosophical or "scientific," which make the world self-originating and self-sustaining, as well against poststructuralist accounts that are unable to "save appearances," Christian theology "re-describes the created world, not as nothing, nor indeed as any self-sufficient something, but as the real testimony and loving expression of God who donates the ideal to the real that we might make it so."[50] In other words: "Understanding nature as God's creation means seeing it as neither divine nor demonic, but viewing it as 'the world.'" It is contingent and it is orderly, so it can be studied. But even that which can be studied by means of the natural sciences is not outside but rather within creation. God is the Creator of "all things visible and invisible," says the creed. Seeing nature as God's creation also reminds us of its enslavement and eager expectation of the final redemption (Rom. 8:19-21).[51]

In this light it seems odd to me that Pannenberg argues for the necessity of speaking of "nature" rather than "creation" in theology. Indeed, he goes so far as to contend that "from many aspects, the word 'creation,' or in any case its usual understanding, is not very appropriate for a theology of nature."[52] I suspect behind Pannenberg's refusal to use creation as a concept lies his wide-

---

48. McGrath, *ScT* 1:88. As will be discussed in more detail, the socially constructed nature of nature has been a cause of headache for environmentalists!

49. The rule-confirming exception is the trilogy by McGrath, *Scientific Theology*.

50. Blond, "Perception," p. 221.

51. Moltmann, *God in Creation*, pp. 38-40; see p. 39.

52. Pannenberg, *Toward a Theology of Nature*, p. 72; see McGrath, *ScT* 1:135-6 for a similar kind of critique.

spread fear of the "ghetto mentality" of much of Christian theology, particularly among the neo-orthodox. Hence, the term "nature" would communicate appropriately to the secular audience. Behind this legitimate concern, however, is a twofold problematic assumption. First, it seems totally oblivious to the contested nature of the category of "nature" and assumes that all in the secular sphere will agree on its meaning. Second, it seems to assume that Christians can bring into the conversation with nonbelievers the theological meaning of creation even though that term is not used — as if theological language would not matter. I doubt both of these premises and therefore recommend a robust use of the category of creation when talking about the theological meaning of nature. Rather than blocking dialogue with scientists, it will facilitate it by making that particular perspective transparent and amenable for debate.

The insight that Christian theology reads nature as *creation* is deeply embedded in tradition. Definitely it was part of the way nature was read in the Middle Ages, as M. D. Chenu has convincingly argued with reference to the importance of signs ("signification"): "All natural or historical reality possessed a *signification* which transcended its crude reality and which a certain symbolic dimension of that reality would reveal to man's mind." This meant nothing less than that this "[g]iving an account of things involved more than explaining them by reference to their internal causes" as the contemporary natural scientific and secular mind-set does, but rather "it involved discovering the dimension of a mystery."[53] Christian theology should not be ashamed of this process of signification — against all postmodern rebuttals of claiming any intrinsic meaning to the signs. As argued above, in itself — apart from a philosophical, theological, or, say, aesthetic interpretation — nature lacks inherent meaning as a sign. It is ambiguous and can be read in various ways. But as soon as nature is read as the handiwork of the loving triune Creator, it assigns — or better, re-cognizes — this inherent significatory meaning in the work of God.[54]

Ultimately, acknowledging nature as creation leads to "thanksgiving for the gift of creation and for the community found in it, and adoring praise of the Creator." The creation psalms (8, 19, 104, among others) provide a marvelous template.[55] While it is questionable whether it is useful to speak of creation as "sacrament,"[56] certainly it has a sacramental ring to it particularly in relation

53. Chenu, *Nature, Man and Society*, p. 102; cited in McGrath, *ScT* 1:194.
54. See further, McGrath, *ScT* 1:194.
55. Moltmann, *God in Creation*, p. 70.
56. See Pannenberg, *ST* 2:137-38, on nature as sacrament.

to the eucharistic celebration. From God's creation we receive gifts and give back to God God's own.[57]

If nature is creation, then it means that traces of the Creator can be discerned therein. Indeed, that is the case. To that effect, a robust trinitarian natural theology was constructed in *Trinity and Revelation* (chap. 8), to which the reader is referred.

Having established nature as creation, before turning to the task of constructing a *trinitarian* theology of creation, let us briefly delve into the ancient problem of how "nature," Christianly understood as creation, relates to "grace," God's saving and healing purposes for what is created. Here our interest in this topic is limited to the implications for the study of nature (as creation).

The Graced Nature and the Opportunity for Scientific Investigation

Over against the efforts to pit "nature" against "grace" — the tendency that of course came to its zenith in Reformation theologies — Aquinas established that "grace does not destroy nature but perfects it" (*ST* 1.1.8). While Thomas did not mean it that way, subsequent scholastic tradition distinguished nature from grace in a way that seemed to leave nature autonomous and devoid of grace, the so-called pure nature concept.[58] It is clear without saying that the concept of "pure nature" "undermines the deepest truth of nature itself — the truth that nature is created *ex nihilo,* and that it bears within itself and expresses the liberality and generosity of the Creator."[59] The result is secularization. No need to mention that these implications are totally foreign to Thomas and the scholastic tradition.

This is where Radical Orthodox theologian Milbank enters the discussion. He outlines two possible theological responses to the nature-grace dialectic. One approach "supernaturalizes the natural," that is, it looks at nature as God's creation, from a theological point of view. The other response, which Milbank believes — mistakenly — to be the legacy of Rahner, "'naturalizes the supernatural.' In its enthusiasm to bring harmony between nature and grace, it empties grace of all real content. Theology has nothing to say to the world, which is granted its own charter of independence. . . . The world has to be analysed by non-theological, non-Christian disciplines such as social science

---

57. See Moltmann, *God in Creation,* p. 71.
58. See Spaemann, *Philosophische Essays,* pp. 26-27.
59. Healy, "Henri de Lubac," p. 546. A useful discussion is Schmitz, *The Gift.*

and psychology. Theology then comes along and adds a Christian gloss to the facts which these sciences uncover."[60] While Milbank makes the valid claim that there are instances in which the secular has taken over and so suppresses the theological interpretation of nature as creation, he errs when he locates that mistake in contemporary Roman Catholic theology. That tendency is to be sought in *secular* sciences, whether humanistic or naturalist. In contrast, the mid-twentieth-century Roman Catholic theology from which Rahner drew great resources, often named *nouvelle théologie* (Henri de Lubac), helped correct the post-Thomas secularizing development of a nature-grace dialectic. Somewhat similarly to the Eastern Orthodox tradition (but more or less independently as far as I can tell), Lubac insisted that nature is always graced, coming from the loving, creative, and sustaining work of God.[61] As gift, nature cannot be autonomous. As an ordered creation, it can be approached with the help of reason, another gift of God.

This holding of nature and grace tightly together has significant implications for the scientific study of nature. Unlike modern, atheistic, and scientific-naturalist views, Christian theology claims that the orderliness that makes possible scientific investigation is embedded inherently in the nature of "nature" as creation.[62] "The universe might have been a disorderly chaos, rather than an orderly cosmos."[63] The Christian view of nature as creation derives from God, the Creator, the built-in rationality of nature that makes possible all scientific study.[64] Rightly, Thomas F. Torrance named it "contingent rationality."[65] For this Scottish theologian, there is an inherent rationality in the order of space and time, and hence, it can be investigated. The biblical teaching on creation, as will be noticed below, insists on the orderly nature of the cosmos, which makes study and reflection on its regularity possible. Thomas F. Torrance's favored notion of "contingent rationality" corresponds to this observation: there is rationality and regularity inherent in the created order of space-time.

The theological construction of nature as creation not only allows but also even calls for a theological account of the beginnings and source, that is, the doctrine of creation. To be more precise, a distinctively Christian theology of creation is trinitarian. To that we turn next, before in the subsequent chapter relating that theological account with the most recent scientific interpretations.

60. As interpreted by Shakespeare, *Radical Orthodoxy*, K #403-10.
61. See the important discussion in Milbank, *The Suspended Middle*.
62. See Heller, "Scientific Rationality," pp. 141-50.
63. Polkinghorne, *Science and Creation*, p. 20.
64. See Pedersen, "Christian Belief," p. 125.
65. Torrance, *Divine and Contingent Order*, pp. 3, 22.

4. A Trinitarian Theology of Creation

In Search of an Authentic Trinitarian Account of Creation

The One Creator as an Eternal Communion of Father, Son, and Spirit

Similar to the rest of the divine economy — God's "outward" works — creation is the united work of Father, Son, and Spirit.[1] This is to follow the ancient rule of the indivisibility of the works of the Trinity *ad extra* as well as the foundational guidelines of contemporary trinitarian theology according to which all human knowledge of God is based on the economy of salvation (as discussed in *Trinity and Revelation,* chap. 11).

Moltmann rightly reminds us that before we ask the question "what does God mean for the world which he creates and sustains?" we should consider: "what does it mean for God to be the Creator of a world which is different from him, and is yet designed to correspond to him? What does this creation mean for God?"[2] Creation is first and foremost a statement about God. Luther famously taught that the words "I believe in God, the Father almighty, CREATOR of heaven and earth" are "the shortest possible way of describing and illustrating the nature, will, acts, and work of God the Father."[3] Materially the Protestant Reformer was following the medieval Catholic mystic

---

1. See Polkinghorne, "Universe in a Trinitarian Perspective," chap. 3.
2. Moltmann, *God in Creation,* p. 72.
3. "The First Article [of the Creed]," in Luther, *Large Catechism,* in *The Book of Concord,* p. 432.

Pseudo-Dionysius the Areopagite, who understood creation to be so deeply infused with the presence of God that it allowed people to be aware of God, the Creator.[4]

As established in *Trinity and Revelation* (chap. 11), the one God of the Bible exists as an eternal communion of love — Father, Son, and Spirit. Trinity speaks of interrelatedness, relationality, dynamic mutual conditioning, communion, community (chap. 12). These are important values that fund the doctrine of creation in relation to our dynamic, evolving, and emerging view of the world in the sciences.

While Christian tradition has always attributed the creation to the God of the Bible, it has not always been successful in establishing a distinctively *trinitarian* account of creation.[5] Even luminaries such as Thomas Aquinas seem to have conceived creation predominantly as the work of the one God as the "first cause."[6] Thomas's approach in this respect differs from those of some of his predecessors, particularly the Cappadocian Saint Basil: "And in the creation bethink thee first, I pray thee, of the original cause of all things that are made, the Father; of the creative cause, the Son; of the perfecting cause, the Spirit; so that the ministering spirits subsist by the will of the Father, are brought into being by the operation of the Son, and perfected by the presence of the Spirit."[7]

As with the trinitarian doctrine itself, theology has to be willing to live in the dynamic tension between modalism that denies true diversity and tritheism that compromises monotheism. In other words, constructive theology must incorporate into its account the valid intuitions of tradition's emphasis on God as "single subject," which bespeaks unity and undividedness, as well as current theology's desire for threeness, which highlights communion, diversity, and multiplicity. To do so, it is essential to see that creation, reconciliation, and consummation as the "action of the one God in relation to the world is not wholly different from the action in his trinitarian life."[8] Creative work is not so "external" to divine life as to be distanced and meaningless. Nor is creative work so "internal" to divine life as to lead to pantheism.[9] When that continu-

---

4. Pseudo-Dionysius, *Divine Names*, p. 53.

5. Luther, *Lectures on Genesis 1–5*; *LW* 1:9; for an important comment, see Prenter, *Spiritus Creator*, p. 192.

6. Aquinas, *ST* 1.44.1.

7. Basil, *On the Holy Spirit* 16.38; for a delightful trinitarian account of creation in Luther, see *LW* 1:9.

8. Pannenberg, *ST* 2:5.

9. This point was made skillfully by John of Damascus, *Orthodox Faith* 1.7.

ing dynamic is kept, it is beneficial — differently from tradition — to speak of the "real multiplicity within the unity of the divine action," which is neither mere appearance nor "proper only to the creaturely side. It is proper to God's own action as well." Just think of the incarnation as an example of the work that is "grounded in the trinitarian plurality of the divine life." Similarly, the whole economy of salvation from creation to sustenance to reconciliation to consummation is a joint work of Father, Son, and Spirit, the trinitarian God.[10]

This is all good as far as Christian theology is concerned. What about other religions, to whom all talk about the triune God is either meaningless or a stumbling block? Although the detailed investigation of myths of origins and cosmologies in four other faith traditions has to wait until the next chapter, a tentative statement is appropriate here before proceeding to the Christian exposition.

Trinity and Interfaith Hospitality?

In terms of interfaith hospitality, we should not assume that Christian theology chooses for the main template a *trinitarian* approach. But is that a choice? Not really. For Christian tradition to stay faithful to its particular identity, and so contribute to interfaith hospitality by making space for true difference between dialogue partners, a trinitarian approach to creation is not so much a choice as a given. While the many details of the trinitarian basis of the Christian confession of God, based on the Jewish Scriptures in light of the coming of Jesus Christ sent by the Father in the power of the Spirit, are worked out in *Trinity and Revelation* (chap. 11), let it suffice to say here that the "first word" of God said in Christian Scriptures, the NT, is Father, Son, and Spirit. The implications of this uncompromising starting point has to be negotiated with both the Jewish and the Islamic confessions.

It is true that, particularly in relation to our two Abrahamic sister faiths, the choice has to be defended. "If the Trinitarian concept of God is distinctive to Christianity, then Islam exists, at least in part, as a decisive rejection of that concept" with its "unitarian thesis" based on the uncompromising confession of *Tawhid,* the unity of God.[11] According to the Sufi philosopher S. H. Nasr, both ancient cosmologies and the (current) Islamic cosmology are based on the uncompromising "idea of Unity" *(al-Tawḥīd).* For Muslims, it is "the most

---

10. Pannenberg, *ST* 2:8-9.
11. K. Ward, *Religion and Creation,* p. 59.

basic principle upon which all else depends."[12] In that sense — ironically from the Christian point of view — Islam's "basic idea of God is a return to . . . the view that God enters into a specific covenant relation with a particular group of people."[13]

What about Hinduism and its alleged trinitarian structure? Would those resources help develop a "trinitarian" Hindu theology of origins? *Trinity and Revelation* (chap. 15) attempts a detailed comparison between the Christian Trinity and Hindu notions of Trimurti or *saccidananda*. The first one has to do with the "trinity" of classical deities, namely, Brahma, Vishnu, and Siva. Hindu theology has not taken to the comparison, if for no other reason than because the worship of Brahma has almost disappeared and the three deities of Hinduism were never conceived as separate but rather as manifestations of the one and same One. A bit more promising is the latter: *sat* means "being"; *cit,* "thought"; and *ananda,* "peace." Hence, both some Hindus and Christians have surmised that herein can be seen Father, Son, and Spirit, respectively, at work. A careful, detailed comparison shows that, ultimately, those seeming similarities are just that — *seeming* similarities. When it comes to Buddhism, the only thinkable pointer to Trinity could be found in the Mahayana tradition's concept of sunyata (emptiness). Our investigation in *Trinity and Revelation* (chap. 15) came to a similar conclusion with Hinduism.

As mentioned, for the sake of an authentic, hospitable dialogue each faith tradition must clarify its necessary identity-forming commitments and, at the same time, let the other do the same. On that basis, a continuing, careful, detailed comparison of notes and dialogue is both meaningful and promising.

With these desiderata in mind, let us first highlight the distinctive work of each of the trinitarian persons, Father, Son, and Spirit. That will save us from overly abstract trinitarian speculation; rather — following the famous "Rahner rule" (the economic Trinity is the immanent and the immanent is the economic Trinity) — we will attempt some modest and grateful insights into God on the basis of what God is doing in the world. We will then be in a place to reflect on the God-world relationship in a trinitarian context, particularly in light of the mediatory work of Christ. An important corollary aspect of that investigation is to inquire into the possibility and conditions of the existence of creation as independent of (yet closely related to) the Creator. Finally, the doctrine of creation should be linked intentionally with the eschatological hope (a theme, naturally, to be discussed in detail in the section on eschatology).

12. Nasr, *Introduction to Islamic Cosmological Doctrines,* p. 4.
13. K. Ward, *Religion and Creation,* p. 59.

The Love and Goodness of the Father

The way the Bible speaks of God is to speak of divine love. Theologically put: with the same love that the Father loves the Son in the Spirit, the world is "loved" into being and sustained until it finds its consummation in the return to the Creator. Summarizing the meaning of the Apostles' Creed in his *Confession concerning Christ's Supper* (1528), Luther presents the theology of divine giving in an integral trinitarian grammar:

> These are the three persons and one God, who has given himself to us all wholly and completely, with all that he is and has. The Father gives himself to us, with heaven and earth and all the creatures, in order that they may serve us and benefit us. But this gift has become obscured and useless through Adam's fall. Therefore the Son himself subsequently gave himself and bestowed all his works, sufferings, wisdom, and righteousness, and reconciled us to the Father, in order that restored to life and righteousness, we might also know and have the Father and his gifts. But because this grace would benefit no one if it remained so profoundly hidden and could not come to us, the Holy Spirit comes and gives himself to us also, wholly and completely.[14]

In contrast to human love, the divine love reaches out to those who are not worthy in order to make them valuable.[15] The contemporary Lutheran theologian Pannenberg aptly summarizes this long tradition: "God had only one reason to create a world, the reason that is proclaimed in the act of creation itself, namely, his own divine being and in distinction from him."[16] Rightly Oswald Bayer, yet another contemporary Lutheran, notes that the understanding of a "generous God" known by the Reformers "who is continuously giving, sharply contradicts the activism that is advocated in the present age, which wants nothing to be given as a gift. But God is categorically the one who gives."[17] Talk about divine hospitality![18] Another way of saying this is to speak of God's goodness. Goodness is God's essential nature.[19] The key message of Jesus in the announcement of the dawning of the righteous rule of the Father

14. *LW* 37:366; WA 26:505-6.
15. For a fine exposition, see Bayer, *Martin Luther's Theology*, pp. 95-119.
16. Pannenberg, *ST* 2:20.
17. Bayer, *Martin Luther's Theology*, p. 98.
18. For discussion of "divine hospitality," see *Trinity and Revelation*, chap. 13.
19. Bayer, *Martin Luther's Theology*, p. 96.

was the unconditional and liberal goodness toward his creation and creatures: "God shows himself to be Father by caring for his creatures (Matt. 6:26; cf. Luke 12:30). He causes his sun to shine and his rain to fall on the bad as well as the good (Matt. 5:45). . . . He lets himself be invoked as Father, and like earthly fathers, and even more than they, he grants good things to his children when they ask (Matt. 7:11)."[20]

In a trinitarian grammar, we can speak of the Father, who "[i]n all the creatures to which he addresses his love . . . loves the Son," and this love is mediated through the Son.[21] Herein is the possibility of creation distinct from God. The Son's self-distinction from the Father "is the origin of all that differs from the Father, and therefore of the creatures' independence vis-à-vis the Father."[22] In this self-distinction — in the mediatorial agency — is the key to the independence of both God from the world and the world from God. From the divine side, "precisely because God the Father is thus intrinsically related to the Son and the Spirit, he is not bound always to have a world around him . . . and therefore can be held to create freely."[23] From the creaturely side, the relative independence — to the point that the creature may also choose to separate himself or herself from the Creator — is conditioned on the distinction from the Father of the Son. As the Reformed theologian Gunton puts it, "to create in the Son means to create by the mediation of the one who is the way of God out into that which is not himself."[24] The same is expressed in the famous words of the Catholic thinker Rahner: "When God wants to be what is not God, man comes to be," and this we can know from the logic of the incarnation.[25] Whereas the eternal Son mediates the possibility of creaturely life vis-à-vis the Father, the earthly Jesus shows humans the true essence of creaturely freedom, namely, reciprocal love and willing submission to the will of the Father.[26]

20. Pannenberg, ST 1:259; so also Luther, The Small Catechism, in The Book of Concord, pp. 354-55.

21. Pannenberg, ST 2:21.

22. Pannenberg, ST 2:22.

23. Gunton, The Triune Creator, p. 67.

24. Gunton, The Triune Creator, p. 143.

25. Rahner, Foundations, p. 225.

26. See Pannenberg, ST 2:22-23.

The Mediating Role of Christ

The Cosmic Christ

There is a link between the NT idea of Christ as Logos and the creative power of the *dabar* of Yahweh. Elaborating on this theme, theological tradition looked not only into the OT background but also — as constructive theology has always done — into the surrounding pagan resources. In Middle Platonism there came to its zenith the development of the ancient *logos* idea according to which things created (fashioned, to be more precise) corresponded to the Ideas or divine *nous*. The obvious Christian contextualization, then, emerged in which "the participation of the eternal Son in the act of creation with the help of the idea that the Logos corresponds to the divine intellect, which from all eternity contains within itself the images of things, the ideas."[27]

Tradition also found in the NT a correlation between the christological Wisdom motif (Col. 2:9) and the OT Sophia.[28] Speaking of Christ, Origen maintains that "all the creative power of the coming creation was included in this very existence of Wisdom"[29] that eternally derives from the Father. This "Wisdom was the beginning of the ways of God . . . forming beforehand and containing within herself the species and beginnings of all creatures, [and] must we understand her to be the Word of God."[30]

Significantly in the OT, this agent of Wisdom is female, Lady Wisdom (Prov. 1:20-33; Sirach 24; Wisdom 1:4-6; 7:22-23; 8:1). Contemporary female theologians have rightly highlighted the importance of the linking in early Christian intuitions of the OT idea of wisdom as Sophia and her female nature. According to Elizabeth Johnson, early Palestinian Christianity envisioned Jesus as God's Sophia.[31] The postcolonial Chinese American Kwok Pui-lan notes how the vision of Jesus as Sophia-God may help people conceive of creation as "an organic model" in search of the healing of creation and how well it connects with some wisdom traditions in Asia and beyond.[32]

The cosmic Christology of the NT (John 1:1-14; Col. 1:15-19; Heb. 1:2-4)

27. Pannenberg, *ST* 2:25.
28. Zimmerli, "Ort und Grenze der Weisheit im Rahmen," p. 302.
29. Origen, *The First Principles* 1.2.2; see also Augustine, *Literal Meaning of Genesis* 2.6; trans. Taylor, p. 54.
30. Origen, *The First Principles* 1.2.3.
31. Fiorenza, "The Sophia-God of Jesus," pp. 264-65.
32. Pui-lan, *Postcolonial Imagination*, pp. 164-65; see also Pui-lan, "Ecology and Christology," pp. 113-25; G. Kim, *The Grace of Sophia*.

points to the integral link between Christ's role in creation and his role in reconciliation. This universal Christology found echoes in patristic theologies but unfortunately was by and large lost by the time of modern classical liberalism and its highly reductionist conception of Jesus merely as a "spiritual" teacher of personal piety. There was a solid cultural reason for the significance of cosmic Christology in early theology, as the world of antiquity in general was cosmocentric and there was the intuition of human life and society being a microcosmic part of and reflection of the macrocosm.[33] In patristic theology, key christological categories such as resurrection — which in later theology were appropriated merely in terms of personal hope, or as in classical liberalism, a fanciful myth belonging to the childhood of humanity — implied hope for the whole cosmos.

Far from being an outdated ideology, the cosmic creation Christology of early Christianity needs to be rediscovered for the contemporary world. The vast cosmic ramifications of scientific cosmologies demand it.[34] This is true as well for the global church: much of the Christianity of the Global South finds cosmic Christology familiar and important. Furthermore, in Eastern Orthodox Christianity the cosmic orientation was never lost. Moltmann rightly envisions the ascended Christ as the *Pantocrator* who encompasses not only the "conquest of enmity and violence and in the spread of reconciliation and harmonious, happily lived life,"[35] but also the world of nature and evolution.[36] Much here resonates with the late Roman Catholic paleontologist-priest P. Teilhard de Chardin's "Christ of Evolution."[37] Even the "normal" Catholic teacher Rahner made great efforts in that direction, speaking of "Christology within an evolutionary view of the world."[38]

Against this wide rediscovery of cosmic categories, the anthropocentrism of classical liberalism and much of subsequent (Protestant) theology seems hopelessly outdated and irrelevant. Out of that reduction emerges the alleged highly problematic difference between the Asiatic religions known for being nature religions and Christian faith proclaimed as "personal" religion.[39]

33. See further, Moltmann, *Way of Jesus Christ*, pp. 46-49.

34. See Moltmann, *Way of Jesus Christ*, pp. 63-72.

35. Moltmann, *Way of Jesus Christ*, p. 279.

36. Moltmann, *Way of Jesus Christ*, chap. 6; see also Farrow, *Ascension and Ecclesia*, pp. 191-221 especially.

37. Teilhard de Chardin, *Christianity and Evolution*.

38. Rahner, "Christology within an Evolutionary View," pp. 157-92; see also Shults, *Christology and Science*, chap. 2.

39. For comments, see Moltmann, *Way of Jesus Christ*, p. 275.

Rightly Moltmann contends: "Yet in its original, biblical form Christianity was by no means personal, anthropocentric and historical in the modern Western sense. It was much more *a way* and a moving forward, in the discovery of 'the always greater Christ.' "[40] For the sake of contemporary constructive theology, it has to be rediscovered. It is only in light of the whole history of Jesus Christ culminating in the cosmic rule in anticipation of the final advent of the righteous rule of God that his role in creation can find perspective. The themes of creation, incarnation, reconciliation, cosmic rule, and eschatological fulfillment should be held together in a healthy trinitarian grammar.

The Mediator of Creation and Reconciliation

Although reconciliation and creation are closely related in the christologically mediated trinitarian economy of salvation, creation should not be subsumed under reconciliation, as was done in OT studies of the past and in Barth's dogmatics. It was common in biblical scholarship until recent years to undermine the independent status of creation as a theological theme and basically subsume it under redemption. In this scholarly consensus, creation theology played no independent role in the OT but rather was seen as subordinate to redemption. In recent years, OT scholars have corrected the earlier bias[41] and have helped make creation its own theme. Similarly, Barth's theology of creation was subordinated under redemption via the link of covenant: creation is the "external" basis of covenant while covenant is the "internal" basis of creation.[42] In this respect, Barth's theology needs reorientation. I wonder if the same applies to the African American liberationist approach of James H. Evans, who claims that rather than being interested in origins, black theology is interested primarily in the relation of creation to soteriology and redemption.[43] Although I may misunderstand Evans's intentions in arguing this way (in order to bespeak liberation), it seems to me that the best way to establish a link between the human and the divine with regard to the doctrine of creation is to consider both origins and the relation to redemption and liberation. Be that as it may, neither should reconciliation be subsumed under creation.

The one who was the agent of creation became in the incarnation part

40. Moltmann, *Way of Jesus Christ,* p. 275, emphasis in original.

41. Westermann, *Creation,* p. 175 and passim.

42. "Creation as the external basis of the covenant" (*CD* III/1, pp. 94-228) and "The covenant as the internal basis of creation" (pp. 228-329).

43. J. Evans, *We Have Been Believers,* p. 74.

of creation. Christian tradition argues on the basis of the incarnation of the Logos that "the same divine rationality or wisdom which the natural sciences discern within the created order is to be identified within the *logos* incarnate, Jesus Christ."[44] Athanasius's *On the Incarnation of the Word* thus argues in the very beginning that it is "proper for us to begin the treatment of this subject by speaking of the creation of the universe, and of God its Artificer, that so it may be duly perceived that the renewal of creation has been the work of the self-same Word that made it at the beginning" (1.1). It is important for Athanasius to establish the doctrine of the incarnation on the basis that the same God who "made the universe to exist through His word" (3.1) also made human beings in his image, "as it were a kind of reflexion of the Word" (3.3). This is a profound expression of the divine hospitality as the divine Logos "submits to the historical and temporal particularities of human existence with all its limitations and exclusions, even to violence and death itself. God's hospitality is . . . a creational and incarnational hospitality."[45]

According to the Reformed American theologian William Dyrness, embodiment is one of the three "normative categories" in the articulation of the theological reality of our life in the world; the categories correspond to the trinitarian approach to life, faith, and theology. The other two are agency and relationality. God as lover of the world is committed to the world and thus seeks to make contact. Relationality and commitment are intertwined. Hence, agency emerges. Love manifests itself not only in speaking but also in doing. God's deeds suggest the third category, embodiment. Having created a world in which human life and life in general is physical — embodied — God's loving reaching out to the world takes the shape of embodiment, incarnation.[46] Embodiment is an underlying Christian principle that goes beyond but of course is not unrelated to the salvific purposes of the "Word became flesh" in Jesus of Nazareth. Moltmann rightly says that in the creative works of God, "Embodiment is the end of all God's works."[47]

The principle of embodiment is not only an essential theological observation but also the way to a right understanding of human life and society on this earth: "These works of God in creation, reconciliation and redemption also surround and mould the living character of created, reconciled and redeemed men and women. . . . We arrive at the theological perception of the

---

44. McGrath, *ScT* 1:188, emphasis in original.
45. Boersma, *Violence, Hospitality, and the Cross,* p. 187.
46. Dyrness, *The Earth Is God's,* pp. 16-24; see p. 21.
47. Title for chap. 10 of Moltmann, *God in Creation;* see particularly pp. 244-45.

truth of the human being in the arc that reaches from his physical creation to the resurrection of the body."[48] The theological import of embodiment funds the desire of constructive theology to forge a link between its and sciences' view of the human being as a fully embodied holistic creature.

Whereas the self-distinction of the Son from the Father is the condition for the existence and relative independence of the created reality from God, the work of the divine Spirit creates the possibility for its unity with the Creator as well as its coming into life and flourishing.

The Life-Giving Spirit

The Rediscovery of Cosmic Pneumatologies

Corresponding to the cosmic vision of Christology, the biblical witnesses present to us the Cosmic Spirit. The *ruach Elohim* "was moving over the face of the waters" (Gen. 1:2).[49] The same Spirit of God that participated in creation over the chaotic primal waters (Gen. 1:2) is the principle of human life as well (Gen. 2:7). This very same divine energy also sustains all life in the cosmos (Ps. 104:29-30).[50] In other words, "all divine activity is pneumatic in its efficacy."[51]

In the Christian East, the linking of the Spirit with creation has been a rule and custom. The Russian-born theologian Sergius Bulgakov puts it succinctly:

> In the Divine life, the Holy Spirit realizes the fullness adequate to this life and plumbs the depths of God by a unique eternal act. In creaturely being, the Holy Spirit is the force of being and the giver of life, but, according to the very concept of creation, this being and this life exist only as becoming, that is, not in fullness but only in the striving toward fullness. . . . This natural grace of the Holy Spirit, which constitutes the very foundation of the being of creation, exists in the very *flesh* of the world, in the matter of the world.[52]

48. Moltmann, *God in Creation,* p. 246.
49. See further, Jenson, "Aspects of a Doctrine of Creation," p. 22.
50. For profound comments, see Calvin, *Commentary on Psalms 93–119,* on Ps. 104:29.
51. Moltmann, *God in Creation,* p. 9.
52. Bulgakov, *The Comforter,* p. 220, emphasis in original.

The Christian tradition at large, however, particularly the Protestant tradition, has been slow to match the "'christological concentration' . . . by an extension of theology's horizon to cosmic breadth" of the Spirit and the acknowledgment of the "indwelling divine Spirit of creation."[53] Like what happened to the cosmic Christology of patristic times, the cosmic divine Spirit was no longer needed as the explanation of the world in modern theology. The Spirit's work came to be associated with salvation fairly narrowly understood, and its sphere was ecclesial rather than cosmic or in relation to nature. As a result, both in "Protestantism and Catholicism, the doctrine of the Holy Spirit, or pneumatology, has to do mostly with private, not public experience."[54]

Paul Tillich's profound discussion "Life and Spirit"[55] contributed significantly to a rediscovery and reformulation of a life-affirming cosmic pneumatology. The Spirit of Life is at work at all levels of the "hierarchy" of creation, from the inorganic all the way to "the spiritual presence"[56] in the human spirit, religion, culture, and morality. Notwithstanding limitations such as the strong modalistic tendency and the placement of pneumatology in the third rather than the first volume of his systematics (thus making the Spirit a second movement to the doctrine of creation, so to speak), Tillich's achievement should be duly noted. Significantly, the Lutheran Tillich's Dutch Reformed contemporary, Hendrikus Berkhof, envisioned the Spirit as the "vitality" of God, "God's inspiring breath by which he grants life in creation and re-creation."[57] With reference to a number of key OT passages from Genesis 1:2 to Job 33:4, he states: "We understand that the same God in action, the same *ruach* working in the deeds of salvation, is also the secret of the entire created world. . . . God's Spirit creates and sustains the life of *nature*."[58] Behind this robust creation pneumatology is the correct understanding that "'Spirit' means that God is a vital God, who grants vitality to his creation," and therefore, Spirit can be defined as "God's inspiring breath by which he grants life in creation and re-creation."[59] Similarly to Tillich, though, Berkhof suffers from a modalistic, unitarian bias.

Pannenberg has famously spoken of the need to overcome the reductionist tendencies in the Christian conception of the Spirit and forge an inte-

53. Moltmann, *God in Creation*, p. xiv; for the "Cosmic Spirit," see further pp. 98-103.
54. McDonnell, "The Determinative Doctrine of the Holy Spirit," p. 142.
55. Part 4 of *ST* 3.
56. Part 4, sec. 2 of *ST* 3.
57. Berkhof, *Doctrine of the Holy Spirit*, p. 14.
58. Berkhof, *Doctrine of the Holy Spirit*, p. 95, emphasis in original.
59. Berkhof, *Doctrine of the Holy Spirit*, p. 14.

gral link with the whole of creation. This is also the way to secure the principle of continuity among the many works of the Spirit: "God's Spirit is not only active in human redemption. . . . The Spirit is at work already in creation as God's breath, the origin of all movement and all life, and only against this background of his activity as the Creator of all life can we rightly understand . . . his role in the bringing forth of the new life in the resurrection of the dead."[60] The title of the most noted current pneumatological work, Moltmann's *The Spirit of Life* — with the original German subtitle, *Eine ganzheitliche Pneumatologie (A Holistic Pneumatology)* — reflects the desire in much of contemporary theology for an all-encompassing life-affirming account of the work of the Spirit. For that to happen, the meaning of the word "Spirit" needs to be clarified: unlike the usage in contemporary Western languages, in the OT "spirit" in no way involves any dualism of "material/bodily/earthly" versus "spiritual."[61] Interestingly, the same point was made in the nineteenth century by Johann Christoph Blumhardt, from whose theology Moltmann, among others, draws. Under the telling heading "The Redemption of the Body," the Reformed theologian states: "*The Spirit must embody itself. It must enter into our earthly life;* it must happen that deity be born in flesh so that it can overcome this earthly world. God is active Spirit only when he gets something of our material underfoot; before that, he is mere idea. The Spirit would govern life."[62] Insightfully, Moltmann also warns us of juxtaposing the Spirit of *Yahweh* (OT) and the Spirit of *redemption* (NT); it is of course the one and the same Spirit — although Christian theology has tended to ignore the former.[63] Berkhof makes the same point with a somewhat awkward expression: "The work of the Spirit in our modern so-called secularized world reminds us of the fact that our exalted Lord is not only the Head of his church but also primarily the Head of the world."[64]

Moltmann rightly notes that a turn to a robust creational pneumatology pushes theology toward panentheism, as it attempts to "discover God *in* all the beings he has created and to find his life-giving Spirit *in* the community of creation that they share."[65] Moltmann dubs it "immanent transcendence,"[66]

---

60. Pannenberg, *ST* 3:1.

61. Moltmann, *Spirit of Life,* p. 40.

62. In Eller, ed., *Thy Kingdom Come,* p. 18, emphasis in original.

63. Moltmann, *Spirit of Life,* pp. 8-9.

64. Berkhof, *Doctrine of the Holy Spirit,* p. 104.

65. Moltmann, *God in Creation,* p. xi, emphasis in original; also pp. 225-26; similarly Johnson, *Women, Earth, and Creator Spirit,* p. 42.

66. Moltmann, *Spirit of Life,* p. 34.

while Berkhof puts it this way: "So intimate is the Spirit to man's life that we sometimes feel ourselves on the brink of pantheism."[67] "The possibility of perceiving God in all things, and all things in God, is grounded theologically on an understanding of the Spirit of God as the power of creation and the wellspring of life" (Job 33:4, 13ff.; Ps. 104:29-30).[68] An important similar contribution to the pneumatological understanding of creation comes from various indigenous spiritualities. Coupled with a holistic way of life, the sensing of the divine everywhere is a needed corrective to much of Christian tradition.[69]

While some forms of panentheism in contemporary theology blur the distinction between the Creator and creation, this project's "classical panentheism" is able to avoid that fallacy and at the same time embrace the intimate presence of the Creator in the Spirit in creation. A pneumatological perspective also helps better construct a viable theology of continuing creation (providence) and the possibility of continuing divine action. How can we best speak of the robust, all-embracing presence of God as spirit in creation? For that task we gain help from both tradition and current constructive theologies.

While constructive theology continues the fruitful task of honing ways of speaking of the Spirit's presence and life-forming activities in creation, contemporary theology also faces the definite challenge of how to best dialogue with natural sciences.

Divine Spirit and Natural Sciences

Early Christian tradition faced major problems in trying to appropriate the biblical idea of God as Spirit and God's Spirit as creator because in Hellenistic thought (Stoicism), *pneuma* was supposed to be made of the finest "stuff," thus linking it with problematic notions of divisibility, composition, extensions, and locality. That led to imagine Spirit as the "will" and "reason."[70] Only the return to the biblical account of the *ruach Yahweh* as the life principle, not detached from but rather energizing and supporting all life of the cosmos, including the physical/material, could help theology correct this reductionism.[71] While theologically not fully satisfactory in all accounts, Hegel's concept of the Spirit comes closer to the biblical understanding as the "term *(Geist)*

67. Berkhof, *Doctrine of the Holy Spirit,* p. 95.
68. Moltmann, *Spirit of Life,* p. 35.
69. For an excellent discussion, see O'Murchu, *In the Beginning.*
70. Pannenberg, *ST* 1:371-73.
71. See the important discussion in Moltmann, *Spirit of Life,* p. 40.

combines the concept of rationality reflected in the English word 'mind' with the dimension of the supermaterial bound up with our term 'spirit' . . . , an active subject, an activity, or a process."[72] Here is an important bridge to how to speak of the Spirit in light of the most recent developments in our dynamic, evolving, evolutionary world. "The authors of Scripture did not rely on the categorical distinction between material and immaterial substance to express their experience of the biblical God. . . . Their experience of the redemptive activity of the biblical God was a being-encountered by a powerful presence that was wholly beyond their finite control. The absolute reality of this intensive presence bore down on them in a way that opened up the possibility of new life."[73] The biblical way of speaking of God in relation to the world is an "incomparable divine *presence.*"[74]

Talk about the divine presence, the presence of God in the cosmos and created reality through his Spirit, makes an important connection with contemporary natural sciences.[75] As different from the theistic worldview of biblical Christianity as the contemporary, basically "naturalist" (atheistic) worldview of the natural sciences may be, it is also necessary to seek connections. Pannenberg has famously argued that the biblical notion of "God as spirit" might have consonance with the current scientific view of life as the function of "spirit/energy/movement," expressed as the concept of (force) field.[76] "The presence of God's Spirit in his creation can be described as a field of creative presence, a comprehensive field of force that releases event after event into finite existence."[77] Pannenberg is of course quick to admit that "[a]t a first glance this biblical view of life is hard to reconcile with modern opinions. For modern biology, life is a function of the living cell or of the living creature as a self-sustaining (above all self-nourishing) and reproducing system, not the effect of a transcendent force that gives life."[78] That said, he notes rightly that the different concepts of force, energy, and field are used to describe interactions, including movement and change. Although Faraday's nineteenth-century field

72. Grenz, *Theology for the Community of God,* p. 82.

73. Shults, *Reforming the Doctrine of God,* p. 35.

74. Shults, *Reforming the Doctrine of God,* p. 36, emphasis in original.

75. For important Pentecostal-charismatic contributions, see "*Science and the Spirit: Pentecostal Perspectives on the Science/Religion Dialogue*" (at http://www.calvin.edu/scs/ scienceandspirit/), with its growing number of publications; Yong, ed., *The Spirit Renews the Face of the Earth.*

76. Pannenberg, "God as Spirit — and Natural Science," pp. 783-94; *ST* 1:382-83.

77. Pannenberg, *Introduction to Systematic Theology,* p. 194.

78. Pannenberg, *ST* 2:77.

theory has been revised dramatically, Pannenberg believes that from a theological viewpoint his basic idea of regarding "bodies themselves as forms of forces that for their part are no longer qualities of bodies but independent realities that are 'givens' for bodily phenomena," in other words "fields" or "force fields,"[79] is useful. While contemporary physics definitely sees no need to resort to the divine Spirit to explain the fields, Pannenberg discerns here (in keeping with the metaphysical origin of the field concept in ancient Greek philosophy of *pneuma*) an opening for a metaphysical, theological explanation.[80] But to do that, theology must also have its own material reasons to consider the divine Spirit as "field" in order to avoid bad apologetics.[81] Those reasons have been given above, most importantly taking root in the biblical account of the Spirit as life principle. Notwithstanding the critique targeted against Pannenberg's use of the outdated field concept of the nineteenth century,[82] the basic intuition is right on point. In calling the Spirit of God a field, we are of course using a metaphor or analogy; this metaphor's justification has to be assessed against its general appropriateness, rather than on whether it exactly fits in all aspects of the scientific explanation.

It seems to me that a conception of the divine Spirit in terms of "incomparable divine presence" goes well with what Tillich hinted at with his evolutionary-driven, dynamic account of the Spirit of Life and which Moltmann makes a full-scale program of Spirit of Life.

While deeply immanentist — following the biblical intuitions (Ps. 139) — the conception of the dynamic work of the Spirit as presence/field is twofold in nature and also affirms God's transcendence: "On the one side the Spirit is the principle of the creative presence of the transcendent God with his creatures; on the other side he is the medium of the participation of the creatures in the divine life, and therefore in life as such."[83] As discussed in the context of the attributes of God (*Trinity and Revelation*, chap. 12), the omnipresence of the triune God in the world God has created takes place through the ever-present Spirit (Ps. 139:7-12). At the same time, the Spirit complements the independence of the creatures from the Creator by uniting them with the Creator.

79. Pannenberg, *ST* 2:80.
80. Pannenberg, *ST* 2:81.
81. Pannenberg, *ST* 2:83.
82. See Polkinghorne, "Wolfhart Pannenberg's Engagement with the Natural Sciences," pp. 151-58. A highly insightful discussion is in Worthing, *God, Creation, and Contemporary Physics*, pp. 117-24. A critique and constructive proposal is Morales, "Vector Fields as the Empirical Correlate of the Spirit(s)."
83. Pannenberg, *ST* 2:32.

Creaturely life can only happen as a function of the presence of the Spirit, as mentioned above.

Because of the presence in creatures of the transcendent God through his Spirit, creatures are "open" by nature. The divine Spirit is not only the principle of openness of creatures to the future but also the principle of self-transcendence, as "the presence of the infinite in the finite imbues every finite thing, and the community of all finite beings, with self-transcendence."[84] That comes to the fore in growth and development as well as in the continuous desire to reach out beyond the limits of finite existence. The religious quest, of course, is a profound expression of this attempt at transcendence.

The Coworking of the Spirit and Son in Creation

While in Christian tradition and contemporary theology the distinctive roles of the Son and the Spirit, along with the Father, in the work of creation are defined in some detail,[85] Pannenberg reminds us of the obvious, yet often neglected, lacuna in theology, namely, how can we understand the cooperation of the two trinitarian members? Perhaps this question has not been reflected on much because of the simple lack of biblical material other than passages that in a general sense have been interpreted by theologians to refer to the joint work of the Son and the Spirit (Ps. 33:6; Gen. 1:2-3; among others).[86] The close connection between Son and Spirit of course comes to a climax in the earthly ministry of Jesus as depicted in the Synoptic Gospels and can be named systematically a form of Spirit Christology. In the trinitarian grammar, the work of the Spirit, the divine energy, the third person of the Trinity, is everywhere linked with that of the Son (as discussed in *Christ and Reconciliation,* chap. 8). But again, how are the two linked together in creation?

Pannenberg makes the novel suggestion that perhaps the concept of information could establish the cooperation between Son and Spirit. If, as established, the Son is the "logos of creation, the origin and epitome of its order," the principle of independence, and the Spirit the life principle of creation and creatures, it can be said that unlike natural laws that presuppose determinism or at least do not manifest constant creativity (even if in an open world the laws may emerge in new ways when given enough time), the "cre-

84. Moltmann, *God in Creation,* p. 101.
85. See Boff, *Holy Trinity,* pp. 22-23, 87, 93-95.
86. Pannenberg, *ST* 2:109-10.

ative dynamic of the Spirit also has an element of indeterminacy." Hence, "it is from the Spirit's dynamic, according to the relations of the Logos, that the distinct, independent, and self-centered form of creaturely operation arises."[87] In other words, the Son guarantees the orderliness and the Spirit, novelty and openness. (Indeterminacy, as will be discussed below, is a feature of the current theoretical quantum understanding of nature, making room for novelty and "divine intervention" without breaking the regularity of the world.) The feminist Elizabeth Johnson highlights beautifully the Spirit as the infinite source of novelty: "From the beginning of the cosmos, when the Spirit moves over the waters (Gen. 1:2), to the end, when God will make all things new (Rev. 21:5), standing still is an unknown stance. The long and unfinished development known as evolution testifies to just how much novelty, just how much surprise, the universe is capable of spawning out of pre-given order or chaos. In every instance the living Spirit empowers, lures, prods, dances on ahead."[88]

The way Christian Aristotelianism used the concept of information is noteworthy although of course very different from contemporary usage: it meant formation of existing matter (cf. in-form). Therefore, Aquinas sharply distinguished this formation from the original divine act of creation that brought into existence both matter and form.[89] Unlike Aristotelianism, in which energy is something independent from matter, in contemporary relativistic understanding of reality, mass (matter) and energy are intertwined to the point of being exchangeable (matter can be seen as manifestation of energy). Related to these developments, the concept of information rather than energy is at the center of scientific explanations of natural processes: "Information now came to denote the unusual or improbable nature of an event that is being caused, or has been caused, by energy. The amount of energy has to be greater, the higher the information content of the event, i.e., its . . . novelty." The concept of novelty is linked with probability rather than with predetermined outcomes and hence is linked also to the openness to the future, a fitting feature of the dynamics of the divine Spirit.[90] Pannenberg summarizes the trinitarian implications:

> The defining of information in terms of probability theory enables modern theology to view information as a measure of the creaturely new that

87. Pannenberg, ST 2:110; see also Staniloae, Experience of God, pp. 6, 60.
88. Johnson, Women, Earth, and Creator Spirit, p. 44.
89. Aquinas, ST 1.45.2.
90. Pannenberg, ST 2:111-12; see p. 111.

through the Spirit proceeds with each new event from the creative power of God. As a measure of the creative workings of the divine Spirit, the concept of information is subject to the Logos. The differing information content of events constitutes their uniqueness by which they are an expression of the creative activity of the Logos. . . .

Theologically one may see in the rise of each particular form a direct expression in creaturely reality of the working of the Logos, of the divine Word of Creation.[91]

Having briefly described the distinctive, yet interrelated, roles of Father, Son, and Spirit in the work of creation, let us focus on how to establish the independent existence of creation alongside the Creator.

The Possibility and Conditions of Creation alongside the Creator

The Sovereign Creator

The main theme of the first biblical account of creation — a liturgical text, tightly structured and ordered as illustrated in its hymnic form[92] — was counter to the Babylonian (and perhaps Egyptian) creation myths, particularly *Enuma Elish,* which conceives "creation" as a battle between Marduk and Tiamat. Whereas in Babylon the heaven and the earth emerge out of the fatal fight between the gods,[93] in Israel creation is the function of the sovereignty of Elohim/Yahweh resulting in an orderly and good world. It is by the power of the divine word (and spirit) that everything comes into being.[94] Part of Elohim's power is to subdue and put in perspective — as created — astral entities such as sun and moon or the gigantic living beings of the deep sea. This is nothing less than their demythologization.

In line with this important biblical theme, contemporary theology should affirm the sovereignty of God as creator: instead of a struggle between deities, there was the sovereign creative command through the Word and Spirit. The particular term used in Genesis 1:1, *bara,* "to create" (as distinct

91. Pannenberg, *ST* 2:112, 114.

92. Its recital in the Israelite congregations generation after generation helped consolidate the faith in the faithfulness of Yahweh, the Creator, who had redeemed his people from the Babylonian captivity.

93. The text of *Enuma Elish* is available in Heidel, *The Babylonian Genesis,* pp. 1-48.

94. Westermann, *Genesis 1–11,* p. 85.

from *asah*, "to make," v. 2), reflects this divine sovereignty. Of course, several other OT texts affirm the sovereignty of God and rule out all notions of a dualistic view of the origin of the world,[95] similar to philosophical views that build on an absolute necessity of philosophical monisms, whether ancient or modern.[96] The point of the *ex nihilo* formula is to envision God's work as "absolute" beginning, rather than as fashioning out of existing materials.[97] The doctrinal formulation of *ex nihilo* was needed to finally establish that truth, as the first Genesis narrative does not necessarily establish it. Hence, "in the beginning" is not a time-bound statement; rather it means to speak of the absolute "beginning" of everything. "Before" this "beginning" there was no-thing.[98] The divine creative act is unique and unrepeatable. "Because God's creative activity has no analogy, it is also unimaginable."[99] In that light Schleiermacher's subsuming the category of creation under that of providence totally misses this point, and hence must be regarded as theologically failing.[100] How can something be preserved that has not been created!

As is well known, process theism rejects *ex nihilo* vehemently, viewing "creation" in terms of a reordering of chaos.[101] Its view of God as merely a persuader (providing the "lure"),[102] working with preexisting materials, can hardly be reconciled with biblical and theological tradition.[103] This is not to deny the correct intuitions behind the rejection of the divine sovereignty, namely, the establishment of divine patience and kindness rather than power and force. Those features, however, should not be purchased at the cost of introducing a dualist conception of creation. "But the patience and humble

95. Pss. 104:14-30; 139:13; 147:8-9; and so forth. For useful comments, see Pannenberg, *ST* 2:15-16, 24.

96. For detailed comments, see Pannenberg, *ST* 2:17-19.

97. Those who accuse *ex nihilo* of a negative (often abusive) establishment of absolute sovereignty as a reason to reject the doctrine, miss the fact that over against God's power in a truly trinitarian theology of creation are also God's love, care, and deep engagement of the world; for criticism of *ex nihilo* in this respect, see Mary-Jane Rubenstein, "Cosmic Singularities," pp. 491-99.

98. We owe to Plato (*Timaeus* 28a) the distinction between *me oun* (relative negation of being) and *ouk on* (absolute negation); the latter is meant. For details, see Tillich, *ST* 1:186-89; see also pp. 253-54.

99. Moltmann, *God in Creation*, p. 73.

100. Schleiermacher, *Christian Faith*, §§39, 40 (pp. 148-52).

101. Cobb and Griffin, *Process Theology*, p. 65; see also pp. 63-79.

102. L. S. Ford, *The Lure of God*.

103. Whitehead's often-cited statement is this: "It is as true to say that God creates the World, as that the World creates God" (*Process and Reality*, p. 348). For Pannenberg's similar harsh critique, see *ST* 2:15-17.

love with which God seeks his creatures are divine in the sense that they do not proceed from weakness. They are an expression of the love of the Creator, who willed that his creatures should be free and independent."[104]

Is it appropriate to consider the triune God the "cause" of the world? While that sounds intuitively correct, it is liable to serious misunderstandings having to do with both theological and scientific/philosophical considerations. With regard to the latter, the whole idea of causality has changed so radically in recent decades that positing God as the "first cause" after tradition creates insurmountable problems (to be discussed in chap. 7). The theological problem arises out of the understanding of causality in traditional philosophy (Aristotle), which was assumed by theological tradition. In that scheme, the cause communicates its own being to the effect; but if so, then an emanationist, graded view of creation would follow. To reject the emanationist view, however, is not to deny the close correlation between God and creation. Rather than *causa efficiens prima*, it is best to think of the God-world relationship with regard to "beginnings" in terms of *analogia relationis*: there is correspondence but not causality.[105] Correspondence retains both relationality and dissimilarity between the infinite Creator and the finite creature.

The Freedom and Love of the Creator

Is the coming into existence of the cosmos a necessary act of God? What is the "reason" for the existence of the cosmos? By and large tradition agreed on the freedom of God in creation although it debated about how to best secure that. Barth vigorously defended the divine freedom and linked it with the equally important idea of God's love as the impetus for creation[106] — a theme robustly argued by Luther much earlier.[107] While materially following the Reformed tradition of "decrees," which made the coming into being of the world a matter of divine will and resolve, Barth also helped correct it by focusing on God's love along with will. Reformed tradition taught that in order to reveal his glory — which is the ultimate goal of the decree — God first decides for the kingdom and only then for creation. Creation is then kingdom's promise and

---

104. Pannenberg, *ST* 2:16.

105. See Moltmann, *God in Creation*, pp. 76-77.

106. Barth, *CD* III/1, p. 95.

107. Heidelberg Disputation #28; *LW* 31:57: "*The love of God does not find, but creates, that which is pleasing to it.* . . . Rather than seeking its own good, the love of God flows forth and bestows good" (emphasis in original).

in the service of the eschatological revelation of God's nature.[108] Barth's theology similarly makes creation a secondary act, but through the framework of covenant rather than the glory of God.[109] Very differently from the Reformed tradition, for Paul Tillich, "God is not creative because he has decided to be so; he is creative because he is God." Here no divine decree is required. Beginning from God's nature — namely, God is "necessarily" creative[110] — rather than from will, this Lutheran theologian not only embraces an emanationist view but also makes the cosmos eternally corresponding to the eternity of God's creative identity. Creation for him is, as Moltmann describes it, "identical" with God's life or God's "destiny."[111]

With Moltmann, I critique both the Reformed view and Tillich's view and turn to the category of love to which Barth pointed but was unable to make the leading theme. "It is more appropriate if we view the eternal divine life as a life of eternal, infinite love, which in the creative process issues in its overflowing rapture from its trinitarian perfection and completeness, and comes to itself in the eternal rest of the sabbath."[112] The category of love helps keep the identity of the divine life and divine creative activity closely linked together, yet without conflating them.

Where I depart from Moltmann, however, is in his making creation "necessary" and thus violating divine freedom. Against Barth, he argues that the idea of the absolute freedom of God[113] leads to "an arbitrary God." According to Moltmann, "when we say that God created the world 'out of freedom,' we must immediately add 'out of love'" because "God's freedom is not the almighty power for which everything is possible. It is love, which means the self-communication of the good."[114] While I partially agree with this criticism of Barth because he fails to utilize trinitarian resources, I find Pannenberg's approach more acceptable because he is able to hold on equally to both divine freedom and love. God's deity does not require the world; rather the world is "the result and expression of a free act of divine willing and doing. Unlike the Son, it is not in eternity the correlate of God's being as the Father."[115] As

---

108. Heppe, *Reformed Dogmatics,* chap. 7, "The Decrees of God"; for comments, see Moltmann, *God in Creation,* pp. 80-81.

109. For comments, see Hielema, "Searching for 'Disconnected Wires,'" pp. 75-93.

110. Tillich, *ST* 1:252.

111. Moltmann, *God in Creation,* pp. 83-84; see p. 83.

112. Moltmann, *God in Creation,* p. 84.

113. See Barth, *CD* II/2, p. 166; see also p. 10 and IV/2, pp. 344-46 particularly.

114. Moltmann, *God in Creation,* p. 75.

115. Pannenberg, *ST* 2:1.

discussed, with the same love that the Father loves the Son, the world is "loved" into existence. There is absolutely no necessity for the world, just pure overflowing divine love. Creation is God's gift, a gesture of immense hospitality. Jonathan Edwards's nuanced musing "Concerning the End for Which God Created the World" makes the same point: God is fully actual in his triune life and hence does not "need" the world.[116] On the other hand, this fully actual triune being is also inherently disposed to increase in actuality, and as a result, the other, the world, brings communal love, beauty, and delight to the divine life. That "increase," as Edwards explains it, can only happen *ad extra*, in time and space.[117] "God creates the world . . . so that God's dispositional essence could now be exercised outside of God's internal fullness."[118]

But could God, then, have been active even without the world? Theological tradition has rightly established that the trinitarian relations in themselves are actions. To these inner trinitarian actions, in the form of the outward action, creation and providence are added.[119] What the outward action in the world means is a new kind of divine activity — not surprisingly since God is the source of all creativity and novelty.[120] The securing of God's independence from the world is not meant to compromise the close and mutual relationship between Creator and creation — a key theme in classical panentheism supporting the current project: "with the act of creation and in the course of the history of his creatures he makes himself dependent on creaturely conditions for the manifestation of his Son in the relation of Jesus to the Father."[121]

This brings me to my second source of uneasiness with Moltmann, namely, the way he negotiates the distinction between the Creator and creation. Moltmann refers to the Jewish Kabbalistic notion of *zimzum*. "Before God issues creatively out of himself, he acts inwardly on himself, resolving *for himself*, committing *himself*, determining *himself*."[122] While tradition has utilized routinely the distinction between "outward" and "inward" actions of God, it has hardly reflected on how an omnipresent God could have any realm "outside" himself! Moltmann's solution is that the omnipresent and infinite

116. J. Edwards, "Miscellanies," no. 104, p. 272.

117. J. Edwards, "Dissertation I," p. 433.

118. S. H. Lee, *From a Liminal Place*, pp. 52-53 (quotation p. 53); see the excellent discussion in S. H. Lee, *Philosophical Theology of Jonathan Edwards*, pp. 170-210. I was also helped by Jenson, *America's Theologian*, pp. 99-110 and all of part 3.

119. See Pannenberg, *ST* 2:1-3.

120. See Pannenberg, *ST* 2:4-5.

121. Pannenberg, *ST* 2:7.

122. Moltmann, *God in Creation*, p. 86, emphasis in original; also pp. 79-80 and passim.

God has made room for a finitude in the divine life. "It is only a withdrawal by God into himself that can free the space into which God can act creatively." This "mystical primordial space," *nihil*, is connected with *ex nihilo*. Furthermore, Moltmann links *nihil* with the self-emptying of God in Christ.[123] What to think of this proposal? Not only is it semimythical,[124] it is also highly speculative,[125] without any witness either in biblical or theological tradition.[126] Nor do I find helpful the similarly speculative, semimythical conception of Barth, *Das Nichtige*, which, ironically, seems to give reality to the "nothing."[127] Even more problematic is his linking it with "opposition and resistance," to which "God asserts Himself and exerts His positive will."[128]

Both Moltmann's and Barth's attempts to reimagine the *nihil* are also unnecessary because the "making room for creation" can be integrally and satisfactorily explained in a truly trinitarian framework through the mediation of Christ.[129] Having established the possibility and conditions of the existence of the world independently from the Creator, while at the same time closely linked to God, we must clarify how to best envision the continuing mutual relationship in a trinitarian grammar. A corollary task is to affirm the value of creation as God's artifact.

The God-World Relationship in a Trinitarian Framework

The Value of CUreation

Only with the turn to a robust doctrine of the Trinity may constructive theology envision the infinitely loving and resourceful God as the Creator of the

---

123. Moltmann, *God in Creation*, pp. 86-93 (quotation p. 86).

124. As noted by Pannenberg, *ST* 2:14-15.

125. I see as similarly speculative Hans Urs von Balthasar's idea of the complete self-giving to the Son (and Spirit) of the person of the Father in *kenosis*. *Mysterium Paschale*, p. viii.

126. Gunton's (*The Triune Creator*, p. 141) criticism of Moltmann includes the charge that shifting the metaphor of *kenosis* from soteriology/Christology to creation is not legitimate. I don't necessarily see why that is the case: If Christ is the agent of both reconciliation and redemption (which Gunton of course wholeheartedly endorses), why couldn't one make this application?

127. Barth *CD* III/3, pp. 289-368.

128. Barth *CD* III/3, pp. 327, 351.

129. I am not quite sure what to think of the concept of "roominess" in God as the way of explaining the independence of the world in Jenson, "Aspects of a Doctrine of Creation," p. 24, citing John of Damascus, *The Catholic Faith* 13.9-11.

world, both transcending it and being deeply embedded in it. Because it is a trinitarian act, creation allows for an authentic personal interaction between the triune God and the world, affirming both intimate connection and real distinction. Furthermore, it safeguards the divine freedom and makes the coming into existence of the created reality the function of the divine love and goodness.[130] At the same time, it honors the God-given limited freedom of creation as distinct but not separate from the Creator: "If the world is too closely tied to the being of God, its own proper reality is endangered, for it is too easily swallowed up into the being of God, and so deprived of its own proper existence."[131] A properly worked-out conception of the way God is related to the world and the world is dependent on, yet independent from, the Creator, has the capacity to establish creation's lasting value. Creation is not God; God is not creation. Creation is *creation* — neither pure nature nor eternal divine "being."

The depiction of the work of creation as the joint work of the triune God best supports two essential theological values: participation and materiality.[132] These were concerns of early patristic theology in its vehement attack on Gnosticism.[133] Because they are created and thus dependent and contingent on the Creator and the creative divine Spirit, creatures are meant to participate in God. While Radical Orthodoxy finds this theme profoundly in Saint Augustine,[134] it is present in biblical testimonies and widespread in Christian tradition. The trinitarian doctrine of participation is capable of saving "the appearances by exceeding them" rather than "dissipating the reality of the immanent, material world."[135] In that sense, and correctly understood, we can speak of "a genuine theological materialism because it affirms what is beyond the material; its affirmation of transcendence funds a proper valuation of immanence — a valuation that is not really legitimate for nihilism, despite all the postmodern theorizing about the body and so on."[136]

---

130. For comments, see Gunton, *The Triune Creator*, pp. 53-55.

131. Gunton, *The Triune Creator*, p. 66.

132. See G. Ward, "In the Economy of the Divine."

133. For combating Gnostic dualism, see Irenaeus, *Against Heresies* 2.2.4.

134. Astonishingly, and in my understanding mistakenly, Radical Orthodoxy finds the metaphysics of participation — of all the thinkers — in Plato, so much so that at times Milbank can speak of "Platonism/Christianity" (*Theology and Social Theory*, p. 290; Milbank, Pickstock, and Ward, "Introduction," pp. 3-4). I seriously doubt!

135. Milbank, Pickstock, and Ward, "Introduction," p. 4. Cf. Butler, *Gender Trouble*, p. 43.

136. J. K. A. Smith, *Introducing Radical Orthodoxy*, p. 76. For an important discussion, see G. Ward, "Theological Materialism."

A component of theological materialism is the desire and capacity "to restore time and embodiment to our understanding of reality."[137] Indeed, by attacking the idea of the eternity of matter as something that "both had a beginning and, for that reason, was not inferior but intended by a good creator,"[138] early theologians helped reaffirm the relative value and goodness of all created reality, including the material, physical, "earthly." Behind this shift lay a marked deviation from the "Greek tendency to attribute the meaning of things to eternal principles underlying an eternal world rather than to a personal creator of a temporal world."[139] A significant further achievement of early tradition was the principle of "ontological homogeneity," that is, while not putting down the remarkable diversity of creation, the Neoplatonist view of degrees of being — based on an emanationist theory of origination — which of course also funds and is funded by dualism of matter and spirit, was rejected.[140] While hierarchy was rejected, difference was celebrated.[141]

As the work of the triune God, creation has inherent value. It is not instrumental. Barth, as he often is, is ambiguous and perhaps internally contradictory. On the one hand, he seems to take many steps toward affirming the value of creation per se, particularly when he speaks of "creation as justification" over which God rejoices;[142] on the other hand, the template of "creation as the 'external' basis of covenant and covenant as the 'internal' basis of creation"[143] without doubt makes creation instrumental. Gunton rightly sees this as an unfortunate reflection of the (Western) tendency "so to subordinate creation to redemption that the status of the material world as a whole is endangered."[144] The atheist Feuerbach's harsh rhetoric may indeed have some substance to it: "Nature, the world, has no value, no interest for Christians. The Christian thinks only of himself and the salvation of his soul."[145]

---

137. Pickstock, "Radical Orthodoxy and the Meditations of Time," p. 64, cited in J. K. A. Smith, *Introducing Radical Orthodoxy*, p. 76.

138. Gunton, *The Triune Creator*, p. 9.

139. Gunton, *The Triune Creator*, p. 25, also pp. 27-31.

140. Gunton (*The Triune Creator*, pp. 71-72) finds this principle best elucidated by Basil in his *Hexaemeron*.

141. For an important comment on this idea in Gregory of Nyssa, see Jenson, *God after God*, p. 120.

142. Barth, *CD* III/1, pp. 366-414.

143. Barth, *CD* III/1, pp. 94-228 and pp. 228-329.

144. Gunton, *The Triune Creator*, p. 165.

145. Feuerbach, *Essence of Christianity*, p. 287, emphasis removed.

"Classical Panentheism": Intimacy and Distinction

The trinitarian account of creation is the key to the burning issue in all contemporary theologies of creation — the relationship between God and creation, between creation and God.[146] Moltmann is correct in contending that "[a]s long as God was thought of as the absolute subject, the world had to be viewed as the object of his creation, preservation and redemption. . . . Through the monotheism of the absolute subject, God was increasingly stripped of his connection with the world, and the world was increasingly secularized."[147] On top of theological problems, sociopolitical implications follow. Feminists, other women theologians, and postcolonialists have correctly "challenged the image of the separate immaterial God for its collusion with the subordination of women and the devastation of creation."[148]

Saint Augustine's in many ways brilliant and important theology of God serves also as an example of warning in this respect.[149] He is deeply concerned, on the basis of Exodus 3:14, that the divine "nature, unchangeable, invisible and having life absolutely and sufficient to itself, must not be measured after the custom of things visible, and changeable, and mortal, or not self-sufficient."[150] While this reflects the central biblical idea of God as Almighty and beyond all transience, his claim also makes the deity abstract, distant, and unresponsive. How can this be reconciled with the equally important idea of God's Fatherly responsive love and deep presence in the world through the Spirit? It is ironic that it is in the middle of the exposition of the Trinity — the embodiment of relationality and communion — that Augustine insists on "God [as] the only unchangeable essence" and "substance."[151] The ontology of the times did not allow the interpretation of "essence" relationally as our contemporary orthodoxy can;[152] hence, Augustine's God in this respect seems more like a "monad" of Leibniz than the caring Father of the Bible. The distance of the Creator from the world is further pronounced in Augustine's (in many other

---

146. See Clayton, "God and World," pp. 203-18.

147. Moltmann, *God in Creation*, p. 1.

148. Rivera, *Touch of Transcendence*, p. 1.

149. Still a highly useful short discussion is Scheffczyk, *Creation and Providence*, pp. 94-105; somewhat one-sidedly critical, though helpful in many ways, is Gunton, *The Triune Creator*, pp. 73-86.

150. Augustine, *Trinity* 5.1.2.

151. Augustine, *Trinity* 5.2.3.

152. For a relational account of transcendence, see Rivera, *Touch of Transcendence*, p. 2.

ways correct) view of time as created, which for him makes God exist "outside time." Add to this the ontologically hierarchic view of creation, a hangover from Neoplatonism.[153]

Thomas's creative reinterpretation of Exodus 3:14 begins to correct earlier tradition and points to a more coherent account of the God-world relationship. Whereas for Augustine, the Exodus passage connotes God's changelessness and immovability, for Aquinas it means God's uniqueness as the sheer act of existence; in God, existence and essence coincide. As a result, God "must be His own Godhead, His own Life, and whatever else is thus predicated of Him." Everything else exists because God exists and causes it to exist.[154] The end result is: "God exists in everything. Paradoxically, God is never really distant from creation, although creatures, since they are unlike God in nature, are necessarily distant from God. The distinction lies in this: God is being, but all created things only have being. And they have being as a participation in what God is fully and perfectly. With this line of reasoning, Aquinas artfully combines likeness and distance."[155]

It is easy to see how closely — against common suspicions — this view of Aquinas is also in keeping with what this project calls "classical panentheism," namely, a "foundationally" close link between the Creator and created reality, although not of course their identification with each other. God's essential presence everywhere in creation was of course affirmed much earlier by Irenaeus: "For no part of Creation is left void of Him: He has filled all things everywhere, remaining present with His own Father."[156] Or, in the words of the contemporary postcolonialist female theologian Rivera: "God is irreducibly Other, always *beyond* our grasp. But not beyond our touch."[157]

In *Trinity and Revelation* (part 2), the vision of classical panentheism was outlined and discussed in detail. Let it suffice to summarize its main results here (with the understanding that full argumentation and documentation can be found therein). Resources for such a reworked conception of God are to be found not only among various contemporary theological orientations, including feminist and other female theologians, other liberationists, and a host of scientist-theologians, but also in biblical and Christian traditions. While a number of standard features of classical theism call for radical revision, the construction of a mutually relational and dynamic God-world relationship

153. Augustine, *Confessions* 12.7.
154. Aquinas, *ST* 1.3.3; 1.44.1.
155. A. M. Clifford, "Creation," p. 218.
156. Athanasius, *On the Incarnation of the Word* 8.1.
157. Rivera, *Touch of Transcendence*, p. 2, emphasis in original.

does not have to mean leaving behind the best of classical traditions. Nor does it have to lead to a radical panentheism in which the world is conceived as the body of God. Instructive here is feminist Kathryn Tanner's distinction between "contrastive" and "noncontrastive" accounts of divine transcendence. Whereas the former contrasts transcendence and immanence inversely, meaning that the more focus on one, the less on the other, the latter "suggests an extreme of divine involvement with the world — a divine involvement in the form of a productive agency extending to everything that is equally direct in its manner." In other words, the "noncontrastive" approach saves God from becoming one being among others and rather supports divine transcendence simultaneously with robust presence and activity throughout.[158] "The God who is transcendent in relation to the world, and the God who is immanent in that world are one and the same God."[159] A merely immanentist account of God makes God sympathetic but powerless; a merely transcendent, on the other hand, distances God from earthly realities. But there is more to it, as Cone continues brilliantly.[160] Even in deepest immanence, God is *in-finitely* present and beyond!

Much help for the conception of classical panentheism has also been gained from the work of some leading feminist thinkers regarding the importance of metaphors and new "models" of God (S. McFague, J. Soskice, E. Johnson, among others).[161] The literalist, patriarchal, male-dominated language for God easily leads to dualistic, hierarchical, and oppressive accounts of the God-world relationship. Metaphors and models of God major on power images such as king or ruler. Biblically based images such as "God as potter who creates the cosmos by molding it, God as speaker who with a word brings the world to be out of nothing,"[162] and "God the creator as mother who gives birth to the universe"[163] are badly needed to balance, critique, and make more inclusive theological imagination and liturgical practice.

The last task of the current chapter is to highlight the importance of continuity in the divine economy of salvation, the development from creation to salvation to consummation.

---

158. Tanner, *God and Creation*, chap. 2; see also Rivera, *Touch of Transcendence*.
159. Moltmann, *God in Creation*, p. 15.
160. Cone, *Black Theology of Liberation*, p. 76.
161. A useful discussion particularly with regard to creation, including theology-science dialogue, is Sallie McFague, *Models of God*, pp. 249-71.
162. McFague, *Models of God*, p. 250.
163. McFague, *Models of God*, p. 249.

Creation, Reconciliation, and Consummation
as the Work of the Triune God

Speaking of a holistic view of salvation and the work of the Spirit among Yoruba Christians in West Africa, Caleb Oluremi Oladipo notes:

> With this understanding of the Holy Spirit, creation, redemption, and sanctification are not different actions of the Father, Son, and Holy Spirit in sequence. Creation does not mean that God set things going at the beginning of time. Rather, creation is an ongoing activity of God. By reconciliation and redemption, Christians mean that the creative activities of God is also a continuous process whereby the disorderliness of existence are healed, its imbalances redressed, and its alienation bridged over. Sanctification is also a continuous activity of God whereby he brings creation to its perfection.[164]

This pneumatological trinitarian theology is fully in keeping with Moltmann's insistence that Christian theology of creation is less interested in "protological creation" and much more focused on "eschatological creation," which on the basis of Christ's resurrection looks forward to the final redemption of not only spiritual but also bodily life.[165] In the NT, "the outpouring of the Spirit and the experience of the energies of the Holy Spirit in the community of Christ belong to the eschatological experience of salvation."[166] Already in the OT, particularly in Second Isaiah, the promise of "new creation" becomes a theological theme. When Yahweh, the Creator, is "doing a new thing" (43:19), nothing less than a cosmic renewal will occur (40:4) and the "glory of the LORD shall be revealed" (40:5). Original creation and *creatio continuata* are put together. More than that: creation and eschatology are linked together, with a view toward the renewal and re-creation of the whole cosmos. Creation and redemption are similarly linked, not subsumed one under the other but rather understood as integral moments of one divine economy.[167]

In the trinitarian grammar, similarly to Christ's mediating work that links together creation, redemption, and eschatological fulfillment, the Spirit's mission relates in its own way to the trinitarian unfolding of the divine economy.[168]

---

164. Oladipo, *Development of the Doctrine of the Holy Spirit*, p. 100.

165. Moltmann, *God in Creation*, pp. 65-69.

166. Moltmann, *God in Creation*, p. 95.

167. R. J. Clifford, "The Hebrew Scriptures," p. 517.

168. Grenz, *Theology for the Community of God*, p. 379.

The Spirit's mission is to complete the program of the triune God in the world. To this end, he is the Creator Spirit. Not only is he the source of life, the Spirit is the power of the eschatological renewal of life. He is the agent who brings into being the new creation (2 Cor. 5:17). He effects the union of believers with Christ and Christ's community, the reconciled people of God. At the consummation, the Spirit's mission will reach its ultimate goal as he establishes the glorious fellowship of the redeemed people living in a redeemed world and enjoying the presence of their Redeemer God. En route to that day, the Spirit nourishes the spiritual life he creates.

Fitting, according to the ancient trinitarian *taxis*, is the role of perfecter: "In the life-giving operations of the Spirit and in his indwelling influence, the whole trinitarian efficacy of God finds full expression. In the operation and the indwelling of the Spirit, the creation of the Father through the Son, and the reconciliation of the world with God through Christ, arrive at their goal. . . . All the works of God end in the presence of the Spirit."[169] Polkinghorne rightly notes that "the sanctifying work of the Spirit is a continuing activity that awaits its final completion in the creation of the community of the redeemed, a consummation that will be manifested fully only at the *eschaton*."[170]

Theologically considered, Irenaeus's "evolutionary" view of humanity's and creation's development, according to which even the first humans were not created perfect but rather imperfect,[171] points to the coming eschatological perfection in the new creation. In contrast to the modernist naive optimism of linear development, the eschatological vision of the process of redemption and perfection "involves a faction, a breaking up. Worldly reality in all its aspects, the material and the immaterial, enters into a situation of fructification and endless bounty precisely by way of participation in the descent and ascent of Jesus."[172]

The hope for the eschatological consummation includes the whole of humanity — but not only that, the whole of God's creation. The main Christian symbol of eschatology, the kingdom of God, should not be reduced to merely the hope of the individual or even the whole people of God, but must also include the hope for the rest of the cosmos, the "integration of the real history of human beings with the nature of the earth."[173]

169. Moltmann, *God in Creation*, p. 96.
170. Polkinghorne, "Hidden Spirit and the Cosmos," p. 171, emphasis in original.
171. Irenaeus, *Against Heresies* 4.38.
172. Farrow, "St. Irenaeus of Lyons," p. 348; cited in Gunton, *The Triune Creator*, p. 56.
173. Moltmann, *God in Creation*, p. xi; see also Finger, *A Contemporary Anabaptist Theology*, p. 563.

5. Nature and Cosmology in Religions' Imagination

For Orientation

In the preface to his discussion of the doctrine of creation, Pannenberg mentions that "[t]he systematic presentation of Christian doctrine does not attempt a comparative evaluation of the Christian and other religious interpretations of the world and human life from the standpoint of the given understanding of the reality of God." Instead, he argues that this is the task of the philosophy of religion.[1] The current project decisively disagrees and rather engages the visions and teachings of four major living faith traditions throughout the theological argumentation.

There is little truth to the mantra that whereas the Asiatic religions are cosmocentric, the Semitic faiths are anthropocentric; this claim is usually made without a detailed engagement of scriptural and theological traditions.[2] In Hinduism's cyclical worldview, worlds and universes succeed each other over an almost infinite time span. That would support the cosmocentric orientation. But the vision of "salvation" in terms of each individual's enlightenment (variously described in Hindu and Buddhist traditions) certainly shifts the focus to anthropocentrism, or even individualism. Furthermore, the appearance nature of reality (on which more below) does not necessarily endorse cosmocentrism per se. While it is true that in Abrahamic faiths cosmogonies

1. Pannenberg, *ST* 2:xiv.
2. A typical recent example is Fuller ("Humanity as an Endangered Species," p. 5), who names the orientations of Abrahamic and Asiatic faiths "anthropic" and "karmic," respectively.

are written mainly from the perspective of humanity, this in no way means that their scriptural traditions lack a cosmic orientation. Indeed, it can also be argued that the Christian vision of eschatological salvation in terms of the renewal of the whole creation particularly supports a robust integrative approach to creation in which both humanity and the cosmos have their own places. Indeed, I suggest that a better term for Abrahamic traditions' relation to nature is "anthropocosmic."[3]

The real differences between Abrahamic and Asiatic traditions have to do with the meaning of history, the intentionality of creation, and the moral dimension. Whereas for Asiatic religions, particularly Hinduism, reality is an "appearance," for Judeo-Christian and Islamic traditions it is the place for "salvation history." Whereas for Buddhism there is no "reason" for the emergence of the cosmos (certainly no divine cause), and for Hinduism creation is a "side effect" (or *lila*, "play"), Jews, Christians, and Muslims hold to an "intentional creation."[4] God creates the world for a purpose. Another noted difference has to do with the emphasis in Judaism, Islam, and Christianity on God as the source of moral order, and hence the importance of loving obedience and covenant. Yet another difference between a Western and an Asian outlook on life is that for Asians the world is more "spirited." The distinction between "material" and "spiritual" is far less categorical. What is spiritual is primary while the material is secondary, a feature that runs contrary to much in the West.

We will begin with a short statement on creation and cosmology in Abrahamic traditions because of the foundational similarities of cosmologies among these "religions of the book" (to be expanded in the following chapters). The bulk of the chapter then delves into the more detailed investigation of Buddhist and Hindu cosmologies and particularly views on origins because those are much less well known among theologians.

Creation Theologies in Abrahamic Traditions

Looking at "[t]he majestic chapters with which the Bible opens could easily give the impression that cosmogony, the question of cosmic origins, was of

---

3. The term comes from the Chinese Confucian scholar Tu Weiming; see, e.g., his "Ecological Turn in New Confucian Humanism," n.p.; Chittick ("Anthropocosmic Vision in Islamic Thought") applies the concept to Islam.

4. Soskice, "*Creatio Ex Nihilo,*" p. 29, with reference to Burrell, "Freedom and Creation in the Abrahamic Traditions," p. 167.

major concern from the beginning to the writers of the Old Testament."[5] That is not the case, however (even if, as discussed, we should not marginalize the theme of creation in OT theology either). Nor should we draw the conclusion that because in the Qur'an references to creation are scattered all over, the themes of creation and providence are not important in that faith tradition.

All three traditions believe in God, loving and Almighty, who has brought about the cosmos and sustains and guides its life from the beginning to the end. The ultimate meaning of the confession of God as Creator is that the whole universe is ontologically dependent on God.[6] Natural order "is not an independent domain of reality . . . its principle resides in another realm of reality, which is Divine."[7] The same Creator guides the creation with the help of the laws of creation he has put in place (Q 30:30).[8] As a result, the cosmos is not blind, but rather, there is purpose in God's creative work.[9] God and world can never be equated or separated. God is infinite; cosmos and creatures are finite.

Like Christian tradition, the Muslim theology of creation can be approached from various perspectives, beginning from the "cosmic verses" in the Qur'an and how they came to be understood by the Prophet and his companions, to philosophically oriented explanations drawing from Greek heritage (flourishing during the eighth and twelfth centuries c.e.), to the subsequent Wisdom or Illuminationist cosmologies that emerged with the shift away from Hellenistic influences, to contemporary modern Islamic cosmologies also engaging the natural sciences.[10]

Foundational to all Islamic traditions is Qur'anic teaching.[11] Like Christian tradition that, adopting the Jewish theology of creation, opposed nontheistic aspects of Hellenistic pagan philosophies, the Qur'anic teaching "replaced the pagan Arabs' conception of nature with a new and vivid" theological interpretation.[12] Similarly to the Bible, the Qur'an describes God as the Creator

---

5. McMullin, "Creation *Ex Nihilo*," p. 11.

6. Nasr, "Question of Cosmogenesis," p. 177; Morewedge, *Metaphysics of Mullā Ṣadrā*, pp. 80-81.

7. Nasr, *Religion and the Order of Nature*, p. 61.

8. See further, Nasr, *Introduction to Islamic Cosmological Doctrines*; O'Shaughnessy, *Creation and the Teachings of the Qur'an.*

9. See Muzaffar Iqbal, "In the Beginning — II," pp. 94-95.

10. Muzaffar Iqbal, "In the Beginning," pp. 381-82.

11. For a highly informative discussion, see Muzaffar Iqbal, *Islam and Science*, chap. 2. As is well known, the Qur'anic cosmology is rich and variegated, including the teaching on Allah's "Throne" and "Footstool," the "Guarded Tablet" and "Pen," and so forth; an interested reader can find a detailed discussion in Muzaffar Iqbal, "In the Beginning," with many more sources.

12. Özdemir, "Towards an Understanding," p. 6. He underscores the importance in

in the absolute sense, that is, God brought into existence that which was not existent "before": "When nothing had yet come into existence, there was the One, the First *(al-Awwal),*" the ineffable one, incomparable (Q 26:11),[13] who never perishes (55:26-27).

Materially close to the Christian view of nature as creation is the Qur'anic interpretation of created order as "muslim." The term means "submission"; its root *(slm)* denotes "to be safe," "to be whole and integral." The idea behind the term is that one who submits to God avoids disintegration.[14] Hence, calling nature *muslim* is based on the idea that "the whole nature works according to divine laws . . . and according to the way God designed and created it. . . . Working according to God's laws, nature submits itself to God's will."[15] The Qur'an testifies that "to God prostrate whoever is in the heavens and whoever is in the earth, together with the sun and the moon, and the stars and the mountains, and the trees and the animals, as well as many of mankind" (22:18). In the same spirit, al-Ghazali renders Q 41:11 as "They [i.e., the heavens and the earth] said, 'We have submitted [to You] willingly.'"[16] Turkish scholar Ibrahim Özdemir summarizes: "Muslims live in a world that is alive, meaningful, purposeful, and more importantly, *muslim* like themselves, even prostrating itself before God."[17]

No wonder Islam has a long tradition of natural theology not unlike Judaism and Christianity. All created realities are considered "signs" revealing the creator (Q 30:22).[18] Hence, the study of nature may draw us nearer to God (41:53). If all creatures are signs, then, "it gives humans the impression that God is within us. If God reveals Himself" through all the created beings, "then it is not difficult to get the idea that wherever humans look we can easily feel the presence of God all around and within us."[19]

Islam of "the metaphysical dimension of nature" as opposed to pagan philosophies' — as well as modern sciences' — conception of purely materialistic and "lifeless" nature.

13. See also the short Sura of Sincerity (or Unity), Qur'an, sura 112.

14. Rahman, "Some Key Ethical Concepts," p. 183.

15. Özdemir, "Towards an Understanding," p. 16.

16. al-Ghazali, *The Jewels of the Qur'an,* p. 57.

17. Özdemir, "Towards an Understanding," p. 19, emphasis in original. This holistic, life-embracing theistic appreciation of nature comes to the fore also in literature. Among the luminaries, none surpasses the fame of the thirteenth-century Jalāl ad-Dīn Muhammad Rūmī (known simply as "Rumi"); for his "ecology," see L. Clarke, "The Universe Alive," pp. 39-65. (*Masnavī* is a 26,000-line "poem" in six volumes, considered by many Sufis as the "Persian Qur'an.")

18. See Baharuddin, "Significance of Ṣūfī-Empirical Principle," pp. 223-42; see also Setia, "*Tashkir,* Fine-Tuning, Intelligent Design," pp. 293-318. According to Özdemir ("Towards an Understanding," p. 20), the term "sign" appears no fewer than 280 times in the Qur'an.

19. Özdemir, "Towards an Understanding," p. 12.

The foundational message signified by creation for Muslim theology is *tawhid,* the unity and oneness of God. Corresponding to — but also distinguishing itself from — the Christian *trinitarian* theology of creation, the Qur'anic "principle of unicity of God *(tawhid)*" serves as the theological framework for both creation theology and the "unification of Sciences and Nature," argues Masudul Alam Choudhury.[20] It also speaks of "unity, peace, and reconciliation," including the unity of the whole of humankind.[21]

Codependent Origination:
The Buddhist Vision of the Origins of the Cosmos

Without engaging here the long-term debate of whether Buddhism is a "religion" at all,[22] and if it is, whether it is theistic (*Trinity and Revelation,* chap. 15), let it suffice to say only that none of the Buddhist traditions consider the Divine as the "Creator" in any sense similar to the Abrahamic traditions, not even those Mahayana traditions that show much more pronounced interest in deities than does Theravada. In that sense, Buddhism is a "naturalist" philosophy closer to contemporary scientific materialism but with the crucial difference that, unlike scientific reductive materialism, even in Buddhism's nontheistic orientation it is the spiritual/mental that is primary. Furthermore, unlike scientific materialism, Buddhism is not atheistic in the contemporary meaning of the term: even the most nontheistic Theravadins acknowledge the existence of deities, even a huge number of deities;[23] it is just that the interest of the Buddhist seeker for liberation is not in the deities but in his or her own pursuit (with the help of Buddha, *dhamma,* and *sangha* [community]).[24] Hence, it would be a fatal mistake in terms of interfaith hospitality to exclude Buddhist tradition from the investigation into religious cosmologies.

An important clue to the Buddhist attitude toward questions of origins comes from the conversation on metaphysical issues between the monk Malunkyaputta and Gautama. Buddha said, "bear always in mind . . . [that] I have not elucidated that the world is not eternal; I have not elucidated that the

20. Choudhury, "The 'Tawhidi' Precept in the Sciences," p. 243.

21. Said and Funk, "Peace in Islam," pp. 156-58.

22. Cf. the somewhat hasty denial in Hudson, *A Philosophical Approach,* p. 16. A more balanced discussion can be found in Steinkellner, "Buddhismus," pp. 251-62.

23. But in no Buddhist tradition is the founder, Gautama, a divine figure in the manner of monotheistic traditions.

24. See insightful comments by Koyama, *Mount Fuji and Mount Sinai,* p. 74.

world is finite; I have not elucidated that the world is infinite; I have not elucidated that the soul is one thing and the body another. . . . And why, Malunkyaputta, have I not elucidated this? Because, Malunkyaputta, this profits not."[25]
This statement sets the tone for the original Buddhist contribution to questions
of origins: speculation into mysteries on which there may be various — even
contrasting — opinions should not occupy the attention of those who seek
liberation from *dukkha.* That said, it is ironic that Buddhist cosmology is rich,
variegated, and highly sophisticated.[26]

What is the world made of according to Buddhist philosophy? The third
part of the Tipitaka, Abhidhamma, the most systematic bringing together of
teaching derived from the Buddha, provides highly sophisticated analyses of
82 or 89 or so constituent elements, *dhammas.*[27] The main point of this discussion is that everything else (81 of 82) is fleeting and conditioned, whereas
the last one (the 82nd) is nirvana, real and unconditioned. That is free from
change and decay.[28] There is thus no absolute "origin." Even the famous mythic
description of the emergence of the cosmos in *Aggañña Sutta*[29] (in which,
after greed arose in luminous primordial beings as a result of which moral
degradation spread, and from the original "butter"-like fragrant substance
more solid beings began to evolve, leading up to humans and others) is not
meant to be an account of absolute beginnings but rather yet another way to
speak of "beginningless" origination and evolution.

This raises the question if in any meaningful sense it can be said that the
world is "created" in Buddhism. Similarly to Hindu traditions, Buddhism does
not speak with one voice. The main response, however, is "no" as stated categorically in *Lotus Sutra,* the "catechism" of the Mahayana tradition: the cosmos
was "not derived from an intelligent cause," nor has it any purpose.[30] Rather,
the cosmos is everlasting and without beginning.[31] Other views also appear
in Buddhist scriptures, but these seem to me secondary.[32] Notwithstanding

---

25. Majjhima Nikaya Sutta 63; see Silva, "The Buddhist Attitude towards Nature," n.p.

26. Two standard English-language primers are Kloetzli, *Buddhist Cosmology,* and Sadakata, *Buddhist Cosmology.*

27. Much less of Abhidhamma is available in English translation. A basic source is *A
Manual of Abhidhamma (Abhidhammattha Sangaha).*

28. For an authoritative statement, see Buddhagosa, *Visuddhimagga* 16.71; p. 522.

29. *Aggañña Sutta: On Knowledge of Beginnings, Digha Nikaya* 3.80-98 (in Walshe, pp.
407-15).

30. Lotus Sutra 5; quotation from 5.80 (*SBE* 21).

31. Lotus Sutra 13.19 (*SBE* 21).

32. See Lotus Sutra 11 (*SBE* 21).

differences (particularly among the Mahayanas), all Buddhist schools agree that dependent origination rather than creation is the key to the coming to existence and nature of the cosmos.

Indeed, according to the leading Theravada teacher of Thailand, the Venerable P. A. Payutto, "dependent origination"[33] (or "causal interdependence") is the single most important principle. Payutto further argues that this is not a heavenly teaching received by the Sakyamuni (the Buddha), but rather, it "describes the law of nature, which exists as the natural course of things." (The Christian theologian with a keen eye on natural theology can't help but hear some familiar soundings here despite the vastly different theological context!) Highly significant theologically is the Theravada teacher's claim that "The progression of causes and conditions is the reality which applies to all things, from the natural environment, which is an external, physical condition, to the events of human society, ethical principles, life events and the happiness and suffering which manifest in our own minds. These systems of causal relationship are part of the one natural truth."[34] This general principle of causation is expressed classically like this:

"When this is, that is."
"From the arising of this comes the arising of that."
"When this isn't, that isn't."
"From the cessation of this comes the cessation of that."[35]

In other words, according to the principle of effect, everything emerges in an interrelated manner — from "ignorance" to "volitional impulses," "consciousness" to "body and mind," "craving" to "clinging" to "birth" to "aging and death" — all the way to "Sorrow, Lamentation, Pain, Grief and Despair." From here begins the release, as "[w]ith the complete abandoning of Ignorance, Volitional Impulses cease, . . . with cessation of Consciousness . . . of Craving, Clinging, . . . of Birth, Aging, and Death," and ultimately, "this whole mass of suffering."[36] "Everything formed is in a constant process of change" as the world is "constantly in a process of undergoing change. In nature there are no static and stable 'things'; there are only ever-changing, ever-moving

33. See *Paticca-samuppada-vibhanga Sutta: Analysis of Dependent Co-arising* (Samyutta Nikaya 12.2) for the famous analysis of Gautama concerning the idea of "dependent origination."
34. Payutto, *Dependent Origination,* "Introduction" (n.p., so chap. is given in referencing here).
35. Samyutta-Nikaya 12.61.
36. E.g., Samyutta-Nikaya 12.2. See also Payutto, *Dependent Origination,* chap. 1.

processes."[37] The world passes through cycles of evolution and dissolution, *ad infinitum,* basically similarly to Hinduism. At the human level, the principle comes to the fore in the doctrine of "no-soul" (to be discussed in part 2).

Now, what are the theological implications of this most foundational Buddhist principle of *pratitya-samutpada?* A common understanding takes it as a world-origin theory, making ignorance *(avijja)* the first cause and tracing evolution through the whole twelve links. If so, then Buddhist cosmology would not be radically different from other religions' imagination, with the exception that God or a supernatural force is missing — but then, it would be quite similar to scientific naturalism. Emergence and evolution would be "normal" processes. As appealing as this interpretation may sound to the religionist and theologian, it clearly contradicts the most foundational Buddhist principle of *interdependence.* In that scheme, there cannot be an originating factor not caused by or having been brought about by others. Therefore, while not totally rejecting this interpretation, Payutto says that its value is limited and secondary in that it "presents a picture of the universe functioning according to the natural processes of growth and decline . . . proceeding according to the flow of causes and effects and bound to the conditions found in the natural process. There is no Creator or Appointer, nor is the world a series of aimless accidents."[38] In other words, this origin-oriented secondary hermeneutics helps the Buddhist to understand and make sense of the process of evolution.[39] However, the main teaching about dependent origination has everything to do with the core insight of Buddhism, namely, the process of the arising and cessation of *dukkha* (the first "Noble Truth").

Rather than using "suffering" (or "pain" or "stress") for *dukkha,* it is best to leave the term without English translation to avoid misunderstanding. It is intentionally an ambiguous word. With all their differences, all Buddhist schools consider *dukkha* to be the main challenge in life and, consequently, extinction of *dukkha* to be the main goal, the *summa* of everything in Buddhism and its scriptures.[40] Suffering is inescapable as long as one is in the circle of life and death, samsara. To be more precise, it is the craving (the second "Noble Truth") that is the real root and cause.[41] Behind the (misplaced) crav-

37. Silva, "The Buddhist Attitude towards Nature," n.p. The Pali term *anicca* is routinely used to describe this.

38. Payutto, *Dependent Origination,* chap. 2.

39. *Dhammacakkappavattana Sutta* 11 of Samyutta Nikaya 56.11.

40. Chandngarm, *Arriyasatsee [Four Noble Truths],* pp. 9-14.

41. Similarly to the notion of *dukkha,* the term *tanhā* ("craving" or "desire") used by Buddha is a multifaceted concept.

ing, according to the Buddha, is ignorance. The logic of the emergence and continuation of suffering rooted in craving due to ignorance is indebted to the law of *kamma*.[42] (More on this in part 2 below in the discussion of the human condition.) The context of *dukkha* and its extinction by overcoming "desire" is thus the main target of codependent origination.

That said, it is not unjustified to raise the question of "ultimate reality,"[43] which seems to arise whenever questions about the origins of the cosmos are penetrated. What might be the Buddhist candidate(s) for the ultimate reality? When it comes to Theravada, I am not quite sure there is one. What unites all diverse Mahayana traditions is the concept of sunyata.[44] Thus says the leading Mahayana theologian Masao Abe (Tokyo School of Japan): "The ultimate reality . . . is neither Being nor God, but Sunyata."[45] Some Buddhist and Christian theologians have wondered if that concept ("emptiness") could serve as the heuristic common point between the Christian view of God and the Buddhist view of ultimate reality.[46]

Notoriously difficult to translate and even more notoriously hard to understand, "sunyata" literally means "(absolute) nothingness." However, it is not "empty nothingness." It is only "empty" in terms of being "entirely unobjectifiable, unconceptualizable, and unattainable by reason or will."[47] According to the classic formulation of the *Prajnaparamita-sutra* ("The Heart Sutra"):

> Form is Emptiness, Emptiness is form. Emptiness does not differ from form, and form does not differ from Emptiness . . . in Emptyness [*sic*] there is no form, no feeling, no recognition, no volitions, no consciousness; no eye, no ear, no nose, no tongue, no body, no mind . . . no ignorance and no extinction of ignorance . . . no aging and death and no extinction of

42. *Kamma* ("the law of reaping and sowing") has two sides in the Buddhist analysis: on the one hand, the "bad" *kamma,* which consists of "unskillful" actions and attitudes such as greed or hatred, and on the other hand, the "good" *kamma,* which consists of "skillful" actions and attitudes such as nongreed, nonhatred, and nondelusion. Good *kamma* produces good while bad *kamma* brings bad effects and results. Payutto, *Dictionary of Buddhism,* p. 60.

43. For an insightful comment, see Nambara, "Ultimate Reality," pp. 117-18.

44. In the focused discussion of the concepts of the "divine" (*Trinity and Revelation,* chap. 15), other less well-known candidates for ultimate reality are also studied, namely, nirvana, Dharmakaya, and "suchness" *(tathata).*

45. Abe, "Kenotic God," p. 50. *Christ and Reconciliation* (chap. 10) presents a sustained dialogue with Abe's linking of sunyata with Christian belief in the *kenosis* of Christ.

46. See further, Yong, *The Cosmic Breath;* and *Pneumatology and the Christian-Buddhist Dialogue.*

47. Abe, "Kenotic God," p. 50.

aging and death; likewise there is no Suffering, Origin, Cessation or Path, no wisdom-knowledge, no attainment and non-attainment.[48]

According to Masao Abe, "Sunyata is not self-affirmative, but *thoroughly* self-negative. . . . [E]mptiness not only empties everything else but also empties itself." And importantly with regard to Christian intuitions: "Sunyata should not be conceived of somewhere *outside* one's self-existence, nor somewhere *inside* one's self-existence. True Sunyata is neither outside nor inside, neither external nor internal, neither transcendent nor immanent."[49] If all that still sounds predominantly negative to Christian ears, Abe goes on to say that, at its core, "in Sunyata, regardless of the distinction between self and other, humans and nature, humans and the divine, everything without exception is realized *as it is* in its *suchness* (in Sanskrit, *tathata,* which may also be rendered as 'is-ness')."[50]

My comment is that whatever the interfaith potential of the concept of sunyata may be (and I tend to be more skeptical than some of my Christian colleagues), it is a remarkable indication of the deeply nontheistic and "naturalistic" approach to origins in Buddhism, another illustration of the principle of dependent origination. Linking sunyata with the Abrahamic faiths' creation out of "nothing" does not seem to be well advised; "nothing" really is no-thing and merely negative. (More on that in the next chapter.)

Hindu Cosmologies of Origins

Rich Diversity of Traditions and Visions

Rich in religious cosmologies and sacred cosmogonies, Hindu traditions understandably speak of "creation" in diverse voices.[51] Just consider how very different are the highly imaginative narratives, symbols, and metaphors of the cosmos in the Rig Veda (the oldest part of Vedic scripture), the highly sophisticated notions of form and numbers in the ritually oriented Yajur Veda (whose focus is on teaching us how to do sacrifices for the cyclical renewals of the cosmos), or the Atharva Veda and its interest in finding the key to balance

48. Heart Sutra (no translator given, n.p.; available at http://www.sacred-texts.com/bud/tib/hrt.htm [11/14/2013]).
49. Abe, "Kenotic God," p. 51, emphasis in original.
50. Abe, "Kenotic God," p. 52, emphasis in original.
51. Menon, "Hinduism and Science," p. 8.

and health in a cosmos filled with evil powers. What is common to all these and the rest of Vedic scriptures is the virtual lack of concern for morality, justice, and equality. This is a marked difference from Semitic faiths, particularly of the Scriptures of Judaism. The Indian revelatory literature's main aim is to help the faithful to see the unity in the cosmos between the divine and all else, somewhat differently defined in various subtraditions. Add to the diversity the rich cosmological heritage of the Bhagavad-Gita and numerous Puranas (most prominently the massive *Mahabharata* and *Ramayana*), the scriptures of the large majority of Indians. Only a tiny elite group of specialists (the Brahmins) have the luxury of studying the vast Vedic literature.[52]

From the Gita, Hindus learn that the Deity is the creator and sustainer of the world.[53] The Lord also resides in all things; he is likened to the taste of water and the light of sun and moon. He is also *Om,* the eternal "echo," the sound originating from the mythic past (similarly Rig Veda 10.190). Not surprisingly, the Gita thus "affirms the interdependence of the spiritual and material nature."[54] With all their differences, the various Hindu scriptural traditions affirm that God and nature are the same.[55] The assertion that the Lord is "creator" has to be understood in a way that does not confuse it with the Semitic tradition's teaching of *creatio ex nihilo*.[56] A telling example of this is Nasadiya Sukta: "Verily, in the beginning this (universe) was, as it were, neither non-existent nor existent; in the beginning this (universe), indeed, as it were, existed and did not exist: there was then only that Mind."[57] The idea of the physical universe having been created out of nothing is absolutely and totally foreign if it means that the cosmos is "not sharing the substance of the Self. Rather, one 'becomes' what one emits from oneself."[58] The description of "creation" in Brihadaranyaka Upanishad (1.4) is a case in point: Brahman first

52. For an introduction to sacred literature in India, see *Trinity and Revelation,* chap. 8.

53. Gita 7; *SBE* 8:74, 76; 13:106.

54. J. Y. Lee, *Theology of Change,* pp. 105-6, 110 (quotation p. 105).

55. Dwivedi, "Classical India," p. 45.

56. This is not to deny the fairly frequent use of the term "in the beginning" in the Upanishads; see, e.g., Brihadaranyaka Upanishad 1.2.1; *SBE* 15:74.

57. Satapatha Brahmana 10.5.3.1; *SBE* 43:374-75. Many Upanishadic statements, when taken in isolation, seem to speak of the nonexistence of the universe prior to creation, such as, "In the beginning there was nothing" (to be perceived). Brhidaranyaka Upanishad 1.2.1; *SBE* 15:74. So also begins the famous "Creation" hymn in Satapatha Brahmana (6.1.1.1; *SBE* 41:143): "Verily, in the beginning there was here the non-existent." These statements, as tempting as it would be for an Abrahamic faith representative to take in terms of *ex nihilo,* must be understood within the unitive system of Hindu thought as explained in this section.

58. See K. Ward, *Religion and Creation,* pp. 79-80.

made himself split into two, bringing about male and female; out of female came cow and bull, out of them mare and ass, and so forth. Out of his body parts, further things were created. Hence, "He knew, 'I indeed am this creation, for I created all this.' Hence he became the creation, and he who knows this lives in this his creation."[59] No wonder the cosmos is sometimes compared to a cosmic being, a living organism, as in the famous hymn to Purusa (Rig Veda 10.90) where, similarly, out of the organs of the deity ("his mouth, his arms . . . his thighs and feet") everything is made.[60]

What is more similar to the Semitic faiths is that "Hindu scriptures attest to the belief that the creation, maintenance, and annihilation of the cosmos is completely up to the Supreme Will."[61] Gita puts it in a way that closely resembles the NT statement about Christ (Rev. 1:8): "I am the beginning and the middle and the end also of all beings."[62] What is different from the Abrahamic traditions is that all Hindu scriptural traditions also affirm rebirth and a cyclical worldview: hence, "creation" does not mean the absolute beginning as in the Semitic traditions. K. Ward adds here a highly insightful observation: "It might be said that the Indian metaphysical framework of an endless repetition of universes, the cycle of samsara and the ultimate futility of action and desire, gives rise to the idea of the Supreme as an unchanging reality which realizes no new values in creation, which is inactive and without passion and which offers no ultimate consummation for the finite order."[63] (That said, ironically, there are important Hindu traditions that look at the emergence of the cosmos as a result of the Lord's love and benevolence toward the creatures and depict a theistic kind of picture![64] These kinds of views, probably, have to be taken as an exception to the rule of monism.)

The most well-known scriptural tradition of Hinduism in the West is that of the Upanishads, the last (latest) part of the Vedas. Among the six clas-

---

59. Brihadaranyaka Upanishad 1.4.5; *SBE* 15:86; so also 1.4.10; *SBE* 15:88.

60. Other explanations as to the "origins" of the universe are offered in the Upanishads, such as "Death" (Brihadaranyaka Upanishad 1.2.1; *SBE* 15:75) and "Death or Hunger" (Brihadaranyaka Upanishad 1.2.4; *SBE* 15:76). Chandogya Upanishad 6.2.1 (*SBE* 1:93), having surveyed these and similar proposals, finally concludes: "In the beginning . . . there was that only which is . . . , one only, without a second." I am indebted to K. Ward, *Religion and Creation*, p. 81.

61. Dwivedi, "Dharmic Ecology," p. 6; see, e.g., Gita 10; *SBE* 8:87: "I am the origin of all, and that all moves on through me."

62. Gita 10; *SBE* 8:88.

63. K. Ward, *Religion and Revelation*, p. 141.

64. Just consider Svetasvatara Upanishad 6.16; *SBE* 15:265: "He makes all, he knows all, the self-caused, the knower . . . the master of nature and of man . . . the cause of the bondage, the existence, and the liberation of the world." See further, K. Ward, *Religion and Creation*, p. 82.

sic schools of Hinduism,[65] by far the best known in the West are the main Vedanta schools, which major in a careful exegetical and theological study of the Upanishads.[66] It is here that the sophisticated philosophical discussions of origins and of the relation of the cosmos to Brahman are carried on. Notwithstanding important internal differences, all Vedanta schools agree with the rest of the Vedic literature, "That Self [atman] is indeed Brahman."[67] Variously translated as "the Supreme" or similar, Brahman is the central concept of the Upanishads. Brahman is beyond all qualities, definitions, limits[68] — or to use the Western philosophical terminology, absolutely infinite. According to the Vedic religion, Brahman consists of all things,[69] "without undergoing any modification, passes, by entering into its effects (the elements), into the condition of the individual soul,"[70] and therefore the divine can be discerned within each person and in everything. "The idea that there is a God totally other than the material universe is foreign to the tradition." Rather, "[b]ecause Brahman consists of all things, all things are one."[71] Highly illustrative of the refusal of Hindu thought to make the Lord a creator and rather insist that the cosmos is an extension, as it were, of the Divine, is the well-known epic of origins in the beginning of the *Laws of Manu*. It teaches that out of his own body the Lord brought forth various kinds of beings. That the Lord "with a thought created the waters, and placed his seed in them," and the seed "became a golden egg" of course finds some parallels in the first verses of Genesis, but then it says something completely different: "in that (egg) he himself was born as Brahman, the progenitor of the whole world."[72] In other words, if God can

---

65. Nyaya, Vaisesika, Samkhya, Yoga, Purva Mimamsa, and Vedanta, also known as "Later" (Uttara) Mimamsa (not to be confused with Purva Mimamsa).

66. For the theology of scripture in Hinduism and its relation to Christianity, see chap. 8 of *Trinity and Revelation*.

67. Brihadaranyaka Upanishad 4.4.5 (*SBE* 15:176).

68. Read the Brihadaranyaka Upanishad 4.4 to get the picture.

69. Brihadaranyaka Upanishad 4.4.5 (*SBE* 15:176): "That Self is indeed Brahman, consisting of knowledge, mind, life, sight, hearing, earth, water, wind, ether, light and no light, desire and no desire, anger and no anger, right or wrong, and all things."

70. Sankara, *Vedanta-Sutras* 2.3.17; *SBE* 38:30. A classic statement of the fact that bringing forth the cosmos does not make the Brahman any less is the Invocation to Isavasyopanishad: "That is infinite. This is infinite. From the infinite, the infinite has come out. When this infinite is taken from that infinite, what remains is infinite." The first word "that" refers to Brahman, and the following "this" to the cosmos. Quoted in K. Brown, ed., *The Essential Teachings of Hinduism*, p. 23.

71. K. Ward, *Religion and Creation*, p. 79.

72. *The Laws of Manu*, 1.8-9; *SBE* 25:5.

be named creator in any sense according to this story, it is as creator of one's self! For all Hindu streams, the "other" (separated from the divine, Brahman) is rather an appearance or the manifestation of the One.[73] In that sense, life is not self-existent (as it is in Buddhism) but rather depends ultimately on some reality beyond itself.[74]

The One and the Many: Debates within the Vedanta Schools

In outline, all Vedanta schools (and more widely, the whole Vedic tradition) embrace this much in common. But on how precisely to speak of the unity of Brahman and the cosmos, there are significant differences. For our purposes, the most noteworthy is the division between the strictly monistic schools, the nondualist *advaita* school represented most famously by Sankara of the eighth century, and the qualified nondualist *(Visistadvaita)* school of Ramanuja of the eleventh century.

For Sankara, Brahman is totally void of all limitations and is identical with *atman* (the "soul" or the "self"). Because of ignorance, the human soul is encumbered with body and mind and thus subject to *dukkha* (sorrow) and continuous samsara, endless cycles of birth and death, unless through knowledge one attains liberation when the identity between Brahman and *atman* is realized. Attaining this realization is the ultimate goal of the study of the Upanishads. One of the fiercest critics of Sankara's strict nondualistic hermeneutics was Ramanuja. His qualified nondualist tradition refutes Sankara's identity between Brahman and *atman*. Rather than identity, Ramanuja argues that the Vedas teach the principle of inseparability. Of course, Ramanuja believed that Brahman was nondual *(advaita),* but for him that belief did not negate but rather affirmed the internal diversity and complexity of the divine.[75] (These two views do not of course exhaust the Vedanta tradition, as there is also the influential thirteenth-century theology of Madhva, a qualified dualism, among others, but for our limited, comparative purposes Sankara's and Ramanuja's theologies suffice.)

The spirituality of the common folk in India, guided by Gita and expressing itself in some form of *bhakti* devotion and spirituality with endless (often

---

73. K. Ward, *Religion and Revelation*, p. 137.

74. K. Ward, *Religion and Human Nature*, p. 11.

75. For the discussion of implications for the doctrine of God, see chap. 15 of *Trinity and Revelation.*

local) customs and colors (to which usually also belong local deities), is not as monistic as *advaita* and so is much closer to Ramanuja's qualified view. The term "inconceivable identity-in-difference" is routinely used to describe this qualified monism. According to this interpretation, everything is simultaneously one with and different from the Supreme Being, Lord (who comes with various names; common folk in India follow either the Siva god [Saivites] or Vishnu [Vaishnavites], the latter being best known through an *avatara* cult, particularly of Krishna).

Advaita's uncompromising nondualism has enormous implications for the nature of reality.[76] Therein "the relation of Ruler and ruled does not exist" apart from the "phenomenal world."[77] The cosmos emerges from the Real in a process that simultaneously becomes the vehicle for the self-expression and manifestation of the divine.[78] This means that the phenomenal world is not the "real" (or truest, as it were) existence. Of course, the phenomenal world exists, but it is "appearance" in the sense that it is not the ultimate.[79] Even the oft-quoted saying of Sankara that "the fiction of Nescience [*avidya*] originates entirely from speech only,"[80] does not mean that talk about the cosmos (as distinct from Brahman) is merely rhetorical but rather that what is ultimately real is Brahman; that alone is self-subsistent. Related to this dualistic view of reality is the distinction between two realities, *para* and *apara*, developed in later Upanishads, that is, between spirit and matter.[81] (In Western philosophy, Plato's idealism has significant parallels: as in his famous cave analogy, what the people consider the real world is not that, but merely a shadow.) That distinction, however, does not posit the kind of categorical dualism present in

---

76. As Sara Grant (*Towards an Alternative Theology,* pp. 39-40) points out, "In India as in Greece, the ultimate question must always be that of the relation between the supreme unchanging Reality and the world of coming-to-be and passing away, the eternal Self and what appears as non-Self" (the study compares Aquinas and Sankara).

77. Sankara, *Vedanta-Sutras* 2.1.14; *SBE* 34:330.

78. K. Ward, *Religion and Human Nature,* p. 12.

79. "The world of appearances is real though not self-subsistent" (K. Ward, *Religion and Revelation,* p. 146). Well-known illustrations of Sankara include mistaking rope for a snake (*Vedanta-Sutras* 1.3.18; *SBE* 34:189) and elephants seen in dreams for real ones (1.2.12; *SBE* 34:123). Sankara's modern interpreter Swami Vivekananda goes quite far as he says: "This universe does not exist at all; it is an illusion. The whole of this universe . . . [is] all dreams." Vivekananda, "Steps of Hindu Philosophic Thought," n.p. For a balancing and correcting statement of Sankara's view, see Lipner, *Hindus,* p. 14.

80. Sankara, *Vedanta-Sutras* 2.1.27; *SBE* 34:352; For comments, see K. Ward, *Religion and Revelation,* pp. 145-47.

81. See Menon, "Hinduism and Science," p. 11.

much of Western thought between spirit and matter: "God, ultimately reality, permeates all material manifestations, and hence . . . there is no fundamental antagonism between matter and spirit, world and God." At all times, Hindu vision seeks to experience "the harmony of dualities."[82]

This idea of the "appearance nature" of the phenomenal world can be understood in a more negative or positive way (to use Western criteria). On the one hand, the world can be considered merely an illusion with no inherent value.[83] On the other hand, "the world can also be seen as the divine play, in which the One, though remaining complete in itself, manifests in diversity so as to realize its infinite potential in endless ways, and to enjoy that self-realization."[84]

Hindu Monism(s) and Abrahamic Faiths

How does this strict monism relate to the Semitic distinction between the Divine and created reality? Sometimes it is argued that in one important sense — namely, with regard to the *ex nihilo* doctrine — Sankara's absolute monism may find a common point with Semitic faiths when we look at the following well-known statement: "(Brahman is that) from which the origin, &c. (i.e. the origin, subsistence, and dissolution) of this (world proceed)."[85] So, it seems like Brahman/the divine is the "cause" of the cosmos. But the commonality may be only *alleged*. It is based on the strange idea (strange at least to Western logic!) that "the effect is in reality not different from the cause,"[86] and that "the creator is non-different from the created effects."[87] I simply don't know how to understand this statement.[88] A much more promising candidate for commonality is Ramanuja's qualified nonduality, particularly as that comes to expression in the Vaishnavite view of Krishna as the "agent" of creation (not

82. Menon, "Hinduism and Science," p. 11.
83. Some of Vivekananda's sayings seem to be stating that having realized his own nature, "the whole world has vanished" for the Vedantist ("Vedanta Philosophy"); for other such sayings, see K. Ward, *Religion and Human Nature*, pp. 13-14.
84. K. Ward, *Religion and Human Nature*, p. 15.
85. Sankara, *Vedanta-Sutras* 1.1.2; SBE 34:15.
86. Sankara, *Vedanta-Sutras* 1.1.25; SBE 34:94.
87. Sankara, *Vedanta-Sutras* 1.4.14; SBE 34:265.
88. I am not convinced by K. Ward's (*Religion and Revelation*, pp. 150-51) effort to understand Sankara in light of Aquinas's saying that "whatever perfection exists in an effect must be found in the effective cause" (ST 1.4.2); the two theologians are speaking of different issues.

totally unlike the Logos in Christian tradition); this popular theology of "creation" is of course closer to the Semitic idea of distinction (but not separation) between God and world.[89]

A highly interesting Upanishadic account of origins seems to suggest an idea of creation as the Lord's consort, not totally different from some Christian thinkers' views (cf. Moltmann). "In the beginning" there was the "Self alone," a "person" who feared as a lonely person does and had no delight. "He wished for a second." To combat loneliness, the Self split himself into man and wife. And then from that, various kinds of beings came into being, as mentioned above.[90] Placed in the uncompromisingly monistic Hindu framework, though, even this kind of epic does not make any break from the unity of creator and created.

In sum, Vedic cosmology at large and *advaita* in particular represent a different understanding of the god-world relationship from that of Abrahamic faiths. Even in the most pan(en)theistically oriented versions of Christian theology, which of course are marginal, the world is not conceived to be a nondifferentiated extension of the Lord. For its integrity, Christian theology must posit a distinction, if not a separation, between God and the world, as the classical panentheism of this project argues. I tend to be convinced by R. C. Zaehner's reasoning that there is an "unbridgeable gulf" between those theistic faiths that see the Creator as infinitely greater than the creatures and those that equate the two.[91]

Sankara's whole project is to help men and women come to the liberating knowledge in which all distinctions are overcome, as truly *atman* is Brahman. If this is not pantheism, what is?[92] Also, Brahman is not other than all things, but "is the same as that Self, that Immortal, that Brahman, that All."[93] Hence, there is also no doctrine of creation *(ex nihilo)* in Hinduism as the world emerges from within Brahman.[94] (Rather than creator, Brahmā is better called Visvakarmā, the "architect.")[95]

89. See further, Dasa, "Ramanujacarya's *Visistadvaita-vada*," n.p.

90. Brihadaranyaka Upanishad 1.4.1-5; *SBE* 15:85-86.

91. Zaehner, *Mysticism, Sacred and Profane,* p. 204, contra K. Ward, *Religion and Revelation,* pp. 152-53.

92. Contra K. Ward, *Images of Eternity,* pp. 18-19.

93. Brihadaranyaka Upanishad 2.5.1 (*SBE* 15:113); the following verses repeat that idea over and over again.

94. Sankara, *Vedanta-Sutras* 1.1.2; *SBE* 34:15. Another important notion in Sankara's thought is that since "the effect is in reality not different from the cause" (1.1.25; *SBE* 34:94) and "the cause virtually contains all the states belonging to its effects" (1.2.24; *SBE* 34:145), Brahman must be imagined as the material cause of the world. See further, K. Ward, *Images of Eternity,* p. 16.

95. See Sharma, *Classical Hindu Thought,* p. 20.

That Ramanuja seeks to challenge the unqualified monism of his famed predecessor is not to introduce dualism but rather to offer a more sophisticated — *qualified* — account of *advaita.* Indeed, as Ward brilliantly notes, the "real distinctions . . . are all distinctions within one basic reality." Hence, "Ramanuja is ironically more of a monist than Sankara, who retains the basic dualism of reality and appearance."[96] In his account, reality consists of three tiers: "the world of material things, the multiplicity of *jīvātmas,* individual living beings, and *Brahman,* who is identical with *īśvara,* who is none other than Visnu. Creation is the body of *Brahman* but not without qualification." When speaking of the world, Ramanuja famously intuits it as the body of God. What is astonishing is that his way of speaking of the world as the body being animated by the divine spirit, being dependent on it, and being guided by Brahman, sounds so strikingly similar to some contemporary Christian, deeply panentheistic conceptions.[97] An important related idea is what Christian and Western philosophical tradition calls "infinity," as "God contains all finite realities, both good and evil, but also transcends them. God is with and without form . . . changing and changeless, is with and without existence in a changing world, is both father and mother of all beings, is incomprehensible and yet reveals himself, is separate from all beings yet united with all beings."[98] While Sankara's monism poses a problem for Christian tradition, Ramanuja's qualified monism comes closer to it.

If a distinction is posited between Brahman and the world, God can act in the world. While that is a great advantage, there is also an unresolved problem related to Ramanuja's agreement with Vedanta tradition that Brahman has "the individual souls for its body."[99] How can they then be under the guidance of Brahman? Ward rightly notes: "The reason why theists make a distinction between souls and God is that souls are finite centres of consciousness, whereas God is infinite; souls fall into error and sin, whereas God is omniscient and perfect,"[100] and so forth. From a Semitic tradition's perspective, this is yet another reason for the need to posit a distinction — even when panentheistically conceived — between God and world, including the divine and human.

Although the aim of comparative theology is neither to soften real dif-

---

96. K. Ward, *Images of Eternity,* p. 31.

97. Ramanuja, *Vedanta Sutras* 2.2; *SBE* 48:261-62.

98. Carman, *Majesty and Meekness,* p. 146.

99. Ramanuja, *Vedanta Sutras* 1.1; *SBE* 48:132.

100. K. Ward, *Images of Eternity,* p. 31; see chap. 2 for an extended discussion of this and related challenges in Ramanuja.

ferences nor to look for a consensus at any price, it is also important for the continuing dialogical pursuit to discern where similar types of intuitions are present even in systems of thought as widely different as Christianity and Hinduism. Ward puts it succinctly: "Though Semitic faiths tend to stress the moralism of the Supreme, and Indian faiths tend to stress the non-dualism of Being, both express a sense of the world as dependent on the Supreme; a sense of alienation requiring moral or epistemic reconciliation; and a sense of final realization of goodness, whether in the Supreme alone or in a community of relational beings."[101]

Having established a distinctively Christian understanding of nature as creation and having constructed a trinitarian theology of creation, followed by a detailed look at cosmologies of origins and nature in other Abrahamic and two Asiatic faith traditions, we now bring all that into a sustained dialogue with contemporary scientific cosmologies. Chapter 6 will focus on the question of "beginnings," whereas chapter 7 will deal with continuing sustenance and the conditions of divine action in the created world.

6. Creation in Evolution:
An Evolving Cosmos and Emerging Life

Whereas chapters 3 and 4 attempted a constructive *theological* account of the cosmos and nature as the work of the trinitarian God, Father, Son, and Spirit — and chapter 5 engaged cosmologies of origins in some living faiths — the current discussion seeks to put the religious and theological interpretations in a wide and deep dialogue with the contemporary understanding of the origins, evolvement, and functioning of the cosmos as interpreted in natural sciences (cosmology, physics, evolutionary biology, and similar fields). If this book were a study in the *science*-religion dialogue per se, it would probably be more pertinent to begin with the scientific understanding and then seek to find correspondences and dissimilarities with Christian and other religions' interpretations. For a systematic theological work, on the other hand, it is useful (and perhaps even necessary) to do it the other way around in order to offer an integrative *theological* account.

The discussion, already begun in the first two chapters, continues with the implications of the dramatically changed worldview and philosophy of science in the twentieth century; hence the investigation of the religion-science relationship carried on in chapter 2 is assumed as the template. Thereafter, the question of the ultimate origins of the cosmos will be investigated through the scientific and theological lenses. The third main part of the chapter will delve into the question of origins and conditions of life and its evolvement in our kind of world and cosmos.

A Changed Worldview and Its Implications for Theology

One of the main reasons why theology of creation is in transition has to do with the vastly changed worldview of contemporary times. Among many significant changes, probably none surpasses the importance of the shift from substance ontology, aligned with dualisms of various sorts, to relationality and holistic explanations (for details, see *Trinity and Revelation,* chap. 10). Significantly, the rise to relationality was also rediscovered in Christian theology with the trinitarian renaissance (chap. 11). Briefly put: both philosophical and scientific — as well as theological (trinitarian) — reasons speak for the need to envision reality as relational, interdependent, and communal. Similarly, the triune Creator is the ultimate divine communion.[1]

In the physical sciences, the most dramatic change since Newton, along with relativity theories (of which more below), is the shift from classical to quantum physics.[2] Quantum theory has helped overcome once and for all the naive mechanism and full determinism that were often assumed in the older paradigm. What quantum theory reveals is that not only at the smallest, subatomic level (where quantum theory primarily functions), but also at the macrolevel, nature reveals surprises, irregularities, and unpredictability. This is not to say that nature acts unlawfully; the laws of nature are still in place and natural phenomena are (relatively speaking) deterministic — otherwise no scientific observations would be possible. What the unpredictability means is that determinism is not ironclad and that — at least according to the major (Copenhagian) interpretation of quantum theory — natural processes and events are probabilistic in nature.[3] The Heisenberg unpredictability principle claims that a lack of exact results is not a matter of weakness of measurement but an inherent feature of the reality studied.[4] Indications of that are well-

---

1. An important discussion is Polkinghorne, *Trinity and the Entangled World.*

2. A standard introduction for nonspecialists is Polkinghorne, *Quantum World;* for a nonmathematical primer, see Polkinghorne, *Quantum Theory.* My exposition in this paragraph draws directly from his essay "The Quantum World," pp. 333-42.

3. "Natural phenomena can be both deterministic and random. For example, the half-life of a given nucleus can be calculated using nuclear theory and quantum mechanics. However, the individual nuclei decay randomly, but if the sample of nuclei is great enough, within the statistical uncertainty associated with random events that are associated with a definite average number, the calculated half-life will be confirmed by an experimental measurement. I call this lawful randomness." Richard Carlson (private e-mail communication, 9/7/2013).

4. While the so-called Copenhagen Interpretation, sometimes called the "standard" theory, following Niels Bohr, Werner Heisenberg, Max Born, and others, is not the only interpretation, it certainly is the mainstream. The biggest challenger is the Bohmian (more)

established phenomena such as the wave/particle duality (that is, light appears both as wave and as particle) and the incapacity to measure both the momentum and position of the particle.[5] Or consider the highly counterintuitive Bell's theorem — which, ironically, also helped put to rest the lifetime resistance of Albert Einstein to the "spooky" nature of quantum reality.[6] Bell showed in 1964 that without any "real" reason the measurement of two chance events — imagine the measurement of the spin of two electrons when they travel as a result of the decay of an atom — shows definite nonlocal correlation, that is, while it cannot be said that these two chance events really influence each other, they are to a certain extent inseparable.[7] This principle of "togetherness-in-separation" or "nonlocalizability"[8] has since been conclusively proven beyond doubt as a feature of the quantum world.[9] The quantum theory also opens up, to say the least, the possibility that consciousness — human observation and "measurement" of quantum processes — has a real effect on how processes go, implying a much more complex interaction of various levels of reality, from physical to mental.[10]

Add to these and related quantum features that bespeak indeterminism, probability, and surprise the whole new field of chaos theory, which shows that, while causality (rightly understood) is of course not to be put aside when observing the events and processes of nature, the more developed the processes, the less *mechanistically* causal they are — even if they are basically deterministic! Consider the famous "butterfly effect": the slightest change affecting climate in one part of the world, when amplified, may cause at the

---

deterministic view of the theory. For a short discussion from a theological perspective, see McGrath, *ScT* 2:283-85.

5. The famous "superposition" principle, roughly speaking, says that a particle can be said to be both "here" and "there," not of course simultaneously but probabilistically, that is, we can never know for sure. Consider also other celebrated quantum examples of indeterminism and counterintuitiveness, namely, the "double-split experiment," that is: imagine a beam of electrons shot through a metal plate with two narrow slits; the results clearly imply that these particles have behaved more like waves as they appear to have entered both slits!

6. For Einstein's well-known resistance to quantum theory (which he, of course, helped originate!), see Polkinghorne, *Quantum World,* chap. 7.

7. See R. Russell, "Quantum Physics," pp. 346-48.

8. So named by Polkinghorne, "Demise of Democritus," pp. 6-7, where he names it "nonlocalizability."

9. For a highly useful resource for contemporary philosophical and theological debates about quantum theory, see *Zygon* 41, no. 3 (2006).

10. See Clayton, "Tracing the Lines," pp. 215-17; see also Chia, "Quantum Nonlocalities," pp. 17-39.

other end of the globe a huge storm! (That is why weather forecasting can never be accurate beyond a very short period of time.) That said, we should mind Polkinghorne's warning that the "strange and counterintuitive" nature of the quantum world "does not license the attitude that everything goes,"[11] nor does it "endorse the essential rightness of Eastern religious thought," as argued in some popular books. The former quantum physicist also rightly notes that while metaphysical questions emerge in the world depicted by quantum theory, the "theory is not of itself a sufficient basis for a universal metaphysics" as is seen in a variety of philosophical approaches by its students.[12]

This kind of world is open rather than closed in nature. Theologically put, Moltmann speaks of the openness in terms of a robust theology of "heaven," which expresses the fundamental openness of creation to God and thus to the future.[13] In the open universe, the process of emergence is constantly at work. The basic definition of *emergence* is "that new and unpredictable phenomena are naturally produced by interactions in nature; that these new structures, organisms, and ideas are not reducible to the subsystems on which they depend; and that the newly evolved realities in turn exercise a causal influence on the parts out of which they arose."[14]

Emergence theories seek to defeat explanatory reduction — also known as "physical closure" — which seeks to explain everything in the world in terms of physical processes and entities.[15] The theologian-philosopher Philip Clayton offers this more refined description of key claims of emergence: (i) ontological monism: reality is ultimately composed of one kind of stuff; (ii) property emergence: the emergence of genuinely novel properties; (iii) the irreducibility of the emergence: the emerged properties and capacities cannot be reduced back to a subvenient base; and (iv) downward causation: there is top-down causation (not only bottom-up).[16] The last point is the most significant and — among reductionist materialists — the most severely contested. While reductionists are open to the idea of "weak" emergence that, while proposing new levels and patterns, still maintains in principle the physical closure (or something close to that), they contest "strong" emergence that, as defined above, speaks of the capacity of new patterns and processes to exert

11. Similarly, Norris, *Quantum Theory and the Flight from Realism.*
12. Polkinghorne, "Quantum World," p. 340; see also Clayton, "Tracing the Lines," pp. 215-17.
13. Moltmann, *God in Creation,* chap. 7.
14. Clayton, *Mind and Emergence,* p. vi; for the history, see chap. 1.
15. For an important discussion, see Murphy, "Reductionism," pp. 19-39.
16. Clayton, *Mind and Emergence,* pp. 4-7.

causal influence.[17] Concerning (i), emergentists can hold several ontological options, from physical monism (that all that there is ultimately is the physical) to ontological monism (reality is made of only one kind of "stuff," but not necessarily material) to dualism (that there are two substances or properties, at least concerning humans, namely, physical and mental). As to how many levels of emergence there might be in reality, of course no one knows. The Yale biophysicist H. Morowitz has found no fewer than twenty-eight![18]

What is crucial is that "[t]rue complexity occurs with the emergence of higher levels of order and meaning."[19] The mathematician John Conway's "Game of Life" has drawn considerable attention in illustrating the importance and unique nature of emergence. By manipulating two options (on and off), it can be easily seen how quickly the matrix gives rise to emerging phenomena and yet, this all happens "deterministically" (that is, it is determined algorithmically and hence is highly predictable) rather than randomly![20] A theologically significant observation is that "[e]mergence at all levels of being, and not just at those of life and mind, requires that nature possess an anticipatory rather than simply a cumulative character. It must be open to a domain of potentiality that makes a quiet entrance — from the future as it were — and thus opens up the otherwise unbending fabric of things to the later-and-more."[21] In other words, "mere transit of time," however long it is, hardly produces anything new.[22] In the created order that is open, there is a curious interplay not only of chance and necessity but also of novelty and entropy. In other words, there is a dynamic tension between increasing entropy and the higher structuring. "In its dependence all creaturely reality is subject to the fate of destructuring, of dissolution according to the law of entropy. Because of the openness of process structures to future events, however, new structures are constantly formed, since processes take place in open rather than closed systems."[23] Moreover, as discussed above, there is the role of the Spirit as the source of novelty.[24]

---

17. See also Clayton, "Conceptual Foundations of Emergence Theory," pp. 1-31.

18. Morowitz, *The Emergence of Everything*.

19. Ellis, "Science, Complexity, and the Nature of Existence," p. 113.

20. For the now classic (first) presentation of Conway's theory to a wide audience, see M. Gardner, "Mathematical Games," pp. 120-23; for an important discussion, see Dennett, *Darwin's Dangerous Idea*, pp. 166-81.

21. Haught, *Is Nature Enough?* p. 86.

22. Haught, *Is Nature Enough?* p. 94.

23. Pannenberg, *ST* 2:112.

24. See Clayton, "Toward a Constructive Christian Theology of Emergence," pp. 315-44; see p. 315.

What about the question of naturalism in relation to emergence? Cannot even the strong, let alone the weak, emergence be explained without reference to any transcendent being? Indeed, even strong emergence does not compel one to opt for a theistic explanation. It is significant that the very first modern emergence theorists at the beginning of the twentieth century already saw various interpretive options: Samuel Alexander was a Spinoza type of pantheist with evolutionary theistic leanings; Lloyd Morgan, a deeply classic theist; and Wood Sellars wished to avoid any particular religious interpretation.[25] In sum: emergence theories, particularly the strong option, can be either naturalistically (nontheistically) or theistically understood. No need to mention that the latter is the case in the current project.

Other important changes in the scientific and philosophical worldview are under way, not least with regard to understanding causality and the nature and role of the laws of nature, to be discussed below. The implications of these and related changes for the doctrine of creation and theology of divine action will be discussed in this and the following chapter. A fitting summary is that of Polkinghorne:

> We are presented with a picture of the physical world that is neither mechanical nor chaotic, but at once both open and orderly in its character. A simple everyday notion of objectivity is too limited an account even for physical reality. The latter displays an elusiveness which is nevertheless rationally structured, though perhaps not exhaustively so. . . . The contingent rationality of the world . . . is consonant with its being the free creation of a reasonable Creator.[26]

The Origins and Conditions of the Universe in Light of Contemporary Cosmology

The Big Bang Cosmology

As an academic discipline, contemporary cosmology faces a number of challenges and opportunities.[27] Not only does it utilize a variety of disciplines in its

25. For a highly nuanced and insightful discussion, see Gregersen, "Emergence," pp. 279-302.

26. Polkinghorne, "The Quantum World," p. 341.

27. A highly readable and reliable primer for nonspecialists is NASA/WMAP Science

study of origins, evolution, and the ultimate fate of the entire universe, such as astronomy (astrophysics), particle physics, gravitation, mathematical physics, and quantum theory, it also crosses the border between experimental science, metaphysics, philosophy, and in some cases even religion.[28]

Undoubtedly the most overwhelming challenge to contemporary cosmology is the simple fact that its "object" is the whole of reality. With this come a number of insurmountable obstacles, quite uncommon to other "hard" sciences, including the following:

- We do not know how "big" the universe is. Even reference to the multiverse theory, that is, rather than one universe, there are a number of them — perhaps even an infinite number — does not get around the basic question, as "universe" basically means all that there is.
- We cannot make "all that there is" our object of study, as we are integrally part of it. Hence, our observations are always those of "insiders."
- Even worse: whatever the "size" of the universe, we already know enough to realize that just our own Milky Way — one among at least 10 billion other galaxies — is so vast that traveling across it even at the speed of light, which of course is possible only for objects (particles) with no rest mass such as the neutrino, would take 100,000 years; even that would not have really made any difference regarding our location in the currently known universe.

What is the most current scientific account of the origins of the cosmos?[29] While one should not expect a full consensus in the global scientific academy regarding what undoubtedly is the most complicated question ever posed to human investigation, it is safe to say that the standard big bang theory is the established natural sciences' view of origins and evolvement. This is not to say that it will never be replaced by another major theory; most likely it will, and there are already indications that a shift will take place in the near future. That said, in the beginning of the third millennium of the Christian

Team, "Cosmology." A useful nontechnical discussion for theologians is Stoeger, "Contemporary Cosmology," p. 219.

28. For "the need for a larger view" in Cosmology (uppercase, indicating the need to go beyond but of course not against the merely scientific cosmology), see Murphy and Ellis, *On the Moral Nature of the Universe,* pp. 59-63 and passim.

29. In addition to the many sources cited here, I am also indebted to R. B. Mann, "Physics at the Theological Frontiers"; Boisvert, *Religion and the Physical Sciences,* has also been constantly open on the desk for quick reference.

era, the global natural scientific community regards the big bang not only as a "theory" in the term's popular sense, which speaks of its tentative and non-evidential form, but also as a "theory" that is established both theoretically (mathematically) and with huge experimental support — notwithstanding a number of heated debates about many issues.

Briefly put, the standard model argues that the cosmos came into being about 13.8 billion years ago from a singularity of zero size and infinite density (usually marked as $t = 0$ in which t denotes time), and has since expanded to its current form. Since the Hubble discovery in the 1920s, we know that the galaxies are receding from us, and therefore that the cosmos is "expanding." Important evidence for this expansion and the big bang came from the discovery in the 1960s of the microwave background radiation that is believed to be an echo from the original big bang.

Two key theoretical principles that have been extensively studied experimentally support the view, namely, relativity theory and the cosmological principle. Whereas Albert Einstein's 1905 special relativity theory linked space and time together in a space-time continuum and thereby made all points of observation relative rather than absolute, the 1916 general relativity theory was able to include gravity. Radically revising the Newtonian theory in which space and time were understood to be some kind of separate backgrounds or "containers" in which matter moved, Einstein established space-time as a four-dimensional manifold (three space and one time dimension) that "can stretch, warp, and vibrate."[30] Furthermore, whereas Newton's 1680s theory of gravity applied only to bodies at rest or moving slowly ("slow" in relation to the speed of light!), Einstein's theory applied to bodies in all conditions. That is because gravitation was thought of no longer in terms of a "field" but rather as a distortion of space and time. As the physicist John Wheeler's famous dictum puts it: "Matter tells space how to curve," and "[s]pace tells matter how to move."[31] Think of the surface of a balloon with colored spots while it is being blown up: it is not that the spots are moving (even though they are) but that the surface of the balloon is expanding!

Now, on this basis the big bang theory builds naturally: observing the galaxies flying apart as indications of constant expansion, it simply looks back in time to the point when the expansion started; finally you come to the "beginning point." But for that to work — in other words, for the general relativity theory to be applied to the study of the cosmos as a whole — we need

30. Spitzer, *New Proofs*, p. 15.
31. Misner, Thorne, and Wheeler, *Gravitation*, p. 5.

an assumption concerning the distribution of matter. Roughly speaking, the assumption of the cosmological principle is that the distribution of matter in the universe is homogeneous and isotropic when averaged over very large scales. An important support to this assumption, besides extensive observational evidence related to the even distribution of galaxies, among others, came from the 1960s discovery of cosmic microwave background radiation, the remnant heat from the big bang: it seems to have a highly uniform temperature over the large scale. Further support for the big bang model has come from the defeat of its onetime challenger, the so-called steady state theory of Hoyle, Bondi, and Gold, of the late 1940s. This theory supposes that although the universe is constantly expanding, new matter is also being created to keep a constant density over time.

Important refinements to the classical big bang theory, originally proposed in the 1920s by the Roman Catholic priest-physicist Georges Lemaître, have been made since. Currently we know that immediately after the big bang, during the extremely short period of time (so-called Planck time, 10^{-43} seconds, the shortest measure of time) named the "inflation period," dramatic developments occurred that help explain many oddities in the composition and processes of the current cosmos, including the Flatness Problem and the Horizon Problem.[32] What is odd is that contemporary science is not able to explain what happened during that immensely short period immediately following the bang, since no known laws of nature apply to it. The current relativistic laws of nature can explain how the cosmos has evolved since, that is, after 10^{-43} seconds till today. What happened "before" that, hence, must be a matter of quantum laws. Here, however, the theologian must exercise great caution: the fact that the initial singularity or big bang "involves infinite temperature and infinite density serves as a warning that this did not actually happen"; it is rather like a "'prediction' of the model which does not represent what really occurred."[33] If it "happened," it is the kind of happening our known laws — and hence also terminology — cannot grasp at all! To speak of this initial singularity as the "beginning" is therefore highly problematic.

Here also is the culmination of undoubtedly the biggest unresolved riddle in contemporary natural sciences: how to reconcile with quantum theory, which studies the tiniest, smallest particles within the atom, the theory of relativity, which is able to explain the functioning of everything big — the big-

---

32. For an accessible explanation to these problems, see "What Is the Inflation Theory?" in NASA/WMAP Science Team, "Cosmology"; Stoeger, "The Big Bang," pp. 156-60 particularly.

33. Stoeger, "The Big Bang," p. 158.

ger, the better![34] Separately, these two theories have been proven true beyond much doubt. However, all mathematical attempts to make them collaborate embarrassingly fail, even in principle. Hence, the continuing search for a "theory of everything"[35] that would be able to explain both the smallest and the biggest. Without that grand unified theory, contemporary science cannot go beyond the Planck-second following the bang (during which time, allegedly the four basic forces of physics — gravity, electromagnetism, weak nuclear force, and strong nuclear force — were unified, that is, there was only one "superforce"). The new quantum cosmologies, superstrings, loop quantum gravity, and noncommutative geometry theories may prove to be the way to the theory of everything, if it can ever be discovered.[36]

Other recent refinements to the original big bang scenario include the discovery of "dark energy" and "dark matter" with profound implications for our understanding of both the nature and the development of the cosmos. Let us ask the simple question: What is the universe made of according to our latest knowledge? All life is basically made of three components: protons, neutrons, and electrons.[37] But what is astonishing is that — totally the opposite of what was believed — the universe overall is not made mainly of this "baryonic matter," as it came to be called. On the contrary, most of the universe is something "dark," namely, "dark matter" (23 percent) and "dark energy"[38] (72 percent), which leaves only a few percent for the "stuff" life is made of.[39] While much is still unknown about both dark matter (a form of matter so dense that it neither emits nor absorbs any light and therefore cannot be detected) and particularly dark energy, the latter is important in helping

34. The problem is often presented briefly as that of unification: How can we give a unified explanation of the four fundamental forces, gravity, electromagnetism, and the strong and weak nuclear forces?

35. Barrow, *New Theories of Everything;* for an important discussion, see Küng, *The Beginning of All Things,* chap. 1.

36. For an excellent discussion, see Greene, *The Elegant Universe;* an accessible guide is also Smolin, *Three Roads to Quantum Gravity.*

37. Protons and neutrons are bound together into nuclei, and atoms are nuclei surrounded by a full complement of electrons.

38. See further, the Berkeley Cosmology Group's site: http://astro.berkeley.edu/~mwhite/darkmatter/dm.html (11/2/2013).

39. We also know nowadays that to use the term "atom" (as a convenient reference to the three above-mentioned components) is technically wrong as the term means "uncut." Each atom in itself is an extremely — perhaps infinitely — complex "microcosm." It is only the limitations of measurement devices that hinder our going beyond "quarks" and similar "smallest" things we can infer currently.

explain the 1998 discovery that the expansion of the universe is speeding up. The slowing down of the cosmos, which indeed happened for billions of years, is due to gravity, which keeps matter from flying apart. The current speeding up, then, presupposes another kind of "matter" or "energy" or "field," which would act differently than gravitation. Dark energy is thus presupposed. It also helps explain the flatness of the cosmos as well as other large-scale features including the distribution of galaxies.[40]

Even with these revisions, the standard big bang scenario presupposes the beginning of the universe and makes it thus "historical" rather than eternal. The famous Hawking-Penrose singularity theorem established the fact. In 1980 Hawking argued that "a curvature singularity that will intersect every world line . . . [makes] general relativity predict a beginning of time."[41] The singularity is of course the big bang, beyond which "it is impossible to extend the space-time manifold."[42]

Beyond the Big Bang Model: Emerging Quantum Cosmologies

Famously, however, Hawking came to radically revise his view of the big bang, shifting from an initial singularity to a boundary-less scenario that still presupposes the "beginning," the finite nature with regard to the beginning, although no beginning in time (no singularity). Why this move? The main reason goes back to the fundamental riddle of contemporary natural sciences, mentioned above — the impossibility of reconciling classical and quantum physics. Everywhere else but in or very close to the singularity classical physics works; in or very near, it does not. Hence, what if the assumption of singularity — which is entailed by classical physics — is not needed in the quantum world? Hartle-Hawking's "no-boundary" model builds on that premise. Its difference from the standard model can be easily depicted with the following illustration: imagine a piece of wood in the shape of a cone. In the standard model there is a sharp edge, in other words, a singularity, $t = 0$.[43] In the no-boundary model the edge is rounded off, smooth; hence, there is no singularity, no beginning in time. Going back to the cosmos, it still is finite — like the surface of a bal-

40. See further, "Universe Overview," in NASA/WMAP Science Team, "Cosmology."

41. Hawking, "Theoretical Advances in General Relativity," p. 149, quoted in Spitzer, *New Proofs*, p. 30.

42. Q. Smith, "Uncaused Beginning," p. 120, quoted in Spitzer, *New Proofs*, p. 31.

43. For the sake of illustration, let us ignore the fact that in reality even in the sharpest edge can one hardly discern singularity.

loon — but no preferred, definite beginning point can be established. This is precisely Hawking's argument, now that

> the quantum theory of gravity has opened up a new possibility, in which there would be no boundary to space-time and so there would be no need to specify the behavior at the boundary. There would be no singularities at which the laws of science broke down, and no edge of space-time at which one would have to appeal to God or some new law to set the boundary conditions for space-time. One could say: "The boundary condition of the universe is that it has no boundary." The universe would be completely self-contained and not affected by anything outside itself. It would neither be created nor destroyed. It would just BE.[44]

Having collaborated with the American physicist Jim Hartle (hence, the Hartle-Hawking proposal), Hawking reminds us that "this idea that time and space should be finite 'without boundary' is just a *proposal*: it cannot be deduced from some other principle."[45] Using "imaginary numbers,"[46] his own invention, makes it possible to make the distinction between time and space disappear completely.[47] Generally speaking in his invoking of quantum gravity, the role of space becomes dominant whereas that of time is being marginalized ("imaginary time").

Hartle-Hawking's revision of the standard model is of course not the only current challenger. There are plenty of them, emerging all the time. For the sake of clarification, we can outline some broad — but in many ways inter-related — tactics among those who, unlike advocates of the standard model, wish to replace the classic with quantum physics/gravity:

(a) Scenarios in which the big bang is still the beginning of the universe, but it is no longer "singular"
(b) Various types of "bouncing" or "oscillating" models in which big bounces rather than one single big bang succeed each other endlessly
(c) Scenarios in which (like option b) the big bang is no longer the beginning, but rather a gateway or portal, if you will, to an era that preceded the big bang or to another "dimension" of reality

44. Hawking, *Brief History of Time,* p. 141.

45. Hawking, *Brief History of Time,* p. 141, emphasis in original.

46. Imaginary numbers, which are different from both positive and negative numbers, yield negative numbers when multiplied by themselves: $1i \times 1i = -1$; $2i \times 2i = -4$; etc. See Hawking, *Brief History of Time,* pp. 139-41.

47. Hawking, *Brief History of Time,* p. 139.

(d) "Multiverse" scenarios in which our universe is but one among many others, perhaps infinite in number

The Hartle-Hawking proposal represents, of course, option a. The "bouncing universe" scenario — known under many names such as "eternal return," or "a cyclic, oscillating, pulsating, or reprocessing universe" (option b) — imagines big bangs in succession, probably without any end. Whereas the standard view speaks of a big bang, these know a big bounce — as well as a big crunch, the collapse of the universe back to infinite density, but not as the final end but rather as an occasion for yet another cycle of big bang–big crunch, *ad infinitum.* This theory has long historical roots in Greek philosophy and among Asiatic faiths, yet it is a marginal view among scientists.[48] Why? The main challenge is the recent finding that rather than slowing down, the cosmos seems to be speeding up, as mentioned above. But if for the sake of argumentation we suppose that a big crunch would happen, would that then make feasible the bouncing scenario? Many doubt that, because of other opposing reasons such as the radiation paradox. Whereas almost all "light" (that is, electromagnetic radiation) is the famous cosmic background radiation stemming from the big bang, only about 1 percent is "light," as in starlight. In the expanding cycle, stars are formed and emit light. If there were a great — perhaps infinite — number of cycles of universes, then in each collapsing phase starlight would be scattered and reabsorbed by matter, and finally the lights would go off in the cosmos! The current ratio between cosmic radiation and starlight is 1/100 rather than, say, 1/100,000, which should have been the figure in the case of 1 million cycles behind us, and so forth. The second consideration conflicting with the bouncing universe's rejection of a beginning of the universe has to do with the entropy paradox. Unless the current "cycle" is the first one — ever! — the amount of entropy at the moment of the big bang could not have possibly been extremely small as we know it to be for the simple reason that every star keeps releasing burning entropy. The final reason for opposing the bouncing universe scenario is an increase in cyclic expansion, that is (without going into technical details),[49] each cycle would be longer than the previous one, which of course disallows an infinite regress; "retrieving the steps" of the cycles would get us to the shortest one, the beginning.[50]

48. A highly interesting theological exploration is Worthing, "Christian Theism and the Idea of an Oscillating Universe."
49. Explained in Q. Smith, "Uncaused Beginning," pp. 108-39.
50. This whole paragraph is based on Spitzer, *New Proofs,* pp. 24-30.

Option c is represented by a number of other quantum cosmology-related proposals. The "island" scenario considers our universe in the analogy of a part of an island, among other islands. Although within any island the same laws of physics apply, "between" the islands that may not be the case. The "superstring" theories imagine the standard four-dimensional universe of ours to be but a slice of a universe with many more dimensions, perhaps ten or so (this is also the assumption of "supergravity" theories); the best-known among these more-than-four-dimensional models is the "ekpyrotic" scenario; our four-dimensional universe is envisioned as a (mem-)brane moving around within a higher-dimensional space-time among other branes.[51]

A family of proposals maintains that while *our* universe most probably has evolved the way theory predicts, ours is not the only one. This is scenario d in the typology. Unlike other cosmological scenarios that apply their theory of origins and development to the whole universe, the "multiverse" alternatives assume a number of parallel universes, perhaps infinite in number. The Everett-DeWitt Quantum "Many Worlds" Hypothesis is routinely mentioned as the first such major proposal, followed by a number of others.[52] Not only are there a number of parallel universes, there is also a constant splitting into ever new universes. As the famed physicist Paul Davies, himself not a subscriber to the view, strikingly puts it: "Whenever a measurement is performed to determine, for example, whether the cat is alive or dead, the universe divides into two, one containing a live cat, the other a dead one. Both worlds are equally real, and both contain human observers. . . . Countless times each second, the universe is replicated."[53] The obvious challenges to various multiverse proposals, similarly to the group of proposals in option c, beyond total lack of any kind of empirical evidence, are the following: opposition to the parsimony principle (Ockham's Razor), that is, the simplest explanation is to be preferred over the complex one unless there is a reason for the latter, and significant problems in relation to cosmological observations regarded reliable and justified.[54] An all-important point for our discussion is that in all the various forms of multiverse theories, "something is supposed to have happened before the big bang, and so the big bang is not in these scenarios

51. For a brief, nontechnical account, see Spitzer, *New Proofs*, pp. 20-21.

52. An accessible account of this and other similar proposals can be found in Spitzer, *New Proofs*, pp. 67-72.

53. P. Davies, *God and the New Physics*, p. 116. The reference to the cat is of course to the (in)famous Schrödinger's cat experiment in which only the measurement tells us, under a 50/50 probability of being alive or dead, the state of the cat.

54. Spitzer, *New Proofs*, p. 68.

the 'beginning of the universe' and the 'beginning of time' as it is in the Standard Big Bang Model."[55]

Before engaging these scientific scenarios philosophically and theologically, let us ask tentatively: What about the future of the cosmos? Three options are available. In the "open model," the cosmos is infinite in size but finite in the beginning, and it continues expanding forever until it cools down to the point that life is extinct. In the "closed model," it is finite in size as well as in the beginning; having expanded to a maximum radius, the cosmos recontracts to the final singularity, the "big crunch." In the "flat" model, the universe expands but almost stops at some point. No one can tell which of these options (or other hypothetical views) is the correct one, but most scientists currently opt for the open model. Some important support for that has come in the observations of supernova beginning in the 1990s.

The Theological Meaning of the "Beginning" of the Universe: *Ex Nihilo* in Abrahamic Traditions

On the Clarification of the Terms of Discussion

The question of the "beginning" of the universe is highly complex. On the religious side, it relates to the question of *ex nihilo* and its interpretations (in all three Abrahamic faiths). On the scientific side, it engages both the big bang cosmologies and their alternatives and how they might relate to Abrahamic faiths' theological doctrine of creation. Obviously, then, this is a question that has to be carried on in a highly multidisciplinary environment that includes biblical, tradition-historical, philosophical, religious, and natural scientific contributions.

We must first ask the foundational question of whether it makes sense to assume any kind of beginning to the universe. What if the universe is eternal, and therefore, there is no beginning? Although the eternity of the universe is a minority position in science nowadays, until the rise of contemporary cosmology, it was the standard position among scientists as well as the widely held philosophical-theological position among three Abrahamic faiths throughout history. That will be our second topic, including its current corollary: whether the universe is infinite or finite.

If the universe is not eternal, however, there has to be some kind of begin-

55. Spitzer, *New Proofs,* p. 21; fittingly, Spitzer calls these models "past-extended big bang models."

ning; but what does that mean? Terminologically and materially, it may mean many different things — as already the discussion of current scientific cosmologies indicates: beginning *of* time; beginning *in* time; beginning as in "origin," the ultimate "source" or "cause" of everything. These alternative hermeneutics have to be worked out in detail. After that discussion, third, we will inquire into the theological value of the most intuitive way of connecting current cosmology with theology, namely, the view in which the big bang means the beginning of the universe in time (and/or beginning of time itself) as the correlate for the Abrahamic traditions' *ex nihilo* doctrine. Fourth, we will investigate what may happen to the theology of creation if, with the leading quantum cosmological alternative of Hartle-Hawking, it can be shown that there is no beginning in time.

Although detailed discussion and argumentation are needed to come to a proper conclusion in the final part of this section, let us set forth the main thesis here in the beginning: for the theistic doctrines of creation (in Abrahamic faiths), the foundational conviction concerns the contingency of the universe on the Creator. In other words, however the question about the relation of time to the big bang or similar scientific view of the "beginning" is negotiated, theology's claim for the ultimate contingency of creation upon the Creator is not thereby absolved.

Ex Nihilo in Abrahamic Traditions

The Slow Establishment of Ex Nihilo *in Jewish Tradition*

As established above, the Asiatic traditions do not subscribe to any (meaningful) form of *creatio ex nihilo* whereas for all three Abrahamic faiths it is a core doctrine.[56] However, it took about a millennium for the Jewish tradition to adopt the *doctrine* of *ex nihilo*.[57] The reason is that Genesis 1:1-2 can be interpreted in terms of God working with "materials" already in existence, and the expressions "Let there be . . ." throughout the first chapter "could certainly be understood as summoning into existence rather than fashioning from something pre-existent."[58] Furthermore, OT writings at large show little concern about metaphysics.[59] The slow development of *ex nihilo*, however, should not be understood as casting

---

56. Cogliati, introduction to *CGA*, p. 1.
57. As discussed in detail in McMullin, "Creation *Ex Nihilo*."
58. See Kellner, *Dogma in Medieval Judaism*, pp. 213-17.
59. Soskice, "*Creatio Ex Nihilo*."

doubt on the uncompromising Jewish confession of Yahweh as the sole origin and sustainer of the cosmos. This deeply held belief was also important in the rebuttal of the Hellenistic notion of *ex nihilo nihil fit* ("from nothing comes nothing"), as that supported an "atheistic" view of the origins of the cosmos. Furthermore, unlike Aristotle, Jewish tradition did not make the world necessary (as it refuted its eternity), as it considered important the defense of God's freedom.[60]

Notwithstanding the lack of historical details concerning the rise of alignment with *ex nihilo* over the centuries, the medieval master Maimonides helped definitely establish *ex nihilo* in Jewish tradition: "Those who follow the Law of Moses, our Teacher, hold that the whole Universe, i.e., everything except God, has been brought by Him into existence out of non-existence. In the beginning God alone existed, and nothing else; neither angels, nor spheres, nor the things that are contained within the spheres existed. He then produced from nothing all existing things such as they are, by His will and desire. Even time itself is among the things created."[61]

Maimonides' description of creation includes the standard elements of the *ex nihilo* view, including the rejection of the eternity of matter, and hence, eternity of the cosmos.[62] Like Augustine, Maimonides understood that *ex nihilo* could not presuppose even the existence of time but rather that time in itself is created. Human language, however, fools us here: "We say that God *existed* before the creation of the Universe, although the verb *existed* appears to imply the notion of time; we also believe that He existed an infinite space of time before the Universe was created; but in these cases we do not mean time in its true sense."[63]

Christian Theological Implications

While the Fathers rightly acknowledged that *ex nihilo* was not directly taught in the Bible,[64] as early as the second century the doctrine was established.[65]

---

60. For details, see Soskice, *"Creatio Ex Nihilo,"* pp. 30-37.
61. Maimonides, *Guide for the Perplexed* 2.13; p. 171. For an important study, see Seeskin, *Maimonides on the Origin of the World.*
62. Maimonides, *Guide for the Perplexed* 2.17; p. 180.
63. Maimonides, *Guide for the Perplexed* 2.13; p. 171, emphasis in original.
64. Tertullian, *Against Hermogenes* 21-22; Irenaeus, *Against Heresies* 2.10.4; Basil of Caesarea, *Hexaemeron* 1.7. For other references, see Pelikan, *Emergence of the Catholic Tradition*, pp. 36-37.
65. A highly useful discussion, with a view toward science-theology dialogue, can be found in T. Peters, "On Creating the Cosmos," pp. 276-82.

It helped reject the Platonic notion of the eternity of matter[66] and the idea of the divine architect fashioning the cosmos out of materials already available.[67] With *creatio ex nihilo*, early tradition also ruled out pantheism, which equates God and matter. Tradition also rejected the necessity of creation as God the Almighty created everything "[b]y the bare exercise of volition."[68]

When speaking of *ex nihilo*, one has to be careful not to make "nothing" something — as happened in Barth's curious and mystical notion of *Das Nichtige*. The expression "nothing" is merely shorthand for saying that there was nothing preceding, whether material or spatial or temporal, out of which God created.[69] Theologians should oppose the tendency in current cosmology to "magically reify the *nihil*."[70]

The doctrine of *ex nihilo*, however, does not rule out the participation of creatures in the evolvement of creation.[71] While this fact did not go unnoticed in earlier tradition, with the rise of modern science it became an urgent one, that is, "the relation between on the one hand the religious claim that God created the world and on the other hand the Enlightenment claim that we human beings are world-makers."[72] Although theologically speaking these two claims do not have to be in contradistinction, to many they appear to be. Constructive theology's task is to put them in a mutually conditioning relationship. Similarly, *ex nihilo* does not rule out the emergence of novelty, surprises — evolution! On the contrary — and in contrast with Deism — Christian tradition teaches that the same Creator who brought about reality from nothing, in *creatio continua* not only maintains but also helps bring about new forms and new phenomena.[73]

---

66. See Wolfson, "Patristic Arguments against the Eternity of the World," pp. 351-67.

67. A detailed, vigorous defense of *ex nihilo* is Copan and Craig, *Creation out of Nothing*.

68. Clement, *Exhortation to the Heathen [Greeks]*, chap. 4 (*ANF*², p. 190); so also Tertullian, *Against Hermogenes* 45. For a fine summative statement of *ex nihilo*, see A. M. Clifford, "Creation," p. 213. For a summary of contemporary critiques of *ex nihilo*, see O'Donnell, *Trinity and Temporality*, pp. 17-21. Perhaps the harshest critique available is that of Catherine Keller's process-driven semipantheistic theology of creation in *Face of the Deep*.

69. For comments, see McMullin, "Creation *Ex Nihilo*," p. 11.

70. Oliver, "Trinity, Motion and Creation *Ex Nihilo*," p. 134.

71. See Watson, *Text, Church, and World*, pp. 142-43.

72. Broadie, "Scotistic Metaphysics and Creation *Ex Nihilo*," p. 53.

73. See T. Peters, "On Creating the Cosmos," pp. 284-91.

Ex Nihilo *in Medieval and Contemporary Islamic Tradition*

During the medieval era, Islamic philosophers differed regarding *ex nihilo* doctrine on the basis that some assumed to have freedom to interpret Qur'anic teaching without a particular cosmology.[74] Whereas al-Kindi (d. 873) subscribed to *ex nihilo* (and thus departed from Aristotle, whose influence was significant on all Muslim thinking), many later philosophers rejected the doctrine (without of course questioning the doctrine of God as Creator per se), such as al-Farabi (d. 950), the famed Turkish polymath and "Renaissance man." Al-Farabi followed the Hellenistic "chain of being" template that proceeds down from the One in successive emanations. Another multi-genius, Avicenna (d. 1037), sought a masterful synthesis of the absolute authority of revelation, Aristotelian philosophy as interpreted by al-Farabi, and (later in his life) Sufi mysticism (without giving up intellectual pursuits). As a result, his doctrine of creation is a hybrid concept with "kinds of creations" (for example, temporary and eternal creatures as well as creation through other agents) with different categories of creatures from angels to "cosmic souls" to heavenly bodies to earthly objects. He also entertains the obscure "idea of creation . . . [as] not compatible with the idea of beginning to exist after non-existence," that is, before any "existence" there is "nonexistence," out of which everything emerges. Hence, "the universe cannot have begun to exist *de novo.*"[75] (In other words, for Avicenna the term "creation" is used only of this ultimate coming into existence from nonexistence.) Averroes, however, although of course gleaning also from Aristotle, was more keen to build on Qur'anic authority. Yet he envisioned an eternal cosmos in constant change or evolution as a result of God's continuing creation. (In contrast to al-Farabi, he rejected the emanationist view.)[76] N. Guessoum rightly notes that "Averroes introduced an interesting new twist to the old concept of unity of the cosmos; he considered it from the viewpoint of change (or lack thereof), concluding that as content and form be dissociated, and both are eternal, the cosmos must be static, even if it evolves." (This view, of course, comes close to what is called Hoyle's steady-state theory of the mid–twentieth century.)[77] The most

74. See Fatoorchi, "Four Conceptions of *Creatio Ex Nihilo.*"

75. Acar, "Creation," p. 78; Acar's essay is a detailed investigation of the complex view of creation (existence, time, and related issues) in Avicenna.

76. The emanationist view also exercised great influence through the Ikhwan as-Safa (the "Brethren of the Purity") esoteric society in tenth-century Shia Iraq. Their encyclopedic "epistles" (letters) mark yet another milestone of early Muslim scientific and philosophical activity. For a brief discussion, see Guessoum, *Islam's Quantum Question,* pp. 196-98.

77. Guessoum, *Islam's Quantum Question,* pp. 194-96, here p. 196.

noted Muslim philosopher of all time, al-Ghazali, had no patience for those who departed from the *ex nihilo* doctrine, and he considered the eternity view as one of the three cardinal heresies[78] (along with the denial of the resurrection of the body and God's knowledge of particulars).[79]

In light of this diversity of views among authoritative philosophers, it is significant that "Muslims and their religious scholars, particularly the Qur'an's interpreters, today take it for granted that the Qur'an refers to the creation of the universe as an *ex-nihilo* act (by God). In doing so, they base themselves on the latest scientific knowledge in order to reconstruct the story of the creation from the verses that deal with the topic, verses that are in fact scattered in the Book, unlike the Bible's Genesis chapter."[80] Qur'an 7:54 is a key verse here: "Lo! your Lord is Allah Who created the heavens and the earth in six Days, then mounted He the Throne. . . . His verily is all creation and commandment. Blessed be Allah, the Lord of the Worlds!"[81] While this and many other Qur'anic passages (2:29; 21:30; 41:9) say at face value that there was a beginning to the universe, several great medieval scholars (Ibn Rushd, Ibn Sina, and others) were open to the eternity of the cosmos.[82] In terms of the future of the cosmos, references to a big crunch can be found among Muslim scholars, on the basis of Q 21:104.[83]

With these insights in mind, we look briefly at why the idea of the eternity of the universe continued to have such an appeal in these three traditions.

Whether the Universe Is Eternal

A common assumption among pagan philosophies was that if God is eternal, then creation is as well. For Aristotle time and movement had neither begin-

---

78. Al-Ghazali's Tahafut Al-Falasifah, *The Incoherence of Philosophers*, "Problem I," pp. 13-53; for a synopsis of his views, see Guessoum, *Islam's Quantum Question*, pp. 228-31.

79. For these early philosophical debates in Muslim philosophy (vis-à-vis Greek thought), I am indebted to Leaman, *Islamic Philosophy*, chap. 2; Wolfson, *Philosophy of the Kalam*, chap. 6.

80. Guessoum, *Islam's Quantum Question*, p. 189.

81. See also Q 41:9 (which says that in two days God created the world); 2:29; 21:30.

82. Behind the Muslim speculations about eternity versus a beginning is the debate about whether the earth was created before (Q 2:29) or after (79:27-30) the heavens. See Guessoum, *Islam's Quantum Question*, pp. 190-91.

83. Q 21:104: "The Day when We shall roll up the heavens as a recorder rolleth up a written scroll. As We began the first creation, We shall repeat it. (It is) a promise (binding) upon Us. Lo! We are to perform it."

ning nor end.[84] While Plato opposed the eternity of time, oddly enough some Christian theologians, particularly Origen, came to believe that on Platonic presuppositions the immutability and eternity of God led to the eternity of the world.[85] By and large, however, early theology rejected the eternity of the world, including the alleged connection between the immutability of God and the eternity of the world.[86] Rather than creation taking place in time, time itself comes into being in creation, as Augustine argued.[87]

During medieval times, Christian Scholastics continued combating the Aristotelian and Neoplatonic arguments against the temporal beginning of the world.[88] These debates were fueled by close contacts with Jewish and Arab philosophies and theologies. Moses Maimonides set forth robust objections to the Aristotelian claim for the eternity of the world because of its incompatibility with scriptural teaching.[89] According to Maimonides, there are "three different theories as regards the question whether the Universe is eternal or not," namely, that of Scripture, which speaks for the temporal beginning from nothing; that of the philosophers, such as Plato, who regards creation as a matter of shaping preexistent matter; and finally that of Aristotle, which bluntly makes the world eternal.[90] Whereas in Jewish philosophy the temporal beginning thus became the normative view, among the leading Islamic thinkers debate continued as al-Ghazali's critique of Aristotelianism's argument was combated by Averroes. On the Christian side the final resolution in favor of the temporal beginning came at the Fourth Lateran Council (1215).[91] Interestingly enough, Aquinas did not find the council's argumentation conclusive even though he granted the possibility of its temporal beginning: for him the only sure thing was that the world is creation, in other words, the product of the divine creative act and hence dependent — even if it might be eternal.[92]

---

84. Aristotle, *Physics* 8.1. This view was common among contemporary philosophers with the notable exception of his teacher Plato, who imagined a beginning for time (*Timaeus* 37d). Plotinus affirmed eternity based on the idea of the derivation of time from eternity (*Enneads* 3.7.6).

85. Origen, *De principii* 1.2.10.

86. For details and references, see Pannenberg, *ST* 2:147.

87. Augustine, *City of God* 11.6; before him, Clement of Alexandria, *Stromata* 6.16.

88. Representative selected texts from Bonaventure, Aquinas, and Boethius (in Latin and German translation) can be found in Nickl, *Über die Ewigkeit der Welt*.

89. Maimonides, *Guide for the Perplexed* 2.13-29.

90. Briefly outlined in Maimonides, *Guide for the Perplexed* 2.13.

91. "Twelfth Ecumenical Council: Lateran IV 1215," canon 1.

92. Aquinas, *ST* 1.46.1, 2; for details, see Pannenberg, *ST* 2:148-49.

Famously Kant revived the idea of the eternity of the world in his first cosmological antinomy. According to him, one had to imagine a sort of "empty time" before the beginning unless one followed the idea of no beginning. Furthermore, this "something" before the "beginning" would not be void of links with a sequence of causes.[93] Hegel noted that Kant's reasoning rested on the presupposition that there can be no unconditioned existence.[94] Hegel rightly argued against Kant that a "limit" is presupposed by the finite nature of being,[95] and hence the idea of an "absolute" beginning (without preceding time or sequence of causes) may be posited. Commenting on this, Pannenberg rightly observes that the main question here is whether the (Hegelian) claim that the very nature of the finite entails a beginning in time can be determined in relation to the whole of the cosmos; in other words, can we establish whether the cosmos is finite or infinite? That is of course a debated question in contemporary science.[96] Furthermore, Pannenberg rightly notes that ultimately this is a matter of empirical verification rather than merely a derivation from general physics or philosophy. Everybody, of course, agrees with that, but few scientists and theologians — I take it — would be willing to say as he does that "for the first time cosmology could now make the whole universe in both its spatial and its temporal extension a subject of empirical research."[97] Without denying the vast developments achieved in contemporary science, in principle — let alone in practice — the empirical research of the cosmos as a whole is of course absolutely impossible, as noted above.

The main opinion of current scientific cosmology does not consider the universe eternal, although in many quantum cosmologies (such as the "oscillating universe" model) that position seems to follow (and of course, the now rejected steady-state theory considered the universe eternal). More importantly, the discussion in current cosmologies has shifted from eternity to the question of whether the universe is finite or infinite. Whereas the closed model considers the universe finite (with finite space and a beginning as well as an end of duration) and thus can be called homogenous, many quantum cosmologies — ironically — come to mix finite and infinite aspects. The "standard" quantum model of Hartle-Hawking presupposes the beginning (albeit not in time) of the universe and in that sense considers it finite, although it

93. Kant, *Critique of Pure Reason*, pp. 262-66.
94. Hegel, *Science of Logic* 21.228-29 (pp. 197-99).
95. Hegel, *Hegel's Philosophy of Nature*, §258 (pp. 34-37, particularly p. 36).
96. Pannenberg, *ST* 2:151; see also pp. 146-51, for which I am indebted.
97. Pannenberg, *ST* 2:154; see also p. 157.

believes that both spatially and in relation to the future the universe is infinite! Which one of these is correct? "No data is sufficient to force us into univocal answers as to its age, size, or future."[98] Here "we stand at the threshold of physics and metaphysics."[99] This means that, on the one hand, we should not expect to receive a final answer — if that even ever can be had! — merely from the consideration of the scientific data; on the other hand, dismissing the current scientific views of the beginning would only make theology obsolete and irrelevant. Hence, discussion must continue in the intersection of cosmology, philosophy, and theology.

Having clarified the theological ramifications of *ex nihilo* in Abrahamic traditions and the defeat of the eternity of the universe (by and large), let us delve into the investigation of modern cosmologies' theological implications. Before that, we again raise the question: What about the end of the universe? While that topic belongs to eschatology (vol. 5), a brief consideration is in order in light of its close connection to the discussion of beginning with a special focus on the question of finitude. By and large, modern science has been even more skeptical about the end of the universe than of the possibility of a beginning. An early modern contribution came from Descartes, who, while attributing to God the world's coming into existence, surmised that God's immutability implied the continued existence of the world, as after creation all events and changes in the reality were attributed to the creatures themselves. Unchanging laws of nature followed.[100]

Only with the second law of thermodynamics has contemporary science faced the possibility of the end in terms of running out of energy. A related factor leading to the scientific possibility of the end has to do with how to think of the "future" of big bang cosmology, whether in terms of expansion to the point that cold-death results or in terms of big crunch, regressing to something similar at the point of $t = 0$, a singularity of infinite heat.[101] Be that as it may, the scientific speculations about the future of the universe are radically different from the vision in biblical eschatologies: whereas in the former the time span would be billions and billions of years, way beyond human presence, the latter relates to human destiny. In eschatology this foundational question is discussed in detail.

98. R. Russell, *Cosmology,* p. 42.

99. Spitzer, *New Proofs,* p. 23.

100. Descartes, *Principles of Philosophy* 2.36, 37.

101. For an accessible account, see Hawking, *Brief History of Time,* chap. 3.

*The Coherence between the Big Bang Cosmologies and
"In the Beginning" Doctrines of Creation*

What are the scientific reasons for considering the big bang as the beginning of the universe? Or, let us formulate the question like this: What are the scientific reasons why the beginning of the universe should be presupposed regardless of the decision as to how this "beginning" is related to time? First, approaching the singularity $t = 0$, "gravitational tidal forces, densities, and temperatures increase without limit."[102] That clearly speaks for some kind of "absolute beginning." Second, entropy, the second law of thermodynamics, basically says that all cosmic (and smaller) processes happen only in one direction. Without energy from outside, equilibrium comes with decay and disorder. The relevance to the question of beginnings is of course simply this: "If the universe did not have a beginning, then it has been around for an infinite time" and would be something like a perpetual motion machine — which seems not to be possible in light of entropy.[103] The third reason is simply the overall superb explanatory power of the big bang model across the scientific fields that study the universe. Russell summarizes: "Physical cosmology gives a unified interpretative scenario through which the universe developed from an embryonic fireball into the present composition."[104] All in all, it looks like the universe as we know it is the outcome of certain initial conditions stemming from the big bang. So appealing is this thought that, surprisingly, some secularists have come to attribute to $t = 0$ some kind of religious implication.[105] A further ironic confirmation is that a stated motive behind Hoyle's steady-state model was to oppose the seemingly theistic-friendly idea of the "beginnings."[106] Below, in the discussion of space-time, we will come back to the issue of "time-arrow."

No wonder some contemporary theologians have been turned on by the seeming consonance between big bang cosmology and Genesis 1. Oft-cited is Pope Pius XII's embrace of the big bang, which makes it all the more astonishing in light of his resistance to evolutionary theory![107] In the words of T. Peters, "we have sufficient consonance with which to proceed further in the

102. R. Russell, *Cosmology,* p. 39.
103. Spitzer, *New Proofs,* pp. 24-27, here p. 26.
104. R. Russell, *Cosmology,* p. 39.
105. See Spitzer, *New Proofs,* p. 13.
106. See R. Russell, *Cosmology,* p. 40.
107. Pope Pius II, "The Proofs for the Existence of God in the Light of Modern Natural Science," Address to the Pontifical Academy of Sciences, November 22, 1951.

discussion."[108] Unlike other theologians who have been more reserved about jumping on the bandwagon, particularly the late eminent British biochemist-priest Peacocke, who considers the big bang basically meaningless to theology, and the American process religion-science expert Barbour, to whom $t = 0$ is relatively unimportant,[109] Peters is concerned about the danger "[t]o reduce *creation ex nihilo* to a vague commitment about the dependence of the world upon God — though accurate — [but which] does not help much."[110] Russell insightfully registers the concerns behind the virtual equation of $t = 0$ with *ex nihilo*. First, scientific results are changing, as has already happened with the introduction of quantum cosmologies. Second, philosophically it is virtually impossible to speak of $t = 0$ as an "event" or process, as it is about an infinite state to which our scientific concepts do not apply. Third, "[t]he identification of *ex nihilo* with t = 0 would seem too narrow."[111]

Notwithstanding these reservations, the theologian should not underestimate the analogical and material importance of the big bang cosmology as one of the ways to correlate theological claims with scientific ones, minding that when scientific theories change, these tentative correlations are subject to change, without compromising the foundational contingency claim. Without in any way equating $t = 0$ with *ex nihilo*, theology would do well to remember Augustine's famous formulation according to which God did not create in time but rather, time was created with the cosmos.[112] That view is of course materially in consonance with the standard model in cosmology.[113] The philosopher McMullin puts it accurately: "What one *could* readily say, however, is that if the universe began in time through the act of a Creator, from our vantage point it would look something like the Big Bang that cosmologists are now talking about. What one cannot say is, first, that the Christian doctrine of creation 'supports' the Big Bang model, or second, that the Big Bang model 'supports' the Christian doctrine of creation."[114]

---

108. T. Peters, "On Creating the Cosmos," p. 291.

109. R. Russell, *Cosmology,* p. 89.

110. T. Peters, "On Creating the Cosmos," p. 288.

111. R. Russell, *Cosmology,* pp. 84-85 (quotation p. 85).

112. Augustine, *Confessions* 11.7.

113. Astonishingly, Chris Isham considers Augustine's solution superior also to those quantum cosmologies such as the fluctuation model that presuppose the existence of a background space-time or something similar filled with quantum fields, as well as laws of nature out of which the material universe arises spontaneously. If time was created with the universe, then the question of what must have happened "before" the emergence of matter/universe does not arise. For details and documentation, see R. Russell, *Cosmology,* pp. 95-96.

114. McMullin, "How Should Cosmology Relate to Theology?" p. 39, emphasis in original.

Going beyond that may not be warranted. Even when consonance or correlation between the big bang cosmologies and the theological doctrine of creation is established, one has to be careful of the differences, as already mentioned. A warning example is the American physicist Frank J. Tipler's recent *Physics of Christianity* (2007), which makes the bold case that in big bang cosmology "singularity" means God.[115] This is bad theology and even worse physics. When it comes to natural sciences, Tipler's claim that physics proves Christianity, or any religion for that matter, is a nonsensical claim. This is a category mistake.[116] Much more nuanced and cautious is American rabbi David W. Nelson's suggestion that perhaps a "metaphorical identity" could be found between the big bang and God.[117]

The Doctrine of Creation and Quantum Cosmologies without a Beginning in Time

The Hartle-Hawking model, as discussed, posits a finite past without an initial singularity as well as infinite space and future. Hawking hastens to draw conclusions that finally there is a theory that makes God obsolete: because there is no beginning, no God is needed, and by understanding the laws of nature we can read God's mind.[118] Hawking is a first-rate scientist but a very poor philosopher-theologian, and he makes several foundational mistakes. The most critical is this: the doctrine of creation in no way restricts divine activity to the beginning of, bringing about, the universe. The doctrine of creation is also about continuing creation, providence, and divine action.[119]

A theological challenge to be taken more seriously comes from quantum cosmology's positing the infinity of the universe (in relation to size and future). Even if this is partial infinity, so to speak, because the past (albeit without a beginning point in time) is finite, it still is a huge statement. Even without this proposal, the seemingly "infinite" size of the observable universe (let alone what is beyond that) is mind-blowing. What to think of that theologically? Let us first make an all-important distinction to clarify the issue. Russell notes that while the past has to be finite for the theistic doctrine of

---

115. Tipler, *The Physics of Christianity*, p. 1: "The Cosmological Singularity is God."

116. For insightful comments, see Sudarminta, "Big Bang Cosmology and Creation Theology," pp. 143-44.

117. D. W. Nelson, *Judaism, Physics, and God*, chap. 2.

118. Hawking, *Brief History of Time*, pp. 140-41.

119. See also similar kinds of responses by R. Russell, *Cosmology*, pp. 97-99.

ex nihilo to work (or else the universe is eternal), that does not necessarily presuppose a beginning in time. That is yet another counterintuitive insight of contemporary scientific thinking. Again we see the significance of Augustine's idea of time coming into existence only with creation, thus making the idea of "unbounded finitute" (more) sensible.[120] Going even further, Russell remarks that ultimately, "we cannot equate contingency with something as loosely defined as finitude,"[121] particularly when the finitude does not relate to the past. After all, in the science-theology dialogue, we should allow for both consonance and dissonance. With that in mind, McMullin's suggestion cited above can be revised like this:

> We may look for *consonance in terms of the temporal past,* so that the Big Bang that cosmologists are now talking about would count as a correlate to the theological concept of finitude in terms of a beginning in time through the act of a creator, but we cannot necessarily expect the future or the size of the universe to show a similar correspondence with the theological concept of finitude. In sum, we must accept the possibility of *consonance over the past but dissonance over the future and size, consonance over the future but dissonance over the past and size, and so on.*[122]

Hypothetically, I believe we can go even further and at least make a thought experiment to test the feasibility of the idea of the universe being truly eternal without even a finite past. Would that be a deathblow to the doctrine of creation? Not necessarily. We can get help from the revised concept of infinity. In *Trinity and Revelation,* the philosophical idea of infinity in relation to God is investigated both in relation to the "proofs" for the existence of God (chap. 9) and in the context of divine attributes (chap. 12). By reading Descartes and Hegel (and even some Church Fathers), it was established that rather than being limited by the finite, the infinite so transcends the finite that it also includes it within itself (otherwise infinity would be compromised when "bordering" on something that is not infinite, namely, finite). Contemporary mathematics, particularly that of George Cantor, has not only distinguished various types of infinities but also helped establish "an unreachable Absolute" (or "Absolute Infinity") toward which all other levels of infinities point. The identification in mathematics of types of infinities accords well with the existence in physics of

---

120. R. Russell, *Cosmology,* pp. 99-100.
121. R. Russell, *Cosmology,* p. 45.
122. R. Russell, *Cosmology,* p. 46, emphasis in original.

all kinds of infinities (such as vacuum fields). Now the current mathematics' concept of Absolute Infinity can be used analogically in theology in reference to God, and therefore, all other infinities, including the universe's age and size, do not threaten the doctrine of creation.[123] The universe's eternity then would be qualitatively different from that of God as much as God's infinity is Absolute.

Be that as it may, a fitting closing statement for this section, before clarifying some key features of contingency, is that of the British theologian Simon Oliver:

> Whether one accepts the Big Bang understood as a temporal boundary to the universe, as in the inflationary theory, or the Hawking model of a beginningless universe which is nevertheless finite, neither approximates to the doctrine of creation *ex nihilo*. Natural science cannot truly think the *nihil*. Scientific cosmology still operates with the Aristotelian notion that *ex nihilo, nihil fit*. The vacuum of modern particle physics which fluctuates to bring the universe to existence through so-called quantum tunnelling is not "nothing," for this "nothing" is apparently subject to fluctuation.[124]

The Theological Significance of Contingency

To repeat, the main claim of *ex nihilo* is about contingency.[125] Robert J. Russell has further clarified the various interrelated aspects of contingency. First, "global contingency" refers to the universe's dependence on the Creator as a whole, including "ontological" contingency (that is, the sheer existence of the cosmos) and "empirical" contingency, "the empirical features that characterize the universe as a whole," such as the laws of nature and cosmic constants.[126] Second, "local contingency" denotes the dependence of each and every part and process of the cosmos on the Creator (which can be similarly divided into ontological and empirical aspects). The third category, "nomological contingency," means the "variety of forms of contingency reflected in the laws of nature." Herein Russell considers the most important facet the "first instantiation contingency," that is, when the laws of nature came into being, which can be

123. A rigorous study is R. Russell, *Cosmology,* chap. 2.
124. Oliver, "Trinity, Motion and Creation *Ex Nihilo*," p. 134; the American physicist W. S. Stoeger concurs (Stoeger, "The Big Bang," p. 169).
125. Pannenberg, "The Doctrine of Creation and Modern Science," p. 9. Materially similarly are Tillich, *ST* 1:196, and Gunton, *The Triune Creator,* p. 113.
126. R. Russell, *Cosmology,* p. 36.

interpreted either in the "mild way," that is, only some basic laws were manifest in the "beginning" and as new forms emerged, new kinds of laws had their first instantiation, or in the "aggressive way," which refers to something as radically new and unprecedented as Christ's resurrection. Those kinds of "miraculous" events point to "a transformation of the present nature *beyond* what emergence refers to."[127] The aggressive form presupposes openness of the created reality and the fact that "the meaning of contingent processes which begin with a first instance in nature will only be fully clear at the end of history (that is, eschatologically)." That will of course make the universe historical in nature.[128]

One of the set of questions that current cosmology raises has to do with time and space. Although time and space were once imagined to be "absolute" (Newton), now, after the advent of the relativity theory, time-space (along with gravity) forms an intertwined continuum. Quantum cosmology further has made the whole notion of time thinner and even more "relative" — a radical move from the time of Newton! What are the theological implications? To that topic we turn next.

Creation's Space-Time in Theological Perspective

Problematic Notions of Time in Tradition

The awkward expression "space-time" reminds the reader of the obvious fact that in the post-Einsteinian worldview neither time nor space has the kind of "absolute" existence it had in classical physics.[129] Rather, we speak of a space-time continuum (of four dimensions or even more, if string theories are correct). To single out either "time" or "space" in the discussion itself is not to forget this basic insight, but rather to make communication more economic and manageable.

Early theology was drawn to the idea of the eternity of creation because of the eternity of God.[130] That belief, as discussed above, was abandoned for good reasons. Augustine, on the other hand, made time a created entity.[131]

127. R. Russell, *Cosmology*, p. 37, emphasis in original.
128. R. Russell, *Cosmology*, pp. 37-38.
129. Reliable nontechnical primers for theologians are Goosen, *Spacetime and Theology*, chap. 3, "What Is Science Saying about Spacetime?" and K. Ward, *Big Questions*, chap. 5.
130. See further, R. Russell, *Time in Eternity*, pp. 94-100.
131. Augustine, *City of God* 11.6. Materially the idea was suggested earlier by Clement of Alexandria, *Stromata* 6.16, and Gregory of Nyssa, *Against Eunomius* 1.26.

The correct insight, however, was coupled with another, highly suspicious supposition that if time has its origin in God, then God somehow must exist "outside" time. There was yet another mistaken notion related to Augustine's foundationally correct insight into the created nature of time. It has to do with Augustine's desire to secure God's immutability in light of the fact that God's transition from eternity to time would imply change if time existed prior to creation of the universe. Although Augustine's idea is problematic in that it sets time in antithesis to "timeless" eternity, the lasting value is that it "opposes any restriction of the divine action in creation to the beginning of the world."[132] As Pannenberg shows,[133] Barth, speaking of creation in time, partially misunderstood Augustine's point in mistakenly believing that by denying the existence of time prior to creation, Augustine would also deny the temporality of creation. Augustine, of course, did not teach that. (Indeed, ironically Barth's insistence on creation taking place in time, albeit as "the first among God's works,"[134] subjects him to the charge that there was time "prior" to creation, the fallacy Augustine avoided — and which Barth also recognized and wished to get around!)[135] Where Barth, however, was more enlightened than Augustine was in his reluctance to set time and eternity in juxtaposition because eternity is the "source of time."[136]

The corollary to Augustine's theory of time — namely, that God exists outside time — led to a highly problematic juxtaposing of eternity and time. There were two ways of understanding eternity and its relation to time, both of which contemporary theology finds wanting. First, one could think of God's eternity as something "timeless."[137] That idea also seemed to be in sync with divine omniscience: God does not have to *fore*know (which he of course could) because all events are "simultaneously" present to him. (Ironically, that view relates well to the contemporary "block view" of time proposed by some physicists, as discussed below.) Second, one could think of eternity as an unending time. Both notions are theologically inadequate, as argued below.

Before getting into the constructive theological discussion, however, we

132. Pannenberg, *ST* 2:39. For Augustine's profound analysis of time as *distention animi* (extension of soul), which highlights the "time-bridging" nature of human experience of time, that is, the interrelation between memory of the past and anticipation of future in the present, see R. Russell, *Time in Eternity,* pp. 98-100.

133. Pannenberg, *ST* 2:38-39.

134. Barth, *CD* III/1, p. 42.

135. Barth, *CD* III/1, pp. 70-71.

136. Barth, *CD* III/1, pp. 67-71; see p. 70.

137. Aquinas, *ST* 1.10.2.

must introduce the most foundational issue relating to religion-science dialogue concerning time: whether to think of the ontological nature of time as tenseless or tensed. It is the question Einstein's special relativity theory brought to the surface.

"Block Time" or "Flowing Time"

Roughly speaking, philosophers divide understandings of ontology of time into two camps, conveniently called A-time and B-time. The former is the commonsense notion in which the present is real and so is also the flow of time from past to present to future,[138] whereas the latter is the majority view among physicists (and Anglo-American philosophers of time as opposed to the Continentals). For scientists, the current understanding of space-time implies that time and space have an equal ontological status, and thus it is unnecessary to distinguish between past, present, and future. Analogically, think of space laid out there completely. In this B-time scheme, the "now" is but a human mind's construction, not a quality of nature.[139] Briefly put, A-time is tensed or flowing time, whereas B-time is tenseless or block time.[140]

That said, a couple of important qualifications are in order concerning the B theory. Strictly speaking, it is not correct to say that all notions of "absolute" time are canceled by relativity. What happens, rather, is that "we lose the sense of a unique universal present and we end up with multiple inertial frames of reference for the relation between past and future and with multiple rates at which time passes."[141] Nor is it correct to say that the theory of relativity and block universe deny change (because of tenselessness). Indeed, most ironically, it is exactly the relativity theory that made it possible for cosmology to move away from the static to a dynamic, evolving universe! But what the block universe is saying is that

138. Subdistinctions in this category usually include "presentism," that is, only the present is real (and the past is "lost"), and "growing-past theory," with further subcategories in which either the future is not real or the future is only potentially real as it is indeterminate and open to more than one option.

139. See R. Russell, *Cosmology*, p. 220; R. Russell, *Time in Eternity*, pp. 7, 22.

140. The distinction between A-time and B-time derives from McTaggart, "The Unreality of Time," pp. 457-74. An excellent nontechnical, short primer to block time is P. Davies, "That Mysterious Flow," pp. 82-88. For theologians, excellent introductions to the discussions of block time and flowing time are Craig, *Time and Eternity*, pp. 32-66 and chaps. 4; 5; R. Russell, *Time in Eternity*, chap. 2.

141. T. Peters, "The Trinity in and beyond Time," p. 269; see also Stoeger, "Faith Reflects on the Evolving Universe," pp. 162-82.

Change takes place in time, that is, along the dimension of the structure which represents time. But there is no change of the structure as a whole. . . . Every event in time is permanently fixed at its location. Indeed, it can be said that while space-time is intrinsically temporal (that is, one of its dimensions is time), it is extrinsically timeless (that is, it does not exist in some embedding hyper-time). Space-time neither changes nor becomes; it just is (tenselessly).[142]

So far the discussion has assumed the commonsense "flowing time" scenario, as opposed to that of "block time." What is at stake for theology in the debate? Much, indeed, is at stake.[143] So much so that this question may be(come) one of the defining and most critical issues in the theology-science conversation for some time. Theology's desire to opt for flowing time is funded by the obvious great problems caused by block time.[144] One of the problems involves the question of authentic human freedom if the future does not mean potentialities. Furthermore, divine freedom in light of the insistence on the openness of the future to God also seems to be at stake. Related, it would be extremely difficult to envision an authentic form of Christian eschatology apart from some kind of reality of unfolding of history and time. In terms of interfaith engagement, it seems that for Abrahamic faith traditions, a block-time model would be a major theological obstacle, whereas the Asiatic faiths' cyclical worldview, eternal emergence and return, points in a different direction from the Abrahamic faiths' emphasis on history and historical time. With these considerations in mind, let us look at several reasons that support the flowing-time template. There are commonsense, scientific, philosophical, and theological reasons.

Perhaps the weakest argument in scientists' hearing is the appeal to folk psychology, common sense. That said, across the cultures and history, flowing time is a basic human intuition. The psychologist William Friedman, who for most of his academic career has studied human consciousness of time, reports that "the division between past, present, and future so deeply permeates our experience that it is hard to imagine its absence."[145] Of course, human intuition

---

142. Craig, *Time and Eternity*, pp. 168-69.

143. See Drees, "A Case against Temporal Realism?" pp. 335-37.

144. Ted Peters ("The Trinity in and beyond Time," p. 266) insightfully notes that although it is best for Christian theology not to envision time as block time, "[t]here is a sense in which we can say the past and the future are not actual. The present is actual. The present provides the perspective for apprehending past and future realities." In keeping with the Hebrew tradition, the Christian view regards time prophetically, time between promise and fulfillment.

145. Friedman, *About Time*, p. 92; see also p. 2, cited in Craig, *Time and Eternity*, p. 272.

cannot serve as the ultimate arbiter — nor can universal intuition (although that is much stronger than a local intuition); there are also things worth believing true that are counterintuitive, such as some basic insights of quantum theory. Nevertheless, the consistent — or to use Einstein's word, "persistent" — human intuition of past-present-future reality has some relative value.

There are scientific reasons to oppose or at least radically qualify the block-time conception. First of all, there is the second law of thermodynamics, entropy, that seems to require unidirectionality and irreversibility of time,[146] as will be discussed in more detail in chapter 8. Similarly, the majority interpretation of quantum physics with its indeterminacy principle makes much less sense (if any) if the future is not potentially true and open for processes to evolve in an indeterminate way. (True, some claim that even block time may be able to account for indeterminacy, but I have a hard time seeing how.) To the same effect speak chaos theory and its effects on the probabilistic nature of nature. These and related reasons lie behind the fact that notwithstanding the reality that a majority of physicists and philosophers of time support the block theory, the issue is far from resolved among scientists, mainly because science alone cannot give the final answer; it is as much philosophical-metaphysical in nature.[147] A telling illustration is Einstein himself, who at first was a proponent of the flowing-time conception and was convinced to the contrary only three years after launching his special relativity theory by the thinking of the mathematician Hermann Minkowski.[148]

This brings us to the importance of philosophical, including metaphysical, considerations — an area often resisted by physicists (particularly in the first part of the twentieth century when analytic philosophy and logical positivism made it a virtue to carve all "nonempirical" notions out of science). The issue of space-time, indeed, is a textbook example of "where physics meets metaphysics."[149] Consider this recent insight of physicist-theologian R. J. Russell: what if the correct insight of block-time theory that past-present-future are "relations" rather than indicators of real time (because tenses cannot be taken as properties of events) were turned upside down epistemologically. Building on the primacy of relationality (as the opposite of substance ontology), it would lead to the argument that tenses are *ontologically constituted by the relations*. Hence, "a modified A-theory of time with tense as relational."[150]

---

146. See T. Peters, *God as Trinity*, pp. 159-63.

147. Isham and Polkinghorne, "The Debate over the Block Universe," pp. 135-44.

148. Craig, *Time and Eternity*, pp. 167-69.

149. For an excellent discussion, see Heller, "Where Physics Meets Metaphysics."

150. R. Russell, *Time in Eternity*, pp. 129-45 particularly. Russell builds here on Pannen-

These are some of the key reasons for constructive theology to continue defending the idea of real "historicity" of the universe and hence the dynamic nature of time. Both the limited space and my lack of training in mathematics and physics prevent a deeper investigation here. Let it suffice to refer the reader to a number of contributions that defend some kind of traditional notion of time: in addition to leading systematicians deeply engaged in religion-science dialogue who basically take that view for granted (such as Pannenberg, Moltmann, and T. Peters), the scientist-theologians R. J. Russell[151] and J. Polkinghorne,[152] as well as philosopher-theologian William Craig Lane,[153] among others, have provided detailed argumentation. At this point, I also leave to others the highly complicated issue of quantum gravity's implications for time.[154]

Eternity and (Space-)Time in a Trinitarian Framework

Although contemporary theology should honor the best intuitions of tradition's desire to defend God's role as the sovereign, transcendent Creator with its appeal to the timelessness of God[155] — which, of course, ironically has some resemblance with block-time theory in some real sense — the traditional way also must be balanced with an equally important insistence on God's omnipresence in and engagement with creation and its time. "What the doctrine of creation requires is that God should transcend spacetime. . . . That does entail that God cannot be limited in spacetime. But it does not entail that God cannot be in time at all, in any sense; and it does not entail that the Divine being contains no analogates of past, present and future." Indeed, both divine omnipresence (that God is present everywhere at all times) and incarnation

---

berg's theology of time and is also looking for analogical insights from particle physics, game theory, and elsewhere.

151. R. Russell, *Time in Eternity,* chap. 2.

152. Polkinghorne, "The Nature of Time," pp. 278-83; Polkinghorne, *Exploring Reality,* chap. 6; Polkinghorne, *Faith, Science, and Understanding,* chap. 7; for a debate, see Isham and Polkinghorne, "The Debate over the Block Universe."

153. For a detailed, accessible consideration of the issue of block time versus flowing time (under the nomenclatures "static" and "dynamic" time), see Craig, *Time and Eternity,* pp. 32-66 and chaps. 4–5.

154. The interested reader may begin with R. Russell, *Cosmology,* pp. 90-94, with guidance for further sources.

155. See Aquinas, *ST* 1.8.2. For the understanding of eternity as nontemporal, see also Augustine, *City of God* 12.17.

imply some kind of temporality in divine life. Furthermore, the openness of the future seems to require some relation to temporality.[156]

R. J. Russell's brilliant and concise summary of the emerging theological consensus concerning the eternity-time relatedness serves well as both a tentative summary and a springboard for detailed discussion: "I understand eternity to be the boundless temporality of the Trinitarian God, a lavishly rich 'supra-temporality' that is both the source and fulfillment of the temporality of creation: the temporality we experience in nature, in our lives, and in history. This is an eternity that flows out of the endless perichoretic dance of the divine persons ceaselessly taking place within the unity of Trinitarian community."[157]

Theologically speaking, eternity is neither timelessness[158] nor lack of movement as Christian tradition surmised. Trinitarian doctrine alone shows the contrary: in the immanent Trinity, an eternal reciprocal loving relationship, there is movement, dynamics, receiving, giving — let alone in the economic Trinity in its outward movement.[159] Christian tradition was not able to link its speculations on the time-God relationship to the concrete trinitarian acts and relations of the triune God, the Creator. Currently, "Rahner's Rule," the unity between the immanent and economic Trinity,[160] helps Christian theology to hold on to both that which is beyond and that which is intimate. Indeed, we can speak of "temporalized eternity."[161]

Eternity — or as Pannenberg lately has called it, "omnitemporal[ity]"[162] — as the infinite source of time both transcends and incorporates it into itself. Therefore, "we find God on both sides of the fence, both as eternal and as temporal."[163] Hence, we should endorse neither the timelessness of God nor God's temporality but rather make room for God's own time[164] because the

156. K. Ward, "God as a Principle of Cosmological Explanation," p. 250. As Peacocke well puts it, referring to Augustine's view of time: "Thus the fundamental otherness of God must include the divine transcendence of time" ("Theology and Science Today," p. 34).

157. R. Russell, *Time in Eternity*, p. 5. In this section, I also glean from Pannenberg, "Eternity, Time and Space," pp. 163-74; Jackelén, *Time and Eternity*, chap. 4.

158. Rightly noted by Rahner, "Further Theology of the Spiritual Life I," p. 162.

159. See Pannenberg, ST 1:405.

160. If not absolute identity, to preserve divine freedom and the reality of historical happenings; see *Trinity and Revelation*, chap. 11.

161. See T. Peters, *God as Trinity*, pp. 146-47, 173-75.

162. Pannenberg, "Eternity, Time, and Space."

163. T. Peters, "Trinity in and beyond Time," pp. 263-64 (quotation p. 264).

164. Cf. Gunton, *The Triune Creator*, p. 92, who (rightly) rejects both God's temporality and God's timelessness but (wrongly) asks us to stop there, in an apophatic position.

former would divorce God from real activity and presence (!) in the world, and in the latter, "God will be conceived by a process of abstraction from the world."[165] In the dynamic trinitarian context of speaking of God's own time — and only in that context — Boethius's oft-cited definition that "Eternity is the simultaneous and complete possession of infinite life"[166] makes the correct point (which is neither about "block time" nor removing God from time). In God's eternity, time is transcended but not "canceled" in the sense that it never had any meaning (that would be an idea closer to the intuitions of the great Asiatic faiths). But doesn't this lead to a self-contradictory statement that in the divine life there is both timely sequence (which implies finiteness) and infinite transcendence of time by eternity? Many contemporary philosophers think so.[167] Again, it seems to me that only the turn to the Trinity may help us avoid paradox: the incarnation of the second person of the Trinity tells us the eternal God has entered time.[168] Why could we not apply the *hypostatic* union template also to the eternity-time relationship?

What are the implications for divine omniscience? Understandably, contemporary theologians have tried several tactics, including the suggestion of the simultaneity of a "temporal" and "eternal" present,[169] as well as the unique omniscient being's "divinely preferred frame of reference."[170] An important insight is offered by Barbour's (self-evident!) observation that the immanent God, existing everywhere in the universe, is hardly prisoner to the limitations of lack of speed.[171] Polkinghorne makes the important point that the "totality of experience" helps God to avoid the impasse set up by the lack of a preferred frame of reference in the relativity theory. As an omnipresent observer of all events, God is able to experience them all rather than having to pick a particular one.[172]

As with creation in general, so with creation's space-time, the ultimate reference is to the eschaton, the final redemption. Participation in God's eter-

---

165. Gunton, *The Triune Creator*, pp. 91-92 (quotation p. 92).

166. Boethius, *Consolation of Philosophy* 5; similarly Augustine, *Confessions* 11.11; for comments, see Pannenberg, *ST* 1:403.

167. For debates, all the details of which are not totally transparent to me, see Stump and Kretzmann, "Eternity," and rejoinder by Helm, *Eternal God,* chap. 2 particularly.

168. So also T. Peters, "Trinity in and beyond Time," p. 269.

169. Stump and Kretzmann, "Eternity."

170. Lucas, *The Future*, p. 220.

171. Barbour, *Religion in an Age of Science*, p. 112.

172. Polkinghorne, *Science and Providence*, p. 82.

nity "can overcome the disintegration of human life"[173] with the "entry of eternity into time."[174] Eternity is not only the source of time, it is also the goal, destiny. Time thus has a teleological nature.[175] This means that the "eternity of the New Creation" is the "gift of true temporality of the Trinity to our world, both as it is to be and as it is being transformed into the New Creation by God's radically new act beginning with the bodily resurrection of Jesus at Easter." It is the time of healing, sanctifying, and bringing to fulfillment of God's purposes for creation; it is also the time of judgment of all that does not stand the standard of eternity.[176]

What Is Space-(Time)?

Much less studied a topic by theologians[177] (although not necessarily by philosophers and scientists), space has been conceived of traditionally in two main ways: as a "receptacle" (or "container"), that is, as container of all objects (named by Einstein "box space"); and as "relational," that is, rather than having its own objective existence, space is a positional quality of material objects (i.e., how they are related to each other).[178] The receptacle idea found its culmination in Newton's "absolute space," of which Leibniz was deeply critical because he rightly saw that space really is nothing else but relations between objects.[179] Insightfully Torrance distinguishes between finite and infinite forms of receptacle space; its theological import is related to Newton's identification of God as the "infinite container" of all objects.[180] That identification, of course, is highly problematic: "If God Himself is the infinite Container of all things, He can no more become incarnate than a box can become one of the several objects that it contains." The Nicene *homoousios* doctrine is of course at stake as well.[181]

173. Pannenberg, *ST* 3:601.

174. Pannenberg, *ST* 3:603.

175. Tillich, *ST* 3:320; see also Goosen, *Spacetime and Theology*, p. 33.

176. R. Russell, *Time in Eternity*, pp. 5-6; see p. 5. For the eschatological importance of Jesus' resurrection, see also O'Collins, *Jesus Risen*, pp. 154-57.

177. As also noted by Moltmann, *Experiences in Theology*, p. 315. The discussion on the theology of space throughout this section is indebted to the work of my former doctoral student Chan Ho Park, "Transcendence and Spatiality of the Triune Creator."

178. This is the classic definition by Einstein in the foreword to Jammer, *Concepts of Space*, p. xv.

179. Jammer, *Concepts of Space*, p. xvi.

180. Torrance, *Space, Time, and Incarnation*, p. 57.

181. Torrance, *Space, Time, and Incarnation*, pp. 39-40.

Fortunately, some Church Fathers rightly saw the significance of the relational idea of space as it would help explain creation, Trinity, and incarnation.[182] Indeed, in Christ God has related to the world and humanity, and Christ is thus the "place" of meeting[183] (note that the concept of "place" is an antecedent to the relational idea of space).

Similarly to absolute time, the concept of absolute space was shattered, if not totally abolished, by relativity theory. Relativity theory basically took away all basic axioms held of space and time in classical physics in which "space and time are separable and absolute. Space is like an empty container in which every object has a definite location. Time passes uniformly and universally, the same for all observers." In the Einsteinian world, "[s]pace and time, then, are not independent but are united in a *spacetime continuum*."[184] In other words, "time is closely interlocked conceptually with space, matter and energy."[185] Theologically speaking, rather than absolute realities in themselves, like the rest of creation, the time-space continuum is a created reality.[186] That said, against naive assumptions, this does not mean that contemporary physics has gotten rid of all "absolute" notions; just consider the speed of light and a number of other cosmic constants.[187]

Toward a Theology of Space-(Time)

Understandably, the Bible speaks of God's presence in the world in economic rather than analytic terms. God is our dwelling place (Ps. 90:1; Deut. 33:27). This, of course, has to be understood metaphorically.[188] Theologically speaking, both God's presence in the world (omnipresence and incarnation) and God's transcendence mandate talk about God's presence and embodiment (incarnation) in the world. In short: both biblical and theological intuitions thus point to the relational notion of space, not to mention scientific considerations (relativity theory). Furthermore, deeply linked with the doctrine of *ex nihilo*

182. For the theological importance of relationality in the space concept, see Pannenberg, *Toward a Theology of Nature*, pp. 65-66.

183. Torrance, *Space, Time, and Incarnation*, p. 24.

184. Barbour, *Religion in the Age of Science*, pp. 177, 178, respectively, emphasis in original.

185. Peacocke, *Theology for a Scientific Age*, p. 130.

186. See Gunton, "The Doctrine of Creation," p. 149.

187. Polkinghorne, *Theology in the Context of Science*, pp. 55-56.

188. See also McFague, *Body of God*, p. 156.

is the insistence on "the absolute priority of God over all time and space, for the latter arise only in and with created existence and must be conceived as relations within the created order."[189]

As mentioned, the idea of relational space can be found in tradition. While I fear Torrance overstates his case and makes the early Fathers advocates of an idea totally unknown to them, his basic insight is still spot-on: "In the light of God's creation of the world out of nothing, His interaction with nature, and the Incarnation of His Creator Word, they [Greek Church Fathers] developed a thoroughly relational conception of space and time in which spatial, temporal and conceptual relations were inseparable."[190]

When relating God to earthly space, in analogy to what was said of time, we *"should accept neither the spacelessness nor the spatiality of the being of God."*[191] The former would separate God from the world, whereas the latter would make God yet another object among other worldly objects. God must have his own space, so to speak.[192] God can use the space of creation, but he has his own space different from that of creatures.[193] As with eternity-time conceptions, the notion of *hypostatic* union can be applied to the divine presence in the world. On the basis of the incarnation we know that "the Lord Jesus Christ, who shares with us our creaturely existence in this world and is of one substance with the Father, is He through whom all things, including space and time, came to be." This is but saying *homoousios* in another way.[194]

Moltmann adds an important note to the discussion of space. Naming it "ecological space," the place created by God for all creatures, he further notes that it is a "perichoretic" space: "Every human person exists in community with other people, and is also for them a living space. Every living thing is as the subject of its own life the object for other life as well. We are at once inhabitants and inhabited."[195] This communal, to-be-in-relation, mutually conditioned conception of space is a great asset to theology.

Because it is created and "inhabited" by the triune God, space-time is

189. Torrance, *Space, Time, and Incarnation*, p. 11.

190. Torrance, *Space, Time, and Incarnation*, p. 58.

191. C. H. Park, "Transcendence and Spatiality of the Triune Creator," p. 78, emphasis in original.

192. Schwarz ("God's Place in a Space Age," p. 367) says the same by speaking of "dimensions": "God would be present in our dimension (i.e., four-dimensional spacetime continuum) without being contained by it and he would transcend it without being absent."

193. C. H. Park, "Transcendence and Spatiality of the Triune Creator," p. 12.

194. Torrance, *Space, Time, and Incarnation*, p. 14.

195. Moltmann, *Coming of God*, p. 301.

redeemed by the incarnation, cross, resurrection, and ascension of Christ. (This theme is developed in chapter 7 of *Christ and Reconciliation.*) The eschatological consummation will bring the redemption to a glorious culmination.

Having clarified the issues of "beginnings" of the universe and its space-time, we now focus on the "beginnings" of life-forms. The much-discussed notion of the "anthropic principle" builds that bridge.

The Conditions of Life: The Biopic (Anthropic) Principle

Because nature in itself is a "blind book," open to various kinds of readings from atheist to Deist to theist, not all scientists acknowledge that the design of the universe calls for a divine Designer. All students of the cosmos of course discern a significant amount of highly nuanced, intelligent, and useful conditions, parameters, and organization. But what that implies is a highly contested issue. Among scientists, there is a group who consider this cosmic "fine-tuning" something significant and worth reflecting on; some of those scholars, while not necessarily committed to any specific religious confession, see the possibility of religious interpretation on the basis of these discoveries.

In its most general form, the argument that considers the universal constants, initial conditions, and other signs of design meaningful goes like this:[196]

1. The values of the universal constants controlling the interrelationship among space, time, and energy in the universe must fall within a very *narrow, closed* range in order to allow any life-form to develop.
2. But the possible values that these universal constants *could* have had that would have *disallowed* any life-form developing are astronomically higher (falling within a virtually *open* range).
3. Therefore, the odds against an anthropic condition occurring are astronomically high, making any life-form (or universal condition allowing a life-form) exceedingly improbable. This makes it highly, highly unlikely that the conditions for life in the universe occurred by pure chance, which begs for an explanation (cause) — physical or metaphysical.

Universal constants include highly "fine-tuned" constants regarding space and time such as "Planck minimums," the speed of light, and so forth;

196. Spitzer, *New Proofs*, p. 50; for a more detailed listing, see McGrath, *Fine-Tuned Universe*, pp. 119-21.

energy (four fundamental forces: gravitational, electromagnetic, strong nuclear, and weak nuclear); and large-scale and fine-structure constants (total visible rest mass and a number of other constants such as Hubble constant and cosmological constant).[197] A critical part of these constants has to do with initial conditions. According to Polkinghorne,

> Cosmic history is a tug-of-war between the opposing tendencies of the contractive pull of gravity (drawing matter together) and the sum of expansive effects (such as the initial velocities after the big bang, together with other effects, such as that due to a non-zero). These two tendencies must be closely balanced if the universe is not to collapse quickly into a "big crunch," or rapidly become so dilute that fruitful process is an impossibility. In fact, if cosmologists extrapolate back to the Planck era, when the cosmos was 10^{-43} seconds old, they conclude that the difference then could only have been one part in 10^{60}.[198]

From a theistic perspective, the principle can also be linked specifically with the emergence of humanity. As the theologian Torrance memorably put it, the import of the principle is "not only that the universe is a home for humanity, but that the personal nature of humankind belongs to the very nature of nature."[199] Or recall the physicist Freeman Dyson's oft-cited note that "the more I examine the universe and study the details of its architecture, the more evidence I find that the universe in some sense must have known that we were coming."[200] This is all good, but recently it has been rightly noted that the idea of "fine-tuning" should not be limited to one species of creatures — to us. It relates much more widely to the possibility of life in its unbelievable diversity. Hence, what came to be called the "anthropic principle"[201] should be extended to encompass all life (conditions) in the universe, and be renamed the "biopic principle."

197. For an authoritative, constantly updated presentation, see "Introduction to the Constants for Nonexperts," in NIST [National Institute of Standards and Technology] Reference on Constants, Unit, and Uncertainty, available at http://physics.nist.gov/cuu/Constants/background.html. Two standard, highly useful sources are P. Davies, *The Accidental Universe*, and Hoyle, *The Intelligent Universe*; for a short yet detailed numerical and verbal summary for theologians, see Spitzer, *New Proofs*, pp. 52-67.
198. Polkinghorne, "The Anthropic Principle," p. 2.
199. Torrance, "The Transcendental Role of Wisdom in Science," pp. 142-44.
200. Dyson, *Disturbing the Universe*, p. 250.
201. Barrow and Tipler, *Anthropic Cosmological Principle*; see also Leslie, *Universes*; Holder, *God, the Multiverse, and Everything*; McGrath, *Fine-Tuned Universe*.

The biopic principle can be found in two forms. Whereas the "strong" principle seems to be saying that the universe is compelled, in some sense, for conscious life to eventually emerge, the "weak" principle much more modestly states almost the obvious, that it takes conscious persons such as us to observe that this kind of world is fit for life. Here one can already discern that behind any notion of "fine-tuning" is a debate about whether that necessitates a Designer. Many scientists, who of course would not necessarily undermine the intricate accuracy of the fine-tuning, are deeply suspicious of any Designer arguments.[202]

For the theist, or someone like the physicist Paul Davies who is sympathetic to theistic interpretations, manifestations of the fine-tuning such as "the numerical coincidences could be regarded as evidence of design," even to the point that they "might be attributed to God."[203] Others do not use such language. For most scientists without theistic belief, even the most sophisticated fine-tuning is merely a matter of happenstance. Another common response to the biopic principle, in many ways philosophically more interesting, is to account for it by the bias or location of the observer (as also the weak interpretation in some sense implies). Yet another way to explain away the need for the Designer, so to speak, is an appeal to the multiverse theory. Among an infinite number of universes, one of them just happens to bring about life. But then, of course, we have not observed any other universe![204] These arguments against the theistic interpretation of the biopic principle are as strong as their explanatory power altogether. For example, concerning the multiverse theory, we noted above many critical questions, not least the lack of any kind of "empirical" observations.

The theological appropriation of the biopic principle and design argument, understandably, is not only the commodity of Christian tradition. Currently, one can find it strongly presented in Islamic tradition as well.[205] The Qur'anic passage from 21:16 is often invoked: "Not for (idle) sport did We create the heavens and the earth and all that is between!"[206] For the medieval philosopher Ibn Rushd, only two proofs for the existence of God were deemed worthy of embrace — both of them already taught in the Qur'an (25:61; 78:6-

202. For a balanced theistic interpretation, see R. Collins, "A Scientific Argument for the Existence of God," pp. 47-75; for a philosophical theistic argument, see Craig, "Barrow and Tipler on the Anthropic Principle," pp. 389-95.

203. P. Davies, *God and the New Physics*, p. 189.

204. These various options are discussed in McGrath, *Fine-Tuned Universe*, pp. 121-24.

205. For an up-to-date discussion, see Guessoum, *Islam's Quantum Question,* chap. 7 (on design) and chap. 8 (on the anthropic principle).

206. Trans. Abdullah Yusuf Ali, at www.altafsir.com.

16; 80:24-33). They are "providence," that is, everything in the universe serves the purpose of humanity, including the earth, sun, moon, weather, and so forth; and "invention," that is, everything in the world bears the mark of being invented (rather than coming from happenstance), for example, plants and animals, conditioned for humans.[207] Even before him, al-Kindi argued that "the orderly and wonderful phenomena of nature could not be purposeless and accidental."[208] The fine-tuning argument can also be found in Jewish theology.[209]

In contrast, it seems to me tentatively that Buddhist cosmology is prone to dismiss the whole argument not only because it finds the term "anthropic" at the center of cosmology foreign but more importantly because it rejects both creation and Creator (in any theistic sense).[210] Of Hindu responses it is difficult to say anything much: one wonders if most Hindu cosmologies' positing of multiple universes may find some resonance with the multiverse explanation; on the other hand, the happenstance ideology of that scientific view is hardly in keeping with theistic Hinduism.[211]

Whatever the religious interpretation, the fine-tuning principle points to the emergence of life on our planet. To its theological meaning we turn next.

The Emergence and Diversification of Life: Tentative Explorations and Remaining Mysteries

The Continuing Mystery of the Emergence of Life: Some Theological Observations

Although the post-Enlightenment ethos of disenchantment has a hard time tapping into anything "super"-natural (that is, beyond nature), it would be good for us to mind that "[l]ife is so unlike the nonliving states of being that our religious ancestors spontaneously attributed its existence to a mysterious divine agency."[212] Even those who are not willing to attribute the mystery to

207. Hillier, "Ibn Rushd (Averroes) (1126-1198)," n.p.
208. In *Routledge Companion to Theism*, p. 69.
209. See Aviezer, "The Anthropic Principle."
210. For Buddhist reservations about speaking of the anthropic principle, see Thuan, "Science and Buddhism."
211. That there are some Hindu "creationists" who value the anthropic principle (mostly though from outside India [such as Cremo, "The Fine-Tuned Universe," chap. 10]) says little of mainline Hinduism's viewpoint in this regard.
212. Haught, *Is Nature Enough?* p. 56.

a transcendent spiritual reality should mind its challenge. Indeed, the mystery of life is even more remarkable in light of science's overall finding that "the universe is *essentially* lifeless,"[213] at least when it comes to any organic life even remotely resembling our concept. Although religious and philosophical traditions have pondered the miracle of the coming to existence of life for millennia, as a scientific field, "origin-of-life" studies, which look at the emergence of life on Earth in the wider context of cosmic evolution, go back only to the first decades of the twentieth century; this investigation also includes the inquiry into the origin of the elements out of which everything is made.[214]

Does the emergence of life speak of design? Counterintuitively, there seems to be much to commend the view that rather than designed, life just emerged randomly. The late and extremely slow emergence of life-forms in itself seems to be pointing to it. From what we know, the random fusion of bacteria with protocells, allegedly the major step in the diversification of elementary life-forms that contributed to the emergence of more developed forms, seems to have had a number of "near misses."[215] After the advent of the most elementary forms of bacterial life, it would take over 2 billion years to have higher forms. Rightly we can ask: "If there were anything other than purely natural agency at work in this story, then why has there been so much randomness, awkward engineering, wasted experiments and 'fooling around' until the cosmos became complex enough to be endowed with life, sensitivity and consciousness?"[216]

What is the theological response? The secular mind-set that believes that the scientific evolutionary account has finally replaced the belief in divine providence misses the point. Theology's task is neither to compete with the scientific account nor to seek an alternative explanation as to *how* the logistics of the emergence and diversification of life-forms took place. Recall that theology and science study the same created reality, albeit differently.[217] Theology's (as well as philosophy's) task is to inquire into the metaphysical implications and conditions. The Creator who in the first place established the natural laws that govern the evolvement and sustenance of the vast cosmos seems to be utterly patient with letting those regularities — combined with accidents — produce ever-more sophisticated life reaching up to the highest that we know, namely,

213. Haught, *Is Nature Enough?* p. 57, emphasis in original.
214. For details, see Chela-Flores, "The Phenomenon of the Eukaryotic Cells."
215. Haught, *Is Nature Enough?* p. 57, with reference to Margulis and Sagan, *Microcosmos.*
216. Haught, *Is Nature Enough?* p. 58.
217. See the thoughtful essay by Numbers, "Science without God," pp. 265-85.

consciousness. For the first time, conscious humans are able to begin to reflect on the wisdom of the Creator in letting such a process take place.

The contemporary thermodynamic theory has helped us dramatically better understand the astonishing capacity of nature to bring about new forms. The seemingly spontaneous emergence of new structures (called "dissipative," and different from the maintenance "equilibrium" structures) leads again and again to the transition from nonliving to living organisms. But how exactly, we do not know.[218] This brings us to the foundational question: What is life? It of course depends ultimately on the definition of "life."[219] We know now quite accurately what kind of biological and chemical processes (which, ultimately, are of course based on the physical-cosmological conditions of the evolving universe), on top of metabolism and capacity to reproduce, are the essential conditions for living beings in contrast to physical objects.[220] Those phenomenological descriptions, however, are hardly more than that — phenomenological descriptions — and therefore offer little in terms of explanation. A significant step that may take us closer to the mystery of life is the highlighting of the capacity to carry information (just think of DNA).[221] No wonder that finding "a natural law that leads to the origin of information" is the stated goal of current biological sciences.[222] (In hindsight, it is astonishing that even the most brilliant current scientific minds could have so rudely missed the critical role of information in the emergence of life, attributing it merely to physical and chemical processes.)[223]

With much justification, the physicist-priest Polkinghorne has argued for years that introducing information into the nonphysical and nonliving realm is a crucial task for theology as a way of speaking of divine action.[224] In doing so, however, it is of utmost importance for theology to avoid making information any more mystical than it already is: even information functions in a regulated, natural law–guided environment.[225] Nor can information of

---

218. An important up-to-date discussion is Hewlett, "True to Life?" pp. 158-72.

219. See Cleland and Chyba, "Defining 'Life.'"

220. For a detailed discussion, see McGrath, *Fine-Tuned Universe*, chap. 10.

221. See Küppers, *Information and the Origin of Life*.

222. Eigen, *Steps towards Life*, p. 12, cited in Haught, *Is Nature Enough?* pp. 64-65.

223. No less luminaries than the inventors of DNA were guilty of that: Crick, *Of Molecules and Men*, p. 10; I am indebted to Haught, *Is Nature Enough?* p. 66.

224. Polkinghorne, "Theological Notions of Creation and Divine Causality," p. 236.

225. Haught's (*Is Nature Enough?* p. 67 and passim) critique of Intelligent Design theory in this regard is justified as that movement has sought to account for the specified information complexity of DNA (as an alternative explanation to normal science).

course be identified with divine action (any more than, say, "fields" of physics), but rather should be considered metaphorically or analogically as a way of referring to divine influence. Resisting the identification helps theology avoid the error Tillich warned us about: adding the divine action to the chain of causal influences produced by science.[226]

It seems to me that the Aristotelian form-matter distinction points in the right direction: only when matter is — literally — *in-formed,* does life emerge.[227] If God is not only the original creator but also the one who continuously creates and acts in the world, it means that "the stuff of the world has a continuous, inbuilt creativity." In other words, "God's relation to the world is perennially and eternally that of creator," in the beginning *ex nihilo,* and thereafter "in and through inherent, inbuilt creativity of the natural order, both physical and biological." Rather than laying aside the laws of nature, God acts more like a musical composer, to use Peacocke's favorite metaphor, utilizing the potentialities of the created universe and thus honoring its relative independence (even in its total contingency).[228]

The Diversity of Creaturely Forms and Their Interrelatedness

Creation is striking not only because of its unbelievably rich diversity — more than two million existing species of plants and animals known, many more to be discovered — but also because of the sheer fact of its multiplicity; yet all organisms are related by common ancestry.[229] In other words, we must speak of the *world* of creatures. Why so? Because a "single creature would be too tiny face to face with God's infinity."[230] This is not to deny the initial singularity out of which, as a result of the big bang (or similar "beginning") the multiplicity of creaturely life emerged; it is just to establish philosophically the basis for the diversity and multiplicity of creation. Theologically expressed, here is the

---

226. Tillich, *ST* 1:24.

227. See further, Haught, *Is Nature Enough?* pp. 67-69.

228. Peacocke, "Chance and Law," pp. 139-42; see p. 139. The investigation into the mystery of life also raises the question of the possibility and nature of artificial life. A reliable, rich resource is the Web site of the International Society for the Artificial Life at http://www.alife.org/. For theological reflections, see Gregersen, "Reduction and Emergence in Artificial Life," p. 285.

229. For details, see Ayala, "The Evolution of Life," p. 21.

230. Pannenberg, *ST* 2:61. Regarding the finite-infinite discussion in dialogue with Descartes and Hegel, see *Trinity and Revelation,* chap. 9.

divine Logos at work, as the principle of not only distinctness but also diversity of creatures. Patristic theology had something like this in mind when speaking of the forms and origins of all creatures being present in Christ, the Wisdom, the Logos.[231]

According to evolutionary theory, the diversity merely serves the principle of adaptation to the environment and hence is the key to the selection process. While theology of course agrees with that, the diversity in itself is also an occasion for the wisdom and creativity of God in the biblical narrative, as beautifully illustrated in Psalm 104 as well as Job 38 and 41, among other passages. Fertility and capacity to produce are hence high values in the biblical outlook.[232] "Theologically we may view the expansion of the universe as the Creator's means to the bringing forth of independent forms of creaturely reality."[233] This is not only about spatial expansion but also, in relation to creaturely life, about the heightening of self-organization and self-guidance. If the minimum definition of autocatalysis is production and self-production, then among more highly developed creatures it culminates in conscious life. Even though we cannot say of merely conscious life that it may be regarded as an end in itself, it certainly takes consciousness, particularly self-consciousness, to even think of a topic like that!

The natural sciences rightly connect the diversity and continuing evolution of creaturely forms to the concept of natural laws. The difference between natural law and theological interpretation of the divine Logos as the basis of diversity is that whereas the former is abstract, the latter is concrete, that is: "In terms of the order of natural law, creatures seem to be interchangeable and thus to be no more than indifferent examples of the validity of the law." On the other hand, the "way in which the divine Logos is the unity of creation in its plurality" is that rather than the "abstract order of the world . . . [t]he working in creation of the Logos . . . includes its entry into the particularity of creaturely reality."[234]

Not only the diversity of creatures but also the regularity and order of events, notwithstanding the utterly complex, even "chaotic nature" thereof, is the basis for the development and evolution of permanent forms. Regularity makes possible duration. Order and regularity do not preclude but rather facilitate and presuppose the continuing creaturely work of God. The christo-

231. Origen, *De principiis* 1.2.2.

232. See further, Pannenberg, *ST* 2:129-31.

233. Pannenberg, *ST* 2:127.

234. Pannenberg, *ST* 2:62-63; materially similar is Torrance, *Reality and Evangelical Theology*, p. 23; for comments, see McGrath, *ScT* 1:189-91.

logically based "upholding the universe by his word of power" (Heb. 1:3) does not lead to uniformity but rather to continuing new forms and expressions of creaturely life — while at the same time the established order is being maintained. "The uniformity of natural occurrence is on the one hand an expression of God's faithfulness and constancy in his activity as Creator and Sustainer, while on the other hand it is the indispensable basis for the development of ever new and more complex forms in the world of creatures."[235]

The created reality is characterized not only by diversity but also by interrelatedness. Creatures form an interrelated web.[236] "On the one hand each individual creature has others before it and with it; on the other hand it has the justification of its own existence in service to the others that live before it."[237] The evolutionary process is marked by "great natural cohesions" that link all creatures together, including human beings.[238] Human beings, like all other creatures, are part of the web of nature. Hence, "[h]umans themselves are to live not only *off* lower creatures but also *for* them as the basis of their own superior life."[239] As a result, we should first ask what links human beings with the rest of creation, rather than what distinguishes us. Before looking at the human being as the *imago Dei,* we should focus on the human being as the *imago mundi* ("the image of the world").[240] That is the task of theological anthropology in part 2. The relationship between humans and the rest of creation is mutual: "Creation has its meaning for human beings, and human beings have their meaning for the community of creation."[241] Consequently, as mentioned in the introduction, a proper theology of creation is at the same time an ecological theology.

The multiplicity and continuously diversifying plurality of forms manifest the Creator's love in giving relative independence to creatures. Theologically speaking, we can say that in the evolutionary sequence of forms, autocatalytic creatures represent an increasing measure of independence granted by the Creator; these creatures produce and reproduce themselves — of course,

---

235. Pannenberg, *ST* 2:72.

236. Feminist cosmologies have importantly stressed this theme. See Howell, *A Feminist Cosmology,* particularly chap. 2. Interrelatedness and participation are also a major theme in Powell, *Participating in God.* I am indebted to that book much more than (the lack of direct) references here may imply.

237. Pannenberg, *ST* 2:115.

238. Moltmann, *God in Creation,* p. 185.

239. Pannenberg, *ST* 2:116, emphasis in original.

240. Moltmann, *God in Creation,* p. 186.

241. Moltmann, *God in Creation,* p. 189.

not out of their own "resources," but as part of the bigger whole. While this is the function of "information-directed structure building and activity" based on the genetic information (DNA), "[w]e cannot understand living processes . . . only in terms of the replication of the bearers of genetic information. Already in the origin of life there is needed the relation to a totality that links the different functions of DNA and proteins in their development. At all stages in the development of life, then, the parts depend on the whole to which they are functionally related."[242] This is the principle of contingency at work as part of continuous creation.

The final task in the current chapter is to put the evolution of the cosmos and life in the wider context of evolutionary theory's reception and appraisal among religions, including the theological assessment of several key philosophical issues that neo-Darwinism raises. Rather than prefacing the main chapter on evolution with the typical Darwinist debates, it makes more sense to consider those debates now after the material discussion of how contemporary science understands the emergence of the cosmos and life has been conducted.

Evolutionary Theory in Religious and Theological Assessments

Darwinism in a Christian Theological Viewpoint

The relation of Christians to the evolutionary theory of Darwin has traveled a long and winding road, from cautious acceptance in the beginning years, to vehement opposition subsequently by many, and finally to its embrace by mainline Christianity in its theistic form — notwithstanding continuing opposition among the conservative churches (particularly in the United States but also elsewhere). Particularly challenging has been the application of the evolutionary scheme to the evolvement of humanity.

Against popular misconceptions, the idea of evolvement and evolution of the created reality is neither a new and novel idea stemming from modern science nor something that is either religious or antireligious in its core.[243] Just consider the first creation story in Genesis chapter 1: it presents creation in terms of a sequence of events and forms, even when its presentation understandably

---

242. Pannenberg, *ST* 2:128, with reference to Wicken, *Evolution, Thermodynamics, and Information,* pp. 41, 104, 106, and 130 particularly.
243. See Ayala, "Evolution of Life," p. 22.

differs in details from contemporary science.[244] The Semitic faiths (Judaism, Christianity, Islam) have always conceived "God's relationship with the world as an intimate one"[245] rather than mechanical or distant; in that view, it is only natural to think of creation as "a dynamically evolving system."[246] Hence, against common assumptions, with all its distinctive features, the basic *idea* of the contemporary scientific theory of *evolution*, generally speaking, is not new.[247]

Darwin was not of course the original modern inventor of what we now call evolutionary theory, although he became its most eloquent public disseminator.[248] The key ideas of his 1859 *Origin of Species by Means of Natural Selection* are well known: random variations among species; the struggle for life due to the increase of populations at a geometrical rate; the best chance of survival for those with the most useful variations; and the passing on of the most useful traits to the next generation by the possessors of those traits.[249]

As is well known, Darwin himself was not an atheist, neither did he see his theory denying the idea of the Creator God. While his remarks in the second edition of *The Origin of Species* on the "grandeur in this view of life, with its several powers, having been originally breathed by the Creator into a few forms or into one"[250] might have been inspired by desire to avoid conflict with religious authorities, they also point to the possibility of a theistic interpretation of evolutionary ideas. No wonder, particularly in the American context, that evolutionism was cast in a theistic framework from the beginning and was not at first greatly resisted by the churches.[251] It was rather

244. For comments on similarities and differences, see Pannenberg, *ST* 2:116-18.

245. McMullin, "Natural Science," p. 49.

246. Hesse, "Physics, Philosophy, and Myth," p. 191.

247. For the tracing of the history of evolutionary ideas beginning from Plato and Aristotle, see chap. 1 in Korsmeyer, *Evolution and Eden*.

248. As is well known, his grandfather, a physician, expressed some key evolutionary ideas. Jean-Baptiste Lamarck's *Zoologist Philosophy*, published in 1809, is based on an evolutionary view of the development of life. The British economist Robert Malthus's *Essay on Population* in 1798 had a definite influence on Darwin's emerging evolutionary theory. Others could be mentioned behind Darwin's thinking, such as the English naturalist Alfred Russel Wallace. See further, Schwarz, *Creation*, pp. 13-15.

249. Following the summary in Schwarz, *Creation*, p. 15. This and the following section are greatly indebted to his succinct exposition on pp. 3-20. There are a number of recent editions of the *Origin of Species* with additions and corrections from the sixth and last English edition (New York: D. Appleton, 1896). The one used here is vol. 49 of Great Books of the Western World. A major resource for the study is *The Cambridge Companion to the "Origin of Species."*

250. Darwin, *Origin of Species*, p. 243.

251. Even the conservative Reformed theologian Charles Hodge's *What Is Darwinism* (1874), with a strongly critical attitude toward the new theory, still acknowledged the theistic

the atheistic, cosmically oriented interpretation by the British philosopher Herbert Spencer just a few years after the appearance of Darwin's first work that helped emerging evolutionary theory take a decidedly antireligious turn. For Spencer, it was no longer God but some kind of elusive unknown power at work in the material world bringing about and facilitating the growth and diversity.[252] Similarly, the influence of the German zoologist Ernst Haeckel, a devoted follower of Darwin's insights, helped disseminate antitheistic orientations with his uncompromisingly monistic philosophy in which the organic and inorganic form an indissoluble unity.[253]

Darwin's subsequent main work, *The Descent of Man in Relation to Sex* (1871),[254] was likely to rouse even more resistance from religious circles.[255] Again, Darwin was not presenting completely new ideas,[256] and the way he presented them was conciliar and modest. In hindsight, it is somewhat ironic that while the resistance to Darwinism soon intensified in the United States, after a fairly smooth embrace of evolutionism, the opposite was the case on the Continent and the British Isles. While at first strongly criticized, evolutionism in a theistic manner came to be embraced not only by mainline Protestant but also by Roman Catholic churches by the mid–twentieth century or so.[257]

While it would be a fatal mistake for Christian theology to oppose evolutionary theory in principle (even if, as is likely, many of its insights and

---

belief of Darwin himself. In his *Systematic Theology* (2:15-19, citation on p. 15), Hodge comes forward more strongly: "[Darwin's] system is thoroughly atheistic, and therefore cannot possibly stand." For Hodge, see Schwarz, *Creation,* pp. 92-93.

252. Spencer, *First Principles* [1867]. For the highly influential "Social Darwinism" stemming from Spencer and others, see Hofstadter, *Social Darwinism in American Thought.* For the influence of evolutionary thinking on the American "Social Gospel" movement (W. Rauschenbusch and others), see Schwarz, *Creation,* pp. 101-2.

253. Haeckel, *Riddle of the Universe* [1899].

254. In vol. 49 of Great Books of the Western World. The original edition as well as subsequent English editions and editions in several other languages are also available at http://darwin-online.org.uk/EditorialIntroductions/Freeman_TheDescentofMan.html.

255. While biased, as mentioned above, still useful for early conflicts is A. White, *History of the Warfare of Science with Theology.*

256. An important precursor whose great value Darwin himself acknowledged (*Descent of Man,* p. 254) was Ernst Haeckel, *Natürliche Schöpfungsgeschichte,* originally published in 1868. Its English translation, *The History of Creation* (1876), misses the important point of the original title: literally, *Natural History of Creation.* While presenting key ideas also presented by Darwin, Haeckel's book is filled with naive optimism of human progress and so also links with Spencerian ideology.

257. For a useful, accessible, and richly documented discussion on both sides of the Atlantic, see Schwarz, *Creation,* chap. 4. This section is indebted to it.

perhaps even presuppositions continue to be changed as a result of careful scrutiny), we should also be mindful of the abuses of the theory. Indeed, evolutionism has emerged as "a secular religion"[258] — "the great cosmogenic myth of the twentieth century"[259] — in the secular cultures of the Global North.[260] Evolutionary theory was — and continues to be — "the perfect instrument for developing a materialist outlook."[261] Social Darwinism has been used as a means of shaping economic and sociopolitical programs deeply antagonistic to the values of human dignity and the equality of all. Most drastically, in the hands of Nazis, some communists,[262] and other tyrants, traces of evolutionism have funded cruelty and violence. Even apart from these kinds of extremes, evolutionary theory tends to fund ideology that makes the whole vast created reality a matter of self-emergence and self-sufficiency. In the hands of atheists of the nineteenth century as well as those of contemporary scientist-atheists such as Richard Dawkins,[263] evolutionary theory's insights are "employed for a comprehensive world view. . . . The world then exists *ex se* [of itself], not *ab alio* [of another]. Divine attributes are ascribed to it. The exponents of evolution do not always realize clearly enough that the ideological application of their theoretical concepts hinders their scientific work rather than promotes it."[264]

Theologically it can be concluded that contemporary evolutionary theory, rather than being an enemy of a theistic view of creation, "has given theology an opportunity to see God's ongoing creative activity not merely in the preservation of a fixed order but in the constant bringing forth of things that are new."[265] Not only in the first creation story but also elsewhere in the biblical narrative, particularly Second Isaiah, the importance of God doing a new thing is highlighted. Contemporary science and philosophy of science use the category of emergence as an umbrella concept to speak of that.

Apart from Christian tradition, how have the other four living faiths related to evolutionary theory?

258. Purcell, *From Big Bang*, p. 115.

259. Denton, *Evolution*, p. 358; I am indebted to Purcell, *From Big Bang*, p. 115.

260. For an insightful critique of Darwinism as a "universal philosophy" and a way of disenchantment, see Cunningham, *Darwin's Pious Idea;* see also Haught, *Making Sense of Evolution*, pp. 34-35.

261. Moltmann, *God in Creation*, p. 194.

262. Not surprisingly, Friedrich Engels and Karl Marx warmly welcomed the publication of Darwin's *Origin of Species* (1859).

263. For various forms of atheism, see *Trinity and Revelation*, chap. 9.

264. Moltmann, *God in Creation*, p. 194.

265. Pannenberg, *ST* 2:119.

Evolutionary Theory and Other Religions

Among the Jews, a basically similar kind of development as happened among Christian communities has taken place.[266] The leading rabbis of the nineteenth century such as Abraham Geiger and Isaac Meyer Wise, along with most traditional communities in the United States, vehemently opposed evolutionism, while the famous Italian Kabbalist Eliyahu Benamozegh (d. 1900) considered evolutionism, if proven as a scientific theory, fully compatible with Judaism.[267] Similarly to Christian theology, mainline Jewish theology nowadays sees no conflict with the theistic interpretation of evolutionism, including human evolution. The highly influential Rabbinical Council of America ruled in 2005 that "evolutionary theory, properly understood, is not incompatible with belief in a Divine Creator, nor with the first 2 chapters of Genesis."[268] Indeed, significantly more Jews in the United States accept evolution than do Christians.[269]

The third Abrahamic faith, Islam, has had the greatest difficulty in finding a constructive way to deal with evolutionism, and the issue is still a huge problem.[270] "There is no doubt that the idea of biological evolution constitutes a major cultural blockage in the Muslim world today . . . [as] even highly educated Muslims expound negative views towards evolution," says a leading Muslim scientist, the Algerian astrophysicist Nidhal Guessoum.[271] So fierce is the opposition that it is not uncommon to find *fatwas* (more-or-less binding legal-religious rulings) on it.[272] What is striking in Muslim countries is that not only a large majority of the general public but also university students and professors strongly and consistently oppose evolution, particularly human evolution.[273] Even among American Mus-

266. For the most comprehensive and up-to-date discussion, see Cantor and Swetlitz, eds., *Jewish Tradition*.

267. Slifkin, *Challenge of Creation*, pp. 245-47; for details, see Faur, "The Hebrew Species Concept," pp. 42-66. For a useful resource, consult Cantor and Swetlitz, eds., *Jewish Tradition*.

268. Rabbinical Council of America, "Creation, Evolution, and Intelligent Design."

269. According to the Pew Research Center's 2008 poll "Religious Differences on the Question of Evolution" in the USA, 77 percent of Jews embrace evolution; among Christians, the figures are the following: Catholics 58 percent, mainline Protestants 51 percent, and evangelicals 24 percent.

270. See Ayoub, "Creation or Evolution?"

271. Guessoum, *Islam's Quantum Question*, p. 273.

272. See the Fatwa Center of America's ruling against human evolution in 2010 at www .askmufti.com (4/21/2013).

273. Guessoum, *Islam's Quantum Question*, p. 274.

lims, fewer than half accept evolutionism.[274] The most important reason for opposition is the question of Adam. For religious leaders, the idea of a pre-Adamic species is still totally unacceptable.[275] Unknown to many — both Muslims and others — and in contrast with the contemporary, nearly unanimous rejection of Darwinism, evolution was not always resisted, as long as a theistic framework was in place. During the classical "golden era" (ninth to twelfth centuries C.E.), intensive debates about evolutionary ideas (long before modern Darwinism, of course) were carried on that resulted in the embrace of organic evolution and transformation of species.[276] Importantly, in the many debates among Muslim scholars immediately after the publication of Darwin's main works in the nineteenth century, a diversity of views was entertained for a while, from total rejection to partial and even full embrace (by some modernists).[277]

Currently, as mentioned, there is almost a global rejection of the theory. Almost all Muslim scholars or religious teachers who advocate evolutionary theory are located in the United States or Europe, but even among them, some leading scholars such as Seyyed Hossein Nasr of George Washington University, perhaps the most noted Islamic intellectual, is ambiguous at best about the whole compatibility of the theory with the Qur'an; at times, he even seems to support Muslim creationism, a growing movement, gleaning also from Christian creationists.[278] Among the very tiny group of scholars who reside in traditional Muslim lands and defend evolutionism, a leading voice is Guessoum, who currently teaches in the United Arab Emirates. His *Islam's Quantum Question* (2011) is a highly sophisticated advocacy of evolutionism and honest self-criticism of grave lacunae in the state and culture of scientific enterprise in Muslim lands. He argues that in the Qur'an can be found passages that could be interpreted in an evolutionary manner, such as the following:

274. According to the 2008 Pew poll, only 45 percent of American Muslims embrace evolutionary theory.

275. Guessoum, *Islam's Quantum Question*, p. 303; for harsh polemic against evolutionism, much of it written by leading Muslim scholars of sciences, see chap. 9.

276. Ziadat, *Western Science in the Arab World*, p. 25.

277. For detailed historical scrutiny, see Howard, *Being Human in Islam*, chap. 1; see also Majid, "The Muslim Responses to Evolution."

278. A leading Muslim creationist, now with a ministry also in the USA, is the Turkish author Harun Yahya (http://www.harunyahyausa.com). For Nasr, Yahya, and Muslim creationism, see the detailed discussion in Guessoum, *Islam's Quantum Question*, pp. 314-23.

". . . verily He created you in stages." (Q 71:14)

"It is He Who created you from clay; then He decreed a term [or era]." (Q 6:2)

"When your Lord said to the angels, 'Indeed I am about to create a human being out of clay. So when I have proportioned him, and breathed in him My spirit, then fall down in prostration before him!'" (Q 38:71-72)

It is yet to be seen how and when the global Muslim community may be willing to take up the issue of evolution and reflect on its implications for views of humanity and human nature.

Interestingly, among the main Asiatic faith traditions, evolutionary theory has hardly caused any concern. Concerning Buddhism, there are a number of reasons for this. First, Gautama considered questions of origins to be secondary and marginal. Second, at least in some key Buddhist scriptural accounts, as discussed above, an evolutionary view (though not in its modern form) can be discerned. Third, the idea of no-self and impermanence leans toward evolvement and evolution.[279] Already at the end of the nineteenth century, the *Buddhist Catechism* of Henry Steele Olcott, when discussing "Buddhism and science," states: "The Buddha's doctrine teaches that there were many progenitors of the human race."[280] It is a common idea among contemporary Buddhists, based on key ancient intuitions, that "[l]ike all species, we too have been formed and conditioned by an immensely long and complex series of transformations." Similarly, there seems to be "common ground between Buddhist thought and evolutionary biology."[281] The 2006 monograph by Robin Cooper, a scientist and Buddhist teacher, titled *The Evolving Mind: Buddhism, Biology, and Consciousness,* is a careful argument not only for the basic correctness of evolutionary theory but also for the potential contribution Buddhism may make to (neo-)Darwinism in its insistence on self-transcendence as the ultimate goal of evolution from the simplest forms to humanity.[282]

Similarly, the Hindu traditions consider the origins and development of the whole reality in terms of evolvement. Unlike Abrahamic traditions and

---

279. See Verhoeven, "Buddhism and Science," pp. 77-97.

280. Olcott, *The Buddhist Catechism,* part V, Q. 329. José Ignacio Cabezón ("Buddhism and Science," p. 44) takes this and other similar statements in the *Catechism* as an indication that "both Buddhism and science teach evolutionism."

281. Waldron, "Common Ground, Common Cause," pp. 153, 156, respectively.

282. R. Cooper, *The Evolving Mind.*

common sensibilities in most societies of the times, the Darwinistic linking of human evolvement with that of animals was simply not a problem to Hindus; generally speaking, Hinduism "presupposed a common ancestry between animals and humans." Moreover, for Hindus, even the gods may assume animal features (and of course, at least in some interpretations, as a result of rebirth, one may turn out to be an animal).[283] In a recent editorial in the influential Indian *Current Science* publication, P. Balaram responds to the question posed to him by a friend: "Why is it that the creation vs. evolution debate rages unabated in the United States, but never seems to be an issue anywhere else in the world, including India?" Surveying some current textbooks in the high schools and the general mind-set, the editorial not surprisingly concludes that evolutionism, either as a general theory or regarding human origins, is not a problem.[284] Although it is difficult to find a Hindu teacher who would oppose evolutionism in general, some are critical of certain aspects of the Darwinian account of human evolvement, including natural selection.[285] On the other hand, there are both Hindus and others who have been very enthused about the alleged similarities between Hindu views of evolvement and scientific evolutionary theory; those attempts, however, probably hardly do justice to either religious or scientific standards.[286]

Theological, Philosophical, and Scientific Challenges to Darwinism

Although there is no basis for discrediting — in light of our contemporary scientific knowledge — the basics of the (neo-)Darwinian view of the evolvement of life, that is not to say that critical discussion of many of the key tenets of the theory is not needed. Questions have to do with issues such as how to conceive evolution: Is it mainly continuous or punctiliar? What is the role of chance and necessity? Is there any purpose in evolution? These are among the

283. Gosling, "Darwin and the Hindu Tradition," p. 348; see also Gosling, *Religion and Ecology*, pp. 40-41.

284. Balaram, "Editorial," pp. 1191-92.

285. See the founder of ISKCON, A. C. Bhaktivedanta Swami Prabhupada's *Life Comes from Life* at http://www.angelfire.com/ego2/prabhupada/life/life_comes.htm (11/24/2013).

286. The noted leader of the Brahmo Saj movement, Keshub Chandra Sen, claimed similarity between the Gita's narration of the evolvement of *avatars* from fish and tortoises all the way to human incarnation (*That Marvellous Mystery*, p. 65); and Michael Cremo *(Human Devolution)* assumes that Hindu tradition may help not only improve but even to some extent replace Darwinism.

most significant ones when it comes to a better understanding of emergence and evolution of life and species.

Continuous or Punctiliar Evolution?

One of the key fallacies of neo-Darwinism is the presumption of gradualism, that is, an assumption of a more or less continuous, smooth development of species and forms. This assumption has come under devastating critique recently. Eugene Koonin opposes gradualism with his illustrative term "biological big bangs," which proposes "that most or all major evolutionary transitions . . . show [that] the 'explosive' pattern of emergence of new types of biological entities correspond to a boundary between two qualitatively distinct evolutionary phases." In other words, "Major transitions in biological evolution show . . . sudden emergence of diverse forms at a new level of complexity."[287]

To address this and related liabilities of Darwinism, a number of improvements have been made to facilitate "the evolution of evolutionary theory."[288] Stephen Jay Gould, a staunch Darwinist, has championed the concept of "punctuated equilibrium," which he sees as "an alternative to phyletic gradualism."[289] His coauthor, Niles Eldredge, explains the emergence of evolutionary change in new species in terms of "tend[ing] to show up abruptly in the fossil record."[290] A related, more recent notion is "evolutionary-developmental theory" (also known as "evo-devo"): "the relatively sudden appearance of new species could be due to underlying changes at the genetic level, causing variation in that species' body plan."[291] Rather than attributing change and emergence of new forms merely to the (adaption to) environment, evo-devo rightly highlights the influence of the internal genetic organization, most profoundly manifested in the emergence of consciousness.[292] One highly significant dramatic change and emergence of new forms among animals is of course the Cambrian explosion, also named "the big bang of animal evolution," which took place some 500-600 million years ago and is evidenced in the Burgess

287. Koonin, "The Biological Big Bang Model," n.p.
288. I draw from Purcell, *From Big Bang*, pp. 125-36.
289. For this now classic essay, see Eldredge, "Punctuated Equilibria," pp. 82-115.
290. Eldredge, *Reinventing Darwin*, pp. 94, 104; I am indebted to Purcell, *From Big Bang*, p. 125.
291. Purcell, *From Big Bang*, p. 126. For the standard text combining punctuated equilibrium and evo-devo, see Gould, *The Structure of Evolutionary Theory*.
292. The programmatic text is Denton, *Nature's Destiny*.

Shale Formation in Alberta, Canada[293] (the darling site of paleobiologists), in China, and elsewhere.[294]

A highly important contribution to our understanding of evolution has come from Simon Conway Morris's notion of "convergence," which seeks to hold on to two foundational principles guiding evolution. On the one hand, there is the well-known principle of biological constancy, the "common architecture"[295] behind all animal body plans, and on the other hand, there is the principle of emergence and nongradualism. Different kinds of developments — as illustrated in the development of the flying capacity in insects, flies, and birds — come together, convergence, to bring about new forms and capabilities. This means that there is a finite number of possibilities and that development is not merely about randomness.[296] This brings us again to the question of the role of chance and necessity, and how these may be related to teleology, purposefulness.

Chance, Necessity, and Purpose

A major debate about evolution focuses on the question of whether any purpose can be discerned. Darwin's idea of the "design without designer" has been embraced by many contemporary well-known advocates, from the French biologist Jacques Monod[297] to the British etiologist Richard Dawkins[298] to the American philosopher Daniel C. Dennett. Dennett has named it "Darwin's dangerous idea," namely, that there are lack of purpose in evolution and lack of meaning in life.[299] Monod goes so far as to make "chance *alone* . . . the source of every innovation, of all creation in the biosphere."[300] Rightly Peacocke observes that the concept and idea of chance have been "apotheosized into a

293. See http://www.burgess-shale.bc.ca/ (11/24/2013).

294. The term "big bang of animal evolution" was coined by S. B. Carroll, *Endless Forms Most Beautiful*, chap. 6.

295. Shubin, *Your Inner Fish*, p. 99; for some details with other useful references, see Purcell, *From Big Bang*, pp. 127-29.

296. Among his many writings, see S. C. Morris, "Evolution and Convergence," pp. 46-67.

297. Monod, *Chance and Necessity*.

298. R. Dawkins, *Blind Watchmaker*, among others.

299. Dennett, *Darwin's Dangerous Idea*, p. 266. A recent rejoinder by a leading American evolutionary biologist is Ayala, *Darwin's Gift*; see also a theological response by Haught, "Darwin's Gift to Theology," pp. 393-418.

300. Monod, *Chance and Necessity*, p. 112, emphasis in original.

metaphysical principle threatening the very possibility of finding meaning in human life."[301] The Greeks' mythical Chance in the hands of contemporary scientists has become a semidivine principle of nature.[302]

Darwin did not of course reject the idea of design for certain purposes; he acknowledged that organisms are functionally organized in a certain way. What he did in extending the Copernican revolution to the world of living things was attempt to explain the origin and adaptive nature of all living organisms with the help of natural laws. Rightly, it was the exclusion of purpose rather than the foundational idea of evolution that at first caused great concern in religious circles.[303]

Conceptually we have to clarify the meaning of the term itself: "chance" can mean either probability (as in tossing a coin) or randomness, that is, "the intersection of two otherwise unrelated causal chains."[304] The latter meaning is in place here unless stated otherwise. While chance plays a role in evolutionary theory, it is not right to say it is totally random. Instead, there is a subtle and complex interplay of chance and law. Monod had a hard time in understanding this as he juxtaposed "chance" and "necessity" in mutations (and more widely, in evolution).[305] Natural selection promotes adaptation that is meaningful, that "makes sense" for the advancement of the species. In other words, the "selection" process (albeit without the Selector, so to speak) is not the outcome of purely random processes. In that sense the popular analogy of monkeys facing the task of writing *The Origin of Species* randomly is not a correct illustration. On the other hand, the metaphor of an artist is not much better either, because an artist has a preconceived idea of the end result; evolution does not. Evolution is a purely natural process, although it has "some appearance of purposefulness because it is conditioned by the environment."[306] The best way to illustrate the foundational intuition of evolutionary theory is to say that "[t]he theory of evolution manifests chance and necessity jointly intertwined in the stuff of life; randomness and determinism are interlocked

301. Peacocke, "Chance and Law," p. 123; for the huge cultural and scientific impact of the chance ideology, see also Bartholomew, *God of Chance*, p. 16.

302. For criticism, see Peacocke, "Chance and Law," p. 127.

303. Illustrative is the Baptist theologian A. H. Strong's comment, "We grant the principle of evolution, but we regard it as only the method of divine intelligence," cited in Ayala, "Darwin's Devolution," p. 103 (without original source); see further, Gregory, "Impact of Darwinian Evolution"; A. M. Clifford, "Darwin's Revolution," pp. 281-302.

304. Peacocke, "Chance and Law," p. 124.

305. A glaring example is Monod, *Chance and Necessity*, p. 110.

306. Ayala, "Darwin's Devolution," pp. 105-7 (quotation p. 107).

in a natural process that has spurted the most complex, diverse, and beautiful entities in the universe."[307]

Without in any way discrediting the concept of natural selection, the key concept of Darwinism, philosophically-theologically we have to say that in itself this principle hardly brings about higher and higher (more complex and developed) forms of life (significantly, already the early opponents of Darwin correctly saw this). Natural selection only tells us the survival of the fittest, but it "does not properly claim that more complex organisms will be favoured."[308] The survivor could of course be a less developed (but more persistent) species. In the final analysis, it takes a value judgment to make, for example, sentient life more developed than other forms of life. But without a theistic or other metaphysical basis, value judgments do not make any sense.

What makes the refusal of scientists (not only biologists but also cosmologists and others) to grant purposefulness to evolution an internally incoherent claim is that the same scientists would never consider the laws of physics merely fortuitous and random![309] Just consider mutations in this light: it is a commonplace among biologists critical of theistic faith to claim that chance as a built-in component of biological processes, including mutations — which can happen spontaneously in DNA or can be caused by human-made activities (such as X-rays or ultraviolet light) — excludes the idea of set purpose. But that is not necessarily the case. Because of the irreducibly statistical (thus probabilistic) character of quantum physics, mutations can also be seen as something entirely consistent with the laws of nature.[310]

But granted there are valid reasons to oppose teleology, what might those be? First, the waste and suffering in nature cast serious doubts on it. A second reason is that many organisms seem to stay as they are without any progress — just consider bacteria. Third, no one can deny that there seem to have been a number of freak accidents in nature such as the collision of Earth with meteorites in the past. Finally, it just seems to contemporary science that notions of vitalism, life force, and "supernatural" explanations in themselves introduce bigger problems than they attempt to solve.[311] Let us put these important challenges in a proper philosophical-theological perspective.

A minimalist account of purposefulness is presented by the philosopher

307. Ayala, "Darwin's Devolution," p. 109.

308. K. Ward, *God, Chance, and Necessity,* p. 69.

309. K. Ward, *More Than Matter,* p. 93.

310. This was argued as early as in 1958 in Pollard, *Chance and Providence,* p. 56. For a detailed defense, see R. Russell, "Special Providence and Genetic Mutation."

311. Adapting K. Ward, *More Than Matter,* p. 93.

Paul Davies' "teleology without teleology" proposal. Building on the "standard uniformitarian view" of divine action, that is, God sustains and acts in the world through and in natural processes (rather than in any interventionist manner), he argues that when creating, God has endowed natural laws in a way that they allow even radical change and make room for openness and novelty. Evolution cannot be explained merely by neo-Darwinism, any more than physics can be explained merely with reference to laws of relativity and quantum physics (although neither laws are to be undermined per se). "The intrinsic creativity is entirely the result of natural processes which are infused with inherent powers of self-organization based on, though not reducible to, these very specific laws of nature." This means that although there is appearance of design and purpose, it can be said that it is the result of natural processes.[312] Davies finds in chess an apt analogy: God has chosen out of innumerable options the set of laws that best facilitate the desired outcome ("these laws are inherently statistical"), yet there is room for the "whims" of the players, including chance at the quantum or chaos level.[313] He believes that having already adopted self-organization and emergent complexity as standard features, neo-Darwinistic biologists should not resist his proposal in principle.

Many scientists *qua* scientists, particularly confessing Christians[314] and those with sympathies for religion,[315] advocate the notion of teleology more robustly (without necessarily demanding that it be seen as "evidence" of the Designer). The evolutionary biologist Francisco J. Ayala argues that "theological explanations are necessary in order to give a full account of the attributes of living organisms, whereas they are neither necessary nor appropriate in the explanation of natural inanimate phenomena."[316] The physicist Stoeger contends that against the opinion of many, as a physicist he cannot help but find directionality. He puts teleology in the wider cosmic framework:

> The scientific account of the directionality of evolution begins really in cosmology with the Big Bang, moves through astronomy with the origin of structure, the stars, and the elements, and enters a rather new phase with the origin of life on Earth. A second transition occurs with the origin of

312. P. Davies, "Teleology without Teleology," p. 151; see also P. Davies, *The Cosmic Blueprint*.

313. P. Davies, "Teleology without Teleology," p. 155.

314. Stoeger, "The Immanent Directionality," pp. 163-90.

315. Ayala, "Darwin's Devolution," pp. 101-16.

316. Ayala, "Darwin's Devolution," p. 101. For an important discussion by a biologist-theologian, see McGrath, *Fine-Tuned Universe*, chap. 14.

human consciousness. . . . In the very first trillionths of a second after the Big Bang, the fundamental laws of physics — those of gravitation, electromagnetism, and the strong and weak nuclear interactions — were determined. Together with them an arrow of time was established, either by the direction of increasing entropy or by the direction determined by the relationship between efficient causes and their effects. Long before stars and galaxies, and even before there was any neutral hydrogen, much less helium or the other elements, these fundamental regularities, which underlie, enable, and constrain all of material reality and its development, were fixed.[317]

These and a number of other developments between a trillionth of a second after the big bang and the emergence and unbelievably rich evolution of life-forms and species — including chemical, geophysical, and biological processes[318] — Stoeger surmises, necessarily raise the question of directionality, particularly in a world that is not fully deterministic but exhibits significant elements of indeterminism at the quantum level (at least). Yet, "the system will evolve in a way yielding configurations within a certain definite narrow range of possibilities." He concludes: "Thus, in a definite sense the series of outcomes — the direction of evolution — *is* coded into both the regularities of nature and the conditions at earlier times." Of course, from the perspective of science or philosophy, there is no way of saying where this obvious directionality originates, but it is hard to contest it.[319] It takes Christian revelation and theological reflection to see God "behind" this directionality and teleology, and as the ensuing discussion on divine action reveals, theology has various tactics available to make an account of it.

To deepen the theological assessment of the chance-purpose relationship, let us take one more focused look at mutations — a showcase for randomness.

What about Mutations and Teleology?

In a fascinating recent essay "Special Providence and Genetic Mutation: A New Defense of Theistic Evolution," the physicist-theologian J. Russell argues

317. Stoeger, "The Immanent Directionality," pp. 166-67.
318. See Stoeger, "The Immanent Directionality," pp. 171-80.
319. Stoeger, "The Immanent Directionality," pp. 168-69 (quotation p. 168; emphasis in original).

that with the help of the "combination of law and chance which characterize physical and biological processes," evolution happens as "God's way of creating life."[320] In keeping with the "ubiquitous" and comprehensive theology of providence developed in the next chapter, it can be said that "God also acts in, with, under, and through these processes as immanent creator, bringing about the order, beauty, complexity, and wonder of life."[321] The combination of determinism and indeterminism (chance, mutation) exactly reflects the kind of natural world that quantum theory has revealed.

"Chance" in evolution can be seen as a "created natural gap," that is, indeterminism inherently belonging to nature. Now, an omniscient and omnipotent God, without any inappropriate "intervention" (laying aside natural laws created by the same God), has the capacity to so guide natural processes as to accomplish goals of continuing evolution. Mostly, we assume, the guidance happens in a mediated way, by the interactions and collaboration of other created processes and events. Chance is not an anomaly but rather a "natural" aspect of the created order.[322] Consider in this context the importance of the time line: during the roughly four billion years over which our planet has evolved, chance and law have had ample time to collaborate. Mutations can happen spontaneously in the DNA or as a result of processes such as X-rays, ultraviolet light, chemicals, and so forth. Combined with the interplay in quantum processes of determinism and indeterminacy (irreversible interactions between quantum systems), the kind of extreme richness of variety characteristic of our world can be imagined to happen.[323] This theistic explanation is in no way a competitor to the standard evolutionary science's variation-cum-natural-selection paradigm, as a result of which the known two billion or so species have evolved over a long period of time.

This discussion has already raised to the surface the question of God's continuing presence and action in the world. Known in theology under the rubric of providence and in philosophical theology under divine action, this topic will occupy us in the next chapter.

320. Chap. 6 in R. Russell, *Cosmology;* citation on p. 212.

321. R. Russell, *Cosmology,* p. 212.

322. See R. Russell, *Cosmology,* pp. 215-17.

323. For a listing of various kinds of "classical" and "quantum" sources of mutation, see R. Russell, *Cosmology,* pp. 218-19.

7. The Trinitarian Form of Continuing Creation and Divine Action

Providence in Theological Tradition: Reaffirmation and Revision

A theist — at least in Abrahamic traditions — is bound to speak of God's intentional, loving care, maintenance, and guiding of the cosmos and its processes. Throughout the biblical narrative, the idea of preservation, sustenance, and guiding makes up part of the texture — from keeping the circle of the earth intact (Ps. 96:10) and the regular order of days and seasons (Pss. 74:16-17; 136:8-9), to preserving God's people, to caring for the animal kingdom and individuals in their various needs (Deut. 11:12-15; Jer. 5:24; Pss. 104; 145:15-20). The theme of caring, fatherly love culminates in Jesus' teaching (Matt. 6:25-34; Luke 12:22-30). The early theologian Theophilus of Antioch took providence as a manifestation of God's deity.[1] Although creation in the first place is a free act of God without any compulsion, having created the world, God cannot be the Lord without providing for its continued existence and maintenance. Only Deists can avoid that — and those religious naturalists who have given up the referential notion of God. Of the latter, Wildman's nontheistic naturalism is a prime example. Because, for him, there is no "Ultimate Reality" (apart from values), "no center of consciousness behind it all," of course "[h]uman beings are thus no longer the object of special divine

---

1. Theophilus of Antioch, *To Autolycus* 1.5: "God cannot indeed be seen by human eyes, but is beheld and perceived through His providence and works." See also Gousmett, "Creation Order and Miracle," pp. 217-40.

purposes and plans but rather explorers in a world of marvels and disasters, making of themselves what they will."[2]

However, any talk about divine providence in the contemporary world poses serious challenges. The move from a (semi)mechanistic Newtonian worldview toward a dynamic view, with current ideas of "chaos theory" and the like, has made quite obsolete the traditional talk about God as the One who guides and perhaps determines the course of the world. As a result, categories in the Christian doctrine of providence must be recast, particularly with regard to divine action in a world ruled by scientific explanations. Furthermore, the two world wars, the Jewish Holocaust, and innumerable other worldwide crises, from poverty and hunger to natural catastrophes, that have occurred in the twentieth century have cast serious doubt on both the existence of providence and its goodness and fairness. In many secular people's minds the idea of providence, far from being a source of safety and protection, seems to be a threat to human freedom.[3] That said, contemporary worldviews offer surprising opportunities to speak of providence. Above, we considered the implications of discerning teleology (purposefulness) in nature, invoking the biopic (anthropic) principle. The move from a deterministic worldview toward a dynamic, emerging, elusive, and indeterminate (relatively speaking) one may also open up new vistas for speaking of a pervasive presence and influence of God in the complex world of nature.

Tradition has made the commonsense distinction between "general" providence, the all-embracing maintenance of the world's order and life, and "special" providence, which encompasses redemptive and saving acts of God as well as particular divine "interventions" related to prayers and miracles.[4] Gunton makes the brilliant remark:

> The incarnation of the Son of God in Jesus of Nazareth provides a way of showing that the distinction of forms of providence is yet embraced within a unity of activity. God's historical action in Christ is . . . the means by which the order of creation is redirected to its original end. "General" providence is maintained by a new and unique — "special" — form of divine interaction with the world, effecting the eschatological destiny of things as a whole by means of particular outcomes involved with and anticipating it: healings, the driving out of demons, the enabling of truth to be spoken and done. Eschatologically conceived, those activities that

---

2. Wildman, *Science and Religious Anthropology,* p. 41.
3. See Schwarz, *Creation,* pp. 184-88.
4. For a typical definition, see Barth, *CD* III/3, p. 185.

are sometimes called "general" as distinct from "special" or "particular" providence are both aspects of the same divine activity bringing the world to its intended destiny.[5]

In keeping with the unity of God's creative and providing activity — which comes to the fore in the incredible diversity of creatures — it must be stressed that God's providential activity, whether "general" or "special," encompasses the whole of creation and not only humans.[6] When making a distinction between various types of providence for pedagogical reasons, we should keep in mind the underlying complex unity at all times.

As does creation, providence in its widest meaning speaks of contingency: creation is not self-sustained; it must be kept in existence and action. Augustine puts it well: "But the universe will pass away in the twinkling of an eye if God withdraws His ruling hand."[7] Descartes rightly opined, following William of Ockham, who "by reason of his concept of the contingency of each individual event consequent on its direct dependence on God,"[8] that there is no absolute way of inferring from an existence at some point the existence of the creature at the next.[9] Providence is the theological answer to that question.

In "general providence" we can distinguish several types of interrelated forms of contingency and dependability:[10]

- Preservation within *nature* is expressed in the regularity of seasons and the cycles of sun and moon, in the predictability of complex processes following certain "rules" (such as chemical reactions), and in the evolutionary process of the cosmos and life at large (in the interplay of chance and law).[11]
- Preservation through *moral conduct* "so as to avoid creation's destruction and self-annihilation" can be seen with the help of conscience, natural law, and a general sense of morality.[12]

5. Gunton, *The Triune Creator,* pp. 176-77.

6. So also Gunton, *The Triune Creator,* p. 177.

7. Augustine, *Literal Meaning of Genesis* 4.12.22 (ed. Quasten, 1:117).

8. Pannenberg, *ST* 2:40.

9. Descartes, *Meditations on the First Philosophy,* meditation III, #36.

10. I am following here the typology of Schwarz, *Creation,* pp. 189-212.

11. Earth's history could have been something totally different but is not; Pollard, *Chance and Providence,* p. 68.

12. Schwarz, *Creation,* p. 193; a meticulous survey of views of natural law is on pp. 194-206.

- Preservation through the *historical* process is the most contested form of providence because the unfolding of history is as ambiguous as, and invites as many opposing interpretations as, nature in itself. From the (Abrahamic traditions') theistic point of view, God is at work and guiding even in the midst of the most complex and disturbing historical events.

In the perspective of this general providence lies the wisdom of Schleiermacher's view of the "miracle": "Miracle is simply the religious name for event. Every event, even the most natural and usual, becomes a miracle, as soon as the religious view of it can be the dominant. To me all is miracle."[13] This statement is not meant to reject the concept of the miraculous but rather, materially echoing Saint Augustine,[14] to rightly note that only a religious interpretation "sees the deeper nature of everyday events, experiencing them as miraculous, as an expression of the providence of God." Hence, "we will find the fact of the order of nature, its regularities and enduring constructs, genuinely astounding. . . . Since it is not self-evident that anything should take place, not merely the emergence but above all the continuation of creaturely forms and states is at every moment miraculous."[15]

To account for the complex unity and pervasiveness of divine providence, theological tradition established three interrelated categories to encompass the various dimensions of preservation: preservation, concursus, and governance (overruling). The doctrine of concursus affirms the invitation for creatures to collaborate with the Creator and thus — against atheistic and other doubts — affirms that the divine preservation does not mean frustrating the relative independence of creatures.[16] On the contrary, the same love and respect God shows to the creatures in making their independence possible in the first place allow the creatures to affirm their independence as well — to the point that the creature who so wishes can go his or her own way, as the biblical narrative testifies. The importance of concursus lies in its highlighting

---

13. Schleiermacher, *On Religion,* p. 88.

14. Augustine, *City of God* 10.12: "Whatever marvel happens in this world, it is certainly less marvellous than this whole world itself, — I mean the sky and earth, and all that is in them, — and these God certainly made. But, as the Creator Himself is hidden and incomprehensible to man, so also is the manner of creation."

15. Pannenberg, *ST* 2:46.

16. Cf. Barth (*CD* III/3, p. 69), who oddly enough suspected that "in the Christian doctrine of preservation, the identity of the creature in its continuity, is wrapped in an unrecognisable obscurity if not completely destroyed."

the relative independence and freedom given to the creatures by the Creator.[17] This independence need not be seen mainly as a way to absolve God from responsibility for any failures and sin in human life. The Creator honors the creaturely freedom to the point that the creature may deviate from his will.

Whereas until modernity the main motif for securing relative independence was the concern not to ascribe sin to the Creator, with the emergence of modern science, theology's concern shifted radically on this issue. Now the theological issue has to do with whether any kind of divine intervention and action in the world — after the initial creating work — could be allowed. It seemed to Descartes that there is no need for God to intervene in the world process after what God did "[i]n the beginning [as] he created matter, along with its motion and rest; and now, merely by regularly letting things run their course."[18] Understandably this view came under atheistic suspicion among theologians as well as the pioneer of modern science, Newton. The irony of this fear on Newton's part is of course that Newton's *Mathematic Principles of Natural Philosophy*, against his own wishes, along with the principle of inertia, helped consolidate a purely naturalistic, mechanistic explanation, a development that did not go unnoticed by atheists of the time![19] Spinoza's formulation of the physical principle of inertia in terms of self-preservation marked the final emancipation from dependence on God.[20] Pannenberg, however, brilliantly notes that "self-preservation alone cannot guarantee the continuation of one's own existence and nature. It is always referred to preservation by another." The reason is simply this: continued existence of a living thing, let alone a person, requires not only bare maintenance but also persistence along

17. While the technical discussions between Lutherans and Reformed scholastic theologians concerning the "timing" of cooperation, whether in terms of simultaneity or in terms of a creative movement on God's part that precedes the creaturely act *(concursus praevius)*, are hardly relevant anymore, it is interesting that Barth takes up the distinction and goes into quite extensive discussions to defend the latter view (CD III/3, pp. 90-154, titled "The Divine Accompanying").

18. Descartes, *Principles of Philosophy*, II, 36.

19. For brief comments, see Pannenberg, *ST* 2:49-50, and more extensively, Deason, "Reformation Theology and the Mechanistic Conception of Nature," pp. 167-91. "Inertia in physics refers to the property of a body (an object) to resist change in its motion. In general, the mass of a body is a measure of its inertia. As a result, inertia does not refer to a body (an object) being free from change, but instead it refers to its resistance to change (in its motion)." Richard Carlson (private e-mail communication, 9/7/2013).

20. Spinoza, *The Ethics*, part 3, proposition 7: "The endeavour, wherewith everything endeavours to persist in its own being, is nothing else but the actual essence of the thing in question."

with change, *"identity in change."* Whereas "inertia" is free from change, persistence is more than that: "it involves an active principle relative to changing conditions of existence."[21] Consequently, from the point of view of theological argumentation we must conclude that "[f]ar from being in opposition to the persistence and self-preservation of finite things, the preserving work of God makes possible the independence of creatures that find expression in the possibility and fact of their self-preservation."[22] The post-Enlightenment secular culture of the Global North of course resists this idea, and it can be established only from the perspective of the Christian theology of creation, including continuing creation.

Along with providence and concursus, tradition also speaks of world governance, loving guidance toward the desired end goal by the Creator. Barth rightly saw that the idea of world governance speaks of God's faithfulness to his creation.[23] According to the biblical testimonies, it first comes to manifestation in Yahweh's dealings with his people[24] and culminates in the announcement of the dawning of the righteous rule of the Father as announced by Jesus, the Son. It is faithfulness rather than immutability, as tradition had it, that secures the preservation, cooperation, and loving guidance of world affairs until reaching the divinely desired goal. As are all God's dealings with the world, faithfulness is funded by trinitarian logic: "God's faithfulness, which proceeds from the mutual faithfulness of the Son to the Father and the Father to the Son, is the basis of the identity and continuation of his creatures."[25]

What is the final goal of providential world governance? For Aquinas it was God himself,[26] and for the Protestant scholastics, the glory of God.[27] We can follow tradition in that from the perspective of the creatures, giving glory to God is indeed the highest calling. From God's perspective, however, we have to say that "the creature was not created in order that God should receive glory from it. God does not need this, for he is already God in himself from all eternity." This notion combats the common atheistic and even religious suspicion that is ultimately guided by a form of self-seeking and self-love. Rather, we have to say that God's love and faithfulness to his creation

---

21. Pannenberg, *ST* 2:51.

22. Pannenberg, *ST* 2:52.

23. E.g., Barth, *CD* III/3, pp. 40-41.

24. Throughout *CD* III/3, §§48 and 49, Barth discusses the OT, particularly the Abrahamic narrative, to illustrate providence and guidance.

25. Pannenberg, *ST* 2:53.

26. Aquinas, *Summa contra Gentiles* 3.17, 18.

27. For Reformed examples, see Heppe, *Reformed Dogmatics,* p. 136.

will become evident in cooperation and governance, the goal of which is the redemption and fulfillment of creation.[28] God does not need the world, but as soon as God — out of his freedom and love — brings about creation, in his faithfulness and love he cannot help but secure its goal. That is not to deny the power of God to work out his eternal plan even in the face of sinful human wickedness and opposition. Ultimately, God will be all in all.[29] In his infinite wisdom, ultimately, God is also able to bring good even out of evil.[30]

Divine Acts in History and Nature

What Is at Stake, and What Are the Challenges for Theology?

In addition to the original work of creation and continuous creation, the Scriptures of the Abrahamic faiths are filled with accounts of divine acts in history, not only in "salvation" history but also in universal history. They are so numerous and varied that there is no need to begin to list them. In Christian tradition, all the way from the Fathers until the advent of modern science, the "mighty acts" of God were taken for granted. The doctrine of providence, particularly special providence, of course rests on that basis, or else Deism follows. So what is the problem contemporary theology faces? It simply is this:

> Physical science, it appears, leaves no place for divine action. Modern science presupposes that the universe is a closed physical system, that interactions are regular and law-like, that all causal histories can be traced, and that anomalies will ultimately have physical explanations. But traditional assertions of God acting in the world conflict with all four of these conditions: they presuppose that the universe is open, that God acts from time to time according to his purposes, that the ultimate source and explanation of these actions is the divine will, and that no earthly account would ever suffice to explain God's intentions.[31]

Although the believing pioneers of modern science such as Newton still felt compelled because of religious reasons to combine the mechanistic-

---

28. Pannenberg, *ST* 2:56-57 (earlier quotation from p. 56).
29. For comments, see Pannenberg, *ST* 2:57-59.
30. A classic discussion of this can be found in Clement of Alexandria, *Stromata* 1.17.
31. Clayton, "Impossible Possibility," p. 249.

determinist view of the world with real divine acts, soon that uneasy relationship completely came apart.[32] Evolutionary theory with its focus on chance further helped make divine acts obsolete. Any notion of free agency in a world ruled by determinism and causal closure (which of course lead to reductionism) is an extremely difficult concept.[33]

Not surprisingly, theologians have reacted in more than one way. Conservatives continued the affirmation of divine acts without concern for science, and liberals virtually left behind any factual notion of divine acts as they were conceived to be merely subjective responses to religious influences (Schleiermacher).[34] Neo-orthodox theologians, with all their resistance to classical liberalism, subscribed to the "nature-history" dualism, thus removing God and his acts from the realm of the sciences.[35] Dissatisfied with these options, yet another growing group of leading theologians are aiming at a third alternative that, while sensitive to the necessity (for biblical-theological reasons) of affirming divine acts, wish to do so in a way that would not contradict physical sciences. Unprecedented theological advances have been made during the past decades, particularly under the leadership of the long-term international Scientific Perspectives on Divine Action interdisciplinary project cosponsored by the Center for Theology and Natural Sciences (Berkeley, California) and the Vatican Observatory (Vatican City).[36] The key theological-philosophical approach advocated by the project is known under the somewhat cumbersome nomenclature Non-Interventionist Objective Divine Action (NIODA).[37] The current project's constructive proposal has learned a great deal critically from that enterprise, even though it also needs theological revision.

So, if any notion of an objective ("real") divine act entails intervention by God in the world, which is supposed to function according to the divinely set laws, it looks like the only alternative is to speak of subjective divine acts, that

32. Well known is Buckley's thesis that the Newtonian mechanistic worldview ironically made God useless and led to modern atheism *(At the Origins of Modern Atheism)*.

33. See further, Peacocke, *Theology for a Scientific Age,* pp. 139-40.

34. For a detailed history and discussion, see Murphy, *Beyond Liberalism and Fundamentalism.*

35. A prime example is Gilkey, "Cosmology, Ontology," pp. 194-205. Other similar interpretations can be found in R. Bultmann, G. Kauffman, and M. Wiles, among others.

36. The landmark project here is *Scientific Perspectives on Divine Action.* The 2008 *SPDA* provides an assessment of the twenty-year interdisciplinary work and six major volumes of publications.

37. See *SPDA;* an up-to-date summary, analysis, and assessment is provided by R. Russell, "Challenges and Progress," pp. 3-56; Clayton, "Toward a Theory of Divine Action," pp. 85-110.

is, personal religious responses. That would certainly not contradict science, but then, theologically speaking, it would make meaningless the whole idea of God's works in nature and history. Is there a way out beyond this "forced option" that has defined Christian responses so far? NIODA advocates argue that this either/or impasse has to be rejected, and instead, a comprehensive and robust theology of divine action must be developed. That proposal seeks to "view special providence as consisting in the *objective* acts of God in nature and history to which we respond through faith *and* we can interpret these acts in a *non-interventionist* manner consistent with the natural sciences." In other words, it is able to "believe credibly that God really did do what the Bible testifies to."[38]

The Conditions and Possibility of Noninterventionist Objective Divine Acts (NIODA)

The goal of NIODA is to reaffirm divine acts without the fear of divine intervention. Particularly, it seeks "to speak about special divine acts in which God acts objectively in an unusual and particularly meaningful way in, with, and through events which serve to mediate God's action."[39] Russell emphasizes that NIODA is not meant as an attempt to explain how exactly God acts, let alone prove that God acts. Rather, NIODA explanations seek to reconcile the conditions of noninterventionist divine acts vis-à-vis current scientific understanding. Nor is NIODA another version of the God of the gaps. Rather than focusing on the gaps in our knowledge (which will probably be filled by new scientific discoveries), NIODA relies on what we currently know.[40]

NIODA's notion of divine action is multifaceted, not only because it encompasses both objective and subjective dimensions as argued, but also because it allows for divine action to happen directly (without God having to perform any prior act) or indirectly (by setting into motion a sequence of events) as well as in either a mediated way (God acting in, with, and through the existing processes) or an immediate way *(ex nihilo)*.[41] The simultaneous establishment of various types of causalities is superior to the tendency to reduce them to only one type, typically the bottom-up approach, which refers

38. R. Russell, *Cosmology*, p. 112, emphasis in original.
39. R. Russell, *Cosmology*, p. 117.
40. See R. Russell, *Cosmology*, pp. 125-29.
41. R. Russell, *Cosmology*, p. 122.

to the effects of the lower level on upper levels. Along with that we need to acknowledge other forms of causality and influence:

- " 'Top-down' refers to God's action at a higher epistemic and phenome-nological level than the level of the effects," such as when mind causally influences brain (and therefore the whole human being).[42]
- " 'Whole-part' causality or constraint refers to the way the boundary of a system affects the specific state of the system," as God is the "boundary of the universe itself," leading up to certain states and processes.
- "Lateral" causality refers to effects at the same epistemic level as their causes, but at the end of the causal chain (as in biology, biological effects).[43]

Along with the top-down, the whole-part influence model is a way to speak of God's influence on the world without interrupting the regularities set up by the same God;[44] this is particularly important in complex systems.[45] The notion of information is useful for speaking of the influence of the environment or a large system on various levels.[46] What is striking is that even in dissipative systems far from equilibrium, large-scale patterns may appear in spite of random motions of the units; this is what is aptly called "order out of chaos."[47] Theologically speaking, the model is based on the recognition that the omniscient God uniquely knows, across all frameworks of reference of time and space, everything that is possible to know about the state(s) of all-that-is, including the interconnectedness and interdependence of the world's entities, structures, and processes. Because the " 'ontological gap(s)' between the world and God is/are located simply *everywhere* in space and time, God could affect holistically the state of the world (the whole in this context). . . .

42. For a thoughtful and cautious clarification and questioning of some of the prem-ises behind Peacocke's and others' use of downward causation (and emergence), see Murphy, "Emergence, Downward Causation, and Divine Action," pp. 111-31.

43. R. Russell, *Cosmology*, p. 124.

44. Peacocke, "Sound of Sheer Silence," pp. 235-40 particularly; Peacocke, *Theology for a Scientific Age*, pp. 157-60; and his essay in *C&C*.

45. For an accessible explanation, see Murphy and Ellis, *On the Moral Nature of the Universe*, pp. 22-32; see also Murphy and Brown, *DMN*, pp. 57-62, with reference to the ground-breaking work of Donald Campbell, among others.

46. Peacocke, "Sound of Sheer Silence," pp. 220-29.

47. Prigogine and Stengers, *Order out of Chaos*. "In dissipative systems order can indeed result from chaos. The requirement is that energy must enter the system in order for this to occur." Richard Carlson (private e-mail communication, 9/7/2013).

This unitive, holistic effect of God on the world could occur without abrogating any of the laws (regularities) which apply to the levels of the world's constituents."[48] Furthermore, Peacocke reminds us that this holistic, unitive divine action can be distinguished from the universal creative act of God "in that particular intentions of God for particular patterns of events to occur are effected thereby — and the patterns could be intended by God in response *inter alia* to human actions and prayers."[49] Theological talk about the Logos expresses the same kind of idea as the scientific concept of information alluded to above.[50] Peacocke further adds an important theological caveat, namely, that God acts in the world as "personal" agent. Speaking merely of the whole-part influence described above would not do justice to the personal and intimate encounter between humanity and God. In that picture, personal predicates of intentions and purposes — as well as emotions such as love, jealousy, concern, and care — should be added.[51]

Along with the multilevel and multifaceted configuration of divine acts, the NIODA project taps into the beneficial resources provided by the major transformations in the scientific perspective itself (as briefly explained above in chapter 6), which may yield meaningful openings for a robust theology of divine action.[52]

One of the openings for divine action is "ontological indeterminism," that is, while regular, natural processes are not totally deterministic, they are rather statistical or probabilistic; chance events also belong to that picture. Hence, *pace* Laplace, there is no way to fully predict all processes of nature, not only because we do not know enough but also because indeterminism describes natural processes.[53] Among science-theology scholars, both quantum theory and chaos theory have been widely investigated concerning indeterminism, that is, their capacity to provide a meaningful opening for divine action. As with all natural processes — and in fact, the whole of nature in itself — it takes an eye of faith to see divine influences therein; in other words, these "openings" have nothing to do with an attempt to "prove" the action of God in the world. We speak of its conditions and possibilities vis-à-vis current scientific understanding of the world. That in the future new theories of how the world functions will undoubtedly emerge does not make theologians' current

---

48. Peacocke, "Sound of Sheer Silence," p. 236.

49. Peacocke, "Sound of Sheer Silence," p. 236.

50. See Peacocke, "The Sound of Sheer Silence," pp. 236-37.

51. Peacocke, "Sound of Sheer Silence," p. 237.

52. For a succinct listing, see R. Russell, *Cosmology*, pp. 117-19.

53. See also R. Russell, *Cosmology*, pp. 120-21.

engagement meaningless. In every generation, new ways of experimenting with religion-science theology are in order. Furthermore, the fact that, even with grand theories such as quantum theory, diverse interpretations compete is no excuse for lack of dialogue; multiperspectivalism is the nature of limited human knowledge, even scientific.[54]

Engaging quantum theory in the discussion of special providence is not new in Christian theology; it goes back to at least the 1950s.[55] Quantum theory helps explain bottom-up causality as it claims (in its major interpretation) that events and processes at the subatomic level are to some extent indeterministic and hence probabilistic. In that sense, the future is ontologically open, "in-fluenced but *under*determined by the factors of nature acting in the present." Hence, we speak of potentialities and actualities.[56] The theologian who utilizes quantum theory is not implying that the subatomic level is the only one at which God works; recall the multifaceted nature of divine action discussed above.[57] Furthermore, the theologian must be careful not to make God a "nat-ural cause." While deeply involved in natural processes, God also supremely transcends the created order, even in the deepest immanence.[58] And again, quantum theory is not creating another form of the God of the gaps. Rather, indeterminacy has to do with what are called "causal gaps" in nature, that is, the lack of total determinism.[59] Rather than "intervening," God works in keeping with nature's indeterminacy. Finally, to avoid occasionalism (that is, the created order merely provides an occasion for God's works, without any true mediatory role), per our discussion above, one needs to speak also of the mediation of divine acts in cooperation with created agents.[60]

Does quantum indeterminacy compromise God's omniscience, as Pea-cocke has repeatedly argued? He considers the limitation "self-limited."[61] I disagree and argue, with Russell, that indeterminacy "does not imply that God cannot know the future," but rather that "God cannot foreknow the future based on God's knowledge of the present just prior to the quantum event." In classical tradition, divine omniscience is based not on the knowledge of the

---

54. For similar comments, see R. Russell, *Cosmology*, pp. 162-63.

55. Heim, *Transformation of the Scientific World View*; Pollard, *Chance and Providence*.

56. R. Russell, *Cosmology*, p. 156, emphasis in original. See also Stoeger, "Epistemological and Ontological Issues," pp. 81-98.

57. See also R. Russell, *Cosmology*, pp. 157, 159.

58. See also R. Russell, *Cosmology*, pp. 155, 169-70.

59. Tracy, "Particular Providence and the God of the Gaps," p. 290.

60. Murphy, "Divine Action in the Natural Order," pp. 340-42 particularly.

61. Peacocke, "God's Interaction with the World," p. 281.

present but instead on God's knowing "the future in its own present actuality."[62] The understanding of the time-eternity relationship developed in this project (chap. 6), in which time derives from the divine futurity (and in that sense, we can "locate" God in the future), supports this claim.[63] Furthermore, while it is true that regarding the quantum system in a superposition (that is, with several potential states to happen represented by the wave function Ψ), we can know only probabilistically what the distinct state will be (that is, when it becomes actual with the "collapse of the wave function"), we also know that the probabilities can be calculated exactly from the wave function. Russell rightly notes that "surely God can know them exactly" if even scientists can do that math.[64] Against appearances, this view, however, does not endorse "divine omnideterminism," but rather establishes a meaningful notion of divine knowledge that is in keeping with the indeterminacy of nature.

Not all scholars agree on quantum theory's compatibility with divine action.[65] Former quantum physicist Polkinghorne has rightly reminded us that, if not carefully done, the employ of indeterminacy may yield an episodic account of divine action by a "hole-and-corner deity."[66] Furthermore, he has wondered how out of lack of order ("chaos") would come something meaningful — provided that quantum processes were chaotic, a claim Polkinghorne rejects. More importantly, he also refers to the well-known "measurement problem" (a hugely complicated issue regarding its meaning and implications). For the sake of this discussion, let me (over)simplify what is the problem for him: when it comes to the "time development" of the wave function Ψ, it follows determinism (of Schrödinger's equation), whereas when it comes to interaction *between* quantum systems, "irreversible interaction" turns out to be indeterministic. Now, on this basis, Polkinghorne rejects the quantum principle as an aid for divine action because it would render it episodic, applying only to the moments of "measurement" and their effects in the macroworld.[67]

62. R. Russell, *Cosmology,* p. 134.

63. R. Russell (*Cosmology,* pp. 219-20) relates this insightfully to the question of God's knowing the effects of chance in mutations.

64. R. Russell, *Cosmology,* p. 171.

65. An outright "global" rejection of not only quantum-theology engagement but the whole NIODA project is Saunders, *Divine Action and Modern Science.* For thoughtful responses and rebuttals, see R. Russell, *Cosmology,* pp. 174-77; Wildman, "The Divine Action Project, 1988-2003," pp. 31-75.

66. Polkinghorne, *Science and Creation,* p. 58; more extensively and precisely in Polkinghorne, *Science and Providence,* pp. 27-28 particularly.

67. Polkinghorne, *Reason and Reality,* pp. 40-41.

Is that so? Not necessarily. Russell has neatly argued that the "measurements" (irreversible interactions) include all kinds of phenomena ranging from "'micro-macro,' 'micro-meso,' and 'micro-micro' interactions" and "are not limited to interactions with the ordinary world around us." Therefore, looking only at those "episodic" moments when the effects of irreversible interactions cause effects at the macrolevel is much too limited. A comprehensive, multi-level understanding alone may yield a "ubiquitous" and "pervasive" character of divine action.[68] A fitting theological summary is thus: "God creates *ex nihilo* and sustains existence of quantum systems as they undergo causal time evolution, governed by the deterministic Schrödinger equation, and as they undergo irreversible and indeterministic interactions (that is, quantum events) with other micro- and macro-systems whose existence God also sustains."[69] (How quantum indeterminacy is related to human freedom will be discussed in chapter 13 of part 2.)

Chaos theory has brought even to the popular consciousness the ex-tremely intricate nature of natural processes, as discussed above. Particularly striking is the "extreme sensitivity to initial conditions displayed by some non-linear dissipative systems."[70] What is ironic about chaos theory is that while the behavior can be modeled by mathematical equations,[71] because of sheer complexity it soon generates a process whose outcome is unpredictable. Mini-mally it can be said that chaos theory "illustrates the insurmountable epistemic limits of any finite intelligence."[72] But not only that: "it also suggests causal relationships where none were previously suspected."[73] So the term "chaos" has to be rightly handled; in scientific understanding it is deterministic and thus compatible with classical physics (otherwise, no equations would be possible). What makes it "chaotic" is that in light of our current knowledge, it relies on probabilities and statistical explanations. In that sense it represents a third alternative between classical and quantum physics, as it combines features of both.[74] Chaos theory has of course everything to do with science's better understanding of an unprecedented complexity of the universe.[75] What is also

---

68. R. Russell, *Cosmology*, pp. 164-67 (165), 171-73. Similarly Murphy ("Divine Action in the Natural Order," pp. 340-42) supports the pervasive nature of divine actions in the quantum world.

69. R. Russell, *Cosmology*, p. 180.

70. Tracy, "Special Divine Action," p. 266.

71. See Wildman and Russell, "Chaos," pp. 49-90.

72. Tracy, "Special Divine Action," pp. 266-67, here p. 267.

73. Crutchfield et al., "Chaos," p. 35; that essay is an accessible primer to chaos theory.

74. R. Russell, *Cosmology*, p. 130.

75. See Küppers, "Understanding Complexity," pp. 93-105.

astonishing is that "chaos" is not merely a limitation to the otherwise regular process of nature; nature (as open) employs "chaos" also for creative, novel, constructive purposes.[76]

Because Polkinghorne expressed grave doubts about quantum indeterminacy's relevance, it is not surprising that he has turned to chaos theory in search of an asset. Somewhat like Peacocke's "whole-part" influence, he surmises that because chaotic systems are extensively linked with other complex processes (and of course, ultimately to the whole), God's influence can be understood in terms of "input of active information" as a way of selecting between alternative paths of development.[77] There are no compelling arguments against the claim that in an "open" world, including an "open" future (without compromising the basically deterministic nature of natural processes), "there is room for the operation of holistic organizing principles, . . . for human intentionality, and for divine providential interaction."[78] Like other theological claims, this kind of holistic and multifaceted divine action is hidden to scientific exploration.[79]

Above we registered that for Peacocke, quantum indeterminacy implied limitations to divine omniscience and the explanation was the self-initiated divine *kenosis*. Polkinghorne applies the same template to chaos theory's caused indeterminacy.[80] My rebuttal is similar to that of Peacocke, explained above. I argue that even with an open future, a meaningful notion of divine omniscience can be had.[81]

Toward a Pneumatological-Trinitarian Theology of Divine Action and Providence

Revising and Reorienting the Noninterventionist Divine Action Approach

Now that we have analyzed the NIODA project's aim and resources, let us attempt a constructive theological statement concerning the conditions and nature of divine action. As a way to a constructive proposal, we will first cri-

---

76. Prigogine and Stengers, *Order out of Chaos*.

77. Polkinghorne, "Metaphysics of Divine Action," pp. 153-54; so also Polkinghorne, *Belief in God in an Age of Science*, p. 62.

78. Polkinghorne, "Laws of Nature," p. 442.

79. See Polkinghorne, "Laws of Nature," p. 446.

80. Polkinghorne, "Laws of Nature," pp. 447-48.

81. In agreement with D. Edwards, "Discovery of Chaos," pp. 170-71.

tique some aspects of the NIODA project and thereafter clarify the meaning of natural laws and causality, key issues related to divine action.

Let me emphasize that the theologically driven critical remarks on the NIODA template should not be taken as undermining, let alone rejecting, its superb achievements. Critique rather arises out of the deep desire to refine it and so make it fit for a systematic/constructive theological work.

First, ironically, NIODA suffers from "dualistic" tendencies in its conception of divine action's conditions in creation. What I mean is this: when listing the scientific obstacles to divine action, the NIODA scholars tend to resort — against their better knowledge, I take it — to an outdated worldview in which "subject" (God) and "object" (world), physical and spiritual, divine and earthly are strictly taken as alternatives.

Coupled with that, second, is the tendency to make determinism (of natural processes) the default position, which has to be qualified at any cost "to make room" for God to act, instead of beginning from the current scientific understanding of the world's processes as regular and law-like, but so utterly complex and probabilistic that openness is to be taken for granted (although, of course, not openness for *divine* action). I fear at times that the NIODA advocates take determinism more seriously than do most scientists![82] On the other side, the whole concept of "indeterminacy," while certainly related to quantum and chaos theory, may be a wider and more complex concept, and (as a default position) calls for a robust analysis.[83] That is closely linked with a better philosophical-theological understanding of natural law: while respectful of the regularities of the world, there is no reason to consider God as prisoner to his own laws![84]

Related, third, is NIODA's almost pathological (or at least exaggerated) fear of "intervention." As N. T. Wright correctly notes, the continuous use of terms such as "invasive," "intrusive," and "interventionist" implies, or even presupposes, "a latent Epicurean framework: the divinity is normally outside the process of the world, and occasionally reaches in, does something, and then goes away again. But in biblical thought heaven and earth — God's sphere and our sphere — are not thought of as detached or separate. They overlap and interlock."[85]

82. For a thoughtful reflection, see Stoeger, "Conceiving Divine Action," pp. 240-44.
83. See further, Gregersen, "Three Types of Indeterminacy," pp. 165-86; K. Ward, "Divine Action in an Emergent Cosmos," pp. 288-89, here p. 289.
84. See "Contingency and Natural Law," in Pannenberg, *Toward a Theology of Nature*, pp. 72-122.
85. N. T. Wright, "Mind, Spirit, Soul and Body," n.p.

Fourth, NIODA is much more sophisticated in scientific-philosophical than in (systematic-)theological argumentation and approach. Indeed, the whole effort so far has been motivated so much by apologetic concerns deriving from (at times somewhat noncritically) listening to natural scientists that the constructive theological work is yet to be done. Part of the weakness is its lack of an integral trinitarian conception of God's works in the world, its lack of trinitarian contours.[86]

Some critics of NIODA have wondered whether its use of various kinds of approaches to "make room" for divine action, namely, whole-part/top-down causation, quantum theory, and chaos theory, is a liability. I disagree with this criticism and wholeheartedly emphasize that multiplicity of tactics is rather a great asset.[87] This is far superior to "uniformitarianism," which reductionistically thinks that "God always and everywhere does the same job of creating-and-upholding an already established universe," after Schleiermacher and contemporary liberals.[88]

Finally, the foundational question that has to be asked in relation to the NIODA project is whether, contrary to all its claims otherwise, it still ends up being a new form of God-of-the-gaps theology. This has to do with its robust use of both quantum theory's and chaos theory's alleged "openings." Although the approach avoids the old-time pitfall of the God-of-the-gaps tactics in which God is needed whenever there are epistemological gaps (because NIODA speaks of permanent, ontological gaps in an indeterministic nature), the divine influence is still pretty thin. Clayton expresses my doubts well: "A gap for divine action that cannot be closed may represent a breakthrough for the theologian, but inserting God into this space, even if it is a permanent opening rather than a gap, may well seem like a sleight of hand to one's scientific partners" and hardly convincing at all.[89] That said, it can be counterargued (and I think Clayton would agree with me) that the whole aim of the Divine Action project is minimalist, to provide the context for theologians to speak of divine acts in a meaningful way in the context of current scientific understanding of the world. How much that may or may not be convincing to nonbelieving scientists is a different matter.

Having affirmed the basic intentions and insights of the NIODA project

86. R. Russell (*Cosmology*, pp. 192-93 and elsewhere), though, notes the need for that. Ted Peters brings the trinitarian aspect into the conversation, but his contributions have been less strictly speaking on divine action.

87. So also Gregersen, "Special Divine Action," pp. 181-83.

88. Gregersen, "Special Divine Action," p. 184.

89. Clayton, "Toward a Theory of Divine Action," p. 108.

with several needed corrections and revisions, before venturing into the constructive theological proposal, we briefly touch on two interrelated issues that have everything to do with God's relation to the world in terms of continuing creation, providence, and action, namely, causality and natural laws.

Divine Acts, Causality, and the Laws of Nature: Theological Clarifications

Since the medieval era, fierce debates have arisen about the relationship between divine and creaturely causality. For the "occasionalists," God is the only cause, and the act of God provides the "occasion" for the creature's activity.[90] Interestingly, the pioneers in the debates were medieval Islamic philosophers. The Asharites were not only strict occasionalists but also voluntarists: they believed the world order was solely dependent on God's gracious will and hence, without contradiction, God could, for example, make rules according to which 1 + 1 equals 3. The Mutazilites strongly rejected the view and "maintained God's wisdom and justice as standing condition of creation without which the created order could not have any meaning and continuity." A few centuries later an even stronger rebuttal of the Asharite voluntarism came through the criticism of Ibn Rush (Averroes), who responded to the then-leading occasionalist al-Ghazali. Ibn Rush was furious about even the idea of God being capable of contradicting himself. On the contrary, God has created the world in a way that has set certain laws in place, and creation obeys those laws. How else could justice and accountability be secured, he also wondered.[91]

On the Christian side, Aquinas sought a solution in the distinction between direct (uncreated) and indirect (created) causality.[92] This double-agency view reconciles *ex nihilo* and continuing creation, and — notwithstanding internal debates in all Abrahamic traditions — in some sense or another is the conviction shared by all.[93] Although this double-agency view is nowadays usually labeled a "Catholic" opinion, one among many views of causality, I rather think that most all commonsense thinking in some way follows this line. One may have detailed debates about finer points, but it is hard to contest the wisdom of the basic concept.

Clayton rightly argues that we need a new and more comprehensive

---

90. Cited in S. Lee, "Occasionalism." That entry is a useful primer to the debates.

91. Kalin, "Will, Necessity and Creation," pp. 115-17.

92. Aquinas, *Summa contra Gentiles* 3.69, 70 particularly; *ST* 1.45.5; see also 1.45.8.

93. See Stoeger, "The Big Bang," p. 170; see further, Pambrun, "*Creatio Ex Nihilo* and Dual Causality"; Tracy, "God and Creatures Acting."

notion of causality in order to account for continuing divine acts in the world. The careful study of nature, indeed, reveals various types of causalities at work, "from classical Newtonian causality, to gravity, to the influence of quantum fields, to the 'holistic constraints' or integrated systems — and on to the pervasive role of mental causes in human life,"[94] to quantum theory's entanglement causality (in which particles or events vastly distant from each other "mysteriously" covary), and so forth. Quantum physics also seems to acknowledge the influence of intentionality (if not otherwise, then at least in measurement and observation).[95] Yet another indication of the complexity of causality is the continuing and complex influence of emergence (of new species, processes, developments) taking place in a multilayered "hierarchy" of the world, leading up to mind and consciousness. Although contemporary science cannot go back to Aristotle's theory of (fourfold) causality, Clayton reminds us that "final causality" is particularly noteworthy for theologians as it relates to what Pannenberg speaks of in the "power of the future" and what some process theologians label the "lure of the future." However one may understand the "eschatological-futurist" cause, *theology* can only to its own detriment ignore its significance, not only for the future but also for today.[96]

Natural laws, their nature and role, are tightly linked with causality. The talk about natural laws established itself in the seventeenth century along with the rise of modern science. While science soon distanced itself from religion, the original intuitions of natural law were deeply embedded in Christian and Deistic notions of the world as ordered and designed by God.[97] Even among the scientists, there hardly is a consensus about the nature of the laws of nature, although most would probably take them without much reflection as "universal" and "absolute" in some elusive sense at least.[98] There are several foundational debates about the nature of laws of nature: Are they ontological and thus truly govern natural processes, or are they just conventional descriptions of typical regularities and the kinds of causal efficacies they represent? Whether they are this or that, theologically speaking we have to say that they "are due ultimately to God's faithful and trustworthy action in creating the world *ex nihilo*. God's action as Creator is accomplished both as a whole and at each moment and, through such faithful and trustworthy action, the world

---

94. Clayton, "Impossible Possibility," pp. 254-55.

95. See P. Davies, *Other Worlds*, pp. 132-33. See also Stapp, *Mind, Matter, and Quantum Mechanics*. I am indebted to Clayton's essay.

96. See further, Clayton, "Impossible Possibility," pp. 256-57.

97. McGrath, *ScT* 1:225.

98. Cf. P. Davies, *God and the New Physics*, p. 209.

is given its natural regularities."[99] Although Christian tradition can have a high view of natural laws, based on divinely set regularities of the world,[100] it is also best not to regard them as "eternal" and omnipotent since that would threaten both the *ex nihilo* nature of creation and divine omnipotence.

The challenge to omnipotence was already noticed in medieval theology, particularly in response to the Islamic philosopher Averroes's deterministic account. "For Averroes, the reliability of God ultimately rested upon God's obligation to respond in certain fixed ways to external pressures."[101] Rightly Scotus and Ockham objected to that logic and anchored the orderliness of nature — hence its "laws" — in the will of God. While their robust voluntarism as the "reason" for creation may need balance and qualification with the primacy of love, for the purposes of the current debate it makes the correct point. Ockham's way of resolving the issue was of course to appeal to the "two powers of God." While originally God was free to do anything *(potentia Dei absoluta)*, after having created the world (out of his own free will), he has made himself honor the laws of nature *(potentia Dei ordinate).*[102]

Whatever one's view of the ontology of natural laws, both scientifically and theologically we should resist the reductionist identification of natural laws with physical laws.[103] Although physical laws most probably are the most foundational, the dynamic, multilayered nature of reality (including a similar view of causality) blocks that kind of identification.

Russell adds several qualifications regarding the "laws of nature." First, scientific theories can only partially and to a certain extent describe the actual laws. Whether the actual laws of nature can ever be discovered is an open question. Because they are created and thus contingent, natural laws cannot be considered "eternal"; God did not create the world following some preestablished laws. The laws, similarly to time, are created.[104]

A Trinitarian Theology of Divine Action

Trinitarian theology is a distinctively Christian framework for conceiving not only the coming into existence of the created order but also the Creator's

99. R. Russell, *Cosmology,* p. 119.

100. Brunner, *The Christian Doctrine of Creation and Redemption,* pp. 24-26.

101. McGrath, *ScT* 1:228-29.

102. For a fine account, see Van den Brink, *Almighty God.*

103. So also Polkinghorne, "Laws of Nature," p. 437.

104. R. Russell, *Cosmology,* pp. 119-20. See also Stoeger, "Contemporary Physics," p. 210.

continuous creation thereof. With the same love that the Father loves the Son, he loves the universe, his creation, by continuously providing for its life, meaning, and hope for the future. The Son as Logos and mediator of all creaturely work of God is the one in whom everything is held together. Through his Spirit the triune God is present in, under, above, and below, so to speak, all natural processes. According to Gregory of Nyssa, "For all things depend on Him who is, nor can there be anything which has not its being in Him who is. . . . [A]ll things are in Him, and He in all things. . . . He Who holds together Nature in existence is transfused in *us;* while at that other time He was transfused throughout *our nature.*"[105] Astonishingly — in light of the cosmologies of his time — Gregory's thinking is so thoroughly participatory and holistic that even heaven for him does not represent merely something transcendent but rather, "pervades all creation and . . . does not exist separated from being."[106] Many other theological witnesses to the same effect can be found in theological tradition.[107] The Australian Roman Catholic Denis Edwards succinctly summarizes the main thrust of a trinitarian theology of providence: "The trinitarian God works in and through the process of the universe, through laws and boundary conditions, through regularities and chance, through chaotic systems and the capacity for self-organization."[108]

Consequently, as already emphasized, theologically we must hold on to the widest and most diverse possible account of divine action in the world, rather than, say, debating whether it is due to quantum or chaos indeterminacy. Furthermore, very importantly, we should not seek to reveal the " 'causal joint' between divine action and created causality," simply because we can't[109] — or else we could read God's mind! At the same time, we should of course consider scientific and theological explanations as complementary.

A key to a ubiquitous and comprehensive theology of divine action is the trinitarian doctrine of divine omnipresence — which also entails divine omniscience: "All things are present to him and are kept by him in his presence,"[110] as classically affirmed in Psalm 139. This is of course not to compromise but rather to establish transcendence as well: "Precisely as the one who incommensurably transcends his creation, God is still present to even the least

105. Gregory of Nyssa, *The Great Catechism* 25, emphasis in original.
106. Gregory of Nyssa, "On What It Means to Call Oneself a Christian," p. 87; I am indebted to Zimmermann, *Incarnational Humanism,* p. 235.
107. Aquinas, *ST* 1.1.8; Luther, WA 23:133; *LW* 37:58.
108. D. Edwards, "Discovery of Chaos," p. 170.
109. D. Edwards, "Discovery of Chaos," pp. 172-73.
110. Pannenberg, *ST* 1:380.

of his creatures. As in the case of his eternity, then, there are combined in his omnipresence elements of both immanence and transcendence in keeping with the criterion of the true Infinite."[111] In this sense, the establishment of divine action with the help of quantum theory (in its ubiquitous form) points in the right direction, "reemphasizing God's operational presence in the most basic processes of nature known to us,"[112] that is, even the subatomic. Here an analogical-metaphorical use of the scientific concept of field of force is appropriate: "the presence of God's Spirit in his creation can be described as a field of creative presence, a comprehensive field of force that releases event after event into finite existence."[113]

In keeping with the scriptural teaching (Pss. 139; 104:29-30), the trinitarian presence in the world is funded by a robust pneumatological doctrine. Moltmann's striking term "immanent transcendence" well captures this dynamic. "Through his Spirit God himself is present in his creation. The whole creation is a fabric woven and shot through by the efficacies of the Spirit. Through his Spirit God is also present in the very structures of matter. Creation contains neither spirit-less matter nor non-material spirit; there is only *informed* matter."[114] In keeping with the complexity of the world — and the infinity of the triune God — the presence of the Spirit is manifested in various forms in every being in the world.[115] Far from being subsumed in the natural processes or acting as yet another natural cause, the Spirit of God is transcendently immanent in all things.[116] Again, this is a theological claim and of course hidden to scientific experiments.

Gunton adds the important note that whatever problems may relate to the interpretation of the Spirit of God in terms of "force field," it has great value on the question of how to understand God's action: the idea of the Spirit's work "as interacting fields of force rather than billiard-ball-like entities bumping into one another, is of extreme importance in showing that the world is open to God's continuing interaction with it."[117]

A robust trinitarian panentheism (classical panentheism) funds a dynamic, multifaceted divine action, providence, and causality. To be the Creator is far more than being the world's cause. While causality should not of course

---

111. Pannenberg, *ST* 1:412.
112. Gregersen, "Special Divine Action," p. 194.
113. Pannenberg, *Introduction to Systematic Theology,* p. 49.
114. Moltmann, *God in Creation,* p. 212, emphasis in original.
115. Moltmann, *Spirit of Life,* p. 34.
116. Moltmann, *Spirit of Life,* pp. 34, 35.
117. Gunton, *The Triune Creator,* p. 175; also p. 176.

be eliminated from the theological thesaurus,[118] the main focus should be placed on the living, dynamic, creative presence of the Creator in the world:

> If the Creator is himself present in his creation by virtue of the Spirit, then his relationship to creation must rather be viewed as an intricate web of unilateral, reciprocal and many-sided relationships. In this network of relationships, "making," "preserving," "maintaining" and "perfecting" are certainly the great *one-sided* relationships; but "indwelling," "sym-pathizing," "participating," "accompanying," "enduring," "delighting" and "glorifying" are relationships of *mutuality* which describe a cosmic community of living between God the Spirit and all his created beings.[119]

Classical panentheism also allows us to hold on tightly to both sides of the activity and relationship between God and the world: the "one-sided" creation and the "mutual" participation of creatures in preservation, perfecting, and final consummation.[120] The divinely given mandate (Gen. 1:26-27) belongs to that invitation for collaboration and vice-regency.

Unlike we humans, the triune Creator is not in a hurry with the universe. Speaking of continuous creation and divine acts in the universe, we need to be reminded of the long time line. If, as we think currently, the universe came into being about 14 billion years ago with extremely fine-tuned conditions, we have a lot of room, so to speak, to consider the breadth and depth of divine action throughout the universe's history. In that framework, talk about multilevel (top-down, whole-part, and bottom-up, among others) causality and influence is both necessary and highly useful.[121]

In light of these theological reflections, and in keeping with the triune God's infinite nature, including omniscience, we should be open to recognizing "the profound metaphysical point that divine causality transcends any other category of causality."[122] This is not an effort to divorce God from the world, nor to make divine action more mysterious than it is. Rather, it is to cash out the implications of God's thoroughgoing, all-pervasive presence through the Spirit in the world created and sustained in and through the Son because of the Father's overflowing love.

118. Contra Moltmann, *God in Creation*, p. 14.

119. Moltmann, *God in Creation*, p. 14, emphasis in original.

120. I am aware that here I modify Moltmann's citation to serve my own, "less" panentheistic and more classical account of the God-world relationship.

121. See also R. Russell, *Cosmology*, p. 160.

122. W. Carroll, "Aquinas on Creation," p. 91, cited in Tracy, "Special Divine Action," p. 254.

An important step toward a comprehensive, ubiquitous theological account of the divine action is to affirm God's exceptional acts along with regular law-like events.

Divine Action, Miracles, and Transcending the Natural

The Miraculous and "Supernatural": A Conceptual-Theological Clarification

While not all NIODA project advocates reject miracles per se, for many of them the noninterventionist divine action does not include miraculous divine action.[123] In that, NIODA follows the canons of the post-Enlightenment worldview. The reason Tillich eschewed what he called the "supranaturalistic" is that he saw such events as violations of nature's laws (although he rightly saw that if "miracles" were allowed, they should be called "sign-events" following Johannine terminology).[124]

What is at issue here is clarified by looking at historical developments. The term "miracle" is linked with the "supernatural." That term (in distinction from "natural"), however, is to be used with great care. For early theology, the supernatural-natural distinction did not exist if it meant, as in modernity, the distinction between two realms, that of God and that of the sciences, respectively. All of reality was governed by God. What we call miracle meant an event for which we do not know the explanation, but it was not contrary to nature.[125] The term "supernatural" did not establish its theological usage until the thirteenth century in Aquinas, to whom it meant — literally — something "going beyond" *(super)* nature, "above the wonted order and course of nature, as to raise the dead,"[126] but not something against nature. Indeed, against modern intuitions, for Thomas, "the natural order is enveloped in the supernatural, which provides origin, sustenance, and a goal for the natural."[127] What makes miracle miraculous is not that it is against nature, but that "it surpasses the faculty of nature,"[128] and hence is God's work, hidden to human understanding.

That said, Aquinas's distinction between natural and supernatural — the latter denoting a more intense, particular presence of God in nature — con-

---

123. R. Russell, *Cosmology*, p. 121.

124. Tillich, *ST* 1:115.

125. Augustine, *Literal Meaning of Genesis* 6.13.24; *City of God* 21.8; Aquinas, *ST* 1.105.6.

126. Aquinas, *ST* 3a.13.2. For the first appearance of the term in the ninth century, see Kenny, *The Supernatural*, pp. 94-95.

127. Schwarz, *Creation*, p. 215, with reference to Aquinas, *ST* 1.105.5.

128. Aquinas, *ST* 1.105.7.

tributed to the important shift toward modernity's juxtaposition of the two. Whereas, ironically, for the medieval scholastics the distinction was meant to defend the supremacy of God,[129] for modern thinkers it meant relegating God to his own realm, separated from nature, which increasingly was explained by science.[130] Soon nature ran on its own powers, and miracles came to be perceived as violations of nature's laws. The naturalistically oriented world explanations of modernity could not tolerate the idea of temporary suspensions of the natural order. Spinoza, hence, opposed the possibility of miracles — not only because in his view the immutability of natural order was necessitated by the immutability of God — but also (in agreement with Leibniz), more importantly, because it would show the weakness of the Creator if he had to intervene to adjust the world's workings.

Samuel Clarke rightly saw that this common eighteenth-century denial of divine interventions altogether "delivers up the world to a materialistic fate by banishing from it the activity of divine preservation and overruling. God's cosmic plan is indeed unchangeable, but it is not achieved in an order of things that is present from the outset, not by a mechanistic functioning."[131] Rather, Clarke surmised, the divine governance happens through a process of disorder and orderly renewal. Human discernment of the process of divine governance and maintenance of the world's order can never capture its complexities; human formulations of nature's laws are mere approximations. Pannenberg rightly notes that in this Clarke harks back all the way to Augustine in that what appears to us a miraculous intervention is not that but rather a matter of our ignorance.[132] For Schleiermacher "miracles" are impossible not only because he (rightly) refuses to consider them as "proofs" of the Deistic god but also because in his (wrongly) subsuming creation under providence and lacking a proper trinitarian theology of mediation, he simply is unable to speak of any "specific" divine acts of providence. He follows the Humean idea of miracles as the violation ("suspension") of nature's laws. He considers whether a meaningful idea of prayer would entail miracles and responds no, as even the answers to prayers are "only part of the original divine plan,"[133] rather than something newly added.[134]

---

129. God alone was capable of doing miracles, strictly speaking; Aquinas, *ST* 1.110.4.

130. Schwarz, *Creation*, pp. 215-16.

131. Pannenberg's understanding of Clarke (*ST* 2:45).

132. Pannenberg, *ST* 2:44-45.

133. Schleiermacher, *Christian Faith*, §47.1 (pp. 178-81, here p. 180); see also §47.2 (pp. 181-83) for further problems with miracles in relation to natural causes.

134. Cf. Dembski, "Schleiermacher's Metaphysical Critique of Miracles," pp. 443-65.

Making miracle the function of human ignorance — as much as human knowledge is likely to have limitations — is as fallible as the God-of-the-gaps logic in general; fewer and fewer incidents are in need of being labeled miracles. That is the liability of the Augustinian-Thomistic tradition embraced by the Roman Catholic tradition. No better is Protestant liberalism's search for natural explanations (so as to, for example, explain Jesus walking on the water or feeding the five thousand with appeal to natural resources)[135] or naive contrasting of the mind-sets of "primitive" disciples and technologically sophisticated twentieth-century persons.[136]

The seriously-to-be-taken challenge to miracles comes from contemporary science's claim for physical closure and determinism and theology's need to avoid the conception of the miraculous as a violation of natural laws. Building on the discussion above, we first investigate why a theist with appeal to good theological reasons might want to reject the category of the miraculous and then construct a contemporary theology of the miraculous.

Theological Objections for the Miraculous?

The theologian — in all Abrahamic traditions — faces a considerable challenge in light of the claim that "[c]learly, Christian theology can never reject the possibility of miracles within the context of God's special providence and remain *Christian* theology."[137] It is not only because of the need to affirm the immanence of God — as emphasized in the discussion of divine action above — but also, and perhaps primarily, for the establishment of the transcendence of God. "A God who cannot in principle intervene 'miraculously' in the universe can hardly be credibly maintained to be its 'wholly other' Creator." The all-important point here has to do with the doctrine of God, namely, that the deepest question about miracles is less whether miracles happen or not and more whether God is allowed to have the capacity to perform them.[138]

135. Reimarus's (*Goal of Jesus and His Disciples*, p. 119) making the disciples fraudulent because of their alleged desire to defend the divinity of Jesus with appeal to miracles represents the all-time low point of dealing with miracles.

136. Bultmann, "New Testament and Mythology," p. 5.

137. Worthing, *God, Creation, and Contemporary Physics*, p. 140, emphasis in original; on p. 142 he cites the classic statement of George G. Stokes (*Natural Theology* [London: Adam and Charles Black, 1891], p. 24): "Admit the existence of a God, of a personal God, and the possibility of miracle follows at once."

138. Worthing, *God, Creation, and Contemporary Physics*, pp. 145-46; see p. 146.

How credible is the Humean claim for the miracle as the violation of natural laws? It has to be revised significantly. First, it is tied to the now-outdated Newtonian-Laplacean strict determinism, and as such has lost much of its key appeal. Second, unlike many theologians, scientists, ironically, are always testing the limits and explanatory power of hitherto known natural laws. How else would radical paradigm changes such as the introduction of the highly counterintuitive quantum theory ever be embraced?[139] Third, at least in principle, current quantum science knows of limits to natural laws as in singularities.[140]

Not all religion-science scholars, however, are willing to embrace the category of the miraculous. The reason why the late biochemist-priest Peacocke opposed the category of the miraculous is theistic naturalism's refusal to "intervene in or abrogate the world's natural regularities."[141] While believing that "God, a supernatural being, has caused, and continues to cause, the whole universe to exist," in response Keith Ward wonders "[h]ow plausible it is, then, to say that such a God will refuse to operate in the world in particular ways." Isn't the Christian bound to believe at least in some miraculous divine acts such as the resurrection, the descent of the Spirit, and so forth? According to Ward, even a minimalist *Christian* account of Christ's significance (provided that many traditional issues such as the virgin birth might be debatable) seems to require the reality of miraculous divine acts, that is, acts that transcend the natural order. Furthermore, Ward continues, anyone who believes in the reality of God also affirms "massive dualism" in terms of God being infinite while the world is finite, as well as God being totally spiritual while the creatures are (also) material. Ward concludes that Peacocke probably would endorse dualism "between a spiritual God and the created universe," but that he would refuse to embrace "any dualism of spirit and matter *within* the cosmos." But even the rejection of the latter type of dualism may not be as strong as Peacocke believes in light of his deep panentheism in which — metaphorically speaking — the world is the body of God. Ward simply notes the obvious, that "the body does not run in accordance with a set of completely autonomous and internal laws." A machine would, but a living organism does not; rather, the body follows the mind. (Here we of course come to the limits and perhaps

139. Worthing, *God, Creation, and Contemporary Physics*, p. 140, with reference to Feynman, *The Character of Physical Law*, p. 159, for a parody of an uncritical belief in physical laws.

140. Cf. Worthing, *God, Creation, and Contemporary Physics*, p. 144.

141. Peacocke, "Prologue," p. 9. Unfortunately Peacocke mistakenly claims to find support for this antimiraculous noninterventionist view in Eastern Orthodox theology by taking out of context a statement from Lossky (*Mystical Theology of the Eastern Church*, p. 70).

internal self-contradiction of the body analogy, as in creaturely life, the mind and body form one being, whereas all who are not pantheists distinguish between the divine and the bodily and do not make the divine "mind" depend on the body as it does with humans.)

The cash value of panentheism, Ward surmises, is something similar to what even classical theism claims: that because of the divine omnipresence, "no part of the physical universe is ever absent from God." If so, then the personal God truly interacts with the world, including being affected by world affairs. Now comes Ward's final challenge, with which I also agree: if God creates the world with an intentional act (as all theists believe), then it has to be said that "[s]ince the bringing of something into being is the strongest possible causal influence upon it, it may seem unnecessary to espouse a theory that denies any particular influence of God upon the universe."[142] Recall our insight above that a theist must assume a true personal — and thus intentional — agency from God, mere "whole-part constraint" or "top-down" causality being not enough.

I would add that in Peacocke's own deeply panentheistic, mutually conditioned theology, to suppose that something comes from "outside" to violate the natural laws seems like an odd fear. Only a Deist could say so, but not a panentheist (nor even a classical theist). Furthermore, when personal beings are in mutual interaction and have causal effects, these influences are not external violations of another person's balance, so to speak. God similarly is believed to be (analogically speaking) a Person, and hence intends to have a personal relationship.[143] Ward also makes the needed observation that unless one thinks of natural laws as reducible to a set of physical laws — which Peacocke's emergent monism of course is not willing to do (nor can any other theist do) — the Humean fear of the violation thereof disappears. This is also supported by the simple notion that we no longer think that nature is totally deterministic (although it is "regular") and that, therefore, the laws of nature "do not cover everything." Furthermore, as said, human choices matter. "If humans have responsible choice, their actions will not be all subsumable under laws. . . . Personal explanations, in other words, allow for alternatives."[144]

Hence, the conclusion is that rather than denying the possibility of miracles, we just have to do away with the mistaken concept of miracles as "arbitrary interferences in an otherwise elegant and lawlike cosmos" — violations

---

142. K. Ward, "Personhood," pp. 153-55, here p. 155.
143. Cf. Wiles, "Religious Authority and Divine Action," pp. 181-94.
144. K. Ward, "Personhood," pp. 156-57, here p. 157.

of the laws of nature. Instead, we have to say that in the kind of created reality we live in, miracles have "their own form of intelligibility and rationality" as the personal God is affected by and responds to the needs, desires, and prayers of his creatures. Recall our conviction that "the divine Spirit interpenetrates the universe at every point." To call these divine "interventions" violations of laws is absurd. That natural sciences are able neither to predict nor to fully investigate them, does not make miracles any less true.[145]

Ward concludes that miracles are neither "immoral," that is, breaches of natural laws, nor "irrational," that is, "emergency interventions" to fix what went wrong in nature. Rather, they are "law-transcending events, extraordinary events manifesting divine causality that modifies the normal regularities of nature with the purpose of manifesting the basis and goal of the physical world in a wider spiritual realm." One of the purposes of miracles is to "show the power of Spirit to relate matter to Spirit" in transcending the typical patterns of interaction.[146] The most profound Christian miracle, the resurrection of Christ, seems to point to freedom from decay and dissolution, "showing the goal of the whole physical process to be the transformation of the physical into an incorruptible vehicle of divine life."[147] Significantly the miracles in the Gospel of John are called "signs" *(semeia)*. Ultimately, miracles thus receive their meaning not from the past but from the future, new creation.

Christ's resurrection as the most profound divine action known to us reveals the ultimate meaning of the miracle. Rather than going against nature, it transcends and lifts up the natural. It points to the eschatological consummation when, according to the biblical promises, creation "will be set free from its bondage to decay" (Rom. 8:21). In resurrection even death will be defeated (1 Cor. 15:55).

Are miracles then a *direct* divine action? Of course, they appear to be so when, for example, a miraculous healing happens in response to prayer. But ultimately, theologically speaking, even healing miracles and the like — unless they are "violations" of natural laws — happen within the fabric of natural causes and thus represent indirect action of God. Finite human beings cannot experience God's works without mediation. We always experience miracles through a created agency. That is, of course, not to deny that such events assure us in a touching manner of the deep love and care of God; in other words,

---

145. K. Ward, "Personhood," p. 160.

146. K. Ward, "Divine Action in an Emergent Cosmos," p. 297.

147. K. Ward, "Divine Action in an Emergent Cosmos," p. 297. On the importance of the resurrection of Christ in this regard, see also Polkinghorne, *Quarks, Chaos, and Christianity,* chap. 6.

even this "indirect"(ly experienced) divine action is a "personal" divine action because God is Father, Son, and Spirit.[148]

In the final analysis, a theological perception of an event as miraculous is just that: *theological.* On the one hand, miracle can only be had through the eye of faith — and therefore, the "miracle does not replace faith by demonstrating the presence of God through sign language."[149] On the other hand, without faith, theological interpretation, even the strangest and most counterintuitive event can also be explained otherwise. Similarly to the book of nature, a "miraculous act by itself is silent" and invites diverse interpretations.[150]

148. See Stoeger, "Describing God's Action," pp. 251-52.
149. Schwarz, *Creation,* p. 221.
150. Schwarz, *Creation,* p. 225.

8. The Suffering and Flourishing of Nature

．

Traditional Theology of Evil and Suffering in Need of Radical Reorienting and Revision

Although the mystery of evil is likely to remain that — a *mystery* — any theistic faith, even those outside the Abrahamic traditions, has to account for the presence of evil in light of God's goodness (if such a claim is issued by the faith tradition). The problem is particularly pressing for Abrahamic faiths that insist on God's fairness, love, and goodness.[1] Rampant suffering and acts of evil in the world, in relation both to humanity (moral evil) and to nature (natural evil), not only constitute a major atheistic challenge concerning the existence of God. Even more importantly, suffering poses the question of what kind of God there is, if there is one. Dubbed "the argument from neglect," the challenge simply is this: Doesn't the nonoccurrence of the kinds of acts that one would expect from a loving, personal God speak for a nonpersonal God who is a malevolent person, if not amoral?[2] Humans' and nature's suffering belong together, but neither one should be subsumed under the other. The Old Testament book of Job's reflection on the justification of God in light of human suffering culminates in what may be the greatest nature passage

1. Linzey, *Christianity and the Rights of Animals*, p. 59. For the (questionable in my mind) distinction between a "defense" and "theodicy," see Tilley, "The Problems of Theodicy," pp. 35-51.

2. The term was coined by Wesley Wildman, himself a naturalist (nonpersonal) theist; see his "Incongruous Goodness, Perilous Beauty, Disconcerting Truth," pp. 277-78. For an important discussion, see Clayton and Knapp, "Divine Action," pp. 179-94.

in Jewish-Christian Scripture, chapters 38–39, a reflection on "natural evil," "natural theodicy" — as well as the beauty and wonder of nature![3]

As universal as the experience of evil is, there is no universally agreed upon definition: "Each value system or worldview defines what it considers to be the good" or the evil.[4] Traditionally, the topic of suffering and evil has been discussed in the doctrine of providence under the rubric of theodicy (that is, how to justify the goodness and power of God vis-à-vis rampant evil and suffering in God's creation). Its focus has been almost exclusively on pain and suffering in human life and the implications for belief in God.[5] In contemporary theology and particularly in this project, the complicated and complex question of evil, suffering, and pain will be reoriented and revised in a number of significant ways.

First, rather than human suffering and pain, the main focus in this context will be on nonhuman creatures and creation. The first part of the chapter speaks of evil and suffering in nature as a "natural" phenomenon, that is, without any direct link with humanity. Whatever our understanding of the entrance (and presence) of evil and suffering in God's creation, only a tiny amount of nature's suffering, decay, and death has any relation to humanity (and of course, nature has been there billions and billions of years before humans). The second part, then, takes up the "pollution" of nature, which for the sake of this discussion serves as an umbrella term and includes all (directly or indirectly) human-caused damage to the environment, whether climate, water, earth, animals, vegetation, and so forth.

That choice raises the question of whether to take up the human-oriented theodicy question, then, in part 2 in the context of theological anthropology. The negative response to that query takes us to the second distinctive feature of our discussion, namely, that the proper place to discuss the theodicy question — the justification of God — is eschatology, the doctrine of last things. This departs from tradition, in which the answers were usually sought from the past, the origins. Only in light of the end of the unfolding of the historical process, in the context of Christian hope for the arrival of the kingdom of God, is it possible to link suffering and evil to God's righteous rule and care for the world God has created. Even in this chapter, the eschatological horizon has to be opened as the only final hope of resolution. And indeed, when the full theological theodicy is attempted in *Community and Hope* (part 2), the

---

3. See Bauckham, *Living with Other Creatures*, pp. 7-9.

4. R. Russell, *Cosmology*, p. 230.

5. An important exception is by the leading worldwide expert Andrew Linzey, *Animal Theology*; see also Murray, *Nature Red in Tooth and Claw*.

discussion of human suffering and pain has to be linked again with the wider context of evil in all of God's creation. Treating natural evil before suffering in human life is a way to begin to balance a rampant omission in Christian tradition. At the same time, the discussion of pollution of nature does not absolve humanity from its God-given responsibility to take care of creation.

Third, the discussion of evil and suffering in nature must be linked tightly with current scientific understandings of the world, particularly with topics such as entropy and the nature of creaturely life as finite. Abstract speculations such as whether God *could* have created another kind of world without evil — while worth asking in a humble and modest spirit — can only be meaningfully discussed while keeping in mind what kind of world it is that we know.

Fourth, as with all other systematic themes in this project, the question of evil and suffering has to be placed in the interfaith context. To make that task manageable — and in light of the vastly differing orientations in cosmology and understandings of nature — three Abrahamic faiths will be put in dialogue here.

Finally, as the heading to this chapter tells us, not only suffering but also the flourishing of nature is in view. The topic of flourishing invites theology to envision ways of helping nature blossom, be healed, and live well under the circumstances that govern our known world. There are a number of things we humans cannot do when it comes to "natural" processes in nature, say, decay and death (including violent death caused by other animals). That said, there are many things we can do — or leave undone — to help turn around the impending eco-catastrophe. In the last chapter of part 2, we will reflect theologically on human flourishing.

Before tackling the meaning of nature's suffering, let us raise a question usually ignored in theological theodicy: whether the universe can be said to be moral in any sense. It all depends on how one defines the issue. Of course, the processes of nature do not bear moral responsibility as do humans. But in a qualified theological sense, we can establish some kind of moral dimension to the universe — and perhaps we humans can learn something of the way nature functions. The important work by the philosopher Nancey Murphy and the physicist George Ellis, *On the Moral Nature of the Universe*, argues that God's way of working in concert with nature rather than violently overriding its law-like functioning may have implications for human morality: "it implies a 'kenotic' or self-renunciatory ethic, according to which one must renounce self-interest for the sake of the other, *no matter what the cost to oneself.*"[6]

6. Murphy and Ellis, *On the Moral Nature of the Universe*, p. xv, emphasis in original; for a detailed discussion, see chap. 6.

Whereas for these authors the paragon of such ethics is Christian Anabaptism, it is to be expected that in other faith traditions similar kinds of intuitions may be found.[7] This insight is one of the steps toward a more unified worldview that links nature, human life, and cosmos together more closely.[8]

In Search of an "Evolutionary Theodicy"

The Theological Meaning of Nonhuman Suffering and Pain

Since the publication of John Hick's definitive monograph *Evil and the God of Love* (orig. 1966), it has become customary to speak of two wide theodicy traditions — or, more elusively, "orientations"[9] — Augustinian and Irenaean.[10] For the Augustinian tradition — which heuristically means the whole Western Church's tradition through Thomas and the Protestant Reformers all the way to Barth — evil is merely a "privation," a lack of goodness. This does not undermine the reality of the empirical *experience* of suffering and pain; it is an ontological statement. Ultimately only good exists. Indeed, not only is the world very good because of God's creation, but the principle of plenitude even helps explain the presence of evil (maximizing its plenitude, the so-called aesthetic principle). Evil's origin is linked tightly with the human abuse of the God-given (in itself good) capacity for making choices. (Ultimately, the "whence" question leads to the precosmic angelic Fall.) With the Fall came not only spiritual death, but also physical death (based on a certain reading of Rom. 5:12).

The major alternative in Christian theodicy history according to Hick is the Irenaean-originated "World as vale of soul-making" tradition. This Eastern Church view of humanity, while of course not evolutionary in any sense, leans more easily toward what Hick calls a "teleological" or "developmental" idea: rather than being perfected beings, humanity begins a long path of development toward maturity. In that process, evil, suffering, and other troubles help cultivate character. Thus, negative experiences serve the higher teleological purposes. An important — albeit historically unrelated — modern development is that of Schleiermacher, who similarly rejects the idea of original per-

---

7. Murphy and Ellis, *On the Moral Nature of the Universe*, p. 7.

8. Murphy and Ellis, *On the Moral Nature of the Universe,* p. 1; see chaps. 3 and 5 particularly.

9. Hvidt, "Historical Developments of the Problem of Evil," p. 2.

10. These two traditions will also be discussed in part 2 (chap. 15) with regard to the Fall and sin.

fection and is not attributing all evil and suffering to human sin. According to Hick, perhaps the most revolutionary contribution of Schleiermacher is that he is "the first great theologian" to affirm openly that God is "ultimately ordaining sin and suffering" and hence bears the ultimate responsibility.[11] Evil is instrumental for testing and maturity to take place. Hick himself takes up the Irenaean-Schleiermachian scheme in order to forge a contemporary version of teleological, developmental theodicy.[12] On the one hand, he critiques the standard features of Augustinian theodicy tradition, including its outdated mythical features (a literalist understanding of the Fall, a precosmic angelic Fall, and so forth), its focus in the past, its abstract nature, its desire to absolve the Creator from responsibility, and its making evil merely a matter of human disobedience.[13] Hick's teleological view is of course in keeping with current cosmic and anthropological evolutionary understandings. Second, the refusal to relieve God from responsibility for evil and sin helps avoid dualism. Third, its loosening of the link between human sin and evil, particularly natural evil, is to be affirmed. What is still lacking in Hick's theodicy is a cosmic, "evolutionary theodicy" in the sense of a robust account of natural evil — although it takes important steps in the right direction. Furthermore, its making *all* evil a matter of maturity is of course limited: there is probably some (much?) evil that has little to do with the maturity of any being. Third, this leads to what is obviously the major challenge to Hick's theodicy: the existence of dysteleological evil, that is, evil ruthlessly destructive and damaging to persons, evil that seems disproportionate as punishment for wrongdoing and that obstructs the soul-making process.[14]

As can be seen, the theological tradition of Abrahamic faiths has focused almost exclusively on the evil and suffering in human life — and to some extent on the way it may affect nonhuman creatures.[15] Suffering, pain, and evil in nature[16] have received remarkably little attention — let alone physical natural evil such as earthquakes, hurricanes, the impact of asteroids, and so forth (apart from the immediate damage caused to humanity).[17]

---

11. Hick, *Evil and the God of Love*, p. 228.

12. Hick, *Evil and the God of Love*, part 3.

13. A useful summative comparison between the two traditions is chap. 12 of Hick, *Evil and the God of Love*.

14. S. Pinnock, *Beyond Theodicy*, p. 6.

15. Linzey, "Is Christianity Irredeemably Speciesist?" pp. xi-xx.

16. Roughly similar to natural evil is "evolutionary evil," a term coined by Christopher Southgate, "God and Evolutionary Evil," pp. 803-21.

17. Terminologically it is useful to include under "natural" evil both (1) biological nat-

Some theological approaches even consider natural evil not really evil by maintaining that natural theodicy is irrelevant, that is, natural evil is just "natural" and constitutive of life, and therefore in no need of explanation.[18] That makes any attempt at natural theodicy only marginally relevant.[19] At the same time, natural evil is made an unavoidable consequence of God's act of creation. What to think of this opinion? It has to be qualified. On the one hand, it is of course true that death and decay are inevitable in our kind of world. That, however, does not make the issue theologically irrelevant; indeed, as the following section on the meaning of entropy indicates, it calls for careful reflection. On the other hand, God as the Creator cares for all creatures. Consider also the compassion and care for animals and nature in Jesus' teaching and practice.[20]

Recall that Augustine's goal was to help absolve the Creator of blame for the entrance of evil.[21] It looks like the order and goodness of creation are so essential to Augustine's ontology of creation that there is no place for natural evil.[22] Furthermore, it seems like his idea of plenitude makes nonhuman creatures and beings merely instrumental to the perfection of the universe.[23] That said, his view of decay and death of nonhuman beings also reflects (unknowingly!) the current evolutionary worldview in that the lower beings are destined to give way to higher ones and to the continuation of the process.[24] What about pain and suffering in nonhuman beings? While Augustine does not deny the existence of pain in animals, its description also follows that of his privation theory.[25] At times, it also sounds like animal pain merely serves the principle of design ("unity") for our benefit.[26] Be that as

---

ural evil such as pain, suffering, disease, and death, and (2) physical natural evil including geological, meteorological, oceanographic, astrophysical, radiative phenomena, and so forth. See R. Russell, "Physics, Cosmology, and the Challenge," p. 109 n. 318.

18. For details, see discussion in R. Russell, *Cosmology*, pp. 253-56. For the inevitability of suffering and death in nature, see, e.g., Peacocke, *Theology for a Scientific Age*, pp. 63, 221.

19. Southgate ("God and Evolutionary Evil," pp. 808-9) aptly calls this simply "The Problem Dismissed."

20. Bauckham, "Jesus and Animals I" and "Jesus and Animals II."

21. G. Evans, *Augustine on Evil*, p. 98.

22. See Augustine, *On Order* 1.7.18; in Borruso, trans., pp. 23-24.

23. Augustine, *City of God* 12.4.

24. Augustine, *City of God* 12.5; see also Augustine, chap. 8, "From the Corruption and Destruction of Inferior Things Is the Beauty of the Universe," in *Concerning the Nature of God, against the Manicheans*.

25. Augustine, *Enchiridion (Faith, Hope, and Love)* 3.11.

26. See Hick, *Evil and the God of Love*, p. 85; Munday, "Animal Pain," pp. 435-68.

it may, it seems to me undeniable that to the extent that Augustine affirms natural evil, including pain and suffering in nature, he links it with the disorder in the cosmos due to the human fall. Or to be more precise: disorder entered the cosmos even before the human fall through the angelic rebellion following Satan's "fall."[27] So, at its best Augustine's natural evil is a result of misuse of freedom of either spiritual or human beings and the accompanying divine punishment for wrong choices.[28] More widely, in Christian tradition the main reason for overlooking animal pain is the nonrational and therefore subordinate and utilitarian view of animals.[29] Furthermore, the relationship between the human fall and the suffering of animals (and the rest of creation) was not appropriately clarified.[30] A summative statement about theological tradition's assessment of animal pain and suffering goes something like this: "avoid cruelty to animals and treat them with kindness; animal lives are not considered sacred and hence they have no significant right to life; as they lack reason, animals may be reasonably used for human benefit (food, companionship, transport, work, recreation and so on)."[31]

Do plants (and other nonsentient entities) feel pain? Science does not speak with one voice at the time of this writing. What we know is that plants seem to have some kind of biochemical injury mechanisms and, for example, may release hormones that could indicate a sensation.[32] Perhaps we should find another term because pain entails a nervous system — or use the term strictly analogically.[33] It seems to me that the theological concern for nature's suffering is not predicated on the difficult question of the nature of animal consciousness, the study of which is highly complicated;[34] common sense says that perhaps only the higher animals are *conscious* of pain in some sense. The question is large: How can a creation and creatures pronounced "good" multiple times in the Genesis narrative be subject to decay, suffering, and pain?[35]

27. Even Satan and the fallen angels are still under God's power and receive their existence only from God. Augustine, *City of God* 22.24.

28. For a detailed study, see G. Clark, "The Fathers and the Animals."

29. Yamamoto, "Aquinas and Animals."

30. See Ickert, "Luther and Animals."

31. Wade, "Animal Theology and Ethical Concerns," p. 1.

32. Frank Kühnemann of the Institute for Applied Physics in Bonn has recently argued that there is some kind of rudimentary sensation of pain in plants ("When Plants Say 'Ouch'").

33. Wildman, "Use and Meaning," pp. 53, 56.

34. See M. S. Dawkins, *Through Our Eyes Only?* pp. 2-3.

35. For a striking statement, see Lubenow, "Pre-Adamites, Sin, Death, and the Human Fossils," p. 225.

Entropy, Evil, and Suffering in Nature

The physicist Richard Carlson reminds us: "Starting with the products of the Big Bang, time, and the development of more and more complex entities, previously developed material in concert with the laws of the universe eventually resulted in the highest level of evolution. On Earth, given its finite size and resources and the need for millions of years to achieve this level, creaturely death is required as part of the process. In fact, it can be said that new life has always depended on the death of the now living."[36] If freedom of will, as tradition correctly argues, helps us understand much of the evil and sin happening in human life, it seems that entropy, the second law of thermodynamics, has much to do with decay, death, suffering, and pain in nature.

It appears that reaching the highest level of evolution, namely, conscious beings capable of making thematic the relationship to the Creator, requires an awful lot of suffering and "waste" over the billions of years.[37] If this version of the developmental good-harm analysis (GHA) is deemed too anthropocentric, a wider biocentric argument would likewise highlight the importance of suffering as entailed by an adaptive fit to the environment. Or, to widen the scope even more: the emergence of complexity and intelligence requires a long process of wastefulness. In that sense, entropy and suffering seem to be instrumental.[38] But understandably, some object to this reasoning. An interesting argument comes from Ruth Page, who is willing to justify the instrumentality of suffering only with regard to every individual being's life but not in the longer range of evolution.[39] While there is certainly a need to consider the individual being, Page's reasoning is completely at odds with how the evolutionary process seems to be working according to our current knowledge. It simply is not possible even to begin to demand that each individual being receives full "reimbursement" during the being's lifetime.[40] This law applies not only to the biological world but also to physics:

> The natural evils of transience, dissolution, death, and the pain, suffering, and loss they induce have their roots in the underlying characteristics of nature, particularly in matter and its interactions, including gravity,

36. Private e-mail communication, 9/7/2013.
37. See K. Ward, *God, Chance, and Necessity,* p. 191.
38. Southgate and Robinson, "Varieties of Theodicy," p. 75.
39. Page, *God and the Web of Creation.*
40. It seems to me that Southgate, "God and Evolutionary Evil," is in material agreement with my argument.

and in the increase of entropy — the second law of thermodynamics — which is always in force. . . . Thus, transience, dissolution, and death are the entropic price demanded for the exploration of new possibilities, the generation of novelty and the support of highly organized systems in our evolving universe.[41]

This remark yields two important lessons. First, it speaks of the need for theology to engage the physical sciences in relation to natural evil — what can be called "cosmic theodicy."[42] Although routinely ignored in theological-philosophical discussions, the biological and physical processes are extremely tightly intertwined; we know now that "[e]volutionary biology requires the macroscopic world of nature as described by classical physics," and on the other side, "[t]he classical world, in turn, requires quantum mechanics and special relativity."[43] Indeed, put in the widest possible framework, we have to speak of "natural theodicy shaped in terms not of evolutionary biology but of fundamental physics, big bang cosmology, and the constants in nature."[44] The second lesson is that only with reference to eschatological overcoming of entropy can final hope be established, as will be discussed below.

It is clear that entropy and evil are related concepts in many ways, yet neither can be subsumed under the other.[45] As costly as life and evolution are to the environment, in that only through the use of (limited) resources and processes of decay and death may life-forms be sustained and evolve, "the value of life and indirectly the value of entropy as a necessary component to life cannot easily be dismissed."[46] Ultimately, "[i]t seems hard to avoid the paradox that 'natural evil' is a necessary prerequisite for the emergence of free, self-conscious beings."[47] A foundational difference between entropy and evil is that entropy can be said to belong to the goodness of creation as it is a necessary requirement for growth and change (at least in our kind of world). Of evil we can hardly say the same, even if God has allowed it and is able to

41. Stoeger, "Entropy, Emergence, and the Physical Roots of Natural Evil," p. 93.

42. R. Russell, "Physics, Cosmology, and the Challenge," p. 110.

43. R. Russell, "Physics, Cosmology, and the Challenge," pp. 113-14 (both subheadings); for accessible technical details, see pp. 114-22.

44. R. Russell, "Physics, Cosmology, and the Challenge," p. 123.

45. A highly insightful analysis of similarities and differences is R. Russell, *Cosmology,* pp. 234-36.

46. R. Russell, *Cosmology,* pp. 236-37 (quotation p. 237); see also p. 240.

47. Peacocke, *Creation and the World of Science,* p. 166, quoted in R. Russell, *Cosmology,* p. 237.

bring good out of bad. Theologically speaking, although it seems like entropy, and its ultimate effect, death, is going to win, the biblical vision has in view the final cosmic redemption with the overcoming of the second law of thermodynamics (Rom. 8:21-22). In Jesus' miracles, including his nature miracles, a sign of this hope was already manifest.[48]

Having established the role and necessity of entropy (and thus suffering and death in nature) and having clarified the relationship between evil and entropy, we now face the most challenging question: How exactly should we conceive the relationship between the good, loving Creator and the existence of entropy/evil in nature? One way to deal with this problem is to use the so-called good-harm analysis (GHA), which has obvious parallels with Hick's twofold distinction of traditional theodicies.[49] It consists of three categories, the first being "Property-Consequence GHA: possessing a certain good or commodity leads to harm for its use for the better,"[50] such as freedom of the will in Augustinian tradition. Well-known examples in nature include the seemingly overviolent killing of sea lions by a certain class of orcas, which, while "evil" in itself (and not necessary but rather potential), also ironically helps the victims develop for the better.[51] What about those many cases when evil in nature is so rampant or dysteleological that it seemingly has no meaning? God's world governance either permits evil to have free rein (relatively speaking) or impedes evil (but because evil is too all-encompassing, it can only be restrained to an extent).[52] In light of GHA, this kind of suffering and evil hardly serves any purpose. Interestingly, there is a parallel in the physical sciences' dysteleological models that involve an ever-increasing entropy; rather than serving any purpose, the entropy just brings about ever-increasing disorder. The once-famous heat death of the universe is a version of that.

The second category is Developmental GHA: to achieve a certain good goal (such as maturity), some harms are inevitable, as in the Irenaean teleological/developmental view.[53] Natural processes offer many examples, including the above-mentioned sea lions' experience. This of course raises the question,

---

48. R. Russell, *Cosmology*, p. 237.

49. Southgate and Robinson, "Varieties of Theodicy," pp. 67-90; for an early example of good-harm analysis, see Aquinas, *ST* 1.22.2.

50. Rolston, "Naturalizing and Systematizing Evil."

51. Southgate and Robinson, "Varieties of Theodicy," p. 84; for others, see pp. 85-86.

52. Appropriately named "Rampant Evil and Dysteleological Cosmological Models" by Worthing, *God, Creation, and Contemporary Physics*, pp. 148-53.

53. In Worthing's (*God, Creation, and Contemporary Physics*, pp. 148-53) template, this relates to the "'Domesticated' Evil and Teleological Cosmological Models" alternative.

"How could a good God intentionally allow the wasteful and horrific deaths of billions of animals over billions of years before man's sin (much less directly will to employ this struggle as his primary means of creating)?"[54] What if this is the only way to have our kind of world — particularly, higher animals with (some) freedom of will? Although one can imagine a world of creatures without pain and suffering,[55] creation with a sequence of forms and generations cannot be imagined without coming to an end of finite life. In that sense, inevitably, "[e]volution is costly business."[56] This reasoning seems to point to the third category, namely, Constitutive GHA: a certain good is inseparable from harm or suffering, as in aesthetics, where beauty entails ugliness as its contrast. On a closer look, however, GHA is no answer to the questions of the teleological/developmental model because rather than "counting the costs" as in the two previous types, here neither goodness nor evil is considered ultimate; rather, the ultimate contains and gives rise to both good and evil. Ultimately, this leads to the abandonment of the weighing of costs altogether (and so the project of theodicy).[57]

Hence, perhaps the best way to deal with this (seemingly) teleological — and "necessary" — suffering and evil is to resort to what philosophers call a "consequentialist natural theodicy" (CNT), that is, natural evils are an unintended by-product or consequence of God's free choice to create the kind of world in which we live, an evolving world. Correctly understood, CNT contends that God had no choice but to permit physical and biological natural evil in our kind of world; this is not to put any external necessity on God but rather to state the obvious, that God freely decided to create the cosmos and *freely* decided to create *this kind of world,* so, in light of our current knowledge, it looks like natural evil could not have been avoided. In a qualified sense, then, it can be said that CNT represents yet another form of "the best of all possible worlds."[58] As to whether other options were available to God, the Creator, we do not know[59] (nor whether in other kinds of universes, should there

---

54. Moreland and Reynolds, introduction to *Three Views on Creation and Evolution,* pp. 21-22.

55. Cf. R. Clark, *Survival of Charles Darwin,* pp. 77, 53.

56. Polkinghorne, *Science and Theology,* p. 77. Similarly, Gould ("Darwin and Paley Meet the Invisible Hand," p. 8) poses this challenge to theists: "The price of perfect design is messy relentless slaughter" (quoted in Munday, "Animal Pain," p. 450).

57. See Kallenberg, "The Descriptive Problem of Evil," pp. 297-322.

58. Murphy, "Science and the Problem of Evil," pp. 131-32; so also Tracy, "Lawfulness of Nature," p. 153.

59. Cf. Aquinas, *ST* 1.25.6.

be any, other kinds of world orders are in place). Other highly speculative, abstract questions to which we are not likely to get any affirmative answers include these: Would slightly different — even extremely slightly (in light of the biopic principle) — constants have produced a cosmos in which natural evil did not happen? Is life (and conscious life) really worth this high a "cost"? And so forth.[60]

Among all these important questions, yet another arises that is not only abstract but also deeply practical: granted that natural evil is necessary for this kind of world, one wonders if *this much* natural evil is necessary. In other words, wasn't it possible for God, if he so desired, to prevent, circumvent, soften some (many would say much) of the suffering rampant in nature?[61] That said, CNT, in itself, is a penultimate answer to the painful problem of suffering. Only with the turn to eschatological consummation can any long-standing hope be gained.

Cosmic Theodicy in an Eschatological Perspective: Preliminary Remarks

All in all, the foundational question to any theistic theology is the dual affirmation of the world created good and its existence in a state of dissipation, decay, and destruction. As mentioned, only with reference to the final overcoming of entropy, hence decay and death, can the theodicy question be handled. The eschatological locating of the question also raises important related questions (which will be more comprehensively discussed under eschatology).

Christian eschatological hope encompasses the whole of creation, not only the destiny of humans. The redemption of time and space, as discussed above, as well as the importance of embodiment (as reflected in the bodily resurrection of Christ) are part of this Christian "earthly" vision for the future.[62] The cosmic renewal for which creation "groans" now in anticipation of the eschatological redemption (Rom. 8:22) includes natural as well as human shalom.

Eschatological hope is anchored in a thick theology of divine suffering, including *kenosis,* which tells us that God, the Creator, is not an uninter-

---

60. See also R. Russell, "Physics, Cosmology, and the Challenge," p. 111; Murphy, "Science and the Problem of Evil," pp. 140-47.

61. So argues strongly Rowe, "The Problem of Evil and Some Varieties of Atheism," pp. 127, 131; for a philosophical rebuttal of Rowe's reasoning, see Wykstra, "The Humean Obstacle," pp. 138-60. These are discussed in Tracy, "Lawfulness of Nature," pp. 167-70.

62. See also R. Russell, *Cosmology,* pp. 262-66.

ested, Deistic "Unmoved Mover," but a loving Father from whose hands even nonhuman creatures receive their sustenance and well-being.[63] The kind of evolutionary world we know entails growth and decay, pain and joy, birth and death. With creatures' joys, God rejoices, with creatures' tears, he sympathizes. Under the neologism "classical panentheism," such a view of the trinitarian God is attempted in *Trinity and Revelation* (chaps. 10–12). The feminist Sallie McFague sees in the narrative of Jesus the pattern for divine immanence, something that cannot be read off from evolutionary history, namely, the direction "toward inclusive love for all, especially the oppressed, the outcasts, the vulnerable."[64] Sharing, inclusion, and resistance to evil deeds, she surmises, run counter to the suffering and waste in nature.[65] That is something that has to be wholeheartedly affirmed. Yet we should also acknowledge the robust tension between that and the inevitable death, decay, and suffering in nature. Naively, we should not expect that even the most sacrificial sharing of resources and work for liberation of all would stop the cycle of entropy — until God's eternity.

Reference to eschatology, however, raises the question of the redemption of individuals. As discussed above, it is not justifiable to expect recompense in this life, either for humans or for other creatures. The Christian eschatological vision includes the renewal not only of the cosmos but also of all creatures. As to how it happens for different classes of creatures, in this case nonhumans, neither biblical nor theological tradition gives much guidance, other than that there are delightful pictures of the messianic peace and shalom, including the flourishing of nature both in the shared portion of Jewish-Christian Scripture and at the end of the NT. This is not to deny that "religious ends" according to mainline Christian tradition are different for humans and nonhumans, and therefore, the same kind of hope of afterlife for nonhuman creatures is not promised as for men and women.[66]

Only in light of the eschatological hope can we say that the "[c]reation praise of God to which the Psalms refer is always in anticipation of the eschatological consummation. In light of this, creation already praises God by its continuation as a finite reality, for in this way creatures are as God willed them to be. They also praise God in their perishing, because this is part of

---

63. For an important application of *kenosis* to the God-world relationship, see Coakley, "Kenosis," pp. 192-210.

64. McFague, *Body of God*, p. 160.

65. McFague, *Body of God*, p. 174.

66. Therefore, I find mistaken the dream of "pelican heaven," an afterlife hope for animals, of McDaniel, *Of God and Pelicans*, p. 45.

their finitude."[67] The eschatological coming of the kingdom of God also brings about the needed monistic resolution: ultimately, Abrahamic faiths can only have one ultimate reality, although prior to that, depending on one's theology, it seems like two powers are in place.[68]

So far, we have discussed suffering, pain, and evil in nature, which by and large seem to occur totally unrelated to human behavior and of course precede it by billions of years (and if extended to the nonsentient realm, go back to the beginnings of the universe). Now it is time to tackle the more imminent issue of human-caused suffering, currently threatening even the whole existence of life on our planet.

The Pollution of Creation: Ecological Resources and Challenges among Religions

The Role of Sacred Traditions in Relation to Nature

The pollution[69] of creation is a well-documented, major crisis threatening not only the well-being but even the *being* itself of our planet. "Environmental pollution is considered to be our world's most dangerous, and constant, threat."[70] As the Catholic ethicist-theologian Daniel Maguire has reminded us, "if current trends continue, we will not."[71] This raises the question of the role of religions in helping overcome the impending eco-catastrophe. This investigation is driven by the conviction that not only "[h]uman beliefs about the

---

67. Pannenberg, *ST* 2:173; for a profound theology of creation's praise, see Bauckham, *Living with Other Creatures,* chaps. 7 and 8.

68. For details, see Hick, *Evil and the God of Love,* chap. 2.

69. Recall that in this discussion "pollution" is used as an inclusive umbrella term denoting all types of harm to the environment and its processes and creatures by humans (whether directly or indirectly).

70. International Conference on Environmental Pollution and Remediation: http://icepr2013.international-aset.com/index.html (11/26/2013). Other resources include those produced by the UN: http://www.un.org/en/globalissues/environment/ (11/26/2013); the National Science Foundation: "Global Climate Change. Research Explorer," http://www.exploratorium.edu/climate/index.html (11/26/2013); NASA: http://climate.nasa.gov/ (11/26/2013). The World Health Organization constantly reports on the health effects of environmental changes: http://who.int/globalchange/environment/en/ (11/26/2013). Other reliable resources include the Environmental Change Institute, University of Oxford, http://www.eci.ox.ac.uk/ (11/26/2013); Houghton, *Global Climate Change;* Justus and Fletcher, *Global Climate Change.*

71. Maguire, *Moral Core of Judaism and Christianity,* p. 13.

nature of ecology are the distinctive contribution of our species to the ecology itself," but that, importantly, "[r]eligious beliefs — especially those concerning the nature of powers that create and animate — become an effective part of ecological systems."[72] Here is a new challenge and opportunity for all religions: in the past they did not have the need to face environmental threats and care; in the contemporary world, they must.[73]

Unlike the past, most religions nowadays make claims to being "green."[74] Constructive theologians, however, should exercise proper caution. To begin with, should we really expect the conservation of the environment to be in the forefront of sacred Scripture? I think it is a foundational mistake to expect a text, say the OT, written (mainly) for an exiled community in search of a national/ethnic/religious identity in a hostile world, to major on the topic of ecology![75] Indeed, it is not so much a matter of what the ancient scriptures of each tradition are saying about nature at face value, but rather, whether — in keeping with the deepest theological and spiritual teachings — an eco-friendly hermeneutics is feasible and available.[76] Rightly the Muslim writer Craig Phillips concludes: "Though we tend to read our scriptures anthropocentrically, we must reflect on the fact that our scriptures are not anthropocentric, and nor are they ecocentric."[77]

A persistent theme in contemporary religious discussion on nature's flourishing is an apologetic against the complaints of religions' devastating influence on environmental attitudes and actions. The (in)famous essay by Lynn White formulated that charge most radically.[78] As flawed — historically, hermeneutically, and analytically — as the essay is, at least it has been able to fuel self-critical soul-searching[79] and constructive responses among religious traditions.

---

72. Sullivan, preface to *I&E*, p. xi.

73. Tucker and Grim, series foreword to *I&E*, p. xvii; Foltz, "Introduction," p. xxxviii.

74. For an important current resource, see the theme issue "Ecology and World Religions" of the *Journal of Dharma*. Continuously updated information, resources, and discussions can also be drawn from the Alliance of World Religions and Conservation official Web site, http://www.arcworld.org/. The organization claims to be "secular" but helping faith traditions to cultivate a keen awareness of the habitat at large.

75. See further, Hütterman, *Ecological Message of the Torah*, p. 11; for a seasoned comment, see McFague, "An Ecological Christology," p. 35.

76. See Foltz, "Islamic Environmentalism," p. 249.

77. Phillips, "Green Creation," p. 6; he refers to Katz, "Faith, God, and Nature," p. 164.

78. L. White, "Historical Roots," pp. 1203-7. For a rebuttal and response from an Islamic perspective, see Foltz, "Islamic Environmentalism," p. 249. From a Jewish perspective, see Lamm, "Ecology in Jewish Law and Theology," pp. 162-85.

79. See Afrasiabi, "Toward an Islamic Ecotheology," p. 281.

One of the most persistent and ill-defined myths concerning religions' role in conservation has to do with the alleged radical difference between Asiatic and Abrahamic traditions. "One of the most common and enduring stereotypes in environmental literature is the idea that Eastern religions promote a sense of harmony between human beings and nature. On the other side of the stereotype stand the religions of the West, promoting the separation of human beings and nature and encouraging acts of domination, exploitation, and control."[80] Without in any way setting up a "contest" between the East and the West, one only has to lament the naivete and superficiality of these statements. The critic would only need to pose this question: How would you scripturally and in terms of general *Weltanschauung* support these claims?[81]

As religions continue to tackle the issue of environmental response, the warning by the postcolonial Indian sociologist Ramachandra Guha should be kept in mind: there hardly is a one-size-fits-all solution. He reminds us that the "official" Western approach to conservation — now the supposed hallmark globally — is but one way of trying to solve the imminent problem.[82] One of the key issues is the participation, or lack thereof, of women in environmental issues with their own distinctive contribution.[83]

Ecology and Environment in Asiatic Traditions

How "Green" Is the Buddhist View of Nature?

To the question of whether, and to what extent, Buddhism is a "green" philosophy, one may expect two kinds of responses. The first one, coming mainly from general cultural (and some less specialized academic) circles, would be "Yes, of course." In support, a number of alleged pillars of the Buddhist eco-friendly attitude include its alleged nonanthropocentrism, its focus on this-worldly ethical pursuit rather than centering on transcendental salvation, Buddha's compassion toward all beings as an example, and so forth.[84] A re-

---

80. Eckel, "Is There a Buddhist Philosophy of Nature?" p. 327; Eckel himself is not condoning the statement.

81. Cf. Snyder, *The Practice of the Wild*, p. 10.

82. Guha, "Radical Environmentalism," pp. 71-83.

83. For an exception to the lack of female Islamic ecologists, see Ammar, "Ecological Justice and Human Rights for Women in Islam," pp. 377-89.

84. The literature promoting this view one-sidedly is vast, including Batchelor and

curring theme in this type of promotion of the green nature of Buddhism is the dualism of Christian tradition and nondualism of its Asian counterpart.[85] The second response, coming from both Buddhologists and those scholars who know Buddhism beyond superficialities, would be far more cautionary and in many cases negative altogether.[86] In a noted analysis of various approaches to ecology among the Buddhists, Ian Harris distinguished four: eco-spirituality, eco-justice, eco-traditionalism, and eco-apologetics. Concerning the last category, he is quite critical and urges sound scholarly scrutiny of claims; for example, what is the tradition's textual basis for the alleged self-evident compatibility with green values and related claims?[87] While Harris seems to believe that Buddhism's ecological advocacy may be redeemed, some experts do not.[88]

Why this hesitancy among scholars to endorse Buddhism as eco-friendly? The most obvious reason has to do with the very "foundations" of Buddhism, particularly in its original Theravada form. Rather than, say, the Christian vision of a new creation that encompasses the renewal of the whole of creation and all creatures, the Buddhist vision of seeking liberation from *dukkha* is — at least from an outsider's perspective — deeply anthropocentric, individualistic, and oblivious of nonhuman beings. In order for that statement not to be taken as inhospitable, let me mention that the main Buddhist traditions include great narratives of the infinite compassion of the Buddha toward all beings;[89] the Mahayana traditions have the idea of helping other people reach enlightenment (and in the Pure Land tradition, even an idea of Amitabha Buddha as "savior"), and so forth. For the purposes of this comparative investigation, however, the importance of the ultimate "salvific vision" (release from *dukkha*) should not be dismissed. "Given this character of the Buddha's message as focusing on human liberation, the question of how Buddhist teach-

Brown, eds., *Buddhism and Ecology;* Badiner, ed., *Dharma Gaia;* Callicott and Ames, eds., *Nature in Asian Traditions of Thought.*

85. Cf. Melin, "Environmental Philosophy in Christianity and Buddhism," pp. 357-74.

86. A prime example is Habito, "Environment or Earth Sangha"; my discussion is deeply indebted to his.

87. I. Harris, "Getting to Grips with Buddhist Environmentalism," pp. 173-90.

88. See Keown, "Buddhism and Ecology," p. 97.

89. One of the darlings of those stories is about Buddha's self-sacrifice to save a tigress as told in *Jatakamala* #1 in *Jātakamālā or Garland of Birth Stories by Āryaśūra,* trans. J. S. Speyer (1895); an electronic version from 2010 is available at http://www.buddhanet-de.net/ancient-buddhist-texts/English-Texts/Garland-of-Birth-Stories/Garland-of-Birth-Stories.pdf, pp. 3-12. (For some reason, this narrative is not included in the vast six-volume Pali Jataka collection.)

ing and practice relates to concern about or caring for 'the environment' can be relegated to a peripheral issue at best."[90]

Unlike in Abrahamic traditions in which nature has intrinsic value as the handiwork of a personal Deity, in Buddhism (deriving from classical Hinduism) and its cyclical view of time/history, nature/the environment is doomed to a repeated cycle of arising–maintenance–annihilation–return to "nothingness"– arising again — *ad infinitum.* The Buddhist expert Ruben L. Habito concludes: "If this universe, which includes our Earth . . . is ultimately going to be annihilated, there is no motivation to take any steps to preserve it from inevitable destruction. In this context, the ecological deterioration of our Earth can be taken as an indication of the oncoming stage of annihilation, seen as an inevitable order of things, and therefore not as a cause for concern calling for action to try to stem it."[91] Ironically, then, it is not only among Christians, past and present, that escapist eschatology has been found an appealing option. Why invest in a world doomed to be annihilated? Interestingly, the Buddhist Pure Land tradition's vision of salvation in the "Land of Bliss" located "west" of the earth, the Kingdom of Amitabha Buddha, is not materially much different from the yearning for heaven among Christians or for paradise by Muslims.[92] (The Jewish this-worldly, noneschatological orientation is much less prone to escapism.)

All in all, these kinds of theological reasons that seem to obliterate or totally frustrate environmental pursuits and ethics among Buddhists are almost never mentioned in the popular promotional literature hailing "green" Buddhism. On the other side, some features of Buddhist scriptural-philosophical and spiritual tradition point to the intimate connection between humanity and the environment, most notably the deeply interrelated teaching of the origins of the cosmos (dependent co-arising). Donald K. Swearer succinctly summarizes: "The compatibility between the Buddhist worldview of interdependence and an 'environmentally friendly' way of living in the world, the values of compassion and nonviolence, and the example of the Buddha's life-style and the early *sangha* are cited as important contribution to the dialogue on ways to live in an increasingly threatened world."[93] Buddhist cosmology is also hierarchical,

90. Habito, "Environment or Earth Sangha," p. 133. Materially similarly, Eckel, "Is There a Buddhist Philosophy of Nature?" p. 340. For a highly nuanced effort to negotiate between the need to pursue one's own enlightenment and at the same time be mindful of the environment, see Sponberg, "Green Buddhism and the Hierarchy of Compassion," pp. 351-76.

91. Habito, "Environment or Earth Sangha," p. 134.

92. See also Habito, "Environment or Earth Sangha," p. 134.

93. Swearer, "Hermeneutics of Buddhist Ecology," p. 21. For important discussions, see Sandell, ed., *Buddhist Perspectives on the Ecocrisis;* S. Davies, *Tree of Life.*

consisting of various levels, from the deities to humans to other living beings to inanimate beings, which also speaks of interrelatedness.[94] Coupled with the above-mentioned tradition of Buddha's compassion toward all and sharing with all Awakened Ones (the so-called Buddha nature), a powerful resource for ecology is the peaceful, harmonious coexistence of all beings, human, other living, and inanimate, as depicted in the highly important Mahayana text *Lotus Sutra*.[95]

Hinduism's Ecological Resources and Dilemmas

The significance of ecological attitudes among the Hindus is immense in light of the huge environmental problems in India and surrounding areas.[96] Apart from China (and parts of Russia), no other major country of the world is facing as catastrophic (near-)future ecological disaster, unless something changes soon. What is Hinduism's capacity to facilitate an eco-friendly, nature-flourishing lifestyle? There is no need to repeat here the warnings expressed above regarding the naive and uncritical praise of Buddhism by many Westerners concerning the "green" resources in Hinduism. Rather, let us ask the same theological question we need to ask with every religious tradition: What are potential obstacles? What are key resources stemming from the philosophical-theological-scriptural-spiritual basis?

There is no doubt that, as in Buddhism, the cyclical worldview of Hinduism potentially leans toward being oblivious to the conservation of the earth here and now. Furthermore, Hinduism's appearance nature of reality or the cosmos as *līlā* ("play," that is, an unintended "by-product") similarly may cause the faithful to consider this earth a secondary, temporary dwelling place, on the way to the "real world." A number of other critical questions await response before the issue of Hinduism's relation to ecological concerns can be even tentatively defined. So far the mainly promotional literature has hardly begun to tackle the issues: Can the strongly ascetic[97] Hindu outlook

94. For various classifications in Buddhist traditions, see Habito, "Environment or Earth Sangha," p. 133.

95. See particularly chap. 5, "On Plants," for an example of harmonious coexistence (*Lotus Sutra [Saddharma-Pundarika or, the Lotus of the True Law]*, in *SBE* 21, n.p.); chap. 20 is a beautiful description of "The Bodhisattva Never Disparaging," who promotes a nonviolent, peaceful lifestyle. An authoritative contemporary exposition is Hanh, *Peaceful Action, Open Heart*.

96. For details, see Dwivedi, "Dharmic Ecology," pp. 3-4.

97. For a highly useful consideration of asceticism in relation to the environment in several faith traditions, see Chapple, "Asceticism and the Environment," pp. 514-25.

(in pursuit of one's own deliverance) contribute to the communal (most widely understood, including nature) good? What is the role of karma, the bondage to the world because of deeds in the past and present, with regard to environmental care? What about the deeply *theologically* based and (originally) divinely sanctioned hierarchic nature of society (the caste system) when it comes to ecological concern?[98] Finally, I am not quite sure what may be the implications for ecology of whether — speaking of Vedanta traditions, which have been the main dialogue partners in this project — one subscribes to absolute or qualified nondualism. From an outsider's perspective, with regard to this particular theme, the distinction between Sankara and Ramanuja seems minute.

These are the reasons for my reservations and cautions, and here I am joined by a slowly growing number of critical scholars, both Hindu and others. What about hopeful resources? There are some beautiful, inspiring scriptural resources extolling the beauty of nature. Just consider the long "Hymn to Goddess Earth" in Atharva Veda,[99] which begins with this lofty statement: "Truth, greatness, universal order (rita), strength, consecration, creative fervour (tapas), spiritual exaltation (brahma), the sacrifice, support the earth. May this earth, the mistress of that which was and shall be, prepare for us a broad domain!" Many other such beautiful nature hymns can be found particularly in Rig Veda (1.115; 7.99; 10.125; and so forth),[100] somewhat similar to the nature psalms in the Hebrew Bible.

The idea of the world as the body of a god or goddess, although not a universal Hindu idea, is important among the Vaishnavites (who follow Ramanuja) — as a consequence of which India by many Hindu traditions is considered a "holy land" — and naturally may lead to great concern for and care of the environment.[101] More widely speaking, some key Vedic scriptural traditions such as the celebrated creation hymn of Rig Veda 10.90 *(Purusha Sukta)* establish an integral connection between deities, humans, and all of nature. In light of these considerations, and even more generally in light of the Indian worldview, there is no dividing line between the sacred and the secular in Asiatic cultures as there typically is in the Global North. "There is no area of

98. These and other questions are also raised by L. Nelson, introduction to *Purifying the Earthly Body of God*, pp. 8-9.

99. Atharva Veda, section X: Cosmogonic and Theosophic Hymns, 12.1, Hymns of the Atharva-Veda together with Extracts from the Ritual Books and the Commentaries; *SBE* 42, n.p.

100. For short commentary, see Patton, "Nature Romanticism," pp. 45-58.

101. See L. Nelson, introduction to *Purifying the Earthly Body of God*, p. 3.

life that is alien to spiritual influence."[102] *Dharma* ("duty" or "righteousness") relates to all of life, not only religious and ethical realms.

Deeply embedded in Hindu religious consciousness is the idea of "common good" *(sarva-bhuta-hita),* the highest ethical standard based on one's *dharma.* A good deed with a view to common good results in good karma.[103] The principle of *dharma* is not only for the individual's good but also for the well-being of all.[104] Not surprisingly, then, almost all Hindu scriptures forbid killing a living being.[105] The reason is that God is in all beings, and therefore, "he who injures living creatures, injures him."[106]

While all Hindus should mind these dharmic principles, some movements seek to take them most seriously, such as the Bishnois, "Defenders of the Environment," a small community in Rajasthan,[107] and the Chipko movement in Uttar Pradesh.[108] Gandhi's role as the spokesperson for the environment is debated; it is safe to say that much in his thinking supported it, but he spoke of it very little.[109] In the final analysis, it is left to Hinduologists and practitioners to navigate the obstacles and resources, similarly to other traditions. A hospitable interfaith engagement certainly may be a key resource.

Ecological Resources in Two Abrahamic Traditions

Although it is true that the liability of Abrahamic faiths, as mentioned, is too anthropocentric a view of nature that may lead to the undermining of nature, there are also vast resources to facilitate the flourishing of nature: the task of vice-regency given by God both in Hebrew-Christian and Islamic scriptures (see chap. 11); the importance of history and time (because of a linear rather than cyclical worldview); the covenant spirituality of the Hebrews that binds human beings to God, other humans, and nature; the incarnational Christology of the Christian Scriptures in which Christ is the agent of creation and

102. Rao, "The Five Elements," p. 24.

103. Dwivedi, "Dharmic Ecology," p. 12.

104. *Mahabharata,* Shanti Parva 109, p. 238.

105. *The Laws of Manu* 5.38.

106. Vishnu Purana 3.8; p. 290; also p. 291.

107. See http://www.nativeplanet.org/indigenous/cultures/india/bishnoi/bishnoi.shtml (11/26/2013).

108. See http://www.indiaenvironmentportal.org.in/category/thesaurus/chipko-move ment (11/26/2013).

109. Lal, "Too Deep for Deep Ecology."

appears within the created reality, as well as the related sacramental theology in which God's grace is embodied; and so forth.[110]

The Emergence of Ecological Awareness among the Jews

Similarly to the others, the Jewish tradition by its own confession has "joined the environmental movement relatively recently."[111] Reasons are many and understandable: the survival of the small dispersed nation particularly in the Holocaust world, including continuing threats from the surrounding Arab nations, let alone the two-millennia-long diaspora, has not facilitated concern for the natural environment. Although secular Jewish eco-minded individuals excelled in green activities beginning from the 1960s,[112] it was mainly among some Jews in the United States that the religiously driven pursuit started.[113]

It is not of course true that nature was absent from Jewish life; just consider the many nature-related blessings and prayers in liturgy, many of them based on OT texts.[114] The annual feast of Sukkot, also known as the Feast of Tabernacles, during which people live in small huts for a week commemorating not only the forty years of survival in the desert but also nature and agriculture, is a great nature event. It is a joyous time of celebration and is rightly called nowadays the "Jewish Environment Holiday."[115] Jewish scriptural tradition also testifies to the faithfulness of the Creator for the sustenance and well-being of nature (Gen. 8:22, among others).[116] On the other hand, similarly to the Muslim tradition, Jews are very careful not to "venerate the natural

110. I was inspired by Tucker and Grim, series foreword to *I&E*, p. xxv.

111. Tirosh-Samuelson, "Introduction," p. xxxiii. See also Waskow, "Is the Earth a Jewish Issue?" pp. 35-37. The highly provocative essay by Schwarzschild, "The Unnatural Jew," understandably stirred up various kinds of responses.

112. For a fascinating reflection on the interface, see Blanchard, "Can Judaism Make Environmental Policy?" pp. 423-48. See also the current broad survey by Mark X. Jacobs, "Jewish Environmentalism," pp. 449-80.

113. For the famous *Shomrei Adamah* ("Keepers of the Earth") organization founded in 1988 by Rabbi Ellen Bernstein, see http://ellenbernstein.org/ (11/26/2013). The quickness with which Jewish awareness picked up the theme is evinced by the forty-page resource by Stenger, "Judaism and the Environment."

114. See further, Gillman, "Creation in the Bible and in the Liturgy," pp. 133-54.

115. See, e.g., the Association of Reform Zionists of America, ARZA Resources for an Eco-Zionist Sukkot Celebration, at http://www.arza.org/_kd/Items/actions.cfm?action=Show &item_id=1424&destination=ShowItem (11/26/2013).

116. See Goodman, "Respect for Nature in the Jewish Tradition," pp. 227-28.

world for its own sake or to identify God with nature . . . [like] the pagan out-look that Judaism rejects as idolatrous."[117] Related to this concern is the debate among some leading eco-theologians whether to consider the earth sacred or not. Those gleaning from the Kabbalah and other mystical sources naturally lean toward linking the divine and earthly closely to each other (without in any way crossing over the border of pantheism),[118] whereas those more traditional (in this regard) refuse to make nature sacred.[119]

What might be the distinctively Jewish sacred resources for the keeping of the earth (in addition to the ones briefly outlined above)? According to Hava Tirosh-Samuelson, the following three are routinely mentioned: "protection of vegetation . . . ; awareness of the distress of animals; and predicating social justice on the well-being of the earth itself." They all belong to and derive from the covenantal theology foundational to all Jewish tradition. The covenant framework also links humans causally to the thriving (or lack thereof) of the environment, as many scriptural passages clearly indicate (e.g., Lev. 26:32, among others).[120] Similarly to Christian tradition, Jewish theology also reflects on the implications for environmental values of two foundational theological dimensions — the immanentist versus transcendentalist controversy and the anthropocentric/theocentric/biocentric polarity.[121]

The Islamic View of Nature as "Sign" and Its Implications for the Environment

Interrupting the long "general indifference to the environmental crisis,"[122] the first leading Muslim intellectual to begin to articulate an Islamic theology and ethics of environment was S. H. Nasr.[123] On the one hand, Nasr was harshly critiquing the technocratic use of nature in the modern West, and on the other hand, he was highlighting the spiritual and moral dimension of the cri-

---

117. Tirosh-Samuelson, "Introduction," p. xxxiv.

118. See A. Green, "A Kabbalah for the Environmental Age," pp. 3-15. Green is not a Kabbalist per se, even though he gleans from those resources, among others.

119. Wyschogrod, "The Sanctification of Nature in Judaism," p. 294. For a good survey of views, see Tirosh-Samuelson, "Judaism," pp. 25-64.

120. Tirosh-Samuelson, "Introduction," p. xxxviii; for a highly interesting typology, see further, Kaplan, "Reverence and Responsibility," pp. 407-22.

121. Sokol, "What Are the Ethical Implications?" pp. 261-82. See also the important discussion in Schwartz, "Judaism and Nature," pp. 437-47.

122. Nasr, "Islam, the Contemporary Islamic World, and the Environmental Crisis," p. 86.

123. Nasr, Man and Nature.

sis. This is fully in keeping with mainline Islamic tradition, which attributes even the environmental crisis ultimately to "the loss of a relationship between humans, the natural realm, and Allah." In Islamic terms, as soon as believers forsake the way of the *Sharī'a,* consequences even to nature follow.[124] (The term *Sharī'a* in popular media and among those who lack any meaningful knowledge of the Islamic tradition has come to mean suppression of rights and return to traditional way of life; in the best Islamic tradition, *Sharī'a* is something like the ethics of the Torah to Jews and of the Sermon on the Mount to Christians.)

Because in Islam "every individual creature or being has its own ontological existence as a sign of God, and by its very being manifests and reveals His majesty and mercy . . . every creature deserves attention and consideration for its relation to the Divine."[125] This theological conviction may have immense ecological impetus. A related ancient Islamic resource is the concept of balance. Similarly to the heavens, which are sustained "by mathematical balance," human beings should be balanced, straight, and honest in relation to each other and natural resources.[126] Oft-quoted is the Prophet's admonition to exercise modesty even with water ablution in the ritual of prayer.[127]

What are the role and place of creation (nature) vis-à-vis humanity? According to Muzaffar Iqbal, "Unlike the worldview created by modern science, the Qur'ānic view of the elements of the cosmos does not make them subservient to humanity; rather they remain in the service of their Lord, Who created them and set on tasks for His Purpose." While natural resources do benefit humanity, they are not under humanity's control as commodities; rather they are God's.[128] The Islamic tradition speaks of humanity's relation to God in terms of *fitrah,* a rough equivalent to the Judeo-Christian conception of the image of God. While part 2 will investigate this concept in detail, suffice it to say here that because *fitrah* assumes "religion true to the primordial nature of humankind," even the environmental message based on the Qur'anic teaching is "part of the instinctive nature of humankind and need not be instilled, but rather awakened."[129]

124. Chishti, "*Fitra,*" pp. 69-71.
125. Özdemir, "Towards an Understanding," p. 11.
126. Comments in *The Holy Qur'an,* trans. Yusuf Ali, pp. 5177-78, cited in Özdemir, "Towards an Understanding," p. 13.
127. Özdemir, "Towards an Understanding," pp. 14-15.
128. Muzaffar Iqbal, "In the Beginning — II," pp. 109-10
129. Chishti, "*Fitra,*" p. 67; see also Baharuddin, "Guardians of the Environment," pp. 41-49.

Adnan Z. Amin summarizes some of the theological, philosophical, and spiritual resources supporting ecological values in Islam:

> The traditional concern of Islam for social justice and care for the poor, the orphaned, and the widowed has a broader relevance that embraces concern for the natural environment as well. Protection of land and proper treatment of biodiversity are now being advocated by Islamic scholars and teachers. In addition, the unity of all reality *(tawḥīd)* and the balance of nature *(mīzān)* as recognized by Islam constitutes an important basis for religious ecology and environmental ethics. Islamic teachings on land management hold great promise for protection of fragile ecosystems, namely, valuing sacred precincts *(harām)* and setting aside land for the common good *(himā).*[130]

Eco-theological Challenges in Christian Tradition

Concern and Respect for Ecology as a Theological Task

The editors of a major compendium of essays titled *Nature in Asian Traditions of Thought* recently outlined the reasons why Judeo-Christian tradition has allegedly contributed significantly to eco-crisis. Wisely the editors exercise a fair amount of critical judgment in putting the blame on one religious tradition alone; yet it is instructive to summarize the main complaints based on their succinct listing: that God is transcendent; that nature is an artifact of a divine male craftsman; that human beings exclusively are in the image of God, therefore separated from the rest; that to human beings have been given dominion; that dominion means subduing nature and multiplying the human species; that relation to nature is hierarchic, based on a divinely sanctioned hierarchy; that beings other than humans do not have any intrinsic value; and that relation to nature is instrumental, rational, and technocratic.[131] Even a cursory reading of the current project tells us that Christian "theology of creation," pejoratively described above, has very little or nothing to do with that kind of alleged "theological" approach. In this light, Lynn White's (in)famous thesis that "the historical roots of our ecological crisis" can be found in Christianity[132] is both exaggerated

---

130. Amin, "Preface to *Islam and Ecology*," pp. xxxiii-xxxiv.
131. Callicott and Ames, introduction to *Nature in Asian Traditions of Thought*, pp. 3-4.
132. L. White, "Historical Roots."

and misplaced. Of course, Christian tradition's contribution to the rise of contemporary science has indirectly influenced the technological abuse of nature, but that effect does not have much to do with the tradition's basic intuitions.[133]

Constructive Christian theology should be able to hold in a dynamic tension an attitude of reverent admiration for the beauty of creation in its endless diversity and creativity, and a deepening concern for nature's vulnerability and suffering from the current global economic-industrial rape. While the beauty of creation may draw us closer to the Creator, it is curious, as Wittgenstein notes, how "we should be inclined to think of civilization — houses, streets, cars, etc. — as distancing man from his sources" and "[o]ur civilized environment, along with trees and plants in it . . . isolated from everything great, from God, as it were."[134]

Theologically, it is highly ironic that it has been hard for traditional Christian theology to embrace the socially constructed nature of nature, as discussed above (chap. 3), but it has been a real problem for the contemporary secular ecological movement as well. The irony is heightened by the simple observation that in their critique of alleged ecological "sins" of Christianity, the green movements have embraced much of postmodern philosophy; the problem is that whereas the "[p]ostmodern cultural theory and criticism have been intensely suspicious of any attempt to reify what is in reality merely a convention . . . [t]he ecological movement . . . has tended to see nature as a conceptually self-sufficient domain of intrinsic value, truth and authenticity."[135] In other words, like the theology of creation (but usually without reference to the Creator), the ecological movement affirms robustly the indispensable value of nature, without even thinking that that assumption is only one way of constructing the meaning of nature! To the ecologically oriented late modern person, it comes as a shock to hear the philosophical colleague bluntly reject any reference to the intrinsic beauty of the "natural environment" as inherently (read: essentially) "natural." Key arguments of the environmentalist movement are being deconstructed one after another as epistemologically implausible![136] In this light, the theological construction of nature as creation, and thus intrinsically valuable and "essentially" good, is a necessary asset to ecological pursuits (chap. 3).

Whereas for the postmodern deconstructionist the value of nature is

---

133. See P. Jewett, *Who We Are*, p. 352; Ellul, *Technological Society*, p. 33.

134. Wittgenstein, *Culture and Value*, p. 50, cited in Kerr, "Modern Philosophy of Self," p. 23.

135. McGrath, *ScT* 1:115.

136. For a short useful discussion, see McGrath, *ScT* 1:115-16.

far from an established fact, and for the secular, ecologically minded person nature's value is taken for granted without any justification, on the other end of the spectrum, namely, among some ecologically minded scholars of *religion*, the virtual divinization of nature is assumed to be necessary to foster an attitude of care. The eco-feminist Starhawk is a striking example. While her call to treat nature as "Goddess" does not mean envisioning "a being somewhere outside of this world," it still is an invitation to see nature as inherently divine.[137] Although particularly the many mystical spiritual traditions of both the Christian East and the Christian West have approached creation with a deep reverence and sense of holiness,[138] it is best for theological argumentation to refrain from speaking of nature as divine. Divinization blurs the boundary line between the Creator and creatures.[139] What about calling nature a sacrament?[140] While there are sacramental elements in nature, calling nature a sacrament extends the meaning of that preferred technical spiritual/theological term in a way that is a category mistake. Rather than a sacrament, the special conveyor of salvific grace, nature — including creatures embedded in nature's web — hopes for the final redemption according to the biblical promise (Rom. 8:19-26).[141] Neither divine nor a sacrament, nature, in theological perspective, "remains sacred in the sense that it belongs to God, exists for the glory of God, even reflects the glory of God, as humans also do."[142] The de-divinizing of nature affirms creation as *creation*, finite and vulnerable, as well as valuable because of its goodness.[143]

The blaming of eco-catastrophe on religion is usually hopelessly one-sided and lacks needed nuances. This is not to deny that the "ecological crisis of the modern world has its starting point in the modern industrial countries," which were shaped by Christian influence.[144] Rather, we are reminded of the obvious: the most critical influence for dominating and exploiting nature comes from secular sources, particularly from the Enlightenment, which in itself was greatly influenced by movements such as (Italian) Renaissance

137. Starhawk, *Dreaming the Dark*, p. 11; see also her *The Spiral Dance*.

138. For medieval mystical reverence toward nature, see Dreyer, "An Advent of the Spirit," pp. 123-62.

139. So also Hall, *Imaging God*, p. 48; see further, Fisher, *Human Significance*, pp. 37-40.

140. Cf. M. Wallace, "Crum Creek Spirituality," pp. 121-37; for discussion, see Daecke, "Profane and Sacramental Views of Nature," pp. 127-40.

141. Materially similarly, Pannenberg, *ST* 2:137-38.

142. Bauckham, *Living with Other Creatures*, p. 13.

143. See further, Bauckham, *The Bible and Ecology*.

144. Moltmann, *God in Creation*, p. 20.

humanism, in which humanity's difference (supremacy) from nonhumans was the stated theme.[145] Recall that Judeo-Christian tradition is thousands of years old whereas the ecological crisis due to science is only a few hundred years old. Furthermore, without any finger pointing, it is beyond doubt that not only other religious traditions but also atheistic cultures are to be blamed for continuing crimes against nature; just consider the extent of the rape of nature in atheistic lands such as Russia (the former Soviet Union), China, and elsewhere. Indeed, as argued above (chap. 2), removing God from the center and introducing anti-Christian influences has caused much of the abuse and distancing of nature.[146]

That said, the mandate in Genesis 1:26-27 for humanity to act as God's faithful vice-regents does not justify abuse but rather is a call to responsible service on behalf of good creation.[147] Regretfully, the command to "subdue the earth" was too often taken in its literal sense in Christian tradition. Although there is the minor alternative "green" tradition in Christianity that includes mystics and saints to whom nature had intrinsic value and human dominion represented stewardship and care for creatures, in the main Christian tradition, greatly influenced by Greek philosophical movements (particularly Stoicism), nature was conceived to have been made for humans and their benefit, and as a result, it was seen through a utilitarian lens; humanity's relation to nature was based on a hierarchical, dualist view emphasizing difference rather than solidarity.[148]

Precisely as the image of God, reflecting the characteristics of the Creator, the human being is placed in the world as steward, accountable to God.[149] Rather than superiority, humanity should exhibit solidarity with creation to which it also belongs.[150] Indeed, says Orthodox theologian John Zizioulas, humanity is called to exercise priestly vocation on behalf of creation, and the "human being is not fulfilled until it becomes the 'summing up of nature,' as priest referring the world back to its Creator."[151] In a Christian vision, "[a]ll

---

145. Bauckham, *Living with Other Creatures,* pp. 47-58; for details, see chap. 3 above.

146. See also Kerr, *Immortal Longings,* p. 163; for a passionate discussion, see Borgmann, *Power Failure.*

147. See Welker, *Creation and Reality,* pp. 60-73.

148. For an excellent analysis, see Bauckham, *Living with Other Creatures,* chap. 2.

149. Pannenberg, *TA,* p. 79; Fisher, *Human Significance,* pp. 40-42.

150. See A. M. Clifford, "When Being Human Becomes Truly Earthly," pp. 173-89; Ruether, *Gaia and God,* pp. 19-22 particularly.

151. As paraphrased by Fisher, *Human Significance,* p. 152, with quotation from Zizioulas, "Preserving God's Creation," p. 2. Cf. S. R. L. Clark, *Biology and Christian Ethics,* p. 269.

creatures on this earth find their way to one another in the community of a common way, a common suffering and a common hope."[152] There is a continuity between the human and nature, and Christ died and was resurrected not merely for humans but for nature as well.[153]

How to Speak of God, the Creator, in an Ecologically Appropriate Manner

In the introductory chapter above, we highlighted the importance of how to speak of creation, focusing on the power of metaphors. The same applies to the way we speak of God, the Creator. Particularly women theologians have reminded us now for many decades that language matters; the way we speak shapes reality for us. Making an important distinction between "conceptual" (that is, propositional) and metaphorical language,[154] the eco-feminist Sallie McFague reminds us of the obvious: the way we name God to a large extent determines how we view God. Traditional theology operates with literalist, patriarchal, exclusive terms, and that leads to a distant and rigid conception of the God-world relationship.[155] Feminist scholars have rightly noted that patriarchalism is not a lone phenomenon: it is linked with dualisms that miss the deep interconnections in the cosmos and life, including its vulnerability.

What is needed is both deconstruction of patriarchal language and reconstruction of complementary, more adequate models of speaking of God and the God-world relationship.[156] The use of new kinds of metaphors of God, such as Friend or Lover, is not to identify God with that particular metaphor, but rather to understand God in light of some of its characteristics.[157] Programmatically, her landmark work *Models of God* is subtitled *Theology for an Ecological, Nuclear Age*. As a leading motif for revising God-talk, she calls for "a new sensibility"[158] toward our earth, especially the threat of nuclear catastrophe.[159] Her call for a new sensibility includes a holistic or ecological, evolutionary view of reality; acceptance of human responsibility for nuclear

---

152. Moltmann, *Way of Jesus Christ*, p. 273.

153. Moltmann, *Way of Jesus Christ*, p. 307, emphasis in original.

154. McFague, *Models of God*, pp. 31-36; see further, chap. 2; McFague, *Metaphorical Theology*, chap. 3.

155. McFague, *Metaphorical Theology*, p. ix.

156. McFague, *Metaphorical Theology*, pp. ix-xi, 25-26.

157. McFague, *Metaphorical Theology*, pp. 22-23.

158. Title of chap. 1 in McFague, *Models of God*.

159. So also Thistlethwaite, "God and Her Survival in a Nuclear Age," p. 135.

knowledge; and an awareness of the constructive character of all human enterprises.[160] This Protestant feminist's call for a nondualistic, nonhierarchical view of reality resonates with the Roman Catholic Elisabeth Schüssler Fiorenza's brilliant statement: "Not the holiness of the elect but the wholeness *of all* is the central vision of Jesus."[161]

In contrast to many secular feminists[162] and some radical theologians,[163] McFague claims to promote not a monistic view of reality in which all distinctions between human beings and other forms of life are leveled, but a view of reality based on a model of the world as God's body that enhances mutuality and interdependence. Although the current project's classical panentheism does not operate with the body analogy,[164] McFague's invitation for a mutual, respectful, caring relationship to creation is fully embraced.

Theological Resources for the Healing and Flourishing of Creation

The task of an ecological, constructive Christian theology is twofold: it has to clarify and help avoid ways of thinking and speaking of nature as creation that are detrimental to her survival and well-being; and it has to search for resources — theological insights, metaphors, approaches — that may help foster flourishing and continuing shalom of God's creation. On the basis of the trinitarian theology of creation developed in this project, two interrelated themes will be brought into conversation here — the Spirit's work for continuous healing of creation, and the eschatological hope for final redemption, culminating in God's Sabbath rest of eternal delight and consummation. It is highly promising that a growing number of theologians and religious communities are engaging the task of both theological reflection and ecologically sustaining activities.[165]

160. McFague, *Models of God,* chap. 1.

161. Fiorenza, *In Memory of Her,* p. 121, quoted in McFague, *Models of God,* p. 7, emphasis in original.

162. See, e.g., Y. King, "Making the World Live"; Griffin, *Woman and Nature.*

163. M. Daly, *Pure Lust* and *Gyn/Ecology.*

164. For details, see chap. 10 in *Trinity and Revelation.*

165. For rich ecclesiastical resources, both theological and practical, see the following: World Council of Churches: http://www.oikoumene.org/en/resources/documents/wcc-programmes/justice-diakonia-and-responsibility-for-creation/climate-change-water.html (11/26/2013); World Anglican Communion Environmental Network: http://acen.anglicancommunion.org/index.cfm (1/14/2014); Roman Catholic (United States Conference of Catholic Bishops): http://www.usccb.org/issues-and-action/human-life-and-dignity/environment/

An Ecological Pneumatology: The Healing and Vulnerability of Creation

Returning to the importance of minding the language of theology, that is, the importance of metaphorical, symbolic, nondiscursive, poetic, imaginary, and aesthetic expressions — along with (but not replacing) the analytic, propositional, and argumentative — links us with the deep intuitions in the Christian mystical traditions. Intuitive for the mystical vision is the link between the Holy Spirit and the flourishing of nature,[166] going back even to biblical traditions.[167] Just recall the medieval Saint Hildegard of Bingen's metaphor of the "greening" of the Spirit, Bonaventure's symbol of the Spirit as the "living water,"[168] or Thomas Aquinas's poem of "warming fire" and "light."[169] Theology still done mostly in the Global North has much to learn in this regard from its counterparts in the Global South. The Korean Methodist J. Y. Lee's distinctive pictures of the Spirit as "cloth" or "weaver" invoke images of protection and care,[170] an aspect of which is supplementing the predominantly masculine God language with female images of the Spirit.[171]

Named in the creed as *vivificantem* (the "vivifier," or life-giver), the Holy Spirit is not only the divine energy-information-life-force that brings about and sustains life; the Spirit is also the source of flourishing, thriving, prospering, blooming, blossoming.[172] Theologically speaking, the "Spirit is the ecstasy that implements God's abundance and triggers the overflow of divine self-giving,"[173] a gift of endless divine hospitality encompassing the whole "fellowship" of creation.[174]

(11/26/2013). An emerging field of exegesis and hermeneutics has to do with ecclesiological sensibilities: Habel and Trudinger, eds., *Exploring Ecological Hermeneutics;* the five volumes of *The Earth Bible* (in process); and Bauckham, *The Bible and Ecology.*

166. For the importance of nature-based metaphors applied to the Spirit, see Fatula, *Holy Spirit,* pp. 2-3 and passim; see also Moltmann, *Spirit of Life,* chap. 12, for an extensive discussion of various nature metaphors of the Spirit.

167. For the beauty of the earth described through the sensibilities of the Spirit's presence at the Day of Pentecost, see Fatula, *Holy Spirit,* pp. 33-34.

168. See Dreyer, "An Advent of the Spirit," pp. 123-62.

169. In Donahoe, *Early Christian Hymns,* pp. 156-59.

170. J. Y. Lee, *Trinity in Asian Perspective,* p. 104; for other metaphors, see K. Kim, *Holy Spirit in the World,* p. 181.

171. Boff, *Holy Trinity,* pp. 92-93; Comblin, *Holy Spirit and Liberation,* p. 49; Müller-Fahrenholz, *God's Spirit,* p. 26. For biblical and historical background, see S. Harvey, "Feminine Imagery for the Divine," pp. 111-40.

172. Johnson, *Women, Earth, and Creator Spirit,* p. 42.

173. C. Pinnock, *Flame of Love,* pp. 49-50.

174. Johnson, *Women, Earth, and Creator Spirit,* p. 44.

Instead of invoking pantheistic, semipagan resources, increasingly utilized in many ecological and "green" pneumatologies of nature, the moderate Catholic feminist Elizabeth Johnson's *Women, Earth, and Creator Spirit* resonates well with this project's classical panentheism in envisioning the role of the Spirit in the healing of the ecosystem:

> [T]he Spirit's encircling indwelling weaves a genuine solidarity among all creatures and between God and the world. . . . [W]hen things get broken, which can happen so easily, this divine creative power assumes the shape of a rejuvenating energy that renews the face of the earth (Ps 104:30). The damaged earth, violent and unjust social structures, the lonely and broken heart — all cry out for a fresh start. In the midst of this suffering the Creator Spirit, through the mediation of created powers, comes, as the Pentecost sequence sings, to wash what is unclean; to pour water upon what is drought-stricken; to heal what is hurt; to loosen up what is rigid; to warm what is freezing; to straighten out what is crooked and bent.[175]

The eco-pneumatologist Mark Wallace wishes to "retrieve a central but neglected Christian theme — the idea of God as carnal Spirit who imbues all things — as the linchpin for forging a green spirituality responsive to the environmental needs of our time." He says: "I believe that hope for a renewed earth is best founded on belief in God as Earth Spirit, the compassionate, all-encompassing divine force within the biosphere who inhabits earth community and continually works to maintain the integrity of all forms of life."[176] As argued above, "spirit" in the biblical understanding is not something opposed to "earth" or "body," but rather is the divine life-energy.[177] Importantly, the Bible uses metaphors of the Spirit that are taken from nature such as the "animating breath," the "healing wind," the "living water," the "cleansing fire."[178] To speak of the "earthen spirit"[179] is not to undermine the divine uniqueness of the Spirit but rather to speak of the divine infinity in which finite and infinite are both transcended and embraced simultaneously.[180]

175. Johnson, *Women, Earth, and Creator Spirit,* p. 43.

176. M. Wallace, *Fragments of the Spirit,* p. 7.

177. Moltmann, *Spirit of Life,* pp. 225-26; see also p. 40.

178. M. Wallace develops these kinds of biblical metaphors from nature in *Fragments of the Spirit;* for a list of others, see also his *Finding God in the Singing River,* pp. 6-9.

179. For this term I am indebted to Mark Wallace, "Christian Animism," pp. 203-6.

180. For "Christian animism," see M. Wallace, "Christian Animism"; M. Wallace, *Green Christianity,* pp. 1-10; Abram, *Becoming Animal.*

In green theology, the Holy Spirit can also be depicted in terms of the "wounded Spirit."[181] Wallace points out that "if Spirit and earth mutually indwell one another then it appears that God as Spirit is vulnerable to serious loss and trauma just insofar as the earth is abused and despoiled."[182] This is all good and useful. Where some eco-theologies take a dangerous and mistaken course is to speak of the cosuffering of the triune God in terms of deicide, the "death of god." Although the rhetoric that "the specter of ecocide raises the risk of deicide"[183] is just that, namely, *rhetoric,* behind it are highly problematic theological and scientific assumptions. In light of current cosmological knowledge, it does not make sense at all to make any kind of link between what happens in one tiny little planet at the margins of one of the galaxies among billions of other galaxies and the almighty Creator! The implications for the Creator of this vast universe of even the most dramatic nucleo-catastrophe are nil! Theologically, after even thousands of qualifications, to imply that the Creator's own creation would be a threat, in any sense of the word, is simply absurd. To maintain the theologically pregnant meaning of the triune God's deep imbuement of the cosmos through and in the Spirit, this kind of suspicious rhetoric should be exposed and corrected.

The Eschatological Sabbath Rest: The Jewish-Christian Vision of Shalom

Common to all Abrahamic traditions is the idea of God, the Creator, being the ultimate source of the harmony, peace, and well-being of nature. In Jewish tradition, the favorite term is "Sabbath," which is a continuous celebration of shalom, peace, harmony, and joy.[184] For many North American First Nation peoples it is "the Harmony Way," which similarly speaks of a holistic, cosmic well-being in which the "whole" is bigger than the sum of its parts.[185] Among Christians in the Global South, the holistic nature-honoring attitude comes through much more easily than among their economically privileged Global North counterparts.[186]

In the biblical testimony, God "completed" creative work on the day of

---

181. M. Wallace, "The Green Face of God," pp. 450-53.

182. M. Wallace, "The Green Face of God," p. 451.

183. M. Wallace, "The Green Face of God," p. 452.

184. See further, Rosenzweig, *The Star of Redemption,* pp. 312-15.

185. Woodley, *Shalom and the Community of Creation,* chap. 1 particularly.

186. For important contributions from African contexts, see Sindima, "Community of Life," pp. 137-47; Daneel, "African Independent Church Pneumatology," pp. 143-66.

Sabbath (Gen. 2:2), having first judged everything very good (1:31). In this light it is highly curious that Christian tradition speaks of six days of creation as if the seventh day, Sabbath, were meaningless. As a result, "[t]he resting God, the celebrating God, the God who rejoices over his creation, receded into the background." And yet, according to the biblical and Jewish intuition, "it is only the Sabbath which completes and crowns creation."[187] Sabbath is not only looking back, it is also an eschatological feast as it opens creation for its true future. As such it anticipates the arrival of the final shalom, "the beginning of that peace with nature which many people are seeking today, in the face of the growing destruction of the environment."[188]

Sabbath reminds us of the need to balance work and rest, activity and leisure, which is a major challenge for the contemporary lifestyle. The Jubilee also reminds us of the need to give rest to the fields and ground. A corollary lesson is the need to mind economic and social justice when thinking of shalom; while the pollution of nature is not solely the function of economic considerations, much of it is.[189] In the chapter on human flourishing (chap. 16 below), the implications of global economy, economic distribution of possessions and goods, as well as work will be engaged theologically.

Sometimes it is surmised that the Christian eschatological hope would lead to the dismissal of the hope for the rest of creation. This is not the case. J. M. Soskice rightly notes that if "there is no hope of the triumph of God's justice on earth, [there is] no point in praying that God's kingdom will come and will be done on *earth* as it is in in heaven."[190] That is because we will be "redeemed *with* the world, not *from* it."[191] It is rather Platonic dualism that has served as the source of gnosticism, escapism, and political irresponsibility.[192] Those dualities[193] should be eliminated and corrected in light of the expectation of the coming of God's universal rule in new creation. Rightly, the American philosopher Kevin Corcoran writes that "we human beings have been made from the mud and dirt — God-blessed, God-loved, and God-embraced mud and dirt — and made for life in an equally earthy envi-

187. Moltmann, *God in Creation*, p. 6 (quotation); p. 276.
188. Moltmann, *God in Creation*, p. 277.
189. See further, Bergmann, *Creation Set Free*, chap. 5 particularly.
190. Soskice, "Resurrection and the New Jerusalem," p. 57.
191. Moltmann, *Spirit of Life*, p. 89, emphasis in original.
192. Moltmann, *Trinity and the Kingdom*, pp. 89-90.
193. The discussion of "dualism" is often hampered by philosophically and historically inaccurate and misleading statements. A major theological study would be needed to give a comprehensive picture.

ronment."[194] God's kingdom includes this whole world inasmuch as "God's reconciling, redemptive, and restorative activity takes place within the natural, material world. This is the theater of God's redemptive activity, the theater of God's kingdom."[195]

The truth that this Christian eschatological and soteriological vision includes all of creation, not merely humanity, however, should not be made a pretext for virtual elimination of the distinctive nature of humanity in God's economy of salvation and the theological importance of God having united Godself with creation in Christ's humanity, as is a tendency in David Clough's systematic theology *On Animals*. It oddly argues that no more can the particularity of the incarnation (Jesus as Jewish male) be interpreted as exclusive of Gentiles and females than it can of nonhuman creatures.[196] Even worse, he opines that the incarnated Christ himself should not be understood as distinctively human because the "flesh" *(sarx)* that the Word became just denotes "created reality."[197] Furthermore, distancing himself from all contours of theological tradition, he surmises that the *need* for redemption of animals is based on their moral responsibility,[198] even sinfulness,[199] and some kind of free will.[200] This reasoning is filled with theological misinterpretations such as these: First, without all these highly dubious turns, the Christian biblical-theological vision of consummation includes all of creation in the eschatological renewal. Second, interpreting incarnation as having no special relation to the *humanity* of the God-man is such a forced exegesis that it hardly warrants correction. We can just mention the numerous Pauline passages in which the incarnated Christ's representation and solidarity with humanity is the leading theme, let alone the whole theological tradition. Third, making animals morally responsible — theologically speaking, sinful — is absurd not only in light of scientific knowledge, but also philosophically and theologically. To be morally responsible is to be able to reflect on the nature of one's deeds, which requires not only the highest level of consciousness and intellectual-emotional resources but also the capacity for self-reflection; for

194. Corcoran, "Thy Kingdom Come," p. 67.
195. Corcoran, "Thy Kingdom Come," p. 67.
196. Clough, *On Animals*, chap. 3.
197. Clough, *On Animals*, chap. 4, particularly Kindle ed. #316-82 (hereafter K).
198. Clough, *On Animals*, K #3953-3965, 4105.
199. Clough, *On Animals*, K #4115, 4165; fortunately, Clough corrects himself a little bit by admitting that responsibility for sin is not equally shared between humans and animals (#4153).
200. Clough, *On Animals*, K #4051.

the lack of those skills we do not regard underaged humans ethically culpable! Fourth, the first part of this chapter made a case for a theologically solid ecological theodicy. All in all, I just hope that a work like *On Animals* would not be counterproductive for the advancement of a responsible, theologically competent animal theology and a wider theological reflection on nonhuman creation because of its neglect of biblical-theological tradition and current evolutionary scientific knowledge.

II. HUMANITY

9. Introduction: Humanity in a Radically Changed Context

Theological Anthropology in a New Environment

Traditionally Christian theology has considered the transition from the discussion of nature to humanity as a disjuncture with the intention to underscore the importance of difference of humanity from the rest of creation. Contemporary theology, on the contrary, considers the transition just that, namely, *transition*, starting with the question of "what links human beings with animals and all other creatures."[1] Before speaking of humanity as the *imago Dei*, let us talk about men and women as *imago mundi* (the "image of the world").[2] Surprisingly, the two creation narratives in the beginning of the OT point to a dynamic mutuality, fellowship, and unity-in-diversity among creatures. The emergence of a sequence of forms — or "generations [*toledoth*] of the heavens and the earth when they were created" (Gen. 2:4a) — culminating in the creation of humanity, makes the creation an interrelated web, a network. The Yahwist narrative makes the creation of human beings a matter of having been "formed . . . of dust from the ground" and having had "breathed into his nostrils the breath of life," as a result of which "man became a living being" (Gen. 2:7). This "spirited," living being, formed of *ha adama* (earth), is called *Adam*. Similarly to all other creatures, the one created "in the image of God" (Gen. 1:27) depends for her livelihood on the "green plant for food" (Gen. 1:30; cf. 29).[3] Moltmann rightly

---

1. Moltmann, *God in Creation*, p. 185.
2. Moltmann, *God in Creation*, pp. 186-87.
3. For comments, see Moltmann, *God in Creation*, p. 187.

concludes: "It is only when we become aware of the things which human beings have in common with other creatures, and the things that differentiate them, that we can understand what the human being's designation to be the image of God really means (Gen. 1:26)."[4]

Not only theological developments but also dramatic changes in the sciences and philosophy have caused previously unimaginable shifts: from a naive cosmology with our planet at the center of reality, astronomy and physics moved it out to the margins of a vast galaxy among billions of galaxies; evolutionary theory and biology definitively linked humans with the rest of creation; "[m]odern psychoanalysis showed that beneath the human being's feeble self-awareness . . . lie worlds belonging to the unconscious — worlds of unrecognized drives and involuntary suppressions";[5] neurosciences revealed astonishing bases of human decisions, emotions, and will in brain functions; and so forth. At the end, the human being "has seemed definitely to redissolve in the common ground of things."[6]

One of the changing factors with regard to theological anthropology is its location in systematic and doctrinal theology. Rather than forming their own locus ("place," i.e., chapter), anthropological questions were scattered among other doctrinal themes. Typically, premodern theology discussed theological anthropology in four loci:

- In the doctrine of creation, both the continuity and discontinuity with other creatures were in the forefront, but the latter was usually emphasized. The defining concept here was the *imago Dei*. Part of the discussion was long-standing debates about how to frame the dualist understanding of human nature, whether as spirit-soul-body (trichotomist) or as spirit/soul-body (dichotomist), as well as the question of the origins of the soul.
- In the doctrine of sin and salvation, the emphasis was placed on the salvation of the "soul." A literal understanding of the Genesis 2–4 narrative was assumed.
- In eschatology, questions related to the "intermediate state" were discussed. While belief in the resurrection of the body pointed to the "material" nature of Christian eschatological vision, a holistic, cosmic

4. Moltmann, *God in Creation*, p. 188; see further p. 189.
5. Moltmann, *God in Creation*, pp. 185-86, here p. 186.
6. Teilhard de Chardin, *Appearance of Man*, p. 186. See also Thielicke, *Being Human*, pp. 29-32.

vision of the new creation was often missed because of a predominantly "spiritual" hope.

- The doctrine of revelation considered the conditions for the reception of divine revelation, under the rubrics "general revelation" and "natural theology."[7]

Rather than lamenting the radical transformation of the context of humanity, constructive theologians should take it as an opportunity. Indeed, this is not the first time Christian tradition has had to revise the assumptions on which it bases theological doctrines. Just consider the revolution from the Ptolemaic to the Copernican solar system. Or consider the far-too-long opposition to evolutionary theory. That said, the church should neither accommodate to the "spirit of the age" nor compromise its deepest theological convictions. Rather, in its conviction that no new discovery of nature can ultimately threaten faith, the church should make its message understandable to new generations of men and women. Furthermore, the task of constructive theology is to provide thoughtful critique of the scientific denial of human uniqueness in its linking of humanity with the rest of creation, or of brain study with a reductionistic denial of the whole concept of human intentions and free will.

Although reductionism among scientists should be resisted, constructive theologians should embrace the significance of sciences. Building on the discussion of science-religion relations (chap. 1), we now add a few further remarks with anthropology in focus, including the views of other religions.

Sciences, Religions, and Theological Anthropology

The biggest scientific challenge — and resource — for contemporary theological anthropology is undoubtedly the standard evolutionary theory.[8] As discussed in part 1, the relation of Christians to Darwinism has taken a long and winding road, from cautious acceptance in the beginning years, to vehement opposition, to finally an embrace of its theistic form by mainline Christianity — notwithstanding

7. See D. Kelsey, *Eccentric Existence,* 1:27-41. For an interesting discussion of how views and foci of theological anthropology have shifted throughout theological history among the main Christian traditions and in the context of new theological breakthroughs, see Bevans and Schroder, *Constants in Context,* chap. 1 (for a summary table, see p. 37).

8. See the 2009 British Council Survey in ten countries among the general population concerning views of Darwinism: http://www.britishcouncil.org/darwinnow-survey-global.pdf (5/22/2013).

continuing opposition among the conservative churches (mainly in the United States). Particularly challenging has been the application of the evolutionary scheme to the evolvement of humanity. Jewish groups have gone through a basically similar kind of development. Leading rabbis of both the nineteenth century and traditional communities in the United States vehemently opposed evolution while the famous Italian Kabbalist Eliyahu Benamozegh (d. 1900) considered evolution fully compatible with Judaism.[9] Similarly to Christian theology, mainline Jewish theology nowadays sees no conflict with the theistic interpretation of Darwinism. The Rabbinical Council of America ruled in 2005 that "evolutionary theory, properly understood, is not incompatible with belief in a Divine Creator, nor with the first 2 chapters of Genesis."[10] Indeed, a higher percentage of Jews accept evolutionism than Christians in the United States.[11]

Among Abrahamic faiths, Islam has the greatest difficulty in relating to evolutionism. "There is no doubt that the idea of biological evolution constitutes a major cultural blockage in the Muslim world today," says the leading Muslim scientist, Algerian astrophysicist Nidhal Guessoum.[12] So fierce is the opposition that it is not uncommon to find *fatwas* (more-or-less binding legal-religious rulings) on it.[13] Not only do the great majority of people in Muslim countries strongly oppose evolution, but so do the academic elite![14] Fewer than half of American Muslims accept evolution.[15] The most important reason for opposition is the question of Adam. For religious leaders, the idea of pre-Adamic species is still totally unacceptable.[16] Unlike this contemporary, nearly unanimous rejection of Darwinism, however, Muslims have not always

9. Slifkin, *Challenge of Creation,* pp. 245-46; for details, see Faur, "The Hebrew Species Concept." For a useful resource, consult Cantor and Swetlitz, eds., *Jewish Tradition.*

10. Rabbinical Council of America, "Creation, Evolution, and Intelligent Design," December 7, 2005, http://www.rabbis.org/news/article.cfm?id=100635 (5/22/2013).

11. According to the Pew Research Center's 2008 U.S. poll "Religious Differences on the Question of Evolution," 77 percent of Jews embrace evolution; the figures for Christians who embrace evolutionism are as follows: Catholics, 58 percent; mainline Protestants, 51 percent; and evangelicals, 24 percent.

12. Guessoum, *Islam's Quantum Question,* p. 273.

13. For the Fatwa Center of America's ruling about evolution in 2010, see http://ask-mufti.us/ (6/27/2013). This *fatwa* is more moderate and open-minded than most such given in Muslim countries. Even the most respected global Islamic databases such as IslamOnline (http://www.islamonline.com/) unequivocally reject evolution, particularly that of humans.

14. Guessoum, *Islam's Quantum Question,* p. 274 and appendix C.

15. According to the 2008 Pew poll, "Religious Differences on the Question of Evolution," only 45 percent of American Muslims embrace evolutionary theory.

16. Guessoum, *Islam's Quantum Question,* p. 303; for harsh polemic against evolutionism, much of it written by leading Muslim scholars of sciences, see chap. 9.

resisted evolution, as long as a theistic framework was in place. During the classical "golden era" (ninth to twelfth centuries C.E.), intense debates about evolutionary ideas were carried on that resulted in an embrace of evolutionary principles "before evolutionism."[17] In the debates immediately after the publication of Darwin's main works in the nineteenth century, for a while a diversity of views were entertained — from total rejection to partial and even full embrace (by some modernists).[18]

Currently the only Muslim scholars or religious teachers who advocate evolutionary theory are located in the United States or Europe, but even among them, some leading scholars — such as Seyyed Hossein Nasr of George Washington University — are ambiguous at best about the compatibility of the theory with the Qur'an. At times Nasr seems to support Muslim creationism (a growing movement, gleaning also from Christian creationists).[19] Among the very tiny group of scholars who reside in traditional Muslim lands and defend evolution, a leading voice is currently Guessoum, who teaches in the United Arab Emirates. His 2011 *Islam's Quantum Question* is a highly sophisticated advocacy of evolutionism and an honest self-criticism of the state of scientific enterprise in Muslim lands. He argues that passages can be found that could be interpreted in an evolutionary manner, such as the following:

". . . verily He created you in stages?" (Q 71:14)

"It is He Who created you from clay; then He decreed a term [or era]." (Q 6:2)

"When your Lord said to the angels, 'Indeed I am about to create a human being out of clay. So when I have proportioned him, and breathed in him My spirit, then fall down in prostration before him!'" (Q 38:71-72)

It is yet to be seen how and when the global Muslim community may be willing to take up the issue of evolutionism and reflect on its implications for views of humanity.

Among the main Asiatic traditions, evolutionary theory has not caused

17. Ziadat, *Western Science in the Arab World*, p. 25.
18. For a detailed historical examination, see Howard, *Being Human in Islam*, chap. 1; see also Majid, "The Muslim Responses to Evolution."
19. A leading Muslim creationist, now with a ministry also in the USA, is the Turkish author Harun Yahya (http://www.harunyahyausa.com). On Nasr, Yahya, and Muslim creationism, see the detailed discussion in Guessoum, *Islam's Quantum Question*, pp. 314-23.

much concern. In Buddhism, there are a number of reasons for this. First, the questions of origins according to Gautama are secondary and marginal. Second, at least in some key Buddhist scriptural accounts, as discussed in part 1, evolutionary intuitions can be discerned. Third, the idea of no-self and impermanence, of course, leans toward evolvement and evolution.[20] Already at the end of the nineteenth century, the *Buddhist Catechism* stated, "The Buddha's doctrine teaches that there were many progenitors of the human race."[21] It is a common idea among contemporary Buddhists that "[l]ike all species, we too have been formed and conditioned by an immensely long and complex series of transformations," and therefore, there seems to be "common ground between Buddhist thought and evolutionary biology."[22] The 1996 monograph by Robin Cooper, a scientist and Buddhist teacher, titled *The Evolving Mind: Buddhism, Biology, and Consciousness* makes this case convincingly.

Similarly, most Hindu traditions consider the origins and development of the whole reality in terms of evolvement. Darwin's linking of human evolution with that of animals was simply not a problem to Hindus; generally speaking, Hinduism "presupposed a common ancestry between animals and humans"; even gods may assume animal features (and of course, at least in some interpretations, as a result of rebirth, one may turn out to be an animal).[23] In a recent editorial of the influential Indian *Current Science* publication, P. Balaram responds to the question a friend posed to him: "Why is it that the creation vs evolution debate rages unabated in the United States, but never seems to be an issue anywhere else in the world, including India?"[24] Although it is difficult to find a Hindu teacher who opposes evolutionism in general, some are critical of certain aspects of the Darwinian account of human evolvement, including natural selection.[25] On the other hand, some enthusiastic attempts to interpret ancient Hinduism in light of current science seem to go far beyond any scientific criteria.[26]

20. See Verhoeven, "Buddhism and Science," pp. 77-97.

21. Olcott, *The Buddhist Catechism,* part V, Q 329. Cabezón takes this and similar statements in the catechism as an indication that "both Buddhism and science teach evolutionism" ("Buddhism and Science," p. 44).

22. Waldron, "Common Ground, Common Cause," pp. 153, 156, respectively.

23. Gosling, "Darwin and the Hindu Tradition," p. 348; see also Gosling, *Religion and Ecology,* pp. 40-41.

24. Balaram, "Editorial," p. 1191.

25. See the founder of ISKCON, Srila Prabhupada's *Life Comes from Life.*

26. Cremo, *Human Devolution,* which assumes Hindu tradition not only can help improve but even to some extent replace Darwinism.

Among those theologians — whether in the church or in other faiths — who seek to construct a theological account of anthropology that embraces contributions from evolutionary theory, neurosciences, and many other fields of inquiry, the greatest challenge is the lack of an integrated vision of humanity. Ironically, already at the turn of the twentieth century, the German philosophical anthropologist Max Scheler lamented: "We have a scientific, a philosophical, and a theological anthropology in complete separation from each other. We do not have a unified idea of man."[27] In the methodological introduction to this volume above, the importance of a transversal interdisciplinary approach was outlined. This second part of the monograph needs such an approach as much as the first one, particularly when we seek to understand more fully the uniqueness of human beings and their nature in the matrix of theological, scientific, and religious wisdom. Wentzel J. van Huyssteen puts the challenge succinctly: "Scientists who treat the issue of human uniqueness as if it were only a biological or anthropological event, and theologians who treat it as only a spiritual or religious issue, want the book of human nature to be written in only one language. No one disciplinary language, however, can ever completely capture every aspect of the complex issue we are trying to understand."[28] Thus, we need an integrally interdisciplinary investigation.

An important contribution of *theological* anthropology is its role of being *critical,* to persistently remind the scientific community of the need to resist reductionism and seek to combine scientific and social, as well as religious, dimensions in the study of humanity. The explosive increase in knowledge about humanity in recent years, rather than making religious and theological reflection obsolete, on the contrary intensifies the need. Merely accumulating scientific knowledge hardly suffices, as necessary as that is. Questions of meaning, purpose, personal feelings, and ultimate destiny call for a sustained interdisciplinary, transversal reflection.[29] Not all theologians, however, are convinced. Astonishingly, the most important recent theological anthropology, the massive two-volume *Eccentric Existence* by the Yale senior theologian David Kelsey, intentionally and purposefully avoids dialogue with the sciences! Having acknowledged the appeal of an interdisciplinary and "intertraditional conversation" as a means of "conceptual bridge-building" between theology

---

27. Scheler, *Man's Place in Nature,* pp. 5-6.

28. Van Huyssteen, *Alone in the World?* pp. 35-36; see also W. S. Brown, "Nonreductive Physicalism and Soul," p. 1812.

29. See also Hefner, *The Human Factor,* pp. 8-9.

and secular thought, he decides to abandon it for reasons only vaguely and briefly explained, including the need to first fully formulate the Christian understanding.[30] It is clear that in order to dialogue with the other, one has to clarify one's own position; that, however, is best done in a dialogical mode that in itself makes a contribution to the Christian viewpoint.

For theology to avoid the temptation of accommodation (instead of critical mutual engagement) or merely serving as maidservant to science, theology should keep in mind its identity. Along with its critical function, what is theology's contribution to the understanding of humanity in the beginning of the third millennium?

What Is *Theological* about Theological Anthropology?

"What does the specifically Christian conviction that God actively relates to us imply about what and who we are and how we are to be?"[31] asks Kelsey, an American. The late Canadian Baptist Stanley J. Grenz elaborates: "The task of theological anthropology is to set forth the Christian understanding of what it means to be human. Christian anthropology views the human person and humankind as a whole 'in relationship to God.' . . . [T]he specifically theological context in which theological anthropology must be developed is that of the confession of the triune God. Hence, Christian theological anthropology is *trinitarian* theological anthropology."[32]

This means there is a mutual, although asymmetrical, conditioning relationship "between an idea of God and a human self-understanding."[33] Indeed, says German Lutheran theologian Pannenberg, "it is presupposed that there are sufficient reasons for regarding the God of the Bible as the definitive revelation of the reality of God that is otherwise hidden in the unsearchable depths of the world and of human life." Consequently, "religion is not dispensable in the search for a proper understanding of human reality. . . . [I]t is not a relic of a past age, but . . . is constitutive of our being as humans."[34] The Austrian Catholic thinker Rahner goes so far as to demand that "[d]ogmatic theology today has to be theological anthropology"[35] — put in a perspective that pre-

30. D. Kelsey, *Eccentric Existence*, 1:6-7, here p. 6.
31. D. Kelsey, *Eccentric Existence*, 1:159.
32. Grenz, *Social God*, p. 23.
33. Pannenberg, *ST* 2:290.
34. Pannenberg, *ST* 2:225.
35. Rahner, "Theology and Anthropology," p. 1.

vents succumbing to classical liberalism's primarily immanentist account of humanity and the world.

Whereas in patristic and subsequent theology the means to knowledge of God was the cosmos and the world, in modern theology an orientation to anthropology became the theme. For modern theologians, "human experience of the world and of the individual's existence in it repeatedly supplied the point of departure for discussing the reality of God."[36] Although in many forms of modern theology, as mentioned, particularly in classical liberalism and its offshoots, anthropology came to dominate and subsume theology under humanity,[37] the "growing anthropocentrism" also has a legitimate and important *theological* basis, namely, the incarnation, the Logos becoming human.[38] In that perspective, Schleiermacher's claim has lasting value: only with the coming of Christ can the creation of human nature be seen as completed.[39] Hence, "Christology is understood as the fulfillment of the anthropology, and the anthropology becomes the preparation for the Christology."[40]

The reference to theology as the ultimate norm helps us put in perspective Linda Woodhead's paradoxical suggestion "that one of theology's most important contributions to the anthropological enterprise is to undermine it." That does not of course mean that theology has nothing to say of humanity, but rather that theology's responsibility is to resist the common tendency to define humanity by reference to humanity alone. Theological anthropology brings the human into the domain of the divine.[41] As in Christology, in theological anthropology these two approaches form an integral, mutual relationship. To avoid generic notions of God — although for the sake of interfaith dialogue that approach may also play some preliminary role — a robustly trinitarian theology of God funds theological anthropology.[42]

To achieve its task in a coherent manner, theological anthropology seeks to locate the human being in two interrelated contexts: "proximate" and "ulti-

---

36. Pannenberg, *TA,* p. 11; see also his "Anthropology and the Question of God," pp. 80-98.

37. Philosophical atheism, ironically, used this theological tendency for its own sake. See Pannenberg, "Speaking about God," pp. 99-116.

38. Pannenberg, *TA,* p. 12.

39. See the epithet of §89 (pp. 365-66) in Schleiermacher, *Christian Faith.*

40. Moltmann, *God in Creation,* p. 218; for "Incarnation as Our Ultimate Context," see D. Kelsey, *Eccentric Existence,* vol. 2, chaps. 18 and 19A.

41. Woodhead, "Apophatic Anthropology," p. 233; see also D. Kelsey, *Eccentric Existence,* 1:28-29, and Grenz, *Social God,* p. xi.

42. See D. Kelsey, *Eccentric Existence,* vol. 1, chaps. 2A; 3A.

mate." The former relates to the immediate physical, social, cultural lives, and the latter refers to relation to God, the Creator — a common theme (at least) for all Abrahamic traditions.[43] The task of considering human persons in their proximate contexts in the contemporary environment pushes theology out of its comfort zone's ecclesiastical contours and into the rapidly globalizing, pluralistic, fragmented, and post-"whatever" world of social, political, economic, and cultural diversities, including sciences and religions.

Until now, Christian anthropologies have been constructed in quite an isolationist way. Engagement of sciences — while not of course a totally new development — has added much to theology's credence and value. The main challenge of the third millennium is to take seriously the presence of religious pluralism and its implications for Christian doctrine. The theology-sciences-religions trilogy not only offers a promising platform for mutual learning and enrichment; it also exposes theology to deep and foundational differences of orientations. Briefly put: whereas contemporary sciences and philosophies advocate a (physically) monist view of human nature, "[w]hat seems to be characteristic of most religious views of human nature is that they relate human life in some way to a supra-material realm of spirit or mind, whether spirit is conceived as one or many, as substantial or as in continual flux."[44] True, even when united in this basic orientation to the "transcendental" dimension as the defining feature of humanity, religions do not speak with one voice about human constitution and relation to the divine.[45] Yet, that said, the conceptions of humanity held by the natural sciences and by the religions differ radically. Add to the equation the current lack of unanimity among Christians concerning human nature, and you begin to capture the complexity of the discourse.

What about theistic naturalism in relation to theological anthropology? Recently, attempts have been made to construct a religion-friendly theological naturalism, a "spiritually evocative naturalist interpretation of human life."[46] Unlike secular naturalism, its theistic counterpart does not reject religion, but at the same time, it declines to accept any kind of metaphysics, anything beyond the natural/nature.[47] Without repeating the reservations about theological naturalism expressed in chapter 1, let me briefly mention my uneasiness

---

43. D. Kelsey, *Eccentric Existence*, 1:4-5.

44. K. Ward, *Religion and Human Nature*, p. 1.

45. See further, K. Ward, *Religion and Human Nature*, pp. 1-2.

46. Subtitle to Wildman, *Science and Religious Anthropology*.

47. For a careful discussion of naturalism in dialogue with the well-known Tillichian distinction between naturalism and supranaturalism (Tillich's own term), see chap. 2.

concerning theological anthropology.[48] It seems to me that rejecting metaphysics (as problematic as the term itself may be)[49] is self-contradictory on two accounts: first, because a "naturalism" in itself is a stated opinion about the "meaning" of human life, it represents "metaphysics" of sorts, just differently; second, because any nonmetaphysical explanation of religion is simply meaningless. A mere naturalistic account of religion leads into such an immanentist reduction that no living faith tradition, not even Buddhism, could take it without radically changing tradition's identity. While one can of course call religion something that "rules out both supernaturalism and all views of ultimate reality as an active, focally aware entity" and only "affirms an ultimate reality in the axiological (that is, valuational) depth structures and dynamics of nature,"[50] that view does not even resemble traditional or contemporary living faiths.[51] On the other hand, it leads to such a widening of the term "religion" — from "existentially potent behaviors, beliefs, and experiences in every domain of life, from wonder at nature to awe in the face of human frailty" — that most everything in life is religion![52]

With these tasks and desiderata in mind, let me briefly outline the plan for the discussion of theological anthropology in this volume.

Orientation to Part 2: Humanity

Following this introductory discussion, chapter 10 engages the evolvement of modern humans in the long line of hominids, focusing on how to define uniqueness and dignity in light of contemporary knowledge of the evolutionary process — the end result of which is a conscious, moral, and spiritual embodied animal called *Homo sapiens*. That discussion will lead to the distinctively theological investigation (chap. 11) of humanity under the classical rubric of the *imago Dei*. The investigation of the image of God seeks to utilize the best of both Christian tradition's and current sciences' insights in order to provide a holistic, embodied view of human persons. At the end

---

48. For similar kinds of criticisms from a theistic (process theology) viewpoint, see Clayton, foreword to Wildman, *Science and Religious Anthropology*, pp. xi-xiii.

49. For a detailed discussion of the kind of metaphysics adopted in this project, see chap. 9 in *Trinity and Revelation*.

50. Clayton, foreword to Wildman, *Science and Religious Anthropology*, pp. xvii-xviii.

51. Wildman's claim concerning "anti-supranaturalism" (*Science and Religious Anthropology*, p. 25) is both unnuanced and overly generic.

52. Wildman, *Science and Religious Anthropology*, p. xv.

of the chapter, the Abrahamic faiths' common intuitions of humanity will also be noted.

Chapter 12 engages current neuroscientific study with the purpose of constructing an alternative proposal of human nature called "multidimensional monism." In an attempt to gain from the latest developments in monistically oriented, nonreductionist interpretations of human nature, the current proposal also critically engages them. The next chapter (13) continues that investigation, focusing on the conditions and nature of human freedom in the world of (relatively speaking) deterministic processes. The primary aim is to defeat the neuroscientific-philosophical reductionist determinism. Having established human freedom, the same chapter also engages the ancient problem of how to best negotiate divine foreknowledge and creaturely freedom, by proposing a novel view titled "Molinist-pneumatological."

Chapter 14 continues the interfaith engagement with a focused look at how humanity and human nature is conceived in four living faiths. The traditional topics of original sin and fall are taken up in chapter 15 under the rubric of "human misery"; it places them both in the context of the diversity of interpretations within the theological tradition itself and particularly in relation to evolutionary theory's obvious rebuttal of many of tradition's key beliefs. The chapter argues that while it is urgent for constructive theology to revise many of the outdated beliefs related to traditional doctrinal formulations, it is also absolutely necessary to hold on to the deepest intuitions concerning what is wrong with us. The chapter ends with a detailed comparison of the Christian theology of sin with the analysis of the human condition in other faith traditions. The last chapter (16) seeks to hold on to the resources gained so far in the investigation of humanity and human nature with the goal of constructing a viable theology of human flourishing, taking careful note of the resources in other religions as well. That chapter continues the discourse started in part 1 on nature's flourishing (chap. 8).

10. An Evolving Humanity: Uniqueness and Dignity in Scientific Perspective

The Evolvement of Human Uniqueness

According to Pannenberg, "[m]odern anthropology no longer follows Christian tradition in defining the uniqueness of humanity explicitly in terms of God; rather, it defines this uniqueness through reflection on the place of humanity in nature and specifically through a comparison of human existence with that of the higher animals."[1] The first task for contemporary constructive theology is to consider carefully the evolvement of humanity in light of scientific insights. In this search, theologians are much helped by the contributions of paleoanthropology, an umbrella term for interdisciplinary work among paleontologists, physical and evolutionary anthropologists, (bio- and cognitive) archaeologists, and geologists, in collaboration with evolutionary biologists and psychologists, as well as those working in the emerging field of evolutionary epistemology.

With justification it is often asked nowadays, what, if anything, marks humanity distinct among other creatures, particularly in light of the 99 percent genetic similarity between humans and chimpanzees; indeed, ironically, this similarity is greater than that between chimpanzees and other higher apes! Furthermore, we know now that the "immediate" evolution of humans has a five- to seven-million-year history. We should also keep in mind that the definition of a "human" depends not only on scientific changes but also on changes

1. Pannenberg, *TA,* p. 27.

in worldviews.[2] However human uniqueness is defined, it is astonishing that among the millions and millions of species that have come and gone, "only one line . . . leads to persons, to self-awareness and consciousness."[3]

The Hominid Lineage

The closest predecessors of modern *Homo*[4] *sapiens* are of course the hominids.[5] The genetic evidence indicates that the oldest group of hominids (somewhat loosely and inaccurately called pre-australopithecines)[6] goes back 5 to 7 million years in history, although until 3.5 million years ago the evidence is rather fragmentary. The australopithecines are routinely mentioned as the first known hominid species; their origin spans a period of 4-5 million to 1.5 million years ago. Classified under half a dozen subspecies,[7] they all walked on two feet and showed evidence of an important growth of brain size.[8] The development of the hominids peaked about 2 million years ago. It may be significant that all hominid fossils older than 1 million years are limited to Africa.[9] Unlike the earlier consensus, it is currently agreed that a number of different types of hominids coexisted, perhaps about twenty different species.[10]

2. See van Huyssteen, *Alone in the World?* pp. 47-48. See also Proctor, "Three Roots of Human Recency."

3. Van Huyssteen, *Alone in the World?* p. 48. See n. 1 with reference to Rescher, *Evolution, Cognition, and Realism.*

4. The term *Homo* is inaccurate and used without precision in paleoanthropology and related discussions. For a bibliographical note, see Purcell, *From Big Bang,* p. 148 n. 3.

5. See Cartmill and Smith, *The Human Lineage;* still highly useful, although no longer up to date, is Klein, *The Human Career.*

6. The common name for australopithecines, "southern apes," is another highly inaccurate and, in this case, even misleading nomenclature: they are neither apes nor confined to southern Africa!

7. The darling of paleoanthropologists is "Lucy" of *Australopithecus afarensis,* based on an important 1976 discovery of tools; see http://humanorigins.si.edu/evidence/human-fossils/species/australopithecus-afarensis (5/22/2013).

8. Paleoanthropological literature uses the measurement called "encephalisation quotient" (EQ), the ratio of the brain to body weight. For a mouse it is 0.5, for an elephant 5.25, and for a dolphin 5.31; Purcell, *From Big Bang,* p. 149 n. 8.

9. Purcell, *From Big Bang,* p. 179, referencing as the source Klein and Edgar, *Dawn of Human Culture,* p. 246. The reference to the descent of the Chinese is based on the research reported in Ke, "African Origin of Modern Humans," pp. 1151-53.

10. The discoveries in 1959 of the 1.8-million-year-old *Zinjanthropus* in Tanzania and

Bipedalism is routinely taken as the first defining mark of the hominid.[11] The expansion of the brain beginning from *Homo habilis* 2 million years ago, followed by *Homo erectus* (about 1.7 million years ago and surviving until about 200,000 years ago), along with the use of tools and a dietary shift to include meat, are other definitive early developments.[12] About a million years ago, out of several species of hominids, all limited to the African continent, only *Homo erectus* remained and started to expand to Europe and parts of Asia. About a half-million years ago, an even more developed form of *Homo erectus* appeared, called "archaic *sapiens*." While definitely not yet *Homo sapiens*, this species is a bridge to the *sapiens*. It is debated whether this evolvement of the hominid that led to the rise of *Homo sapiens* was gradual or punctual.[13]

A continuing debate among paleontologists concerns whether the "Out of Africa" or the "Multiregional Evolution" hypothesis is correct; the former seems to win the day.[14] Be that as it may, we know that the final decisive stage of development on the way to the emergence of the modern human being happened in (western) Europe. The history of modern humans is fairly short when compared to that of the hominid, and in that shift the presence of *Homo neanderthalensis* plays a role; that species is dated to the Middle Paleolithic era (400,000/200,000–45,000 years ago).[15] The problem, however, is that there is nothing like scholarly consensus about their capacities and nature. It is agreed that they lacked artistic capacities and their intellectual skills were far from those of modern humans; despite their long existence, they made virtually no progress in the use of tools. The most dramatic development, called the "creative explosion" or "cultural big bang," took place with the shift from the Middle to the Upper Paleolithic era 45,000-35,000 years ago: "it is during this time that human consciousness and intelligence emerged, and with it creative, artistic, and religious imagination."[16] Here a significant role is played by the

---

Homo habilis in the same area in the early 1960s were the first scientific reasons for abandoning the one-species hypothesis.

11. For a definitive statement, see Schwartz and Tattersall, *Human Fossil Record,* 4:469.

12. The Turkana Boy from about 1.6 million years ago is the famous first early *Homo erectus.*

13. Van Huyssteen, *Alone in the World?* pp. 60-62, based mainly on Lewin, *Origin of Modern Humans,* pp. 15-32.

14. For a now classic statement, see Klein, "Behavioral and Biological Origins of Modern Humans."

15. The Lower Paleolithic period is long, from 3 million to about 220,000 years ago, and it is the period of the hominid, as discussed above.

16. Van Huyssteen, *Alone in the World?* p. 64; see also p. 66. For an insightful, nontech-

rich and important reservoir of cave paintings that also point to the emergence of religion and sense of transcendence.

There are both continuity and discontinuity in the evolvement of humanity. There has been a shift in the determination of the relation of the hominids to *Homo sapiens* as they are now seen as "less human."[17] Recent research has found some of the assumptions of their closeness to contemporary humans to be inadequate.[18] Ian Tattersall and Jeffrey H. Schwartz, the two leading paleoanthropologists, summarize it well: "*Homo sapiens* is not simply an extrapolation or improvement of what went before it . . . our species is an entirely unprecedented entity in the world, however mundanely we may have come by our unusual attributes."[19] This emerging scholarly consensus helps critique the earlier linear view of development — on which, ironically — much of the theologically based critique of human evolution is often based![20]

Human Uniqueness in Contemporary Scientific Understanding:
Preliminary Considerations

The determination of human uniqueness is a debated issue for many reasons; among paleoanthropologists and other scientists, notwithstanding an emerging consensus at a general level, no canonical opinion has yet been reached of the criteria. The question in itself is ultimately philosophical in nature[21] — and includes metaphysical considerations. The standard paleoanthropological definition of human uniqueness lists features such as development in tool production, increased technological changes, use of ornaments, significant changes in economic and social organization, and so forth. These kinds of lists compiled by paleoanthropologists should be amplified and expanded by neuro- and brain scientists and psychologists to include such as the following:

1. *Language:* the capacity to communicate a potentially infinite number of propositions; to relate regarding complex, abstract ideas, as well as about the past and the future

---

nical discussion of the importance of the Blomco's cave discovery (in South Africa) for the "cultural big bang," see Klein, "Suddenly Smarter."

17. For a definitive statement, see Schwartz and Tattersall, *Human Fossil Record,* 4:510-11.

18. Van Huyssteen, *Alone in the World?* pp. 51-54.

19. Tattersall and Schwartz, *Extinct Humans,* p. 9, cited in Purcell, *From Big Bang,* p. 173.

20. See Cela-Conde, "Hominid Evolutionary Journey," p. 59.

21. DeSalle and Tattersall, *Human Origins,* p. 45, cited in Purcell, *From Big Bang,* p. 174.

2. *A theory of mind:* an ability to consider the most likely thoughts and feelings of another person

3. *Episodic memory:* a conscious historical memory of events, persons, times, and places (i.e., more than memory for actions and their consequences)

4. *Conscious top-down agency:* conscious mental control of behavior; the ability to modulate ongoing behavior in relationship to the conscious process of decision making

5. *Future orientation:* ability to run mental scenarios of the future implications of behaviors and events

6. *Emotional modulation* by complex social and contextual cognition that serves to guide ongoing behavior and decision making[22]

Even this fairly sophisticated list requires amplification with features such as the capacity to discern beauty in its various forms; the importance of feelings such as falling in love or deep disappointment; the gift of imagination that "travels faster" than the speed of light; and other somewhat mysterious but no less "real" mental capacities.[23] As much as some rudimentary forms of "consciousness" may be found in some animals, these are a far cry from human consciousness and lack the human mind's capacity for self-transcendence.[24] Similarly, as much as higher animals may be able to "learn" to use — or imitate — words taught by humans, that skill has little to do with human symbolic behavior, including syntax and semantics.[25]

The philosophically and theologically essential question has to do with the negotiation between (neo-)Darwinian gradualism and its more recent challenger, the "relatively sudden and once-off emergence" view (supported by the Out of Africa interpretation). In the latter view, "the human revolution" took place in Europe about 40,000 years ago (in the aftermath of the migration from Africa beginning about 50,000 years ago) and had much to

22. W. Brown, "Cognitive Contributions to Soul," pp. 103-4; this list is repeated, e.g., in J. Green, *Body, Soul, and Human Life,* p. 42. See also Carruthers, *Architecture of the Mind,* pp. 155-57.

23. For theological reflections on humor, will, and consciousness as expressions of self-transcendence, see P. Jewett, *Who We Are,* pp. 69-89.

24. The attempts (such as that in J. Green, *Body, Soul, and Human Life,* pp. 39-40) to diminish the uniqueness of human consciousness in light of reports by scientists of the subjective awareness of pain among fish and of mammalian capacity for some emotional feelings, look to me very limited. For critique, see Gazzaniga, *Who's in Charge?* p. 9.

25. Henshilwood, "Fully Symbolic *Sapiens* Behaviour," pp. 123-32.

do with "the creative explosion" seen in the outburst of cave paintings and sculpted and carved ivory and other materials.[26] Although the details of this view are being redefined constantly in light of archaeological findings, it is now the dominant scholarly opinion. Most recently, in terms of dating, the emergence of modern *Homo sapiens* most probably needs to be pushed back, but on exactly how much, there is no final opinion yet — probably somewhere around 70,000-80,000 years back in history.[27] (The discovery of evidence of intentional symbolic activity at Pinnacle Point, South Africa, about 160,000 years ago seems to be the extreme point.)[28]

Uniqueness and Human Genetics

Since the discovery in the 1950s of the structure of DNA[29] and subsequent discoveries, genetics has become a massive enterprise in our society[30] — for two main reasons. First, notwithstanding misinterpretations in the popular imagination of the meaning of mitochondrial DNA (mtDNA) in terms of "mitochondrial Eve," an *ur*-mother of all,[31] it has considerable scientific value. Transmitted only by the mother, mtDNA tells us that the human race shares a common origin in terms of maternal origins, although, not a single human person.[32] (In contemporary estimation, it takes at minimum a group of about 10,000 people to give rise to a lasting population.) Astonishingly, the variation

26. Consider book titles such as *The Human Revolution: Behavioural and Biological Perspectives on the Origins of Modern Humans,* and Pfeiffer's *The Creative Explosion: An Inquiry into the Origins of Art and Religion.*

27. See McBrearty and Brooks, "The Revolution That Wasn't," pp. 453-63.

28. Purcell, *From Big Bang,* p. 181. For a brief statement and sources for the Pinnacle Point discovery, see Marean et al., "Early Human Use of Marine Resources," pp. 905-8.

29. Of course, DNA itself was known much earlier, beginning from the end of the nineteenth century.

30. For the Human Genome Project (ended in 2003) of the U.S. Department of Energy and the National Institutes of Health, see http://www.ornl.gov/sci/techresources/Human_Genome/home.shtml (5/22/2013).

31. Krzysztof and Kimmel, "Alternatives to the Wright-Fisher Model," pp. 165-72.

32. See, e.g., Willoughby, *Evolution of Modern Humans in Africa,* p. 145. Cf. the comment by Justin L. Barrett: "I think it is important to be clear about what is and isn't being claimed by the rejection of a mitochondrial 'eve' or genetic 'eve': many readers will have heard that science has demonstrated the extreme improbability (or even impossibility) of humans being descended of a common ancestral pair. That is simply false. What does seem improbable from the science is that we are all descended from one and only one ancestral pair." E-mail communication to the author, 8/30/2013.

in the mtDNA among humans is almost zero, while among other mammals it may be significant — and that despite the much wider geographical diversity of humans. Also remarkable is that "the greatest genetic diversity of a species is found in the region where it originated."[33] The simple conclusion is that the whole of humankind has evolved from one group of ancestors.[34] A second factor confirming human genetic commonality is the Y chromosome that is inherited only from the father. In light of recent studies, the same kind of uniqueness that characterizes the maternal DNA applies here as well.[35] In sum, the genetic commonality among all human beings has significant implications for determining not only human uniqueness but also the common "brother-hood" and "sisterhood" of all. As mentioned, genetically, racial differences are absolutely meaningless, indicating that all human beings belong to the same species. This is accentuated by the fact that there are no subspecies in our species — unlike hominids and other mammals.

But what about the genetic commonality among humankind in relation to the fact that 98-99 percent of our genetic heritage is shared with chimpanzees? What should we think of best-selling books such as Jonathan Marks's *What It Means to Be 98% Chimpanzee: Apes, People, and Their Genes*? In the popular imagination, a title like that demonstrates the "scientific evidence" that humans are only more advanced mammals — yet this conclusion doesn't stand up under closer scrutiny. The structure of DNA, to begin with, allows a maximum 75 percent diversity. Furthermore, genetic similarity in itself only explains so much. Consider this: humans and dandelions share about 25 percent of their DNA, and humans and daffodils no less than 33 percent.[36] Indeed, Marks wishes to expose "the central fallacy of molecular anthropology," namely, the desire to explain everything in terms of genes, a fallacy of our current cultural consciousness.[37] Consider that there is 99 percent DNA similarity between whales and dolphins, and only a few percent less between whales and hippopotamuses![38] Hence, the genetic similarity between humans and chimpanzees is not what matters, but rather, "just how strange we are compared to all other living species on this earth."[39]

---

33. Fairbanks, *Relics of Eden*, p. 108, cited in Purcell, *From Big Bang*, p. 193.

34. Stringer and McKie, *African Exodus*, p. 113, cited in Purcell, *From Big Bang*, p. 192.

35. Tattersall and Schwartz, *Extinct Humans*, p. 230; Oppenheimer, *Out of Eden*, p. 41; for a reliable nontechnical presentation, see Willard, "Genome Biology," pp. 810-13.

36. See Marks, *What It Means to Be 98% Chimpanzee*, pp. 29-31 and passim.

37. Marks, *What It Means to Be 98% Chimpanzee*, pp. 41-43 and passim, here p. 41.

38. Fairbanks, *Relics of Eden*, pp. 126-27.

39. Purcell, *From Big Bang*, p. 191.

The genetic commonality, along with a number of unique human characteristics listed above, supports the "sudden outburst" of *Homo sapiens* view without in any way downplaying the evolutionary connectedness with the whole lineage of the emergence of other animals. In part 1 (chap. 6) the Darwinian and neo-Darwinian "phyletic" gradualism was subjected to critique, and the significance of the emergence of new forms and species, both continuously and (relatively speaking) discontinuously, was established. Furthermore, we reaffirmed the notion of purpose against its critics. One way of speaking of the newness of *Homo sapiens* is to call the transition between the archaic *Homo* and *Homo sapiens* a "punctuated speciation event"[40] (or "punctuated equlibria").[41] The leading anthropologist Ian Tattersall boldly announces that humanity represents a "totally unprecedented kind of being."[42] At the threshold of the appearance of modern human beings (about 50,000 years ago), anatomy and behavior, so to speak, parted ways. Whereas until then they progressed in tandem, thereafter behavioral and cultural change began to accelerate in a dramatic way.[43]

With all these considerations in mind, it seems to me that theologically and scientifically the most fruitful way of thinking of the emergence of humanity is to balance and correct the "standard Darwinian adaptive gradualism, governed by natural selection," with due emphasis on the newness and unprecedented nature of human development.[44] This approach raises the question of in what ways, more precisely, we should think of the role of genes and culture (behavior, environment) in the emergence of humanity.

Genetics, Determinism, and Culture

Since the discovery of DNA and vastly developed insight into the human genome, genetic (and biological) determinism has taken the upper hand in many questions about human life. Neo-Darwinism and sociobiology in particular have advanced this determinism. The problem, however, is that "a world where everything blindly obeys instructions coded in its DNA is precisely

40. Lieberman and Bar-Yosef, "Apples and Oranges," p. 289.
41. Tattersall, *World from Beginnings*, p. 6.
42. Tattersall, *World from Beginnings*, p. 100. See also his *Monkey in the Mirror*, p. 141, where he calls the question of the emergence of humans "the most baffling" question "in all biology"; cited in Purcell, *From Big Bang*, p. 185.
43. Milner and Tattersall, "Faces of the Human Past."
44. Purcell, *From Big Bang*, p. 182.

what science does *not* find."[45] While there is of course no reason to undermine the importance of the laws of nature (however they are understood) and the regularity of cosmic and human functioning, it is also necessary to consider the importance of the emergence of new forms and features. The mathematician Ian Stewart has famously argued that even though the organic world is no less mathematical in its growth and form than the inorganic world, "the mathematical basis of *living* things is just more subtle, more flexible, and more deeply hidden."[46] Hence, genes matter, but they do not determine everything in human evolution — just consider the importance of "random" mutations.

The paleontologist Simon Conway Morris has famously critiqued the prevailing determinism among the neo-Darwinists.[47] He argues that we need to hold on to both novelty and surprises in the evolution and the phenomenon of "convergence," that is, seemingly independent developments coming together to produce new forms and capacities. With regard to a highly significant question concerning human intelligence, Morris argues — against Stephen J. Gould, who believes that were evolution to be repeated, the probability of the emergence of humanity would be virtually zero[48] — that the emergence of humanity and human intelligence is "inevitable" unless we believe we live in a world without any purpose and goal.[49]

Both from the scientific and philosophical, as well as the theological, perspective, as much as the evolution of *Homo sapiens* is a matter of "natural" (and happenstance) evolution, the capacity for self-transcendence also marks human beings as distinct from the rest of creation.[50] Consider the evolution of the human brain; its evolution can certainly be understood in terms of biological and other "natural" factors. But the "inner" or "subjective" experience *(qualia)* made possible thereby can hardly be reduced to biological or genetic reasons alone, any more than can higher mental activities.[51]

The highlighting of the significance of human self-transcendence, self-

45. Van Huyssteen, *Alone in the World?* p. 55, emphasis in original, paraphrasing a key thesis of Stewart, *Life's Other Secret.*

46. Van Huyssteen, *Alone in the World?* p. 55, emphasis in original, based on Stewart, *Life's Other Secret* (see particularly pp. 8, 14).

47. See particularly S. C. Morris, *Crucible of Creation;* S. C. Morris, *Life's Solution.*

48. Gould, *Wonderful Life,* p. 289: "Replay the tape a million times from . . . [the] beginning, and I doubt that anything like *Homo sapiens* would ever evolve again."

49. S. C. Morris, "We Were Meant to Be . . . ," p. 26; see also the important discussion in Barbour, *Nature, Human Nature, and God,* pp. 39-70.

50. Van Huyssteen, *Alone in the World?* p. 58.

51. Van Huyssteen, *Alone in the World?* p. 59.

reflection, and cognitive as well as symbolic skills as capabilities that cannot be reduced to biological and genetic factors is not to attempt to sever human evolvement from its biological and genetic basis. Rather we highlight these to show that the human is more than that.[52] No doubt human knowledge is deeply embedded in biology, and in that sense all living things share cognitive capacity at various levels as they seek to fit in their environment in their process of survival, that process we call adaptation.[53] Whereas instincts lead to immediate, nonreflective responses, rationality gives rise to reasoned, reflective, and delayed patterns of behavior. Because human behavior — more than that of other animals — is guided by rationality, its evolution is not determined by genes but is rather the function of epigenesis — "the notion that development is not a simple and inevitable unfolding or growing process, but instead is highly variable within certain constrained limits."[54] The genes constrain and shape but do not determine human knowledge, which is the result of the complex interaction of genetic, psychological, and cultural factors.[55] While deeply embodied, knowledge is not merely "biological knowledge," and therefore no "universal Darwinism" provides the way to explain it. Importantly, "once intelligence has evolved in species, self-conscious brains have a causal force equal to that of genes. Self-consciousness, self-transcendence, and culture come to play an important role." Hence, the importance of culture and its influences: "Cultural evolution requires explanation beyond the biological theory of evolution in its strictest sense," part of which is not only arts and language but also religion.[56] We also know now (thanks to Richard Nisbett and others) that culture shapes even cognitive and intellectual capacities and differences such as those between Asians and Westerners.[57] A fitting way to describe the unique nature of humanity is to speak of the "two-natured animal." The genetic and cultural information comes together in an absolutely unique way in *Homo sapiens*. "Since the genetic and cultural have coevolved and coadapted together, they are one reality, not two."[58]

52. Cf. the title of K. Ward's *More Than Matter: Is Matter All We Really Are?*

53. Van Huyssteen, *Alone in the World?* pp. 79-80.

54. Van Huyssteen, *Alone in the World?* p. 81.

55. For a thoughtful and balanced discussion along these lines, see V. E. Anderson, "A Genetic View of Human Nature," pp. 68-69 particularly.

56. Van Huyssteen, *Alone in the World?* pp. 86-87.

57. See Nisbett, *Geography of Thought;* see also Gazzaniga, *Who's in Charge?* pp. 239-43.

58. Hefner, "Biocultural Evolution," p. 330; he refers to Goldsmith, *Biological Roots of Human Nature.*

Here we come to a significant, unique feature of the human being: unlike other animals whose lives are guided and supported from very early on by instincts, the human being is extremely vulnerable when left alone, and it takes a very long time for her to learn even the basic skills of survival, let alone higher skills. Hence, humans have a long childhood and youth.[59] Also, at the other end of life, only among human females do we find menopause, which implies that rather than continuing bringing about new babies, seasoned females may concentrate on teaching and transmitting cultural skills.[60]

The early-twentieth-century "philosophical anthropologist"[61] Arnold Gehlen highlighted the importance of the "inhibition of evolution" that makes humans "deficient beings"[62] demanding slow growth, constant care, and much cultural shaping in order to mature. Even with regard to birth, "human beings are born a year too soon and in a still unfinished state," not only socially and mentally but also "physiologically premature."[63] Without social culture and care, human children are totally vulnerable.[64] Human beings develop in the "social womb."[65] Ironically, human development is facilitated rather than hindered by the deficiency of instincts, unlike other animals; hence, in human life a "hiatus, a gap, between perceptions and impulses" is productive. Human beings must compensate for these "deficiencies" — including utter vulnerability in early life to the threats of the environment — by language and culture. This way they are able to "convert the disadvantages of their initial biological condition into advantages."[66] As Gehlen noted, human beings are therefore by nature cultural beings.[67]

59. Purcell, *From Big Bang,* p. 195. The more rapid development of the Neanderthal (and their shorter life span) is well documented in current literature; see, e.g., Mithen, *Singing Neanderthals,* p. 241.

60. R. Alexander, *How Did Humans Evolve?* p. 12; R. Dawkins, *Selfish Gene,* p. 13. For a recent important study on the "grandmother hypothesis" (that is, the significant roles of grandmothers for making humans distinctively who we are among other animals), see Kim, Coxworth, and Hawkes, "Increased Longevity Evolves from Grandmothering."

61. The classic work is Scheler, *Die Stellung des Menschen im Kosmos* (ET: *Man's Place in Nature*).

62. Gehlen, *Man,* pp. 93-109, here p. 109.

63. Pannenberg, *TA,* p. 38.

64. Pannenberg, *TA,* p. 39.

65. Attributed to Adolf Portmann; Purcell, *From Big Bang,* p. 196.

66. Pannenberg, *TA,* p. 39.

67. Gehlen, *Man,* p. 72.

The Evolvement of Mental and Cultural Capacities

The Symbolic and Rational Species[68]

Linguistic and symbolic capacities are essential elements of our cultural adaptation. While all higher animals communicate in some way or another, only humans use language.[69] This is made possible by the extraordinary development of human brain capacity and aided greatly by the specifics of the vocal tract. Not only the size of the brain matters (although its significance in human, including hominid, evolution should be duly noted),[70] but also specifics about the brain. At a weight of only three to four pounds in adults (with a man's brain slightly heavier), the brain contains 10 billion neurons communicating with each other through synapses that number about 10^{12}. Less than 2 percent of the body in size, it consumes one-fourth of the body's oxygen. As extremely "high-tech" as it is, recall how "earthed" and embodied it is also: just deprive the brain of glucose and oxygen and the lights go off immediately![71] What is amazing about brains — if it were not so obvious that we are prone to miss it — is simply that "though they're obviously material, important parts of them make sense only in terms of activities that transcend matter, like seeking the truth and choosing what's good in itself." As the great Russian neurologist Alexander Romanovich is claimed to have said, "the brain is dumb" as a physical organ.[72]

A useful way to consider the function of a brain is to look at it as a nested, hierarchic action loop in constant interaction with the surroundings. While the lower parts of the hierarchy of the action loops (spinal cord, brain stem, and midbrain) are nested within and modulated by higher-level loops, the higher and more complex actions are processed and executed in the higher loops (diencephalon, particularly thalamus, and cerebral cortex).[73] The cere-

---

68. See Deacon, "Symbolic Threshold." I will first look at the development of the brain, and thereafter, language.

69. Hagoort, "Uniquely Human Capacity for Language Communication," p. 45.

70. DeSalle and Tattersall, *Human Origins,* p. 192. "[T]he degree of connectivity, particularly of frontal cortical systems, is now considered as important as cortical size in differentiating cortical brain systems of humans and other primates." Private e-mail from Warren S. Brown, 8/2/2013.

71. Spence, *Actor's Brain,* p. 17.

72. Purcell, *From Big Bang,* p. 198.

73. I am helped here by Jeeves and Brown, *Neuroscience, Psychology and Religion,* chap. 4. For anatomical details, I draw mainly from Spence, *Actor's Brain.*

bral cortex "on top" of human brains is what matters most, but even here, specification is needed, as its size in chimpanzees is only slightly smaller than in humans. It is the "top" parts of the cerebral cortex that are the critical domains and are relatively large in humans. The phylogenetically youngest neocortex (or isocortex) is the largest and most complex part of the cerebral cortex and in humans occupies four-fifths of the brain's size (with primates slightly less and with other mammals significantly less). The cerebral cortex plays a key role in the functions of memory, attention, thinking, language, and consciousness. A particularly important role in human brains is played by the Broca and Wernicke's areas, which facilitate speech reception and production, respectively; these areas are significantly less developed in higher apes.[74]

When it comes to crossing over the symbolic threshold, seemingly elementary ways of "communication" such as the use of ocher for red pigment to paint one's body as far back as about 160,000 years ago are noteworthy,[75] although firmer evidence comes from about 75,000 years ago.[76] Clearly, anthropologists discern in these kinds of early finds "the origin of modern thought and behavior — and, by implication, language." Some of them show patterns that are not merely the result of chance, particularly when there is repetition of the same design.[77] What is significant about even these earliest artistic signs is that "we can easily find symbolizations of experiences that reach beyond our needs for mere survival or mere utility, beyond our space-time universe." As mentioned, they also thereby refer to religious and other metaphysical notions.[78]

The capacity for language requires also proper development of the vocal tract. Although the anatomy and basic mechanics of voice production are broadly similar in humans and in primates, there are important differences between the production of human speech and nonhuman vocalizations that make human speech and communication possible[79] (the details of which are not needed here).[80] The slow but decisive shift from elementary ways of sym-

---

74. For details, see Spence, *Actor's Brain,* pp. 83-90.

75. Edgar, "Letter from South Africa"; see also K. Brown et al., "An Early and Enduring Advanced Technology," pp. 590-93.

76. Henshilwood, d'Errico, and Watts, "Engraved Ochres," pp. 27-47; Henshilwood, "Modern Humans and Symbolic Behavior," pp. 78-85.

77. Mithen, *Singing Neanderthals,* pp. 250-51, cited in Purcell, *From Big Bang,* pp. 224-25.

78. Purcell, *From Big Bang,* p. 273.

79. See Lieberman, *Uniquely Human.*

80. For details, see Ghazanfar and Rendall, "Evolution of Human Vocal Production," pp. R457-60.

bolization to the complex and nuanced use of language in modern humans is a major distinguishing feature of humanity.[81] The "thing" about human language is not vocalization, articulation, even making up words "according to precise rules," although it is essential in crossing over the "symbolic threshold" and making us "the symbolic species," to quote Terrence Deacon.[82] Language has opened the window into reality, so to speak, and the possibility of sharing those experiences with other people — present and future. What is highly significant about language is not that we have to understand it "as something on its own, but rather as the means by which being, reality, reveals itself to us." Therefore, "any attempt to reduce language to communication at an animal level would miss out on its primary task, which is to literally put words on our experience of being."[83] As promising and important as the experiments with higher apes' capacity for learning some rudiments of speech may be, primates at their best stay on the lexical level and are not capable of acquiring syntax.[84] While the hominids — somewhat like human infants — can use some kind of communication, "proto-language," they lack the essential elements of human language, namely, syntax and meaning (semiotics).

The move from proto-language to human language is so tremendous that many biolinguists and cognitive archaeologists relate it to the "human revolution." Says Derek Bickerton: "In the absence of any other convincing cause for this development, we may assume that it resulted from the emergence of syntax, an agency just as powerful in its manipulation of thought as in its manipulation of words." Thereafter, he notes that " 'the Syntactic Species' perhaps more accurately distinguishes us from all the species that preceded us."[85] No wonder, along with the birth of consciousness, that the origin of language is dubbed "the hardest problem in science."[86]

In other words, the foundational difference between human language and the proto-language of higher apes is simply the unlimited nature of the

81. For a recent (nontechnical but accurate) discussion, see Tattersall, "Language and the Origin of Symbolic Thought," pp. 109-16.
82. Deacon, "Symbolic Threshold," pp. 79-92.
83. Purcell, From Big Bang, p. 226. This discussion neither requires nor has the space to go into the much-debated question of the specifics of the origin of language; for a primer, see Purcell, pp. 226-31.
84. Purcell, From Big Bang, p. 236. "There is doubt about the inability of chimps to comprehend syntax. Kanzi could differentiate the meaning of some sentences based on syntactic differences alone." Private e-mail from Warren S. Brown, 8/2/2013.
85. Bickerton, "Did Syntax Trigger the Human Revolution?" p. 104.
86. Knight, "Language, Ochre, and the Rule of Law," p. 282; Knight speaks only of language, not of consciousness; I am indebted to Purcell, From Big Bang, p. 230.

former: human language "knows no limitations of space or time," whereas animal communication is time- and space-limited.[87] This openness of course is linked with the openness of humanity to the future and beyond physical (and other) limitations, as will be discussed in the following section in reference to religion. Openness may also help explain the unbelievable drive for continuing innovation, improvement, and inventions in human culture — a feature unknown even among the hominids, let alone other animals.[88] No wonder the difference between humans and other species is "not just a difference of degree. It is a difference in kind."[89]

These reflections on the seemingly unlimited capacities inherent in modern human communication and language take us to the complicated question of what makes human understanding and knowledge distinctively human. Is cognitive capacity also the product of evolution? And if so, how exactly? To these questions we turn next. (The focus on understanding and intelligence in no way means to undermine the critical importance of other mental features such as the sense of beauty, goodness, and truth.)[90]

The Evolution of Human Knowledge

The mystery of understanding — simply put: How can a biological-material basis give rise to understanding and truth claims? — did not go unnoticed by the pioneers of modern evolutionary theory, as the oft-quoted statement from Darwin illustrates: "But then with me the horrid doubt always arises whether the convictions of man's mind, which has been developed from the mind of the lower animals, are of any value or at all trustworthy. Would any one trust in the convictions of a monkey's mind, if there are any convictions in such a mind?"[91]

An important emerging field that may contribute significantly to clarifying the role of the evolution of human knowledge in general and hence, also of religious and theological intuitions in particular, is evolutionary epistemology. The basic claim of evolutionary epistemology is simple and profound: evolution relates to the emergence and development not merely of species

---

87. Bickerton, *Language and Human Behavior,* pp. 12, 17.
88. See Bickerton, *Language and Human Behavior,* pp. 46-48; Purcell, *From Big Bang,* pp. 237-38. Cf. Lonergan, *Insight,* p. 520.
89. Tattersall, *World from Beginnings,* p. 101.
90. A highly important discussion is McGrath, *Open Secret,* part 3.
91. F. Darwin, ed., *Charles Darwin,* p. 64.

but also of thoughts and ideas.[92] It is argued that not only are human mental capacities constrained and shaped by the mechanisms of biological evolution but that "the thoughts and ideas that we have in our heads" are also similarly attributed to evolution.[93] In other words, epistemology is taken to be a product of biological evolution.[94]

Genetic and biological factors, however, only explain so much. Human knowledge and rationality are a function of complex genetic and cultural factors. If understanding, use of symbols, and imagination are "material" in any sense of the word, it certainly seems that they must be a quite different type of "material"! That said, it is amazing how hard reductionism dies among many sociobiologists, evolutionary psychologists, and others.[95] A reductionist evolutionary epistemology makes meaningless the whole project of human knowledge and other meaningful mental capacities. If reductionism were true, then not only does it deny the meaning and truthfulness of all statements made by humans, but it also denies the whole idea of human freedom and responsibility. Therefore, it is important to highlight the distinctive nature of mental capacities such as the use of language, symbolic thought, consciousness, and understanding for a proper understanding of human uniqueness. While theologians are interested in these topics in themselves, the next section also links them with the question of the emergence and the legitimacy of religion. Without a nonreductionist account of the rise of mental capacities, the notion of religion and other higher cultural phenomena can hardly be upheld.

Avoiding naive reductionism, a seasoned interpretation of evolutionary epistemology should seek to steer a radical middle course between two extremes. On the one hand, the standard evolutionary epistemology's emphasis of considering all human knowledge so deeply embedded in its biological-genetic basis that it becomes meaningless (and "content"-less) is to be rejected, if for no other reason than its internal inconsistency (that is, that statement in itself cannot be taken as "true"). On the other hand, the reluctance of the tradition (whether philosophical or theological) to acknowledge the evolution-bound nature of human knowledge — including its cultural products, whether

92. See Radnitzky and Bartley, eds., *Evolutionary Epistemology.* See also van Huyssteen's extensive discussion in *Alone in the World?* pp. 75-110; and van Huyssteen, *Duet or Duel?*

93. Van Huyssteen, *Alone in the World?* p. 76. The following exposition is based on van Huyssteen's lucid and insightful exposition. The main sources he is building on are Plotkin, *Darwin Machines,* and Wuketits, *Evolutionary Epistemology.*

94. Gontier, "Evolutionary Epistemology."

95. For famous — or infamous — such statements, see Blackmore, *Meme Machines,* p. 246; quoted in Purcell, *From Big Bang,* p. 245.

art or science or religion — cannot be followed either even though theologians (and a few philosophers, I suppose) would understand well such hesitancy. In other words, there is no reason for theology to resist the idea of the evolutionary/evolving nature of human insight into reality at large and religion in particular as long as this perspective is not made a pretext for explaining away the meaning of religion and hence also theological intuitions.

The nonreductive evolutionary epistemology builds on the conviction that while rooted and embedded in biological evolution, human "consciousness, self-awareness, reflectiveness, and rationality . . . have the ability to take on cognitive goals and ideals that cannot be justified in terms of survival-promotion or reproductive advantage only" (or for that matter, do not have to be a function of physical deprivation or drugs or the like). In other words, rational knowledge, aesthetic appreciation of beauty, and moral sensibilities "transcend our biological origins," even though they do not have to be separated from them.[96] Whether we speak of "transcendental experiences" (Rahner)[97] or "openness to the world/exocentricity" (Pannenberg)[98] or use any other similar terms, it seems uncontested that human imagination always seeks to reach beyond physical and finite limits.

This discussion takes us to the highly complex and multifaceted question of the relation between human religiosity and evolution, theologically speaking, the apex of human development.

Evolution and Religion

To the question of why humans seem to be "incurably religious" (Pannenberg), nontheological scholars have of course given various types of answers. Two wide paradigms of study are important for the sake of this theological discussion. For the sake of clarity, let me name them in the following way:

- The "evolutionary biological adaptationist" (EBA)[99] model understands religion as a biologically based evolutionary product that aids in the adaption to the environment to meet needs (and avoid threats). Obviously, this approach is keen on evolutionary epistemology's power of explanation.

96. See van Huyssteen, *Alone in the World?* p. 95.
97. Rahner, *Hearers of the Word,* pp. 92-93; Küng, *Does God Exist?* pp. 438-39 particularly.
98. Pannenberg, *TA,* pp. 34-42.
99. This nomenclature is my invention.

- The "cognitive science of religion" (CSR) model considers religion a by-product of nonreligious cognitive systems and patterns (working in different domains rather than in one, the "religious domain").

In many ways the advocates of these two paradigms often see them as alternatives. Because the latter is a much younger approach (no older than fifteen to twenty years at the time of this writing), it is customary to find CSR representatives critiquing EBA for its obvious difficulties in accounting for those many cases in which religion has not been an aid in adaptation but rather has functioned maladaptively, say in relation to morality, xenophobia, otherworldliness, and so forth. Of course, on the other side, counterarguments such as that religion serves group cohesion, gives meaning and strength in life under difficult circumstances, and other similar functional reasons have been offered.[100] Furthermore, it is quite astonishing that much of CSR investigation is done without any focused attention on evolutionary considerations, not even evolutionary epistemology. Without going into those complicated debates, for the sake of this theological discussion I will carefully assess both paradigms' contributions and weaknesses from a theological perspective. No theological account of humanity can be adequate without a careful consideration of religiosity. (In *Trinity and Revelation,* chapter 9 looks at the question of the origins of religions from the philosophical and religio-cultural point of view, particularly with regard to the rationality of God-talk.)

Briefly stated, the theologian faces these main challenges in these two paradigms: EBA tends to adopt uncritically the prevailing reductionist model of explanation of evolutionary epistemology and thus considers — without much detailed investigation — religious beliefs and claims merely as "blind" products of evolutionary adaptation. The main challenge coming from CSR is its naive adoption of naturalist epistemology that in principle does not allow for the truthfulness of religious beliefs and claims as they are considered merely by-products of nonreligious factors.

Evolutionary Biological Adaptationist Model

The EBA model takes religion (and transcendental beliefs) mainly as a means of adapting to the environment and its challenges. The paleoanthropologist Franz Wuketits argues that the need for metaphysics is a common human

---

100. The now classic work arguing for adaption is E. O. Wilson, *Sociobiology.*

characteristic; metaphysical explanations relate to the origins of the world and life after death. The importance of burials is routinely noted as a sign among early humans of acknowledging the tension between the lasting and passing, as well as the beginning of hope beyond death; particularly, the habit of putting food with the deceased (probably not before the Upper Paleolithic period)[101] indicates belief in an afterlife.[102] These acts help humans cope with the world and its unknowns. But that is not all paleoanthropologists are saying specifically about *religious* beliefs. By making them adaptationist strategies, anthropologists take it for granted that they cannot therefore have any factual basis. They are illusion, imagination. Evolutionary epistemology and neuro-scientific study of religious phenomena fund naturalist reductionism, which is becoming the semicanonical "scientific" view[103] — so much so that at its extreme, mental states (including metaphysical and religious states) are said to be "as integral to the human body, as, say, the digestive system."[104] If true, reductionism would of course undo religion as any kind of meaningful human cultural activity and hence make theology merely an archaeology of mistaken beliefs, nothing more than fantasies, dreams, or illusions.

In response to reductionism, the theologian van Huyssteen notes: "But if metaphysical beliefs . . . do not really tell us anything about 'first causes' or 'last purposes' (i.e., God), but rather about our own *propensity* for such beliefs . . . why did they evolve on such a massive scale in the history of our species?" In other words: On what scientific basis can it be assumed uncritically that because religious/metaphysical beliefs assist in adaption, they must necessarily be merely that — "adaptionist" devices without any real epistemological validity?[105] To repeat myself, making religious beliefs factual would not of course "prove" the existence of God, any god; rather, it would make God-talk "natural" and rational.

Behind the attempts of evolutionary sciences and philosophy to debunk religion lies a deep but pervasive methodological assumption that has to be subject to critique. Currently often named the "evolutionary debunking argument,"[106] the assumption is that as soon as you discover the "origins" and

---

101. So, e.g., Tattersall, *Becoming Human,* p. 10.

102. Hegel famously argued for the connection between burial rites and belief in immortality; see further, Pannenberg, *TA,* pp. 73-74, 360, 417.

103. Atran, *In Gods We Trust,* p. 10.

104. Lewis-Williams, *Conceiving God,* pp. 137, 158, cited in Purcell, *From Big Bang,* p. 211.

105. Van Huyssteen, *Alone in the World?* pp. 94-95, here p. 94, emphasis in original.

106. Kahane, "Evolutionary Debunking Arguments," pp. 103-25; Leech and Visala, "Cognitive Science of Religion," pp. 301-16.

evolvement of religion (or morality),[107] you have thereby proved that there is nothing factual about religion. This is a "genetic fallacy," that is, one seeks to explain away a phenomenon by tracing its origin even when such an appeal to origins is irrelevant.[108] Consider this simple example: we do not reject the habit of wearing a wedding ring just because it originally symbolized the custom of ankle chains worn by women to prevent them from running away from their husbands.[109] The implication is simple: the naive use of the debunking argument must be put under critical scrutiny.[110]

Without in any way dismissing the basic insights of paleoanthropology and evolutionary epistemology, theologically one may put forth an alternative hermeneutics: what if the "universal" human search for the transcendent helps explain religious beliefs in terms of

> our drive toward something transcending human powers as reflected in the fabric of the universe, a reality that is greater than, and transcends, empirical reality. Religious belief, therefore, implies that there is this transcendent aspect to reality, and that we humans are part of, and related to, this dimension of transcendence. For religious believers it will be natural to interpret the emergence of consciousness and self-consciousness as revelatory of something deep in the universe, something inexplicable by physics, something behind the material face of the world.[111]

In sum, rather than trying to reduce religion in biological evolution (without, at the same time, severing religion from its evolutionary basis), a reasonable case can be made at least for its rationality, which facilitates careful investigation thereof.[112]

The nonreductionist human openness-to-the-world — beyond (but not separated from) biological-genetic conditions — makes room for the possibility of religion as something meaningful and "rational." Just consider

---

107. Ruse, "Is Darwinian Metaethics Possible?" pp. 13-26.

108. See, e.g., Waller, *Critical Thinking*, p. 5.

109. Example given by Damer, *Attacking Faulty Reasoning*, p. 100.

110. For a classic statement about the need to be more cautious when explaining religion, see Hume, *Natural History of Religion* (1775), p. 1.

111. Van Huyssteen, *Alone in the World?* p. 97; he builds here on O'Hear, *Beyond Evolution*; O'Hear, however, does not engage Plotkin and Wuketits, whose work van Huyssteen critically utilizes.

112. See Rolston, *Genes, Genesis, and God*.

how difficult it would be to explain otherwise "the persistence of the transcendent,"[113] the propensity to religious belief at all times and in all places throughout the history of *Homo sapiens*. Rightly, the Lutheran American theologian Ted Peters notes that "[b]ehind, underneath, or above what we see and hear is a transcendent yet present reality that is suprasensory, supranatural, spiritual, divine, or all of these."[114] This is what the sociologist of religion Peter Berger names "a rumor of angels."[115] Again, the marshaling of the evidence of the persistence and universality of religion among humanity is not an attempt to "prove" the existence of any god, let alone a particular God; rather "the function of anthropological proofs [is] to show that the concept of God is an essential part of a proper human self-understanding, whether in relation to human reason or to other basic fulfillments of human existence."[116] In other words, the anthropological argument is based on the existence and force of a religious disposition as part of human structure, so much so that we speak of "incurable religiosity,"[117] as the failed atheistic-totalitarian experiments in China, the former Soviet Union, and elsewhere have shown.

Enter the CSR paradigm and materially similar kinds of challenges, though in different types of methodological and material arguments, which now face the theologian.

The Cognitive Science of Religion Model

A new and rapidly growing field, cognitive science of religion (CSR)[118] is an interdisciplinary, pluralistic, and elusive network of approaches. While dominantly naturalistic and often perceived as antitheistic,[119] it also allows theistic

113. Title of chap. 2 in McGrath, *Open Secret*.

114. T. Peters, *God — the World's Future*, p. 83.

115. For a discussion of many such examples in science and arts, see Polkinghorne, *God of Hope*, pp. 30-36.

116. Pannenberg, *ST* 1:92-93. Justin L. Barrett (private e-mail, 8/30/2013) makes this highly insightful comment: ". . . the adaptiveness of religion would be surprising if religious claims were totally false (e.g., no supernatural agents) but predictable if these claims were tracking on some truths."

117. Pannenberg, *ST* 1:157.

118. J. Barrett, "Cognitive Science of Religion," pp. 768-86; see also J. Barrett, *Why Would Anyone Believe in God?*; J. Barrett, *Cognitive Science, Religion, and Theology*.

119. Nielsen (*Naturalism and Religion*) seems naively following the opinion that once religion is "naturalistically" explained, by definition its truth claims cannot be true.

interpretations.[120] CSR approaches religion piecemeal rather than from an essentialist viewpoint, and thus seeks to avoid defining religion.[121] "CSR's central idea is the religion as a byproduct thesis according to which religious beliefs and practices are informed by our nonreligious cognitive systems working in different domains."[122] In other words, there is no "God-gene" or specifically religious domain.[123] A related "big" claim in CSR holds that religion is not a *sui generis* phenomenon (as nonreductionist religionists such as Mircea Eliade and Clifford J. Geertz argue) but rather can be naturalistically explained.[124] That, however, does not mean that religiosity is not "natural." On the contrary, CSR marshals empirical evidence that we are all "born believers," to cite Justin Barrett's recent title.[125] Deborah Kelemen has even suggested that children may be "intuitive theists,"[126] and Paul Bloom has proclaimed that, according to the developmental evidence, "religion is natural."[127] Wide evidence demonstrates that children have a strong bias to see the natural world as purposeful even in ways that religiously committed adults would never (deliberately) teach their offspring.

CSR argues that because religion is natural, it is easy for human beings to learn and transmit. That claim, however, should be refined. Certain types of religious beliefs and representations are particularly apt to be transmitted, namely, "minimally counterintuitive representations" (MCI), that is, those that are not merely intuitive (so as to fail to be interesting) but on the other side, not overly counterintuitive (so as not to load the cognitive system too much).[128] There is solid experimental evidence supporting the MCI thesis.[129] Related is the "theological correctness" thesis: while believers tend to give the "correct" answer (with regard to their belief system, say Mahayana

---

120. See chap. 5 in Visala, *Naturalism, Theism;* he himself sees CSR as compatible with theism.

121. For introductions to the field, see J. Barrett, *Why Would Anyone Believe in God?;* Boyer, *Religion Explained;* Pyysiäinen, *How Religion Works;* Pyysiäinen, *Supernatural Agents;* Murray and Schloss, eds., *Believing Primate.*

122. Visala, *Naturalism,* p. 9, emphasis removed.

123. See further, Atran, *In Gods We Trust,* pp. 13-15.

124. Visala, *Naturalism,* p. 19.

125. J. Barrett, *Born Believers;* see also Banerjee and Bloom, "Would Tarzan Believe in God?" pp. 7-8.

126. Kelemen, "Are Children 'Intuitive Theists'?" pp. 295-301.

127. Bloom, "Religion Is Natural," pp. 147-51.

128. Visala, *Naturalism,* pp. 56-59; for the classic definition, see Boyer, *Religion Explained,* p. 65.

129. E.g., Barrett and Lawson, "Ritual Intuitions," pp. 183-201.

Buddhism or Roman Catholic Christianity) to theological questions when given time to reflect, they tend to depend on folk intuitions when responding to immediate needs or events. Consider God's omnipresence: because the believer knows that according to Christian teaching God is "everywhere" rather than "somewhere," he or she may intuitively respond as if God were right now here![130]

The important theological question to be asked here is whether the distinction between "intuitive" and "counterintuitive" by definition implies the nonfactual nature of religious beliefs. Many CSR advocates take that position for granted[131] (and it is of course in keeping with the naturalist epistemology and methodology of the paradigm). "The home of religions, so it is argued, is social life rather than metaphysical or cosmological speculation." Hence, for example, "supernatural agents" ("divine beings," religiously named) have to do with moral intuitions or other social functions — but they are not real or existent.[132] That conclusion, however, is neither necessary nor — theologically — satisfactory. One can argue that the objects of religious beliefs such as God, Christ, and angels are both existent *and* serve societal and cultural roles. At the same time, they can be counterintuitive, like, say, the insights of quantum physics.[133]

In sum, the validity of the reductionist and "strict naturalism"[134] approaches to explaining (away!) religion is as strong as are the two foundational epistemological-metaphysical claims, namely, those related to reductionism and naturalism (with the corollary view of causal closure, that is, ultimately a physical cause must be found, and top-down causation is denied). While the latter was discussed and qualified above (chap. 1), the former will be defeated in the following chapter (11). Furthermore, I have already defined "nature" as "creation" (chap. 3) and so allow for the existence of "supernatural" (not in terms of antinatural but as something transcending nature) and divine action (as defined in chap. 6). All these resources more than defeat the strictly nat-

---

130. Hornbeck and Barrett, "Refining and Testing 'Counterintuitiveness' in Virtual Reality."

131. Atran and Norenzayan, "Religion's Evolutionary Landscape"; for an important critique, see J. Barrett, "Counterfactuality in Counterintuitive Religious Concepts." I am indebted to Barrett for guiding me in this discussion.

132. Visala, *Naturalism*, p. 65 (reporting, against his own opinion).

133. As argued by a leading experimental CSR advocate, J. Barrett, *Why Would Anyone Believe in God?* pp. 122-23. See also Näreaho, "Cognitive Science of Religion," pp. 83-98; Visala, *Naturalism*, pp. 83-84.

134. So named by Visala, *Naturalism*, p. 86.

uralist program of explaining religion merely as an adaptation or by-product (if that means bracketing out its truth claims).

Next we will focus on the most distinctive theological resource, namely, the theology of the *imago Dei*. That discussion, however, does not take place apart from the results reached in this chapter. On the contrary, talk about the image of God presupposes and is not in conflict with the evolutionary theory among the sciences, although, as discussed in chapter 9, particularly in Abrahamic faiths, for a long time the theological and evolutionary interpretations were seen as alternatives. (For the Islamic tradition, that is still a huge and wide challenge.) The image of God investigation is also greatly helped by other important scientific insights, particularly those related to the sociality, embodiment, and emotionality of human beings — values inherent in biblical intuitions but not thematically developed in theology until recent times. At the end of the next chapter, the Christian talk about the image of God will also be put in dialogue with the other two Abrahamic faiths.

11. Humanity as the Image of God: A Theological Account

Introducing the Theme: The Constitution of the Self and the Image of God

Christian theology's most significant anthropological concept, *imago Dei,* claims to provide a foundational account of the human person and humanity in relation to the Creator, other creatures, and the cosmos as a whole. Notwithstanding the scarcity of direct references to the concept in the biblical canon — after three occurrences in the beginning (Gen. 1:26-27; 5:1; 9:6), the concept disappears until it is picked up in a couple of NT passages (1 Cor. 11:7; James 3:9)[1] — from early on theological tradition made it an umbrella term. Everywhere in the Fathers, Genesis 1:26 plays a significant role when commenting on humanity and human destiny.

That said, not every contemporary theologian is convinced that *imago Dei* is the proper starting point for constructing theological anthropology. As mentioned, Kelsey's monumental work dismisses the image of God, along with the creation theology of Genesis 1-3, and instead turns to the Wisdom literature of the OT. The grounds for this surprising move are both exegetical and theological. He builds on the groundbreaking work of the OT scholar Claus Westermann, particularly his insight that the exodus narrative (Exod. 1–18) is at the center of the Pentateuch as the basis of the history of Israel as a people and that Genesis 1–3 as an independent narrative is merely assumed rather

---

1. The apocryphal literature contains allusions to the image: Ecclesiasticus 17:3; Wisdom 2:23.

than looked upon as the story of the origins. Wisdom literature focuses on the continuing providential care of God and the quotidian rather than mythical origins, whereas the canonical creation theologies (Genesis, Isaiah, and some NT passages) subordinate creation under redemption. Kelsey further argues that Wisdom theology avoids the anthropocentrism of creation theologies' existentially oriented accounts.[2] Wisdom literature (which does not know "image of God" traditions) focuses on the quotidian, life here and now.[3] To his credit, Kelsey acknowledges that Wisdom literature represents "one voice among many in canonical Holy Scripture."[4]

My objections to Kelsey, very briefly put, are the following: First, I do not think that pitting one section of the canonical Scriptures against another is the best way to follow the canon. Rather, utilizing both Genesis and Wisdom traditions does better justice to the process of revelation in the Bible. Second, although it is true that the image of God as a technical term plays a minor role in the canon, making a term a theological "umbrella concept" that employs a number of biblical themes is nothing new in theological construction and growth of tradition. Third, avoiding negative values such as anthropocentrism does not require omitting Genesis 1–3 (the current project defeats anthropocentrism and yet upholds the image of God tradition). Fourth, the question of origins is a key area of interest not only in Judeo-Christian tradition but also in other religious traditions; therefore, ignoring it and focusing on the quotidian sounds reductionist. The conclusion thus holds that there is every reason to consider carefully the meaning of the image of God and gain every possible benefit from the wide range of canonical teaching, including Wisdom literature and the NT.

The main challenge — and opportunity — for constructive theology is whether "it be possible to revision the canonical core of the *imago Dei* in such a way that it might again function as a gravitational force in contemporary theological anthropology, while at the same time facilitating interdisciplinary reflection."[5] To use Paul Ricoeur's words, "[e]ach century has the task of elaborating its thought ever anew on the basis of that indestructible symbol" of the image of God.[6] A key interdisciplinary challenge has to with how to link the ancient theology of the image of God with the currently most vigorously

---

2. D. Kelsey, *Eccentric Existence*, vol. 1, chap. 4A (main argument); chap. 4B (technical discussion). Among key publications of Westermann, see his *Genesis 1–11* and *Creation*.

3. D. Kelsey, *Eccentric Existence*, 1:190-91 and passim.

4. D. Kelsey, *Eccentric Existence*, 1:161.

5. Van Huyssteen, *Alone in the World?* p. 116.

6. Ricoeur, "The Image of God and the Epic of Man," p. 110.

debated issue of the self. Let us first look at the conversation about the constitution of self beginning from modernity.

From the Modern Stable Identity to the Postmodern Loss of Self

The turn to self in modernity is well known and well documented.[7] Its implications for theological anthropology, however, have been more intensely reflected upon only lately, although, ironically, "the picture of the self-conscious and self-reliant, self-transparent and all-responsible individual which Descartes and Kant between them imposed upon modern philosophy may easily be identified, in various guises, in the work of many modern theologians."[8]

Generally speaking, in modernity the notion of self has been characterized by a turn to inwardness.[9] That said, the turn to inwardness is of course a far older phenomenon. As routinely noted, Saint Augustine played a crucial role here.[10] For him, however, the turn inward was deeply theologically motivated: he was not in search of his own soul as much as his God.[11] In contrast to Augustine, the modern turn inward was funded by the desire to be distanced from God and to affirm autonomy, which resulted in an "unprecedented uncertainty about human identity."[12] On the way to the modern concept of self, Boethius's well-known definition is a milestone: "Nature is the specific property of any substance, and Person the individual substance of a rational nature."[13] Unfortunately, it is too often read out of context. Like Augustine's, Boethius's interests were theological, in this case christological; he needed to distinguish "nature and person" to negotiate between Eutychians (Monophysitism) and Nestorianism ("two-nature" Christology). On the basis of (then) contemporary substance-ontology, personhood seemed to be steady and fixed and its focus rationality. His definition makes sense particularly against the Aristotelian philosophical tradition with its scale of definitions and the task at hand to resolve a christological problem. The way "individual substance" was understood implied indivisibility, which of course can be found

---

7. See D. Kelsey, *Eccentric Existence*, vol. 1, chap. 2B.

8. Kerr, "Modern Philosophy of Self," p. 24; see also his *Theology after Wittgenstein*.

9. C. Taylor, *Sources of the Self*, pp. 111, 113.

10. See LaCugna, *God for Us*, p. 250.

11. Augustine, *The Happy Life* 2.11; for comments, see C. Taylor, *Sources of the Self*, p. 130.

12. Janicaud, *On the Human Condition*, p. 1.

13. Boethius, *Treatise against Eutyches and Nestorius* 4.

in the mental, rational "soul."[14] This commonly held philosophical notion was picked up by modern thinkers, and it facilitated the anchoring of self in the "inner self"; it also helped form, as a response, the expressivist concept of self in Romanticism.[15]

Fittingly, Grenz names modernity's view "the world-mastering rational self": "the self takes charge of the world it inhabits . . . so as to constitute itself and determine its identity," particularly relying on the powers of reason.[16] Herein lies the wisdom of Foucault's famous observation that "man" was an invention of modernity[17] (rather than, say, of classical humanism). A related implication from the "sovereignty of the 'I' " is its effort to displace God from the center of the universe.[18] Yet another development is the self-sufficient self related to the victorious rise of psychological sciences from William James to Abraham Maslow with its focus on (self-)consciousness. With the establishment and consolidation of the central role of psychology in society, the turn inward, particularly self-consciousness — as well as to emotions — led to "the triumph of the therapeutic self." Yet, "accepting this role, psychology is transformed into the image of Enlightenment instrumental science, even to the point of becoming its ultimate exemplar." The end result is that "[t]his pilgrimage netted a self-assured, self-sufficient, centered self that constituted a stable identity in the midst of a chaotic world."[19] Although this thoroughly modern concept of self-sufficiency is the dominant force in the Global North (and influential among the intelligentsia of the Global South trained in the West), its global appeal should not be overrated. Consider, for example, that the pan-African *ubuntu* (or *ubuntunse*)[20] means that "[t]here is no independent existence without the creative act of God. Just about all African myths of creation clearly indicate the link between humans and God as their creator and provider of what was needed to sustain life."[21]

14. The rationality of the soul was the key to Aquinas (*ST* 1.29.1), who borrowed from Boethius. As is often the case, Gunton's critique of Thomas is overstated; *Promise of Trinitarian Theology,* p. 94.

15. Grenz, *Social God,* p. 66. In the background lies the ancient philosopher Porphyry's "Tree," which places beings with minds at the top of the scale, distinct from others, e.g., animals that lack rationality (at least in the human sense).

16. Grenz, *Social God,* pp. 67-70, here p. 67.

17. Foucault, *Order of Things,* p. xxiii.

18. See Seo, *Critique of Western Theological Anthropology,* p. 71.

19. For details, see Grenz, *Social God,* pp. 86-97, here p. 97.

20. Mnyandu, "Ubuntu as the Basis of Authentic Humanity," pp. 77-86.

21. Kapolyo, *Human Condition,* p. 35. For a massive, now classic study, see Mbiti, *Concepts of God in Africa,* part 4: "God and Humans."

The Western modern conception of self shifted drastically with the advent of postmodernism. Whereas Christian tradition and classic humanism were "grounded . . . on the notion of an ontologically given human nature," postmodernity saw it merely as a cultural and linguistic construction without any "foundations."[22] Consequently, the "reign of the modern self . . . [was] short-lived, for the centered self of the modern era appears to be one of the casualties of the postmodern dethroning of all ruling monarchs."[23] The postmodern deconstruction of the self was prepared for much earlier and did not happen overnight. Grenz goes as far back in history as the sixteenth-century "pre-Freudian" French Romantic essayist Michel de Montaigne's turn to autobiography as the means of self-discovery. Whereas Descartes and other (early) modernist-driven thinkers relied on stable identity, Montaigne and some others were already discerning the loosening of the "foundations" on which to build identity. Discontent with the rationality of the Enlightenment led to the search for self in terms of self-expression reaching its zenith in Romanticism.

Historical details aside (which are masterfully charted by C. Taylor and others), the definite disintegration of self seemed to be inevitable. While few went as far as the "nihilist" Nietzsche, at least he was honest; rejecting all transcendental grounds for belief and morality, he also helped expose the thinness of Romanticism's effort to find any alternative ways of completing self from the Enlightenment. Whether it is the dissolution of self (as in structuralism after F. de Saussure) or the death of self (M. Foucault), all such notions herald the destruction of a confident, steady self. But not only that: "The postmodern ethos is characterized not only by the loss of the self but also by the *embrace of its demise*." Hence, with these postmodernists we are at the radically opposite end from the modernists to whom the loss of self was a great tragedy. "Preference" and "self-referentiality" are the key ingredients of the move of (self-)constructed, fleeting, ever-changing selves within "webs of interlocution." Identities, if there are any, are in the making; rather than "foundations," there are narratives.[24]

Now, the challenge — and opportunity — for constructive Christian theology of the image of God is that neither modernity's self-affirmed, self-

22. McGrath, *ScT* 1:111, with a reference to Barthes, *Mythologies*, p. 108. In this section I am indebted to McGrath's incisive and richly sourced discussion (pp. 111-12 particularly).

23. Grenz, *Social God*, p. 97; see also Martin and Barresi, *Rise and Fall of Soul and Self*, pp. 255-64.

24. Grenz, *Social God*, pp. 98-137, here p. 133.

sufficient identity, nor postmodernity's self-constructed, self-referential identity, is an option. Instead, a robustly God-referential, holistic, and communion-driven account based on trinitarian resources will be attempted. In that account, rationality, physicality, emotions, and sociality all play key roles particularly when the deepest biblical intuitions are rediscovered and put in conversation with current neurological, behavioral, and other scientific fields of study, all done with a willingness to learn from theologies of the Global South and female theologians and other liberationists.

Image of God as Divine Destiny: A Theological Reading of the Growth of Tradition

From Structural to Relational Interpretation

There is a definite hermeneutical development in the history of interpretations of *imago Dei*. Whereas in early theology, the structural[25] view — the idea that there is something within the structure of human beings that makes us the image of God, whether reason or will or something similar — was in the foreground, by the time of the Reformation, the relational view came to be preferred. In relational interpretations, what is crucial about the image of God is humanity's placement in reference to God (and derivatively, other human beings). Without necessarily leaving behind either one of these approaches, in modernity, influenced also by the emerging evolutionary theory, the dynamic view came to dominate. In that outlook, human beings are considered to be on the way, so to speak, to their final destination. The image of God is the divinely set destiny as much as a present reality.[26] This hardly was a new invention. Just consider Irenaeus, who linked the image to the eschatological vision at the end of his discussion of the recapitulation theory.[27]

The diversity of interpretations is understandable because the biblical materials themselves do not explicitly elaborate in a significant way on the phrase "image of God."[28] Historical, cultural, philosophical, religious, and sociopolitical factors have all played roles in determining what the image is.[29]

Notwithstanding differences among the patristic interpreters, reason

25. So named in Brunner, *The Christian Doctrine of Creation and Redemption*, p. 59.
26. I am indebted to Grenz, *Social God*, particularly chap. 4.
27. Irenaeus, *Against Heresies* 5.36.3.
28. For OT, see Jónsson, *Image of God*; for NT: Schnelle, *Human Condition*.
29. See Harrison, *God's Many Splendored Image*, pp. 30-33.

came to dominate the structural view,[30] often coupled with will.[31] While both rationality and will obviously belong among the central features of the human being, it was not from the Bible but rather from Hellenistic philosophy that they were borrowed.[32] That alone is not a problem; theology gleans all the time from the context. What is problematic is if the external influence is not in keeping with biblical intuitions. In the Bible, it is not rationality or will but rather the placement of humanity in relation to God that is central. That said, the linking of reason and will with the image is of course not all mistaken. Reason and will are necessary for the establishment of freedom, including moral freedom, the potential of becoming what God intended the human being to be.[33] An important related implication of human freedom (granted by virtue of the image) is the equality of all human beings, including both sexes.[34] Indeed, freedom also related to the slaves[35] and even lepers.[36] Furthermore, freedom of religion was established on the same basis.[37] We conclude that while neither reason nor will should be taken as *the* meaning of the image, the necessity of both for the freedom of humanity is to be maintained.

No single feature or "commodity" or characteristic, not even "soul" (as Augustine first thought because of the Manichean influence),[38] can be named

30. This came to culmination in Augustine; see, e.g., *Confessions* 13.32; *City of God* 12.24; *On Christian Doctrine* 1.22; for detailed discussion, see Grenz, *Social God,* pp. 152-57.

31. Representative is Justin Martyr, *First Apology* 28; *Dialogue with Trypho* 141.

32. The background to the centrality of reason lies in the Aristotelian idea of the human person as "rational animal." Aristotle, *On the Soul* 3.3.

33. Gregory of Nyssa, *On the Making of Man* 4.16; Irenaeus, *Against Heresies* 4.37.1, 4. Cf. the comment by Joel B. Green (private e-mail, 9/28/2013): "It isn't that patristic interpreters focus on 'reason.' It is that many patristic interpreters focus on 'the soul,' which they define as a 'reasonable soul,' and this 'reasonable soul' would then be equated with the immortal soul (over against the 'animal soul' shared with other creatures)." For details, see J. Green, *Practicing Theological Interpretation,* chap. 3 particularly. While I endorse Green's critique of the patristic focus on reason, I also give more credit to the rational capacity in humanity, as the subsequent discussion reveals.

34. Augustine, *Literal Meaning of Genesis* 3.22.34; for passages in Clement of Alexandria, Basil of Caesarea, and others, see Harrison, *God's Many Splendored Image,* pp. 92-96.

35. Gregory of Nyssa, *Greater Catechism* 5; for other testimonies, see Harrison, *God's Many Splendored Image,* pp. 97-99.

36. See Harrison, *God's Many Splendored Image,* pp. 99-102.

37. See the important passage "Of the Freedom of Religion in the Worship of God" by Lactantius, *The Epitome of Divine Institutes* 54. For a detailed discussion of freedom in these and other Fathers, see Harrison, *God's Many Splendored Image,* chap. 1. For implications for the political sphere, see Rist, "Augustine on Free Will and Predestination," pp. 420-47.

38. Augustine, *Confessions* 5.10.19. As late as the nineteenth century, the Lutheran John

as the meaning of the image. Slowly patristic theology came to the conclusion that the whole human person is the *imago*.[39] Indeed, the Fathers rightly intuited that the final eschatological vision of God cannot be had without the body.[40] Although body-soul dualism still continues, the linking of the image with embodiment was an important benefit. The Fathers also reminded us that with all our rational investigation into the meaning of the image of God, ultimately human personhood remains a mystery, not only because we do not know enough but also because that is the nature of "person," reflecting the mysterious personhood of God (Rom. 11:34).[41]

The structural interpretation continued to dominate in medieval theology, culminating with Aquinas, whose "two-story anthropology" came to refine the patristic image-likeness distinction;[42] therein, the "supernatural gifts" (faith, hope, love) have been lost with the Fall, but the "natural" gifts, including reason and will, are (almost) intact.[43] By the time of the Reformation, "[t]he relational understanding of the *imago Dei* moves the focus from noun to verb," focusing on the relationship between the Creator and creatures. This means "the birth of the relational imago."[44] Calvin's covenant theology and Luther's *coram Deo* (before God) are hallmarks of that turn. Calvin's vision of relation as the "mirror of divinity"[45] clearly expresses the relation to God as the key to understanding *imago*.[46] Restoring the "rectitude" makes it possible for the human person to fully mirror the Creator.[47] Similarly to the Genevan Reformer, to the Wittenbergian, soteriological concerns were in the forefront. The main point to Luther is that even reason and will (which he otherwise affirms as the key to the image)[48] only matter insofar as they function in terms of directing us to God.[49] Restoration can only happen "through the Word and the Holy

---

Theodore Mueller (*Christian Dogmatics*, p. 207) located *imago* in the soul and only in the body insofar as it is "the organ of the soul"!

39. Irenaeus, *Against Heresies* 5.6.1; Gregory of Nyssa, *On the Making of Man* 29; for examples from Maximus the Confessor, see Wilken, "Biblical Humanism," pp. 25-26.

40. Augustine, *Literal Meaning of Genesis* 12.35.68; Irenaeus, *Against Heresies* 5.6.1.

41. Gregory of Nyssa, *On the Making of Man* 11; similarly, Augustine takes up this theme often, e.g., in his musings on the mystery of mind and memory in *Confessions* 10.15-25; 8.13, 14.

42. See Grenz, *Social God*, pp. 186-90.

43. Aquinas, *ST* 1.93.1, 9; Grenz, *Social God*, pp. 157-61.

44. Grenz, *Social God*, p. 162; see also Ramsey, *Basic Christian Ethics*, p. 255.

45. Calvin, *Hebrews*, 9:3.

46. Torrance, *Calvin's Doctrine of Man*, p. 36, quoted in Grenz, *Social God*, p. 166.

47. Calvin, *Institutes* 1.15.3; Calvin, *Galatians and Ephesians*, Eph. 4:24.

48. See Luther, *Disputation Concerning Man*, theses 4, 5, 6, 9; *LW* 34:137.

49. Luther, *Lectures on Genesis 1-5*; *LW* 1:90.

Spirit."[50] As a result of the rediscovery of relationality in contemporary (to us) scientific worldview and philosophy in general and Christian theology in particular (related to the trinitarian renaissance and rise of communion theologies), relationality and sociality have become a key theme in current theological anthropology, albeit somewhat differently conceived than in tradition (to be discussed below).

"Humanity in the Becoming": The Rise of the Dynamic View

While the relational view continued to be supported by several luminaries among modern Reformed thinkers, including S. Kierkegaard and E. Brunner,[51] the dynamic view emerged as the dominant one beginning in the nineteenth century. As mentioned, its roots were in strands of patristic theology, particularly Irenaeus. Although contemporary exegesis cannot maintain Irenaeus's distinction between image and likeness of God (the former remained after the Fall whereas the latter was lost), Irenaeus's view materially establishes the future-oriented dynamic interpretation.[52] Importantly, he also linked the image with Christ;[53] by virtue of the divine incarnation we are "shown" what the true image means.[54] Christ became incarnate with the will "to bring the fullness of the divine image and likeness to humankind, a fullness that encompasses all dimensions of human existence."[55] Consequently, "the image of God is not something to be found in man, but is rather the direction in which we are to grow."[56] An important asset to Irenaeus (and the subsequent Eastern Orthodox tradition) is the dramatically different understanding of the Fall. Rather than a catastrophic fall of a perfect human person, it is rather an unfortunate and tragic stumbling of yet immature "children" in their walk toward maturity and perfection.[57] Although humans are created in God's image and are free, they are not created perfect, but rather immature, with the "capacity for growth that enables them to respond to God's invitations and come to maturity."[58]

50. Luther, *Lectures on Genesis* 6–14; *LW* 2:141.
51. For details, see Grenz, *Social God,* pp. 173-77.
52. Irenaeus, *Against Heresies* 5.6.1, commenting on the meaning of "perfect" in 1 Cor. 2:6.
53. Irenaeus, *Proof of the Apostolic Preaching* 22; in Smith, trans., p. 54.
54. Irenaeus, *Against Heresies* 5.16.2.
55. Grenz, *Social God,* p. 146.
56. González, *History of Christian Thought,* p. 165, cited in Grenz, *Social God,* p. 147.
57. Irenaeus, *Against Heresies* 3.22.4; 3.23.5; 4.38.1-2.
58. Donovan, *One Right Reading?* p. 129. For the classic statement, see Irenaeus, *Against Heresies* 4.38.3; Clement of Alexandria (*Stromata* 6.12) materially agreed.

An important pre-Darwinian advocate of the "evolving image of God,"[59] the philosophical anthropologist J. G. Herder echoed the Irenaean ideas by surmising that God has implanted the direction in human hearts toward future self-improvement and ultimate destiny, which — unlike those Enlightenment thinkers to whom the destiny was totally human-made — has to do with religion.[60] Similarly, the nineteenth-century theologian I. A. Dorner related the image to future destiny, communion with God. The image "is to be viewed partly as original endowment, partly destination."[61] Herder's goal was "to describe the unfinished humanity of human beings in such a way as simultaneously to counter the difficulty that the fulfillment of human destiny cannot be thought of as the accomplishment of the very ones in whose lives that destiny is to become a reality."[62] Only by virtue of capacity for self-transcendence — which, "Christianly" speaking, has as its reference God — can the hoped-for (and implanted, so to speak) destiny be achieved. Among some leading twentieth-century theologians, particularly Rahner and Pannenberg, the idea of transcendence, variously named ("openness to the world," "exocentricity," or even "spirit"), was made a key *theological* anthropological concept.[63]

The American Lutheran theologian Ted Peters has made the exocentric, future-driven interpretation the leading motif: "In the proleptic framework . . . I will view the image of God in humans as the call forward, as the divine draw toward future reality. We are becoming."[64] Building on Irenaeus, Peters speaks of *pre*capitulation: "Christ established ahead of time what it is that will define who we as humans shall be."[65] That is because "[b]ecoming human, in the last analysis then, is not really a restoration to a prefallen state of grace that humans once possessed and then lost. It is not a return to the old generation. It is rather a future arrival for the first time. It is participation in the new creation."[66]

As mentioned, the three main hermeneutical traditions of the *imago Dei* (structural, relational, dynamic) are not to be taken as alternatives but rather taken as complementary. That said, the pendulum has clearly shifted

---

59. Pannenberg, *TA*, p. 50.

60. Herder, *Outlines of a Philosophy*, IV.6 (pp. 98-105); see Grenz, *Social God*, pp. 179-80.

61. Dorner, *System of Christian Doctrine*, 2:78.

62. Pannenberg, *TA*, pp. 47-60, here p. 60.

63. See Pannenberg, *TA*, pp. 60-74.

64. T. Peters, *God — the World's Future*, p. 147. Before him, for example, Macquarrie, *Principles of Christian Theology*, p. 76; Orr, *Christian View of God and the World*, p. 140.

65. T. Peters, *God — the World's Future*, p. 152.

66. T. Peters, *God — the World's Future*, p. 156.

toward the dynamic while holding on to the importance of sociality as well. The constructive proposal will build on this basic result won from the theological reading of history. The dynamic view will be developed in the trinitarian framework — for the simple reason that if humanity reflects God and God is triune, Trinity and image are integrally related.

A Trinitarian Theology of the Image of God

The Triune God and Humanity in Relation

Whatever else the image of God means, it means that humanity is referred to God. "In disclosing himself as the God-who-has-made-us-for-himself, the Creator discloses to us that we are the creature-uniquely-related-to-him."[67] We are referred *theologically* — and *christologically,* as the NT teaching on the image reveals. Indeed, in that light, we have to conclude that we humans are "copies" of the image, whereas Christ alone is the "original" image (2 Cor. 3:18).

The trinitarian conception of God in Christian tradition tells us that the creation of humanity is based on self-giving love of the Father. The creative act of the Father through the Son means "that God's creating is rooted in an eternal dynamic relation in which Godself is given and received as God's intelligibly wise self-expression, God's 'Word' in which is expressed God's glory, incomprehensibility, and holiness — the fullness of God's mystery." Absolutely free and uncontrollable (John 3:6), the gift of life is given to human beings,[68] who as creatures are "living on borrowed breath."[69] If the Son is God's self-expression, then it means that in some real sense humanity also expresses God and divine qualities.

Among the number of suggestions concerning the meaning of the plural ("Let us . . .") in Genesis 1:26,[70] the most likely is not only the plural of majesty but also — from a Christian trinitarian perspective — "a plural of deliberation" or "a communing with his own heart."[71] Communion theology is at work here. Having been created in the image of God, then, is linked with

---

67. P. Jewett, *Who We Are,* p. 18; see further, Weber, *Foundations of Dogmatics,* 1:529-33.

68. D. Kelsey, *Eccentric Existence,* 1:123-24, here p. 123.

69. D. Kelsey, *Eccentric Existence,* vol. 1, title for part 1.

70. For other suggestions, see Westermann, *Genesis 1–11,* pp. 144-47. See also Middleton, *Liberating Image,* pp. 55-60.

71. Moltmann, *God in Creation,* p. 217.

personhood, communion, relationality, belonging.[72] There is a deep social reference here.[73]

In sum: the basic statement about humanity is relatedness to God. That is the only way to ensure that all human beings, regardless of their capacities — whether rational, emotional, relational, or other — exist in the state of the image of God. Or else, for example, the intellectually disabled could not. Even when it comes to relationality, the basis has to be God relating to the human being, rather than the measure of the human person's capacity to relate. Namely, there are people who do not have the capacity to reciprocate relationality.[74] Here Pannenberg's observation that the human person "has a centre not only in itself but also beyond itself"[75] is useful. The Spirit's role comes to the fore here. It is only through the Spirit of God — the source of life and growth — that true existence, self-transcendence, can happen. True freedom — contrary to the utopian vision of atheism, based on human independence — can only be reached through opening up to the freedom to the Spirit. (From a theological perspective, the "beyond itself" is God, as it clearly was for Jesus.)[76]

While not without its challenges, Calvin O. Schrag's quest for "the self after postmodernity" makes the valid point that concerning personhood, the *who* question should replace the Cartesian *what* that pursues "an abstract universal nature."[77] I depart from Schrag in that, rather than the quest becoming that of the "questioner," which still is subject-oriented, the quest is put in relation to God and covenantal relationship. That gives meaning even to the *who* question and points to the ultimate destiny of humanity. Eschatologically oriented — and in keeping with the evolving nature of identity development in general[78] — "[t]he story of the self is a developing story, a story subject to

72. For details of divine communion and its implications, see *Trinity and Revelation*, chaps. 11 and 13 particularly. For the dynamic intertextuality of the singular and plural in divine self-address in Gen. 1:26-27, see Moltmann, *God in Creation*, pp. 217-18.

73. See Cairns, *Image of God in Man*, p. 44.

74. See Reinders, *Receiving the Gift of Friendship*, p. 274. Wolterstorff's *Justice: Rights and Wrongs* (p. 352), which anchors the image in "human nature" rather than capacities, makes a similar point, although I am not quite sure what this generic term "human nature" may mean.

75. As explained nontechnically in John Macquarrie's review of Pannenberg's *Anthropology in Theological Perspective*, "What Is a Human Being?"

76. Pannenberg, "The Christological Foundation of Christian Anthropology," p. 99. This is of course the implication of the classical christological concept of *enhypostasis*, that is, Christ's "personality" is in Logos/God.

77. Schrag, *Self after Postmodernity*, p. 22.

78. For theological reflections on identity formation, see Pannenberg, *ST* 2:201-2 and 51-52; more widely chap. 5 in Pannenberg, *TA*.

a creative advance, wherein the past is never simply a series of nows that have lapsed into beings, but a text, an inscription of events and experiences, that stands open to new interpretation and new perspectives of meaning."[79] As the theologian Michael S. Horton observes, "[i]n this narrative construction, the self is neither wholly self-determined . . . nor wholly determined by the past or by the present but is relatively open to the future."[80] It is easy to see how well the relational-dynamic view reconciles with evolutionary theory in sciences. And it is difficult to see how any new insight in sciences could frustrate this trinitarian theological account.[81] "Our evolutionary derivation does not rule out the immediacy of our relation to God . . . [particularly because] our relation to God is an express theme as a condition of our own creaturely life and our survival. We humans deal thematically with something that is a fact for all creaturely existence" (namely, the reference to Creator/God).[82]

Pannenberg rightly notes that "If our creation in God's image means that we are to seek God, to honor him as God, . . . and to thank him as the Author of life and of every good gift, then we may assume that there is a disposition to do so in every human life, no matter how little we see of it in a given case."[83] This capacity and inclination is internal to us — against Barth's misguided protestations.[84]

Although rationality, as mentioned, cannot be the defining factor in a truly trinitarian grammar, it plays an important role. If creation happened in and through the Logos, the divine "reason," then it means that rationality is deeply embedded in reality. In humanity, as the most developed form of creaturely existence, reason has come to its highest expression. Rahner put it succinctly: "human beings are bodily creatures who have a fundamentally unlimited transcendentality and unlimited openness to being as such in knowledge and freedom."[85] Christian theology should hold fast to both the capacity for transcendence, which also enables a personal relation to the triune God, and the embodiedness of transcendence in materiality, the bodily nature of humanity.

---

79. Schrag, *Self after Postmodernity,* p. 37, cited in Horton, "Image and Office," p. 197.

80. Horton, "Image and Office," p. 198.

81. See Nietzsche, *On the Genealogy of Morals* (1887), III.25, p. 591.

82. Pannenberg, *ST* 2:135. One is reminded here of the naming of the human being as "sacred animal" *(sanctum animal)* in Lactantius, *Divine Institutes* 6.20.

83. Pannenberg, *ST* 2:227.

84. Thereby Barth also defended the idea that the image cannot be lost if in the first place it did not belong to us (*CD* III/1, p. 200).

85. Rahner, *Theological Investigations,* 21:42.

An essential feature of the Jewish-Christian understanding of the image is its universal nature: not only each human person but also humanity as a whole exists in the image of God.[86] If the human destiny is referred to the Creator, then it means that it cannot be achieved alone. The same Creator has set the same destiny for all of humanity. Furthermore, in reference to the royal connotations of the term "image,"[87] it is not illegitimate to see it as a form of "democratization," as the royal language was applied to common folks, unlike in (then) contemporary cultures.[88] Universality is also further consolidated by the conviction that however one negotiates the relation of the *imago* to sin, there is a wide agreement that likeness-to-God was not lost as a result of the Fall.[89]

An important implication of the relatedness to the Creator is the mandate and responsibility to serve as God's vice-regents. The God-given task to name the creatures points to this (Gen. 2:19-20). In the ancient world — as in some cultures in our day — naming means exercising power and authority. In evolutionary history, the development of language is of course needed for naming.[90] The capacity and feature of humanity, unique among creatures, that makes it possible is "exocentric transcendence," the capacity to reach beyond the immediate horizon, all the way to making a distinction between the finite and the infinite. The capacity to define the individuality of things is the basis for human comastery of nature.[91] This mandate does not justify any abuse or objectification of nature but rather is an invitation to a responsible and faithful service on behalf of God's creation.

The divine mandate raises the question of whether the *imago Dei* is limited to only one species in the vast creation, namely, humanity.[92] Gilkey surmised that the whole of creation rather is meant by the image.[93] That view would have the benefit of noting not only human relation to God but also

86. Contra Wilken, "Biblical Humanism," p. 20 (who misunderstands Augustine's point about memory being "my" memory instead of someone else's). Cf. Hegel, *Lectures on the Philosophy of History*, pp. 18-19.

87. Westermann, *Genesis*, pp. 36-37.

88. Wenham, *Genesis 1–15*, pp. 30-31.

89. Westermann, *Genesis 1–11*, p. 148.

90. See further, Ayala, "Human Nature," pp. 41-45; for Jewish comments, see Cohon, *Jewish Theology*, p. 294.

91. Pannenberg, *TA*, p. 36.

92. Considering angels as the bearers of the image of God, Aquinas went so far as to wonder whether angels are "more" in the image of God than humans! *ST* 1.93.3. I am indebted to Dr. Olli-Pekka Vainio for reminding me of Thomas's view.

93. Gilkey, *Nature, Reality, and the Sacred*, pp. 175-92.

human relation to the rest of creation, it has been argued.[94] As appealing as that view is, it cannot be affirmed without much qualification. Of course, it is true that human destiny is deeply embedded in the destiny of all created reality; just consider Romans 8:22-23.[95] However, the point of the biblical narrative is to stress the uniqueness of humanity among the creatures. The *theological* importance of the statement of the image of God is further accentuated by the observation that, on the one hand, the human being comes into existence by a special divine resolve rather than a general creative word, as does the rest of creation, and that, on the other hand, humanity is addressed directly by the Creator in a way no other creatures are. In this context, we also have to appreciate the "direct transfer of the divine breath" (Gen. 2:7) belonging to the uniqueness of human creation[96] (not in terms of setting us apart from other creatures as all life is the function of the divine Spirit, but in terms of special intimacy and directness of God's act). Moltmann rightly notes that in this divine resolve, there is also a hint of self-humiliation as "God 'implants' his image and his glory in his earthly creation, the human being, which means that he himself is drawn into the history of these creatures of his."[97]

The Image of God and the Economy of Salvation

There is an integral trinitarian grammar of the economy of salvation, including the redemption of the whole of creation, in the *imago* theology. Moltmann offers a useful template for outlining the course of the economy of salvation in terms of three interrelated facets of the image of God:[98]

1. as the original designation of human beings: *imago Dei;*
2. as the messianic calling of human beings: *imago Christi;*
3. as the eschatological glorification of human beings: *Gloria Dei est homo.*

While Christian theology begins the consideration of the image of God from the first creation story, it is only in light of Christ's coming that the full

94. Peterson, "Are We Unique?" pp. 159, 177; I am indebted to Fisher, *Human Significance*, p. 178.
95. See further, Moltmann, *God in Creation*, p. 189.
96. Eichrodt, *Theology of the Old Testament*, 2:121.
97. Moltmann, *God in Creation*, p. 217.
98. Moltmann, *God in Creation*, p. 215.

meaning is known. This is not to leave behind what the Jewish Torah says; it is rather to maintain it in a way that also integrates the image into the meaning of Israel's and Christians' Messiah. The fulfillment of humanity does not come by way of return to the mythical paradisal beginning but rather by the historically anchored and eschatologically fulfilled christological end (2 Cor. 3:18).[99] Irenaeus famously said: "For the glory of God is a living man; and the life of man consists in beholding God."[100] The glory of God is seen fully in Jesus Christ, the archetype of the image of God (2 Cor. 4:4). The eschatological hope for the believers who are continuously being conformed into the image of Christ (2 Cor. 3:18) is to see Christ face-to-face (1 Cor. 13:12); then, and only then, they shall be like him (1 John 3:2). That marks the final culmination of the fulfillment of the image of God. This is of course the essence of the ancient patristic and even current Eastern Orthodox vision of *theosis.*

The linking together of creation, Christology, and eschatology raises an important systematic question, namely, whether the divinely set destiny is pertinent to this life or to the life to come.[101] Under the tutelage of Kant and modern liberal theologians, the former position — moral life in the present world — became the focus, although reference to the future eternal life was not thereby denied, particularly among thinkers such as Herder.[102] Conservative theology counterattacked. For constructive theology, however, there is no reason to see present and future as alternatives. They presuppose each other as part of the unfolding of the historical salvific acts of the triune God from creation to redemption to the coming of the new creation.

An essential implication of the reference to the Creator as the "foundation" of human life and personhood is the establishment of human dignity. Let us delve more deeply into this theme that has already been present in the argumentation implicitly.

The Dignity of Human Life

Christian tradition routinely located the uniqueness and dignity of human life in the immortal soul. While understandable, that move is hardly supported by the biblical data; what is, however, affirmed in the biblical teaching is the link

---

99. Moltmann, *God in Creation*, pp. 225, 227.

100. Irenaeus, *Against Heresies* 4.20.7.

101. Importantly, Pannenberg entitles the section that discusses the image of God "Human Destiny" (§2; *ST* 2:202-31).

102. See further, Pannenberg, *ST* 2:222-23.

between the image of God and the inviolability of human life (Gen. 9:6).[103] In keeping with the discussion above, the locus of the dignity is the whole human being (and humanity at large) set in relation to God.[104]

While not uniquely a biblical or Christian idea,[105] only the image of God and, as a result, the "destiny of fellowship with God confers inviolability on human life in the person of each individual."[106] Pannenberg correctly concludes: "A feature of the dignity that accrues to us by virtue of our being destined for fellowship with God is that no actual humiliation that might befall us can extinguish it. In a special way, because they have nothing else that commands respect, the faces of the suffering and humbled and deprived are ennobled by the reflection of this dignity that none of us has by merit, that none of us can receive from others, and that no one can take from us."[107]

While Christian theology should give full support to human attempts to establish human dignity on "natural grounds," particularly as it is affirmed by the United Nations,[108] it also has to highlight the necessary reference to God, including the eschatological hope for the life everlasting in union with the Creator. In this respect, even the establishment of the irreducible dignity of each human person based on the "humanism of the other" by the Jewish thinker Emmanuel Levinas in itself is not sufficient, although necessary from the viewpoint of Christian theology. Merely calling the ethical responsibility toward the other "holy" is not able to sustain dignity apart from God.[109] Modern theology too often missed this point in its separation of the dignity from God altogether — as noted in the discussion of the formation of self above, culminating in the conception of an independent substantial self.[110] Indeed, some contemporary Protestant theologians came "often to rely upon unexamined secularized notions of human dignity, or to reject dignity altogether as an unbiblical and therefore unhelpful concept."[111] (On

103. Some early theologians rightly saw this: Theophilus of Antioch, *To Autolycus* 2.18; Gregory of Nyssa, *On the Making of Man* 3, among others; Ambrose, *De dignitate conditionis humanae* (PL 17:1105-8), also Lebech, *On the Problem of Human Dignity,* pp. 64-68.

104. See comments on Ps. 8:4 by the OT scholar Eichrodt, *Theology of the Old Testament,* 2:120-21, 126.

105. See, e.g., Cicero, *De officiis* 1.30.106, who anchored dignity in rationality.

106. Pannenberg, *ST* 2:176.

107. Pannenberg, *ST* 2:177.

108. See *Charter of the United Nations* (June 26, 1945), preamble.

109. See Cohen, introduction to *Humanism of the Other,* p. xvi.

110. Soulen and Woodhead, "Introduction," p. 9; see also Gushee, *Sacredness of Human Life,* chap. 7.

111. Soulen and Woodhead, "Introduction," p. 2; see also Witte, "Between Sanctity and Depravity," p. 121.

the contrary, current Roman Catholic theology has been far keener on securing the dignity and has reflected extensively on its significance.)[112] This oblivion is supported by a number of voices coming from some feminists with the suspicion that dignity is a statement about male prominence, from postcolonial theorists with the assumption of its link with unjust and illegitimate power structures in the world, and so forth.

The atheological detachment of human dignity from God was ironically prepared by some earlier theologians, most prominently the fifteenth-century Pico della Mirandola. His humanistically flavored *De dignitate hominis* (1486) located the ultimate dignity in the human capacity to choose one's own destiny, to be "the molder and maker of thyself," indeed, capable to "sculpt thyself into whatever shape thou dost prefer," even to "grow upward . . . into the higher natures which are divine."[113] Of course, the ultimate vision of being united with the Divine is deeply Christian, but Mirandola's mythical vision seems to be detached from its christological and theological roots and made a "natural" human project.[114] Herein of course he anticipated Kant's view of rationality as the asset for establishing human autonomy and freedom.[115] Kant was instrumental in helping turn the tables in modern philosophy and theology: whereas in the past the dignity of humanity was dependent on God, in this new world, the "idea of God is dependent on human dignity as its source and norm." In other words, having established the dignity on its own account, Kant reintroduced the concept of God to ground morality *(The Critique of Practical Reason).*[116]

In Nietzsche we see the tragic effects of the turn away from any reference to God in relation to affirmation of human dignity and the virtual loss of the concept altogether.[117] The modern atheists following him all the way from Marx took the insight of human autonomy and refused to reintroduce the concept of God altogether; the contemporary "scientific" atheists such as Dawkins have made this a major project.[118] The critical task of constructive

112. See Pope Benedict XVI's encyclical *Caritas in Veritate* (2009) and the *Dignitatis Humanae* of Pope Paul VI (1965). For current statements, see the United States Conference of Catholic Bishops, "Human Life and Dignity."

113. Mirandola, *On the Dignity of Man,* p. 5, quoted in Soulen and Woodhead, "Introduction," p. 10. Notwithstanding scholarly debate about Mirandola's view in this regard (cf. Zimmermann, *Incarnational Humanism,* pp. 136-38), it seems to me it is uncontested that his ideas were used in later tradition to fund a secular view of humanity.

114. For comments, see Soulen and Woodhead, "Introduction," p. 10.

115. See Kant, *Fundamental Principles,* section 2.

116. Soulen and Woodhead, "Introduction," p. 11.

117. For a detailed discussion, see Gushee, *Sacredness of Human Life,* chap. 8.

118. For critical discussion, see *Trinity and Revelation,* chap. 9.

theology is to rediscover the derivation of human dignity from its reference to God and thus critique modernity's call for autonomy. Contrary to secular opinion, "once removed from theological and ecclesial context, the concept of human dignity proves remarkably fragile — insufficient to sustain the ethical and metaphysical weight that modern rights-talk would place upon it."[119]

What about the biblical teaching that all creatures, not only humans, are related to God (Ps. 104:21) and praise the name of the Lord (Ps. 150:6)? Only human beings can be said to have "learned to see divine reality in its distinction from everything finite." Therefore, "[o]nly humans . . . have religion." Again, this is not to deny the deep linking of humanity with the rest of creation, nor the biblical intuition that in some way — but not intentionally, so it seems — even other animals are referred to their Creator in some real sense (Ps. 104:21).[120]

So far we have used the concept "dignity" as if we knew its meaning. A minimalist, yet robust, definition like the following serves us well here: "[E]ach and every human being has been set apart for designation as a being of elevated status and dignity. Each human being must therefore be viewed with reverence and treated with due respect and care, with special attention to preventing any desecration or violation of a human being."[121] The reference to the Creator does not of course mean that only those who acknowledge the Creator can be granted full dignity. The universal nature of humanity as the image of God relates the dignity to all. This is also the theological basis for the equality of all — a conviction that was reached already in early Christian tradition (often in criticism of pagan thought),[122] although its many implications, say in relation to sexism and slavery, took a long time to be fully grasped.

Although the conviction that humans represent the most highly developed creatures has been used in Christian tradition to dissociate humans from the rest of creation, that claim does not necessarily have to imply separation. It can be reasoned, rather, that exactly as the most highly developed creatures, men and women have the biggest responsibility to be mindful of their deep links with the rest of the life of the cosmos and the well-being of the planet in which they find their dwelling place.

Is the conclusion then that humanity is the ultimate goal of evolution and the cosmos? The response to this question includes several considerations.

119. Soulen and Woodhead, "Introduction," pp. 14-15.
120. Pannenberg, *ST* 2:134.
121. Gushee, *Sacredness of Human Life*, pp. 16-36, here p. 24.
122. See Minucius Felix, *Octavius* 16.

First of all, I agree with the Jewish authority Maimonides that each creature of God has its own intrinsic value that is not to be derived from humanity.[123] Second, even if in light of our current knowledge humanity represents the highest level, in principle it does not follow that therefore a higher type of being could never evolve (although currently no empirical evidence exists).[124] Third, in light of the incarnation of Jesus Christ, it has to be said that humanity — or something similar with which the divine may be hypostatically united — represents the apex of evolution.[125] That statement, however, is not about the nobility of human creatures; it is about the divine initiative to establish the union in this unique way.

But does the ultimate grounding of the dignity and value of human life in reference to God threaten — or perhaps totally deny — human freedom, as philosophical atheism has argued since Feuerbach? Theological tradition's answer is *no*. That is because God the Creator has granted the creatures, most notably the human being, true and real independence. The theological significance of the sequence of the forms in the evolution of the cosmos has to do with the culmination of the gift of creaturely independence graciously granted by the Creator. As independence increases incrementally as we go higher up in the sequence,[126] it is justified to conclude that (in light of our current cosmological knowledge) humanity represents the culmination of that process. The independence of creatures does not mean separation from the Creator, not only because creaturely life by definition is not self-sustaining, but also because only by virtue of independence can the reality of the creature's life be ascertained. Only in distinction from the Creator can the creature affirm his or her own life.[127] A gracious gift of God, independence does not have to be won from God;[128] therefore, the atheistic charge of the lack of freedom as a result of faith in God/ religion does not follow. An important corollary is that therefore, in the domain of religion (and other such ultimate beliefs), no coercion should be allowed.[129]

We have established human uniqueness and dignity in the relatedness to God, so the next task becomes constructing a more detailed and comprehen-

---

123. Maimonides, *Guide for the Perplexed* 3.13-14; he also reminds us (1.59) that ultimately God is the final purpose of everything, the end of all ends.

124. Cf. Pannenberg, *ST* 2:132-33.

125. Pannenberg, *ST* 2:137.

126. Pannenberg, *ST* 2:127.

127. Pannenberg, *ST* 2:133-34.

128. Pannenberg, *ST* 2:135.

129. A classic contemporary statement is Pope Paul VI's encyclical *Dignitatis Humanae* (1965).

sive account of the human being as a relational, holistic, embodied creature. In that constructive task, we will also utilize the insights from evolutionary science and other sciences that study humanity. That investigation, in turn, will lead to a focused investigation of the nature ("composition") of human nature in the following chapter.

The trinitarian, "participatory ontology" of Christian theology — also named recently "incarnational humanism" — undergirds a comprehensive, holistic, and multidimensional view of humanity that laid the foundation for the major ideals of Western culture. "Our understanding of personhood (balancing the individual and social self), of human dignity and rights, of freedom conceived as responsibility, of the value of language, of the importance of literature and art for self-knowledge, of the correlation of faith and reason (indeed of the spiritual and the material), and, finally, of education as character formation were decisively shaped by the Christian doctrine of the incarnation."[130] Let us reflect more carefully on the implications of a trinitarian account of humanity for a holistic and embodied view of human personhood.

Sociality, Emotions, and Embodiment: Toward a Holistic Account of Humanity

Both biblical scholars and neuroscientists are telling theologians that critical values shaping human personhood include sociality, embodiment, and emotionality, along with rationality of course. These values go back to the fundamentals of a biblical view of humanity and the implications of a trinitarian, relational theology of the human being as the image of God. According to the biblical scholar Robert Di Vito, in biblical perspective the human person

> 1) is deeply embedded, or engaged, in his or her social identity, 2) is comparatively decentered and undefined with respect to personal boundaries, 3) is relatively transparent, socialized, and embodied (in other words, is altogether lacking in a sense of "inner depths"), and 4) is "authentic" precisely in his or her heteronomy, in his or her obedience to another and dependence upon another.[131]

130. Zimmermann, *Incarnational Humanism*, p. 163; Harrison, *God's Many-Splendored Image*, chap. 8.
131. Di Vito, "Old Testament Anthropology," p. 221, quoted in J. Green, *Body, Soul, and Human Life*, p. 12. See also Di Vito, "Here One Need Not Be One's Self," pp. 49-88.

If so, then the goal of constructive theology is to reestablish and "return to embodied notions of humanness where our embodied imagination, sexuality, and moral awareness are directly linked to the fully embodied self-transcendence of believers who are in a relationship with God."[132] Let us first continue reflecting on the implications for our understanding of the human person through the lens of relationality.

A Communal and Relational Account of Personhood

As mentioned repeatedly, dynamic relationality has replaced the hegemony of a static substance ontology. In theological anthropology, commensurately, we view the human being as a relational being, in relation to God, to fellow human beings and creation, as well as to oneself. Importantly, these relations are not considered external but rather internal, formative to the human being.[133] The turn to relationality has helped theological anthropology think of the human person as *person* rather than as individual.[134] Rather than isolated, personhood is relational, communal, networked. It is not a statement against the unique personhood of each individual but rather a way to save us from the perils of rampant individualism in the Global North — unlike the cultures of the Global South.[135] In this relationally based, communion-driven theological anthropology, based on the trinitarian communion logic, "human and divine relationality [come] together in a mutually informing manner."[136] The Orthodox theologian John Zizioulas's combination of two classic theological/christological terms, *ekstasis* and *hypostasis,* is in turn meant to secure that to relationality, full personhood, and integrity: *ekstasis* — literally "standing-outside-of-one's-self" — means "openness of being . . . a transcendence of the boundaries of the 'self' which leads to . . . *freedom,*" whereas *hypostasis* speaks of human (and divine) personhood as "the bearer of its nature in its totality . . . the totality of human nature."[137] Pannenberg's "exocentricity" speaks of the same reality. These affirmations are needed for true personhood.

132. Van Huyssteen, *Alone in the World?* p. 267.
133. See Schwöbel, "Recovering Human Dignity," p. 47.
134. See the important work by McFadyen, *Call to Personhood.*
135. Carr, *Transforming Grace,* pp. 156-57. See also Yu, *Being and Relation.*
136. Grenz, *Social God,* p. xi; similarly Ratzinger, *In the Beginning . . . ,* p. 47; Pannenberg, *TA,* pp. 84-85.
137. Zizioulas, "Human Capacity," p. 408, including n. 3, emphasis in original.

Relationality and communion theology are the way to defeat the modernist Cartesian individualism, critiqued so harshly by theologians,[138] philosophers,[139] sociologists,[140] and others. Feminists of various sorts, other liberationists, and some postcolonialists say the same thing using different nomenclature. Herein constructive theology also has much to learn from our colleagues in the Global South. For example, in African settings, authentic humanity is defined in terms not of individuality but rather of commonality, and hence such terms as "caring, humble, thoughtful, considerate, understanding, wise, godly, generous, hospitable, mature, virtuous, and blessed" are at the center.[141]

Although theology has its own reasons for constructing a communion theology of human personhood, the importance of sociality in current scientific study of the evolution and development of humanity should not be understated. Sociality is deeply embedded in human development[142] and its evolutionary history.[143] Relationality's importance is acknowledged currently in a new way in the neuroscientific research as opposed to the individualist paradigm of the past. We know now that mental life is shaped and formed by social context,[144] including socialization and language.[145] Particularly important in this regard is the uniquely human capacity to discern other people as persons with their own subjectivity. Human persons are also capable of noticing other persons' intentions and activities (facilitated by "mirror neurons") as well as imputing mental states to others and predicting their behavior (the "Theory of Mind" [TOM]).[146] On the other hand, even the individual's access to one's own self works via others as we experience ourselves "indirectly" in the context of the reflected standpoints of the community.[147] The capacity to

138. J. Green, "Bodies," p. 158; for a brief, useful comparison between individualistic and relational approaches to personhood, see Gregersen, "Varieties of Personhood," pp. 2-4.

139. W. Barrett, *Death of the Soul.*

140. Bellah et al., *Habits of the Heart;* W. Barrett, *Death of the Soul.*

141. Kapolyo, *Human Condition,* p. 39.

142. For neuroscientific and behavioral research on "social mind," see Gazzaniga, *Who's in Charge?* chap. 5. For the classic social psychological work, see Mead, *Mind, Self, and Society,* and on its implications for theological anthropology, see Pannenberg, *TA,* chap. 4.

143. For a short useful discussion, see Brothers, "Neuroscientific Perspective on Human Sociality," p. 67.

144. See Arbib, "Towards a Neuroscience of the Person," pp. 79-80.

145. Brothers, *Friday's Footprints.*

146. See further, Murphy and Brown, *DMN,* pp. 31-34. TOM is missing in other animals: Call and Tomasello, "Does the Chimpanzee Have a Theory of Mind?" pp. 187-92.

147. Mead, *Mind, Self, and Society,* p. 138; on Mead, see Pannenberg, *TA,* pp. 185-90.

discern others and oneself in relation to others is deeply connected also with embodiment: "Persons are bodies with a first-person perspective."[148]

So, is all talk about the "inner life" then but a reintroduction of the Cartesian "ghost in the machine"? Not really. While acknowledging the value of many scholars' criticism of the lack of balance in the Augustinian turn inward[149] and particularly the Cartesian idea of the mind as an "inner theater," even here one has to resist reductionism and seek a radical middle. It simply is not true that all talk about inner life is mistaken or useless, particularly since "human life is experienced as an inner life expressed through embodied relation to other persons and the cosmos itself."[150] Hence, turning inward is not necessarily a flight from the rest of one's world, nor is it a visit to the only "true" self. Nor is the experience of God in one's inner spiritual life, when rightly conceived, in any way antisocial or "nonearthed" because "the place for the experience of God is not the mystical experience of the self; it is *the social experience of the self* and *the personal experience of sociality*."[151] If the development of mental life, including sociality, is a deeply embodied process, and if emotionality and imagination, along with rationality and intellect, form an essential part thereof, a promising holistic view of the human person as the image of God is in view.

Embodied and Emotional Human Personhood

The Body among Religions

The attitude toward the body among religions is confused and complex[152] — similar to problematic attitudes in philosophy, sociology, anthropology, and society at large.[153] The Jewish appreciation of and focus on the body are

148. Murphy and Brown, *DMN*, p. 30 n. 41, with a reference to the important book by Lynne Rudder Baker, *Persons and Bodies: A Constitution View.*

149. Augustine, *Confessions* 10.8; see Cary, *Augustine's Invention of the Inner Self.*

150. R. Anderson, *On Being Human*, p. 182. See also the helpful note by Farrer (*Freedom of the Will*, p. 90) that even in talking to oneself, the subject of the experience is the whole person.

151. Moltmann, *Spirit of Life*, p. 94, emphasis in original.

152. For a useful short orientation, see Coakley, "Introduction."

153. For a masterful accessible orientation, see Culianu, "Introduction," pp. 1-18; see also the essays by Turner, Assad, and Midgley in *RB*, part 1, "Contemporary Western Perspectives: Secularism and Body."

distinctive among religions due to their this-worldly focus on salvation and eschatology. That said, it is not correct to say that whereas Judaism is interested in the body, Christianity is interested in the soul; the doctrine of the resurrection of the body (let alone the incarnation) makes that merely a generalization. And recall that even among Jewish traditions there are different orientations: whereas the Hellenistic Judaism of Philo placed an accent on the immortality of the soul, the mainline rabbinic Judaism expected the resurrection of the body at the end. On the other hand, in the rabbinic literature (especially the Mishnah and the Talmud), soul-body dualism is prevalent, not unlike in Christian tradition. This is quite astonishing in light of the accent on embodiment in the OT — Holy Scripture for both Jews and Christians!

That said, the Jewish tradition has a number of valuable lessons to offer about embodiment. In the influential Kabbalah theosophic tradition that emerged in the twelfth century, the image of God is centered on body and bodily actions. The human body mirrors the image of the Godhead. Louis Jacobs also argues interestingly that the Sabbath system, while forbidding manual work, indirectly "constitutes in itself worship with the body, albeit by negation." In keeping with that, "the satisfaction of bodily needs and appetites on that day is enjoined as a religious duty," even to the point of indulgence. More generally, Jacobs argues that many other key religious rituals such as burial rites and priestly blessings, while keeping in tension the concentration on striving for spirituality and the need to keep religion earthbound, refrain from undermining, let alone stigmatizing, the body.[154]

The Islamic scriptures share the idea of human beings created of dust and returning to dust and that the dead will be resurrected on the judgment day. Somewhat like (Orthodox) Judaism but unlike Christianity, Islam does not distinguish between the religious and the secular; hence, the body is always looked at from a religious perspective, as is everything else. The Islamic law then regulates in much detail the right and wrong use of the body. What I have a hard time believing is that, as is often claimed, even among the Abrahamic faiths, Islam as "natural" religion regards everything in the human body natural and hence does not consider the body unclean or, for example, a handicap as something unnatural or a problem.[155] As an outsider, it also seems to me that the Qur'anic promises of heavenly life in terms of sensual pleasures including not only rest and plentiful food, as well as drink (forbidden in this

---

154. L. Jacobs, "The Body in Jewish Worship," pp. 71-89 (pp. 77, 78, respectively).

155. Consider, e.g., the well-known Qur'anic rule (5:6) concerning uncleanliness and "seminal pollution" with regard to prayers.

life), but also the enjoyment of virgins with beautiful eyes and the service of young boys (suras 44, 52, 55, 76, among others) have very little to do with an affirmation of the body per se (as in Christian tradition's bodily resurrection hope).[156]

In the various Hindu scriptures, as can be expected from such a wide array of traditions, many diverse attitudes can be discerned, "starting with the *Rg Veda* (which celebrates the body exuberantly) and the Upanisads (which warn of its treachery), through Sanskrit love poetry (predictably pro-body and libertine) and the Yogic texts (also pro-body, though in a rather different key, and certainly not libertine)."[157] The highly influential *Laws of Manu* exhibit diversity of attitudes toward the body, from contempt for its uncleanliness and uneasiness with its nature, including harsh misogyny (6.76-7), to acknowledgment of its "natural" nature and value (with regard to conception and birth, 9.31-42), to the affirmation of the body of both men and women (10.70-72).[158] In the midst of the diversity of views among Hindu movements, it is fair to say that fundamentally that tradition can hardly be taken as body-affirmative for many reasons, such as the appearance nature of reality (more of that below), the salvific desire of achieving release from all earthly matters in a purely spiritual realm, the denial or undermining of individual personality (apart from which one has a hard time in imagining embodiment), and so forth (these issues will be taken up in some detail in chapter 14).

In keeping with Hinduism, Buddhism in the main not only is dualistic in a general sense (body-soul) but also believes the body will come to an end at death. Like other ascetic teachings, Theravada Buddhism's canonical texts that deal with monastic life and spiritual exercises not only reject all bodily sexuality but also depreciate it.[159] Mahayana traditions' appraisal of the body is more complex for several reasons. First, unlike Theravada, it is not monastic in its orientation and therefore pays much less attention to the need for a particular kind of "taming" of the body to attain enlightenment. Enlightenment is

156. For the well-known explanation by the medieval Ibn al-Nafis according to which the Prophet's eschatological teachings are to be understood in terms of accommodation to the people's inability to grasp a more spiritual form of hope, see Meyerhof and Schacht, eds., *Theologus Autodidactus*, p. 57.

157. Doniger, "The Body in Hindu Texts," pp. 167-84, here p. 168.

158. *The Laws of Manu, SBE,* vol. 25; I am indebted to Doniger, "The Body in Hindu Texts," pp. 169-73.

159. Basic rules are set out in the last chapter (19) of Parivara (of Vinaya Tipitaka), of which it is very difficult to find an English translation. For representative passages, see S. Collins, "The Body in Theravada Buddhist Monasticism."

available — at least in principle — to all who desire it, and in many Mahayana traditions it can be voluntarily postponed for the benefit of others. Second, the whole concept of *kaya,* "body," is polyvalent, somewhat similar to the English term; it may mean flesh, a collection (as in "body of literature"), or the essence (as in "body of the text"). Not only that, but it is one of the key terms in theology, related to the famous *trikaya,* three bodies, doctrines of Buddha (the "transformation body," the "enjoyment body," and *"dhamma* body"). As discussed in chapter 10 of *Christ and Reconciliation,* there are some common themes and signs of what in Christian tradition is called incarnation, which may have implications for how to think of the human body.[160] That said, in authoritative scriptural texts a similar kind of depreciation of the body as unclean and frail can be found, similar to that of the original form of Buddhism.[161] In general, in all main Buddhist traditions, clinging to the body is a hindrance to enlightenment and should be renounced; body is impermanent, disposable, while the soul is "eternal," or at least qualitatively radically different from body. The ultimate goal of renouncing the body also means depreciation of desire for the opposite sex, another form of bodily want.[162]

The Theological Rediscovery of Body and Emotions

Philip Clayton reminds us of the necessity of a holistic, multidimensional account of human personhood of embodiment:

> We have thoughts, wishes, and desires that together constitute our character. We express these mental states through our bodies, which are simultaneously our organs of perception and our means of affecting other things and persons in the world. . . . [The massive literature on theories of personhood] clearly points to the indispensability of embodiedness as the precondition for perception and action, moral agency, community, and freedom — all aspects that philosophers take as indispensable to human personhood and that theologians have viewed as part of the *imago dei.*[163]

160. See also S. Hamilton, "From the Buddha to Buddhaghosa," pp. 46-63.

161. See *Siksā-samuccaya,* pp. 216-17.

162. For an important discussion, see Paul Williams, "Some Māhāyana Buddhist Perspectives on the Body," pp. 205-30. It seems to me that even in Tantric traditions, with their more celebratory attitude toward the body and sexuality, the idea of impermanence and turning away from the body still holds; for that, see pp. 220-28.

163. Clayton, "The Case for Christian Panentheism," p. 205.

While carefully learning from philosophers, scientists, and others, constructive theology also has its own integral reasons to speak for embodiment and holism.[164] Indeed, a number of key theological convictions fund embodiment, including the incarnation, the resurrection of the body,[165] and the "sacramental principle," that is, the Divine continuously appearing in "flesh" (symbolically in the Eucharist).[166] Appealing to the incarnational divine embodiment and the pronouncement of everything created as "good," including the material,[167] contemporary theology should robustly embrace the indispensable value of the bodily and corporeal, not only the "soulish" and "spiritual." Rather than flight from the body, a Christian view of creation funds intimacy, closeness, mutuality — values of whose importance some female and postcolonial theologians often remind us.[168]

Constructive theology should also follow the persistent "critique of dualistic metaphysics — including body/soul, matter/spirit, intelligible/sensible" by many female theologians and others.[169] One of the unfortunate effects of traditional dualisms one-sidedly favoring rationality as the key to the *imago*, as liberationists untiringly remind us, is the downplay of praxis, action, and experience.[170] Recall the American Reformed theologian William A. Dyrness's inclusion of embodiment, along with relationality and agency, among the three "normative categories" in the articulation of theological reality of our life in the world. Theology at large is yet to learn this simple but profound lesson: indeed, theologically we can say that, against the common suspicions, *"God as Creator is no closer to spirit than God is to physical matter."*[171] In this area, particularly the European American, white, male-dominated theological tradition is in need of correction from other Christian "cultures." Unlike many European American cultures, in black culture "[t]he body is not a hindrance but a vehicle for the true expression of the spiritual." Hence, it is understandable that particularly in traditional African cultures the bodily — and communal — nature

164. For a highly useful discussion of some leading contemporary theologians' views on embodiment, see van Huyssteen, *Alone in the World?* chaps. 3 and 6. For general orientation, consult Solomon, *The Passions.*

165. T. Peters, "Resurrection of the Very Embodied Soul?"

166. Ross, "God's Embodiment and Women," p. 193.

167. D. Kelsey, "Personal Bodies," p. 151.

168. Rivera, *Touch of Transcendence*, p. 7.

169. Rivera, *Touch of Transcendence*, p. 8; see also Ruether, "Dualism and the Nature of Evil," pp. 26-39.

170. Sobrino, "Spirituality and the Following of Jesus," p. 234; I am indebted to Fisher, *Human Significance*, p. 66.

171. D. Kelsey, *Eccentric Existence*, 1:56, emphasis in original.

of human person is in the forefront, and dualistic-individualistic accounts are far less known.[172]

To the bodily life belong emotions, passions, and desires. Damasio reminds us that "the mind derives from the entire organism as an ensemble," which simply means that mind is embodied. Indeed, one of the most far-reaching discoveries of current cognitive science is cognition's embodied nature.[173] More recently, researchers have come to talk about the "rationality of emotion"[174] and emotions as an essential part of rationality. What has recently been named "Descartes' error" was his failure to highlight the role of emotions at the expense of reason (ironically, I have to say, in that his last book was titled *The Passions of the Soul,* 1649!) and making emotion the servant of reason. For Descartes, reason and emotion operated in different provinces of the brain, and the former took the lead.[175] In light of current neuroscientific research, the opposite is the case. Recently we have also discovered that emotional (and moral) states such as empathy, shame, trust, regret, and detecting the emotional states of others are not only tightly linked with certain neural activities but also embodied and socially shaped.[176] With all its great gains, cognitive science has only recently realized the implications of its ignorance of noncognitive topics, particularly emotion, and begun to change that.[177] We know now that separating reason and rationality from emotionality is simply not justified: emotions support and underlie proper functioning of reason.[178] We also know now that emotion plays an important role, for example, in moral judgment.[179] Similarly, emotions play a role in religion. One of the reasons why Christian tradition — often following the general cultural drive — has been slow to embrace emotions is their equation with "passions,"[180] which, often

---

172. See J. Evans, *We Have Been Believers,* p. 101. See also D. S. Williams, "A Womanist Perspective on Sin," pp. 130-49.

173. Damasio, *Descartes' Error,* p. 225.

174. See further, Watts, "Psychological and Religious Perspectives on Emotion," pp. 243-60; for general orientation, consult Solomon, *The Passions.*

175. See Damasio, *Descartes' Error,* p. xi.

176. For the role and significance of these "Von Economo neurons," see, e.g., Allman et al., "Intuition and Autism," pp. 367-73.

177. See further, LeDoux, *The Emotional Brain;* H. Gardner, *The Mind's New Science.* In recent years, a subdiscipline of neuroscience has emerged: cognitive affective neuroscience; see Siegel et al., eds., *Healing Power of Emotion;* Panksepp and Biven, *Archeology of Mind.*

178. See Damasio, *The Feeling of What Happens,* chap. 2 particularly.

179. Koenigs et al., "Damage to the Prefrontal Cortex," pp. 908-11; Haidt, "The Emotional Dog and Its Rational Tail," pp. 814-34.

180. For general orientation, consult Solomon, *The Passions.*

by definition, have been conceived as sinful and opposite to rationality. That, however, is a misunderstanding and should be corrected. Finally, not only are the emotions and intelligence tightly linked with each other, but linked also with them is embodiment, as illustrated in the subtitle of a recent widely acclaimed book by Antonio Damasio: *Body and Emotion in the Making of Consciousness* (1999). Indeed, add to the equation sociality, and we can envision the human being in her wholeness and complexity.

Consider also the critical implications of embodiment to a holistic account of engendered human existence: "Because we are embodied, we are gendered, sexual beings; we speak and express ourselves; we can view a painting and listen to a symphony; we can relate to others in a community. Downplaying embodiment (emphasizing the soul over the body, the spiritual over the sensible) is to devalue these modes of being-in-the-world."[181] Before delving into the complex search for an understanding of human nature in such an embodied-social account, let us concentrate on the importance of our gendered form of existence as male and female in light of the image of God theology.

"Male and Female He Created Them"

Not only embodiment but also the male-female relationship has been a problem among most religious traditions. For example, Islam's depreciation of women, coupled with deep body-soul dualism, is well known.[182] Similar examples can of course be found in other faith traditions — and secular ideologies.

What is unique about the (second) biblical creation narrative is the account of the creation of the woman, not only of humanity in general or of man, as in other creation myths of the time.[183] The theological implication is that sexual distinction belongs to the essential and formative nature of human creation. Sexuality, then, is deeply social in nature.[184] Sexuality is also integrally linked with embodiment: only embodied beings can be either sex.[185] This is not to say that woman "needed" to be created to respond to the immediate feeling of loneliness of the man; she was created to establish the deeply social

181. J. K. A. Smith, *Introducing Radical Orthodoxy,* p. 77.

182. See, e.g., Q 2:223, 228. The allowance of polygamy, notwithstanding rules concerning fair treatment of wives, also points to subordination (see Q 4:3).

183. V. Hamilton, *Book of Genesis,* p. 157.

184. Westermann, *Genesis 1–11,* p. 227; Grenz, *Social God,* p. 270; for details, see chap. 7 of Grenz.

185. For comments, see Grenz, *Social God,* p. 277.

nature of humanity.[186] Nor is the designation of woman as "helper" (Gen. 2:18) a way of making the female subordinate or the servant of man; the use of the Hebrew term *('ezer)* in the biblical narrative does not warrant that.[187]

As it has regarding the environment,[188] Christianity has traveled a long road to establish the full equality of all human beings.[189] The denigrating sayings about women by leading theologians from Augustine to Aquinas all the way to modernity are too well known and need not be repeated once again here.[190] In this regard Christian tradition has a sorrowful track record.[191] Regretfully, the same applies not only to other Abrahamic faith traditions but also to other religions.[192]

What is highly curious is that even the Enlightenment philosophy did not have resources to rehabilitate the equality of women. While Descartes in principle opened up the life of reason for all of humanity, his denigration of the body as opposed to the soul, the "true self," continued hierarchic subordination.[193] Rather than equality, Kant advocated the idea of complementarity, assigning features such as "beauty, delicacy, modesty, compassion, sympathy, and feeling" to the feminine as opposed to "nobility, depth, reflectiveness, learning, profundity, and the ability to be principled" to masculinity.[194] Much work, thus, awaits the theologian.[195]

186. Vawter, *On Genesis,* p. 74.

187. The term is also used of Yahweh as Israel's helper (Exod. 18:4; Ps. 33:20; etc.). Importantly, LXX translates it as *boethos,* which refers to a strong helper. Higgins, "Anastasius Sinaita and the Superiority of Woman," p. 255.

188. In fairness one has to admit that the male dominance evident in the biblical canon and much of Christian history is of course not a Jewish-Christian idea. It was a norm also in leading Greek philosophers, including Aristotle; just see *Politics* 1254b, 1260; *On the Generation of Animals* 729b.

189. It is of course true that in the minds of the authors/editors of the Genesis text, there hardly were any egalitarian impulses (as rightly noted by A. M. Clifford, "When Being Human Becomes Truly Earthly," p. 183). That, however, does not mean that we shouldn't reinterpret this text in light of the developing revelation toward a more inclusive view.

190. For a careful and balanced historical discussion, see Johnson, *She Who Is,* pp. 104-20 particularly; also useful is Gonzalez, *Created in God's Image,* chap. 2.

191. Gonzalez, *Created in God's Image,* p. ix.

192. See further, Kvam, Schearing, and Ziegler, eds., *Eve and Adam;* Paul, *Women in Buddhism;* Altekar, *Position of Women in Hindu Traditions.*

193. Lloyd, *Man of Reason,* p. 45; I am indebted to Gonzalez, *Created in God's Image,* p. 56.

194. "Immanuel Kant," p. 145, cited in Gonzalez, *Created in God's Image,* p. 58; see also Schott, ed., *Feminist Interpretations of Immanuel Kant.*

195. See S. Jones, *Feminist Theory and Christian Theology,* p. 11.

What I find problematic — and embarrassing — is that as late as in Barth's theology, a *theological* justification is attempted for the subordination of women on the basis of creation order. Barth claims to find in the first creation narrative a hierarchic dualism that he then applies to male-female relationships.[196] Mentioning first that "God wills to rule him [the human person] but he may serve God," thus establishing the God-humanity subordinationism, he continues to apply it first to Christ's relation to the church and then finally to male-female relationships.[197] Moltmann's harsh criticism is not off-target: "In his account of these analogous structures of domination, Barth is following the ancient metaphysicians, especially Aristotle, who even then treated heaven and earth, soul and body, man and woman, according to the same patterns. . . . A world with an 'order' of this kind can hardly be called a peaceful one."[198]

While rejecting Barth's approach, we have to ask: What, then, is the theological significance of the sexual distinction? Too often Christian anthropology has treated Genesis 1:26-27 as "gender-free" — but then ended up either assuming male dominance[199] or the much-vilified complementarity approach.[200] Although the essentialist idea of womanhood may not appeal to many (any more than the thoroughly constructivist idea, as famously represented by Simone de Beauvoir),[201] common sense says that maleness and femaleness are something "real."[202] Complementarianism essentializes human identity, let alone social roles, in a sense that does not allow full equality and complementary diversity. It makes one-half of humanity receiver, the other half giver. It makes the woman the "other" and object, dooming the female into immanence.[203]

The radical middle position between essentialism and constructivism can be called "critical essentialism." *Critical* essentialism does not deny the commonsense intuition of real differences between male and female. Rather, it argues that "such differences — whatever they may be — will not be ac-

196. Barth (*CD* III/2, p. 368) also finds the hierarchic order in cosmology, in the relation of heaven to earth (p. 368).

197. Barth, *CD* III/2, p. 427.

198. Moltmann, *God in Creation,* p. 255.

199. See Børresen, "God's Image, Man's Image?" p. 187; see also Díaz, *On Being Human,* chap. 4; Plaskow, *Sex, Sin, and Grace.*

200. For a sharp critique, see O'Neill, "Mystery of Being Human Together," pp. 139-60.

201. Beauvoir, *The Second Sex,* p. 301: "One is not born, but rather, becomes a woman."

202. For a useful, balanced discussion of essentialism, see S. Jones, *Feminist Theory and Christian Theology,* chap. 2. For different approaches to sexual distinction among various types of feminist theologies (with a rich bibliography), see Teevan, "Challenges to the Role of Theological Anthropology," pp. 582-97.

203. Beauvoir, *The Second Sex,* p. lix, cited in Rivera, *Touch of Transcendence,* p. 6.

cepted as warrants for social systems which grant men in general authority and power over women in general."[204] The philosopher Sister Prudence Allen sets "integral" in opposition to "fractional" sex complementarity. Whereas the latter looks at the female as missing something that comes from the male, the former heartily affirms the full humanity of both sexes (including their bodies).[205] Significantly, Allen's essay in which she presents these ideas is titled "Integral Sex Complementarity and the Theology of *Communion* [emphasis added]," reminding us that "self-defining" is not to be understood in terms of deviating from deep relationality and mutual belonging.[206]

To Barth's credit, he at least saw it necessary to reflect on sexual distinction from a theological perspective. (In)famously, Barth, and before him Bonhoeffer,[207] linked the divine saying in Genesis 1:26 ("Let us make . . .") with the following statement of having been made male and female. Barth discusses the theme under the topic of covenant and links it with the trinitarian relationship between Father and Son.[208] That linking, however, hardly is at the heart of the saying after Barth's forced exegesis,[209] although in a general sense the idea of juxtaposition and relationality of course is there.[210] The lasting theological meaning of having been created as male and female is that "to be human means being sexually differentiated *and* sharing a common humanity; both are equally primary."[211] That said, I do not find convincing Moltmann's proposal that it is exactly in the sexual distinction and polarity that the real likeness to God and human uniqueness is to be found.[212] Rather, as already established, it is in the unique relation to God (and having been directly addressed by the Creator) that human uniqueness can be found. It is on this basis (rather than on the basis of sexual distinction after Moltmann) that it

204. Cahill, *Sex, Gender, and Christian Ethics*, pp. 1-2. See also Dallavelle, "Neither Idolatry nor Iconoclasm," p. 30.

205. Allen, "Integral Sex Complementarity," p. 540; see also Oduyoye, *Introducing African Women's Theology*, p. 70.

206. Cf. Cahill, *Between the Sexes*, pp. 99-100.

207. Bonhoeffer, *Creation and Fall*, pp. 60-67.

208. Barth, CD III/1, pp. 191-207; III/2, pp. 232-34. Barth has been followed by Trible, *God and the Rhetoric of Sexuality*, p. 19. For exegetical comments, see Westermann, *Genesis 1-11*, p. 232.

209. Rightly critiqued by Bird, "'Male and Female He Created Them,'" pp. 129-59.

210. This is the way Moltmann (*God in Creation*, pp. 222-23 and passim) rightly interprets it.

211. Moltmann, *God in Creation*, p. 222.

212. Moltmann, *God in Creation*, p. 222. This is of course not to undermine sexuality's importance; see Welker, *Creation and Reality*, pp. 62-69.

can be said: "Likeness to God cannot be lived in isolation. It can be lived only in human community. This means that from the very outset human beings are social beings." Consequently, "person and community are two sides of one and the same life process."[213] Where I agree with Moltmann is that because God's image can be reflected fully by females and males, it means that it is wrong to think of God in masculine terms.[214] God is asexual, and hence can never be abused to further male (any more than female) dominion.

Before continuing the theological anthropology with the focus on human nature, let us briefly widen the discussion to include the two other Abrahamic traditions, which also have the image-of-God teaching in their traditions. A more comprehensive account of humanity and human nature among religions will be offered in the next chapter.

The Image of God among Abrahamic Traditions: Jewish and Islamic Views

In all Abrahamic faiths the discussion of humanity is placed "in the dual reality of the . . . eternity and permanence of God, and the mortality and finitude of humankind."[215] Deeply embedded in the Jewish tradition is of course the belief shared with Christians of humanity having been created in the image of God. Jewish tradition, however, speaks with reservations about the *tselem*, "image of God," in order to avoid speaking of God too anthropomorphically. Even contemporary Jewish theology does not devote too much space to it[216] (interestingly, the leading classical theologian Moses Maimonides' fairly detailed reflections on the two Hebrew terms, translated "image" and "likeness," take place in the context of speaking of God).[217] Jewish exegetes, like their Christian counterparts, usually highlight the importance of rationality and intellect as well as moral capacity.[218] A major difference is of course that where Christian tradition speaks of *imitatio Christi*, Jewish tradition speaks of *imitatio Dei*.[219]

Although in the Qur'an there is no direct statement about humanity being created in the image of God (as there is in the Hadith), the corresponding

213. Moltmann, *God in Creation*, pp. 222-23.
214. Moltmann, *God in Creation*, p. 223.
215. Siddiqui, "Being Human in Islam," p. 15.
216. For a fine contemporary discussion, see Schofer, "The Image of God."
217. See, e.g., Maimonides, *Guide for the Perplexed* 1.1, pp. 12-14.
218. Maimonides, *Guide for the Perplexed* 1.1, pp. 12-14.
219. See van Huyssteen, *Alone in the World?* p. 293.

idea is there. The well-known passage of 30:30 comes close to it: "So set your purpose for religion, as a *hanīf*[220] — a nature given by God, upon which He originated mankind. There is no changing God's creation." Here the term *fitrah* (nature) is used, which clearly has resemblance to the image in Christian-Jewish vocabulary. Somewhat similarly to the biblical testimonies, the human being is made of clay in the Qur'an (Q 23:12-14). Not only that, but the one made of clay is also breathed into by the Spirit of God, and therefore even the angels prostrate themselves before him (15:26-30). In the Hadith, the idea of the image of God appears: "Allah, the Exalted and Glorious, created Adam in His own image."[221]

The technical term *fitrah,* used of human nature — "an inborn natural predisposition which cannot change, and which exists at birth in all human beings"[222] — has a number of interrelated meanings, including moral intuitions and religious instinct. According to the well-known Hadith statement:

Everyone is born according to his true nature and the command pertaining to the demise of the children of the infidels and of the children of the Muslims. There is none born but is created to his true nature (Islam). It is his parents who make him a Jew or a Christian or a Magian quite as beasts produce their young with their limbs perfect. Do you see anything deficient in them? . . . The nature made by Allah in which He has created men there is no altering of Allah's creation; that is the right religion.[223]

On the basis of this teaching, in Muslim tradition *fitrah* is universal, not limited to Muslims alone, and is an immutable feature of humanity. Very closely resembling the Christian idea of the innate knowledge of God, it "is the faculty, which He has created in mankind, of knowing Allah." As a result, belief in Allah (the confession of *tawhid*) is "natural" to human beings.[224] Even the children of polytheists have this quality and are blessed until they reach the age of accountability.[225] Indeed, there is the teaching in Islamic tradition that

220. The exact meaning of the term is somewhat unclear (hence left without English rendering here). A number of times it refers to "faith" (of Abraham) and also has the connotation of a nonpolytheistic faith. See Jeffery, *Foreign Vocabulary of the Qur'ān,* p. 112.
221. *Sahih Muslim,* 40, #6809.
222. Mohamed, *Fitrah,* p. 13.
223. *Sahih Muslim,* 33, #6423 (the last sentence is a citation from Q 30:30); similarly *Sahih Bukhari,* 60, #298.
224. Mohamed, *Fitrah,* p. 16. See also *Ibn Taymiyyah Expounds on Islam,* pp. 3-4.
225. *Sahih Muslim,* 33, #6430.

already before having been born into the earthly existence, Allah allowed the human soul to recognize the true God (7:172).[226] Therefore, Islam is at times called *dīn al-fitrah*, the religion of human nature, that is, religion that is in keeping with natural human instincts and inclinations (believed to be confirmed by Q 3:17)[227] — a claim shared by Christian theologians regarding their own tradition. This explains why Muslim theologians say, on the one hand, that there is no compulsion in religion (2:226), and on the other hand, that submission and obedience do not entail loss of freedom, because "freedom is to act as one's true nature demands."[228] The prophets who preach the message of Allah are not introducing something "new" but serve as reminders.[229]

Indeed, the freedom of will — similarly to Jewish tradition — is an essential part of the teaching of Islam and a major reason, along with *fitrah*, to categorically reject the Christian doctrine of original sin. Because of the innate knowledge of *tawhid*, each individual is held accountable for submitting to God. However, only Muslims who have acquired the needed teaching and knowledge are responsible for living according to *Sharī'a*, the religious and sociopolitical law of Islam. For polytheism or other deviations from *tawhid*, there is no excuse; for lack of knowledge of Islamic law there is.[230]

All three Abrahamic traditions affirm the dignity of humanity in relation to God, the Creator. The belief in the creation of humanity in the image of God (even when that term is not used extensively in the Muslim tradition) forms the basis for inviolable dignity. "When any one of you fights with his brother, he should avoid his face for Allah created Adam in His own image."[231] "Whoever sheds the blood of man, by man shall his blood be shed; for God made man in his own image" (Gen. 9:6).

A common theme for all three traditions is the idea of humanity as God's viceroy on earth. This idea is deeply embedded in Jewish tradition based on the biblical teaching.[232] In Islam, the idea of vice-regency is typically described in terms of caliph. According to Qur'an 2:30, when God announced to the angels, "Lo! I am about to place a viceroy [*khalīfah*][233] in the earth," they demurred

226. Q 7:172; see further, Bowering, *Mystical Vision of Existence in Classical Islam*, pp. 156-57.

227. For important comments, see Al-Attas, *Islam, Secularism*, pp. 57-58.

228. Mohamed, *Fitrah*, p. 19; see also Q 51:56.

229. See Mohamed, *Fitrah*, p. 47.

230. Mohamed, *Fitrah*, p. 24.

231. *Sahih Muslim*, 32, #6325.

232. See Cohon, *Jewish Theology*, p. 287.

233. The only other occurrence of the singular form of "caliph" in the Qur'an is in 38:26

and wondered if God knew the risks involved because of the frailty of human nature! In response the Lord taught them how to name the creatures, and that was a cause of marvel among the angelic beings. By extension, key figures such as Noah are appointed as a caliph as God's prophet and servant (10:71-73). A highly significant implication of the comprehensiveness of the vice-regency is the curious saying of 33:72: "Indeed We offered the Trust to the heavens and the earth and the mountains, but they refused to bear it and were apprehensive of it; but man undertook it." Importantly, the saying continues that the vice-regent is "wrongdoer and ignorant" and that God is on the lookout for those who act wrongly (v. 73).[234]

Taking careful notice of this wide consensus among the three Abrahamic faiths concerning the uniqueness of humanity because of the relation to God, we have many more opportunities in the following chapters to investigate in more detail other aspects of anthropologies, highlighting both commonalities and divergences; that discussion is widened to include the contributions of the two Asiatic traditions as well. Before that, the next chapter will take up the complex question of the nature of human nature, building on the evolutionary and theological results reached so far and engaging in some detail the results and approaches of neuroscience.

---

in a divine address to David. In the plural, the term is used a number of times. It is hard to see, however, how the Qur'anic teaching would in any way support the political institution of the Muslim caliphate, as interpreted, e.g., in Rosenthal, *Political Thought in Medieval Islam,* p. 26.

234. For details, see Cragg, *Privilege of Man,* chap. 2.

12. "Multidimensional Monism": The Nature of Human Nature

Introduction: The Confused State of Thinking about Human Nature

Indeed, it is "a strange fact about our culture that we are operating with a variety of radically different views of the basic nature of human beings." As if that were not enough, "[e]ven stranger is the fact that so few people seem to notice."[1] Not only is this true of society at large, but perhaps even more surprisingly, it is true of theology! No wonder inquiry into human nature has been compared to a "labyrinth" where there are "blind alleys" and where it is difficult to "find one's goal."[2]

Add world religions into the equation, and the complexity only intensifies. At one end there is the view that only the spiritual dimension of humanity matters, not the bodily, nor individuality in any sense (*advaita* Vedanta of Sankara). Thus, the whole point of the spiritual quest is to overcome the illusion of dualism. While the other major Vedanta school allows for some form of duality (the qualified nonduality of Ramanuja), the basic view of humanity is not radically different. Even the Sankhya Yoga school, which aims at realizing one's own individual existence instead of being immersed in the ocean of cosmic unity, represents a flight from the body. While radically different in many ways, the main schools of Buddhism, with their denial of the persistence of "self," envision "salvation" in terms of transcending embodiment and thus

---

1. Murphy, *Bodies and Souls,* p. ix; she reports that no fewer than 130 different views of the human person were present in a recent book she read (pp. 3-4)!

2. Kraschl, "Das Leib-Seele-Problem," p. 399, translation mine.

also individuality. Although very rare, almost nonexistent among religions, an essentially material (rather than spiritual) view of human nature can be found in one of Hinduism's main schools, namely, Carvaka, with its virtual atheism. Between these two extremes — essentially spiritual or material conceptions of human nature — stand the three Abrahamic faiths. Despite all their differences, originally they all envision human nature as embodied soul or spirited body. They also make human existence finite and thus not immortal. Particularly in Jewish-Christian traditions, embodiment/materiality is an essential part of human nature, either because of a "this-worldly" eschatology (Judaism) or because of life in the resurrected body in the new creation (Christianity). However — and this is extremely important in relation to the religion-science dialogue — all religious traditions (perhaps with the exception of Carvaka Hinduism and some form of current Christian naturalism) "relate human life in some way to a supra-material realm of spirit or mind," that is, transcendence, and hence relate "salvation" to life to come (less so in Judaism).[3] Their differences from the sciences and "scientific worldview" are thus considerable.

In contrast, among scientists studying human nature and nonreligious philosophers, by far the most common notion of human nature is physicalist (materialist) monism. Apart from a minority of scientists,[4] (conservative) theologians and philosophers,[5] as well as some other nonconformist thinkers,[6] in academia nondualistic explanations rule (notwithstanding the many internal debates among the monists regarding details). While in Christian and some other religious traditions the focus of human uniqueness used to be the soul, in contemporary science and culture it is the brain![7]

Historically and globally speaking, however, this state of affairs is astonishingly strange: most common people, regardless of religious, geographical, and racial features, have intuitively stuck with some sort of dualist (nonmonist) way of thinking of human nature.[8] The developmental psychologist

3. K. Ward, *Religion and Human Nature*, pp. 1-6, here p. 1.

4. Among them the leading voice is Sir J. C. Eccles; among his many contributions, see the volume he edited, *Brain and Conscious Experience*.

5. Important current defenses of dualism include Swinburne, *Evolution of the Soul*; J. Cooper, *Body, Soul, and Life Everlasting*; Moreland and Rae, *Body and Soul*.

6. Baker and Goetz, eds., *The Soul Hypothesis*.

7. Recall that the 1990s were declared by the U.S. government "The Decade of the Brain"; see the official Web site, which also lists several important publications: http://www.loc.gov/loc/brain/. Murphy, "Human Nature," p. 1; Murphy refers to Flanagan's (*Science of the Mind*, p. 318) witty saying that it is the brain that is the *res cogitans*, the thinking thing (rather than mind, as Descartes had it).

8. For the importance of body-soul belief in folk psychology, see the discussion of a

Paul Bloom says that "[w]e can explain much of what makes us human by recognizing that we are natural Cartesians — dualistic thinking comes naturally to us."[9] There is a growing literature of empirical and historical research by psychologists[10] and (cognitive) anthropologists[11] to indicate that "[m]ost people, at most times, in most places, have believed that human beings have some kind of soul." This means that even though most people have also believed in the existence of the body and its importance to human existence, "when it comes to their thoughts and experiences, humans also seem to inhabit a rich world of beliefs and desires, goals and purposes, pleasures and pains, sights and sounds, joys and sorrows whose nature has little or nothing to do with ordinary physical objects and the forces that act on them."[12] Not surprisingly, both historical and current Christianity throughout the global church take dualism as the received tradition.

The talk about "*scientific* orthodoxy" is in need of some nuancing, particularly in its philosophical implications. Neuroscientific results and insights are not "brute facts"; they call for interpretation. "Evidence" in itself hardly explains the meaning of any study. Consider this ironic fact: three leading scholars in the field, namely, Sir John Eccles, Francis Crick, and Roger Sperry — all of them Nobel laureates — look at the same evidence and draw different conclusions: one is dualist, another reductive materialist, and yet another nonreductive physicalist, respectively![13]

What about Christian theology in this respect? What is at stake in the contemporary theological reflection on the "composition" of human nature?[14] Unlike any philosophical view that considers the human being merely as a physical entity, without any "real" mental life or consciousness, Christian "interpretation of human reality must take into account the fact that we live and lead our

---

number of recent studies by the Irish cognitive anthropologist Bering, "Folk Psychology of Souls," pp. 453-98. For (traditional) African views of humanity that assume the necessity of the (nonphysical) spiritual reality, see Kapolyo, *Human Condition*, pp. 36-37.

9. Bloom, *Descartes' Baby*, p. xii; see also p. 191.

10. Bloom, *Descartes' Baby;* Wellman and Johnson, "Developing Dualism," p. 3; Richert and Harris, "Ghost in My Body," pp. 409-27.

11. See Astuti, "Are We All Natural Dualists?" p. 431; E. Cohen et al., "Cross-cultural Similarities and Differences," pp. 1282-1304. I am indebted for these references to Dr. Emily Esch's presentation "Scientific Evidence for Dualism."

12. Baker and Goetz, "Introduction," p. 1. Undoubtedly one of the reasons behind the belief in "soul" is the out-of-body experiences widely reported. For a theological and interdisciplinary discussion, see J. Green, "Three Exegetical Forays."

13. Murphy, "Nonreductive Physicalism," p. 127.

14. See Metzinger, "Introduction," p. 6.

lives consciously" and that "[a]t all events the fact of consciousness is a basic one in human life for which any anthropology must find a suitable interpretation." Religion in any meaningful sense would not of course be possible apart from these higher mental capacities. That said, contemporary theology faces more than one option to continue affirming that foundational belief. While in the past, body-soul dualism was assumed to be the default position, in light of the current scientific knowledge, theology has also come to a new appreciation of the fact that "we know conscious and self-conscious life only as bodily life . . . bodily functions condition all psychological experience. This is true even of self-consciousness." As a result, not only for scientists but also for a growing number of contemporary theologians, "traditional ideas of the soul as a substance that is distinct from the body and that is detached from it in death" have lost much of their credibility.[15]

While the shift toward a unified, monistic, and holistic view is usually attributed to changes in philosophy and particularly (neuro)sciences, Pannenberg reminds us that the shift is "in line with the intentions of the earliest Christian anthropology." Too often the investigation into the history of the body-soul relationship ignores the fact that, unlike Platonism (which by the end of the second century had become the dominant philosophy), important early patristic thinkers defended the psychosomatic unity even when they continued distinguishing between body and soul (spirit). However, that attempt to hold on to the idea of body-soul unity soon gave way to dualism for the simple reason that, in keeping with the times, even those theologians who championed the psychosomatic unity did not thereby reject the idea of soul as an independent entity.[16] Pannenberg's judgment is that "[t]his process illustrates the acceptance by early Christian thinking of ideas that the Hellenistic culture of the age took for granted," and hence "is not an interpretation that has any essential place in Christian anthropology."[17] (Consider that Pannenberg himself is not a physicalist but rather represents an integral holistic property-dualist type of view.) Even with their dualism, early theologians critiqued key aspects of pagan philosophy. A case in point is the belief in the immortality of soul. Although it was affirmed by some early theologians,[18] the preexistence of the soul (and corollary idea of transmigration of the soul) was rejected,[19]

15. Pannenberg, *ST* 2:181-82; see also J. Green, *Body, Soul, and Human Life,* p. 16.

16. Tertullian is an illustrative case in point.

17. Pannenberg, *ST* 2:182; for "The Triumph of Dualism" in early theology, see Martin and Barresi, *Rise and Fall of Soul and Self,* pp. 61-74.

18. Tertullian, *A Treatise on the Soul* 22; Irenaeus, *Against Heresies* 2.34.

19. With the exception of Origen, for whose view see *De principiis* 2.9.6-7; for a more detailed exposition of the topic of "soul," see 2.8.

as well as the soul's divinity.[20] Furthermore, the belief in the resurrection of the body[21] — an anathema to Hellenistic thought — trumped the immortality of the soul; hence, the body was not the prison of the soul as in Plato, neither was death liberation.[22]

Three times in Christian history thinking about human nature has become the focal point of reflection: in the shift from the Hebrew to the Greek-Hellenistic milieu in early Christian theology; during the Aristotelian revival in the Middle Ages; and with the rise of biblical criticism and modern science during modernity.[23] Special attention will be devoted to these turns in the following critical scrutiny of the main historical developments of Christian anthropological intuitions.

Human Nature in Theological Tradition:
A Generous Critical Assessment

The Rise to Dominance of Dualisms

The roots of the body-soul dualism can be traced back to Hellenistic philosophy (which in itself was not a unified tradition but rather a constellation of many).[24] Typically in that tradition, *soma* (body) denoted something alien.[25] It is significant that Plato's idea of death as "the separation of the soul from the body" is contrasted with the immortality of the soul.[26] Soul is eternal and remains while the body is decaying and fleeting.[27] Soul is the higher aspect of humanity: soul directs, rules, and masters, and body serves and is ruled.[28] Platonism influenced significantly particularly the earliest Christian anthropologies, although not uniformly. The Platonic-type dualistic account of Tertullian, influenced by the Stoics, argued for the corporeality of the

20. See Justin, *Dialogue with Trypho* 5, 6.

21. According to Athenagoras (*On the Resurrection of the Dead* 15), resurrection of the body is necessary because eternal life is meant for the whole person.

22. In this section, I am indebted to Pannenberg, *ST* 2:183-84.

23. Murphy, *Bodies and Souls,* p. 7.

24. See Bremmer, *The Early Greek Concept of the Soul,* pp. 13-69 particularly; Martin and Barresi, *Rise and Fall of Soul and Self,* pp. 9-38.

25. Schweizer, "*Soma*," 7:1024ff.

26. Plato, *Phaedo* 64c.

27. Hence, Plato considers highly *meditatio mortis* of the body, mindfulness of the mortality of the body; e.g., Plato, *Phaedo* 80e-81a.

28. Plato, *Phaedo* 79e-80a.

soul.[29] While gleaning from Hellenistic philosophers, he also combated their errors such as the preexistence of the soul: because "soul originates in the breath of God, it follows that we attribute a beginning to it."[30] While distinguished from each other, soul and body also belong together as they are brought about simultaneously at birth.[31]

Plato's pupil Aristotle's conception of the soul is markedly different from his teacher's. For him, the soul is the "form" (or actuality) of the body.[32] Rather than an entity, soul is more like a life principle, "that aspect of the person which provides the powers or attributes characteristic of the human being," but not only the human being but also all other living entities, such as animals and plants.[33] Unlike in Plato, where it seems like soul and body can "live" separately, for Aristotle "the soul is inseparable from its body."[34] To properly understand this hylomorphic account of reality, one has to leave behind the contemporary (to us) notion of "form" as something secondary and "thin"; instead, for Aristotle, form denotes something like actuality-having-reached-potentiality. "Form is an immanent principle that gives things their essential characteristics and powers."[35] Hence, it is doubtful whether Aristotelian anthropology (later adopted by Thomism) is essentially dualist at all;[36] if named as such, it is markedly different from other dualisms.

What is common to all ancient Greek notions of humanity is the "recognition that human beings have some remarkable capabilities all their own (such as doing mathematics and philosophy) and others that they share with animals (sensation). It did not seem possible to attribute these powers to matter — to the body — and so philosophers developed theories about an additional component of the person to account for them. Since living persons have all these powers and corpses do not, the soul is also taken to be the life principle."[37] This intuition was by and large shared by Christian tradition.[38]

By the time of Augustine, the shift toward a more robust dualism along

29. Tertullian, *On the Soul,* chap. 7; in chap. 5 he acknowledges the Stoic background of the view; see chap. 6 for rebuttal of the Platonic view of the incorporeality of the soul.

30. Tertullian, *On the Soul,* chap. 4.

31. Tertullian, *On the Soul,* chap. 27.

32. Aristotle, *On the Soul* 2.1-3; here "actuality" is used for "form"; on the importance for Christian tradition, see Kelly, *Early Christian Doctrines,* p. 171.

33. Murphy, *Bodies and Souls,* p. 13.

34. Aristotle, *On the Soul* 2.1.

35. Murphy, *Bodies and Souls,* p. 13.

36. So also, Murphy, *Bodies and Souls,* p. 13.

37. Murphy, "Human Nature," p. 4.

38. See Tertullian, *On the Flesh of Christ,* chap. 12.

with the stronger hierarchic view of soul and body (the former higher than the latter)[39] had taken the upper hand. In his psychological analogy, Augustine focused on the "soul" as the seat of the image of God.[40] The key aspect of the soul is rationality, indeed, "the image of God is to be sought in the immortality of the rational soul."[41] The mature Augustine, however, began to correct himself, mentioning that the "soul having body does not make two persons, but one man."[42]

Aquinas followed Augustine in locating likeness to God in rationality,[43] but with the help of Aristotelianism, he also took important steps toward rediscovering key aspects of the original biblical unity of human nature. His baptizing of Aristotle's idea of the soul as the "form" of the body[44] became church dogma at the Council of Vienna (1312).[45] "On this view the soul is not just a partial principle but that which makes us human in our bodily reality. Conversely, the body is the concrete form in which our humanity, the soul, finds appropriate expression."[46] True, this is not yet a satisfactory account of human nature, but it points in the right direction of expelling dualism that makes soul and body separate substances.[47]

The third major turning point in Christian — and secular — thinking on human nature had to do with the rise of modernity and modern science. Galileo is not only to be acknowledged for his role in the Copernican revolution; his introduction of an atomist-corpuscular conception of matter that replaced the Aristotelian hylomorphism brought about an unprecedented scientific and philosophical revolution. Whereas in the past, the idea of teleology (purpose) had been taken for granted, in the emerging mechanistic worldview there was

39. The idea of the supremacy of the soul over the body was already present in Tertullian (*On the Soul,* chap. 13), but he also emphasized their interrelatedness, as discussed above.

40. Quoted in Moltmann, *God in Creation,* p. 236 (*Trinity* 10.19).

41. Augustine, *Trinity* 14.4, chapter title. Augustine, however, qualifies the talk about "immortality," reminding us that the souls of those who do not enter blessedness will die (14.4.6); hence, his idea of immortality is not that of Plato. See also Augustine, *On the Morals of the Catholic Church* 27.52.

42. Augustine, *Tractates on the Gospel according to John* 19.15 (on John 5:19-30); so also Augustine, *Trinity* 15.7.11.

43. Aquinas, *ST* 1.93.4, 6.

44. Aquinas, *ST* 1.76.1; indeed, in art. 4, he clarifies that it is the only essential form of the body.

45. Decree 1; http://www.ewtn.com/library/councils/vienne.htm (10/24/2012).

46. Pannenberg, *ST* 2:184.

47. For contemporary hylomorphistic accounts, see Leftow, "Souls Dipped in Dust," pp. 120-38; Haldane, *Reasonable Faith;* Stump, "Non-Cartesian Substance Dualism," pp. 505-31.

no room for that.[48] The Newtonian principle of inertia also replaced the idea of the Prime Mover.[49]

The prime architect of the modern account of human nature is of course René Descartes, whose thought marks the zenith of body-soul dualism. Building on the Platonic heritage, the modern French philosopher[50] also significantly transformed it: whereas in "Plato, the anthropological dualism of body and soul belonged within the framework of the ontological dualism of non-transient Being and transient existing things[,] . . . [f]ollowing the Christian tradition in its Augustinian form, Descartes no longer understands the soul as a higher substance: he sees it as the true subject, both in the human body and in the world of things. He translates the old body-soul dualism into the modern subject-object dichotomy."[51] However, he goes further into dualism than Christian tradition in the mainline, even Augustine, had been willing to go:

> And although I may, or rather, as I will shortly say, although I certainly do possess a body with which I am very closely conjoined; nevertheless, because, on the one hand, I have a clear and distinct idea of myself, in as far as I am only a thinking and unextended thing, and as, on the other hand, I possess a distinct idea of body, in as far as it is only an extended and unthinking thing, it is certain that I [that is, my mind, by which I am what I am] [am] entirely and truly distinct from my body, and may exist without it.[52]

A "nonthinking thing," the body, is to be compared to a machine.[53] Unlike the Aristotelian-Thomist view in which the soul served a number of purposes, including the "vegetative and nutritive," that is, life-sustaining task, the Cartesian body needs no soul to animate it.[54] Furthermore, herein soul's only task is cognitive (inclusively understood, and hence "mind" and "soul" became synonymous).[55] Counterintuitively, Cartesian dualism (or any other form of dualism, for that matter) is not saved from the problem of mental causation;

---

48. See chap. 8 in Martin and Barresi, *Rise and Fall of Soul and Self.*

49. For details, see Murphy, *Beyond Liberalism and Fundamentalism,* chap. 3; Murphy, *Anglo-American Postmodernity,* chap. 1.

50. See the dedication to his *Meditations.*

51. Moltmann, *God in Creation,* p. 250.

52. Descartes, *Meditations on First Philosophy: Sixth Meditation,* p. 9.

53. E.g., Descartes, *Sixth Meditation,* p. 17; for comments, see Searle, *Rediscovery of the Mind,* p. 25.

54. Aquinas, *ST* 1.78.1; see Murphy, *Bodies and Souls,* pp. 56-69.

55. See Murphy and Brown, *DMN,* pp. 15-16.

its challenge is just different from other theories. Ironically, the mind's capacity to work on matter/the physical had become a major problem with the rise of modern science as hylomorphism was left behind (in which "mind/soul was but one instance of form" and thus could be thought of as having causal effects).[56] In modern sciences, inertia was in place unless physical forces caused movement; immanent forms or other nonmaterial explanations seemed to be totally at odds with the mechanistic-atomistic-corpuscular view of reality.[57]

Jumping to the twentieth century, we discern that, somewhat surprisingly, Karl Barth, with all his critique of modernism, came to affirm materially — although distinctively — the modernist dualism.[58] The epithet to the *Church Dogmatics* section titled "Man as Soul and Body" says it all: "Through the Spirit of God, man is the subject, form and life of a substantial organism, the soul of his body — wholly and simultaneously both, in ineffaceable difference, inseparable unity, and indestructible order."[59] Although he seems to express Thomistic leanings ("the soul of his body"), he is indeed firmly Platonic in a soul-dominated, hierarchic view. Expressions such as "the soul rules and the body serves" (p. 421), "the soul precedes the body . . . [and] the body follows the soul" (p. 417), and similar, leave no doubt about that.[60] Unlike the biblical testimonies in which the divine spirit is the life principle of all creatures, whether humans or animals or plants, Barth curiously and problematically surmises that the "Spirit stands in a special and direct relationship to the soul or soulful element of human reality, but in only an indirect relationship to the body. The soul therefore is the life of the body, and therefore the human life as such which man may not only have but be when he receives the Spirit. He may be soul. Thus it is the besouled body that the Spirit chooses and occupies as His dwelling" (p. 365). A highly troubling conclusion of Barth's dualistic anthropology is that "[t]he human being is the ruling soul of his body, or he is not a human being. . . . This is the first thing which we have to say theo-

56. Murphy, "Human Nature," p. 7.

57. Flanagan, *Science of the Mind*, p. 21.

58. Contra interpretations that take Barth's theological anthropology as supporting a holistic view: e.g., R. S. Anderson, *On Being Human*, pp. 210-11; Hoekema, *Created in God's Image*, pp. 216-17; McLean, *Humanity in the Thought of Karl Barth*, p. 46. Oddly, Daniel Price claims that "Barth does not . . . deal in his anthropology with endopsychic structures" (*Karl Barth's Anthropology in Light of Modern Thought*, p. 247). For an important discussion, see Cortez, "Body, Soul, and (Holy) Spirit," pp. 328-29.

59. Barth, *CD* III/2, p. 325. Page numbers to this work have been placed in the following text.

60. That Barth places the whole discussion in the context of speaking of the two natures of Jesus Christ does not materially change the meaning of his statements; it is, after all, theological anthropology that he is doing here and claims to be doing!

logically concerning man as a rational being" (p. 425). This statement fails in more than one account because of the advocacy of dualistic hierarchy, overemphasis on reason, and so forth. One of the unfortunate implications of Barth's type of hierarchic dualism is its potential use for the legitimation of racism: a "higher" class of persons is identified with soul whereas the "lower" class with the physical, including physical work. A related potential defect has to do with a perverted disposition toward the earth, as that is considered to be of lower value, an attitude funded by and leading to escapism.[61]

Dualisms under Theological Assessment

Constructive theology has a twofold task here. First of all, it is essential to discern and continue affirming the legitimate intuitions that lie behind the dominant dualisms of tradition. Second, their liabilities and failings should be affirmed and corrected, which calls for a new account of human nature in critical dialogue with sciences and other religions.

Let us begin with problems and liabilities,[62] building on insights won in earlier chapters. Dualisms (as much as they also differ from each other, particularly Platonic-Cartesian and Aristotelian-Thomist versions) locate humanity (human uniqueness) in the soul rather than in the human person as a whole. Second, dualisms tend to speak of soul in terms of intellect *(anima intellective),* which elevates rationality as the vital principle. That was because early the soul (Gen. 2:7) or spirit was equated with reason (unlike its initial meaning of life principle).[63] Third, contrary to the Bible, where the divine Spirit *(ruach)* is the principle of life, life-force,[64] even the Aristotelian-Thomist account relegates that to soul. In Genesis 2:7, "the soul is not merely the vital principle of the body but the ensouled body itself, the living being as a whole. Hence, it does not have the autonomy expressed by the Aristotelian-Thomistic concept of substance."[65] The existence of human life (Job 34:14-15) — along with all life of all creation (Ps. 104:29, 30) — is the function of the life-giving force of the divine Spirit. Hence, human life is eccentric, referred to beyond itself; it is a life of dependence on the Creator.[66] In contrast to the Hellenistic philosophy and

61. See González, *Mañana*, pp. 129-30.
62. See N. T. Wright, "Mind, Spirit, Soul and Body."
63. See Pannenberg, *ST* 2:188.
64. See Wolff, *Anthropology of the Old Testament*, p. 22.
65. Pannenberg, *ST* 2:185.
66. See Pannenberg, *ST* 2:186 particularly.

occasional tendencies in early theology, even reason/rationality is contingent on divine breath and has no autonomy.[67] Fourth, the dualisms suffer from the downplaying of the body, emotions, and passions. The critical question then is, "If the body does not belong to the *imago Dei,* how can the body become 'a temple of the Holy Spirit'?"[68] Finally, dualisms seem to run against much of current neuroscientific knowledge (of which more below).

The important intuitions behind dualisms of Christian tradition are well worth preserving and cultivating, even if dualisms per se should be left behind: that there is "more" to human life than just the material;[69] that there is something "more" than merely material processes that explain the uniqueness and dignity of human life;[70] that affirming morality and an ethical base calls for "more" than material explanation;[71] and that there is hope for life eternal, and therefore, even at the moment of my personal death, I am not forgotten by God.[72] Contemporary theology must hold on to these intuitions and assess its constructive proposal for its capacity to be able to meet that need. On the way to the constructive proposal, it is mandatory first to take stock of how human nature is understood in current sciences and then look at its many philosophical implications relevant to theology.

Human Mind and Nature in Current
Scientific and Philosophical Perspectives

Constructive theology faces the necessary task of engaging neurosciences, philosophy of mind, and related fields in its search for a coherent account of the human being. In keeping with the methodological orientations discussed

67. See Pannenberg, *ST* 2:190-91.

68. Moltmann, *God in Creation,* p. 239. This problem did not go unnoticed by the Reformation theologians, as can be seen in Calvin, *Institutes* 1.15.3.

69. See K. Ward, *More Than Matter.*

70. In his classic history of European morality throughout ages, Lecky argues strongly that there is an essential link between Christianity's establishment of the dignity of each human person and belief in the soul (*History of European Morals,* pp. 18, 34). This is of course not limited to Christian tradition, as discussed with regard to Hindu and Jewish views in Post, "Moral Case for Nonreductive Physicalism," pp. 199-201.

71. E.g., Rickabaugh, "Responding to N. T. Wright's Rejection of the Soul"; so also Moreland and Rae, *Body and Soul.*

72. In this regard I find too harsh and unnuanced N. T. Wright's ("Mind, Spirit, Soul and Body," n.p.) somewhat pejorative dismissal of K. Ward's nuanced way of defending idealist monism in his *More Than Matter.*

in the introduction to this volume (chap. 1), the "critical mutual interaction" model seems to be most fruitful. While that scheme honors the rationality and independence of both sciences and theology, it also acknowledges that this does not mean their separation from each other. If "God is the all-determining reality" (Pannenberg), then it means that, on the one hand, theology needs neurosciences to better understand the nature of humanity, and neurosciences need the critical task of theology to avoid reductionism(s) so prevalent in sciences studying humanity.[73]

The Integral Connection between Brain Events
and the Mental in Human Behavior

In the current scientific study of the human being, the activities of the brain are of course in the forefront; not for nothing were the 1990s named the "Decade of the Brain" by the U.S. government.[74] Consider that as recently as the late eighteenth century, even among the leading physicians, no causal link between, say, the capacity of speaking and brain activity was discerned! Only in the following century was speech localized in the frontal lobes.[75] Later in the nineteenth century it took dramatic events such as the oft-referred-to Phineas Gage instance to wake up society to the tight link between the brain and human behavior. In 1848 an explosion caused a tamping iron to pierce the skull, exiting from the top of the head, of this twenty-five-year-old New England railroad worker. This led to a serious change in his personality, making this once stable person emotionally and socially bankrupt — yet without any visible effects at all! The obvious lesson from this poor rail worker's incident is simply that brains and neurons have much to do with emotions, sociality, and thoughts![76] A recent counterpart to Gage is the widely reported instance of the schoolteacher in the U.S. state of Virginia in 2000. He was caught collecting and using child pornography, facilitating prostitution, and molesting a child. Having had his brain examined before criminal sentencing, he was diagnosed with a tumor in the right orbitofrontal lobe, routinely associated with moral-knowledge acquisition and social integration. Upon removal of

73. See W. Brown, "Nonreductive Physicalism and Soul," p. 1813.

74. The official U.S. government Web site with links and publications is http://www.loc.gov/loc/brain/.

75. For historical notes, see Jeeves, "Brain, Mind, and Behavior," p. 77.

76. A celebrated account and analysis can be found in Damasio, *Descartes' Error,* chaps. 1; 2.

the tumor, the teacher's behavior returned to normal — but amazingly, after a couple of years, the immoral traits returned, and the reason was the return of the tumor.[77]

More recently rapid developments in experimental psychology, comparative neuropsychology, and brain-imaging techniques have yielded an amazing array of results, insights, and information about the deep and wide connections between the brain and human behavior at all levels. Notwithstanding complicated philosophical interpretations of neuroscientific results,[78] currently there is no denying the tight link between the functioning of the brain and human behavior. Even though the exact localization of specific brain activities has to be handled with great care, certain regions or systems have been shown to be linked with particular mental and physical activities,[79] such as language capacities,[80] types of memory functions (whether declarative, that is, remembering names and events, or procedural, that is, how to do things),[81] or error detection and compensation.[82] Highly interesting, and often mentioned, is blindsight. Simply put, this means that people (totally or partially) blind due to brain damage in a certain area can still detect objects or stimuli shown to them without being able to "see" them — and surprisingly accurately, for that matter! While known for some time,[83] this phenomenon attracts further study and sheds light on related questions of the linking of various types of visual functions to certain areas of brain activity.[84] Another highly significant evidence of the neural basis of human behavior is "mind reading," related to "mirror neurons" that facilitate the human capacity to engage a number of mental activities hitherto found mysterious but also, even more importantly, help the person observe another person engaged in the same activity.[85] Hence, generally speaking, the "theory of mind" makes it possible for us to understand others as intentional agents, a capacity found in a rudimentary form in other higher animals as well.[86] Similarly, human experiences such as psychological

77. Reported in Burns and Swerdlow, "Right Orbitofrontal Tumor," pp. 437-40.

78. An emerging discipline is "neurophilosophy"; see P. S. Churchland, *Neurophiloso-phy*; a nontechnical sequel is Churchland's *Brain-Wise*.

79. Still a worthwhile presentation is Posner et al., "Localisation of Cognitive Operations," pp. 1627-31.

80. See Posner et al., "Localisation of Cognitive Operations."

81. Mishkin and Appenzeller, "The Anatomy of Memory," pp. 80-89.

82. Dehaene, Posner, and Tucker, "Localization of a Neural System," pp. 303-5.

83. A standard work is Weiskrantz, *Blindsight*.

84. Celesia, "Visual Perception and Awareness," p. 62.

85. Ramachandran, "Mirror Neurons and Imitation Learning."

86. Call and Tomasello, "Does the Chimpanzee Have a Theory of Mind?"

pain of social loss or capacity for moral appraisal or trust have all clearly identifiable neural correlates.[87]

There is also quite a lot of evidence that what is sometimes called a "sick will," that is, "inactivity, lack of ambition, autistic behavior, depressive motor skills, and behavioral inhibition," correlates with abnormal activity in the prefrontal cortex.[88] Not only behavioral, cognitive, and emotional functioning and activities but also "the tight link between neuronal processes and moral decision-making — including, but not limited to, reviewing past decisions and their consequences, weighing options and potential rewards, and envisioning the future" — has been empirically demonstrated.[89]

Perhaps as a surprise to many comes the linkage between observed neural activity and the exercise of spiritual and religious activities.[90] We know, for example, that epilepsy has been linked with intensified religiosity and mysticism,[91] and that patients with Alzheimer's disease often struggle with their faith.[92] While it would be naive to exclude other factors present in these cases, the neuronal basis can be experimentally established. Or consider these experimental discoveries: correlation between changes in cerebral activity in charismatic Christians' glossolalia (speaking in tongues), or Tibetan Buddhist meditation, or Franciscan nuns' silent prayer, or Carmelite nuns' mystical experiences with God.[93] Joel Green concludes: "Whatever else such studies indicate, they point clearly to the biological substrate of spiritual experience."[94] An emerging discipline of "neurotheology" intentionally seeks an interdisciplinary account of the meaning and implications of these and numerous other

87. Reported in J. Green, *Body, Soul, and Human Life,* pp. 44-45, with original references.

88. Reported in J. Green, *Body, Soul, and Human Life,* p. 83, based on Libet, Freeman, and Sutherland, eds., *Volitional Brain,* an interdisciplinary collection of essays.

89. J. Green, *Body, Soul, and Human Life,* p. 84, with reference to Tancredi, *Hardwired Behavior.*

90. Groundbreaking interdisciplinary work is being done at the Institute for the Bio-Cultural Study of Religion founded by the neuroscientist Patrick McNamara and philosopher of religion Wesley J. Wildman; see the Web site for research and resources: http://www.ibcsr .org/. A massive collection of essays on evolutionary and neurological bases of religion, including neurotheology, as well as related issues, is the three-volume *Where God and Science Meet: How Brain and Evolutionary Studies Alter Our Understanding of Religion,* edited by Patrick McNamara. For an insightful critique of neurotheology and neurology of religion, see W. Brown, "The Brain, Religion, and Baseball."

91. Persinger, "People Who Report Religious Experiences," pp. 963-75.

92. See "The Neuroscientist and the Theologian."

93. Reported in J. Green, *Body, Soul, and Human Life,* pp. 107-8.

94. J. Green, *Body, Soul, and Human Life,* p. 108.

religion-neuroscience connections.[95] (Another related emerging discipline is "theobiology," which, against the nomenclature, is pursued as much by psychologists as by biologists and other natural scientists;[96] unlike neurotheology, that discipline has not so far progressed significantly, and it looks like neurotheology is becoming the main paradigm.)

What are the implications for philosophy and theology of this close linkage between neural/brain events and human behavior/mind? A particularly important issue has to do with whether the mental is not only a "real" property but also that it can exercise any causal influence downward. This is the question that has occupied philosophy of mind for the latter part of the twentieth century. To that discussion we move next, before beginning the investigation of a constructive theological proposal.

The Possibility and Conditions of Mental Causation

The phenomenon of mental causation — either the mental causing the physical or the mental causing other mental events — is a deep and universal common intuition. It is absolutely fundamental to our concept of actions performed intentionally (as opposed to involuntarily); otherwise, how could we envision meaningful human agency, free will, and moral responsibility? Yet, ironically, the causal interaction between the bodily and mental is one of the unresolved problems — or so it seems — in contemporary philosophy and science. The challenge "is to see how reasons — our beliefs, desires, purposes, and plans — operate in a world of causes, and to exhibit the role of reasons in the *causal* explanation of human behavior."[97] A crucial issue for theologians — and many philosophers — is what the British neuropsychologist Donald MacKay used to call "nothing-buttery,"[98] namely, the identity theory according to which all mental phenomena, whether intellectual, emotional, or moral, are but brain/neural states.[99]

---

95. The standard introductory source is Newberg, D'Aquili, and Rause, *Why God Won't Go Away;* the most recent major work is Newberg, *Principles of Neurotheology.* A useful interdisciplinary collection of essays is Joseph, ed., *NeuroTheology.*

96. See Rayburn and Richmond, "Theobiology," pp. 1793-1811; see also Helminiak, "Theistic Psychology and Psychotherapy," pp. 47-74.

97. Dretske, *Explaining Behavior,* p. x, emphasis in original.

98. MacKay, *The Clock Work Image,* p. 21. See the now-classic argument in Armstrong, *Materialist Theory of Mind,* for the view that mental states are nothing but brain states.

99. Precursors to the current identity theories, the psychophysical monist views, variously conceived, were already represented among early modern scientists such as Thomas

The identity theory rules among a number of scientists of various fields who study human nature. Recall Francis Crick's "astonishing hypothesis" that contemporary science has not only expelled "soul" but also discovered that we are *nothing but* a pack of neurons."[100] Along with the identity theory, several other (related) theories of the mind-body relationship reject or severely minimize the possibility of the mind's causal powers, such as psychophysical parallelism, in which physical events are caused by physical causes and mental events by mental causes. Any appearance of mental to physical causality is just that — *appearance*.[101] According to epiphenomenalism, "conscious mental life is a causally inconsequential byproduct of physical processes in the brain."[102] Furthermore, the obvious question to this view is, why should the causality from mental to physical — at least in principle — be any more difficult to conceive than vice versa? Yet another view, known as "eliminativism," bluntly states that mental events do not exist,[103] and the related interpretation (that similarly attempts to deal with the nonexistence of mental events) called "fictionalism" claims that it is "wise" to live one's life as if they were true![104] The once-dominant paradigm of (American) behaviorism, gleaning from logical positivism's naive demand for "empiricist" verification, similarly reduced all mental states to "external" behavior.[105]

All these theories of the mind-body relationship not only challenge theologians but also — if shown to be true — fatally defeat anyone holding on to the commonsense (and necessary) intuition of the reality of mental life and its

---

Hobbes and George Berkeley; the former was materialist and interpreted both thinking and emotions accordingly in terms of "movements" of head and heart, whereas the latter was idealist.

100. Crick, *The Astonishing Hypothesis*, p. 3, emphasis in original. Similarly, Pinker, *The Blank Slate*, p. 224.

101. With reference to God and divine action, G. W. Leibniz's monadology argued that there is harmony established and sustained by God between the physical and mental and hence the appearance. Famously Owen Flanagan (*Science of the Mind*, p. 64) has ridiculed this tactic as a way of introducing "a big Spirit in order to get rid of the perplexities of a world of little spirits." See also the discussion and critique in Murphy, *Beyond Liberalism and Fundamentalism*, chap. 3.

102. Murphy, "Human Nature," p. 9.

103. Classically argued in P. M. Churchland, "Eliminative Materialism and the Propositional Attitudes," pp. 67-90; a book-long defense is Stich, *From Folk Psychology to Cognitive Science*. A thoughtful and robust rebuttal is Horgan and Woodward, "Folk Psychology Is Here to Stay."

104. See Dennett, "True Believers," pp. 57-80 [1975].

105. Philosophical behaviorism is classically argued by Hempel, "Logical Analysis of Psychology," pp. 164-73; Ryle's *Concept of Mind* is the most well-known monographic presentation. A devastating critique is offered in Putnam, "Brains and Behavior," pp. 24-36.

effects. In other words, can human mental activities be understood merely in biological and physical terms?[106] Particularly the existence of consciousness poses an urgent question. Sometimes among the philosophers of mind the question is raised whether we could envision a human person who would be exactly like us but without consciousness, a zombie.[107] In contrast to a zombie, a defining characteristic of human consciousness is the capacity to have *qualia,* an internal personal feeling about what it is like for me to have a certain experience of something (like smell, sound, touch).[108]

Whereas among neuroscientists, as mentioned, the reductionist identity theory still seems to be the prominent view,[109] regarding Anglo-American philosophy of mind, nonreductive physicalism/materialism in its various versions seems to hold the dominant position.[110] The minimalist description of nonreductive physicalism simply is that in its attack on reductionism it considers the mental as an emergent novel property (or capacity or event) that "supervenes," that is, is dependent on the subvenient base, but that cannot be reduced to its base. Each of these terms, namely, "reductionism" (and its defeat: nonreductionism), "emergence," "supervenience," as well as "multiple realizability," is widely used and even more widely debated among various types of philosophers of mind. Let us take them briefly one at a time to establish the contours of discussion for the subsequent theological assessment and constructive proposal.

How to defeat reductionism is obviously the main target of those who oppose identity theory and its siblings.[111] Terminologically, an important distinction has to be made between "methodological reductionism," that is, "a research strategy of analyzing the thing to be studied into its parts," and "causal reductionism," "the view that the behavior of the parts of a system . . . is determinative of the behavior of all higher-level entities" (also called "parts on whole" and "bottom up"), as well as "ontological reductionism," which claims that "higher-level entities are 'nothing but the sum of their parts.'" The last two are of course related, but regarding the latter, one needs to make yet another distinction. Whereas ontological reductionism claims that "as one goes up the hierarchy of levels, no new kinds of metaphysical 'ingredients' need to be

---

106. Purcell, *From Big Bang,* p. 245.

107. For the now classic definition, see Dennett, *Consciousness Explained,* p. 73.

108. Cf. the programmatic essay by Nagel, "What Is It Like to Be a Bat?"

109. For an important current defense of type identity, see Gozzano and Hill, *New Perspectives on Type Identity.*

110. Bickle, "Multiple Realizability."

111. An important current statement and defense of reductionism is J. Kim, *Physicalism, or Something Near Enough,* chap. 4.

added to produce higher-level entities from lower," for "reductive materialism," the higher-level processes are not only the function of the lower but they are not even "real." That is accurately called "reductive materialism." That is the target of all nonreductivists.

A critical step in the defeat of the identity theory/reductive materialism is the theory of emergence.[112] Recall (from discussion in chapter 1 above) that emergence is the view that new structures, capacities, and processes will come to existence; that these cannot be reduced to the lower level; and that they can exercise a causal influence downward. This means that the mental, most prominently, consciousness, is derived from the biological/physical basis but is not to be reduced to it, and that it may have causal influence on the subvenient base.[113] Now, in keeping with the principle of emergence, supervenience negotiates the relationship between brain and mental events, unlike the identity theory and dualism. Already in 1970, the philosopher Donald Davidson (who famously spoke of mental events as anomalous because they do not follow "strict deterministic" laws that would allow their prediction, without wanting to give up mental events either) stated that supervenience means that "mental characteristics are in some sense dependent, or supervenient, on physical characteristics."[114]

But not any form of supervenience necessarily helps defeat the identity theory, as there are also reductionist interpretations thereof.[115] The one needed for an antireductionist program is one that claims there are a number of ways a particular supervenient property may be instantiated and that it is context specific. In other words, it has to be the case that mental properties (against the covariation thesis, that is, if there is a change in mental event, there is also a change in the physical) could change without the change in the base property due to contextual factors.[116] For example, a rich lady giving money to help a poor man on the street corner can be a genuine token of generosity, while the same kind of gift by this married lady to her secret lover would not be. In other words, supervenient properties can be multiply realizable and therefore are not identity relations.[117] This is called the principle of multiple realizability[118] and

---

112. For a now classic essay, see Popper, "Natural Selection and the Emergence of Mind."

113. See Clayton, *Mind and Emergence*, p. vi.

114. Davidson, "Mental Events," pp. 208, 214, respectively.

115. For a reductionist version, see J. Kim, *Physicalism, or Something Near Enough*, p. 14; see further, McLaughlin, "Varieties of Supervenience," pp. 16-59.

116. See Murphy and Brown, *DMN*, p. 204.

117. Murphy, "Nonreductive Physicalism," pp. 132-35.

118. The key scholars in the development of the concept have been Putnam, "Nature of Mental States," and Fodor, "Special Sciences."

can be illustrated with the help of an important distinction made in philosophy of mind between two types of identity: "token" identity states that every mental event is identical with some physical event or another, and the stronger version, "type" identity, according to which every mental event is identical with a particular physical event. Type identity makes it possible to reduce every mental event to a particular type of physical event, like "pain" to "C-fibers," whereas token identity allows the realizability of a particular mental event with more than one kind of physical event. Type identity would of course lead to the reduction of psychology (and related fields of the study of humanity) to neuroscience,[119] a goal pursued by eliminative materialists.[120] Nonreductive physicalism utilizes the token identity relationship between the physical (brain functions) and the mental.[121] Consider this often-quoted analogy: the property of "good," as in an ethically good person, can be said to supervene on a collection of personality and behavior traits such as benevolence, temper, and kindness.[122] An added value of the multiple-realizability type of understanding of supervenience is that various levels of the hierarchy of reality such as ethical, aesthetic, and, say, religious are not in danger of being reduced to the brain and neurological level (and thus under physical laws) even though, as mentioned, these higher levels can also be said to emerge from the physical, which is the only "stuff" that exists.

Now we are in a place to explain how exactly the antireductionists seek to establish the possibility of the mental causation, top-down (and whole-part) causation. The most persistent critic of nonreductive physicalism, Jaegwon Kim, himself a staunch reductionist, ironically makes a valid point as he claims that

> the emergentist and nonreductive physicalist are mental realists, and Mental Realism, via Alexander's dictum,[123] entails causal powers for mental

119. See Flanagan, *Science of the Mind,* p. 218. Importantly, Jaegwon Kim has become a critic of type-identity theory even though he remains a staunch reductionist (of a functional type); see chap. 5 in J. Kim, *Physicalism, or Something Near Enough.*

120. See, e.g., P. S. Churchland, "Perspective on Mind-Brain Research," pp. 185-207.

121. The type-token distinction has some relation to a distinction made sometimes between "weak" and "strong" emergence. Whereas the weak version speaks of the dependence of the higher (mental) on the lower (physical) in the general sense, the strong version argues for a determination of the supervenient by the subvenient. Strong supervenience virtually makes the mental epiphenomenal.

122. Indeed, this example goes back to the original definition of supervenience by Hare, *The Language of Morals,* p. 145.

123. That is, to speak of mental property (or any property for that matter) is to speak of

properties . . . [as] mental properties, on both positions are irreducible net additions to the world. And this must mean . . . that mental properties bring with them *new causal powers, powers that no underlying physical-biological properties can deliver.* . . . To be real, Alexander has said, is to have causal powers; *to be real, new, and irreducible, therefore, must be to have new, irreducible causal powers.*[124]

Kim rightly concludes that apart from downward causation, mental causation is not explicable. Because of this — and two related reasons, namely, rejection of causal overdetermination[125] (that is, there cannot be two simultaneous causes on the mental, the physical and the mental) and causal closure[126] (that is, ultimately the physical is the causal explanation) — Kim rejects as incoherent the whole notion of nonreductive physicalism.[127] By doing so, as said, he clarifies helpfully the main resources available and necessary for the antireductionist program.

Let us now turn from this general philosophy of mind conversation to investigate in detail the potential of a nonreductive physicalist proposal as set forth by some leading Christian scholars.

The Promise and Liabilities of the Nonreductive Physicalist Account of Human Nature

The Defeat of Reductionism

As observed, philosophers and theologians are intensely seeking a middle way between dualisms and reductive materialism, known as "nonreductive physicalism." (Many other more-or-less synonymous terms are used, including "[pluralistic] emergent monism," "constitutional monism," "open-system

---

causal efficacy (in other words: if mental events do not "do" anything, why speak of them at all!). It was formulated by S. Alexander, *Space, Time, and Deity*, 2:8.

124. J. Kim, *Supervenience and Mind*, p. 350, emphasis in original; see also J. Kim "Making Sense of Emergence," p. 5.

125. J. Kim, "Non-Reductivist's Troubles," p. 208.

126. J. Kim, "Non-Reductivist's Troubles," p. 209.

127. J. Kim, "Myth of Nonreductive Materialism," pp. 242-60; J. Kim, "Non-Reductivist's Troubles," p. 208. Later in his evolving thinking Kim came to grant the possibility and even need of a kind of mental causation — as long as the reductionist program is not thereby thwarted (*Physicalism, or Something Near Enough*, p. 9). He calls this view "conditional physical reductionism" (p. 5).

emergence" or "deep physicalism," "dual aspect monism," and "emergent dualism.") Most (but not all) of these terms are monist in a particular way, namely, *physically/materialistically* (while not denying the reality of the mental, including, in most cases, even religiosity). In this section, I am engaging the nonreductive physicalism proposed by its leading Christian advocates (the philosopher N. Murphy and neuropsychologist W. Brown, among others). Even when my own formulation of the nature of human nature is not identical with that proposal, it is indebted in many ways to its insights.

Obviously, nonreductive *physicalism* takes seriously physicality. In keeping with emergence theory, it believes that a nonreductionist approach with a focus on a "hierarchy of levels of complexity" saves human sciences and higher human capacities.[128] In nonreductive physicalism,[129] explains Murphy, "we are our bodies — there is no additional metaphysical element such as mind or soul or spirit. But . . . this 'physicalist' position need not deny that we are intelligent, moral, and spiritual. We are, at our best, complex physical organisms, imbued with the legacy of thousands of years of culture, and, most importantly, blown by the Breath of God's Spirit; we are *Spirited bodies.*"[130] For *Christian* and other theist nonreductionists, then, the viewpoint does not entail atheism.[131] It affirms "ontological reductionism" (that there are no nonphysical ultimate elements) but rejects vehemently both "causal" and "reductive" materialism, that is, physics is able to explain everything and beyond the material/physical there is nothing "real" such as the mental.[132] Nonreductive physicalism also insists on the possibility of free will.[133]

As mentioned, multiple realizability and then token identity are key aspects of nonreductive physicalism. Furthermore, a satisfactory *non*reductive account can be had only if atomism, bottom-up causation, and determinism can be replaced with self-direction of systems (including the human person as a system) and top-down causation, that is, the higher-level system exerting causal influence on its parts. The well-established principles of quantum nonlocality and entanglement speak for top-down and whole-part causality

128. Murphy and Brown, *DMN*, p. 9, emphasis in original. For a somewhat pejorative and mistaken statement about nonreductive physicalism, see Midgley, "Soul's Successors," p. 53.
129. An exact nomenclature (though too cumbersome for frequent usage) would then be "nonreductive neurophysiologicalism." Murphy and Brown, *DMN*, p. 9.
130. Murphy, *Bodies and Souls*, p. ix.
131. See Murphy and Brown, *DMN*, p. 7.
132. Murphy, "Nonreductive Physicalism," pp. 129-30; for a more extensive analysis of types of reductionism, see Murphy and Brown, *DMN*, pp. 47-48.
133. Murphy, "Nonreductive Physicalism," p. 127.

instead of the Newtonian one-way causality (from the bottom up).[134] Furthermore, regarding human life, the "cognitivist paradigm" coupled with the notions of emergence and two-way supervenience, as it were, gives a fuller and more adequate picture: "new, previously nonexistent, emergent properties, including the mental . . . interact causally at their own higher level and also exert causal control from above downward. . . . Mental states, as emergent properties of brain activity, thus exert downward control over their constituent neuronal events — at the same time that they are being determined by them."[135]

In their effort to defeat reductionism, Murphy and Brown take as the strongest asset the idea of mental events as *contextualized* brain states and supervenience. They surmise that in order to defeat the "Cartesian views of the mind as 'inner' and essentially contemplative or passive" (still rampant even in neuroscientific accounts), it is essential "that supervenient mental states be understood to be co-determined by subvenient neural events *along with* social, environmental, and historical *context.*"[136] In other words, "mental states are *contextualized* brain states," which means that "brain states constitute specific mental states only insofar as they bear appropriate interactive relations to the things in the world and to the agents' ongoing processes and actions."[137] The reason why "[m]ental events are not reducible to brain events . . . [is that] mental events are largely constituted by relations to actions in the environment."[138]

Higher animals, let alone humans, act as agents. In that purposeful human activity, a number of mental capacities make a joint contribution: symbolic, linguistic, cognitive, aesthetic, emotional, moral, and other such capacities. As discussed above, the unique brain capacity in humans, particularly the large prefrontal cortex, makes possible the superior cognitive functioning (including memory) with flexibility, evaluation, and anticipation.[139] While higher animals act according to reason, humans act also for a reason (to borrow the philosophers' distinction).[140]

Even with mental top-down causality resolved, a remaining problem, common to all physicalists, is "how can neural nets mean"[141] — the mys-

---

134. Murphy and Brown, *DMN*, p. 49; see G. Ellis, "Quantum Theory and the Macroscopic World," p. 270.
135. Sperry, "Psychology's Mentalist Paradigm," p. 609.
136. Murphy and Brown, *DMN*, p. 21, emphasis in original.
137. Murphy and Brown, *DMN*, p. 40, emphasis in original.
138. Murphy and Brown, *DMN*, p. 209.
139. For details, see Murphy and Brown, *DMN*, pp. 131-33.
140. See further, Murphy and Brown, *DMN*, p. 145.
141. Chapter title in Murphy and Brown, *DMN*, p. 147.

tery of meaning. Language and words are *about* something. Mental states have intentionality. How can these come from the physical?[142] Many doubt whether it is possible. This includes not only dualists of different sorts[143] but also, somewhat ironically, bioanthropologist Terrence W. Deacon, the author of *Symbolic Species*.[144] Murphy and Brown, however, are optimistic and believe that "the 'mysteries' involved in language use disappear when we consider meaning not as the product of inner mental acts, but as a result of engagement in adaptive action-feedback loops in the world — especially in the social world." This entails paying attention to the *context* of the brain states because mental states are contextualized brain states.[145] "Sense is a product not of an inner mental act, but rather of *communally shared* semantic networks"; "Language hooks *onto the world* as we use it in our socially constructed (i.e., contextually constrained) embodied activities *in the world*."[146] In their pluriform and sophisticated approach to seeking to establish meaning and rationality as genuinely novel and "real" processes, they also utilize the Wittgensteinian idea of language games and the Lakoff-Johnson idea of concepts as "embodied metaphors."[147]

The Liabilities of the Nonreductive Physicalist Account

There are lasting values in nonreductive physicalism that need to be carefully preserved. The foundational key value simply is the importance of physicality.[148] Beyond that, nonreductive physicalism is fairly successful in negotiating between the full embrace of the most recent scientific data concerning human behavior and the essentials of Christian (religious) intuitions.

That said, it is not difficult to see the basic philosophical dilemma of nonreductive physicalism and that its claim for *physicality* as the ultimate base

142. This is the key concern and challenge in Owen Flanagan's nonreductive materialism (*Consciousness Reconsidered*), which denies that high-level concepts of self can be understood in natural terms; rather they have to be constructed over the life span.

143. For a substance-dualist defeat of physicalists' claim that the physical state has intentionality, see Moreland and Rae, *Body and Soul,* pp. 164-65. For an emergent dualist's doubts, see Hasker, *Emergent Self,* p. 32.

144. See Deacon, *Symbolic Species*, pp. 51, 61.

145. Murphy and Brown, *DMN*, pp. 150-51, at p. 150; chap. 4 is devoted to this topic.

146. Murphy and Brown, *DMN*, p. 191, emphasis in original.

147. For the discussion of these matters, see Murphy and Brown, *DMN*, chap. 4.

148. See W. Brown, "Conclusion," p. 223.

and explanation is its Achilles' heel: "say yes, and you seem to end up with a reductive physicalism; say no, and you aren't really a physicalist after all."[149]

In this context one cannot avoid — again — facing the problem common to all physicalists, namely, that of the higher mental capacities, consciousness. Wittgenstein's challenges to materialists still call for a response: "The idea of a process in the head, in a completely enclosed space, makes thinking something occult."[150] One way to highlight the distinctive nature of mental life is to speak of "intentionality,"[151] that is, "aboutness," referring to something else. This aboutness relationship is dramatically different from a causal relationship.[152] It is hard to contest what the philosopher of mind Jerry Fodor observed: "Nobody has the slightest idea how anything material could be conscious."[153] Titles such as *How Matter Becomes Imagination*[154] — even though written by senior neuroscientists, one of whom is a Nobel laureate — simply promise too much.

Although I think the reference to the contextuality and sociality is a needed asset in helping us understand how the "neural" may mean, it still is far from clear how exactly this wider context may resolve the issue. To give a simple example: I simply do not understand how the meaning of these two sentences, namely, that the "[s]ense is a product not of an inner mental act, but rather of *communally shared* semantic networks" and that "[l]anguage hooks *onto the world* as we use it in our socially constructed (i.e., contextually constrained) embodied activities *in the world*,"[155] emerges (if it does) from the associations and functions of countless neurons in my brain. I hasten to say that I would be the last person to dismiss the importance of sincere efforts to understand the "meaning of meaning." What I am saying is that with all its sophistication, we are far from understanding how the meaning emerges from the physical. To name the problem (or indicate the locus of the action) is hardly an explanation. In other words: until much more light is shed on how meaning and aboutness may emerge from "meaningless" and "dumb" matter, mere reference to supervenience theory, even in terms of multiple realizability, does not offer an explanation of how the mental and physical interact. It merely

---

149. Clayton, *Mind and Emergence*, p. 130. No wonder J. Kim *(Mind in a Physical World)* considers nonreductive physicalism internally incoherent.

150. Wittgenstein, *Philosophical Grammar*, §64. Similarly, Wittgenstein, *Zettel*, §605.

151. The phenomenologist philosopher Edmund Husserl wrote the groundbreaking work on intentionality; see Spear, "Husserl on Intentionality and Intentional Content."

152. Clayton, "Neuroscience, the Person, and God," p. 191.

153. Fodor, "The Big Idea," pp. 5-7, quoted in Clayton, *Mind and Emergence*, p. 112.

154. Subtitle in Edelman and Tononi, *A Universe of Consciousness*.

155. Murphy and Brown, *DMN*, p. 191, emphasis in original.

shows covariation.[156] Reference to emergence is hardly an explanation (it looks more like an observation).[157]

These cautions are not meant to undermine, let alone reject, supervenience or emergence, but rather, to show the limitations with regard to explanatory power. Nor is this reservation meant to imply that because of the radically different logic between causal and referential relationships, our study of human behavior (psychology) should not be tightly integrated with neurosciences.[158] Many have the nagging feeling that "[t]o know everything there is to know about the progression of brain states is not to know what it is like to be you, to experience your joy, your pain, or your insights. No human researcher can known, as Thomas Nagel so famously argued, 'what it's like to be a bat.'"[159]

Furthermore, as surprising as it may sound, it seems to me that from a (natural) scientific perspective it is less than clear that physicalism is the right or even the best choice. First, to claim to establish a metaphysical claim on the basis of scientific observation is a category mistake: science, to be science, cannot go beyond its limits (although scientists, often even in the name of science, break this law all the time!). Second, it seems to many that current science is moving away from what "physical" used to mean. The physicist Arnold E. Sikkema notes that a key problem of nonreductive physicalism is "that it elevates the *composition* of entities as though what things are made of is of ultimate concern to a discussion of their ontology." As is well known, in the theory of relativity mass is nothing but a form of energy (in relation to the speed of light); in quantum mechanics, treating subatomic entities as particles is complementary to regarding them as probability waves; and so forth.[160] The point here is that matter/physicality has become very elusive, virtually "nonmaterial." And even if nonreductive physicalists would respond (as I guess they might) that the point of nonreductive physicalism is not about the composition, I think Sikkema's question calls for an answer.

---

156. This is the lasting value of J. Kim's critique of supervenience (of which he advocates the strong form); *Mind in a Physical World*, pp. 9-15, 38-47.

157. So also Gazzaniga, *Who's in Charge?* p. 105.

158. The unfortunate implication of Fodor's, as well as H. Putnam's, legitimate concern for the distinctive nature of the mental and refusal to demand methodological strictures from humanistic studies as strict as those of natural sciences is the virtual severance of psychology from the neurosciences. See, e.g., Fodor, "Special Sciences," pp. 97-115; Putnam, "Philosophy and Our Mental Life," pp. 291-303.

159. Clayton, *Mind and Emergence*, pp. 111-12.

160. Sikkema, "Physicist's Reformed Critique," pp. 23-24, here p. 24, emphasis in original.

The bottom line is this: What is matter/physicality? Is it totally different from the mental? No one would probably wish to contest the general point that "the twentieth century, which began with what could be regarded as an empirical demonstration of the materialistic atomistic vision of Democritus, saw a progressive 'dematerialization' of physics. . . . Modern physics, then, has something quite different in view regarding the structure of the universe than the ordinary parlance used by the 'nonreductive physicalist.'"[161] If mental events, particularly consciousness, morality, and religiosity, are but materially based processes, then the "matter" we speak of has little or nothing in common with our current scientific understanding! It may be, as the Jesuit scientist William Stoeger surmises, that the neuroscientific investigation pushes us to radically reconsider and change what "physical/material" and "nonphysical/nonmaterial" may mean.[162] In any case, as is well known, "matter" is not a well-defined scientific concept (whereas "mass" and "energy" are).[163] We even need a new vocabulary to speak of the mind and the mental. We probably cannot say the mental is "immaterial" or "nonphysical" because that would cut off its deep integration with the brain (any more than we can say the mental is material). Would terms such as "trans-material/-physical" communicate that best?

The main point for my purposes is simply this: perhaps the premature jump onto the physicalist bandwagon by Christian scholars is not as philosophically and scientifically advantageous as previously thought. There are also some urgent religious and theological reasons for continuing the quest. Beyond the obvious, that from the theological and religious point of view many would find it very difficult to think of ontology merely in terms of a staunch physicalist claim,[164] is the deeper claim that even for nonreductive physicalists who are not atheists, physicalism is only the penultimate option. All theistic traditions consider the Ultimate to be spiritual; certainly that is the case for all Abrahamic faiths. In this light, I feel sympathy for the philosopher-theologian Philip Clayton's preference for a "monism" that is not physicalist in itself, although it takes physicality most seriously. He argues that we should not assume that the "entities postulated by physics complete the inventory of what exists" while he insists that "[r]eality is ultimately composed of one basic kind of stuff."[165]

161. Sikkema, "Physicist's Reformed Critique," p. 25.

162. Stoeger, "Mind-Brain Problem," p. 132.

163. Stoeger, "Mind-Brain Problem," pp. 133-35; see also Heller, "Adventures of the Concept," pp. 15-35.

164. Sikkema, "Physicist's Reformed Critique," p. 22.

165. Clayton, *Mind and Emergence,* p. 4.

What would be the benefits of replacing physicalism with a revised notion without going back to dualism? It would allow for a more holistic and diversified ontology of things in creation characterized, or qualified, by the various modal aspects. Thereby it would not try to say the last word on a topic that in light of current scientific knowledge is still open-ended (and might remain so for a long time!). On the other hand, it would help both metaphysical materialists and idealists work out a (more) common account of human nature — namely, a nondualistic, unified monistic one — along with allowing each party to hold on to its dearest "ultra-metaphysical" intuitions (or leave the question open). Furthermore, this move would also help to better combat the prevailing reductionist tendency (not absent even from the nonreductionist physicalist accounts). Finally, it seems to me that it would fund a more robust and hopefully more appropriate multidimensional and pluralist approach in sciences: "recognizing the physical as one aspect among others will help develop a more fully orbed philosophy of science, recognizing the importance of the different methodologies of inquiry that rightfully play roles in the other scientific disciplines, rather than focusing on what some regard as the highly problematic ontology of the entities of mechanics due to their lying so far beyond imagination."[166] With these cautions and insights in mind, let us try our hand at a tentative constructive proposal for how to best understand the nature of human nature in light of theological, philosophical, and scientific contours.

"Multidimensional Monism": Toward a Holistic, Pluralistic, and Unified Account of Human Nature

The insights won from the careful tracing of the rise of dualisms in Christian tradition and its critique, as well as the establishment of deep interrelationships between human mind/behavior and neurological-physiological-biological process, guide our endeavor here. The engagement of nonreductionist physicalism helps us position our investigation against identity theory's reductionism and defeat of the mental. Throughout we have tried to keep in mind the holistic, relational, and embodied-emotional account of human personhood based on image-of-God discourse. Let us continue the constructive work by first looking at the latest developments in biblical studies and how they may point to a holistic, elusive, and multidimensional direction as a further preparation for the more detailed look at the proposal itself.

166. Sikkema, "Physicist's Reformed Critique," p. 26.

Biblical Insights into Human Nature

By the beginning of the twentieth century, critical scholarship had come to question the prevailing body-soul dualism. Particularly significant was the recovery of the holistic, unified, and nonanalytic view of humanity in the Hebrew Bible.[167] As early as in 1911, H. Wheeler Robinson's *Christian Doctrine of Man* conceived the Hebrew idea of personality as an animated body.[168] However, while monistic, Robinson's account differed radically from the later twentieth-century scholarship's emphasis on physicalist monism (his was an idealist philosophy). Some other important works in the early twentieth century argued against dualism, rightly noting that what is called "soul" in the OT *(nephes)* rather means "life" or "living [being]."[169] However, other works continued to advocate dualism,[170] thus indicating a lack of consensus.[171]

A decisive shift in biblical scholarship toward acknowledging the monistic account of the human person came from Rudolf Bultmann's influential interpretation of *soma* as denoting the whole person in the NT.[172] His interpretation, however, suffered because it undermined the physical connotation of the term *soma*,[173] and was in need of correction.[174] Also contributing to the rise of the importance of physicality has been the balancing of the overly Hellenistic reading of Pauline theology with the acknowledgment of deep Hebrew influences.[175] As a result, "a number of more recent, extensive studies have led to verdicts similarly supportive of Paul's essential wholism" and "emphasis on embodied life in this world and the next, while combating body-soul dual-

---

167. An important work was Wolff, *Anthropology of the Old Testament.*

168. H. W. Robinson, *Christian Doctrine of Man.*

169. "Soul," in *A Dictionary of the Bible.*

170. Beckwith, "Soul and Spirit," 11:12-14.

171. I am indebted to Murphy, *Bodies and Souls,* pp. 8-9; J. Green, *Body, Soul, and Human Life,* pp. 14-16, 54-61.

172. Bultmann, *Theology of the New Testament,* vol. 1, §17, pp. 192-203 particularly. His famous statement reads, "Man does not *have* a *soma;* he *is soma*" (1:194).

173. That was correctly critiqued by Gundry, *Sōma in Biblical Theology.* Where Gundry's approach, however, is problematic and in need of correction is that in the end he came to limit the meaning of *soma* in physicality and nothing else; as a result, he also affirmed dualism. Importantly, a more recent commentator on Bultmann's marginalization of physicality (in the meaning of *soma*), Schnelle (*Human Condition,* p. 58), agreed with Gundry's criticism but did not thereby come to affirm dualism. I am indebted to J. Green, *Body, Soul, and Human Life,* pp. 6-7.

174. Kümmel (*Man in the New Testament,* p. 47) speaks of the *soma* as the "complete" person in Paul, and Robert Jewett (*Paul's Anthropological Terms,* p. 447) speaks of it to emphasize "the somatic basis of salvation." Both quoted in J. Green, *Body, Soul, and Human Life,* pp. 6, 7.

175. See J. A. T. Robinson, *The Body,* p. 11.

ism."[176] Murphy summarizes accurately the situation in the biblical scholarship on human nature:

> A survey of the literature of theology and biblical studies throughout the twentieth century, then, shows a gradual displacement of a dualistic account of the person, with its correlative emphasis on the afterlife conceived in terms of the immortality of the soul. First there was the recognition of the holistic character of biblical conceptions of the person, often while still presupposing temporarily separable "parts." Later there developed a holistic *but also physicalist* account of the person, combined with an emphasis on bodily resurrection.[177]

While the "liberal" theological traditions have by and large owned this shift in biblical scholarship, the "conservative" ones for the most part have resisted it and continued to stick with dualism.[178]

As mentioned, the Hebrew term *nephes* refers to the whole person rather than to mere "soul."[179] At times it simply means "person" (Lev. 2:1; 4:20; 7:20). What is striking is that it can also be used to denote animals (Gen. 1:24; 2:7; 9:10). A related Hebrew term, *basar* ("flesh[ly]"; Ps. 119:73; Isa. 45:11-12), may be used in parallel to (but not in contrast to) *nephes*. These two terms "are to be understood as different aspects of man's existence as a twofold unity."[180] The same applies by and large to other terms used in the OT *(gewiyya, leb,* even *ruach)*; they "speak of humans from the perspective of their varying functions."[181]

Regarding the NT, it was a commonplace to claim that whereas the OT

---

176. J. Green, *Body, Soul, and Human Life,* pp. 7-8.

177. Murphy, *Bodies and Souls,* p. 10, emphasis in original; Murphy illustrates the shift in noting that "in *The Encyclopedia of Religion and Ethics* (published between 1909 and 1921) there is a lengthy article on 'soul' and no entry for 'Resurrection.' In *The Anchor Bible Dictionary* (published in 1992) there is no entry at all for 'soul' but a very long set of articles on 'Resurrection'!"

178. An influential advocate of dualism has been philosopher J. Cooper, and his biblical study, *Body, Soul, and Life Everlasting,* who has been followed by other philosopher-theologians and even some conservative biblical scholars.

179. The term occurs about 800 times in the OT and has as its etymology the meaning of "throat" or "gullet"; hence, it denotes human need (as a thirsty throat) and physicality; see further, J. Green, *Body, Soul, and Human Life,* p. 57.

180. Bratsiotis, *"Basar,"* p. 326, quoted in J. Green, "Bodies," pp. 157-58. This paragraph is indebted to Green.

181. J. Green, "Bodies," p. 158. Note Moltmann's subheading: "Thinking with the Body in the Old Testament" (*God in Creation,* p. 256).

is holistic, the NT is dualist. This generalization is just that, a *generalization*, and thus in need of careful reshaping. First, the monist orientation of the OT does not rule out duality or plurality in its presentation of the human being, as even a casual reader notes. Second, more importantly, we know now that the Hellenism of NT times was far from uniform (any more than was the Judaism of that time). Third, the version of Hellenism that was also influential on early Christianity was linked with Judaism — Hellenistic Judaism that gleaned from both Hebrew and Greek sources; its influence on Saint Paul was considerable, rabbi as he was by training.[182]

On the basis of these recent developments, Joel Green, who advocates strongly a monist-physicalist interpretation of the NT data, tests his hermeneutics with some of the most obviously dualistically sounding passages such as Matthew 10:28 ("And do not fear those who kill the body but cannot kill the soul; rather fear him who can destroy both soul and body in hell"). While he takes it as probable that *psyche* (soul) here means the disembodied soul capable of living beyond physical death (a Hellenistic influence on Judaism, as evident in *Testament of Job* 20:3), on the basis of the parallel passage of Luke 12:4 ("Do not fear those who kill the body, and after that have no more that they can do"), he surmises that the point Jesus makes is not a lesson in dualist anthropology but a lesson in the assurance that even martyrdom is not the end.[183] Regarding 2 Corinthians 5:1-10 — "undoubtedly, the most pressing evidence in Paul for a body-dualism" — he acknowledges the possibility of a dualistic reading in terms of the "thanatology concerned with the freeing of the soul from the body for a higher destiny" in which the current state in the body is compared to living in a tent, to be followed by the intermediate state of nakedness, in anticipation of the final abode. However, he finds more convincing in the context of the letter the focus on "the frailty of human existence and the concomitant possibility of denying that one has been clothed in Christ if one suffers as Paul has suffered." In that reading, the metaphor of clothing would refer to baptism, common elsewhere in the Pauline corpus; Paul, then, would be speaking of "longing for the completion of his salvation (i.e., his being 'clothed over' and therefore not found naked in the final judgment)." In sum: this passage would be about the eschatological tension between now and then, rather than an intentional lesson in anthropology.[184] In Green's survey of biblical materials,

---

182. For the complexity of Hellenistic anthropologies, see J. Green, "Bodies," pp. 159-63, on which this paragraph is based.

183. J. Green, "Bodies," p. 162.

184. J. Green, "Bodies," pp. 171-72, with reference to Firnish, *II Corinthians*, pp. 292-95.

"the Old Testament does not locate uniqueness in a doctrine of a (potentially disembodied) soul, but emphasizes instead the character of humanity as God's covenant partner, his counterpart relationship," and in relationship with the rest of humanity as well as the rest of the cosmos. Regarding the NT writers, he notes that they "are more variegated than normally thought, but that, on the question of anthropological monism or dualism, there is greater accord between the traditions represented in the Hebrew Bible and some strands of Greek thought than is usually allowed."[185]

Green's way of reading the biblical data is useful in that it warns us against fixating too easily on a preconceived notion about a dualistic-sounding expression — even if it implies a dualistic understanding. That said, I also think it important to add two critical remarks to put that reading in perspective. First, I don't think that the many clearly dualistic passages, particularly in the NT, could be forced into a monistic hermeneutic. Second, more importantly for my purposes: it seems to me the most sensitive reading of the biblical data points to a multidimensional, elusive, open-ended conception of human nature among various authors and traditions of the Bible. Even dualism, as prevalent as it is, is not the main point, as there are so many ways of speaking of human nature in two- or three- or four- or how-many-dimensional ways. Yet the overall picture seems to be that as important as physicality is, there is the "deeper" or "more-than-physicality" facet to humanity, that is, transcendence or relation to God. With that in mind, I find NT scholar James D. G. Dunn's suggestion of "aspective" and "partitive" NT accounts regarding human nature quite instructive:

> [W]hile Greek thought tended to regard the human being as made up of distinct parts, Hebrew thought saw the human being more as a whole person existing on different dimensions. As we might say, it was more characteristically Greek to conceive of the human person "partitively," whereas it was more characteristically Hebrew to conceive of the human person "aspectively." That is to say, we speak of a school *having* a gym (the gym is part of the school); but we say I *am* a Scot (my Scottishness is an aspect of my whole being).[186]

Using linguistic philosophy's sources, Keith Ward's way of referring to "soul" and "body" (not as substances but) as a way of employing differing lan-

---

185. J. Green, "Bodies," p. 172.
186. Dunn, *The Theology of Paul the Apostle*, p. 54, emphasis in original.

guage and their functions in human life makes a similar point.[187] Some kind of elusive property dualism probably best describes what I am trying to say here.

Beyond the question of dualism versus monism, the most current scholarship has illuminated some central ideas in biblical anthropology related to the questions of identity and personhood. Particularly important here is the contribution of Robert Di Vito, who also takes notice of the significance of these themes in contemporary discussion of the loss of self in postmodernity, discussed in the previous chapter. He puts the biblical, particularly OT, conception of human nature in dialogue with that of modernity with its "location of dignity in self-sufficiency and self-containment, sharply defined personal boundaries, the highly developed idea of my 'inner person,' and the conviction that my full personhood rests on my exercise of autonomous and self-legislative action."[188] On the contrary, the biblical view of the human person, as noted in the previous chapter, is embodied, relational, decentered, and undefined with respect to personal boundaries.[189] Clearly one can see that the current biblical scholarship has shifted the focus from substance dualism toward a more holistic and monistic view of humanity; from individualism to relationality and communion; from isolation from the rest of creation and cosmos to a deep connection and being-embedded-in "nature." My proposal — "multidimensional" monism — seeks to do justice to those features.

Multidimensional Monism: A Proposal for
Conceiving the Nature of Human Nature

The first statement about human nature is that human beings are "psychosomatic unities rather than dual beings composed of a spiritual soul housed within a material body."[190] Indeed, as Tom Wright reminds us, we should talk about "differentiated unity": "Paul and the other early Christian writers didn't reify their anthropological terms. Though Paul uses his language with remarkable consistency, he nowhere suggests that any of the key terms refers to a particular 'part' of the human being to be played off against any other.

187. K. Ward, *Defending the Soul.*
188. As paraphrased by J. Green, *Body, Soul, and Human Life,* p. 12, with reference to Charles Taylor's account in *The Sources of the Self,* which Di Vito utilizes.
189. Di Vito, "Old Testament Anthropology," pp. 217-38.
190. Polkinghorne, "Anthropology in an Evolutionary Context," p. 93; so also materially González, *Mañana,* pp. 125-29.

Each *denotes* the entire human being, while *connoting* some angle of vision on who that human is and what he or she is called to be."[191]

But isn't a proposal like that still dualist? Or to put it in another way: Are all notions of dualism to be carved out once and for all? I doubt it. It seems to me that all views that take the mental as real (existent) and that also therefore assume its causal efficacy, end up being property dualisms of a sort. Certainly nonreductive physicalism is, as is emergent monism. It seems to me the Thomistic view, although it has by and large funded substance ontology,[192] can be tweaked to express the best intuitions of property dualism. What also comes to mind here is the physicist Roger Penrose's idea of the mental as "conscious substance"; it speaks of consciousness (which he also dares to call "soul") in a way that clearly belongs under property dualism.[193] Somewhat similarly, the philosopher of mind David Chalmers's idea of the "information states" in terms of "the double-aspect principle" that is based on the "observation that there is a direct isomorphism between certain physically embodied information spaces and certain *phenomenal* (or experiential) information spaces"[194] represents property dualism of some sort.[195]

In systematic theology, Moltmann's vision of "a *perichoretic* relationship of mutual interpenetration and differentiated unity"[196] and Pannenberg's "personal unity of body and soul"[197] speak the same language. The ethicist Niebuhr's associating the "self" with body but his reluctance to reduce self to the bodily reflects the same intuitions.[198] If I understand correctly "emergent dualism," it argues that having had the mental to emerge, it becomes a property on its own.[199] With all its deviations from classical Christian tradition, American process philosophy's monistic dipolarism represents yet another

191. N. T. Wright, "Mind, Spirit, Soul and Body," n.p., emphasis in original.

192. Just consider this statement from *Summa contra Gentiles* 2.69.2: "body and soul are not two actually existing substances; rather, the two of them together constitute one actually existing substance."

193. Penrose, *Emperor's New Mind*.

194. Chalmers, "Facing Up to the Problem of Consciousness."

195. Chalmers, *Conscious Mind*, p. 305, cited in Barbour, "Neuroscience, Artificial Intelligence, and Human Nature," p. 274. In response to Chalmers's proposal, see the rejoinders in Shear, *Explaining Consciousness*.

196. Moltmann, *God in Creation*, pp. 258-60, here p. 259; he also speaks of the unity between body and soul in terms of covenant (p. 260).

197. Main heading in Pannenberg, *ST* 2:181.

198. See Niebuhr, *The Self and the Dramas of History*, p. 26.

199. See Hasker, *Emergent Self*. Cf. the "integrative dualism" of Taliaferro, *Consciousness and the Mind of God*.

form of property dualism.[200] In sum: for every nonreductionist, the distinction, yet not separation, between the physical and the mental is unavoidable in philosophical, theological, and scientific discussion.

Furthermore, I argue that the reality of mental life cannot be had without a (strong) theory of emergence, as explained in this project. It not only saves the mental but also helps establish its causal efficacy. This "radical kind of emergence"[201] holds robustly to the mind's downward and whole-part causation. Strong emergence "is consistent with the neuroscientific data and the data with the constraints on brain functioning. At the same time, it has the merit of conceiving of mental activity in terms of mental causation, which accords well with our own experience of mental agency."[202] A good example here is how to best speak of human "personhood"; it can never be a matter of merely analyzing and investigating biological and physical processes. The physical explanation never captures "me," the person, *qua* person, but rather as an object of study.[203]

With the tight, in many ways indistinguishable, interdependency and communion between the physical and the mental in mind, Polkinghorne suggests "dual-aspect" monism as a fitting concept to describe the holistic account of human nature. The emphasis on *monism* indicates that the classical metaphysical options of materialism, idealism, and Cartesian dualism are unsatisfactory in light of the current multilayered, complex, and dynamic understanding of reality, including human nature. Dual-aspect monism "acknowledge[s] the fundamental distinction between experience of the material and experience of the mental but . . . would neither impose on reality a sharp division into two unconnected kinds of substance nor deny the psychosomatic unity of human beings." A useful way for him to illustrate the nature of dual-aspect monism is quantum theory's idea of complementarity (superposition principle), which allows for two different/distinct states simultaneously. The main point about the *dual-aspect* nature is that "there will be entities, such as stones, whose nature is located wholly at the material pole, and other entities, such as ourselves, who are 'amphibians,' participating in both kinds of polar experience," namely, mental and material.[204] Polkinghorne also reminds us of the obvious difference between the material and the noetic/mental: whereas

200. See further, Harthstone, "Compound Individual," pp. 193-220; for a short discussion, see Barbour, "Neuroscience, Artificial Intelligence, and Human Nature," pp. 275-80.

201. Gulick, "Reduction, Emergence."

202. Clayton, *Mind and Emergence*, p. 139.

203. For comments, see the section titled "Person-Based Explanations and the Social Sciences" in Clayton, *Mind and Emergence*, pp. 144-48.

204. Polkinghorne, *Faith, Science, and Understanding*, pp. 95-97, here pp. 95, 97.

the former is "a world of process, characterized by temporality and becoming," the latter is "everlasting, in the sense that such truths just *are* and do not evolve." These two "worlds," however, are "complementary aspects of a larger created reality" and hence illustrate the duality that goes beyond material versus mental: "it must also embrace becoming/being and everlasting/temporal." Humanity belongs to both, and therefore, "a fully integrated metaphysics" is needed in which "the multiplicity of experience leads us to an account of considerable richness and subtlety."[205] The potential liability of the dual-aspect monism is that it may make the mental less than real and merely a matter of perspective or experience.[206] The dual-aspect monist, however, doesn't have to be liable to this weakness.

That is not yet the whole story. The basic intuition of the undifferentiated psychosomatic unity and dual-aspect monism implies more, as Clayton puts it: "We need multiple layers of explanatory accounts *because* the human person is a physical, biological, psychological, and (I believe also) spiritual reality, and because these aspects of its reality, though interdependent, are not mutually reducible." The term "ontological pluralism" may best describe this approach.[207] Moltmann's creative nomenclatures "spirit-body," "spirit-*Gestalt*," "spirit-soul," as complementary metaphors, echo this.[208] The German systematician Michael Welker warns us of the reductionism with regard to fixating on one particular aspect, either physicalist or mentalist. Whereas scientists fear the latter, humanists tend to fear the former. "There are simply too many anthropological insights and burning questions in social and cultural studies and in the natural sciences that cannot be hosted by this model." Not only the sciences but also biblical theology point to multidimensionality.[209] Prophetically, one may want to say, already decades ago in Paul Tillich's theology, multidimensionality came to the fore — the inorganic, organic, psychic, and spiritual as the fundamental dimensions of the human.[210] Similarly, the practical theologian Don S. Browning has for years developed a robust theology of the multidimensionality of human nature (with a view to discerning moral goods and values).[211]

---

205. Polkinghorne, *Faith, Science, and Understanding,* p. 98, emphasis in original.

206. This is clearly the case in Velmans, "Making Sense of Causal Interactions," p. 75.

207. Clayton, *Mind and Emergence,* p. 148, emphasis in original.

208. Moltmann, *God in Creation,* pp. 262-64.

209. Welker, "Theological Anthropology versus Anthropological Reductionism," p. 319; so also Barbour, "Neuroscience, Artificial Intelligence, and Human Nature."

210. Tillich, *ST* 3:22-23.

211. D. Browning (*A Fundamental Practical Theology,* pp. 94-109, 139-70) lists the di-

Is my proposal something similar to "neutral monism"?[212] Not only because that term carries a philosophical history that I do not want to identify myself with but also because in the final analysis it leaves so much unexplained (such as, how do we then have the multiplicity of features and properties we have?), I find Clayton's "emergentist monism"[213] quite a comfortable label. It may also be named "property pluralism."[214] Peters's "emergent holism" would also fit the bill.[215]

What Kind of Monism?

But why not physical monism? Above I have expressed my reservations about nonreductive physicalism and will not repeat them here. While I greatly appreciate Jaegwon Kim's honesty when, as a staunch physicalist, he admits, "Physicalism is not the whole truth, but it is the truth near enough,"[216] I also think any authentic physicalism ultimately leads to "ontological physicalism," according to which all there is, is physical[217] — and that I do not take as a credible option. Unlike some theistic naturalists (W. Wildman, among others), I am convinced that only *non*theistic materialist naturalism can stay content with physicalism all the way. The reason is simply this: strictly speaking, ontological physicalism can only be penultimate for a theist. Hence, it seems to me that multidimensional monism, as argued in this project, fits better the key belief in Christian faith (and I guess, other theisms as well) of the complex unity of the finite world as God's creation. While exhibiting various properties as a result of rich creative divine work, the notion of the "unity of nature," as distinct from the infinity of the Creator God (who is Spirit), tells us that all creatures share a common nature (however complex and multidimensional that may be).[218]

More precisely: What does theology have at stake in this debate on ontology? Clayton rightly notes that "[i]f one holds that all mental phenomena

mensions into which there is no need to go in detail here. For a short statement, see his "Human Dignity, Human Complexity," pp. 299-316.

212. For a useful discussion with sources, see Stubenberg, "Neutral Monism."

213. That is also the view of Peacocke, "Sound of Sheer Silence," p. 219.

214. Clayton, "Neuroscience, the Person, and God," p. 212; Sperry means something similar in *Science and Moral Priority.*

215. T. Peters, "Resurrection of the Very Embodied Soul?" p. 305.

216. J. Kim, *Physicalism, or Something Near Enough,* p. 6.

217. J. Kim, *Physicalism, or Something Near Enough,* p. 150.

218. See also Clayton, "Neuroscience, the Person, and God," pp. 209-10.

are only expressions of physical causes or are themselves, at root, physical events, then one has (at least tacitly) advanced a theory of the human person that is pervasively physical. It then becomes extremely unclear (to put it gently) why, *from the perspective of one's own theory of the human person,* a God would have to be introduced at all (except perhaps as a useful fiction)."[219] Now, that does not of course mean that a Christian physicalist couldn't introduce God. But the point is that a truly physical *anthropological* account does not make it any easier than any other version of human nature; God has to be introduced "from outside," after all. Clayton lays out the options well: "If a theologian espouses physicalism, she may be forging an alliance with the majority worldview within the neurosciences, but she may also be giving up the most interesting rapprochement between theology and the sciences of the person just as she approaches that debate's most decisive issue." (Similarly, of course, traditional dualism may easily stall the dialogue with sciences.)[220] Perhaps, then, even in terms of dialogue (although theological convictions can never be primarily based on their usefulness), the best way for theology is to insist on the necessity but insufficiency of physical explanation. That would be in keeping with the "mutual critical dialogue" template adopted in this project.

Refusal to consider the physical explanation as the final one leads the theologian to wonder if "one finds in the mental some sign of a new type of phenomenon within the world." The implication is that "then one has thereby introduced at least the *possibility* that there is something inherently mental or spiritual within the one world that we find around us." If one is not willing to go with this opening, one has to resist all true notions of emergence, which after all is necessary for anyone wishing to continue theology-science dialogue (unless one goes with substance dualism).[221] Any theist (except the natural theist), at least in Abrahamic traditions, believes that the ultimate is Spirit(-ual).

When it is viewed from a historical perspective, not only the *opening* but also the full endorsement of nonmaterialist, in other words, idealist, ontology has been the dominant position among Christians and other theists (both mono- and polytheists). The late American Reformed theologian Paul K. Jewett expresses succinctly this sentiment: "To be materially conditioned as conscious selves is not to be materially constituted as such."[222] Not only idealist

---

219. Clayton, "Neuroscience, the Person, and God," p. 204, emphasis in original.
220. Clayton, "Neuroscience, the Person, and God," p. 204.
221. Clayton, "Neuroscience, the Person, and God," p. 204, emphasis in original.
222. P. Jewett, *Who We Are,* p. 9, emphasis removed.

philosophers such as Kant, Fichte, Hegel, Schelling, and numerous others,[223] but virtually all such thinkers from antiquity to recent times, have been idealists of a sort; similarly most cultures in the Global South, particularly in Africa;[224] so also are the *advaita* (nondualistic) schools of Indian philosophy; and so forth. This suggestive listing alone would justify keeping the door open to nonphysicalist monism.

It seems to me that Christian theology would do well to be a bit more cautious in going full-blown into physicalism, not because physical is "bad" or "sinful," neither because only the soul matters, nor for any such reason (all of which have been defeated in this project), but because "we are in great danger of phrasing the discussion in such a way that the deepest and most significant issues of human existence simply never appear on the screen." It is significant that these words were penned by the leading American science-religion expert, the theologian Philip Hefner, with direct reference to Paul Tillich's *Spiritual Situation in Our Technical Society.* He is deeply concerned that is happening in the conversation of brain and mind, in which "the most basic issues that the human tradition has associated with mind are not so much disproven or rejected, [as] they are simply denied a place in the discussion."[225]

Ward has recently suggested another version of dual-aspect theory that he names "dual-aspect idealism" and situates between Cartesian dualism and physicalisms of all sorts (while taking physicalism very seriously). A student of Gilbert Ryle, who coined the term "ghost in the machine" ridiculing Descartes's dualism and turn to the inner self, Ward, however, "strongly object[s] to this description . . . [because] mind and consciousness are different from, something over and above, molecules and matter, and . . . they are not at all ghostly."[226] Indeed, he reminds us how radically different idealism is from the physicalism/materialism of contemporary naturalism, in its claim that "the material world . . . exists as an environment created by a primordial mind in which finite minds can exist in mutual self-expression and interaction. . . . It totally reverses the modern myth that minds are by-products of a purely material evolutionary process, completely determined by physical events in their bodies and brains."[227] At the same time, he also reminds us how vastly different contemporary materialism is through the lens of force fields, quantum theory,

---

223. For an important discussion from the perspective of anthropology, see Martin and Barresi, *Rise and Fall of Soul and Self,* pp. 185-90.

224. See Kapolyo, *Human Condition;* Mbiti, *Concepts of God in Africa.*

225. Hefner, "Imago Dei," p. 81; Tillich, *Spiritual Situation in Our Technical Society.*

226. K. Ward, *More Than Matter,* p. 10.

227. K. Ward, *More Than Matter,* p. 57.

and string theory.[228] Now, as mentioned, Ward is not drawn to dualism per se; instead, he represents a property dualism of a sort.

What process philosophy is calling the "inner" life of the physical, Polkinghorne names dual-aspect monism, and the Oxford philosopher Horace Romano Harré, dual-side theories (of monism), all of which point in the same direction. While not idealist thinkers per se, they do think that even "material" processes somehow are not completely void of some kind of teleology and that the universe is more like an organism than a machine.[229] Ward refers to the human embryo: as much as current science eschews any notions of vitalism or (Aristotelian) teleology, we expect it to become an adult person, a highly complicated, obviously purposeful process.[230] Like Nagel, Plantinga and some others (as discussed in chap. 2 above) see it necessary to speak of the "composition" of the human person in light of the "composition" of the whole cosmos. Whatever "material" and "spiritual" there is in the cosmos, small or big, it all has to be integrally connected.

Behind the insistence on the newness of consciousness should not be the fear — all too common particularly in religious circles — not to acknowledge the deep connection of the mind with nature; indeed, "knowledge has emerged within the history of nature and represents a form of nature's own coming-to-knowledge."[231] Whatever the form of the final suggestion of the nature of human nature may be (after all, we need to speak of *suggestions* rather than fixed definitions), constructive theology would do well to follow these desiderata expressed by Clayton:

> We need a study of mental phenomena which allows us to focus on higher-order units as (sometimes) genuine existents, not just composites of the parts of which they are composed. In particular, it is necessary to think of persons as distinctive units of activity, as agents capable of forming intentions, making references, and having subjective experiences. . . . *We therefore need a "science" of the person of which neuroscience is one, but only one, contributing part.* Such a study of the emergent person is genuinely holistic . . . without insisting that the whole story can be told in terms of neuronal firings.[232]

228. K. Ward, *More Than Matter,* chap. 2.
229. K. Ward, *More Than Matter,* pp. 81-83, here p. 81.
230. K. Ward, *More Than Matter,* pp. 83-84, here p. 84.
231. Hefner, *The Human Factor,* p. 61.
232. Clayton, "Neuroscience, the Person, and God," p. 194, emphasis in original.

This kind of thinking means that, on the one hand, the monistic nature of reality is honored — as explained above, neither nakedly physical nor idealist but rather in its pluriform unity — and on the other hand, that in the hierarchy of levels, not only the relations between levels (say, from physical to mental and mental to physical), but also on each level, are appreciated. For this kind of dynamic, suggestive multidimensional monism, new forms of explanations and terminology are not yet available.[233] The minimalist statement about human nature, going back to the beginning of this section, is then psychosomatic pluralistic unity. The nomenclature "pluralistic unity" also points to the need to dare to "confuse" and go beyond established categories (while holding to the best insights of each) such as idealism, physicalism, and monism.[234] Multidimensional monism is one such emerging proposal for continuing discussion and critique. How this proposal relates to visions in other living faiths will be looked at below in chapter 14.

With the shift away from traditional substance dualism (notwithstanding property dualism of some sort), the question arises of whether to continue using the term "soul" at all.

What about "Soul"?

Among the current advocates of nondualist accounts of human nature, including Christian nonreductive physicalists, the term "soul" has become a virtual anathema. By implication, it also happens often that all uses of that term, even if not used in the substance dualistic context, are deemed suspicious. While that attitude is understandable, constructive theologians should also exercise some critical faculties here. I do not consider it wise, let alone necessary, to leave behind the ancient term "soul," even if traditional dualism is let go. The reasons to continue using the term are the following: First, the theologians' task is to help the faithful to grasp its redefinition, as they have for many other terms whose meanings have changed. Consider the term "creation." The reality that contemporary theology conceives the "logistics" of the bringing into existence of the cosmos by God radically differently than does tradition has not made us reject the concept altogether. That said, theologians also must be careful not to change the term's meaning at their own wish, as often happened

233. I am inspired here by Clayton, "Neuroscience, the Person, and God," pp. 196-97 particularly.
234. See K. Ward, *More Than Matter*, pp. 102-3.

in classical liberalism when, say, the whole possibility of Jesus' bodily resurrection was categorically denied (because of modernist epistemology), and still preachers continued speaking of resurrection as if something had really happened![235] Second, the term "soul" is so widely and frequently used in the biblical canon — and consequently, everywhere in Christian tradition — that its dismissal seems to be totally unfounded and counterproductive as it may cause the rejection of the proposal itself without further investigation. Third, there is also the interfaith consideration: although different religious traditions may mean different things when using the term, the cancellation in Christian tradition would not only look awkward and confusing to others but it would also seriously hinder dialogue. Similarly to terms such as "god" and "prayer" and "salvation," theologians working in a pluralistic world should have minds open enough to tolerate various types of definitions and conceptions of one and the same term. Fourth, blaming the use of "soul" (because of its close connection with substance dualism) for all kinds of ills in Christian life, say an antibody attitude or isolationist spirituality or escapist eschatology, misses the main point, which is that most any conception of human nature may foster negative or positive spiritualities or orientations of religious life (just differently).

The late American Reformed theologian Ray S. Anderson offers useful guidelines for the systematic use of the term "soul." Although my own constructive proposal of human nature does not exactly match his, these guidelines serve well regarding the term. First, "soul" does not denote a "substance or entity residing in the body" but rather denotes the "whole person, especially the inner core of human personal life as created and upheld by God" (to which should be added that no less are body and other aspects of the multidimensional human being also upheld by God). Second, the terms "body," "soul," and "spirit" are not analytic distinctions but rather are functional and overlapping with each other. Third, even though Christians have a firm hope for life eternal in the resurrected body as the gift of God, soul — no more than anything else in the human being — is not immortal by nature.[236] Fourth, as a result, rather than saying that the human person "has a soul," it is better to say that the "person is soul."[237]

What about substituting "spirit" in place of "soul," as some current theo-

---

235. The discussion of the use of metaphors in theology has many parallels in this regard; see *Christ and Reconciliation*, pp. 324-27.

236. R. S. Anderson, *On Being Human*, pp. 182-83, here p. 182. See M. Harris, *Raised Immortal*, p. 237.

237. R. S. Anderson, *On Being Human*, p. 186.

logians are prone to do? This new dichotomy (body-spirit) carelessly used may replace the older one (body-soul) with troublesome implications: it sets "spiritual" over against the physical and "secular." "When the life of the spirit becomes detached from one's embodied existence, spirituality lacks ethical content with respect to how one views the body, with all of its needs, instincts, drives, and potentialities."[238] That said, there is also a theologically legitimate way of using the term "spirit." I have in mind the use Rahner advocated: "Human beings are bodily creatures who have a fundamentally unlimited transcendentality and unlimited openness to being as such in knowledge and freedom." Here "spirit" is not used to establish a dichotomy between bodily and mental, but rather as a way of speaking of the deep embodiment of the human being who, however, is "more" than just the physical, namely, the one who reaches out to the transcendent, even to God.[239] While integrally intertwined, the difference between matter and spirit is that spirit is able to "reflect upon itself and its world, and then again place its world over against itself."[240] To repeat myself: this does not mean anthropological dualism (which Rahner persistently opposed), because with regard to the human being, "[n]ature found herself in him, in spite of all the physical powerlessness of the individual man." Therefore, it is wrong to envision "the material world as a kind of exterior state";[241] even in redemption the spiritual and material are inextricably bound.

Regardless of the terminological choice, all deviations from traditional dualism face the important questions of how to speak of an afterlife and continuation of personal identity. Although full discussion belongs to eschatology, short notes are in order here.

What about Afterlife and Identity?

So, how to think of afterlife in the post-Cartesian-dualism world? In other words, does leaving behind traditional talk about the soul and its disembodied existence mean leaving behind the idea of life everlasting? No, it does not.

---

238. R. S. Anderson, *On Being Human*, p. 187.

239. Rahner, *Theological Investigations*, 21:42. In his idiosyncratic terminology, he names this unlimited transcendental openness to God "supernatural existential" (see 2:240).

240. Rahner, *Theological Investigations*, 21:50; materially this is similar to what Keith Ward (*In Defence of the Soul*, p. 155) says of reason. Others speak of the emergence of consciousness.

241. Rahner, *Theological Investigations*, 5:151, 169; I am indebted to Fisher, *Human Significance*, pp. 95-96.

Christian tradition never affirmed the immortality of the soul (as in Platonic philosophy) nor that only one part of the human person will be saved for eternity. In fact, in early theology, notwithstanding terminological (and at times, material) inconsistency, the divinity of the soul and, hence, its intrinsic capacity to survive beyond death were rightly rejected and replaced by belief in eternal life as the gift of God.[242] Furthermore, the hope for the resurrection was established for the whole person, not only for the soul.[243]

What about the continuity of personal identity? This has to be looked at from two complementary perspectives. Theologically speaking, guaranteeing the identity is God's task, not ours.[244] Scientifically and philosophically speaking, identity is a task belonging to the human person, lasting all of one's life, embedded in growth and development in all areas, including personal development and social context. Embodied memory serves here an important role.[245] Whereas in this life there is always the form of a timely sequence with its broken moments, when God's eternity comes to swallow the finite life, that "will represent the *totality* of our earthly existence."[246]

Polkinghorne correctly notes that in itself the soul's "role as the carrier of human identity is almost as problematic within life as it is beyond death." The continuity cannot be a matter of material continuity since atoms are in constant flux through wear and tear. Perhaps the best way to speak of the continuity of identity is in terms of "the almost infinitely complex, information-bearing pattern in which the matter of the body is organized at any one time. This surely is the meaning of the soul."[247] Referring to the basic intuition of the image of God meaning relatedness to the Divine, we have to say that "[w]hat gives us an identity that does not die is not our nature, but a personal relationship with God."[248] Embodied, the soul does not carry in itself the powers of natural immortality. "As far as science can tell the story, the pattern that is a person will dissolve with that person's death and decay."[249]

242. Pannenberg, *ST* 3:571.

243. See T. Peters, "Resurrection of the Very Embodied Soul?" pp. 322-25.

244. T. Peters, "Resurrection of the Very Embodied Soul?" p. 316.

245. Pannenberg, *ST* 3:562; for the importance of memory, see Augustine, *Confessions* 10.17.

246. Pannenberg, *ST* 3:561, emphasis in original; see also T. Peters, "Resurrection of the Very Embodied Soul?" p. 324.

247. Polkinghorne, "Anthropology in an Evolutionary Context," p. 98; see also his "Eschatology," pp. 38-41.

248. Zizioulas, "Doctrine of the Holy Trinity," p. 58.

249. Polkinghorne, "Anthropology in an Evolutionary Context," p. 99.

This proposal seems to correspond to contemporary scientific understandings of information or the way complex systems could be understood — and all living beings are systems of some kind.[250] Aquinas's hylomorphic account of human nature is also based on these intuitions.

Now, seen from the theological point of view, this does not, however, mean that therefore when the person dies, that is all there is. Utilizing the concept of information, the older soul theory rightly intuited that "the faithful God will remember the pattern that is me and re-embody it in the eschatological act of resurrection." I couldn't agree more with Polkinghorne, who continues: "In making this assertion, I want to affirm the intrinsically embodied character of human being, without supposing that the flesh and blood of this world represents the only possible form that embodiment might take."[251] While I understand why Christian nonreductive physicalists — with justification — underline the importance of death's finality to combat the obvious misconception in which the soul were to possess natural powers of immortality and its independence, I also find the "gap" theory — that is, that between my personal death and the final resurrection there is "nothing of me" — problematic from the systematic theological point of view. Not that I have any doubts whatsoever concerning the capacity of the Creator to re-create *ex nihilo* the resurrected person who has faced physical death (that belief is no more difficult than believing that in the first place the person was given the gift of life). Nor do I think that positing a "soul" is needed to guarantee continuity between this life and the life to come, because, simply put, making the soul the locus of continuity doesn't really explain much in the first place! My reservations lie elsewhere, namely, in the complex and mutually conditioned continuity versus discontinuity relationship between life on Earth and life in the resurrected body as well as between my own personal eternal destiny and that of the whole cosmos. If the gap theory is followed, both of these themes, crucial as they are to a systematic theological negotiation of eschatological consummation, may be frustrated.

One of the key issues arising from the results and insights of neurosciences has to do with the alleged defeat of all meaningful notions of human freedom, freedom of the will. Because of the importance of that question — including the long-standing debates in theology and philosophy — the topic will be taken up in the next chapter. Thereafter, chapter 14 links the whole discussion of human nature (including the freedom of the will) with the teachings of some Jewish, Islamic, Buddhist, and Hindu traditions.

250. Polkinghorne, *God of Hope,* chap. 9.
251. Polkinghorne, "Anthropology in an Evolutionary Context," pp. 99-100.

13. Freedom and Determinism — Divine and Human

For Orientation: The "Necessity" of Human Freedom and Responsibility

This chapter continues the investigation of human nature by focusing on freedom in two interrelated contexts: in relation to current rebuttals of freedom in neurosciences, and in relation to the long-standing theological investigation of freedom in relation to God's foreknowledge and omniscience. It goes without saying that this distinction is only made for the sake of pedagogical clarity and because of the limits of our human minds. Ultimately, *all* talk about human freedom — *creaturely* — is intimately related to God, the Creator.

Arguing for the existence of human rationality and responsibility is not needed for the simple reason that it would not make sense to write a book without assuming them. Nor am I going to spend ink in trying to establish free will per se because (at least in some relative and modest sense) its necessity is so obvious[1] and it is such a deep human intuition;[2] even the deniers of freedom, luckily, do not live according to their belief. Indeed, curiously, even most deterministic scientific accounts are often prefaced by passing remarks on the necessity of free will for a meaningful personal or social life.[3] Be that

1. For the oft-quoted "consequent" statement (that is, what are the consequences if free will is denied) by a premier contemporary defender of free will, see Inwagen, *Essay on Free Will*, p. 16.
2. Much research has been conducted on folk psychology of free will, e.g., Nahmias et al., "Surveying Freedom," pp. 561-84.
3. The essay by Haggard and Libet, "Conscious Intention and Brain Activity," opens with this sentence: "Voluntary action is fundamental to human existence" (p. 47).

as it may, it is pertinent for constructive theology to tackle the complicated and complex issues related to human freedom, including its implications for moral judgments.

Both in philosophy and in theology there are several interrelated issues concerning free will, networked with a number of problems, from moral agency and responsibility, to compulsion, addiction, weakness of will, to criminal punishment, all the way to a number of metaphysical issues.[4] Add to this matrix the deep disagreements about the meaning of the term itself: Is it primarily about whether one is able to act as one chooses without compulsion or whether one is able to choose freely? Curiously the question of freedom *from* (necessity, fate, divine predestination) has dominated the discourse of free will, leaving the issue of freedom *for* (pursuing the good, acting for a reason) with much less attention.

Historically the relation of determinism (necessitarianism) to free will has operated with the question of whether it is "up to us" to act or not.[5] To affirm both or either one (acting or not acting), determinism had to be avoided. Some modern theologians, however, came to split the "determinist question" into two parts, namely, whether determinism is true in the first place, and if it is, whether free will can still be affirmed. The "compatibilist" option allows determinism along with free will, whereas the "incompatibilist" view (a subgroup of which, and sometimes synonymous with, is "libertarians") demands that (at least in principle) the person should have been able to choose otherwise (hence, the view can also be called "counterfactual free will").[6]

So much for the terminology and clarification of the issues. Let us first consider the issue of freedom in relation to neurobiological determinism, the most burning issue in contemporary theology-philosophy-religion discourse. Recall that reductionism as well as hard determinism have been defeated above, and instead, emergence and supervenience (understood the way it was argued) are assumed, including mental causation.

---

4. See further, Kane, introduction to *OHFW*, pp. 3-4.

5. Kane, introduction to *OHFW*, p. 5. Famously defined by Aristotle, *Nicomachean Ethics* 1113b6: "For where we are free to act we are also free to refrain from acting, and where we are able to say No we are also able to say Yes."

6. A more sophisticated typology of views is offered in Murphy and Brown, *DMN*, pp. 270-72, making a distinction between "hard" and "soft" determinism.

Free Will, Determinism, and Neurosciences

Neurosciences and the Threat of Freedom

"Free will represents a frontier for Neuroscience," notes the British neuroscientist Patrick Haggard.[7] The word is out there that finally — after millennia-long debates — neuroscience has "brought scientific method to a question that had previously been purely philosophical," and its main results "deeply undermine the concept of conscious free will."[8] As Christof Koch succinctly concludes: "The brain acts before the mind decides!"[9] Some enthusiastic popularizers go so far as to say that current science has made all talk about free will obsolete and wrong: "Free will is an illusion."[10] While an overstatement — and a big one, for that matter — the challenge to traditional philosophy and theology is considerable.

Scientifically and philosophically more noteworthy (as mentioned above) is that even among those "hard-core" scientists who categorically deny human freedom (and by implication responsibility), the denial dies hard; it looks like what is taken out the front door will be soon smuggled in the back door. Dawkins is illustrative: speaking of "replicators," that is, genes (DNA) that "created us, body and mind," he argues that therefore we as human beings are nothing more than "their survival machines."[11] Having established this uncompromising genetic determinism with no chance of human freedom, in a highly surprising move, he still wishes to support a real notion of freedom and responsibility, in terms of "a capacity for genuine, disinterested, true altruism." The human being is able to avoid "the worst selfish excesses of the blind replicators," even "the selfish genes of our birth and, if necessary, the selfish memes of our indoctrination." How is this all possible, one is left wondering! Dawkins further announces that "[w]e are built as gene machines and cultures as meme machines, but we have the power to turn against our creators."[12] What an internal contradistinction!

So, what exactly is neuroscience saying about volition, freedom, and free will? In the early 1980s, the neuroscientist Benjamin Libet with his colleagues conducted the now classic experiment using EEG (electroencephalography)

7. Haggard, "Does Brain Science Change Our View of Free Will?" p. 7.
8. Haggard and Libet, "Conscious Intention and Brain Activity," p. 48.
9. Koch, "Finding Free Will," pp. 22-27.
10. S. Harris, *Free Will*, p. 5, emphasis removed.
11. R. Dawkins, *Selfish Gene*, p. 20. For Dennett's recent account of replicators, see "New Replicators."
12. R. Dawkins, *Selfish Gene*, p. 20, quoted in Purcell, *From Big Bang*, p. 259.

to measure the brain's electrical activity to study the antecedents of voluntary action, that is, what happens in a brain just before one "chooses" to act voluntarily. Subjects were asked to flex spontaneously their finger or wrist at their choosing. The result was that some milliseconds before flexing signals could be discerned in the vertex (midline of the skull).[13] What made Libet's research noteworthy is that "the *shape* of the movement varied according to whether his subjects felt that they had spent some time 'planning' their movement or had, instead, acted truly 'spontaneously.'" With the element of "planning," the signal was slower to emerge, and with spontaneity, the opposite was the case.[14] In subsequent studies,[15] the pattern was confirmed, leading to the apparently counterintuitive sequence (concerning "voluntary acts"): brain event–intention to act–action. Thus, the research concluded that the "cerebral initiation of a spontaneous, freely [chosen] voluntary act can begin unconsciously, that is, before there is any (at least recallable) subjective awareness that a 'decision' to act has already been initiated cerebrally."[16] Many of the criticisms against the research design are quite self-evident.[17] The circumstances in the laboratory are highly specific and exacting. More importantly, the tasks performed are totally arbitrary and meaningless; not only that, but the nature of the "voluntary" act was utterly short-term as well. Even more, the subjects were highly compliant and preprepared for the "voluntary" act. Hence, they were in a much better place to deliberate about their intentions than most persons in real life. Hence, the most that can be said under these limitations is that the "findings are valid . . . but that they 'only' describe a special case" as described above. Furthermore, in light of our current knowledge of the embodied nature of human behavior, including neural events, what else could one imagine other than that simultaneous brain event?[18]

Behind these important methodological limitations lies a significant philosophical issue. It has to do with the sort of concept of free will Libet's study is designed around. It assumes the idea that "what distinguishes some of our conduct as voluntary is a certain antecedent (seemingly causal but perhaps

13. Libet et al., "Time of Conscious Intention," pp. 623-42.

14. Spence, *Actor's Brain*, pp. 4-5, emphasis in original; on pp. 1-6 is an accessible account of the experiment and implications.

15. See Libet, *Mind Time*, pp. 33-122.

16. Libet et al., "Time of Conscious Intention," p. 623.

17. For a seasoned critique with rich documentation, see Bayne, "Libet and the Case for Free Will Skepticism," pp. 25-46.

18. Spence, *Actor's Brain*, pp. 8-10, here p. 9; see further, Spence, "Free Will in Light of Neuropsychiatry," pp. 75-90; Young, "Preserving the Role of Conscious Decision Making," pp. 51-68.

epiphenomenal) (conscious) mental event." That assumption in itself, however, is questionable. If so, then the research design hardly can deliver the result it claims.[19] This kind of understanding of will behind Libet's study[20] follows the British empiricist tradition (represented, among others, by Hume, for whom the will was "nothing but *the internal impression we feel and are conscious of, when we knowingly give rise to any new motion of our body, or new perception of our mind*")[21] and should be subjected to criticism. The neuroscientist Jason Runyan's critique is right on target: "The presence or absence of a particular mental event is not what we rely on to distinguish some of our conduct as voluntary — it is irrelevant to whether what we do (or do not do) is willfully and freely done. That a kind of mental event is needed to distinguish voluntary conduct is the illusion under which neuroscientists and experimental psychologists interested in the topic frequently work."[22]

Yet another reason why Hume-Libet's assumption is untenable is that "action" is more than behavior, and therefore, making voluntary action a bodily motion caused by a kind of mental event misses the point.[23] Real "action" is part of a large network of factors, including language (-games after Wittgenstein). For an action to be truly voluntary, it is usually required that it freely conform to "a characteristic pattern, or range of patterns, of [action]," and not that it be accompanied by "any very definite sensation or experience."[24] True, some actions may be accompanied by a mental event, but others clearly are not — another reason for rejecting an antecedent mental event as the criterion.[25] We should rather envision "multifarious patterns [to] our voluntary conduct,"[26] including, very importantly, the capacity for refraining from action.[27]

In sum, for these scientific-methodological and philosophical reasons I reject Libet's efforts to dissolve free will. Rather, we need to see that (in keeping with the "contextual" approach adopted in this project regarding mental

19. Runyan, "Freewill," pp. 1-2, here p. 2.

20. Libet et al., "Time of Conscious Intention," p. 627.

21. Hume, *Treatise of Human Nature* 2.3.1, ed. Selby-Bigge, p. 391, emphasis in original. Materially similarly, Locke opines that voluntary conduct is preceded and distinguished by some sort of mental act of willing. Locke, *Essay concerning Human Understanding* 2.21.15.

22. Runyan, "Freewill," p. 5.

23. Wittgenstein reminds us that bodily motion may happen even though we do not act; we can just sit back and observe.

24. Strawson, *Individuals,* pp. 111-12, cited in Runyan, "Freewill," p. 8.

25. Consider Wittgenstein's warning not to apply the same criterion (presence of mental event) to all cases when considering action (*Blue and Brown Books,* §150).

26. Runyan, "Freewill," p. 9.

27. See further, G. Wright, *Explanation and Understanding,* p. 91.

events) "[l]ike our actions in general, our voluntary actions — as a subset of our actions — conform to a certain pattern in relation to the surrounding circumstances that differentiates them from actions that are not voluntary."[28] Therefore, rather than paying attention to fleeting, millisecond-long (or short!) mental events, in real voluntary action we should speak of a mental *state* that consists of awareness, knowledge, reflection, emotions, imagination, and other mental events[29] — by a fully embodied person, in the network of one's community/communities, life experiences, and so forth. One wonders if any empirical research can even come close to capturing this kind of wide spectrum of factors.

Rejecting neurobiological determinism that represents reductionism based on the fatalistic view that human behavior is based on "subpersonal" causes, the emergentist approach chosen in this project argues that during the course of evolution new kinds of mental properties arise and they can have causal efficacy.[30] Rather than bottom-up causation alone, there is a two-way street between the physical and the mental, as established above.

My argument here, needless to say, has nothing to do with an attitude that would undermine the importance of neuroscientific research for the better understanding of human behavior in cases of choosing and exercising responsibility. Not at all. Rather, my point is that

> what we find is that, instead of revealing that neurophysiological causes cause all we at least naively think we do, our neurophysiological observations are consistent with the view that we, as psychophysical agents (i.e., complex entities who are the bearer of certain psychological and physical attributes), are causal agents that bring about *certain* changes, for which there are no sufficient neurophysiological causes, by purposively acting, refraining, deliberating, deciding, etc. In this case, our neurophysiological observations allow a more precise description of a psychophysical agent in action.[31]

28. Runyan, "Freewill," p. 16.

29. The Aristotelian account of deliberating on and weighing options in deciding on a course of action is much more appropriate than that of British empiricism when it comes to discerning what makes a voluntary action; see *Nicomachean Ethics,* book 3, chap. 5.

30. I am indebted to Runyan, "Anatomy of Will," p. 10.

31. Runyan, "Anatomy of Will," pp. 248-49, emphasis in original. While I do not subscribe to the "causal-agency theory" (if not for other reasons, because I am simply not sure if I truly understand it!), I find highly useful O'Connor, "Agent-Causal Theories of Freedom," pp. 309-28.

With these insights in mind, let us go back to the question of determinism.

On Negotiating Determinism and Free Will

No doubt, "[i]n most contemporary philosophical approaches, the question as to whether deterministic ideas about the world threaten the notion we have freewill is in the foreground."[32] When speaking of the defeat of *hard* determinism, the question has to be taken seriously. The question with regard to neurobiological threat to freedom is not about whether neural processes and events are deterministic (relatively speaking, they are, of course, as illustrated for example by the Hodgkin-Huxley neuronal laws),[33] but rather whether neurobiological *reductionism* is true. The reason is simply this: "On our account of downward causation, . . . it makes no difference whether the laws of the bottom level are deterministic or not; higher-level selective processes can operate equally well on a range of possibilities that are produced (at the lower level) by either random *or deterministic* processes."[34] That defeating merely or primarily determinism is not the crux of the issue of freedom is illustrated well in reference to the radically changed situation in the twentieth-century physical sciences where, in contrast to the hard-core determinism of modernity,[35] quantum theory (in its major Copenhagen interpretation) introduced indeterminism; later on "chaos theory" further undermined determinism (without totally leaving it behind).[36]

That development, however — ironically — did not do away with the threat of determinism with regard to human will, nor did it help to totally settle the issue of the conditions of freedom. The philosopher Robert Kane insightfully observes that "while universal determinism has been in retreat in the physical sciences, determinist and compatibilist views *of human behavior* have been thriving while traditional anti-determinist and incompatibilist views of free will continue to be on the defensive."[37] But how can one explain this apparent irony? There are several considerations (beyond the continuing debates about the interpretations of quantum theory): the indeterminate be-

---

32. Runyan, "Anatomy of Will," p. 18; see further, Balaguer, *Free Will as an Open Scientific Problem*, chap. 1.

33. Laws that govern the movement of ions in a nerve cell during an action potential.

34. Murphy and Brown, *DMN*, p. 273, emphasis in original.

35. As famously defined by Laplace, *Philosophical Essay on Probabilities*, pp. 3-4.

36. Murphy and Brown, *DMN*, p. 276; see also pp. 100-102.

37. Kane, introduction to *OHFW*, p. 6, emphasis in original.

havior of the particles may have very little to do with human behavior (i.e., the inference from micro- to macrolevel); the insights that indeterminacy in itself does not of course guarantee *freedom* of will, just its randomness; and perhaps most importantly, the fact that "[w]hile determinism has been in retreat in the physical sciences, developments in other sciences — biology, neuroscience, psychology, psychiatry, social and behavioral sciences — have been moving in the opposite direction."[38] In particular, contemporary neuroscience, for several decades now, has been dominated by determinism and identity theory.

What the defeat of determinism has achieved, however, is to establish the modest and minimalist account of free will with its claim that human behavior is not totally biologically/physically determined.[39] But that is only the first part of the meaning of freedom, the *from* aspect. What about freedom's *for* aspect? As mentioned, some physicalists (on the libertarian[40] side) have set their hopes on quantum indeterminacy:[41] if underdetermined brain events could be established, then room for the freedom to choose was made, the claim goes, reductionism could be maintained (namely, reduction of mental events to neuronal processes after identity theory).[42] But that is a suspicious move for several reasons, not least because of the reductionist agenda's defeat above but also because it is a category mistake in mixing free choice with a physical process (brain events). In reality, as argued, it is the whole person (in his or her environment) that is the agent of freedom rather than one tiny part.[43]

That said, the turn to quantum indeterminacy is neither totally mistaken nor useless.[44] Leading libertarian Robert Kane's proposal takes us a long way toward a satisfactory account of free will vis-à-vis current scientific and phil-

38. Kane, introduction to *OHFW*, pp. 6-8, here p. 8; see also Hodgson, "Quantum Physics, Consciousness, and Free Will," pp. 57-83; Bishop, "Chaos, Indeterminism, and Free Will," pp. 84-100.

39. See Bishop and Atmanspacher, "Causal Closure of Physics and Free Will," pp. 101-11.

40. There is of course more than one type of libertarian version. The one I am interested in here and that is relevant in the context of neurosciences and quantum theory is usually named "causal indeterminism" (and its most noted representative is Robert Kane). Other libertarian versions are "agent-causation," which makes agent the undetermined "prime mover" of free actions (if this sounds somewhat mysterious, it probably is!), and "simple indeterminism," which assumes that a simple, uncaused mental action (volition) is at the center of every causal action.

41. See Loewer, "Freedom from Physics," pp. 91-112.

42. Rather than deterministic, it is probabilistic causation that is in view here; see Anscombe, "Causality and Determination."

43. Murphy and Brown, *DMN*, pp. 277-78; see also Gazzaniga, *Who's in Charge?* p. 105.

44. For benefits, see also Murphy and Brown, *DMN*, pp. 277-80.

osophical challenges. The libertarian's desire to trace the causal chain of action to human agency is a correct intuition.[45] Similarly, it seems to me that Kane's notion of "self-formed agencies" defined as "undetermined, regress-stopping voluntary actions (or refrainings) in the life histories of agents that are required if U[ltimacy] is to be satisfied, and for which the agent is personally responsible"[46] — while somewhat mysterious, to be sure — contains the important insight that human freedom is tightly linked with one's personal narrative, development, and maturation under certain circumstances; we call it character development or the practice of virtues. Furthermore, Kane's emphasis on what he calls "self-networks"[47] — that is, any choice (and its neural constitution) is embedded in a network of goals, desires, deliberations, and feedback from actions — reminds us of the importance of the *contextuality* of human action. Finally, Kane rightly shifts the focus from the alternative possibilities criterion (that is, whether the ability to have done otherwise is an essential condition for free will) to the question of ultimate responsibility, or to be more modest and precise, primary responsibility.[48] Now, the way freedom-from determination can be had for this libertarian is to find a "swerve" of atoms in brain events as a result of quantum indeterminacy[49] (a claim expressed long before modern science by the Epicureans!) or by virtue of chaos theory.[50] How this indeterminacy in the brain processes translates into freedom of choice (to avoid the category mistake) can be explained with the help of conflict of will, difficult and complex situations of choosing:

> In effect, conflicts of will . . . stir up chaos in the brain and make the agents' thought processes more sensitive to undetermined influences. The result is that, in soul-searching moments of moral and prudential struggle, when agents are torn between conflicting visions of what they should become . . . the outcomes are influenced by, but not determined by, past motives

45. Kane, *Significance of Free Will,* p. 4: "Free will . . . is *the power of agents to be the ultimate creators (or originators) and sustainers of their own ends or purposes*" (emphasis in original).

46. Kane, *Significance of Free Will,* p. 75.

47. Kane, *Significance of Free Will,* pp. 141-42 and passim.

48. Kane, *Significance of Free Will,* chap. 5; for the need to replace Kane's "ultimate" with "primary" responsibility, see Murphy and Brown, *DMN,* pp. 285-88.

49. Kane, *Significance of Free Will,* p. 17; for details, see chaps. 8–10.

50. Skarda and Freeman, "How Brains Make Chaos," pp. 161-95. Rebuttals and critiques of the use of quantum indeterminacy and chaos theory as the ways to negotiate free will can be found in Dennett, *Freedom Evolves,* chap. 4; O'Connor, *Persons and Causes,* chap. 2 especially.

and character. The uncertainty and inner tension that agents feel at such moments are reflected in the indeterminacy of their neural processes.[51]

It seems to me that placing the effects of indeterminacy and chaos in the person's choice process (in the context of self-formed agency) may save us from merely introducing randomness and arbitrariness into the process (which, as mentioned, are not able to explain at all).

All these features of Kane's libertarian proposal should be affirmed. What are the challenges? As a materialist reductionist, Kane is neither able nor willing to grant top-down causation. I disagree. Top-down causation is necessary for freedom of choice. Murphy and Brown rightly conclude that at the most Kane presents "a downward *interpretation* of the quantum event in terms of the higher-level systems of drives and goals, but not downward *causation* of the patterns of micro-level events by those higher-level goals."[52] With some overstatement, it can be said that any reductionist account in the final analysis makes "free choice" a matter of a network of indeterminate quantum events that somehow in the process will be endorsed by the human subject. I couldn't agree more wholeheartedly with Murphy and Brown regarding the need for fine-tuning and correcting this libertarian's account of free will: "recognition of the limitations of neurobiological reductionism and replacement with a recognition of the role of downward causation in cognitive and brain processes would allow all of these other valuable pieces of Kane's work to fall into a set of new relations."[53] Only a robust top-down/whole-part nonreductionist and embodied form of causation could save this skewed strategy and make it a fully *personal* act, a volitional event.[54]

Mental Causation, Free Will, and Moral Responsibility:
A Modest Theological Proposal

Recall that the human person is a "two-natured animal" and therefore both conditioned and free. The conditionedness is of course based on the long evolutionary development and current environmental context (most widely

51. Kane, *Significance of Free Will*, p. 130.
52. Murphy and Brown, *DMN*, p. 281, emphasis in original. It appears that in a more recent writing Kane himself admits that at least some kind of top-down causation ("constraint") is to be supposed. Kane, "Rethinking Free Will," p. 396.
53. Murphy and Brown, *DMN*, p. 282.
54. So also Murphy and Brown, *DMN*, p. 283.

understood). Now, what is remarkable is that "[w]ithin this deterministic evolutionary process, freedom has emerged." As startling as it may sound, freedom is produced by determinism![55] As mentioned several times, determinism in itself is not the problem. That is not to say that nature acts fully deterministically but that determinism — regularity of events — *relatively* speaking, applies even to quantum theory and chaos theory. Determinism understood this way can be seen as a divine gift, a sign of hospitality, to ensure the relative independence of creation and creatures. In this "regular" world, the creatures, most profoundly, human beings *qua* creatures, have been granted relative, gracious freedom to ensure their independence, yet not separation, from God. Not only that, freedom born out of determinism also entails a task: "freedom refers to the condition of existence in which humans unavoidably face the necessity both of making choices and of constructing the stories that contextualize and hence justify those choices." Indeed, human persons cannot avoid the freedom to make and justify choices.[56] How else could you live your life as friend, partner, spouse, child, parent, colleague?

This gift nature of (relative) freedom also helps combat the most ultimate riddle of (any form of) the libertarian freedom theories, namely, the infinite regress. The compatibilists (and others who oppose libertarianism) rightly note that human freedom cannot be had because it would entail the source beyond the creature and thus lead to infinite regress. For a theologian, infinite regress is solved with reference to the Creator, the infinite source of freedom.

Practicing human life is a lifelong project and is essentially just that, a *practice*. It is important to make the self-forming actions ubiquitous rather than merely occasions of deep moral or other struggle. All organisms, let alone human beings, "are constantly re-forming themselves" in active correlation with the environment, their desires, their goals, and their beliefs, and as a result, the formation of habits and development of character happen constantly, which also leads to minor effects on neural structures over time. Thus, it is not enough to limit morality to mere decision-making events. Instead, human behavior, morality, and the good life are a matter of patient character formation, practicing of virtues, and formation of habits in constant interaction with other people and communities.[57]

Practicing human freedom and moral responsibility is not only a long-term continuous process but also is holistic and embodied. Therein the entire

55. Hefner, *The Human Factor*, chaps. 6, 7 (quotation p. 30).

56. Hefner, *The Human Factor*, p. 38.

57. Murphy and Brown, *DMN*, p. 283. See McClendon, *Ethics*; MacIntyre, *After Virtue*.

physical organism is the locus of actions and moral judgments, as opposed to the primarily inner orientation of Cartesianism. Consequently, the locus of moral responsibility is the whole person, the identity and moral character during the course of her entire life. The entire human *person* bears the responsibility for the choices. Again, recall, it is only the gift nature of human freedom that can ultimately fund this view.

What about divine action? Can we think of the maintenance of relative human freedom of will in relation to divine presence and divine action? On the basis of the noninterventionist, pneumatologically loaded trinitarian account — speaking of the world in which the divine and creaturely, including human, existence is fully intertwined although of course not equated with each other — it is hard to see why the divine influence could not be deeply embedded at all levels of human existence, "through every fibre of our beings, not least our bodies." Therefore, Wright concludes: "That is why I am not afraid that one day the neuroscientists might come up with a complete account of exactly which neurons fire under which circumstances, including that might indicate the person as responding to God and his love in worship, prayer and adoration."[58] None of that would be out of the reach of the Creator who has created us in the first place.

To establish the possibility of human freedom is one thing (it suffices only for accounts that operate with merely immanentist explanations). To posit human freedom *theologically,* in relation to God, is another thing. To that theme we turn next.

Divine Foreknowledge and Human Freedom: A Mediating Proposal

Setting the Parameters of the Discussion

While in principle freedom might be available for a human person, that freedom either is "bound" because of sinfulness or is totally determined because of divine foreknowledge and will. It is to the latter theological challenge that this conversation seeks to make a contribution (as the question of the relation of human freedom to divine will in the context of human sinfulness/the Fall is discussed under the topic of election in *ordo salutis,* in the future volume *Spirit and Salvation*). This is a problem noticed already by the Stoics in antiquity, and it has occupied the best minds of both Christian and Muslim theologians for

---

58. N. T. Wright, "Mind, Spirit, Soul and Body," n.p.

centuries.[59] (Jewish theologians by and large have taken for granted freedom of the will.)[60]

The problem of the possibility and conditions of human freedom arises as soon as one sets forth the theological claim that all that happens is not only foreknown by God but also divinely determined. Classically Augustine's interlocutor Evodius wondered "how God can have foreknowledge of everything in the future, and yet we do not sin by necessity." Evodius is stuck between a rock and a hard place because "[it] would be an irreligious and completely insane attack on God's foreknowledge to say that something could happen otherwise than as God foreknew."[61]

For all those who wish to affirm some kind of libertarian form of human freedom, two key questions emerge, fittingly named "source question" and "reconciliation question," that is, the way God obtains knowledge of the future and the possibility of reconciling the divine foreknowledge and free will, respectively.[62] Let me first rehearse briefly and critically the classic discussion and thereafter present and defend my own constructive proposal named elusively a "Molinist-pneumatological" approach.

In many ways the simplest and most commonsensical solution to the problem is what can be called the "simple foreknowledge view." Although it has some contemporary advocates, it is the Thomistic view, building on Aristotelian resources, assuming that because God is a simple being (that is, there is no "composition" such as that between essence and existence), God's "act of understanding must be His essence."[63] Since God's knowledge of everything is simple, it means there is no room for contingency (at least ultimately): God's knowledge never changes, and therefore, more or less divine determinism must be assumed. The Augustinian-Calvinistic view materially represents this ancient tradition.[64] Should one wish to speak of human freedom, compati-

---

59. Hasker, "Divine Knowledge," p. 39.

60. For the Jewish affirmation of freedom of the will, see Cohon, *Jewish Theology,* pp. 309-44; for the central concept of *yetzer (ha tov* or *ha ra'),* "inclination" (toward good or evil, respectively), see pp. 297-302.

61. Augustine, *On the Free Choice of Will* 3.2.

62. As formulated by Freddoso, translator of de Molina, *On Divine Foreknowledge,* part 4 of the *Concordia,* p. 1; I am indebted to Hasker, "Divine Knowledge," p. 40.

63. Aquinas, *ST* 1.14.4.

64. For current advocacy, see Hunt, "Simple-Foreknowledge View," pp. 65-103. Luther's *Bondage of the Will* strongly advocates this view; p. 106 states: "It is then essentially necessary and wholesome for Christians to know that God . . . foresees, purposes and does all things according to His immutable, eternal and infallible will."

bilism seems to be the only option. As to *how* compatibilism is possible, this view does not usually offer any sophisticated explanations.[65]

One who sought to provide at least some kind of explanation of how the simple foreknowledge view might work is Boethius, with his "eternity solution": because God is timeless ("eternal" in this specific understanding), the question of who/what decided certain events in a particular human being's life does not arise; there is no interval between, say, t_1 and t_2 (t = moment of time). Apart from the difficulty with that concept of time (and eternity), which I cannot accept, as discussed in part 1, there are other theological (for example, concerning the possibility of God's action in time/history) and logical (the confusion of "conditional" and "natural" necessity in relation to divine foreknowledge)[66] reasons to reject the eternity view it espouses. Nor do I see much promise in Jonathan Edwards's argument in his 1754 *Freedom of the Will* that, notwithstanding ironclad divine determinism and, as a result, total rejection of all forms of libertarianism, God's foreknowledge per se does not determine events because everything simply happens as it happens, whether God foreknows it or not[67] (and of course, God is behind all happenings!). While that may be true rhetorically, I don't see how it could bring any more consolation than strict compatibilism.

Hence, more appealing intellectually has been William of Ockham's "way out," that is, "there are some truths about the past that do not share in the necessity generally attributed to such truths," namely, "truths about God's past beliefs [which] are not accidentally necessary."[68] The technical term "accidentally necessary" simply means that the past is "necessary" in the sense of being beyond our control (having taken place).[69] Although the Ockhamist

65. Cf. Hunt, "Simple-Foreknowledge View," p. 67.

66. Briefly put: in my understanding divine foreknowledge does not necessarily rule out freedom because it only establishes "conditional necessity" rather than "natural" necessity. Only natural necessity would rule out all notions of real freedom. For this and other issues in Boethius, see Rich, "Boethius on Divine Foreknowledge."

67. Famously formulated by J. Edwards, *Freedom of the Will*, p. 123.

68. Hasker, "Divine Knowledge," p. 44. Ockham's own theory is laid out in detail in his *Predestination, God's Foreknowledge and Future Contingents*. A contemporary advocate of Ockham's solution is Adams, "Is the Existence of God a 'Hard' Fact?"

69. Consider this example of being "accidentally necessary": Having turned down an offer for a full scholarship from a prestigious college so that it goes to another interested person, the student "must" work while in school (or have a rich uncle) to finance his education. It is only after the refusal to receive, that this "accidental" event (at least for the next academic year) is "necessarily" ruled out (although in itself the event is not necessary). For a current important discussion, see A. Plantinga, "On Ockham's Way Out"; for the critique of salvaging

distinction certainly is useful (and would have helped Edwards in his attempt to make a distinction between philosophical and "vulgar," that is, ordinary, necessity), even this view is more rhetorical than substantial.[70]

Before we launch into the constructive proposal, a brief comparison with another Abrahamic tradition, Islam, is in order. Although Islam by and large affirms human freedom, not surprisingly there are different schools of thought.[71] The oldest hermeneutics of *fitrah*, "human nature," tended to be predestinarian in orientation. They applied the cause-and-effect relation evident in creation to human actions as well and attributed both right and wrong to Allah. As a result, *fitrah* does not guarantee goodness; a particular human can also be evil, somehow decreed by God.[72] In many ways, this currently marginal Islamic view resonates with the stricter deterministic interpretations of Christian tradition. The "neutral" view came to the fore after the mid–eighth century (c.e.), and was supported by the libertarian criticism of the "classical" view. Rather than divine determinism, God's justice and fairness came to the forefront. This school interpreted the ambiguous Qur'anic passage, "And God brought you forth from the bellies of your mothers while you did not know anything" (16:78), to mean that the newly born infant is like a blank slate, devoid of either good or evil. Only in the course of growth does either inclination take over. The neutral hermeneutics thus put an emphasis on free will and its implications. This view, then, shifts toward what in later tradition became a highly influential Muslim interpretation, namely, the "positive" view, which basically takes *fitrah* as a state of intrinsic goodness. For that mainline Islamic tradition, two foundational affirmations must be held in balance: belief in the sovereignty of God, and his power behind everything that happens in the world.[73]

---

divine knowledge from under accidental necessity, see Zagzebski, *Dilemma of Freedom and Foreknowledge,* p. 76; for the seemingly absurd denial of the necessity of the past, see Mavrodes, "Is the Past Unpreventable?"

70. For a state-of-the-art conclusion (that none of these options above has won wide support), see Hasker, "Divine Knowledge," p. 49.

71. For a detailed discussion, see Mohamed, *Fitrah,* chap. 2.

72. For details, see Wolfson, *Philosophy of the Kalam,* pp. 602-3.

73. It is in light of a strong view of God's omnipotence that many Islamic philosophers came to support an occasionalist interpretation of human freedom (although at first glance, occasionalism, the view that assigns all causal power to God, seems to block any human freedom); for details, see Muhtaroglu, "An Occasionalist Defence of Free Will," pp. 45-62.

A Molinist-Pneumatological Solution

In light of the inadequacies and continuing unresolved problems of the views briefly mentioned above, I turn to what I have suggestively named the "Molinist-pneumatological" approach. I call it Molinist in a heuristic, suggestive way and have no interest in trying to defend the Molinist "system" at large (if there is something like that). Hence, my discussion is not dependent on a number of historical debates (most prominently, the origins and the real advocates) nor on continuing present-day disputes around that movement. Furthermore, my use of Molinism is guided by my larger trinitarian-pneumatological approach to creation and providence.

Molinism seeks to reconcile two claims long thought to be incompatible, namely, that God is the all-knowing governor of the universe and that individual freedom can prevail only in a universe free of absolute determinism.[74] The Molinist concept of middle knowledge holds that God knows, though he has no control over, truths about how any individual would freely choose to act in any situation. Given such knowledge and then creating such a world, God can be truly providential while leaving his creatures genuinely free.[75] Molinism goes further than compatibilism (without leaving behind compatibilist intuitions), which merely holds together divine determinism and human freedom.[76] Molinism seeks to explain *how* God knows the contingent future. Whereas "natural knowledge" is the knowledge of necessary truths (and all logical possibilities), and "free knowledge" encompasses the actual world as it is, "middle knowledge" is the knowledge of the "counterfactuals" of all feasible worlds, that is, what humans might do in any given context. It is best to understand the "moments" in God's knowledge as *logical* rather than temporal moments.[77] The promise of the proposal is that it makes it possible to be "an incompatibilist about causal determinism and human freedom (in the relevant sense), but a compatibilist about God's omniscience (foreknowledge) and such freedom."[78]

In reference to divine foreknowledge, one can see the difference from

74. For leading current Molinist philosophical accounts, see Flint, *Divine Providence;* Dekker, *Middle Knowledge;* Craig, *The Only Wise God.*

75. See Perszyk, introduction to *Molinism,* pp. 4-5. An accurate, nontechnical introduction to Molinism is Craig, "Middle Knowledge View," pp. 119-43.

76. See Fischer, "Putting Molinism in Its Place," p. 209.

77. Craig, *The Only Wise God,* p. 127; see also his *Divine Foreknowledge and Human Freedom.*

78. Fischer, "Putting Molinism in Its Place," p. 209 (not Fischer's own opinion).

the recent open theistic "free will" theory, which seeks to reconcile divine foreknowledge and human freedom by seriously redefining foreknowledge: while "omniscient," God can only know those future events that are possible to be known, but not those that are so much contingent on human choices (or nature's events) that it does not make sense to speak of their knowledge yet.[79]

The current Molinist solution begins with the acknowledgment of the necessary but insufficient role of divine foreknowledge. Foreknowledge is necessary for God's proper governance (providence) of the world, including foreseeing the future, but not after Augustinian-Calvinist determinism in which God's foreknowledge secures the future by knowing and *determining* his decrees.[80] Briefly put, the "twin pillars" of Molinism are then a belief in the traditional notion of providence (the idea that everything that happens is "specifically" intended or else permitted by God) and libertarianism.[81] Of ecumenical interest, it was suggested recently that Molinism (of Catholic origins) may have influenced Arminianism (and by derivation then, I suppose, Wesleyan holiness traditions and those under their purview).[82] "What makes Molinism 'strong' libertarianism — as opposed to any so-called libertarian substitute for 'Thomists' — is the thesis that the sum total of *God's* activity prior to and at the time of our action cannot determine that action if it is free."[83] Molinists claim that their view best accounts for the multiplicity of the biblical teaching — although that is the case with virtually any other option as well! Molina himself regularly referred to three texts in support of middle knowledge: 1 Samuel 23:6-10, Proverbs 4:11, and Matthew 11:23.[84]

Now, before clarifying my use of Molinism from a pneumatological-trinitarian perspective, let me briefly acknowledge some relevant objections.[85] Even though Molinism goes several steps further than compatibilism in trying

---

79. The philosophically most astute defense is Hasker, *Providence, Evil, and the Openness of God,* among other publications. For a critique of Molinism, see Hasker, "Middle Knowledge."

80. See Perszyk, ed., *Molinism.*

81. The standard account is Flint, *Divine Providence;* cf. Perszyk, "Molinism and Compatibilism."

82. So argues Muller, "Arminius and the Scholastic Tradition," pp. 263-77. Molina and his contemporary rivals also opposed Luther's and Calvin's apparent denial of our freedom (to choose or do otherwise). See also the interesting essay by a Calvinist: Tiessen, "Why Calvinists Should Believe in Divine Middle Knowledge." In his *Providence and Prayer,* part 2, Tiessen even speaks of middle knowledge Calvinism!

83. Perszyk, introduction to *Molinism,* p. 4, emphasis in original.

84. See Craig, "Middle Knowledge View," pp. 123-25.

85. A highly useful, succinct account of standard objections can be found in Laing, "Middle Knowledge."

to "explain" the reconciliation problem (between divine foreknowledge and human freedom), it will not offer a total solution. My observation is simply this: Of course it does not, but how could it? To demand a total solution is way too much to expect. What about the rejection of counterfactuals, as was classically done by Schleiermacher (whose view, however, I do not find interesting because it is based on an understanding of divine action and omniscience that is deeply suspect).[86] A weighty objection concerning counterfactuals, to be taken seriously, is the so-called grounding objection, that is, counterfactuals seem not to be based on any categorical facts about the world.[87] While I leave debate of this complicated and thorny question to expert philosophers, I can't help but be persuaded by the commonsense objection of A. Plantinga: "It seems to me much clearer that some counterfactuals of freedom are at least possibly true than that the truth of propositions must, in general, be founded in this way."[88] Similarly, I leave aside the related, less common objection that, while not categorically denying the existence of counterfactuals, denies that counterfactuals of *freedom* can be posited.[89]

My use of key Molinist intuitions is guided by a solid pneumatological-trinitarian framework. I have attempted a robust trinitarian-pneumatological approach based on a relational (trinitarian) account in which the Spirit's universal presence makes possible, permeates, sustains, and guides the life of creation to which a relative independence has been given by the grace of God. In that approach, the possibility of continuing creation (divine action) is nothing dualistic or external but rather an essential part of God's continuing presence in the world. If all creative life, including human life, is a function of and is being constantly energized, sustained, guided, and "lured" by the ever-present Spirit, then also human freedom happens within the framework created by the Creator. In such a pneumatological context, the omniscience

---

86. Schleiermacher, *Christian Faith*, §55.2 (pp. 222-26).

87. Behind the objection is the long-term debate about whether "truth makers" are needed to make a statement true, that is, a statement's truth claim needs a reference to another "fact" or "state of affairs" (B. Russell, J. L. Austin), or whether "truth supervenes on being," that is, any two possible worlds alike with respect to what exists and what properties are exemplified are alike with respect to what is true (see D. Lewis, "Truthmaking and Difference-Making"). A Molinist reply is Merricks, *Truth and Ontology*.

88. A. Plantinga, "Reply to Robert M. Adams," p. 374.

89. Hasker ("The (Non-)Existence of Molinist Counterfactuals") sets forth these objections (which I do not find convincing): counterfactuals cannot exist because they fail to be grounded in reality, the so-called grounding objection; if we assume the existence of counterfactuals, their existence turns out to be incompatible with libertarian free will (thus, they are not counterfactuals *of freedom*).

(full foreknowledge, as it were) of the triune God is understood as the divine omnipresence in creation (as detailed in *Trinity and Revelation,* chap. 12), and thus no event or process evades it. Rather than curtailing the freedom — independence — of creation, that omnipresence constantly makes room for it (mediated by Christ; chap. 4). As argued above, freedom is not something that has to be won from God. Freedom is a gracious gift, a hospitable "necessity" (determined by the Creator) for creaturely life to exist. As such it also allows for its misuse, the creature's fleeing away from the Creator or setting one's will against God. Rather than fully determining the choices and life of humans, the omnipresent-omnipotent-omniscient triune Creator prepares and determines the creaturely environment for such conditions that make possible certain types of free choices but do not determine them, although they are known to God. Even if the human person does not freely choose the ideal option(s), the Creator's will is not thereby frustrated, or else only strict determinism follows. The triune God honors the choices of the creatures, although those choices never come close to frustrating the eternal divine economy of salvation ("salvation" most inclusively understood, encompassing all of creation, the cosmos).

My proposal defeats the strict determinism and lack of freedom of Augustinian-Calvinist-Lutheran and Aristotelian-Thomistic compatibilisms, although it does not leave behind compatibilism correctly understood, nor the basic intuitions of the "simple view" of foreknowledge. My account just puts them in a given perspective. Similarly, my proposal defeats open theism's thin (some would say diminished) account of divine foreknowledge and omnipotence, which basically argues that God knows only those things that are logically possible to know at the moment;[90] for these free will advocates and some others to say that God's omniscience entails the knowledge of events contingent on free choices is neither meaningful nor necessary.[91]

That said, one should be modest about a constructive proposal with regard to an ancient dilemma. Even though the problem is not solved, perhaps the general framework and some guidelines suggested here will help us better live as responsible persons.

---

90. Sanders, *The God Who Risks.*

91. Inwagen, "What Does an Omniscient Being Know about the Future?" pp. 216-30. The most that open theists (and, I guess, Inwagen) are ready to grant is that God's future knowledge (of contingent events based on free choices) may be probabilistic. Hasker, "Divine Knowledge," p. 52.

14. Humanity and Human Nature in Religions' Teachings

For Orientation: The Diversity of Anthropological Visions

What I am attempting in this volume in general and in the chapter at hand in particular is similar to what Keith Ward had as a goal in his celebrated *Religion and Human Nature,* namely, writing "from a particular Christian viewpoint, I have tried to locate Christian ideas of the nature of the human person and its ultimate destiny in the context of . . . [the] range of religious beliefs, and to develop a Christian view which is sensitive and responsive to the concerns which the other traditions express. . . . My interest is to formulate a Christian view about human nature, informed by other religious views which both contrast with it and, at many points, converge with it."[1] A corollary task — and hope — is to let my own Christian understanding critique, challenge, and inspire Jewish, Islamic, Buddhist, and Hindu theological anthropologies.

A useful way to map the diversity of views of human nature among religions[2] is to classify them under three inclusive groupings, the first of which, roughly speaking, is Asiatic traditions. Sankara's *advaita* represents the most "spiritual" (philosophically: idealist) view in which the essence of humanity is spirit(ual) or soul that can exist apart from embodiment and individuality (at least as that is understood in the West). In that outlook, writes Ward, "the Supreme-Self, *Sat-Cit-Ananda,* unfolds into the illusion of separated and conflicting individuality. Spiritual practice consists in overcoming the illusion of

---

1. K. Ward, *Religion and Human Nature,* pp. 8-9.
2. A useful recent guide is Kupperman, *Theories of Human Nature,* part 2 particularly.

separateness, and achieving a sense of nonduality, the pure unity" (p. 1). Another version of this Indian interpretation of humanity is Ramanuja's qualified nonduality in which human nature is conceived essentially in spiritualist (idealist) terms but not in the manner of absolute unity. Through rigorous spiritual practice, the aim is to get rid of all materialist hindrances and so reach pure consciousness of (qualified) "individual" liberation. Somewhat ironically, even the Buddhist vision of reaching liberation from not only all material but even from the "clinging" to life itself is yet another representative of the first group. The second grouping is diametrically opposed, namely, materialist philosophy that is very rare among the religions. Of the six Hindu schools, Carvaka, with its focus on the ritual and social code, is one such. And of course, the materialist naturalism of contemporary sciences belongs there. Third, there is the group of Semitic faiths with their idea of humans as "embodied souls." Even in their traditional dualistic versions with a focus on the "soul" and the spiritual, the necessity of embodiment is acknowledged. Unlike the other two groups, all Semitic faiths refer the existence and life of humanity to the personal God (which is not to deny the theistic orientation of much of Indian tradition). Enlivened by the life-giving Spirit of God, the Judeo-Christian and Muslim traditions look at humanity as made of "dust" and returning to it; however, the creature's dignity and uniqueness depend on God.[3] Mind also that similarly to Christian tradition, each of the other religious traditions includes a diversity of views of human nature.

In this chapter I am continuing the comparative theological discussion (without repeating the Abrahamic faiths' shared views of the image of God treated at the end of chapter 11) and will continue it in several chapters below. I wish to lay out briefly the vision of humanity and human nature in each of four living faith traditions and build on this presentation in dialogical comparing and contrasting. I wish to secure the integrity and inner logic of each tradition's understanding of anthropology by laying out these preliminary visions. We will begin with Abrahamic traditions and then move to the Asiatic faiths.

The Embodied Ensouled Human Being: The Jewish Vision

As counterintuitive as it may sound at first, during the early periods of OT history "the Jews were materialists," that is, they hardly had a developed es-

---

3. I was helped in this typology by K. Ward, *Religion and Human Nature*, "Introduction," although I treat it somewhat differently.

chatology and, therefore, even the blessings of God were mainly regarded in terms of earthly goods. When with the book of Daniel the belief in resurrection emerged, the Talmudic tradition, gleaning from Platonism, came to affirm both resurrection of the body and immortality of the soul. Of course, the Sadducees denied resurrection and afterlife, whereas the Pharisees, along with growing popular belief, affirmed (at least something of) immortality of the soul. In Philo, the Hellenistically driven philosophically oriented approach came to its zenith, including the preexistence of the soul and immortality.[4] After a long hiatus, Jewish philosophy revived not earlier than the tenth century or so; it was then in contact with both Hellenist and Muslim thought.

A number of older Jewish traditions were influenced deeply by Platonic tradition, although its belief in transmigration was rejected and its view of the preexistence of the soul was interpreted in terms of God as the source and end of human life. Wisdom of Solomon seems to most closely follow the pagan tradition as it regards matter eternal (11:17) and the body evil (1:3; 8:20; 9:15; 15:8). It affirms the preexistence of the soul, although it comes from God — or God's wisdom (8:13). According to 2:23, "God created man for incorruption, and made him in the image of his own eternity." Resurrection is not affirmed, as it is only the soul that continues forever, namely, that of the righteous (5:15-17; 6:18-19). As mentioned, Philo also adopted the Platonic view, although he added sophisticated speculations concerning the habitation of incorporeal souls in the air, living before creation in the continued contemplation of God, and so forth.[5] The Book of the Secrets of Enoch combines preexistence of the souls with the hope that there is a prepared place for the souls in the future (2 *Enoch* 23:5; 49:2; 58:5). And so forth. Unlike this apocryphal tradition, Hasidim (mystic-spiritualistic Orthodox tradition) and the Pharisees affirm resurrection of the body — grounded in the doctrine of *creatio ex nihilo* (2 Maccabees 7:20-23). The general resurrection of all came to be affirmed first, and derived from it was personal bodily resurrection.[6] The Essenes believed in immortality but rejected resurrection.[7] All these views had to be checked against the normative rabbinic theology, and they underwent revisions accordingly.

Among several thinkers (such as Saadia Gaon and Isaac ben Solomon Israel), the Spaniard Solomon Ibn Gabirol (a.k.a. Avicebron) creatively engaged

4. Martin and Barresi, *Rise and Fall of Soul and Self,* pp. 42-43.
5. See Cohon, *Jewish Theology,* p. 387.
6. 2 *Enoch* 83–90; Josephus, *Antiquities of the Jews* 18.1.3-6 (the Pharisees also believed in judgment and retribution) (Josephus's main works are available at www.sacred-texts.com).
7. Josephus, *Wars of the Jews* 2.8.11.

the Hellenistic (and also to some extent Islamic) tradition and contributed significantly to issues of self, soul, and personal identity. His *Fountain of Life*[8] suggests a novel form of "materialism" in which, except for God, all substances, whether spiritual or physical, are composed of matter and form. The human soul (like that of the angels) is a kind of "spiritual matter." "It does not really reside in the body like an Aristotelian substantial form in unformed matter, producing a single unified substance, for it already is a single unified substance." Avicebron's hylomorphism, thus, is a creative combination of Aristotelianism and Platonism; as in Plato, the soul acts something like the captain of the ship.[9]

The leading medieval Jewish philosopher Moses Maimonides set the tradition firmly in the Aristotelian camp (with his stated desire to purge Aristotle of all traces of Neoplatonism).[10] His *Guide for the Perplexed,* written in Arabic, is the embodiment of Aristotelianism cum Jewish theology; in its Latin translation it had a huge influence on Christian scholarship, particularly on the Dominicans. On the one hand, Maimonides builds on the Hebrew Scriptures' emphasis on the nonanalytic, integral relationship between body and soul (material and immaterial), and on the other hand, he continues the religious/ philosophical tradition of allowing some kind of independence to the soul, particularly after death.[11] Importantly, in his later work *Essay on the Resurrection,*[12] he came to endorse definitively the resurrection of the body (which he either denied or was vague about in the early part of his career).[13] Maimonides' theology by and large follows and develops the normative rabbinic teaching.

According to the Russian-born American rabbi and theology professor Samuel S. Cohon, "[t]he Jewish conception of human nature reaches its fullest expression in the belief that man is endowed with a divine soul." The immortal soul (immortality given by God) in the rabbinic teaching is "the life-principle and innermost self of man, [which] reveals and praises God, the abiding principle, the life and mind of the world."[14] Judaism thus operates

---

8. http://www.sacred-texts.com/jud/fons/index.htm.

9. Martin and Barresi, *Rise and Fall of Soul and Self,* p. 85.

10. For details, see Cohon, *Jewish Theology,* pp. 379-82.

11. Maimonides, *Eight Chapters of Maimonides on Ethics,* pp. 37-46.

12. Maimonides, *Essay on the Resurrection,* pp. 211-45.

13. In his commentary on the Mishnah, one tenet (#13) in the Thirteen Articles of Faith (*Shloshah-Asar Ikkarim*), based on 613 commandments traditionally found in the Torah, includes belief in the resurrection of the dead. See Fordham University's Medieval Sourcebook: "Maimonides: The 13 Principles and the Resurrection of the Dead," http://www.fordham.edu/ halsall/source/rambam13.asp (3/1/2013).

14. Cohon, *Jewish Theology,* p. 346.

dualistically, making a distinction between the material and immaterial (spirit, soul) without in any way implying moral dualism of good and evil; indeed, says Cohon, any depreciation of the body in later Judaism is a foreign influence from Gnostic and Neoplatonic sources, going all the way back to Plato himself and to the way Philo adopted his stark dualism.[15] Postmedieval rabbinic theology in particular came to rediscover not only the anthropomorphic orientation of early tradition[16] but also the importance of the bodily nature of the human being to the image of God.[17] Cohon quotes the saying from *Shomea Tefillah* (Yom Kippur Eve Service): "The soul is Thine; the body, too, is Thy handiwork." Furthermore, "[w]hile distinguished from the body, *ruah, neshama,* and *nefesh* are not wholly divested of materiality in early thought." The same divine *ruach* gives life to all life on earth, whether of beasts or plants or humans.[18] The normative rabbinic view of human nature regards the human person as body and soul, the former linking with the earth, the latter with heaven. While closely related to the body, the soul is also independent and continues after death.[19] The rabbinic tradition affirms resurrection of the body and usually combines it with a creationistic theory of the origin of the soul (with Zech. 12:1 often used as a supporting text) rather than the belief in the preexistence and/or eternity of the soul. As said, Maimonides' constructive theology is a faithful representation and development of the normative tradition.[20]

The Christian commentator may note several things about Jewish anthropology. First, as discussed in previous chapters, the OT anthropology, while employing a number of nonanalytic terms, majors in a holistic, embodied view of human nature with due acknowledgment of community and the link with earlier generations. Second, this is in keeping with not only the OT but also later, particularly current Jewish emphasis on "salvation" in this life, with much less stress on future eschatology than Christian tradition. Third, like its Christian counterpart, Jewish anthropology was heavily shaped throughout history by influences from philosophical and religious traditions. In sum: it seems to me that a highly integrated hylomorphist account of humanity with the acknowledgment of soul and belief in the resurrection of the body is an important current

15. For a careful critique of Plato and Philo's dualism, see Cohon, *Jewish Theology,* pp. 373-79.

16. The formative work here is Marmorstein, *Old Rabbinic Doctrine of God,* vol. 2, *Essays in Anthropomorphism.*

17. Gottstein, "Body as Image of God," pp. 171-95.

18. Cohon, *Jewish Theology,* pp. 348-49.

19. For details and references, see Cohon, *Jewish Theology,* pp. 389-90.

20. Cohon, *Jewish Theology,* pp. 398-406.

Jewish view (with the caveats that the emphasis is not on the future and there is a wide variety across the spectrum from orthodox to moderate to liberal views).

The Human Being as Body and Soul: The Islamic Vision

Islam and the other two Abrahamic traditions agree not only on the creation of the human being as "God's image" (the quotation marks indicate that while the Qur'an does not use the term, the idea is there) but also on humanity's common origin. The Qur'an puts it this way: "O people, fear your Lord, Who created you of a single soul, and from it created its mate, and from the pair of them scattered many men and women; and fear God by whom you claim [your rights] from one another and kinship ties" (4:1). This statement links human persons not only with their Creator but also with each other; in Abrahamic traditions, humanity forms one family.[21]

Although the Islamic view of humanity is realistic, acknowledging many limitations and failures of human nature, the principle of *fitrah*, as discussed in chapter 11, elevates the human person to a unique place among the creatures.[22] Notwithstanding some exegetical disputes, a number of sayings point to the divinely given status, for example, "Verily We created man in the best of forms" (Q 95:4), and "He formed you and perfected your forms, and provided you with [all] the wholesome things" (40:64). Humanity's status also appears in her inviolable dignity and invitation to serve as Allah's viceroy, discussed above. The Qur'anic creation accounts contain several references to humans having been presented before angels before they were created and having been assigned the lofty status of God's coregents (20:21 and so forth). God's blessings and providence have been lavished upon humanity (7:10; 31:20; 17:70). The reason why the Qur'an (unlike Hadith) dares not to use the Jewish-Christian expression of the image of God is to safeguard the utter transcendence of Allah (42:11). The transcendence of God, however, does not mean distance; somewhat counterintuitively, the Qur'an says of the human being that the Creator is "nearer to him than his jugular vein" (50:16). This is understandable in light of the conviction, shared by the two other Semitic traditions, that the human being made of clay is also breathed into by the Spirit of God (15:26-29).[23]

21. See Syed, "Nature of Soul."

22. Q 4:28; 10:12; 14:34; 16:4; 17:11; 33:72; 70:19; 96:6; 103:2; etc. For details, see Scudder, "The Qur'an's Evaluation of Human Nature," p. 75.

23. For comments, see Siddiqui, "Being Human in Islam," pp. 16-17.

Islamic anthropology is deeply dualistic. As does Jewish-Christian tradition, the Qur'an and subsequent Islamic theology speak of the soul everywhere. In keeping with Abrahamic faiths, the normative Islamic tradition rejects the eternity and preexistence of the soul: "The human soul is something created and originated."[24]

Aristotle (often coupled with Neoplatonic influences) became the guiding philosophical influence in Muslim anthropology. Whereas Avicenna (Ibn Sina) also reflected some Platonic ideas, Averroes was an even more faithful follower of Aristotle, and in every main aspect of anthropology agreed with the Master. Avicenna was a dualist; body and soul are separate substances, and personality is located in the soul and has its total independence from the body.[25] Gleaning from Platonic sources, he viewed soul as "an immaterial substance, independent of the body," spiritual in its essential nature.[26] In his famous "flying [or floating] man" thought experiment (anticipating the Cartesian *ergo sum* scheme of six hundred years later), he imagined a person in a perfect state, blind and suspended in the air and therefore unable to have any sense experiences. Would that person be able to affirm the existence of the self? Avicenna said yes, and saw that as a ground for envisioning the soul's (nonbodily part of human nature) independence.[27] Not surprisingly, he did not believe in the resurrection of the body, although he believed in the immortality of the soul. As in earlier influential medieval philosophers in his tradition, al-Kindi and al-Farabi, reason and intellect are for him the key aspects of the soul's capacities.[28] The Avicennian tradition was of great importance to Thomas and other scholastics; his ideas also shaped the al-Ghazali and Maimonides traditions.

The twelfth century — when a number of Islamic, Jewish, and Greek (Plato, Aristotle) works were translated and disseminated — was a fertile time for continuing interfaith debates about the soul-body problem.[29]

24. *Ibn Taymiyyah Expounds on Islam*, p. 333. That's why in Islamic interpretation even Jesus, as highly regarded as he is, is created rather than eternal (p. 334). For a sharp criticism of those marginal Islamic movements that took the soul to be eternal (although usually not divine), see p. 335.

25. For an exposition of Avicenna's view, see Rezazadeh, "Thomas Aquinas and Mulla Sadrá," pp. 420-21.

26. *Avicenna's Psychology*, p. 3.

27. The thought experiment can be found in the beginning of *Avicenna's Psychology*.

28. Martin and Barresi, *Rise and Fall of Soul and Self*, pp. 82-84.

29. For an important study, see Rezazadeh, "Thomas Aquinas and Mulla Sadrá," pp. 415-28.

Thomas Aquinas and Mulla Sadra were united in criticizing the Neoplatonically based body-soul dualisms in which the body is a mere instrument in the employ of the soul. They put forth a hylomorphic account. Unlike Avicenna, Sadra worked toward a highly integrated body-soul connection.[30] "Sadra regarded the soul and the body connection, somehow as the 'witness' *(ma'iyyah)* of the matter and form, in which there is no inseparability between the two."[31]

In many ways, the Muslim theology brings to the current reflection of the nature of human nature the same kinds of resources that the Aristotelian-Thomist tradition offers Christian philosophy. How would a Muslim scholar respond to the current philosophical and scientific view of a "psychology without a soul"?[32] The Iranian philosopher Mahmoud Khatami critiques as inadequate those views in which "conscious life is only a succession of phenomena, and the ego has no reality beyond that of these phenomena."[33] For him, something more permanent and stable should be assumed of human personhood. On the one hand, he seems to support strongly the traditionalist view that teaches the soul as substance; that he sees primarily for the sake of being able to establish "the spiritual character of the human being."[34] He appeals to Islamic tradition in support of envisioning the human soul without the material/physical side, and in keeping with Aristotelian tradition, assigns to the soul tasks such as knowledge, self-transcendence, will, and morality.[35] On the other hand, in a somewhat surprising move — mindful of current scientific views and some Muslim traditions, particularly Mulla Sadra — he goes on to emphasize that "the soul's acts depend upon the body" even when "acts of thought and will are immaterial." The clue to attempting to resolve these two obviously divergent, if not contradictory, accounts is the Sadraean theory "that the soul has a corporeal generation and bodily emergent [*sic*] in its origin (although it remains spiritual in its survival)." Hence, "the higher manifestations and creativity of the soul, intellectual cognition and intellectual volition, never occur without corresponding phenomena of the sensible order accompanying them." This looks quite similar to some forms of nonreductive

30. For a full discussion of the soul-body problem according to Sadra, see Abdulaziz, "Mulla Sadra and the Mind-Body Problem."

31. Rezazadeh, "Thomas Aquinas and Mulla Sadrá," p. 422.

32. So named by Gruender, *Psychology without a Soul.*

33. Khatami, "On the Transcendental Element," p. 121.

34. Subheading in Khatami, "On the Transcendental Element," p. 122.

35. Khatami, "On the Transcendental Element," pp. 123-25. For the simplicity of the soul, see pp. 125-26.

physicalism. Importantly, Khatami uses the term "emergence" several times and means with it what is meant in current philosophical discourse.[36] However, he surmises that the dependence of "spiritual activity" (that is, all mental life, including also self-transcendence/religious) "is not an intrinsic, subjective one but an extrinsic, objective dependence." That is because the subject of the "psychical life" is immaterial.

So, the mental life entails both "subjective" independence and "objective" dependence upon the physical.[37] Somewhat counterintuitively, he now attacks strongly the Cartesian dualism that in his mind compromises the "unitary nature of man." But how can he advocate nondualism in the context of what looks like a substance dualism? Here is the way it is: the physical and mental, although two substances, come together in the human person in such a way that "together [they] constitute by their union a single complete substance." On this basis, epiphenomenalism is to be rejected as it considers the mental as something less than real. Similarly, physicalism is not accepted because, for Khatami, it tears away the reality of the mental and spiritual. Finally, monism is rejected for obvious reasons: it does not allow for the "substance" nature of the two entities (notwithstanding that in humanity they form one substance). The "substantial unity of body and soul," he concludes, is the correct view in light of Islamic tradition and in the context of current scientific and philosophical thought.[38]

While many questions, including the meaning of "subjective" and "objective," require clarification, it seems to me that Khatami wants both to ensure the uniqueness of mental life, including its nonphysical continuation after death, and to account for physicality as much as he can — all in a substance dualistic framework shaped by Aristotelian hylomorphism. In many ways, he is much closer to the intentions of Christian nonreductive physicalists and emergent dualists than he is to traditional Christian substance-dualism. His accounting for the mental as something derived from the physical (Mulla Sadra) is both bold and innovative. That said, I do not understand how one could presuppose that and still think of the "soul" as independent from the body. Furthermore, I wonder why he sticks with substance ontology, particularly with the idea of the human person as one substance. These questions and critical remarks are not meant to downplay the dialogical importance of Khatami's work, but rather to invite continuing conversation.

36. See Khatami, "On the Transcendental Element," p. 137 particularly.
37. Khatami, "On the Transcendental Element," p. 127.
38. Khatami, "On the Transcendental Element," pp. 128-30.

The Many Hindu Visions of Humanity

Hinduism at large envisions *jīva,* "the living being" (sometimes also translated as "soul"), in terms of three bodies, namely, a physical ("gross"), a subtle, and a causal body. The causal body is a kind of "blueprint" that causes the human being to be what it is. The "subtle" body is the "mental" part of human nature with mind, intellect, activity of sense organs, vital energy, and so forth. As long as the human being falsely assumes separate individuality because of *avidyā,* "ignorance," and has not yet grasped the insight of the identity of *atman* with Brahman, the subtle body represents the continuity in the process of transmigration (at death, the physical body is left behind and decays).[39] Roughly speaking, on this much the orthodox Hindu schools most well known in the West agree. Not so, however, on the details. Recall that among the Vedanta traditions, Sankara's *advaita* school argues for an absolute, uncompromising nondualism and hence, identity of Brahman (god, divine, "spirit") and *atman* (self or soul), whereas Ramanuja's *Visistadvaita* allows for a qualified nondualism that refutes absolute identity between Brahman and *atman,* although it insists on their inseparability. This distinction has everything to do with the nature of humanity. Consider also the importance of the appearance nature of reality in Hindu cosmology and imagination. Envisioning the visible world as merely an appearance of the "real" world of the spirit (ultimately everything is *atman,* that is, Brahman) is of course not to say that therefore the world does not exist; the world exists but as appearance, and can easily mislead men and women to cling to what is *maya,* transitory and impermanent. Although one has to be careful in maintaining that the Semitic faiths are historical and Hinduism is not, it is also the case that history or embodiment certainly is not at the center of Indian vision.

In light of the appearance nature of reality, it is understandable that foundational to a Hindu understanding of humanity and human nature is the sharp distinction between the *real* self and the *empirical* self that lives in the phenomenal world. Whereas the latter is made of "stuff" such as earth, water, and light, and includes the "subtle body" of vitality (breath, mind, intelligence), it is not the "real" me, contrary to common intuitions. The real self is the *atman,* the eternal and formless, indeed the Brahman ("Spirit," "God," the Divine). This does not of course mean that "I" would not exist at all; even appearances, or dreams, or illusions exist in some sense. What the mainline Hindu philosophy is saying is that I do not exist "ultimately" or "really." Here

---

39. See Sharma, *Classical Hindu Thought,* chap. 10. The classic passage "Ātman is Brahman" can be found in Brihadaranyaka Upanishad 4.4.5, 25 (*SBE* 15:176), etc.

we come again to the main goal of pursuing the true knowledge of God: "the cognition of the unity of Brahman is the instrument of final release," as the person understands " '[t]hat Self is to be described by No, no [*neti, neti*].' "[40]

Sankara's *advaita* vision of humanity is the best-known form of Hindu anthropology in the West. An important modern *advaita* advocate whose writings still are influential was Swami Vivekananda, the keynote speaker at the 1893 World Parliament of Religions in Chicago. He affirms the identity of the divine and the human.[41] Ward reminds us that the saying "you are all Gods" cannot mean that each person is actually divine because then no distinction could be made between human persons and, say, *avataras* (Krishna and others). Rather, this statement has to be understood in terms of a divine spark in each person. What can be said is that this spark of divinity is "the true self, *atman,* which is one and the same in every distinct individual. It is not me, in distinction from anyone else. It is the 'me' which is identical with the 'me' in everyone else."[42] Perhaps so. It still presses the question, in light of the non-duality principle, Am I Brahman, the one nondual reality? Or am I a distinct individual soul, with particular duties to perform and a particular limited consciousness? Ward answers this in a way that seems to me pointing in the right direction: "It must be the case that I am both, but that the particular soul is only a transient appearance of the one enduring reality in which all dualities are transcended."[43] This is what Vivekananda seems to be saying — in a way reminiscent of the Buddhist idea of *dukkha:* "The apparent man is merely a struggle to express, to manifest this individuality which is beyond."[44]

Unlike *advaita,* other forms of Hindu philosophy (following more or less closely Ramanuja's qualified nondualism), particularly Vaishnava traditions, based on the teachings of the Bhagavad-Gita, teach the eternity of each individual self.[45] This is taken to mean the existence of an infinite number of selves with no beginning and no end. The relation of these selves to the

40. Sankara, *Vedanta-Sutras* 2.1.14; *SBE* 34:327. K. Ward (*Images of Eternity,* pp. 21, 24) correctly notes that there is, though, inconsistency in the way Sankara speaks of this "unspeakable" *nirguna,* as he at times seems to attach some qualities to it, most prominently "bliss" (1.1.19; *SBE* 34:76) and also "one mass of knowledge" (1.4.22; *SBE* 34:281).

41. Vivekananda, "Is Vedanta the Future Religion?"

42. K. Ward, *Religion and Human Nature,* p. 12.

43. K. Ward, *Religion and Human Nature,* p. 11.

44. Vivekananda, "The Real Nature of Man," chap. 2 in *Complete Works,* vol. 2, n.p.

45. Bhagavad-Gita, chap. 2; *SBE* 8 (p. 44): "Never did I not exist, nor you . . . ; nor will any one of us ever hereafter cease to be." Also, speaking of the spirit: "It is not born, nor does it ever die, nor, having existed, does it exist no more. Unborn, everlasting, unchangeable, and primeval, it is not killed when the body is killed" (p. 45).

Lord is conceived in terms of "inconceivable identity-in-difference" (as discussed above). This interpretation differs from that of *advaita,* according to which only the Absolute Self exists and all other "selves" are but appearances thereof. This view also differs from the "atheistic" understanding of Sankhya, which considers the selves as intrinsically omniscient and perfectly blissful, thus making the existence of God unnecessary. The Vaishnavites believe that the souls are created by God, the Absolute Soul, and have only a tiny part of the perfect bliss fully present in the Lord. The souls are to serve the Lord.[46] In this sense, there is some commonality between how the souls are related to Krishna with the relation of individuals to Christ in Christian tradition. And somewhat similarly, Krishna is both unchanging and changing in nature and considers the devotees dear to him.[47] While the devotion to Krishna seems to require a continued personal life and some form of embodiment, even the Vaishnava view rejects the idea that the self is to be identified with the material body — and it seems like not all among the infinite selves ever come into contact with the material realm. "Those that do must seek to free themselves from all attachment to both their gross and subtle bodies, and obtain release from matter." Hence, at the end, nothing like the incalculable value of human personhood that exists in this particular embodied state in history after the Semitic faiths can be affirmed even in Vaishnava tradition. "Such a value can only belong to the self which is never born and never dies, and which is not to be identified with any particular historical embodiment."[48]

Concerning Hindu traditions at large (particularly those not of the *advaita* school), in which souls exist as distinct from the Lord, the doctrine of rebirth is the foundational belief. According to it, human life is a function of (more or less and variously understood) "eternal" souls taking a place of dwelling temporarily in an embodied state. Apart from religious and theological questions, there is a deep conflict with current scientific understanding according to which everything about humanity (including "soul") emerges either from the physical base or (as in property dualistic views) in close correlation with the physical. The Vaishnava tradition must categorically reject

46. See K. Ward, *Religion and Human Nature,* pp. 37-38. One of the distinguishing features of Hinduism is the presence of several "atheistic" schools (atheistic in the sense of not acknowledging gods), among whom Sankhya is one. The classic passage of Rig Veda (10.129.6) seems to be teaching that gods came later than creation.

47. The classic passage of devotion is in Gita 18 (p. 128): "Dedicating in thought all actions to me, be constantly given up to me, (placing) your thoughts on me"; for mutual devotion, see also chaps. 12 (pp. 99-102) and 18 (see K. Ward, *Religion and Human Nature,* pp. 39, 43).

48. K. Ward, *Religion and Human Nature,* p. 49.

the evolutionary view of a gradual emergence of humanity from the midst of other creatures given its belief in eternal souls descending into matter over long periods of time.[49] If so, then there is an irreconcilable conflict between the otherwise positive embrace of evolutionary theory virtually by all Hindus and a certain kind of interpretation of the origins of humanity as an "eternal" soul.

Notwithstanding a wide variety of views among Hindus, it seems to me that Hindu anthropology is deeply dualistic. Consider this summative statement by the late Swami Adiswarananda, the Ramakrishna-Vivekananda tradition leader who also summarizes the bulk of the discussion above: "According to Hinduism, man is essentially a soul that uses its body and mind as instruments to gain experience. What is the nature of the soul? Hinduism maintains that the macrocosm and the microcosm are built on the same plan, and that Brahman is the soul of both."[50] Part of this teaching is the separation between the apparent and real self as well as the eternity of the "soul." Clearly, these tenets are in deep conflict with all current notions of the natural sciences. Against some common assumptions, in this regard, I have a hard time imagining how an authentic Hindu view could be reconciled with the sciences in the way nonreductive physicalism (and perhaps also my multidimensional monism) could be.

The *advaita* view seems irreconcilable to Abrahamic theistic belief due to its ultimate conflating of the divine and the human (pantheism in Abrahamic traditions). Furthermore, Christian anthropology that resists body-soul dualism and lifts up the importance of embodiment and sociality definitely looks in the opposite direction from any attempt to divide human nature between the apparent and the real, and to consider the bodily only as the temporary "tool" of the eternal spirit. The Jewish-Christian belief in the resurrection of the body in a renewed cosmos puts lasting value on the whole of human nature. Finally, whether *advaita* or another form, I can't see how the inviolable dignity of each human life could be affirmed in a Hindu context. As discussed below (chap. 16), the religious establishment of the caste system alone raises critical questions in this regard.

Interdependence, No-Soul, and *Dukkha:* The Buddhist Vision

It is somewhat ironic that whereas Buddhism and Christianity at large have began to engage each other only in the twentieth century (without, of course,

---

49. K. Ward, *Religion and Human Nature,* p. 70.
50. Adiswarananda, "Hinduism," part 2.

denying some occasional earlier contacts), of all possible topics, the "dialogue seems to founder on the shoals of theological anthropology."[51] If so, this is good news for this project!

Three foundational and wide-reaching Buddhist principles govern talk about human nature: the principle of *dukkha,* interdependent origination, and the no-self teaching. Recall that the most foundational principle in Buddhist cosmology is dependent origination and that this principle of causal interdependence is not limited to the physical. Says the venerable P. A. Payutto: "All facets of the natural order — the physical world and the human world, the world of conditions (dhamma) and the world of actions (kamma), the material world and the mental world — are connected and interrelated, they cannot be separated."[52] With all their differences, all Buddhist schools consider dependent origination and *dukkha* (suffering), including the rest of the "Noble Truths" (the origin and way of extinction), as the *summa* of everything in Buddhism and its scriptures.[53] While typical textbook presentations of Buddhism rightly begin from this foundational basis, as authoritatively pronounced in the very first sermon of Shakyamuni (Gautama) after the enlightenment in which he became the Buddha, they also fail to see the integral and necessary connection between the principle of *dukkha* and the nature of the human being. Buddha's foundational insight was this: "Birth is *dukkha,* aging is *dukkha,* sickness is *dukkha,* death is *dukkha,* association with the unpleasant is *dukkha,* dissociation from the pleasant is *dukkha,* not to receive what one desires is *dukkha* — in brief the five aggregates subject to grasping are *dukkha.*"[54] The point is this: Buddha himself relates *dukkha* and *pañcakkhandā,* the five aggregates "making" the human being. What we call a human being is but a combination of conditioned processes that form the physical and mental continuum. According to the most common analysis, it consists of five constituents *(pañcakkhandā):*

- *Rūpakkhanda:* various bodily organs, faculties, and other things the human being needs for being a living body
- *Vedanākhanda:* "feelings" or "experiences," classified usually according to whether they are agreeable, disagreeable, or neutral
- *Saññākhanda:* faculty of apperception and conception of ideas

---

51. Burns, " 'Soul-Less' Christianity," p. 87.

52. Payutto, *Dependent Origination,* "Introduction."

53. Chandngarm, *Arriyasatsee,* pp. 9-14.

54. *Dhammacakkappavattana Sutta* 11 of Samyutta Nikaya 56.11.

- *Samkhārakkhanda:* faculty that has desires, cravings, volitions, and intentions
- *Viññānakkhanda:* faculty of awareness of things, a particularly important asset needed for the right insight[55]

Dukkha and the five aggregates are not only interrelated. According to the Buddha, "the five clinging-aggregates are stressful [*dukkha*]."[56] In keeping with the Buddha's teaching on the dependently originated or conditioned *(samkhata)* nature of all things, not only humans but everything else is impersonal or selfless (*anattā,* "no-self"). "What we call a 'being,' or an 'individual,' or 'I,' according to Buddhist philosophy, is only a combination of ever-changing physical and mental forces or energies."[57] There is no "self" or "soul" that is permanent (the no-self principle applies also to the rest of reality).[58] Calling the person a "self" is just an elusive, conventional way of referring to that fleeting combination of elements. To be liberated from the illusion of being permanent and hence clinging on to something, the "salvific" insight into the true nature of reality and being is needed (release from samsara, the cycle of rebirths). As a result, self or individual or person does not exist in Buddhism in the way it is conceived in other traditions.[59] Therefore also, "[t]here is no doer of a deed."[60] The goal of nirvana is opposite to the desire and clinging: "there is neither coming, nor going, nor staying; neither passing away nor arising: unestablished, unevolving, without support (mental object). This, just this, is the end of stress [*dukkha*]."[61]

Dependent origination can be applied to humanity in two distinct ways, either as a demonstration of the evolution of the world at large or as a demonstration of the arising and cessation of individual life or individual suffering. The latter is in focus here. Concerning the individual life, the principle can be approached in terms of demonstrating the process over a very long period

---

55. An authoritative presentation can be found in *Visuddhimagga,* chap. 14.

56. *Dhammacakkappavattana Sutta* of Samuytta Nikaya 56.11; this truth is repeated a number of times in the Buddha's teachings.

57. Rahula, *What the Buddha Taught,* p. 20.

58. See *Cula-Saccaka Sutta: The Shorter Discourse to Saccaka* of Majjhima Nikaya 35.

59. An authoritative study is S. Collins, *Selfless Persons.*

60. *Visuddhimagga,* chap. 19, pp. 627-28, here p. 627.

61. "Nibbana Sutta: Total Unbinding (1)" (*Udana* 8.1); for an important contemporary discussion, see Dharmasiri, *A Buddhist Critique of the Christian Concept of God,* pp. 177-214. The discussion includes the relation to the Hindu use of the concept as well as critique of Christian responses and interpretations.

of time, from lifetime to lifetime, or a process that is continually occurring; this hermeneutics is supported by teachings in numerous Suttas and in the Abhidhamma Pitaka, where the entire dependent origination process is one mind moment.[62]

How would a Christian respond to the Buddhist teaching of no-soul?[63] I have to agree with K. Ward that "[f]rom a theistic viewpoint, it will seem to be false that there is no enduring Self and that there is no permanent and noncontingent reality — for God is precisely such a reality." In that sense, "the whole Buddhist world-view and discipline leads away from theism."[64] Indeed, in the absence of self, it is impossible — at least for the Western mind — to imagine "who" is the one who clings to life due to desire, suffers from the effects of karma, and particularly comes to the enlightening realization (if it ever happens) that the samsaric cycle is now overcome. This also has to do with what seems to me a deep and wide difference of orientation between Semitic faiths and Theravada Buddhism, namely, the notion of individuality and the individual's relation to others. Ward nicely summarizes the Theravadin's understanding: "The goal seems to be, not a creative community of agent-subjects, but the calm of the limpid pool wherein all sense of individuality has been long transcended, and all activity has ceased in complete freedom from desire. There is no enduring individuality, and the succession of thoughts, feeling, and sensations that we call a 'self' comes to an end with the realization of pure, objectless bliss."[65]

Furthermore, I cannot think of ways to affirm the dignity of human personhood if there is nothing "permanent" (relatively speaking, because all theistic traditions consider only God permanent). As is often rightly noted, it is also difficult to understand what the talk about rebirth may mean when there cannot be identity between the person who passed away and the one who reappears.[66] In other words, how should we conceive the principle of *kamma* when the "[a]ggregates produced in the past with kamma as condition ceased there too" and "there is no single thing that has come over from

---

62. Payutto, *Dependent Origination*, chap. 2.

63. See W. King, "No-Self, No-Mind," pp. 155-76.

64. K. Ward, *Religion and Revelation*, p. 166.

65. K. Ward, *Religion and Human Nature*, p. 106. For thoughtful reflections from a religious studies perspective, see S. Collins, "What Are Buddhists *Doing?*"

66. I do not know what to think of the idea of "life principle," a kind of vitality and consciousness, dependent on the body but not identical with it, that survives beyond death, claimed to be based on Buddha's teaching. It seems to me that positing such a principle begins to eradicate seriously the idea of no-self. Cf. Burns, " 'Soul-Less' Christianity," pp. 93-94.

the past becoming to this becoming"?[67] In other words, how can "collections of impersonal elements"[68] ever amount to any notion of personal and moral accountability?

What about the Buddhist notion of the nature of human nature in terms of body-soul/physical-spiritual distinctions? The Buddhist view of humanity is deeply holistic and resists dualisms. In keeping with the interrelatedness principles of Buddhist cosmology, all five *khandhas* interrelate and collaborate; for example, our body *(Rūpakkhanda)* has experiences *(Vedanākhanda)* that are recognized and identified *(Saññākhanda)* and of which we are aware *(Viññānakkhanda)*. Hence, we can say that "they function together as the psychophysical continuum for an 'individual,' and they work together in our everyday experience."[69] Therefore, Buddhism does not make a distinction between "spirit" and matter after most other religious traditions.[70] That said, unlike physicalist outlooks of contemporary sciences, it cannot be said that in Buddhism the mental — passion, desires, thoughts — originates in the physical, the body. On the contrary, the mind, particularly as cultivated through the practice of mindfulness *(sati)*, is the origin and control. Just consider this scriptural saying: "This is the only way, monks, for the purification of beings, for the overcoming of sorrow and lamentation, for the destruction of suffering and grief, for reaching the right path, for the attainment of Nibbana, namely, the four foundations of mindfulness."[71] This tells us that "neither Buddhism nor Christianity can accept a mechanistic reduction of self/soul/mind to the physical" after contemporary scientific reductionism.[72] In sum: it seems to me that the Buddhist anthropology is holistic and nondualistic but not in the way of current neuroscience-driven physicalism.

What about the soul? Is there any place for that in the Buddhist understanding? Although it is not difficult to establish the usage of the term "soul" in the Buddhist thesaurus, it is difficult to determine what is its meaning in relation to the typical terminology in Abrahamic faiths and Western philosophical traditions. For example: What is the meaning of "the soul of all

---

67. *Visuddhimagga* 19.22 (p. 628).

68. S. Collins, *Selfless Persons,* p. 160 and passim. I am not sure what K. Ward's (*Religion and Human Nature,* p. 80) statement about personal identity being "a matter of degree" may mean. Common sense tells us that one can either be a person or not be one.

69. S. Hamilton, "From the Buddha to Buddhaghosa," p. 49.

70. Rahula, *What the Buddha Taught,* p. 21.

71. *Satipatthana Sutta,* introductory verses; see also S. Hamilton, "From the Buddha to Buddhaghosa," pp. 49-53.

72. Burns, "'Soul-Less' Christianity," p. 94.

sentient beings . . . that constitutes all things in the world"?[73] Is it something similar to what the Hindu concept of *atman* means? Or is it something like an abstract, cosmic soul/spirit of idealist philosophies? Is there any convergence with the traditional meaning of the term "soul" of an individual person? If so, how is this related to the no-soul principle? Hard to tell.

It is often assumed that the Buddhist notion of humanity is pessimistic and gloomy. Is that true? The important link between *dukkha* and dependent origination is that one of the three aspects of *dukkha* (along with ordinary suffering and suffering produced by change) is "*dukkha* as conditioned states," which is the key to the First Noble Truth and to the question of the human person naturally desiring to affirm one's own self or I. That said, the focus on *dukkha* does not imply that for Buddhism life is pessimistic (any more than it is optimistic, for that matter). The Buddhist vision of life is rather realistic. As is well known, Gautama gave a long litany of things in life that are enjoyable and should be enjoyed, from economic security to enjoyment of wealth to happiness on account of living a good life.[74] Indeed, says Rahula, "a true Buddhist is the happiest of beings" because he or she has no fears or anxieties.[75]

With all their differences, living faith traditions all seek to explain and overcome the effects and roots of evil and "sin" in human life. How that may happen, we turn to next, focusing first on Christian tradition and then engaging the others.

73. See, e.g., Asvaghosa, *Awakening of Faith*, II, pp. 53-54.

74. See, e.g., *Anana Sutta: Debtless* (Anguttara Nikaya 4.62).

75. Rahula, *What the Buddha Taught*, p. 27. There are two important collections of texts by Buddha's students expressing joy and happiness found in the Buddha's teaching: *Theragāthā* and *Therigāthā* (both available at www.accesstoinsight.org).

15. The Misery of Humanity

Challenges to the Doctrine of Original Sin in Current Theology

Although the sinfulness of humanity, as Richard Niebuhr succinctly put it, is "one of the best attested and empirically verified facts of human existence,"[1] it is customary nowadays to begin theological talk about sin with either an apology or a humorous saying. Undoubtedly, one reason for the obscurity and marginality of the doctrine has to do with the dissolution of many of the traditionally held beliefs related to the doctrine of original sin and the Fall, beginning from modern theology in the nineteenth century. Along with that, the whole foundational intuition of the universal and radical nature of sinfulness has become obsolete. The final deathblow against the doctrine came from evolutionary theory, in light of which any defense of the idea of sin imputed to all of humanity stemming from one human person seemed doomed, apart from raising ethical objections concerning the fairness of God in holding people responsible for sinfulness that precedes them.

Notwithstanding many disagreements among the Christian traditions concerning the hermeneutics of "fall" and "original sin," there is no denying the simple fact that while "no religious vision has ever esteemed humankind more highly than the Christian vision," no other tradition has also "judged it more severely."[2] That the *doctrine* of original sin is distinctively Christian, hence, is understandable in this light; it is highly significant that the uni-

---

1. Niebuhr, "Sin," p. 349.
2. P. Jewett, *Who We Are*, p. 57.

versality of sin was not taught until Christianity, not even in Judaism.[3] That said, the *interpretations* of the doctrine of original sin in Christian tradition are far from unanimous. The difficulty with handling the biblical data itself greatly complicates the common task. Ironically, even Jewish and Christian interpreters dramatically differ in the interpretation of one and the same biblical narrative. Jewish readers did not find the doctrine of original sin at all in the First Testament.[4] The obvious reason for the Jewish conclusion is that in the OT Adam virtually disappears after the opening pages. One has to wait until 2 Esdras (7:48) to know that Adam's fall has universal effects (but that each individual may also win over sin [7:57]). To further complicate the picture, even among Christian readers of the Genesis narrative and the rest of the canonical story, radically different interpretations emerged, as the ensuing discussion reveals.[5]

Whatever faults one may find in Christian tradition's hermeneutics of original sin and fall, it is of utmost importance for contemporary constructive theology to be able to make a distinction between those features and the basic intuitions to which the doctrine points, namely, the radical and universal nature of sin that "meets" the human person as soon as one becomes part of that family[6] and the affirmation that all humans have a "universal solidarity in sin."[7] R. Niebuhr's word is worth hearing again: "A theology which fails to come to grips with this tragic factor of sin is heretical both from the standpoint of the gospel and in terms of its blindness to obvious facts of human experience in every realm and on every level of moral goodness."[8] Contemporary constructive theology should also note that evolutionary theory in itself does not necessarily raise questions about our current state of sinfulness; it raises questions only about how and when the first sin occurred, and how this fallen state was transmitted to all people.

Although sinfulness may be an empirically tested fact, it is also a "mystery" (2 Thess. 2:7) — as long as one wishes to hold on to two opposite biblical intuitions about humanity: her goodness (Gen. 1:27, 31) and her sinfulness (Rom. 3:23). "There is nothing in our created nature that would dispose us to

---

3. Pannenberg, *TA*, p. 134.

4. Telushkin, *Jewish Literacy*, pp. 27-90.

5. See Pagels, *Adam, Eve, and the Serpent*, chaps. 5; 6.

6. See Rauschenbusch, *Social Gospel*, p. 5.

7. McFadyen, *Bound to Sin*, p. 17. Similarly, the revisionist Dutch Catholic theologian Schoonenberg, "Sin and Guilt," p. 1584. For thoughtful reflections, see Wiley, *Original Sin*, pp. 37-38.

8. Niebuhr, *Christianity and Power Politics*, pp. 17-18, cited in Wiley, *Original Sin*, p. 138.

sin, yet we invariably fall into sin as we make our own way in the world."[9] In that sense, sin is, as Barth named it, "impossible possibility."[10] That said, theologians should not major in making an already mysterious and complicated doctrine even more mysterious or ethereal, as happened with Barth's obscure idea of evil as "nothing."[11] The OT virtually refuses to offer any reason for the presence of evil in human life, and even the NT, apart from some well-known Pauline references, is silent about its origins (notwithstanding ample references to the deeds and effects of sin). Last — but certainly not least — there is the challenge coming from other faith traditions. How do Muslims, Hindus, Buddhists, and Jews conceive the misery of humanity (if, in the first place, they think such a state exists)?

An Appraisal of the Growth of Traditions

Even if in Pauline theology (recall that in the Gospels, Adam and the Genesis narrative are totally missing) the universality of sin is traced back to Adam (Rom. 5:12), there is not yet an idea of sin "as a fated universal legacy that proliferates generation after generation like a congenital disease."[12] And although Paul teaches the universal occurrence of death (Rom. 5:12, an idea familiar also to Jewish tradition), he does not speak of inheritance of sin in any technical sense. Rather, individuals suffer as a result of their sins.[13] Greek theology followed that tradition in understanding the example and sin of Adam as representing the whole race instead of linking this notion to the idea of inheritance of sin.[14] Pannenberg rightly comments that "[t]he thesis of the universality and radicalness of sin would not have required for its proof the acceptance of a *transmission* of the *individual* sin of the first parents of the human race."[15]

Highly significant for the purposes of contemporary constructive theology of sin is the observation that, on the one hand, patristic theology for centuries did not have a developed doctrine of sin (other than a deep intuition

---

9. Bloesch, *Jesus Christ*, p. 41.

10. Barth, *CD* IV/2, pp. 403-4.

11. Barth, *CD* IV/2, pp. 415-16.

12. Pannenberg, *TA*, p. 121.

13. Pannenberg, *TA*, p. 122.

14. J. Gross, *Geschichte des Erbsündendogmas* I (1960), pp. 92-93, cited in Pannenberg, *TA*, p. 122.

15. Pannenberg, *TA*, p. 123, emphasis in original.

of the fallen and sinful nature of humanity),[16] and on the other hand, doctrinal developments of original sin and the Fall took dramatically divergent paths among Christian traditions. Furthermore, particularly among the apostolic fathers, all kinds of interpretations were offered as to the "origins" of sins, along with differing interpretations of the Genesis narrative, from demons stemming from the fallen angels and daughters of humans, to devils teaching astrology, to the role of Satan, and so forth.[17] Some early writings such as the *Epistle of Barnabas* strongly argue that the souls of children are innocent and born without sin.[18] As discussed, freedom, including moral freedom, was of high value to early theologians. With that they opposed forms of fatalism, Gnostic determinism (that assumed the evil nature of all things physical/material), and other views that seemed to undermine responsibility and self-determination. Ironically, according to Pelikan, the Gnostics alone had an explicit doctrine of original sin![19]

In early theology, sin and guilt were not in the forefront, but rather the redemptive and reconciliatory work of Christ was.[20] Importantly for our purposes, the reflection on the redemptive work itself displayed a lot of diversity and employed a plurality of metaphors and images (as discussed in detail in chapter 11 of *Christ and Reconciliation*). The diversity of metaphors speaks of different facets of salvation. Mortality and power over evil rather than guilt and condemnation placed high in the Fathers' list of salvific intuitions. As is well known, for the first Christian millennium or so, the *Christus Victor* models of atonement, with a focus on recapitulation, resurrection, deification, eternal life, and freedom from underpowers, were the "mainstream" theologies of salvation, and only in the second millennium did more judicial-forensic metaphors (particularly in the West) take over. Pelikan makes the brilliant observation that the doctrine of original sin has by and large "developed a posteriori, by a process which, proceeding from the salvation in Christ and from infant baptism, made the diagnosis fit the cure"![21]

While in the Latin West the Augustinian doctrine was consolidated particularly in opposition to Pelagianism (a version of the Eastern traditions),[22]

16. Rondet, *Original Sin*, p. 70.

17. Justin, *Second Apology* 5; Tatian, *Address to the Greeks* 7; Theophilus, *To Autolycus* 29. See further, Rondet, *Original Sin*, p. 122.

18. See Wiley, *Original Sin*, p. 39.

19. Pelikan, *Emergence of the Catholic Tradition*, pp. 282-83.

20. For useful notes, see Korsmeyer, *Evolution and Eden*, pp. 25-26.

21. Pelikan, *Emergence of the Catholic Tradition*, p. 204.

22. Pelikan, *Emergence of the Catholic Tradition*, p. 316.

the Christian East took a decidedly different standpoint: the human person was regarded as mortal even before the Fall, and hence death per se could not be punishment for the Fall; concupiscence, rather than punishment for sin, was its cause; human nature was intact even after the Fall and was good by virtue of existing as the image of God, and free will was not destroyed by the Fall. Hence, sin was rooted in human freedom.[23] The East followed the Hebrew mind-set in which even the concept of original sin was not standard.[24] According to Eastern theology, we do not inherit sin but inherit its consequences, particularly mortality and corruption, effects more severe than guilt alone. While the universality of sin was affirmed by the Cappadocians, it was often described in terms of woundedness or sickness. As did early tradition, they denied that infants were born in sin — even when establishing the link between the narrative of the Fall and our current state of existence.[25] Recall also that the Antiochene theologian Theodore of Mopsuestia's *Against the Defenders of Original Sin* — a telling title — forcefully argued that only human nature can be inherited, not sin.[26] According to the definitive teaching of Athanasius, the first couple, placed in paradise to contemplate constantly the Word and be shaped spiritually,[27] were tempted by the material world and so "returned" to their natural state, which led to corruption, ignorance, and idolatry. This is the Fall.[28] Freedom of will, however, remained.[29] Because of freedom of will, a "return" to the state of grace is open at all times, although after the Fall moral and other weaknesses in us abound. Rather than being annihilated, the likeness (to God) is obscured or tainted.[30] Irenaeus had already established the powerful vision of Adam and Eve as yet immature "children" undergoing growth and development toward perfection.[31] Along with Eastern teachers, Irenaeus rejected the interpretation of the Genesis 3 narrative in terms of a cosmic fall and regarded it rather as a sign of disobedience of persons in need of growth.[32] No doubt, early Eastern

23. Hefner, *The Human Factor,* p. 128; Pelikan, *Emergence of the Catholic Tradition,* pp. 285-86; Gregorios, *Cosmic Man,* pp. 165-68.

24. Paraphrased by Gregorios, *Cosmic Man,* p. 168.

25. See further, Wiley, *Original Sin,* pp. 50-51.

26. See Pelikan, *Emergence of the Catholic Tradition,* p. 285.

27. Athanasius, *On the Incarnation of the Word* 3; 4; 11 particularly; see also *Contra Gentes* 35. See also Kelly, *Early Christian Doctrines,* p. 346.

28. Athanasius, *On the Incarnation of the Word* 4; 6; 7; *Contra Gentes* 3.

29. Athanasius, *Contra Gentes* 4.

30. Athanasius, *On the Incarnation of the Word* 14.1.

31. Irenaeus, *Against Heresies* 3.22.4; 3.23.5; 4.38.1-2; for comments, see Steenberg, "Children in Paradise," pp. 1-22.

32. See further, Wiley, *Original Sin,* pp. 40-41.

tradition reflected upon paradise. However, its view does not follow the established Western doctrine of a perfect first state.[33]

The Christian East looks into the future, the ultimate goal of perfection (deification). Furthermore, although the Greek Fathers trace the sinfulness back to Adam, Athanasius (no more than others) "never hints that we participate in Adam's actual guilt, i.e., his moral culpability, nor does he exclude the possibility of men living entirely without sin." The Fall is conceived in the East more as a wound inflicted in our nature.[34]

The definite *doctrinal* formulation of original sin was established in the Latin West no earlier than the fourth and fifth centuries. Ambrose laid the foundation for Augustine's doctrine of original sin.[35] Ambrose further idealized the blessedness of life in paradise, making Adam virtually a "heavenly being," able to resist mortality by eating from the tree of life, and without any defects.[36] Pride was the reason for the Fall, which resulted in concupiscence and death. Western writers also deemed it necessary to establish in a more rigid way the theory of the transmission of sin, which eventually led to the Augustinian notion of hereditary transmission. Behind Augustine's sustained interest in the Fall, original sin, and guilt were a number of factors, including his past dealings with sexual sins, his continuing fight with Pelagianism,[37] the hermeneutics of the virgin birth of Jesus (making ordinary conception the source of sin), and his defense of the necessity of infant baptism.[38]

The freedom Adam had before the Fall was the ability not to sin (*posse non peccare,* in distinction from *non posse peccare,* that is, not able to sin, available only in the heavenly state of blessedness)[39] and a will subject to God. The fall "from grace" was complete and disastrous[40] — but God is not to be blamed, only the human being, more precisely, his wrong choice, fueled by pride.[41] When Adam sinned, we participated in it. This interpretation was supported by the faulty Vulgate translation of Romans 5:12, which translated the Greek *eph ho*

33. For details, see Kelly, *Early Christian Doctrines,* pp. 348-49.

34. Kelly, *Early Christian Doctrines,* pp. 347-48.

35. Another influence on Augustine is the pseudonymous Ambrosiaster.

36. Ambrose, *Paradise,* pp. 287-356.

37. See TeSelle, *Augustine the Theologian,* pp. 260-62.

38. Hefner, *The Human Factor,* p. 126; Pelikan, *Emergence of the Catholic Tradition,* pp. 279-331. In my exposition, I was informed by W. Mann, "Augustine on Original Sin and Evil," pp. 40-48.

39. Augustine, *City of God* 14.11.

40. For the listing of heinous effects and sins stemming from the Fall, see Augustine, *Enchiridion* 45.

41. Augustine, *City of God* 14.12, 13; also 12.8.

as "in whom."[42] That means we all participate in Adam's guilt.[43] Sinfulness is propagated by virtue of sexual union, even in the case of baptized parents[44] — an interpretation consistently rejected by the Eastern Church.[45] An asset in the hereditary interpretation of sin came from the traducianist view of the origin of soul, coined by Tertullian and somewhat hesitantly adopted by Augustine[46] (in its "spiritualist" form, as he was critical of his predecessor's materialist theory of soul).[47] An obvious question to Augustine, of which he was well aware, was how can an infant be blamed for participation in Adam's sin when she obviously had not yet developed the powers of choice? Augustine dismisses the question by saying that because it derives from the free act of the first parents, it can also be attributed to every new infant.[48] Only redemption in Christ can save the human being from this *condition* of sinfulness derived from Adam.[49] The Pelagian opposition to the Augustinian doctrine was rejected, and Augustinianism was ratified by the ecclesiastical decrees and became the mainstream Western tradition.[50] Tradition came to speak of original sin in two interrelated ways: *peccatum originans,* that is, the primordial sin, act of disobedience, of Adam and Eve; and *peccatum originatum,* the state or condition caused by that (the effect of which is *concupiscence,* the universal inclination to sin).

Behind the Anselmian-Thomist continuation and modification of the Augustinian doctrine is the "two-story" anthropology, based on a nature-grace dialectic. Whereas intellect and will belong to the realm of nature, the supernatural gift of "original righteousness" (as well as supernatural "virtues" of faith, hope, and love) belongs to that of grace. As a result, the latter can be removed (as happened as a result of the Fall) without destroying the "natural" endowments (even though they, too, were hampered severely because of sin). For Anselm of Canterbury, then, followed by Thomas, the main idea of the

---

42. Augustine, *Treatise on the Merits and Forgiveness of Sins, and on the Baptism of Infants* 1.11; for details, see Kelly, *Early Christian Doctrines,* pp. 353-54.

43. Augustine, *Treatise on the Merits and Forgiveness of Sins, and on the Baptism of Infants* 3.14.

44. Augustine, *On Marriage and Concupiscence* 2.36; *Treatise on the Merits and Forgiveness of Sins, and on the Baptism of Infants* 2.11.

45. Meyendorff, *Byzantine Theology,* p. 145.

46. See Kelly, *Early Christian Doctrines,* pp. 363-64.

47. Among the Greeks, Gregory of Nyssa (*On the Making of Man* 28; 29) seemed to have a similar kind of view. See also Kelly, *Early Christian Doctrines,* pp. 345-46.

48. Augustine, *Retractions* 1.15.2; Bogan, trans., p. 72.

49. Augustine, *Enchiridion* 49.

50. For a nontechnical, yet accurate, discussion of Pelagianism as well as the Councils of Carthage (411-418) and Orange (520), see Wiley, *Original Sin,* pp. 66-75.

Fall is privation of original righteousness.[51] This is a less radical account of the effects of the Fall. Clearly, at the center of Thomas's theology is not fall but rather the supernatural destiny of human nature.[52] In opposition, for Luther, who thought it important to stress the serious and radical nature of the Fall, the Thomistic theory of original sin as privation of original righteousness seemed too thin and "passive." Instead of privation, Luther defined original sin as concupiscence,[53] following the Augustinian idea of sin ultimately deriving from pride and perverted love.

Protestant tradition at large took over the Augustinian interpretation, claiming that "since the Fall of Adam all humans who are propagated according to nature are born in sin," and this "vice of origin is truly sin, which even now damns and brings eternal death on those who are not born again through Baptism and Holy Spirit."[54] For Luther, the Fall meant the loss of the image — "But if you sin, you will lose this image, and you will die"[55] — albeit not totally, because intellect and will in some capacity (as "bound") still remained.[56] This became the official Lutheran position.[57] Following tradition, it identifies *imago* with "original righteousness"[58] and teaches that only in the gospel is there the restoration of that image.[59] In the Reformed tradition the identification of the image with original righteousness continued,[60] although in Calvinistic and other Reformed theologies the idea of the perpetuity is more in the fore.[61] Similarly, Calvin followed — and perhaps even radicalized — Luther's idea of the thick negative effects of the Fall by speaking of "natural depravity which we bring, from our mother's womb, though it brings not forth immediately its own fruits, is yet sin before God, and deserves his vengeance."[62]

While on the basis of mere terminology ("concupiscence," "original righ-

---

51. Aquinas, *ST* 2a.82.3; for Anselm, see Wiley, *Original Sin,* pp. 77-82; a more technical essay is McMahon, "Anselm and the Guilt of Adam," pp. 81-89.

52. So also Wiley, *Original Sin,* p. 83.

53. Luther, *Lectures on Romans* (on chap. 5); *LW* 25:299-301.

54. Augsburg Confession 2, in *The Book of Concord,* ed. Tappert, p. 29, Latin version.

55. Luther, *Lectures on Genesis* 1-5; *LW* 1:62-63, here p. 63.

56. Luther, *Lectures on Genesis* 1-5; *LW* 1:64-65.

57. Formula of Concord, Solid Declaration, art. 1, in *The Book of Concord,* p. 510.

58. As also presented in Melanchthon, *Loci Communes,* p. 48.

59. Luther, *Lectures on Genesis* 1-5; *LW* 1:67.

60. Indeed, in the Heidelberg Catechism, the only reference to *imago* (Q. 6) identifies it with "true righteousness and holiness"; similarly, the Westminster Confession, chap. 4; for details, see Horton, "Post-Reformation Reformed Anthropology," pp. 62-63.

61. For comments, see Horton, "Post-Reformation Reformed Anthropology," pp. 66-67.

62. Calvin, *Romans,* on 5:12 (n.p.), http://www.ccel.org.

teousness") no great distinction appears between the Catholic and Protestant views, one must put this in perspective, particularly after the Council of Trent's repudiation of the Reformers' views[63] and Protestants' strengthening of the opposition to the Thomistic tradition in return. Although clearly overstated and materially mistaken, Luther's charge of Pelagianism concerning the Thomistic Catholic view of sin illustrates the contrast.[64] Luther's collapsing into one "original sin" and "concupiscence" with the important twist (and deviation even from Augustine) that concupiscence remains sin even after baptism (in contrast to Thomas's view that concupiscence is not a sin of guilt after baptism but rather its negative effect), further speaks of his need to radicalize the effects of the Fall.[65] Regarding "original righteousness," of course Luther also believed (with Thomas) in its privation, but Luther did not conceive it as a "supernatural gift" in the Anselmian-Thomistic sense and, more importantly, argued that making it privation alone was not "enough" to be said of the Fall. The Fall is "a propensity toward evil. It is nausea toward the good, a loathing of light and wisdom, and a delight in error and darkness."[66] Even more pronounced is the Reformation tradition's opposition to Eastern Orthodoxy's "ontological realism," that is, that the image "is both ontic and actual."[67]

This selective scrutiny of a fairly well known history of tradition yields the following broad insights and several tasks for revision. Let us begin by listing tradition's beliefs in need of correction and revision in light of current scientific, philosophical, and theological intuitions.

- The literal reading of Genesis 2–3 with its corollaries: the origins of humanity in one couple and their perfect state of innocence and immortality
- The hereditary view of the transmission of sin
- The concept of original sin as entailing guilt and condemnation in relation to human responsibility and self-determination
- The overly individualistic account of sinfulness

63. "Decree concerning Original Sin," in Schaff, ed., *Creeds of Christendom,* 2:83-88.

64. Luther, *Lectures on Romans; LW* 25:261-62.

65. For details, see Lohse, *Martin Luther's Theology,* pp. 70-72, 248-57. The Lutheran slogan *simul iustus et peccator* only makes sense if, even after baptism, the Christian remains both just and sinner.

66. Luther, *Lectures on Romans; LW* 25:299.

67. Berkouwer, *Man,* p. 50, cited in Horton, "Post-Reformation Reformed Anthropology," pp. 67-68. For a highly useful summative comparison between Protestant and Catholic perspectives on original sin and the Fall, see Wiley, *Original Sin,* pp. 93-99.

Let us consider these in light of several broad insights. First, the elusive and diverse nature of Christian reflection on "what's wrong with the world" and with us both justifies and mandates continuing constructive work. One has to be very careful when wishing to define *the* Christian orthodox position on sin. Second, apart from all the hermeneutical differences among the main Christian traditions, until modernity all believed in a more or less literal reading of the biblical narrative, the historicity of Adam and Eve, as well as corollary precritical cosmological views. Incorporating post-Enlightenment advances in science and history into a contemporary account of original sin, without thereby losing the deepest intuitions, is of utmost importance. Third, thinking on the meaning of sin and the Fall in contemporary theology is a deeply ecumenical task and cannot be contained within one tradition. As the reader can easily notice, in the following discussion my own instincts are often more on the Eastern Church's side and in sympathy with much of the Catholic tradition, although I am a Protestant.

No need to mention here that some elements in the Augustinian conception of original sin, apart from the radically changed scientific questions, are highly problematic in themselves, particularly the linking of sexual procreation with transmission of sin and the blatant pronouncing of guilt and condemnation for a human person just by virtue of being born.

Toward a Contemporary Christian Theology of Sin

A Terminological Reorientation

As feminist scholars untiringly remind us, speech makes a difference in life and theology. Concepts shape reality. Hence, I wish to suggest "misery"[68] as an umbrella term for speaking of original sin and the Fall, as well as its effects. The term "original sin" leans too heavily on speculation about the origins, of which we know precious little, and is loaded with assumptions that in popular piety are taken as *the* orthodox doctrine of sin. Other terms used, particularly "total depravity," suggest too stark a picture of human nature that was pronounced good after creation. This choice is not motivated by the desire to eliminate the term "sin" from the theological thesaurus, nor even "original sin," but rather to help redefine them and also locate sin terminology in the wider context of speaking of humanity.

68. So also Pannenberg, *ST* 2, chap. 8.

Further caution with terminology is in order when speaking of terms related to the discourse of misery. An example suggested by female theologians makes the point. It has to do with the Augustinian heritage of finding the ultimate motive for disobedience in pride. While justification for that interpretation can be found in the Genesis 3 narrative, contemporary women theologians have come to question the overemphasis on pride. Rather than pride and "will to power," for women, temptation and vulnerability to sin may be better suggested in dependence, negation of self, undermining one's own capacity, and so forth.[69] The lesson is not to drop from usage the Augustinian idea but to be mindful of the way it is heard in the contemporary context; it needs to be balanced and amplified (in this case) with perspectives from women and minorities.

Only in light of the dignity of humanity by virtue of the *imago Dei* can we meaningfully speak of the misery. That, however, does not mean a return to the idyllic idea of a perfect original state, not only because the biblical narrative does not mandate it but also because it is scientifically untenable. Instead, as argued above, the image of God is a task as much as a current state and therefore points to the future.[70] Speaking properly of the misery of humanity means speaking of sin robustly, yet not in a way that would make it "natural," a liability of many modern accounts of sin — to which we turn next.

The Liability of "Thin" Accounts of Sinfulness

In the aftermath of the Enlightenment, modern theology rejected, for scientific and cultural reasons, a number of traditional beliefs about sin. At the same time, the deepest theological intuitions were in danger of being lost.

Strongly opposing Blaise Pascal's fairly traditional Augustinian-based account of an original perversion of humanity as the cause of the misery of humanity,[71] another French thinker, Jean-Jacques Rousseau, unabashedly affirmed the original goodness of humanity, that is, humans are good by nature although they often do not behave well in society.[72] Categorically rejecting the Christian interpretation of the Fall, he maintained the idea of innocence and gradual falling into moral evil in the course of history. Education and civili-

---

69. Saiving, "The Human Situation," p. 37; so also Dunfee, "The Sin of Hiding."
70. Gunton, *The Triune Creator*, p. 56.
71. Pascal, "Of Original Sin."
72. Rousseau, "Discourse on Inequality," pp. 125-201.

zation were the means to tackle the challenge. Not surprisingly, Rousseau was expelled from the Catholic Church after he published his most well-known pedagogical work, *Emile* (1762).[73] Although less radical in its approach, Kant's reinterpretation in *Religion within the Limits of Reason Alone* (1793) proposed a thoroughly rational-ethical account of human goodness and inclination to evil. He could only take symbolically the intuitions of the Genesis narrative.[74] Schleiermacher's highly revisionist theological account of original sin in terms of arresting the God consciousness (as he puts it in his awkward manner, "an arrestment of the spirit, due to the independence of the sensuous functions"), as he himself notes, can hardly be reconciled with the traditional belief in "sin as a violation of the divine law."[75]

Closer to the deepest Christian intuitions goes Kierkegaard's identification of the main problem of humanity with despair: "There lives not one single man who after all is not to some extent in despair, in whose inmost parts there does not dwell a disquietude, a perturbation, a discord, an anxious dread of an unknown something."[76] That account alone, however, can also be read in a way that makes it primarily a matter of existential feeling and bypasses the question of its relation to the divine destiny set for humanity by the Creator. While the more contemporary existential hermeneutics of the Fall, common among many theologians particularly in the second half of the twentieth century, contain an abiding kernel of truth, namely, anxiety and frustration as results of sinfulness, they similarly end up saying too little. Langdon Gilkey's description of "original sin" is illustrative: "self forms itself, when the self, through its own freedom and choice of itself, constitutes its own existence."[77] Apart from the obscurity of the statement, it naively adopts as its basis the "turning-to-self" axiom of modern thinking.

Similarly, I find limited and reductionist (although, again, not without some merit) the proposal of American process theologians Charles Birch and John Cobb. Rightly refusing to juxtapose biological and cultural evolution, they present an ecological model in which the two are deeply interrelated. The problem, however, is that the talk about a fall "upward" in the process of

---

73. For comments, see Wiley, *Original Sin*, pp. 112-13.

74. For exposition and comments, see Wiley, *Original Sin*, pp. 113-15.

75. Schleiermacher, *Christian Faith*, §62 (p. 273). Note that Niebuhr (*Nature and Destiny of Man*, 1:245-48) considers Schleiermacher Pelagian; materially similar is the judgment of Barth, *Theology of Schleiermacher*, pp. 118-22.

76. Kierkegaard, *Sickness unto Death*, p. 17.

77. Gilkey, "Protestant Views of Sin," p. 159, cited in R. Collins, "Evolution and Original Sin," p. 494.

"the occurrence of a new level of order and freedom bought at the price of suffering" (from the lowest level to animal life when suffering is introduced but apparently without any value, to emergence of human life when suffering is intensified, but with an experience of value) hardly captures Christian intuitions of original sin and fall![78]

As much as Christian tradition is in need of correction regarding its tendency to limit sinfulness merely to the relationship between God and humanity and making it largely an individualistic matter[79] (thereby not always considering its implications for other human beings and creation),[80] the Godward orientation should not be compromised for the sake of accommodation. Making sin merely or primarily a human affair does not suffice.[81] Nor is it legitimate to dismiss the whole concept of "original sin" as irrelevant merely because at times it is used (or abused) in a way that "undermines the guilt of oppressors by universalizing the guilt of humanity";[82] that kind of misuse just needs to be corrected! A distinctively Christian — along with Jewish and Islamic — doctrine of sin can only be constructed when it is not made merely a matter of immanent ethics and creaturely relations, as integral as those values are.[83] The American Reformed thinker Cornelius Plantinga's delightful (if I may say so!) primer *Not the Way It's Supposed to Be* sets forth the foundational claim that, above all, sin at its core is simply the frustration of God-intended shalom, integrity, meant for humanity and the rest of creation.[84]

At the same time, even a robust theology of sin should resist the Augustinian-Protestant tradition's tendency to make sin in some sense part

78. Finally, the construction of more and more developed cultures required enormous sacrifices, in terms of finance, labor, and human lives. Birch and Cobb, *Liberation of Life*. Materially quite similar is Gabriel Daly's (*Creation and Redemption*, pp. 131-47) view of the Fall as a movement from one level of evolution to another, seeking peace at a new level.

79. Still worth hearing is the classic observation of the "introspective conscience of the West" in the discussion of sin and redemption by the Swedish theologian Stendahl, "The Apostle Paul and the Introspective Conscience of the West."

80. This applies by and large even to the important rediscovery of the doctrine of sin in neo-orthodox theology (Barth, Bultmann, Tillich, the Niebuhrs). Consider this: whereas Reinhold Neibuhr's *Moral Man and Immoral Society* clearly moves toward a social hermeneutics of sin, his two-volume magnum opus in theological anthropology, *Nature and Destiny of Man*, develops the theme almost exclusively in individualistic terms.

81. As is done by the feminist Ruether, *Introducing Redemption*, p. 71.

82. A. Park, *Wounded Heart of God*, p. 79. In an alarming way, Park (p. 95) also rejects categorically the traditional redemptive vision of Christianity, namely, justification by faith — again, just on the basis of a potential misuse of that doctrine.

83. See the strong statement in McFadyen, *Bound to Sin*, p. 19.

84. C. Plantinga, *Not the Way It's Supposed to Be*, chap. 1, "Vandalism of Shalom."

of human nature. Christian theology should hold fast to the insight that it does not really take sin to make an authentic human being! Sin does not belong to human nature; sin is an intrusion.[85] Furthermore, constructive theology should learn from the mature Bonhoeffer, who vehemently opposed linking sin with the natural, beautiful, and good enjoyments of earthly life.[86]

Affirming a robust theology of sin is necessary, but it is not a sufficient condition for contemporary constructive theology. A viable theological account should allow a form that incorporates the best of current scientific understanding. This is definitely not an effort to naively accommodate theology under science but rather — in keeping with theology's goal in attempting a coherent account of God and God's relation to the world — is a way to refuse to insulate Christian claims from the rest of the created reality.

Original Sin and the Fall in Light of Current Evolutionary Theory

How can we conceive of the Fall in light of the current scientific knowledge of the long hominid line that has culminated in modern humanity?[87] Current knowledge of human development clearly conflicts with the traditional view that all humans descended from a single pair.[88] The Genesis narrative sets Adam and his immediate descendants in a farming culture that can be traced not much further back in history than about 6,000 years. Furthermore, there is also a city culture; the oldest known examples are less than 10,000 years old. Both of these markers locate the Genesis narrative in the Neolithic period.[89] With the emergence and rise of a distinctively human culture, the symbolic, mythical, and ritual also developed to help cope with life and give it explanation and meaning. From the perspective of Christian-Jewish history

85. In that sense, Tillich's interpretation of "fall" as transition from essence to existence is theologically harmful. Not only does it seem to make the "Fall" necessary, but even worse, in a Platonizing manner, it also imagines some kind of "ontological fall" before its happening in human life. See Tillich, *ST* 2:29-44, fittingly titled: "The Transition from Essence to Existence and the Symbol of 'the Fall.'"

86. While in his early writings *(Creation and Fall* and *The Cost of Discipleship)* this Lutheran pastor followed closely received Protestant tradition, later in his career *(Ethics* and *Letters and Papers from Prison)* he began to appreciate the goodness and promise of the natural order.

87. Even in the current *Catechism of the Catholic Church* (§390), the literal interpretation is assumed.

88. Cf. Warren, *Original Sin Explained?*

89. Hurd, "Hominids in the Garden?" p. 223.

of revelation, it is from around 5,000 years ago that we have evidence from developed mythic and symbolic materials pertaining to what came to be called original sin in tradition.[90]

What about the idea of the perfect estate, the cornerstone of the traditional idea of original sin? Is that taught in the biblical narrative? And if it is, how could it possibly be reconciled with science? Happily for theologians, a plain reading of Genesis 3 hardly leads to the idea of the perfect state. Nor does the biblical narrative teach that as a result of disobedience, human nature was changed; it merely states that the first humans were banished from the garden. The positive and lasting foundational intuition behind the idea of innocence and perfection, a vision not unknown in other cultures,[91] is to be interpreted in terms of a goal for the future, in other words, as an "ideal" state that was never *yet* achieved but sets the standard and orients imagination (as in the Irenaean vision).[92] Albrecht Ritschl rightly noted that to hold on to original perfection would mean to "miss the point that our destiny as creatures is brought to fulfillment by Jesus Christ."[93]

Long before the emergence of the questions posed by modern science, beginning with the Fathers, biblical expositors have been aware of many problems with the literal understanding of Genesis 2–4, including the fact that while Genesis 2–3 speaks of a couple (Adam and Eve), Genesis 4 refers to a larger population of humans interacting, with Cain raising the question of whence Cain's wife, and so forth. While traditional exegesis took Genesis 3 as actual history (etiology), most contemporary scholars consider it in some way a description of the present state of humanity,[94] perhaps as a universal symbol of the whole of humanity and/or history of every person.[95] Already in the nineteenth century, Schleiermacher rejected the historicity of the Genesis story and emphasized the collective, universal meaning of original sin, not propagated biologically — although there is an evolutionary basis in human self-preservation that leads to violence without the influence of the "Re-

90. See Hefner, *The Human Factor,* p. 124.

91. The longing for a "golden age" back in the distant past is of course common to human cultures. Eliade, *Myth and Reality,* pp. 50-51.

92. See R. Collins, "Evolution and Original Sin," p. 470. This "ideal" view, however, should not make Christian eschatological hope a matter of "eternal return" but rather a forward-looking future-drive hope for the coming of the new creation.

93. Paraphrased by Pannenberg, *ST* 2:210; Ritschl, *The Christian Doctrine of Justification and Reconciliation,* pp. 324-25 particularly.

94. Westermann, *Creation,* p. 109.

95. Tillich, *Dynamics of Faith,* p. 29.

deemer" — but rather, culturally.[96] Another contemporary option is to view Genesis 2–4 as an allegory in which Adam and Eve symbolize the large group of human ancestors. All these interpretations are in keeping with the name "Adam," which means humanity or human person in general.

One promising way to consider the biblical Fall narrative is to take Adam and Eve both as symbols of everybody and as representatives of a collective of "last" hominids in their transition to modern *sapiens* in terms of the capacity to exercise free will and self-consciousness (which also facilitates the distinction between the finite and infinite). Polkinghorne hence names the Fall in this respect the "fall upwards," as with the new deeper self-awareness, a new awareness of God dawned.[97] This view proposes that these "first" humans also became aware of God and God's requirements, but more often than not rejected them. One could even imagine that this awareness was "particularly clear, uncluttered by the spiritual darkness that eventually clouded the minds of the human race because of its turning away from God."[98] Herein lies the wisdom of Pannenberg's note that this "fall" or failure of the self was "a necessary phase in the process whereby human beings are liberated to become themselves."[99] That would be a way to do justice to the biblical teaching and traditional intuition that "these first ancestors were in what could be considered an original state of 'justice and holiness,' free from bondage to sin." But this does not have to mean any kind of perfect knowledge after tradition nor perfect innocence, let alone immortality. On the contrary, they were subject to temptations, the desire to turn away from the "voice" of the Lord, inclinations they had inherited from their evolutionary past, including also vulnerability to all kinds of perversions, violence, abuse, self-centeredness, and the like.[100] Analogous to the way humanity inherits all other traits and capacities in an integral genetic-cultural matrix, the spiritual darkness and bondage, including associated violence, can be said to be spread throughout generations.[101] (This does not, however, need a semimechanistic traducian doctrine after Augustinian tradition.) It seems to

96. Schleiermacher, *Christian Faith*, §§70-72, pp. 282-304. However, he also taught that "In all men, original sin is always issuing in actual sin" (§73, p. 304).

97. Polkinghorne and Beale, *Questions of Truth*, p. 68.

98. R. Collins, "Evolution and Original Sin," p. 470.

99. Pannenberg, *TA*, p. 152.

100. R. Collins, "Evolution and Original Sin," p. 470; materially similarly, Jenson, *Systematic Theology*, 2:59.

101. R. Collins, "Evolution and Original Sin," p. 471; materially similarly, Polkinghorne, *The Faith of a Physicist*, p. 15.

me that this kind of elusive outline of the Fall is in keeping with Paul's teaching in Romans 1, which, curiously, has not loomed large — and at times, not at all — in tradition's theological hermeneutics, as chapter 5 has dominated the discussion. Yet it seems like Romans 1:18-32 is meant to present Paul's "fall" narrative. Without any theory of how or when, Paul simply states that human persons, who knew God through the divine presence and traces in nature, turned away from following God and thus were given into darkness and perversion of behavior.[102]

What about Romans 5:15-19,[103] which seems to assume a literal interpretation of Adam as "one man" (repeated several times)? Let me make three important points. First, it would be foolish to deny that Paul (and even Jesus) shared the (then) commonly held beliefs about the biblical narrative, including Adam's historicity. In this regard, I find the philosopher Richard Swinburne's distinction between the "statement or assertion" and "presupposition(s)" useful: "The statement is whatever the speaker . . . is seeking to add to existing beliefs of the hearers," while presuppositions are just that, what is commonly *presupposed* between the speaker and audience in the particular context of the discourse.[104] The implication thus is — similar to, say, what the biblical narrative teaches about the beginnings — that although the presuppositions change over the course of time, the deepest intuitions (in this case, that something has gone wrong with humanity) remain.[105] In other words, the affirmation that Paul regarded Adam as historical (and contemporary theology cannot) in no way frustrates the basic theological teaching of Paul.

Second, when this passage is placed in the wider context of the Epistle to the Romans, it is clear that "Paul does not *begin* with Adam and move *to* Christ,"[106] as is often assumed, but that it is the other way around. The whole reasoning in Romans happens in the context of (and has its beginning and end in light of) Christ and his salvific work.[107] "Adam, read as 'the first human,'

102. So also R. Collins, "Evolution and Original Sin," p. 476.

103. Adam of course also plays a role in 1 Cor. 15:21-22, 44-49, but there Paul's main focus is on the future resurrection of believers, contrasting Adam (the physical) and Christ (the spiritual).

104. Swinburne, *Revelation,* pp. 28-33, here p. 33, cited in R. Collins, "Evolution and Original Sin," p. 477.

105. For details, see R. Collins, "Evolution and Original Sin," pp. 477-79, for which I am greatly indebted; for similar hermeneutical views, see also Inwagen, *God, Knowledge, and Mystery,* pp. 141-42; Dunn, *Romans 1-8,* p. 289.

106. Enns, *Evolution of Adam,* p. 82.

107. Ricoeur (*Symbolism of Evil,* pp. 238-39) rightly saw that Paul indeed was mainly interested in Christ rather than Adam and Eve's status here.

supports Paul's argument about the universal plight and remedy of humanity, but it is not a *necessary* component for that argument."[108]

Third, the way Paul uses Adam goes well beyond the OT contours, if for no other reason than because his frame of reference is Christ. Even when he assumes the individuality of Adam, Paul contrasts Adam with the Last Adam and thus treats both as corporate representatives. Not only that, but Paul is also putting Adam to a different use from the OT. Not only is Adam missing in the rest of the OT, as mentioned, but nowhere does the OT make Adam responsible for the sinfulness of humanity. The curses following the disobedience in Genesis 3:14-19 speak of pain in childbearing, rule of husband over wife, and burden of daily work, but not of death and eternal condemnation. Against common intuitions, not even the subsequent narrative in Genesis 4 of the murder of Abel is attributed to the "Fall" but rather to Cain's freedom of choice (4:7), in keeping with the general tenor of the OT's appeal to choose either the way of the Lord or the way of evil. This all is to say that "Paul's reading of Genesis is driven by factors external to Genesis," and that is the point I wish to make here.[109] Paul's basic reasoning about the universality of sin, human solidarity therein, and the need for Christ's reconciliation is not founded on a literal reading of Genesis 3 but rather on the Christ event.[110] Indeed, as Pannenberg persuasively argues, the importance of Adam to Paul, unlike the OT, is based on the link between universality of sin and universality of redemption.[111]

How to establish the universality of sinfulness in a way that avoids both the "biological" hereditary theory and elimination of human responsibility is a crucial task for current theology. That is our next focus.

Sinfulness and Misery as Universal but Not Hereditary

If sin is connected with the naturally transmitted concupiscent structure of behavior, so that human beings are sinners from their birth and before any individual actions of their own, then they can hardly be responsible for their sinful actions with the kind of responsibility that is based on the principle of

---

108. Enns, *Evolution of Adam*, p. 82.

109. See Enns, *Evolution of Adam*, pp. 82-87, here p. 87.

110. Already in the Jewish theology of Paul's time, a number of different uses of Adam had emerged, similarly going beyond the teaching of Genesis (or the rest of the OT); see Enns, *Evolution of Adam*, pp. 99-103.

111. Pannenberg, *TA*, pp. 120-21.

causality.[112] Tradition's response in the mouth of Augustine that Adam could have chosen otherwise hardly settles the issue. Pelagius's classic question as to how God who forgives sins committed by individuals themselves could impute them to other people still remains unanswered.[113]

Sin is not a fate that comes upon human beings as an alien power against which they are helpless. The concept of sin is inseparable from the ideas of responsibility and guilt. It is this fact that gives rise to the most serious objection against linking the idea of sin to the natural conditions of human existence. It would seem that individual human beings cannot be held responsible for the condition in which they begin to live their lives, since these conditions are not the result of their choice and decision.[114] Still worth hearing is R. Niebuhr's objection that "[t]he Christian doctrine of sin in its classical form offends both rationalists and moralists by maintaining the seemingly absurd position that man sins inevitably and by a fateful necessity but that he is nevertheless to be held responsible for actions which are prompted by an ineluctable fate."[115]

Not surprisingly then, as a result of the rejection of the hereditary doctrine of transmission of sin and its incapacity to account for responsibility, modern theology sought to find other ways of affirming the universality of sin. Kant's concept of "radical evil" played a crucial role here. According to him, we are bad by nature in subordinating the moral law under self-love, which for him meant primarily sensuality in search of happiness.[116] Somewhat similarly to Augustine, Kant speaks of "perversion" that causes a shift in the focus of the desire, although for Kant it is purely in the subjectivity of the person. The radical difference from Augustine and the rest of tradition is that for the Enlightenment thinker God is no longer the standard; rather, the standard is adherence to the moral maxim. This opens the way for the divorcing of morality from God, as of course happened in modernity.[117] Adopting the Kantian view would then replace God by the ethical principle, and that is not permissible.

Theologically solid is Pannenberg's locating the origin and spreading of sin in the tension between "centrality" and "exocentrism."[118] While the former

112. Pannenberg, *TA,* p. 123.

113. For details and documentation, see Pannenberg, *TA,* pp. 123-24.

114. Pannenberg, *TA,* pp. 109-10, here p. 110.

115. Niebuhr, *Nature and Destiny of Man,* 1:241.

116. Kant, *Religion within the Limits of Reason Alone,* p. 27; see also the whole section titled "Man Is Evil by Nature," pp. 27-34.

117. See Pannenberg, *ST* 2:246-48.

118. See Pannenberg, *TA,* p. 84.

is shared with other creatures, the latter is uniquely human;[119] hence, only in human consciousness can it become a moral and religious theme.[120] Exocentrism, the unique human feature, can easily undergo perversions as, rather than being present to the other as other, "[p]resence to the other becomes a means by which the ego can dominate the other and assert itself by way of his domination."[121] Or, with regard to the mandate of human dominion over creation (Gen. 1:26-27), it may become "unscrupulous exploitation and oppression."[122] This conflicts with the human exocentric destiny beyond oneself, in relation to God.[123] It can be named "radical evil" (Kant), "covetousness/concupiscence" (Augustine), or "sin"[124] — as long as it is related primarily to God (even if its effects are felt among the creatures). The turning of exocentricity into centrality, egoism, means not only missing the will of God but also missing true human destiny, which can only be had in something beyond one's self.[125]

The Augustinian view seems to make this a necessary event because of the corruption of nature, concupiscence. In correction we have to say with Pannenberg that "even if human beings are in this sense sinners *by nature*, this does not mean that their nature as human beings is sinful." An important distinction has to be made to get the point. Whereas the first reference to "nature" (in the previous sentence) means something like "natural condition" of human existence, the second means nature as "essence" (which is exocentricity). Only that distinction does justice to the "ought" aspect and relative freedom of will[126] (as Eastern tradition insists). As a consequence, unlike other animals with whom humans share egocentricity, only to humans can it be attributed as guilt, on the basis of divine revelation and our special direct relation to God.

Pannenberg's creative reworking maintains the best of Christian tradition relating sin to our relation to God and other human beings, as well as to evolutionary development. In his opinion the weakened power of the will "precedes and underlies individual decisions and actions." This allows us to

---

119. Pannenberg, *TA*, p. 105.

120. Pannenberg, *TA*, p. 109.

121. Pannenberg *TA*, p. 85.

122. Pannenberg *TA*, p. 80.

123. Tillich (*ST* 2:48-50) materially similarly explains sin as "estrangement from God in the center of his being" (p. 48), "outside the divine center to which his own center essentially belongs," having become "the center of himself and of his world" (p. 49).

124. See Pannenberg, *TA*, pp. 85-86; for Augustine, pp. 87-96.

125. See Pannenberg, *TA*, p. 106.

126. Pannenberg, *TA*, pp. 107-9, here p. 107, emphasis in original.

affirm the key intuitions of original sin in tradition while correcting its time-bound problematic notions in tradition: human beings are sinful before they commit a sinful act (notwithstanding the fact, mentioned above, that guilt will be imputed only in light of personal responsibility); sin, therefore, is located at a deeper level than any individual act; and the universality of sin is the presupposition for the universality of redemption in Christ.[127] These insights I see necessary to a robust and balanced current doctrine of sin.[128]

The main theological point is that sinfulness is a bigger thing than just each human person because humanity forms one family. As Kierkegaard robustly put it: every human being "is at once himself and the whole race, in such wise that the whole race has part in the individual, and the individual has part in the whole race."[129] It is only in the post-Enlightenment Global North that this basic feature of human existence has been missed, but it is now being slowly rediscovered with the help of our colleagues in the Global South. Although the highlighting of the social context and sociality is an important insight, it should not be understood as placing the "guilt" of sin on society per se; that would mean ignoring the biblical idea of the indwelling of sin in each human person (Rom. 7:17).

The Australian Catholic theologian Denis Edwards rightly notes that "[t]he sin of others is intrinsic to and partly constitutive of the situation of our human freedom. The sin of others is a universal and permanent part of the human condition and is in this sense original." As a consequence: "Original sin consists of the fact that human beings have a history of refusal and radical rejection of God's self-communicating love, and this history of personal and communal sin enters into and becomes an inner dimension of each person's situation."[130] In other words, humanity is *bound to sin*.[131] If so, then sin cannot be conceived merely as a personal matter. It is both personal and collective.

---

127. Pannenberg, *TA*, pp. 119-20.

128. Another Lutheran theologian, the American Philip Hefner *(The Human Factor)* has similarly done careful work in trying to understand the deepest intuitions of the traditional doctrine of sin in the context of the evolvement of humanity and, in his case, in the matrix of genetic and sociocultural factors that together shape humanity, including the sense of guilt and sinfulness. Yet another noteworthy work in this respect is P. A. Williams's *Doing without Adam and Eve: Sociobiology and Original Sin*. Studying that monograph, however, I am less confident than with Pannenberg and Hefner that (in this case) the sociobiological framework allows for reaffirmation of tradition's deepest intuitions.

129. Kierkegaard, *The Concept of Dread*, p. 26.

130. D. Edwards, "Original Sin and Saving Grace," p. 377.

131. McFadyen, *Bound to Sin*.

Sin as Personal and Structural

One of the formative shifts in the theology of sin during the second half of the twentieth century had to do with the balancing of highly individualistic interpretations with communal, structural, social, and relational interpretations — in other words, extending the meaning beyond the personal.[132] Illustrative of this move is the new listing by the Vatican of seven deadly sins that focuses on bioethical, moral, and other sins related to community and communal responsibility.[133] Women theologians, postcolonialists, and other liberationists from various global contexts are on the forefront in pushing theology to consider sociopolitical sins, in many cases even environmental sins, as an integral part of the Christian doctrine of sin.

The senior Peruvian liberationist Gustavo Gutiérrez reminds us that "[s]in, the breach with God, is not something that occurs only within some intimate sanctuary of the heart. It *always* moves into interpersonal relationships, and hence is the ultimate root of all injustice and oppression — as well as of the social confrontations and conflicts of concrete history."[134] Mainline theology, according to Gutiérrez, is to be blamed for stopping in its definition of sin with the personal aspect; the social aspect is always there as well.[135] What is theologically significant about this Peruvian liberationist's standpoint is that sin in terms of breaking relationship with God and one's neighbor is "according to the Bible the ultimate cause of poverty, injustice, and the oppression in which persons live," in other words, the *personal* sin is causal.[136]

Not all liberationists are content with interpreting social sin as caused by personal sin. Some will reverse the relationship in one way or another. The Brazilian theologian Leonardo Boff describes human existence as a "fundamental project" in which the "human person is intimately bound up with the

132. A highly useful, globally/contextually representative discussion beginning from the nineteenth century is D. R. Nelson, *What's Wrong with Sin*. See also Ray, *Do No Harm*.

133. See "Vatican Bishop Points to Modern Social Sin" (http://www.catholicnewsagency.com/news/vatican_bishop_points_to_modern_social_sins). For a harsh criticism of the individualist notion of sin as unbiblical, see the Spanish-born Mexican Juan Alfaro's *Christian Liberation and Sin*, p. 13.

134. Gutiérrez, *The Power of the Poor in History,* p. 147, emphasis Gutiérrez's, cited in D. R. Nelson, *What's Wrong with Sin,* p. 86; so also Gutiérrez, *A Theology of Liberation,* p. 24.

135. See Gutiérrez, *The Truth Shall Make You Free,* p. 136.

136. For comments, see D. R. Nelson, *What's Wrong with Sin,* pp. 88-89. For all its excesses (and many would say, antiliberationist impulses), this is the valid concern of the Vatican's response to liberationists: International Theological Commission, "Declaration on Human Development and Christian Salvation," pp. 205-19.

fundamental project of the culture in which he or she lives."[137] Which direction, good or bad, the human person is turning (like the culture, which can also take different paths) is a function of the grace of God at work. Obviously this grace ought to be social in character then. Here, Boff argues, is the necessary contribution of the liberationist orientation to theology. The response of yes or no to God with regard to the fundamental option is not merely individualistic, as is usually conceived in tradition, but also social and contextual, and thus dynamic. The individual person's choice, while not determined by the context, is deeply influenced by it because "[t]he social dimension of the human being is ontologically rooted in the very core of the human being as a person." Indeed, the "social dimension is fundamental," and hence cannot be taken as optional.[138]

The Uruguayan theologian Juan Luis Segundo's "hypostatization of social into individual sin"[139] represents a creative mixing of evolutionary theory (Teilhard de Chardin) and liberationist orientations. By analogy with the principle of entropy, sin becomes resistance to and obstruction of evolvement of higher forms of order, the human fulfillment. As in evolution in general, there are both "positive" and "negative" forces at work simultaneously. Redemption means overturning and overcoming this "entropic" development as we are freed from the dominion of sin (cf. Rom. 6:12, 14, 20).[140] What is ultimately decisive is not human effort but God's redemptive work, although the human response is continuously called forth.[141] The problem with Segundo's reinterpretation of sin is that it may make sin an essential part of human structure (to be more precise, its "lower levels") and so also an integral part of the social structures into which one is born. The strength of the traditional hermeneutic of sin is that although sin is universal, it is not necessary. What must be avoided at all costs is fatalism, namely, the idea that "[w]hen sinful social structures are in place, personal sin must necessarily result, and there's nothing we can do about it."[142]

137. Citation given in D. R. Nelson, *What's Wrong with Sin,* p. 121 (with reference to Boff, *Liberating Grace,* p. 141).

138. Boff, *Liberating Grace,* pp. 141-42. While not always made explicit, behind this kind of reasoning is the widely acknowledged concept of the "situated freedom" of the Dutch Catholic Schoonenberg, *Sin of the World.*

139. Named so by D. R. Nelson, *What's Wrong with Sin,* p. 98.

140. Segundo, *Evolution and Guilt,* pp. 79-80; for comments, see McDermott, "The Theology of Original Sin."

141. See Segundo, *Evolution and Guilt,* p. 64.

142. D. R. Nelson, *What's Wrong with Sin,* pp. 99-105, here pp. 104-5.

For the African American theologian Garth Kasimu Baker-Fletcher, sin "means becoming aware of the ways in which Afrikans [*sic*] (male and female, rich and poor) are engulfed in a demonic system of whiteness/Euro-domination/oppression that has colonized both their bodies and their innermost thoughts, desires, and feelings."[143] Women theologians have developed the doctrine of sin in the context of abuse of the body and sexual crimes. Mary Potter Engels speaks "from the perspective of the liberation of the vulnerable from sexual and domestic abuse" and notes that evil is "systemic" and forms "structures of oppression; patterns larger than individuals and groups."[144]

Constructive theology should welcome these important attempts to widen the domain of sin — and hence also the Fall — beyond the individual. The integral connection between the personal and the social is needed to do justice to the all-pervasiveness of sinfulness and redemption. At the same time, the problem with envisioning sin primarily (let alone exclusively) as social is that "[r]ather than seeing liberation as the dynamic overcoming of sin by grace *within* each person, it becomes merely a new arrangement *among* people."[145] Furthermore, a related difficult question has to do with how to understand the agential role of (inanimate) structures. How can they act or function? How are they related to personal (including persons acting in concert) agency? Finally, the question has to be clarified concerning the mutual role of personal and structural agency (if the latter can be established in the first place). Until these questions are clarified, talk about structures doing something stays vague and — against the advocates — may ironically end up eschewing personal responsibility.

What about some women theologians' attempts to conceive "sexism as original sin"?[146] Mary Daly not only considers sexism "original sin" but observes that it leads to internalization of blame and guilt, and that is inherited through socialization processes. Now, for Daly, these processes are nothing less than representations of demonic power structures that induce individuals to internalize false identities.[147] While there is of course no denying the severity of the oppression of women because of sexism, naming one particular sin, albeit universal in its manifestation, is a category mistake — unless one uses the term "original" merely rhetorically. African Americans could name racism as original sin; First Nations' peoples, the exploitation of land; and so forth.

---

143. Baker-Fletcher, *Xodus*, p. 86.

144. Engel, "Evil, Sin, and Violation of the Vulnerable," pp. 154-55.

145. D. R. Nelson, *What's Wrong with Sin*, p. 91, emphasis in original.

146. Fulkerson, "Sexism as Original Sin." For a clearly rhetorical use of "original sin" in relation to gender construction, see S. Jones, *Feminist Theory and Christian Theology*, p. 117.

147. M. Daly, *Beyond God the Father*, pp. 49-54 particularly.

The problems here are twofold. First of all, the description of "original" sin becomes entirely parochial and contextual. Second, even worse, it dichotomizes the world in two classes — good and bad. It is rather the case that all men and women are sinful, just differently.[148] On the other side of the discussion are those women theologians such as Rita Nakashima Brock who reject the whole concept of original sin (even as a rhetorical device) and invite us to merely attend to the sad effects of damaging actions, attitudes, and structures. Part of the total turnover of the discourse is that ultimately, "[s]in is not something to be punished, but something to be healed."[149] My problem with this move is twofold. First, the human mind — let alone the theological mind — is hardly satisfied without probing into whence the damaging, degrading, hurtful attitudes and acts come. Second, without sounding too penal, it seems to me that any *theological* doctrine of sin must also locate sin as something against the will of God, and hence under the judgment of the divine holy and righteous will. Yes, sin's effects need healing. But sinfulness as a universal human phenomenon also needs divine redemption (along with reconciliation and restoration at the human level).

Sin and Finitude of Life

What about death? Until modernity, the church consensus was that death is the result of (first) sin.[150] Only with the rise of evolutionary theory has this belief changed to the "naturalness" of death because of finitude.[151] The traditional position of course claimed biblical support. Even contemporary exegesis must grant, it seems to me, that for Paul "it is not possible to exclude so-called natural death as not being cointended" in passages such as Romans 5:12 and 1 Corinthians 15:44-48.[152] Be that as it may, we know that death is "natural" in

148. Engel, "Evil, Sin, and the Violation of the Vulnerable," pp. 155-56; see also Volf, *Exclusion and Embrace.* Also worth nothing is the oft-quoted statement by Bauman (*Postmodern Ethics,* pp. 227-28) according to which victims are no better than perpetrators, they just lack opportunities!

149. Brock, *Journeys by Heart,* p. 7.

150. Representative examples are the Council of Trent, Session V, "Decree concerning Original Sin"; June 17, 1546; (Melanchthon's) Apology of the Augsburg Confession 2.47, in *Book of Concord,* ed. Tappert, p. 106.

151. Schleiermacher (*Christian Faith,* §76.2; p. 319) correctly notes the presence of death everywhere in nature and thus that it is not the result of sin.

152. Pannenberg, *TA,* p. 129.

the sense that all individuals of all species must die to make room for the next generation. It simply belongs to the nature of the *finite* being, and having been created as such cannot be sin! Nor do we really find solid basis for the idea of immortality before the Fall of humanity in the biblical narrative itself.[153]

In modern theology, a terminological distinction was made between "natural" death that is not related to sin but to finite nature and death of "judgment" that manifests intensification of the personal feeling toward death in light of the possibility of being cut off from the life of God.[154] Granting the naturalness of death, however, should not be interpreted as meaning some kind of fulfillment of human life in death as Rahner said (gleaning from the existentialist philosopher Martin Heidegger).[155] That view is contrary to both the biblical view of death that regards it as an "enemy" (1 Cor. 15:26), never idealizing it, and basic human intuition that death ends the life-drive and prevents life's fulfillment.[156]

Having constructed an outline of a contemporary Christian theology of human misery and sin, we bring the views of four living faiths into the conversation. On the one hand, all religious traditions surmise that there is a problem in the current human condition. On the other hand, as can be easily imagined, various faith traditions do not speak of the misery of humanity in similar terms. To that matrix of issues we turn in the next major section of this chapter, building on the investigation of religions' anthropologies above.

Human Misery in the Vision of Abrahamic Faiths

Sin and Fall in Abrahamic Traditions

Among the Semitic faiths, there is no unified conception of human misery. As noted, the traditional Christian doctrine of original sin (however that is formulated) is not shared by Jewish and Islamic traditions. The two sister faiths understand sin in terms of "incurring the 'punishments' or disadvantages of ignorance of God, lack of self-control, and short-sighted restriction

153. In Israel's postexilic wisdom and apocalyptic writings the idea of Adam's immortality before the Fall was affirmed (*1 Enoch* 69:11; Wisdom 1:13); see Pannenberg, *ST* 2:213 for details.

154. For details and documentation, see Pannenberg, *TA*, pp. 138-39.

155. See Rahner, *On the Theology of Death*.

156. Similarly Pannenberg, *TA*, p. 138. Even Phil. 1:21 is not a way to glorify death but rather an expression of Paul's intense longing to be with the Lord.

of moral concern." Jewish and Muslim theologies insist on human freedom to choose and responsibility for the choice.[157] The divide within the Abrahamic house, however, may not be as deep as it appears to be. Particularly the view of sin and the Fall developed in this project shares much common basis with Judaism and Islam. This mediating view captures the essence of all three traditions' conception of human misery by thinking of sin in terms of a disease or incapacity rather than as a crime or external force automatically leading to damnation. Moral freedom (relatively speaking) is upheld by all three traditions, combined with the impossibility of fully meeting the demands apart from divine help. "To choose the good expresses one's moral will. To recognize its impossibility admits the corruption of that will, located as it is in a web of corrupted social and environmental relationships." The only resolution is the relatedness to God.[158]

Indeed, the placement of humanity before God is the defining feature of Abrahamic faiths' conception of human misery. All of them, though somewhat differently, consider the "origin" of sinfulness in the deviation of humanity from the Creator. Not surprisingly, all three scriptural traditions therefore share the common narrative of the Fall and its consequences even when their interpretations differ from each other quite dramatically. In many ways, Jewish and Muslim interpretations share more in common with each other than Christian interpretations do with the other two.

Good and Evil Inclinations: The Fall and Sin in Jewish Tradition

As do contemporary Christian theologians, Jewish theologians rightly acknowledge that in the Genesis 3 story there is "no doctrine of the fall of the race through Adam, of the moral corruption of human nature, or of the hereditary transmission of the sinful bias."[159] Indeed, the Jewish reading also serves Christian tradition in a constructively critical way, including rejection of Adam's immortality before the Fall.

Instead of original sin, the Jewish (rabbinic) tradition speaks of two tendencies or urges in every human being, namely, *yetzer ha tov* and *yetzer ha ra‘*, for good and evil, respectively. Importantly, the "inclination" to evil in itself is

---

157. K. Ward, *Religion and Human Nature*, p. 175.

158. K. Ward, *Religion and Human Nature*, pp. 175-76.

159. Cohon, *Essays in Jewish Theology*, p. 220; Cohon discusses in some detail similar etiological accounts of evil in the surrounding cultures (pp. 221-22).

not evil but rather a necessary impulse of life. Indeed, according to the rabbinic midrash, without *yetzer ha ra'* one could not even build a house or marry![160] It is a matter of which of the two is the guiding force in life. Hence, the main term for repentance from evil is *teshuvav,* literally "turning."[161] "Man is engaged in constant struggle against the evil within him but he can control it if he so desires. The means of control are provided by the Torah and its precepts."[162]

This is not to undermine the seriousness of the sinful tendency, which is "not an isolated act, but a state of consciousness, so that one sin leads to others." Indeed, it is the goal of the Yahwist account to highlight the wide diffusion of moral evil (Gen. 4; 6:5-12; 8:21; 9:20-27; 11:1-9).[163] According to the biblical testimonies, human wickedness is great, and even the imaginations of the heart are evil (6:5; 8:21). In other words, the evil urge is present at birth. But each person is responsible for sinful behavior; such responsibility is not inherited. Although the evil inclination plagues the human person, it does not rob the person of all moral integrity, nor cause lostness as in Christian tradition. Each person has the responsibility to keep it in check with the resources of the good urge. Although 4 Esdras speaks of the "fall" in stark terms, likening it to a serious disease affecting the whole of humanity (3:21-22), Jewish theology did not develop it in the way Saint Paul did. Ezekiel's teaching of the personal responsibility alone would have prevented the Christian kind of original sin in terms of inherited condemnatory guilt. It is of utmost importance for Judaism to affirm the freedom from depravity and innate evil of human nature despite the serious inclination toward evil. *2 Baruch* (54:15, 19; 19:3; 48:42-43; 59:2) teaches that even after Adam's sin that brought about death, each new generation has to choose their own path. The rabbinic consensus is that it is only the "physical" effects (namely, death) but not the spiritual (moral and religious depravity) that derive from Adam's first sin.[164]

Theologically it is important to see that even before the beginning of Christianity, in the Jewish apocryphal traditions, the effort to use the paradise story to locate the origin of sin and death began.[165] Indeed, at the beginning of Christianity at least three somewhat different conceptions of sin fought for recognition in rabbinic theology: first, corruption of humanity as hereditary;

160. *Bereshit* [*Rabbah* or *Genesis Rabbah*] 9.7 in *Midrash Rabbah,* 1:68.

161. See L. Jacobs, *A Jewish Theology,* p. 243.

162. L. Jacobs, *A Jewish Theology,* p. 245.

163. Cohon, *Essays in Jewish Theology,* p. 225; see also L. Jacobs, *A Jewish Theology,* pp. 246-47.

164. See further, Cohon, *Jewish Theology,* pp. 302-5.

165. See Cohon, *Essays in Jewish Theology,* 228-34.

second, a vague connection between Adam's sin and subsequent generations' liability to punishment; and third, all sin as the fruit of the human person's own actions. Whereas the rabbinic tradition operated mainly, though not exclusively, with the third paradigm, Pauline and subsequent Christian tradition went with the first two (with the exception of Eastern Christianity, which also wanted to include key elements of the third).[166]

Both Jewish and Christian traditional ways of reading the Genesis narrative have undergone radical revisions as a result of the scientific advances concerning human evolution. Both traditions can still hold tightly to the underlying theological intuitions about the misery of humanity. At the same time, for the continuing dialogue to be meaningful, the differences between *theological* interpretations of the effects and the "source" of human sinfulness should be acknowledged. On the one hand, as mentioned, the different hermeneutics of the same core biblical texts of the Fall by the Jewish tradition has helped Christian theology to put the Genesis narrative in a proper perspective — although it has taken a long time! On the other hand, because of the christological framework, Christian theology should also acknowledge that in its authoritative Scripture, the former Jewish rabbi Saint Paul develops Genesis traditions in a way that goes beyond the Jewish reading. Although even now these two sister faiths envision human misery differently, these differences are understandable and can be tolerated for the sake of hospitable coliving.

Free Will and Human Disobedience: The Islamic View of Adam's Fall

The Islamic tradition never envisioned Adam and Eve in terms of perfect paradise imagery after Christian tradition. Its account of humanity is realistic, as illustrated in Qur'an 95:4-6: "Verily We created man in the best of forms. Then, We reduced him to the lowest of the low, except those who believe and perform righteous deeds, for they shall have an unfailing reward." In a number of places the Qur'an speaks of weaknesses, frailties, and liabilities of humanity.[167] That said, according to mainline Muslim teaching, human nature is, generally speaking, good — or, at least, it is not sinful and corrupted as in Christian teaching. This remark holds even though (as discussed above) the oldest inter-

---

166. Cohon, *Essays in Jewish Theology*, p. 240. That said, the rabbinic tradition was no more uniform than the Christian, and it contained a number of debates, for which see the detailed discussion on pp. 240-70.

167. Q 4:28; 10:12; 14:34; 16:4; 17:11; 33:72; 70:19; 96:6; 103:2; etc. For details, see Scudder, "The Qur'an's Evaluation of Human Nature," p. 75.

pretation of *fitrah*, predestinarian in its orientation, allowed for the possibility of evil human nature among some persons due to the decision of Allah. This is put into perspective by two points. First, even the evil inclination does not mean lostness after the Christian predestination view. Second, this classical view is by no means the mainline historical or contemporary interpretation. It was soon overruled by the neutral view that takes the beginning of human life as a blank slate, thus emphasizing the role of free will — not unlike Christian Pelagianism. The mainline teaching in tradition and contemporary Islamic theology is by and large the "positive view"[168] of human nature. It argues that *fitrah* means the state of intrinsic goodness. The authoritative medieval scholar Ibn Taymiyyah established this view, although its roots go back much further in history. "Every human being is born in the nature of Islam. If this nature is not subsequently corrupted by the erroneous beliefs of the family and society, everyone will be able to see the truth of Islam and embrace it. . . . *Fitrah* is the original nature of man, uncorrupted by subsequent beliefs and practices, ready to accept the true ideas of Islam."[169]

That the Qur'an does not know the doctrine of original sin nor the idea of moral depravity[170] does not mean that the concept of "fall" is not part of the Muslim tradition. The fall narrative can of course be found in the Qur'an — indeed, several narratives can.[171] But its implications (like Judaism's) are different from those of Christian theology. Chronologically the earliest narrative is 20:115-27. After becoming forgetful of the covenant, all angels were invited by God to prostrate themselves before Adam, and they did, but Satan (named Iblis), who then promised to take Adam and Eve to the tree of immortality and knowledge, declined. They ate the fruit, became ashamed, and tried covering themselves with leaves. "And Adam disobeyed his Lord and so he erred" (v. 121). God called Adam again and advised him to leave the garden that had now become an "enemy" (obviously because Satan was said to be there, v. 117). God promised to guide the human or else blindness would follow for the one who previously was able to see. The punishment of blindness would be revealed on the day of resurrection, and even more severe forms of

168. I am following the typology in chap. 2 of Mohamed, *Fitrah.*
169. *Ibn Taymiyyah Expounds on Islam,* p. 3.
170. See Muhammad Iqbal, *Reconstruction of Religious Thought in Islam,* p. 85. A leading contemporary Islamic scholar, Sayyid Qutb, calls the Christian doctrine of original sin a "hideous schizophrenia." "That Hideous Schizophrenia," p. 79.
171. For a detailed discussion, see Löfstedt, "Creation and Fall of Adam," pp. 453-77. He notes (p. 453) that there are striking similarities between Qur'anic and later Christian Pseudepigrapha narratives (as in *The Gospel of Bartholomew*).

punishment might follow. The later account in 2:30-38 repeats very closely the Genesis 3 story with a few significant deviations: again, the angels are invited to bow down before Adam, Satan does not bow and becomes the tempter; after the disobedience, the Lord shows mercy. The third major passage, 7:10-25 (chronologically probably in between the two previous ones), speaks of the disobedient nature of Adam in starker terms and also mentions the going out of the garden in more certain terms (v. 27). Furthermore, all the accounts speak of enmity and distress as a result of the disobedience of which Adam himself (rather than Satan or Eve) is mainly responsible (albeit tempted and lured by Satan).

What is missing in Islamic theology of sin is the idea of *transmission* of "original sin" from one generation to another and its punitive effect on the progeny. Adam (along with Eve and Satan) himself is to be blamed for disobedience, not later generations.[172] Importantly, the Qur'anic narrative does not link the Fall with lostness, as does Christian tradition. On the other hand, although Allah is merciful (a teaching dear to Muslim tradition, as is also evident everywhere in the Qur'an), salvation is by and large in the hands of the human being, who may or may not be willing to submit to the will of God. "The emphasis in the Qur'an is less on human transgression than on the imperative to turn to God for forgiveness."[173] Because Muslims categorically reject the doctrine of original sin and radical sinfulness of all, they do not envision redemption in the way Christian tradition does, namely, as a divine gift. There is absolutely no doctrine of atonement in Islam resembling that of the Christian (or, differently, Jewish) teaching.

In sum: with the anathematizing of Pelagianism, the Christian tradition — before the rise of Islam — ruled out the Muslim type of interpretation of the Fall that considers the human being in too positive terms and, in the final analysis, leaves the salvific initiative to the human being, although of course not totally. Although Jewish theology certainly feels more affinity with the Islamic theology of sin, even it cannot totally embrace it. For Christian tradition, conceiving the human condition through the lens of Christ's salvific work on our behalf, the acceptance of the Qur'anic hermeneutic is not possible. That said, what unites the Abrahamic faiths' imagination of human misery and its "origins" is significant and facilitates a continuing hospitable dialogue and comparing of notes. The difference from the Asiatic traditions, however, is wide and deep, as the ensuing discussion clearly shows.

---

172. I am indebted to Scudder, "Qur'an's Evaluation of Human Nature," pp. 71-80.
173. Siddiqui, "Being Human in Islam," p. 21.

The Human Condition in the Vision of Asiatic Faiths

Craving and Dukkha: *The Buddhist Analysis*

Gautama once used the simile of cloth to illustrate the difference between the pure mind and the defiled mind. The impure cloth absorbs all bad into its fabric, the end result of which is "an unhappy destination [in a future existence]," whereas a happy future awaits the pure minded. Particularly dangerous, so Buddha teaches, is the appeal of sensuality in its many forms.[174] With right knowledge and true effort the purification from all defilement can be attained. Even when the devotee may "go to Master Gotama for refuge, and to the Dhamma, and to the Sangha," those are not to be looked upon as "saviors" but rather as aids.[175] It is easy to see that the defilement of the mind is serious, but not intrinsic or transmitted after the Christian doctrine of original sin.

Everything we discussed above about human nature in Buddha's vision, namely, the principles of *dukkha,* impermanence, and no-self, covers that tradition's response to the question of human misery and its resolution. Malcolm David Eckel helpfully suggests a summative nomenclature that may help us capture the essence of the Buddhist analysis of the human condition: the "beginningless ignorance," reminding us of the (relatively speaking) first step in the karmic cycle of *dukkha.*[176] As a result, as taught everywhere in the Theravada canon, there is the persistent force of craving *(tanhā),* which not only clings to life in general but is also accompanied with greed, hatred, and delusion. Consider the famous fire illustration of the Enlightened One, which speaks of the power of craving:

> Monks, the All is aflame. What All is aflame? The eye is aflame. Forms are aflame. Consciousness at the eye is aflame. Contact at the eye is aflame. And whatever there is that arises in dependence on contact at the eye — experienced as pleasure, pain or neither-pleasure-nor-pain — that too is aflame. Aflame with what? Aflame with the fire of passion, the fire of aversion, the fire of delusion. Aflame, I tell you, with birth, aging & death, with sorrows, lamentations, pains, distresses, & despairs.[177]

174. Analyzed in detail in *Maha-dukkhakkhandha Sutta: The Great Mass of Stress* of Majjhima Nikaya 13, and *Cula-dukkhakkhandha Sutta: The Lesser Mass of Stress* of Majjhima Nikaya 14.

175. *Vatthupama Sutta: The Simile of the Cloth* of Majjhima Nikaya 7 (7.2; 7.18); 7.3 is a list of forms of defilement, from covetousness to anger to vanity, etc.

176. Eckel, "Beginningless Ignorance," pp. 49-72.

177. *Adittapariyaya Sutta: The Fire Sermon* of Samyutta Nikaya 35.28.

Many other such dramatic pictures can be found to make the point that behind the human misery, *dukkha,* is the yearning to cling to what is merely fleeting, decaying, impermanent.[178] The craving makes the human person put "I" at the center without realizing that there is no permanent "I."[179]

Whence this (evil) craving? As with all other topics, Buddha declined from speculating and rather focused on "putting an end to suffering and stress."[180] That said, in the Pali Canon there are mythical stories that give some hints. According to the most well-known Buddhist story of "evolution" of the cosmos and humanity, the appearance of greed predates the emergence of the current world. Among the luminous and joyful primordial beings, a moral degradation took place that eventually had effects not only on humans but also on the rest of the world. Along with the emergence of new forms finally leading up to humans, greed, conceit, and other moral blemishes also grew. Humans were initially genderless; sexual differentiation happened at the end, leading to sexual reproduction.[181] The point of the story, I take it, is that craving, so to speak, is waiting for each new person who is (re)born into the world. In that sense, there is some important commonality with the Jewish-Christian tradition: they all speak of human misery in universal and pervasive ways, as a condition. However, the Buddhist notion is not to be taken in a way similar to the Genesis narrative "of a fall from purity into dis-ease and dislocation."[182] (This is the more important in light of the Buddha's reluctance to address metaphysical questions and his concentration on the healing of the disease rather than its etiology.) The only thing these traditions have in common is the universal human condition as something requiring liberation, insight, or salvation.

Importantly, "[i]n Buddhist thought, however, this state of bondage is not conceived as an ontologically substantial state, essentially unchanging until a supernatural power intervenes."[183] Not only is there no permanent "I" who would be ontologically "sinful," but the whole Buddhist (particularly Theravadan) path is about helping each person gain the needed insight to be liberated (and in most Mahayana movements, helping another enlightened person to take another one to the "bank" of the river). Salvation in Buddhism is ultimately a matter of one's own pursuit: "One is one's own refuge, who else could

---

178. See particularly the famous *Tanha Sutta: Craving* of Samyutta Nikaya 4.199.

179. Anguttara Nikaya, ii.212 [Pali Text Society numbering], p. 226.

180. *Alagaddupama Sutta: The Water-Snake Simile* of Majjhima Nikaya 22.

181. An accessible reliable translation is *Aggañña Sutta.*

182. As opined by E. Harris, "Human Existence in Buddhism and Christianity," p. 36.

183. Makransky, "Buddhist Analogues of Sin and Grace," p. 2.

be the refuge?"[184] The Buddhist John Makransky makes the point succinctly by comparing Augustine's and Gautama's views of the human condition and hope for release: "Whereas Augustine understood such bondage through the lens of Genesis as an ontologically substantial fallen state, Buddhists have viewed it as a continual, momentary process of construction by habits of thought and reaction so profoundly habitual that they seem ineluctable."[185] Yes, there is some — but only *some* — similarity here between the Christian and Buddhist hope for "salvation." Both look for a "transcendent" cause in terms of the divine intervention of grace (Christian) and the *bodhi:* transcendent knowing, "enlightenment" (Buddhism), but the latter not in terms of "divine revelation" or God's grace but in terms of "direct, embodied knowledge of the unconditioned, Nirvana."[186] The key to understanding this is the well-known and foundational distinction Buddha made between the "conditioned" and "unconditioned" existence. The former is the *dukkha* existence, under the power of craving, leading to samsaric rebirth over and over again; the latter is the release from *kamma.*

> In egocentered life, conditioned processes of mind and body, dominated by confusion and self-clinging, obscure the unconditioned aspect, Nirvana. But the Buddha, it is said, having realized the unconditioned in the fullest possible way, taught practices to re-pattern mind and body so as to permit the unconditioned to dawn for others. All such practices as taught by the Buddha (and generations of his followers) are referred to as the "Dharma," the holy pattern, the path to enlightenment. Put another way, the Dharma is the communication of the unconditioned through a Buddha's mind and body, imparting practices by which others' minds and bodies may be similarly opened to the unconditioned, so as to communicate the way to freedom afresh, again and again, from the Buddha's time to our own.[187]

This is the meaning of taking refuge in Buddha and *dhamma* (as well as *sangha,* the community). Buddha is not a savior but rather a necessary

---

184. *Dhammapada* 12.4; *SBE* 10 (in some other versions, 12.160, when verses are numbered from the beginning of the work, rather than from the beginning of each chapter). The English translation of this passage varies; I have followed here the one adopted by Rahula, *What the Buddha Taught,* p. 1. Similarly, *Dhammapada* 20.4 (20.276) puts it: "You yourselves must strive; the Buddhas only point the way."

185. Makransky, "Buddhist Analogues of Sin and Grace," p. 4.

186. Makransky, "Buddhist Analogues of Sin and Grace," p. 5.

187. Makransky, "Buddhist Analogues of Sin and Grace," pp. 5-6.

"transcendent" resource that every human person living under the conditioned existence needs in order to gain liberative insight. Here there is also the difference between the Buddhist and Hindu *advaita* vision, without denying some material similarities: the latter ultimately trusts the divine revelation, the Vedic teaching. And its difference from the Christian vision has already been indicated.

Another interesting question arises here: whether in both the Christian and Buddhist understanding of human nature, there is a "link" or an aid to help tap into the liberative, saving influence. In Christian (and Jewish) theology it is of course the image of God. I do not think there is such a universally shared principle in Buddhism, but I wonder if the early Mahayana concept of *Tathāgatagarbha* (Buddha nature) may point to the same kind of phenomenon. It means that the innermost being of each human person is replete with developing buddhahood at least potentially.[188] Buddhist theology at large, however, does not speak much or with one voice of this, so it has to be left for further investigation.

Ignorance and "Superimposition": The Hindu Diagnosis

The beginning point for the generic consideration of "sin" — human misery — in Hinduism at large is the notion of *dharma* that represents the positive standard against which all deviations must be compared. It is the "duty," the correct way of life, including all activities and spheres of life. Its opposite is *adharma*.[189] Somewhat similar to Buddhism, Hindu traditions have developed detailed lists of vices to avoid, including delusion, greed, and anger, the roots of all vices.[190] Not unlike most religious traditions, Hinduism makes a distinction between great and lesser sins. The most grievous offense is the killing of Brahmin, which is unforgivable and occasion for the death penalty. Other examples of a great sin include drinking intoxicating beverages and stealing. In principle all great sins are unpardonable, with no possibility for atonement. For lesser sins penance and atonement may be available. In keeping with the caste system, killing a person of a lower caste might be a less severe crime

188. Bodhi, "Arahants, Bodhisattvas, and Buddhas," p. 22; see also Makransky, "Buddhist Analogues of Sin and Grace," pp. 6-7; section 7.

189. See Khan, *Concept of Dharma in Valmiki Ramayana*, p. 34. This is the context for the well-known Gita passage (4:7) of Krishna taking *avatara* where there is an increase of *adharma*.

190. Bhagavad-Gita 16.21.

than slaughtering a cow![191] Although there is some commonality with the Abrahamic faiths' conception of sin, the difference is also deep. Whereas sin is ultimately transgression against God, *adharma* is basically a deviation from the "impersonal" law of the cosmos, reality.[192]

The ultimate beginning point for the investigation of human misery in Hinduism — similarly to Buddhism — however, cannot be based on the analysis of wrong deeds, behavior, or attitudes. *Adharma* is to be put in the wider context of Hindu philosophy of human "bondage" to *avidya*, "ignorance" (called by Shaivists *anava*, "congenital ignorance concerning the ultimate"). Ignorance makes one cling to *maya*, "fiction," and thus subject to effects of karma, leading to rebirths over and over again. Only with the removal of this "ignorance" can souls' essential nature as pure spirits be restored.[193] This is the general principle that applies to most Hindu traditions. That said, different Hindu traditions understand the meaning and implications of *avidya* in their own distinctive ways. I will focus here on the *advaita* notion.

According to Sankara's analysis, the most foundational error is the identification of "object" and "subject" — "which are opposed to each other as much as darkness and light are." What do these terms mean? "The subject is the universal Self whose nature is intelligence (*kit*[194]); the object comprises whatever is of a non-intelligent nature, viz. bodies with their sense organs, internal organs, and the objects of the senses, i.e. the external material world."[195] Attributing the features of the one to the other is the foundational mistake, named by Sankara as "superimposition" *(adhyâsa)*. In other words, the human predicament stems "from this wrong knowledge" (nescience) that is not able "to distinguish the two entities (object and subject) and their respective attributes, although they are absolutely distinct, but to superimpose upon each the characteristic nature and the attributes of the other, and thus, coupling the Real and the Unreal."[196] In contrast, in the *advaita* vision, the "true Self is not the mind-body complex; rather, it is the light of consciousness that shines deep within the mind."[197] The Real self is conscious, changeless, and does not

191. Klostermaier, *Survey of Hinduism,* pp. 168-72.

192. I have some reservations about the way the relationship between *adharma* and sin is explained in Bharati, *Understanding Hinduism,* p. 23.

193. See further, Klostermaier, *Survey of Hinduism,* chap. 13.

194. More typically spelled *cit.*

195. Sankara, *Commentary on Vedanta Sutras,* part I, 1.1.1; *SBE* 34:3 (the definition is n. 1, trans. George Thibaut).

196. Sankara, *Commentary on Vedanta Sutras,* part I, 1.1.1; *SBE* 34:4.

197. Thatamanil, *Immanent Divine,* p. 31.

act. The unreal self is made of body-mind and sensations, takes human agency for granted, and is under decay. (The Western reader must be warned of not identifying "consciousness" and "mind" in Sankara's texts, although in contemporary [neuro]scientific analysis mind and consciousness are conflated. For Sankara, "consciousness" belongs to Brahman, "mind" to humans.) As a result of the superimposition (that is, assigning the attributes of the Self to the object and vice versa), humans envision themselves as finite, vulnerable, and decaying (thus, not identical with the changeless, eternal Brahman) and — even worse — attribute finite characteristics to the Absolute.[198]

To leave the analysis here, however, would be badly wanting. The counterintuitive teaching of Sankara is that as mistaken as superimposition is, it is virtually necessary for this simple reason: the "conventional" (nonenlightened) form of life would be actually impossible if the human being were not to assume (some kind of) real agency and "consciousness" (mind). Indeed, only slowly and with the help of the divine revelation (Vedic teaching, particularly the Upanishads)[199] may one develop a grasp of the liberating knowledge, in other words, release from under the ignorance and the power of the superimposition. An essential part of the liberating insight is that, against the common assumption of real human agency, "we ascertain from scripture that the Lord is a causal agent in all activity."[200] How else could it be in the final analysis — or else the foundational principle of the *advaita* would be negated (namely, identity between Lord and humanity)? Because the Lord is partless, human agency cannot of course be anything but part of the undivided divine action; human agency, thus, is an illusion.[201]

What are the implications for the comparative theological discussion of the Hindu *advaita* analysis of the human condition? First, the misery is necessary in the sense that without ignorance, leading to superimposition, purposeful and meaningful human life was hardly possible. Second, there is absolutely no sudden "fall" either in the life of humanity at large or in the life

198. I am helped here by Thatamanil, *Immanent Divine,* chap. 2 (although, as will be evident, I do not agree with all his conclusions).

199. For a detailed discussion of the understanding of divine revelation in Hinduism in general and in Sankara in particular, see *Trinity and Revelation,* chap. 8; against the common (modern liberal) assumption, the main Vedanta traditions uphold an absolute reliance on divine revelation — and certainly Sankara does.

200. Sankara, *Commentary on Vedanta Sutras,* part II, 2.3.41; *SBE* 38:59; for finding the citation I am indebted to Thatamanil, *Immanent Divine,* p. 34 (who quotes from another version).

201. For comments, see Thatamanil, *Immanent Divine,* pp. 35-36.

of every human person; "rather, ignorance is the root cause of the very process of beginningless transmigration and so is a congenital inheritance carrying with it accumulated results generated by innumberable actions performed over countless lifetimes"[202] in the samsaric cycle of rebirths. Mere action perpetuates rebirth/transmigration, until one comes to the liberating insight of the illusion of human agency because of the identity with the Brahman. Third, while not the "cause," embodiment is the obstacle to be removed before the liberating insight. There is an absolute distinction between consciousness (of the Real Self) and body-mind-senses composition of the illusionary self. With that in mind, for me it does not make much sense to still claim that Sankara does not endorse body-mind (or soul) dualism; merely naming it "the distinction between *consciousness* and the mind-body complex" hardly undoes the dualism.[203] "Consciousness" is absolutely removed from the embodiment (and historicity). Fourth, what is the ultimate cause of human misery, ignorance? Like Gautama, Sankara strictly refuses to address the question because he does not wish to give ignorance an ontological status.[204] Like the Buddha, Sankara merely wishes to resolve the dilemma. My response is that Sankara has already made ignorance a really existing reality as it necessarily governs all human life and it calls for an answer about its origins.[205] It does not suffice to avoid the question with mere rhetoric as the advaitic teacher seems to be doing.

Beyond these questions, the major dilemma facing the credibility of the *advaita* analysis of the human condition, as is often noted (and of which Sankara was aware),[206] has to do with the seeming impossibility to imagine evil and ignorance. The reason is simply that the human person is identical with the Lord in whom there is no ignorance or evil. If everyone is already divine, how can one be sinful, fallen, and corrupted?[207] The leading modern *advaita* advocate Swami Vivekananda categorically puts it this way: "If you are the Lord God, I also am the Lord God. So Vedanta knows no sin. There are mistakes but no sin; and in

202. Thatamanil, *Immanent Divine*, p. 36.
203. This is the opinion of Thatamanil, *Immanent Divine*, p. 43. Even the fact that according to Sankara even gods are embodied (p. 43), particularly when *avataras*, hardly changes the situation: even gods are identical with the Lord, to be true "gods," and the Lord is nonembodied.
204. This is the thesis of the influential essay by Ingalls, "Sankara on the Question," pp. 69-72.
205. Cf. Thatamanil, *Immanent Divine*, pp. 54-57.
206. See Sankara, *Commentary on Vedanta Sutras*, part II, 4.1.3; SBE 38:337-40.
207. I find it highly unexpected and confusing that the famed Hindu expert Francis X. Clooney, S.J., fails to tackle this basic issue in his otherwise highly useful case study of a classic *advaita* tradition: "To Be Heard and Done, But Never Quite Seen," pp. 73-99; cf. Thatamanil, *Immanent Divine*, p. 27.

the long run everything is going to be all right. No Satan — none of this non-sense." (He continues somewhat ironically that there is only one sin that Vedanta acknowledges, and that is that one believes in one's sinfulness!) The implication thus is: "You see, Vedanta proposes no sin nor sinner. No God to be afraid of."[208]

The only evil Vivekananda is willing to admit is ignorance. Commenting on this, Ward rightly notes, "that is more plausible when said to an audience of basically well-intentioned but rather self-doubting seekers after truth, than when said to a rally of the National Socialist Party or the League of White Supremacists."[209] One way to negotiate this — although not appealing to many critics, I guess — is Vivekananda's claim that the assertion of one's divinity cannot be made with regard to the phenomenal life, only the noumenal life.[210] But doesn't that make the issue even more complicated? It still begs the question: What are humans in this life? And: Whether they are divine or not now, whence the universal evil in human life? So, is there any evil then, according to Vivekananda? His response: "The Vedanta says that you are pure and perfect, and that there is a state beyond good and evil, and that is your own nature. It is higher even than good. Good is only a lesser differentiation than evil. We have no theory of evil. We call it ignorance."[211] Even if we think that each person is only potentially divine (because of ignorance and superimposition), on the way to release, the question of the reality of ignorance remains. Sankara certainly is not willing to go with Barth's type of allusion to evil as "nothing" that ends up being something "real"! My reading of Hindu sources leaves me wondering if that tradition simply leaves be this deep inconsistency. Although the Abrahamic faiths' reference to the ultimate responsibility of God in allowing evil and sin raises complex theodicy questions, it at least attempts a solution.

Living faith traditions not only envision human misery and liberation therefrom but also imagine what would make a good life. Let's call it human flourishing and pick up the conversation started at the end of part 1 that focused on the flourishing of nature. While constructing a viable Christian theology of human flourishing, including issues such as health and sickness, race and racism, work and economics and globalization, we will also continue interfaith examinations of some of these issues, investigating what kind of liberative impulses religious traditions may have in common.

208. Vivekananda, "Is Vedanta the Future Religion?" Similar kinds of sayings can be easily found in his teaching, e.g., "The Vedanta recognises no sin, it only recognises error." "Practical Vedanta, Part I," in *Complete Works*, vol. 2.
209. K. Ward, *Religion and Human Nature*, p. 19.
210. Vivekananda, "On the Vedanta Philosophy," vol. 5.
211. Vivekananda, "On the Vedanta Philosophy," vol. 5.

16. Human Flourishing in Theological Perspective

The Beauty and Ugliness of a Good Human Life:
The Context for Flourishing

Life in the Quotidian

It might sound counterproductive to begin the discussion of human flourishing by the reminder of the quotidian, the proximate context of humanity as finite and hence ambiguous. It belongs to the nature of finite existence that there are hurdles, riddles, unresolved problems, potential for growth, "fallings down," and so forth. "Creaturely being is limited being. This is an ontological claim."[1] As Archbishop Williams puts it brilliantly: "The existence of the world is not a puzzling fact, as opposed to other, straightforward facts . . . it is all the facts there are."[2]

To creaturely, finite life belong physical limitations, the most dramatic of which is the ultimate disintegration of our lives over the years.[3] Along with these intrinsic limits, we as creatures are also subject to extrinsic ones.[4] To the ambiguity of the quotidian also belongs the existence of evil, moral and natural. Thus, "the real and authentic human being is the ordinary, everyday

---

1. D. Kelsey, *Eccentric Existence*, 1:201.
2. R. Williams, "On Being Creatures," p. 68, quoted in D. Kelsey, *Eccentric Existence*, 1:201.
3. See further, Schloss, "From Evolution to Eschatology," pp. 65-85.
4. D. Kelsey, *Eccentric Existence*, 1:202.

human person."[5] What a powerful critique of the "values" of the consumer society with ideals of lasting fitness and beauty, economic security, and everlasting health.[6] God's gracious relating to human beings in their quotidian, in their everyday-life ambiguity, is thus a true gift, a manifestation of divine hospitality.[7]

An urgent challenge to Christian theology, Kelsey reminds us, is "to develop conceptual and argumentative strategies by which to show that, properly understood, human flourishing is inseparable from God's active relating to human creatures such that their flourishing is always dependent upon God."[8] Only that kind of theology of flourishing may be credible that does not shy away from the ordinary realities of daily life. Moltmann incisively remarks that "the more unreservedly and passionately he loves life, the more intensely he also experiences the pains of life. . . . [T]he more a person loves, the more intensely he experiences both life and death."[9] Without value is thus the late British feminist-pantheist Jantzen's judgment that Christian tradition is not capable of facing death as a "natural" result of finite life because of its hope for eternal life.[10] On the contrary, Christian vision of life has the capacity to fund even "flourishing as dying life."[11]

If life in the quotidian is the "good" life, that means life in all its experiences, both in health and sickness, can be a flourishing life.

Life in Health and Sickness — as Gifted or Disabled

Human personhood does not admit degrees. One cannot be more or less human person. One either is human, or is not.[12] Defining the image of God in terms of being related to God saves theology from anchoring human dignity in the possession of a quality or commodity, such as intelligence or health. One's relation to the Creator is not affected in the least by one's disabilities, not even intellectual ones. That persons like the intellectually disabled are not able to manifest rational capacities to the extent that "normal" persons can, is

---

5. D. Kelsey, *Eccentric Existence*, 1:204.
6. D. Kelsey, *Eccentric Existence*, 1:205.
7. See D. Kelsey, *Eccentric Existence*, 1:212-14.
8. D. Kelsey, "On Human Flourishing," p. 1.
9. Moltmann, *God in Creation*, p. 268.
10. Cf. Jantzen, *Foundations of Violence*, p. vii and passim.
11. Subheading in D. Kelsey, *Eccentric Existence*, 1:314.
12. D. Kelsey, *Eccentric Existence*, 1:204.

a nonissue in this foundational sense.[13] Similarly, the gifted are no more the image of God, not even the intellectually highly gifted.[14]

To the affirmation of life belongs also its affirmation in health and sickness. Definitions of health and sickness vary from time to time. As Moltmann notes, in the contemporary world health easily becomes an idol, but that idolatry may rob the human being of the true strength of her humanity if every sickness endangers full humanity. "Only what can stand up to both health *and* sickness, and ultimately to living *and* dying, can count as a valid definition of what it means to be human."[15] Hence, the secular definition as an index of human flourishing in terms of functionality — meaning that opposite to healthy is "dysfunctional" — is highly problematic.[16] This is not to deny that healthy life is preferred over sickness; of course it is. Rather, "Love for life says 'yes' to life in spite of its sicknesses, handicaps and infirmities, and opens the door to a 'life against death.'"[17]

What about the promise of healing that was part of Jesus' ministry and mandate to his followers? True, healing is there, but so is the continuing suffering, and ultimately death. Every healed person will later die of another cause. Even the resurrected Lazarus saw his life come to an end. Hence, to the Christian gospel belong both the expectation of the healing of the sick, as the sign of the coming of God's kingdom,[18] and the celebration of the "charisma of the handicapped life."[19] Speaking of the disabled in such a manner has nothing to do with glorification — nor subtle stigmatization[20] — of the ones who suffer but rather with resisting the cultural tendency to celebrate success, health, and youth.[21] "My power is made perfect in weakness" (2 Cor. 12:9). In that light, the World Health Organization's definition attempts too much and makes each and every one "sick": "Health is a state of complete

13. For comments, see P. Jewett, *Who We Are*, p. 67. Jewett's remark that even though the disabled "possess the image as given by the Creator . . . [albeit] not as actualized by the creature" materially, says it correctly but contains the unfortunate expression of "possession." Strictly speaking, human beings *are* the image of God; therefore it cannot be lost.

14. Edward Gibbon rightly notes that overestimation of rationality goes all the way back to Greek cultural heritage. *History of the Decline and the Fall of the Roman Empire*, 3:75.

15. Moltmann, *God in Creation*, p. 273, emphasis in original.

16. See D. Kelsey, *Eccentric Existence*, 1:317.

17. Moltmann, *Spirit of Life*, p. 86.

18. See Moltmann, *Way of Jesus Christ*, pp. 104-16; Moltmann, *Spirit of Life*, pp. 188-92.

19. Moltmann, *Spirit of Life*, pp. 192-93.

20. See Iozzio, "Thinking about Disabilities."

21. For antidisability attitudes among female theologians, see Betcher, "Becoming Flesh of My Flesh"; for a Jewish perspective, see Belser, "Returning to Flesh."

physical, mental and social well-being and not merely the absence of disease or infirmity."[22]

The Christian tradition's track record of speaking of disabilities is checkered and problematic. It does not make the state of affairs any more acceptable that not only ancient cultures but also other living faith traditions by and large share the same lacuna.[23] Just consider the OT Levitical laws that obviously exclude from the priestly arena the various kinds of disabled persons (Lev. 21:16-21). Theologically, it has to be seen that the ceremonial law had everything to do with the holiness of God — understood in Israel, and widely in surrounding cultures — in terms of separation from everything imperfect or unclean, rather than with the value (or lack thereof) of a human being. Indeed, to counterbalance, the same legislation also allows the disabled to "eat the bread of his God, both of the most holy and of the holy things" (v. 22).[24]

As with slavery and race, it has taken a long time for Christian tradition — and other faith traditions as well — to catch up to the vision of full equality of all on the basis of God's creative work. Yes, there were some blessed exceptions,[25] but by and large, all the way to the twentieth century prejudices, omissions, and negative attitudes prevailed. It is the task of contemporary constructive theology to "acknowledge and confront the conventional understandings of disability manifest in the biblical text . . . but yet proceed to subvert conventional antidisability readings of the Bible by reading beneath and between its lines." That is the way toward a "redemptive theology of disability."[26] A related new challenge to Christian churches, as well as to other faith traditions, is to stand for and unwaveringly affirm the full humanity and dignity of HIV/AIDS patients, a problem easily forgotten now that some modest medical advances are in use and development.[27]

---

22. From the preamble to the Constitution of the World Health Organization as adopted by the International Health Conference, New York, June 19-22, 1946 (Official Records of the World Health Organization, no. 2, p. 100), entered into force on April 7, 1948. Available at http://www.who.int/about/definition/en/print.html.

23. For a detailed discussion, see Yong, *Theology and Down Syndrome,* chaps. 2; 5. See also Larsson, "Islam and Disability," pp. 367-68.

24. For comments, see P. Jewett, *Who We Are,* p. 41.

25. For the affirmation of lepers as bearing the image of God by Basil and Gregory of Nyssa and Gregory of Nazianzus, see Harrison, *God's Many Splendored Image,* pp. 99-102.

26. Yong, *Theology and Down Syndrome,* p. 42. For a creative discussion of "deconstructing and reconstructing disability" in late modern discourses, see chap. 4. For the now classic work, see Eiesland, *The Disabled God.*

27. See the important Christian response by the World Council of Churches, *Churches' Compassionate Response to HIV and AIDS,* 2006.

The Pursuit of Human Flourishing and Liberations as a *Theological* Task

All Theology Is "Liberation" Theology

Not only humanist reasons — which in themselves are indispensable in light of the dignity and value of humanity as the divine image — but also *theological* reasons impel the continuing Christian pursuit of justice, equality, and community. Indeed, pursuit of justice and liberation is an essential part of the theological task. Philip Hefner reminds us that "the questions Who are we? and What are we here for? are not to be confined to the realm of philosophical and religious meditation. They are questions whose answers influence every aspect of our human existence — war and peace, political and economic justice, hunger, poverty, education, child-rearing, career, sexuality, the conception and birth of new life, as well as the conditions of dying and the breadth of medical practice."[28]

Rightly the senior African American theologian James H. Cone laments that, by and large, theologians — white theologians, for him — have trusted the innocence of their use of the doctrine of creation and so failed to see the many implications for social issues such as racial equality.[29] Similarly, he reminds us that the concept of the image of God, rather than being about rationality or spirituality, "is human nature in rebellion against the structures of oppression. It is humanity involved in the liberation struggle against the forces of inhumanity."[30] An essential task for constructive theology, hence, asks, "What concrete notions of personhood, of human dignity and of freedom emerge from these beliefs that can guide our social and environmental policies?"[31]

These considerations are funded by the insight that liberation is not a theme external to theology — and therefore, cannot be relegated conveniently to "liberation" theologies — but rather is an integral component of the systematic/constructive theological task: "Christian theology is a theology of liberation. It is a rational study of the being of God in the world in light of the existential situation of an oppressed community, relating the forces of liberation to the essence of the gospel, which is Jesus Christ."[32]

Not only is contemporary constructive Christian theology called to reflect on the implications of anthropological beliefs in practices, it is also, on the basis of the divine mandate (Gen. 1:26-27), to seek a lifestyle facilitating

28. Hefner, *The Human Factor,* pp. 4-5.
29. Cone, *Black Theology of Liberation,* p. 75.
30. Cone, *Black Theology of Liberation,* p. 94.
31. Zimmermann, *Incarnational Humanism,* p. 47.
32. Cone, *Black Theology of Liberation,* p. 1, emphasis removed; so also p. 5.

the flourishing of creation. Nothing less is expected of human beings, who "are God's created co-creators whose purpose is to be the agency, acting in freedom, to birth the future that is most wholesome for the nature that has birthed us — the nature that is not only our own genetic heritage, but also the entire human community and the evolutionary and ecological reality in which and to which we belong. Exercising this agency is said to be God's will for humans."[33] The task that lies ahead of constructive theology in this respect is wide and complex. An indication of the pluriform nature of the task is that even a theologian such as James Cone, whose agenda has been liberationist from the start, in hindsight lamented that a number of key issues went unnoticed in the first part of his career: the problem of sexism and a global analysis of oppression, including economy and social class.[34]

With these challenges in mind, as argued above, it is given to constructive Christian theology to set forth boldly and humbly a distinctively Christian account of liberation, equality, and dignity with implications in all spheres of human life. The German systematician Christoph Schwöbel outlines this task of public theology in a compelling manner: "By making transparent how its views on human dignity are rooted in a specific view of what it means to be human and how this, in turn, is grounded in a comprehensive view of reality in relation to God, Christian theology makes its vision of reality publicly contestable, and thereby offers the invitation to proponents of other views of reality to make explicit the implicit assumptions on which their views rest."[35]

If liberation is an essential task for theology, one may assume it also applies (at least in some sense) to other faith traditions. The purpose of the next section is to investigate *theological* resources as well as potential hindrances with regard to such work.

Liberative Impulses among Religions

The three Abrahamic traditions share not only the idea of the inviolable dignity of human nature because of the relation to God, but also the equality of both sexes and all races. That these traditions have not always upheld these ideals — and more often than not, have outright acted contrary to these beliefs — will not make nil this foundational belief.

33. Hefner, *The Human Factor*, p. 27.
34. Cone, *Black Theology of Liberation*, pp. xv-xviii.
35. Schwöbel, "Recovering Human Dignity," p. 46.

While the Qur'an does not know the later concept of "race," it affirms the equality of all using different terminology: "And of His signs is the creation of the heavens and the earth and the differences of your tongues and your colours. Surely in that there are signs for all peoples" (30:22; similarly also 49:13). The term "sign" is of course a technical term speaking of creation as "God's book."[36] Therefore also all share the same divine destiny: "And whoever does righteous deeds, whether male or female, and is a believer — such shall be admitted into Paradise, and not be wronged, the dint in a date-stone" (4:124). Even gender does not count as a criterion of superiority. In Islam, women are as human as men. They are not evaluated on the basis of their gender, but on the basis of their faith and character. That said, authoritative Islamic tradition also includes well-known teachings that contradict these Qur'anic teachings[37] and are used as resources for the submission of women. It is the task of prophetic Muslim theology to negotiate this tension for the sake of liberation.

There is an intriguing irony built deeply into the structure of the Buddhist faith with regard to its liberative potential. On the one hand, comparable to the Judeo-Christian Ten Commandments and Jesus' Sermon on the Mount, Buddhism lists its key ethical principles and actions — the Eight-Fold Path — at the center of its faith. On the other hand, particularly Theravada's nontheistic human-centered soteriology and the principle of *kamma* (according to which each reaps what each has sown and others should not be quick to interfere) clearly point toward isolationism rather than social activism. A related ambiguity about the tradition is that although Gautama by and large was a pacifist — and that Nagarjuna, the founder of the Madhyamika ("Middle Way") tradition, served also as royal counselor for peace[38] — the Buddhist category of soldiers emerged claiming that true detachment (the main aim of all Buddhist practices) had freed them to fight without any anxiety about either their own lives or the lives of others.[39] As in other faith traditions, in modern times attempts to rediscover and creatively reinterpret tradition to fund work for liberation has emerged among some Buddhists.[40]

An intriguing case study is provided by a comparison of the Vietnamese

36. For an important, accessible discussion, see Cornell, "Islam and Human Diversity," pp. 33-40.

37. See, e.g., Q 2:223, 228. The allowance of polygamy, notwithstanding rules concerning fair treatment of wives, also points to subordination (see Q 4:3).

38. See Thurman, "Nagarjuna's Guidelines for Buddhist Social Action."

39. See Smith and Burr, *Understanding World Religions*, p. 39. For twentieth-century warriors, see Victoria, *Zen War Stories*.

40. K. Jones, *New Social Face of Buddhism*.

Buddhist Thich Nhat Hanh's and Peruvian Roman Catholic Gustavo Gutiér-rez's commitments to liberation deeply embedded in their respective faith traditions.[41] Both liberationists speak of the importance of awareness and transformation of consciousness.[42] Both Gutiérrez's[43] and Nhat Hanh's visions of liberation are deeply anchored in their own spiritual tradition: "'Awakened' people are certainly going to form small communities where material life will become simple and healthy. Time and energy will be devoted to the enrich-ment of spirituality. . . . In them the sickness of the times will be cured and spiritual health will be acquired."[44] Gutiérrez's call to reread history and the Bible from the perspective of the poor[45] is paralleled by Nhat Hanh's use of Scripture and doctrine "as a method, as a guide" to the works of liberation.[46]

As a Christian theologian, I cannot help but oppose the divinely sanc-tioned caste system in Hinduism. It forms a major challenge to that tradition's liberative potential, particularly because of its violent and unjust exclusion of masses of people like the Dalit. The caste system goes back to the hierarchical division of society into four classes *(varna)*[47] during the Aryan conquest of India. The division is based on Eternal Dharma as taught in the Upanishads. There is the famous Vedic hymn *Purusa,* a narrative of deities creating the cosmos from the sacrifice of the body of Purusa, including the four castes.[48] This means there is a divine determination of castes. One's placement in the hierarchy is determined by karma accumulated in past existence.[49] Under the four classes (with innumerable subclasses), there is the bottom caste, namely, the "Untouchables" — named by Gandhi the "Friends of God" *(Harijan)*. The self-designation of the "Untouchables" is Dalit, which means "oppressed, ground down." In sum: deeply engrained in the caste system is the ontological

---

41. In this section, I am indebted to the insightful discussion in Lefebure, *The Buddha and the Christ,* chap. 8.

42. For the importance of awakening to life, see, e.g., Hanh, *Our Appointment with Life,* p. 35.

43. Gutiérrez, *On Job,* p. 102.

44. Hanh, *Zen Keys,* p. 158.

45. Gutiérrez, *The Power of the Poor in History,* p. 20.

46. Hanh, *Zen Keys,* p. 47.

47. The four classes are Brahmans, Kshatriyas, Vaishyas, and Shudras. Etymologically referring to "color," *varna,* was related to different skin colors.

48. Rig Veda 10.90; for short comments, see B. K. Smith, *Classifying the Universe,* pp. 27-28.

49. The foundational scriptural basis is found in *Laws of Manu.* Bhagavad Gita 18.41-48 outlines briefly the basic tasks of each caste. For an authoritative study, see B. K. Smith, *Classifying the Universe.*

difference of people, some privileged, others less so. Being divinely sanctioned, it is essentially a *theological problem.*

One of the earliest modern Indian reformists was Ram Mohan Roy (d. 1833), who spoke strongly against what he considered abuses of the Hindu system, including the neglect of women's education and the practice of burning a widow alive at her husband's cremation *(tee* or *suttee).* Gleaning from Christianity and Vedic religions, he founded in 1828 Brahmo Samaj, which later, under the leadership of Debendranath Tagore (d. 1905), broke away from Vedic authority in preference of reason and conscience as the ultimate authority. A similar kind of vision for purifying Hinduism motivated the founding in 1875 of Arya Samaj by Swami Dayananda Sarasvati (d. 1883). Unlike the practice of Brahmo Samaj, he accepted only the authority of the Vedas (earlier ones, to be more precise), including their use as scientific authority as well, and rejected Western influences.[50] Sharply differing from Sankara, the Ramakrishna Mission[51] founded by Vivekananda was totally focused on social service; opposed the caste system, particularly the exclusion of the Dalit; and championed the rights of women.[52]

There is, however, a deep theological problem here. Vivekananda speaks of the human being as divine, and therefore "the only God to worship is the human soul in the human body."[53] This clearly bespeaks for equality and dignity of all (although, as mentioned, Sankara did not think so). But if so, then it means that it does not make sense to speak of suffering, ignorance, or inequality — if all are divine by nature! And according to the original vision of Sankara (similarly to that of Theravada Buddhism), one cannot help others achieve the needed insight for release. In other words, it seems like we should honor a murderer or rapist as much as Gandhi or Mother Teresa.[54] It can be said, of course, that this dilemma can be solved by considering the rapist and murderer only potentially divine; divinity is not yet achieved.[55] Many, myself among them, however, are left wondering if this seemingly deep inherent contradistinction cannot be avoided.

50. Ludwig, *Sacred Paths,* pp. 86-87.

51. For current activities and beliefs, consult the official Ramakrishna Math and Ramakrishna Mission Web site at http://www.belurmath.org/home.htm (8/13/2013).

52. For details, see K. Ward, *Religion and Human Nature,* pp. 15-23.

53. Vivekananda, "Practical Vedanta, Part II," in *Complete Works,* vol. 2; see also "The Spirit and Influence of Vedanta," in *Complete Works,* vol. 1.

54. As Vivekananda is saying in Nikhilananda, "Trip to America." I am indebted to K. Ward, *Religion and Human Nature,* p. 18 (although I use a different source).

55. K. Ward, *Religion and Human Nature,* pp. 16-19.

By far the most influential Hindu reformist way is the *Satyagraha* life-style championed by Gandhi, including nonviolence *(ahimsa)*. In advocating nonviolence, these key principles should be followed, which gain support from Christian tradition: self-reliance rather than dependence; initiative, active dissemination of ideas; importance of truth and integrity; advance by stages (patience); constant self-examination; respect for the opponent; and holding on to essentials.[56] Gandhi's most famous successor, Vinoba Bhave, continued the "constructive program," initiating land distribution and other social improvements. Importantly, he taught that when the Gita teaches the presence of God in all of creation, particularly in every human being, it means that the Lord's service includes service to the neighbor, especially to the vulnerable ones. To that also belongs willingness to serve without personal gain.[57] Needless to say, these values are strongly supported by Christian theology.

Dehumanization and Desecration

On Forms of Dehumanization and Humiliation

Leading patristic teachers built on the scriptural traditions to find a theological basis for affirming the equality of all human beings, whether men and women were equally created in the image of God, or even freedom from slavery. They established the freedom of religion on the same basis. Furthermore, particularly prior to Christendom, the church stood against war, abortion and infanticide, judicial torment and killing, and the bloody mayhem of the arenas. The reason was that each human being "God willed to be a sacred animal," and therefore Christians should "regard men as truly sacred."[58] Fittingly, the Canadian theologian Jens Zimmermann names this "the beginnings of incarnational humanism," which lays the foundation for the best of Western culture's values.[59] In that light, the modern critics of Christianity who "have

---

56. Summarized in Smith and Burr, *Understanding World Religions,* p. 17; for details, see Gandhi, *Non-violent Resistance.*

57. See B. Wilson, "Vinoba Bhave's Talks on the *Gita,*" pp. 110-30.

58. Gushee, *Sacredness of Human Life,* chap. 4; citations (p. 128) from Lactantius, *Institutes* 6.20 (p. 129), and from Clement of Alexandria, *Exhortation to the Heathen* 2.201, respectively. For abolitionist and anticolonialist impulses in Maximus the Confessor's christologically driven theology, see Carter, *Race,* pp. 343-69.

59. Zimmermann, *Incarnational Humanism,* chap. 2 title, and quotation on p. 52. See also the classic study by Jaeger, *Humanism and Theology.*

argued that this religion devalues the human (Nietzsche), fails to change human conditions (Marx) and weakens human responsibility by detracting attention from this world (new atheists)"[60] simply miss the point and manifest their own historical ignorance.

Although this biblically based vision was seriously frustrated by "the fateful transition to Christendom,"[61] faithful witnesses even during the darkest times were never missing. There was Francis of Assisi against the slaughter in the Holy Land, Bartolomé de Las Casas against the Spanish conquistadors, and early Baptists against the systematic rejection of the Jews.[62] Even though it is "a tragically mixed legacy,"[63] it nevertheless reminds Christians of the right way.

Regretfully, one need not go too far back in history to find horrific examples of desecration of human life, particularly of the most helpless and vulnerable. While Nazi crimes usually first come to mind with 12 million, mainly Jewish victims, the volume of human lives lost is even greater in other twentieth-century systemic crimes against humanity: just recall Mao Zedong's elimination of 50-70 million Chinese culminating in the Cultural Revolution, Stalin's slaughter of over 20 million Russians, and so forth.[64]

Dehumanization, however, is not only about genocide and such horrific crimes; it may be related to ethnicity, race, and immigration. Dehumanization takes many forms; it often likens people to animals in pejorative ways: depending on the cultural context, apes, dogs, pigs, rats, parasites, insects, and so forth.[65] It may present women (or children or even men) as mere sexual objects in pornography.[66] The objectification of women (and girls) may also take place in bright daylight, as it were, in the culture's presentation of what makes femininity[67] — coupled with wide use of sexual symbols in marketing. A subtle way of dehumanization in the form of objectification can even be found in such an "innocent" field as medicine in terms of "the denial of qualities associated with meaning, interest, and compassion" to

60. Zimmermann, *Incarnational Humanism*, p. 79.

61. For a detailed discussion, see Gushee, *Sacredness of Human Life*, chap. 5. See also Stephenson, "Imperial Christianity and Sacred War."

62. For details, see Gushee, *Sacredness of Human Life*, chap. 6.

63. Gushee, *Sacredness of Human Life*, pp. 212-13.

64. For statistics, see Scaruffi, "Worst Genocides"; for discussion, see Gushee, *Sacredness of Human Life*, chap. 9.

65. Haslam, "Dehumanization," p. 252.

66. For a sophisticated analysis, see Nussbaum, *Sex and Social Justice*.

67. See Fredrickson and Roberts, "Objectification Theory."

patients treated as mere objects.[68] We could continue the list of how human vulnerability[69] in various forms can be exploited and persons humiliated and dehumanized.[70]

Judeo-Christian theological tradition stands firmly against this and makes every effort to reclaim the immense value of each human being having been created in the image of God. At the same time, it insists that no amount of humiliation, torture, blaming, degradation, or other inhumane treatment can remove the humanity of a human being. Joining forces against dehumanization is a task not only for the whole global ecumenical church but also for joint interfaith work. This is also the right way to repent from innumerable acts of dehumanization done — and still under way — in the name of religion.

Not only blatant dehumanization but also — in most cases, well-meant — efforts to enhance human capacities with the help of rapidly developing technologies should interest theologians, not merely ethicists whose area of specialty it is. Because Christian theology does not admit degrees of humanity, it has to invest careful thought on what to do with various types of enhancement techniques and procedures.

Humanity and the "Posthuman Condition"

So, what about posthuman bodies?[71] Is the way we speak of humanity in an age that has opened the possibility of not only cloning but also creating a "posthuman condition" any different from the past?[72] When you add to the equation genetic manipulation, it is not only the question of "what are we *doing* with our technology?" but also, "what are we *becoming* with our technology?"[73] In its more inclusive sense, "posthuman condition" refers to "a world in which humans are mixtures of machine and organism, where nature has been modified by technology, and technology has become assimilated to form a functioning component of organic bodies." Obvious dangers include

---

68. Barnard, "On the Relationship," p. 98, quoted in Haslam, "Dehumanization," p. 253.

69. Brennan, *Dehumanizing the Vulnerable*.

70. For an important discussion of ways of humiliating and dehumanizing, see the interdisciplinary collection edited by Neuhaeuser, Webster, Kuch, and Kaufmann, *Humiliation, Degradation, Dehumanization: Human Dignity Violated*.

71. Halberstam and Livingstone, eds., *Posthuman Bodies*.

72. Graham, "Liberation or Enslavement."

73. Hefner, *Technology and Human Becoming*, p. 9.

not only dehumanization but also "creation out of control," the tendency to "play God," and technocracy in its various forms.[74]

Behind biogenetics, posthuman bodies, and "transhumanism" is a definite cultural shift to which Christian theology has failed to respond. This shift has to do with Western culture's conception of health, sickness, and the good life: whereas in the past health and sickness were placed within the wider moral framework in which "[h]ealth was regarded as a good but not as the supreme good, illness as a woe but not as the supreme woe," in contemporary thinking health and physical excellence have been elevated on a pedestal.[75] Contemporary bioethics quite uncritically serves that goal. Better, faster, more sophisticated goals are pursued regardless of their moral (and religious) value. Human dignity can hardly be established in such a vision. The goal of contemporary bioethics is in keeping with the original vision of what used to be called eugenics, coined by Darwin's cousin Francis Galton in 1883, the goal of which was to use "our understanding of the laws of heredity to improve the stock of humankind."[76] While much has changed in terms of rapid technological development including molecular genetics and medically assisted reproduction, little has changed in the ultimate pursuit.[77]

As a way of theological response, R. Kendall Soulen summarizes succinctly the differences between "new eugenics" and Christian theology. Whereas eugenics seeks "replacement" for enhancement, theology seeks redemption of all kinds of life; whereas in eugenics, "interrogation for existence" is the leading motif, theology looks for God, who is "calling into existence the things that are not"; whereas in eugenics "the last shall be eliminated," in theological vision "the last shall be the first"; and whereas in eugenics everything is about "counting traits," in theology it is about "beholding name and face."[78] Of course, these are extreme positions that need to be put in their place. Similarly, this juxtaposing is not meant to say no to all forms of health-oriented and life-saving enhancement, improvement, or replacement. It is the theologian's task to serve as critical inquirer into the motives and hidden — and less hidden — agendas, and to relate them to the foundational

74. Graham, "Liberation or Enslavement," n.p.

75. See Soulen, "Cruising toward Bethlehem," p. 105.

76. Wikler, "Can We Learn from Eugenics?" p. 183, cited in Soulen, "Cruising toward Bethlehem," p. 108.

77. For preimplantation genetic diagnosis, see D. King, "Preimplantation Genetic Diagnosis."

78. In Soulen, "Cruising toward Bethlehem," pp. 113-20.

teaching of creaturely life as a gift from a hospitable God to whom we all give account at the end.[79]

Yet another form of dehumanization relates to race and ethnicity in a globalizing world, to which we turn next.

Identity, Race, and Belonging in a Postcolonial World

The Challenge and Promise of Liminality

The *context* of the quotidian has dramatically changed in the twenty-first century due to a number of factors, including "globalization" — however that debated concept is understood. The term "hybrid" has been launched by postcolonial thinkers to speak of the bewildering diversity of societies and communities of the third millennium in terms of cultures, nationalities, races, identities, and other markers. Boundary lines are blurred: "The international blurs into the national. 'We' do not quite know who is 'us' and who is 'them.' Neither race nor language can any longer define nationality."[80] The postcolonial theorist Homi K. Bhabha's term "interstitial perspective" speaks of the in-between spaces and borderlands.[81] The Korean American theologian Sang Hyun Lee speaks of the marginality of his own people in terms of "liminality," which refers to "the situation of being in between two or more worlds, and includes the meaning of being located at the periphery or edge of a society."[82] The Vietnamese American Peter C. Phan uses the phrase "to be betwixt and between," that is, "to be neither here nor there, to be neither this thing nor that."[83] The Japanese American Rita Nakashima Brock's preferred expression to describe the in-betweenness of Asian American women is Bhabha's term "interstitial."[84] In Latin American and Hispanic cultures, the term *mestizaje* refers to the mixture of native people and Caucasians, and *mulatez* to the mixture of Caucasians and black people;[85] and so forth. What makes these types of marginalization and liminality particularly challenging is that — unlike,

79. For responses of various churches, including the World Council of Churches, to these issues, see T. Peters, "Playing with Our Evolutionary Future," pp. 498-502.
80. Keller, Nausner, and Rivera, introduction to *Postcolonial Theologies*, p. 1.
81. Bhabha, *The Location of Culture.*
82. S. H. Lee, *From a Liminal Place*, p. x.
83. Phan, "Betwixt and Between," p. 113.
84. Brock, "Interstitial Integrity."
85. For comments, see Isasi-Díaz, *Mujerista Theology,* pp. 64-66.

say, the blatant racism toward blacks in the United States or (former) South Africa — at work here is often an "invisible" racism, rejection, oppression. The "subtle discrimination" may be "invisible, but potentially lethal," like carbon monoxide![86]

The main point is that rather than being an occasion for the celebration of diversity, hybridity usually leads to marginality, which comes in many forms, from social to cultural to economic and beyond. Constructive theology should have something to say on this issue of liberation, not because this is a good and honorable thing to do, but rather because it is theologically funded.[87] These are not new questions for theology, although they are now more urgently formulated. The ancient church in many ways represented hybridity, beginning with the blending of Jewish and Greek-Roman ethnicities and cultures; currently, hybridity features particularly among the Christians in the Global South, who are the majority of believers.[88]

Liminality is not only a hindrance to flourishing and justice. It also has creative possibilities. Following the social anthropologist Victor Turner's theory of social change, Sang Hyun Lee discerns three stages in the process of change toward flourishing: separation, liminal period, and reassimilation. Just consider a typical immigrant or migrant: one is first separated from one's own, the social structure and networks. As a result, one lives in the "no-man's-land," "in-between," but only for the time being; liminality cannot persist forever. Finally, one may be *reincorporated* into a structure, *communitas* (Turner's term), with a new perspective, new identity, new structures. Liminality, hence, contains opportunities, not only threats.[89] Faith's role comes to the fore in that it "is related to identity construction . . . it provides the courage to face the bewildering space of liminality and to do the work of constructing a hybrid identity without relying upon the false security of an essentialized finite principle." Faith "is the unshakeable foundation of one's sense of dignity and self-esteem" in a highly complex and often confusing environment.[90] In the

86. S. H. Lee, *From a Liminal Place*, pp. 14-21, citation (p. 18) from Sue et al., "Racial Microaggressions," p. 72.

87. In *Trinity and Revelation*, chap. 13, I seek to construct a trinitarian theology of hospitality in pursuit of equality, justice, and communion — based on divine hospitality.

88. Keller, Nausner, and Rivera, introduction to *Postcolonial Theologies*, p. 4.

89. S. H. Lee, *From a Liminal Place*, pp. 5-11. Turner, *Ritual Process*, chap. 3 particularly. Turner's theory is based on the nineteenth-century anthropologist Arnold van Gennep's creative work on the theory of rites of passage, among others. For a highly useful, succinct discussion, see La Shure, "What Is Liminality?"

90. S. H. Lee, *From a Liminal Place*, p. 117.

words of the Japanese American thinker Fumitaka Matsuoka, faith makes us willing and confident to experiencing liminality in "holy insecurity."[91]

Churches and other communities should not only tolerate, much less babysit, the liminal groups, but rather let their distinctive critical and constructive prophetic speech instruct and challenge. From a theological perspective, "The good news of the Christian faith for liminal and marginalized Asian Americans [and others] is that the liminal place of marginality is precisely where God is to be found. God chooses the liminal margins of this world as the strategic place to begin God's decisive work of carrying out God's own end in creation. God chooses to work through liminal/marginalized people in order to love and redeem all fallen humanity."[92] Jesus' place of ministry, including the calling of his disciples, from Galilee — the place of liminality of the times[93] — is a concrete manifestation of the divine desire for human flourishing for all. The NT scholar Gerd Theissen's important work in the sociological-cultural ramifications of Christian faith reminds us that, at its best, religion plays a crucial role in culture's helping in the "protest against the principle of selection"[94] that also marginalizes and separates. "Selection" comes to represent everything contrary to the gospel, namely, aggression, sticking only with one's own, abuse of power, and so forth. The opposite is "solidarity." The heart of Christian faith is that the principle of selection is replaced by that of solidarity, which comes to the fore in Christ.[95] The self-*kenosis* in the incarnation is the ultimate assumption of liminality and marginality into the divine life by the triune God.[96]

Overcoming Racism as a Theological Task

As established above, according to current paleontological knowledge, all human races share a common origin. Racial differences are minute and form no basis for ranking people groups.[97] Even the most brilliant Enlightenment

---

91. Matsuoka, *Out of Silence,* p. 62, cited in S. H. Lee, *From a Liminal Place,* p. 118.

92. S. H. Lee, *From a Liminal Place,* p. 35.

93. S. H. Lee, *From a Liminal Place,* chap. 2, citation (p. 44) from Freyne, *Galilee, Jesus, and the Gospels,* p. 54; for "The Way of the Liminal Jesus as the Christ," see Lee, chap. 4.

94. Theissen, *Biblical Faith,* p. 112.

95. Theissen, *Biblical Faith,* p. 87.

96. See further, S. H. Lee, *From a Liminal Place,* pp. 59-61.

97. For the definitive statement, see "The Race Question," UNESCO, July 1950. For an important although debated discussion, see West, *Prophesy Deliverance!*

thinker Immanuel Kant's division of humanity into four races — white, "Negro," "Mongol," and "Hindustani" — that ultimately boils down just to two, namely, whites and Negroes, is filled with not only ignorance of details but also strong prejudices. The white race is the "noble" one, and the skin color of the others, in descending order, so to speak, is explained in relation to that one![98]

Although ethnocentrism — the belief in the supremacy and unique value of one's own group — is an ancient and universal phenomenon, racism is a modern phenomenon. Racism builds on ethnocentrism but also radicalizes it "when the in-group seeks to keep its 'blood' pure."[99] Often this is coupled with violence and harassment. Although racism is more than that, it has everything to do with one's skin color, as too often "color means rejection and humiliation."[100] Racism is a network of effects including "ethnocentrism, religious intolerance, economic expansionism, and the power to suppress effectively those not of one's own group."[101] Furthermore, deeply held assumptions about rationality and intelligence form the fabric of racism.[102] When coupled with colonialism and slavery, as has happened with blacks and the First Nations[103] of America, it means making human beings a commodity.[104] In the vicious apartheid system of South Africa, the process of making persons a commodity and disposable came to its zenith.[105] In South Korea the *minjung* were not only treated as nameless and faceless but also treated as persons without rights and dignity.[106] In India, the Dalit similarly have been the objects of harsh racist and dehumanizing actions.[107] Racial markers form a wide network of assumptions, prejudices, and attitudes: "Spanish-speaking people are characterized as lazy, Asians as untrustworthy, and black people as criminals."[108]

So, whence racism? The African American theologian J. Kameron Carter

98. Kant, "Of the Different Human Races," pp. 8-22.

99. G. Kelsey, *Racism and the Christian Understanding of Man*, p. 20. See further, Garcia, ed., *Race or Ethnicity?*

100. Cone, *The Spirituals and the Blues*, p. 123.

101. J. Evans, *We Have Been Believers*, p. 105.

102. West, *Prophesy Deliverance!* pp. 49, 64.

103. For the less often talked about cruel treatment of the First Nations, see D. Brown, *Bury My Heart at Wounded Knee*.

104. Cone, *The Spirituals and the Blues*, p. 22.

105. See Balasuriya, "World Apartheid."

106. Ahn, "Minjung," pp. 75-78. See also Bretzke, "Minjung Theology and Inculturation."

107. For invaluable insights, see Clarke, Manchala, and Peacock, *Dalit Theology*.

108. J. Evans, *We Have Been Believers*, p. 100. The now classic psychological work is Allport, *Nature of Prejudice*. For the Asian American context, see A. Park, *Racial Conflict and Healing*.

suggests the provocative thesis that behind racism lies not merely the modernist (Kantian-inspired) essentializing of race as a biological-cultural "thing" but also Christian tradition's severing of its links with Jewish faith as a result of which whiteness and allied Western culture were identified with Christianity (and Judaism was relegated to the inferior status of Orientalism). In other words, "modernity's racial imagination has its genesis in the theological problem."[109] In addition to severe sociopolitical implications, Carter argues that at stake is the whole "foundation" of Christian theology, the "inner transformation that theology itself underwent in giving itself over to the discursive enterprise of helping to racially constitute the modern world as we have come to know it."[110] Although it is premature to judge the accuracy — theologically and historically — of Carter's thesis (published in 2008) of "the theological problem of whiteness,"[111] the main point for this conversation is that acts and attitudes such as those of racism are not theologically innocent.

No wonder, then, that too often racism is deeply linked with faith, whether Christian or Muslim or another. Ultimately, it results in making God a custodian of racist attitudes.[112] Even theology is not innocent of racism,[113] although theologians have the mandate to proclaim that "in a racist society, God is never color-blind."[114] More than that, renouncing and trying to overcome racism is not just a good thing, it is the gospel thing to do: "The task of black theology . . . is to analyze the nature of the gospel of Jesus Christ in the light of oppressed blacks so they will see the gospel as inseparable from their humiliated condition, and as bestowing on them the necessary power to break the chains of oppression."[115] The great African American scholar and social activist of a former generation, W. E. B. Du Bois, brought to light American culture's deep dehumanizing tendencies based on race by calling blacks a *ter-*

---

109. Carter, *Race*, p. 4; see also p. 372. For philosophical-theological reasons behind the cruel treatment of the First Nations, see Drinnon, *Facing West*.

110. Carter, *Race*, p. 3.

111. Carter, *Race*, p. 4.

112. Indicative of this tendency, the printed form of the address before the Mississippi Synod of the Presbyterian Church (November 1954) by G. T. Gillespie, "A Christian View of Segregation," circulated in hundreds of thousands among the White Citizen Council advocates (P. Jewett, *Who We Are*, pp. 101-2 n. 4). See further, W. Jones, *Is God a White Racist?*

113. Cone, *Black Theology of Liberation*, p. xiii. The racist-supporting argument based on Gen. 4:15, Cain's "mark," is as far-fetched as it could be. First of all, there is nothing in the text that directly relates the mark to skin pigmentation. Second, the mark is rather an act of mercy by God to protect Cain's life; see P. Jewett, *Who We Are*, p. 110.

114. Cone, *Black Theology of Liberation*, p. 6.

115. Cone, *Black Theology of Liberation*, p. 5.

tium quid, a third kind, as it were, between cattle and (white) people.[116] So far, however, few theologians other than black liberationists such as Cone and Evans have spoken with passion for full equality and liberation.[117]

Although theologically speaking the extreme rhetorical devices such as *"I am Black because God is Black"*[118] are clearly extreme rhetoric (and somewhat counterproductive, being easy targets of criticism), the legacy of black racism in the United States is deplorable.[119] Behind racism are highly problematic assumptions. According to George Kelsey, first, racism is a form of naturalism, that is, "Nature has condemned inferior races and blessed the superior race"; second, racism is a plan of action, whose end is disastrous: "the logic of racism is genocide"; and third, it is philosophy of history in that "the quality of the superior race is the absolute determinant of history and that quality is biological."[120]

As debated as the concept of "white privilege" may be in American culture,[121] it is hardly contested that "[p]eople of African descent in Europe and North America have not been able to address the question of what it means to be human without, first, wrestling with what it means to be black."[122] White skin color in most cases is not even discerned as a color! Hence, we speak of "colored" people when referring to nonwhites. But of course, white is a color! Evans makes the important observation that — ironically — the question of one's skin color was not minded (it was just assumed) before the factor of race was elevated to a normative status in relation to the human being; in preslavery Africa, for example, the question of blackness never arose.[123]

A highly counterproductive tactic for tackling racism is either to make the oppressed the "chosen people" (as happened in some groups of Africans taken to the United States) or to idealize the victims.[124] It also seems to me that defining

116. See J. Evans, *We Have Been Believers,* p. 74; for the now classic essay, see Du Bois, "The Conservation of Races" (1897).

117. For the importance of the "passionate language" of liberation, see Cone, *Black Theology of Liberation,* pp. 17-20. It is significant that the late white Presbyterian theologian Paul K. Jewett devoted no fewer than 30 (out of about 480) pages, in the beginning part of his theological anthropology *(Who We Are),* to "Human Dignity and Racial Prejudice," including a number of autobiographical narratives by the victims.

118. Cone, *Black Theology of Liberation,* p. 75, emphasis in original.

119. Jordan, *The White Man's Burden.*

120. G. Kelsey, *Racism and the Christian Understanding of Man,* pp. 29, 32, 35.

121. See McIntosh, "White Privilege and Male Privilege."

122. J. Evans, *We Have Been Believers,* p. 99.

123. J. Evans, *We Have Been Believers,* p. 99.

124. For a classic philosophical critique of such notions, see B. Russell, "The Superior

blackness merely in terms of being "victims of oppression who realize that the survival of their humanity is bound up with liberation from whiteness"[125] is only one aspect of liberation, albeit an important one in the contemporary American context. First of all, among blacks there are a number of issues to be resolved for life to flourish, particularly those related to sexism between African American men and women.[126] As womanist scholars remind us, "black experience" is not an unnuanced, generic phenomenon; it may be different for *women* than for men.[127] Similarly, the experience of women in different locations is different.[128]

Theology's response to all forms of racism, whether explicit or subtle, is an unwavering no. For the human being having been created in the image of God, racist attitudes toward another person or group is a twofold sin: the perpetrator commits a sin against another human being; and the perpetrator arrogantly denies the permanent value of the Creator's work of humanity. Furthermore, the perpetrator is dividing one united humanity into two classes, those fully human, and others only partially human.[129]

Toward an Anthropology of the Other

Whether it is the experience of liminality of an immigrant and otherwise marginalized person or the oppression due to skin color or "foreign" language, the same violence of colonialism is at work: it is about the subjugation of the other under the power of the dominant group or culture. The postcolonialist critique persistently reminds us that colonialism goes beyond the issues of racial discrimination, economic poverty, and political marginalization, although those are symptoms. Colonialism "encompasses the whole person, especially how she perceives and thinks about herself,"[130] because it is related — on top

---

Virtue of the Oppressed," pp. 58-64; for theological discussion, see J. Evans, *We Have Been Believers,* pp. 107-9.

125. Cone, *Black Theology of Liberation,* p. 7.

126. For harsh critique of black (male) theology's obliviousness to sexism, see J. Grant, "Black Theology and the Black Woman," pp. 418-33. Similarly, some leading Asian women theologians lament the ignorance of the suffering of women in Asian liberation theologies. Kyung, *Struggle to Be the Sun Again.*

127. See Barbara Smith, *The Truth That Never Hurts.*

128. Isasi-Díaz, *Mujerista Theology,* pp. 18-19.

129. For an important Christian response, see "A Theological Challenge to the Persistence of Racism, Caste-Based Discrimination, and Other Exclusionary Practices. Statement from the WCC Conference on Racism Today."

130. Seo, *Critique of Western Theological Anthropology,* p. 1.

of military, economic, and cultural power abuse — to the underlying anthropology of "the other as non-person."[131] What I mean with this concept is simply this: in colonialism one does not honor the otherness of the other but rather imposes one's own identity on the other and suppresses the possibility of the other being a person (or community of persons). (A related tendency in modernist anthropology is setting up humanity against nature.)[132]

Although perhaps a bit overestimated (and lacking needed nuance), the Korean theologian Bo-Myung Seo's thesis that Western modernity's turn to subjectivity and establishment of "self/I" as a means of setting up one's own subjectivity over against the other(s) is the ultimate force of colonialism, is worth serious theological reflection. On the other side, only the articulation of theological anthropology as "anthropology of the other" may save us from continuing perpetuation of the cycle of oppression and violence.[133]

The Jewish philosopher Emmanuel Levinas's "philosophy of the other" is the most massive effort to make space for and affirm the "infinite" otherness of the other. With the term "infinity," Levinas seeks to confront the modernist desire to reduce and eliminate the absolute otherness of the other (within "totality") and underline its boundless nature.[134] The other can thus not be known or made an object. Ultimately, only "face-to-face" encounter can facilitate an encounter in which true "presence" happens.[135] For Levinas, absolute honoring of the other is of course not merely a nice mental gesture; it is philosophy as "first ethics." Truly "facing" the other "puts me in question and obliges me."[136] Building critically on the work of Levinas and others, the late Russian literary critic Mikhail Bakhtin sought to replace the "monologic solipsism" and subjectivism of Western modernity[137] with the "dialogical principle"[138]

---

131. For commentary on such developments in the conquest of America, see Todorov, *Conquest of America.*

132. Seo, *Critique of Western Theological Anthropology,* p. 62,

133. Seo, *Critique of Western Theological Anthropology,* chap. 3 particularly.

134. Levinas, *Totality and Infinity,* pp. 51, 68.

135. "The face is a living presence; it is expression. . . . The face speaks." Levinas, *Totality and Infinity,* p. 66; see also pp. 50-51; for "face's" resistance to be objectified, see pp. 194, 197.

136. Levinas, *Totality and Infinity,* p. 207. For useful reflections on Levinas's implications for theological anthropology, see Seo, *Critique of Western Theological Anthropology,* chap. 6. The Latin American Enrique Dussell, in *Philosophy of Liberation,* similarly utilizes resources from Levinas to construct an anthropology of the other.

137. Recall his oft-quoted statement that "I" has no "alibi in existence." Bakhtin, *Toward a Philosophy of Act,* p. 41. For finding this source, I am indebted to Seo, *Critique of Western Theological Anthropology,* p. 96.

138. See the useful study by Todorov, *Mikhail Bakhtin.*

and honoring of otherness. Bakhtin rightly saw the importance of the other in the Christian tradition. He confessed that in Christ's teaching there was the appearance of an "infinitely deepened I-for-myself — not a cold I-for-myself, but one of boundless kindness toward the other; and I-for-myself that renders full justice to the other as such."[139]

An urgent task for constructive theology, in collaboration with other faiths, is to work out some details of the anthropology of the other. Not unimportant in that reflection is the choice between hospitality or violence.

Violence or Hospitality

Religions and Violence

Even a cursory look at the latest "World Report on Violence and Health" by the World Health Organization is sorrowful reading concerning the pervasiveness of violence against and abuse of people, including children, youth, women, and others of the most vulnerable.[140] In light of these alarming reports, one wonders if sociobiologists are right about "war as humanity's hereditary curse."[141]

Of most concern here is that the history of religions is full of violence.[142] According to Martin Marty, "[t]he collisions of faiths, or the collisions of peoples of faith, are among the most threatening conflicts around the world in the new millennium." This is because people of different faiths frequently divide themselves and others into competitive and suspicious groups of "belongers" and strangers.[143]

Although the link between religion and violence has been extensively studied, few theories on the origins of the link have been offered. The most ambitious — and widely contested and disputed — is Hector Avalos's the-

139. Bakhtin, "Author and Hero," p. 56, cited in Seo, *Critique of Western Theological Anthropology,* p. 96.

140. "World Report on Violence and Health," 2002.

141. E. O. Wilson, *Social Conquest of Earth,* pp. 62-76, 57-61, respectively; see also the classic essay by James, "The Moral Equivalent of War."

142. See Juergensmeyer, *Terror in the Mind of God;* Kimball, *When Religion Becomes Evil;* Nelson-Pallmeyer, *Is Religion Killing Us?* For important discussions of the relation of religion and its rites, particularly sacrifice, to violence, see Vries, *Religion and Violence;* Lefebure, *Revelation, the Religions, and Violence.*

143. Marty, *When Faiths Collide,* pp. 1-4, here p. 1.

sis that it is scarcity of resources, real or perceived, that lies beneath the violence; positing scarcity as a motive for violence is of course a standard sociological, sociobiological, and economic view. What makes Avalos's proposal unique is not only the link with that and religion, but even more, he claims that at times religions have "created new scarce resources," and that propels violence. More exactly, these resources created by religion are miracles, promise of eternal life, healing, communion with spirits, and so forth, in other words, immaterial and "nonreal" (at least empirically considered) "resources." By controlling the scarcity, religion leads to conflict. Hence, religion is not only immoral but also a waste of time.[144] Avalos's theory has a number of problems, however. If religion is but a human projection after Feuerbachian projection theory, Avalos's view may be plausible. If religion has to do with the existence of and relation to God, the Creator of the world, then religion — or its advocates, even priests — has no ownership, let alone privilege of blocking access to the truth, goodness, and beauty it offers. Hence, *theologically*, Avalos's theory is severely handicapped.[145] Furthermore, when speaking of the role of religions in violence, in many (perhaps most) cases it is very difficult to discern what other factors are involved — ethnic, economic, and sociopolitical.

The greatest challenge to all Abrahamic faiths with regard to violence is the concept of holy war. In Judaism,[146] holy war has important limits: war must be carried on as ordered by and meant for the glory of Yahweh; it is not by human force of arms but rather by the power of Yahweh that victory is won; not only are enemies but at times even the people of Yahweh are being defeated by Yahweh, as in exile, and Yahweh at times uses enemies as an asset. Very problematic is the concept of *herem,* total annihilation of enemies and their goods (the Amalekites being the prime example). Jewish tradition does not speak with one voice here: whereas current liberal Jews consider *herem* merely a theological principle (of total devotion to God), religious Zionists apply the principle to Palestinians and other nearby Arabs. Similarly to Christian hermeneutics, mainstream Jewish scholarship considers this a matter of development of revelation in Scripture.[147] In marked difference from the OT,

144. Avalos, *Fighting Words,* pp. 18, 29.

145. For an insightful critique of Avalos from a religious studies perspective, see Wellman, "Introduction," pp. 5-8. Other current theorists of the origins of violence in relation to religion include R. Girard, M. Juergensmeyer, and Scott Appleby. I have responded to them in *Trinity and Revelation,* chap. 12.

146. For details, see Dobkowski, "A Time for War and Time for Peace."

147. Smith and Burr, *Understanding World Religions,* pp. 75-76.

the Talmud by and large supports peace and active peacemaking, without advocating pacifism.[148] In contrast to political Zionism (Theodor Herzl), the *cultural* Zionism represented by Ahad Ha'am (d. 1927) denounces the use of violence against Arabs by Jews and advocates peaceful coexistence in the Holy Land; a similar approach was taken by the philosopher Martin Buber.[149] The unique context for all contemporary Jewish reflections on war and violence is the haunt of the Shoah (Holocaust).[150]

For Islam the key violence-related challenges are not only holy war but also the way *jihad* is interpreted, whether as "the greater *jihad*," a personal struggle over spiritual obstacles and temptations, or as "lesser *jihad*," a call to a holy war.[151] Like the OT, the Qur'an sets out fairly unambiguous rules for just war, including holy war: after seeking spiritual guidance from Allah, war should be resorted to only as the last means; *jihad* should be led by an imam or at least a Muslim leader; the enemies should be given an opportunity to accept Islam first — or if other Abrahamic faith followers, merely Islamic political rule with a special tax and *zakat,* "almsgiving."[152] On either lesser or greater *jihad,* Muslim tradition does not speak with one voice.[153] A number of contemporary reformists from various Muslim locations have spoken for the nonviolent way.[154] Similarly, some revisionist scholars and clergymen have advocated for a pluralistic, tolerant, and democratic Islamic theory of society.[155] The influential international group of Islamic scholars and clergy participating in the Muslim-Christian "A Common Word" project strongly advocated the greater *jihad* as the only accepted form of interpretation, denounced terrorism

148. Gordon and Grob, *Education for Peace,* chap. 3.

149. For details of these and other twentieth-century Jewish progressives, including Etty Hillesum, see M. Ellis, *Toward a Jewish Theology of Liberation.*

150. See Rubenstein and Roth, *Approaches to Auschwitz.*

151. For a highly nuanced discussion, see Hussain, "Confronting Misoislamia"; the neologism "misoislamia" refers to the shift from islamo*phobia* (*phobia,* "fear") to "hatred of Islam" (*miso,* "hatred").

152. Smith and Burr, *Understanding World Religions,* pp. 136-38. The well-known Qur'anic passages (2:90-93, 256) clearly state that no one should be forced to convert to Islam.

153. See "Muslim Scholars Recast Jihadists' Favourite Fatwa"; see also Troll, Reifeld, and Hewer, eds., *We Have Justice in Common.*

154. Khan Abdul Ghaffar Khan of Afghanistan, Gandhi's close associate; Giasuddin Ahmed of Bangladesh; Fatima Mernissi of Morocco; Chandra Muzaffar of Malaysia, among others. For a short discussion with references, see Smith and Burr, *Understanding World Religions,* pp. 141-42.

155. Most well known is Sachedina, *The Islamic Roots of Democratic Pluralism;* for an important theological study, see Winkler, *Contemporary Muslim and Christian Responses to Religious Plurality.*

and violence in the name of *jihad,* and urged interfaith activities. The document begins with these important words:

> Muslims and Christians together make up well over half of the world's population. Without peace and justice between these two religious communities, there can be no meaningful peace in the world. The future of the world depends on peace between Muslims and Christians. The basis for this peace and understanding already exists. It is part of the very foundational principles of both faiths: love of the One God, and love of the neighbour. These principles are found over and over again in the sacred texts of Islam and Christianity.[156]

To an outsider, Hinduism offers a highly complicated case with regard to violence. The topic of *himsā* (harm) has been reflected on since the beginning of the Vedic religion. And currently, *ahimsa* ("noninjury," "nonviolence") is the most well-known trademark of Hindu reformism (although its roots go back to centuries before the common era).[157] As in other traditions, the scriptural texts exhibit a confused approach to violence, both condoning and restricting (at times, even rejecting) it.[158] On the one hand, the Vedic sacrifices (*yajña*) are considered necessary for the establishment and maintenance of the order of the cosmos (Rig Veda 1.162; 10.90). On the other hand, as early as in Chandogya Upanishad (3.16-17; 8.5, 8.15; also Kausitaki Upanishad 2.5), qualms about sacrificial violence were expressed,[159] and even justified violence was regulated.[160] On the other hand, it seems like war is embedded in the Hindu system, as one of the four main castes of people are soldiers. It is the *dharma* of the Kshatriya to carry on with that profession.

Somewhat similarly to Christian tradition, *ahimsa* (nonviolence) does not apply to (just) war (neither to sacrificial cult). Again, as in the Christian Bible, the Bhagavad-Gita does not reconcile into a coherent vision seemingly different notions of violence and its relation to war.[161] Indeed, in its famous

---

156. "The ACW Letter," http://www.acommonword.com/the-acw-document/ (10/16/2013).

157. Pennington, "Striking the Delicate Balance," pp. 24-25.

158. Particularly difficult have been the human sacrifices of the Purushamedha rite, as stipulated in *White [Shukla] Yajurveda,* pp. 30-31.

159. E.g., Bhagavata Purana 7.15.

160. As in "King's Dharma," in the context of necessary royal affairs; *Laws of Manu* 7. I am indebted to Pennington, "Striking the Delicate Balance," p. 26.

161. See Smith and Burr, *Understanding World Religions,* p. 12.

epic (often dramatized in popular films in India), Arjuna consults Krishna, one of the many avatars of Vishnu, about whether he should refrain from fighting in a battle against the group that includes his uncle and other relatives. Arjuna is told he should fight because he is a soldier, and failing to do so would mean failing the *dharma*. Not only that, but Krishna reveals that the soldiers Arjuna kills will not really die — only their physical bodies will die — whereas *atman* will persist. Finally, even if the soldiers escape death today, later they will die according to their divinely set fate.

All the arguments in favor of violence are deeply problematic for Christian tradition. While it knows just war — as much as the details are debated — divinely authorized killing of one's kin seems never fitting under that rubric. Even more importantly, whatever one's particular view of the body-soul relationship, all Christians believe death is simply death. Even if every Christian hopes for the life everlasting, that hope never justifies the killing of another person — or oneself.

A noted spokesperson for peace and nonviolence, Mohandas Gandhi also, curiously, supported the caste system. He sought to reinterpret Gita's support for war and violence in the following way: first, it is a spiritual message concerning the inner struggle of each believer; second, the long and detailed narration of war and violence of the *Mahabharata* epic at large (of which the Gita is a part) shows the futility of war as a means of establishing peace; and third, in critique of Arjuna's attitude, which was not opposed to killing others but rather one's own kin, we should be able to transcend selfish favoritism and apply *ahimsa* to all.[162]

Not only is the popular picture of Buddhism as a peaceful, inward, world-rejecting, and meditation-focused religion unnuanced,[163] but Buddhist history, against common assumptions, knows the use of violence,[164] and even some of its key concepts such as karma and rebirth have been used to legitimate violence; the former in terms of justifying all kinds of diseases and ills as "judgment," and the latter as a way of helping ease an evil person's karmic effects by ending life.[165] Consider the main historical figure, Asoka, the great ruler of India (third century B.C.E.), who was converted to Buddhism and became its enthusiastic advocate as part of his military conquests. Like Constantine, he was active in helping organize basic elements of religious insti-

---

162. Summarized by Smith and Burr, *Understanding World Religions*, pp. 13-14. See the introduction to Gandhi, *The Bhagavad Gita according to Gandhi*, pp. 6-12.

163. For useful comments, see Victoria, "Teaching Buddhism and Violence," pp. 74-76.

164. Keyes, "Monks, Guns, and Peace," p. 145.

165. On Gautama's doing so, see Victoria, "Teaching Buddhism and Violence," pp. 77-87.

tutions and teachings.[166] As beneficial as the "Two Wheels of the Dhamma" governmental system (that is, lay ruler as the equally important disseminator of Buddha's teaching along with *sangha*) has been in Theravada lands, from the beginning it has also given rise to conflicts, wars, and violence.[167] In the contemporary world, Buddhist nationalisms and fundamentalisms are well known among scholars.[168] The Sinhalese Buddhist nationalism in Sri Lanka at the turn of the twentieth century was deeply nationalistic and carried out "holy war" against Tamil Hindus, Tamil Muslims, and other non-Buddhists. (In 1959 Bandaranaike was assassinated by a Buddhist monk.) While Cambodia's tragedy is even more complicated than that of Sri Lanka, recent research shows that "the ideology of the Khmer Rouge has unequivocal roots in a version of reformist Buddhism."[169] In other words, against common suspicions, even the followers of the Lotus flower have resorted to violence. It is also well known that even His Holiness the Dalai Lama, earlier in his career, gave approval to the use of violence against the true enemies of the people.[170] The difference, however, from the Abrahamic faiths is that in Buddhism, even in Mahayana, there is no equivalent to the conception of the wrath of Allah or Yahweh, the Father of Jesus Christ,[171] which is a particular challenge to all Abrahamic faiths.

A Theological Defeat of Violence

Milbank is bold enough to go beyond the conventional wisdom and argue strongly that even secularism and late modernity cannot save us from violence. On the contrary, associating secularism with paganism, he contends that paganism is ultimately about the worship of sheer power and fosters violence. Furthermore, secularism/paganism accepts the basic forces of the world as brute givens of fate, fortune, and chance. The self-interest of nation-states, the

166. See the important source, *The Edicts of Aśoka*.

167. Reynolds, "The Two Wheels of Dhamma."

168. The extent to which these "modern" (to Buddhism) developments stem from colonialism is a widely debated issue. On another note: in this discussion, I am not engaging the complex question of how to explain fundamentalism as a pan-religious phenomenon transcending particular boundaries (if, indeed, that is the case).

169. Keyes, "Monks, Guns, and Peace," p. 156, with reference to his "Communist Revolution and the Buddhist Past in Cambodia."

170. Victoria, "Teaching Buddhism and Violence," pp. 82-83.

171. See Keyes, "Monks, Guns, and Peace," p. 160.

individual's drive for survival, the impersonal working of market forces — all these are like the will of the gods in pre-Christian Greek myth.[172] Furthermore, Radical Orthodoxy is convinced that the diversity and plurality of different traditions and viewpoints in postmodernity lead necessarily to competition, fights, and ultimately violence — already anticipated by Nietzsche much before postmodernity.[173]

So, what is the theological response to violence? In *Christ and Reconciliation* (chap. 12) I respond in some detail to the typical charges against the violent nature of Christian theology of reconciliation, particularly the suffering and death of the Messiah, as well as the underlying logic of sacrifice (in critical dialogue with Girard). Furthermore, the suspicion of violence linked to the classical affirmation of the uniqueness of Christ is engaged therein. In *Trinity and Revelation* (chap. 13), a detailed response is offered to the widely held assumption that by definition belief in God/gods and the consideration of certain scriptures as authoritative revelation necessarily entail violence and "tribalism." While the myth of a God-violence link is by and large that — *myth* — all religious traditions should continue careful work toward leaving behind all notions of unjustified and illegitimate violence and strive toward "living the hospitality of God."[174] Finally, *Community and Hope* will carefully consider the potential violence embedded in the Christian eschatological vision, defeating the common assumption that God's righteous judgment of evil and bringing about the victorious kingdom of shalom necessarily entail use of illegitimate violence. I will not repeat these lengthy discussions here, but rather discuss in a very focused and limited way the theological parameters for considering violence in the context of the doctrine of creation and anthropology and how that may be defeated by hospitality.

All ideologies based on the ontology of violence should be defeated. The representations of such ontologies in living faiths similarly should be subjected to criticism. The French thinker René Girard's theory of religion is a philosophical version of an ontology of violence, against its own intent. Since I engage it elsewhere, suffice it to say here that because of its fixation on a certain type of interpretation of religion's link with the scapegoat (sacrifice), it is unable to ultimately defeat violence (other than by naively assuming that

---

172. Shakespeare, *Radical Orthodoxy,* Kindle #312-15. Highly interesting is the thesis that triumph and force, even in the religious ritual, are the long-standing ingredients of Rome's identity. See Stroup, "Making Memory."

173. Milbank, *Theology and Social Theory,* p. 5; see also "Postmodern Critical Augustinianism" pp. 227-37.

174. Heading taken from Richard, *Living the Hospitality of God.*

by exposing the cycle of violence due to the scapegoat mechanism, people suddenly refrain from violence!). On the contrary, the biblical creation story is free from violence, and hence, the Christian vision of the world is that of peace and hospitality. The Creator God is not fighting other deities or powers but rather, out of sheer love, in his power he brings about the world. That is a marked difference from the ancient Near Eastern myths, as well as some traditions of Asian religions.[175]

The way later Greek philosophy sought to redeem the inherent violence was to resort to dualism. "In place of a conflict of equals, or near equals, Parmenides generated a dualism of higher and lower forms of being. For him reality was not flux, but by definition that which did not change at all. The real is the totally unchanging." While ingenious, this solution is totally unacceptable to Christian tradition.[176] Christian tradition's way of combating violence is based on the covenant love. The faithfulness of the covenant God will be manifested in the providence and reconciliation of the world and creatures. As Radical Orthodox thinkers rightly argue, the Christian trinitarian vision in its celebration of rather than opposition to multiplicity/diversity in unity is far superior in establishing peace and reconciliation over the secular ontology of immanence, which is nothing less than "ontology of violence," inherently "conflictual."[177]

Christian theology of creation based on the divine pronouncement of the goodness of creation (Gen. 1:31) refuses to ontologize violence, war, and conflict. Diversified unity, loving and accepting embrace of the other, and peace are ontologically founded in the triune God. Unlike in some religious traditions and in secularism, as Milbank notes, a host of traditional Christian thinkers from Dionysius the Areopagite to Augustine to Scotus Erigena exhibit theologically founded attitudes of peace.[178] In this light, the late British feminist Grace Jantzen's charges of Christianity's (as part of Western culture's) enduring fascination with death and violence with its glorifying of violence, loss of beauty, and fear of the body and sexuality are totally misplaced.[179] While it is of course true, unfortunately, that at times Christian tradition has been dominated by males, violent acts have been committed in the name of religion, beauty has not always been appreciated the way reason has been,

---

175. Ricoeur, *Symbolism of Evil*, pp. 182-83, cited in Gunton, *The Triune Creator*, p. 26. See also Noegel, "Dismemberment, Creation, and Ritual."

176. Gunton, *The Triune Creator*, p. 27.

177. Milbank, *Theology and Social Theory*, pp. 376, 296 (quote in the latter).

178. For a short statement, see McGrath, *ScT* 2:105-6.

179. Jantzen, *Foundations of Violence*, pp. vii, 36.

and the body and sexuality have been marginalized, it is also true that those dispositions are neither unique to Christian tradition nor a necessary part of its inner logic.[180]

Acting on the basis of hospitality rather than violence, Christians should therefore be guided by the spirit of openness, inclusion, and welcoming the other. We can either "embrace," receive the other with outstretched arms that also, if need be, "struggle against deception, injustice and violence," or we can "exclude," go with these evil dispositions and acts, and be unwilling to make space for the other.[181] The will to embrace is based on and derives from the self-donation of the triune God that comes to its zenith on the cross. Embrace means making space, turning to the other, seeking strangers, and joining in pursuit of equality, justice, and fairness. There are hopeful signs among churches and in the ecumenical world of constructing hospitable, peaceful theologies and combating violence in all its forms.[182] While they are still limited, their importance should not be missed.

What about capital punishment? Any consideration of the justification of putting to an end the life of another person must happen within the context of relating the human person to the Creator and affirming the inviolable dignity. What are the *theological* ramifications and conditions? What are the implications of the widely agreed position according to which the one (perpetrator) who takes away another human person's (right to) life, renounces the right from oneself as well? The late theologian Paul Jewett frames the issue in a useful way. Concerning the conclusion that once the murderer has taken away another person's life and thus put himself or herself under the judgment of death, he says: "(i) That such judgment is just, we grant; (ii) that it is the only judgment that is just, we doubt; (iii) that it can be justly implemented in a sinful society, we deny."[183] According to Genesis 9:6, any human person who has killed another who is created in the image of God, has pronounced judgment on his or her life. This is the justification for (i). (What is not justified is the abuse of that principle in Christian tradition when, for example, refusal to be baptized resulted in capital punishment.)[184] But that (i) is not the only way to deal with human shedding of blood is manifested in other biblical ways of dealing with the issue like placing the mark on Cain, the murderer of his brother, for his protection

180. For an important argument of the primacy of beauty in Christian cosmology, see Garcia-Rivera, *Garden of God.*

181. Volf, *Exclusion and Embrace,* p. 30.

182. See "Nurturing Peace, Overcoming Violence."

183. P. Jewett, *Who We Are,* p. 123 (numbers added).

184. See P. Jewett, *Who We Are,* p. 124.

(Gen. 4:8-16). These kinds of biblical perspectives affirm (ii). Regarding (iii), there is hardly debate, not only in terms of wrong persons having been executed but also with regard to motives, circumstances, fairness, and so forth. Furthermore, justifying capital punishment primarily to protect members of society hardly convinces, as nowadays there are extremely safe ways of containing the perpetrator. On top of everything, "why may we not suppose that life imprisonment without parole is an 'exemplary vengeance' to inflict on those who are condemned for murder? . . . [T]o have this freedom-in-community forever taken away by incarceration is surely a heavy price to pay for one's offense."[185] In sum: while the possibility of capital punishment in principle cannot be ruled out within the framework of Christian (and perhaps Jewish) tradition,[186] many weighty reasons speak for its severe limitation or abolishment.

Yet another arena of human flourishing has to do with work, economics, and finances — particularly in the globalized world. This is the last topic for this chapter.

Work, Economy, and Land

Toward a Theology of Work

Volf wonders why theologians have devoted so many pages to matters of the Eucharist — which takes place on Sunday — and so few pages to the topic of work, which fills our lives between Monday and Saturday.[187] Not that theological reflection on work is totally missing — consider the papal encyclical *Laborem Exercens* by Pope John Paul II,[188] or the important ecumenical study *Christianity and Economics in the Post–Cold War Era: The Oxford Declaration and Beyond* (1994),[189] or the recent Pentecostal initiative *Flourishing Churches*

185. P. Jewett, *Who We Are*, p. 127.

186. At the same time, theologians should sharply oppose any attempts by so-called Reconstructionist (a.k.a. dominion theology, theonomy) movements, mainly located in the United States, that seek to reestablish the literal following of Mosaic Law as the basis of contemporary "Christian" states. As an example, see Rushdoony, *Institutes of Biblical Law*. For a useful up-to-date discussion, see "Christian Reconstructionism, Dominionism, Theonomy, Dominion Theology, etc."

187. Volf, *Work in the Spirit*, p. 69.

188. "On Human Work" (1981) building on the 1891 encyclical by Pope Leo XIII, *Rerum Novarum*.

189. Based on the 1987 Oxford Conference that led to "The Oxford Declaration on Christian Faith and Economics."

and Communities with its focus on work and economics[190] — but that by and large work has not been deemed a topic worthy of biblical-theological reflection. Yet a number of factors in the beginning of the third millennium speak to the theological significance of work: unemployment and loss of a sense of meaningfulness in employment; the fatigue of many who are overworked; a sense of alienation; and effects of work on one's family life and other aspects of social life.[191] Add to these viewpoints the effects of globalization and global markets; the growing gulf between the haves and the have-nots; increasing migration for economic (and sociopolitical) reasons; and new forms of slavery, including sexual slavery.

Why do we work? Is it merely an effect of the Fall — and a sad one, for that matter (Gen. 3:17b-19)? Or, as Adam Smith believed, are humans made for work to advance "the happiness of all"?[192] Or, perhaps, as the Reformers taught us, is work a Christian vocation? One of the lasting contributions to the understanding of work by Christian theology is its realistic (Gen. 3) but appreciative and reaffirming standpoint; unlike the depreciating attitude prevalent in the ancient world, early theology denied any disgrace to work and made it respectable (often referring to Adam's example in paradise; Gen. 2:15). On the basis of biblical injunctions (1 Thess. 4:11; 2 Thess. 3:10), the necessity of working was affirmed. Often work was connected with the doctrine of sanctification with a belief that new life in Christ would manifest its fruit in everyday labor and lifestyle. That, of course, funded ethical pursuit as well as good practices and virtues.[193] The Reformers' understanding of work as vocation, albeit in need of clarification and correction, further contributed to a proper view of work.[194]

Volf further suggests both eschatological and pneumatological resources as assets to a comprehensive theology of work. If work is related to the divine purpose of creation that points to new creation, then work gains its ultimate meaning from God's future; work is not only a matter of the present world. Essential to Christian vision "is the anticipatory experience of God's new creation and a hope of its future consummation."[195] To secure the lasting value of

190. Self, *Flourishing Churches and Communities.*

191. For an inclusive discussion of "crisis of work," see Volf, *Work in the Spirit,* pp. 35-45.

192. A. Smith, *Theory of Moral Sentiments,* pp. 153-54, here p. 154.

193. Volf, *Work in the Spirit,* pp. 69-74.

194. For an explanation and reinterpretation of work as vocation, see Volf, *Work in the Spirit,* pp. 105-10. While I endorse Volf's critique and revision, I do not see the dangers such as indifference toward alienation or its inapplicability to modern/contemporary work life as integral to the Reformers' theology of vocation, as Volf does.

195. Volf, *Work in the Spirit,* 79; see also pp. 76-87.

work with a view to God's eschatological future, Volf wishes to leave behind the traditional *annihilation mundi* view, total annihilation of the world "by fire" and subsequent re-creation of new creation *ex nihilo* (2 Pet. 3:10), and instead opts for a *transformatio mundi* vision of eschatological transformation (Rom. 8:19-25). Only then will "the results of the cumulative work of human beings have intrinsic value and gain ultimate significance, for they are related to the eschatological new creation. . . . [T]he noble products of human ingenuity . . . will be cleansed from impurity, perfected, and transfigured to become a part of God's new creation."[196] Human work thus is a form of cooperation with the Creator (Gen. 1:26-27). While I fully endorse the principle of continuity, I also see it important to offer a more nuanced negotiation between the present and the future, judgment and cleansing. I discuss this in detail in my work on eschatology *(Hope and Community)*, and argue that both of the biblical intuitions, "annihilation" and "transformation," belong to the hope for the coming of God's new creation.

In view of the new creation, work is energized and gifted by the Spirit of God, as the Spirit is not only the principle of life but also an eschatological Spirit (Rom. 8:23). Although the category of charisma has not played any role outside its ecclesiastical usage, we can also link the charismatic energies with work. The NT knows various kinds of charisms, both extraordinary and ordinary (Rom. 12:6-8; 1 Cor. 12; 1 Pet. 4:11), and the OT gives examples of charismatically endowed handicraft work (Exod. 35:2-3; 1 Chron. 28:11-12) or execution of leadership (Judg. 3:10; 1 Sam. 16:13).[197] This is all relevant for theology of work.

This modest attempt to outline briefly a theology of work is not necessitated in the least by a desire to idealize work — to make it a new form of the "opiate" (Marx). It is rather to include this essential human theme under the theological lens. At the same time, theologians must be reminded of the harsh, complicated, and tiring circumstances and conditions under which work is often done — along with the rest of our lives in the quotidian. Globalization and the global economic system with all its diverse effects are a key influence.

The "Economy of Grace": A Theological Consideration of Global Economics

In the midst of the bewildering complexity of current issues and influences relating to work, two observations are in order. On the one hand, we have

196. Volf, *Work in the Spirit*, pp. 88-102, here p. 91.
197. Volf, *Work in the Spirit*, pp. 102-19.

to confess that to its detriment at large, Christian theology has tended to be silent about the sinful nature of evil structures that either support or at least tolerate economic evils. It has been left to "liberationists" to diagnose and critique economic and political structures[198] that make masses of the poor and require the underprivileged to live on "less than two dollars a day."[199] On the other hand, every critic of the injustice and cruelties of global economics and markets has to be reminded that "[t]he modern market system undoubtedly should be extolled as the most successful human instrument in modernity. Even beyond its effect in the astonishing growth in living standards, its most winsome and weighty claim is that it coordinates and governs masses of human beings peacefully, without command or coercion."[200]

What is globalization and what are its effects? This is a notoriously complex topic that not only economists, sociologists, and politicians but also some theologians seek a proper understanding of.[201] It can be seen as either a positive or a negative force, and it certainly has both sides to it.[202] An essential part of "hypermodern" globalization has to do with "culture industries," perhaps the most subtle and most powerful influence worldwide. These cultural industries are about consumption, backed by massive advertising and marketing.[203] While a number of globalization theorists speak of the consequences of global economy in terms of "calculations of risk"[204] (of medical, social, ecological, and other side effects), theologians should concentrate on effects on human persons.[205]

Unlike the agrarian societies of the past, currently we only have a "risk society,"[206] in which "desire to live one's own life has become the guiding impulse for people in the Western world. . . . The ethic of individual self-interest and self-fulfilment have been given free rein in economic globalization and

---

198. See the Mexican Catholic Juan Alfaro's "God Protests and Liberates the Poor," pp. 27-35; the Argentinian Methodist Aldo Etchegoyen's "Theology of Sin and Structures of Oppression," pp. 156-66; the Cuban American Methodist Justo L. González, "The Alienation of Alienation."

199. Van Til, *Less Than Two Dollars a Day.*

200. Meeks, "The Economy of Grace," p. 197. So also Lindblom, *The Market System.*

201. Bauman, *Globalization.* A highly useful discussion is Muthiah, *Priesthood of All Believers,* chap. 4.

202. See Giddens, *Runaway World,* p. 81; see also pp. xvi, 19; so also Goudzwaard, *Globalization and the Kingdom of God,* p. 20.

203. Budde, *The (Magic) Kingdom of God,* pp. 34-37.

204. See Hutton and Giddens, eds., *On the Edge;* see also the pamphlet (originally lectures) by Giddens, *The Consequences of Modernity.*

205. See Botman, "Covenantal Anthropology," p. 77.

206. Beck, *Risk Society.*

have become the most powerful currents affecting human beings."[207] Ironically, rather than belonging, globalization has fostered "social atomism."[208]

Globalization goes far back in history. Think of the massive occupation of land and resources in the majority world by the Western powers beginning at the end of the eighteenth century, and also of colonialism's ideological, cultural, and epistemological violence and oppression. Even the terminology used, such as "expansion" or "inferior" or "authority," betrays this blatant violence.[209] Lest it be mistakenly assumed that this only happened from the West to the "rest" (as dominant as that was), the same hegemonic abuse of power was in play, for example, in the subjugation of Korea by Japan in the early twentieth century[210] and in the expansion of China over some of its neighboring territories. Though old, colonialism is alive and well — adopting also new forms such as "McDonaldization."[211]

What could theology say to global economics? Beginning from a minimum set of conditions for an economic system that is fair, the following three conditions probably gain wide acceptance: freedom and dignity of individuals; satisfaction of the basic needs of all people, with special reference to the weak; and protection and flourishing of nature.[212] These conditions are based on creation theology's stewardship principle, the inviolability of each human person as the image of God, and communion of human persons with the rest of creation, as well as the greatest commandment. They do not of course dictate details of economic systems or planning — nor is theology supposed to be in that role in a truly pluralistic society — but they guide the thinking and work of Christians in charge. The economic theorist Adam Smith's advocacy of the division of labor primarily on the basis of pursuit of self-interest and self-love, although probably true as an empirical statement, cannot be endorsed uncritically on the basis of gospel values.[213]

Theology should also critique the hegemony of desires. We are beings of desires — unlimited desires! Modern economic theory exploits that basic human orientation as it claims that in the midst of limited resources, everybody has to compete. Theology says that true good is given only by God and

207. Botman, "Covenantal Anthropology," pp. 77-78, here p. 77, engaging the ideas of Waters, *Globalization*.

208. G. Ward, *Cities of God*, pp. 52-77; see p. 75.

209. Said, *Culture and Imperialism*, pp. 6-8.

210. For commentary, see Seo, *Critique of Western Theological Anthropology*, pp. 72-73.

211. Ritzer, *The McDonaldization of Society*.

212. Volf, *Work in the Spirit*, pp. 15-17.

213. For a succinct exposition of Smith theory, see Volf, *Work in the Spirit*, pp. 48-55, esp. 53.

that desire is no god.[214] Theology speaks of "Sabbath economics: the theology of enough."[215] That will also help us negotiate the "paradox of abundance" (Walter Brueggemann): for us humans, security in abundance depends upon the wisdom of knowing that we are dependent upon God and that in our well-being, we rely on the health of the created order.[216] This is a contingent, dependent security, creaturely existence in the quotidian. Rather than glorifying abundance, theology should take a lesson from Jesus, who practiced "downward economic mobility": "Apparently unemployed, he seems to have been sustained by the generosity of others (Luke 8:3), homeless, having 'nowhere to lay his head' (Matt. 8:20; par. Luke 9:58)." Not only that, but he consistently associated with the marginalized, the liminal, the outcasts.[217]

A Christian response to economic matters can be named an "economy of grace" or an "economy of God."[218] Despite the many similarities between the market system and Christian ethics such as the valuation of work and industry, personal and communal responsibility, demand for fairness, and so forth, there are a number of "bones beneath the flesh"[219] such as competition, greed, and maximization of foreign profit. Let us look at some of the contrasts and what might be a proper theological response. While both view the human being as a creature of desire, "Christian anthropology imagines the end of the human being as praise of God; the market system views the end of the human being as maximized utility." The market calls for unending pursuit of the satisfaction of needs. In the Christian vision, true "enjoyment" (Augustine's *fruit*) can only be had in God and "in participation in the abundance of God's communion through God's grace."[220] The vicious circle of the market system's constant creation of "artificial scarcity,"[221] creating constantly new needs and products to fulfill it, coupled with massive ubiquitous advertising, can be broken only by desiring God and the moderate fulfillments that God the Creator graciously grants to creatures.

214. Shakespeare (*Radical Orthodoxy,* Kindle #114), expositing the critique of modern economics of Stephen Long, *Divine Economy.*

215. G. Browning, "Sabbath Reflections 5"; see also, J. Taylor, *Enough Is Enough;* Myers, *Biblical Vision of Sabbath Economics.*

216. Brueggemann, "Liturgy of Abundance."

217. D. Kelsey, *Eccentric Existence,* 1:629.

218. I am following here Meeks, "The Economy of Grace." For a more detailed discussion, see his *God the Economist.*

219. Lindblom, *The Market System,* pp. 52-60 and passim.

220. Meeks, "The Economy of Grace," p. 205.

221. See Meeks, *God the Economist,* pp. 17-19; and Long, *Divine Economy,* pp. 242-45 particularly.

Whereas the market system depends exclusively on the logic of exchange (currently handled with the help of money), the Christian vision (while not of course naively denying the great value of a fair and moderate system of commodity exchange) also knows the logic of gift giving, sharing, even altruistically, echoing the triune God's free gift-giving.[222] Instead of an anonymous logic of exchange, flourishing life requires personal sharing and giving of gifts that foster interdependence, friendship, and mutuality rather than debt, competition, and distance.

Whereas Christian vision supports freedom and liberty rightly understood, the market system's indiscriminate worship of individual property rights and conceiving of freedom primarily in terms of freedom of choice with regard to commodities that best serve one's individual needs must be subject to theological critique. Instead, hospitality and concern for other human beings' and communities' well-being and flourishing are true Christian values. Instead of *exclusive* property rights, the Christian vision funds *inclusive* rights in which all we have is acknowledged as a gift from God, of which we are to be good and responsible stewards in order to find fulfillment as God's servants and in service to others. Ultimately, in Christian vision, "God's grace is the being of the human; the human is the gift of God."[223]

The triune God has called a people to live in the world to reflect the values of justice, equality, and sharing. Faithfully acknowledging their debt to the Creator, the church is supposed to stand on the side of those who are oppressed and marginalized. Not only to feed the hungry and offer a cup of water to the thirsty but also to stand up against injustice as did the OT prophets, and at times Jesus of Nazareth. The discussion of ecclesiology will look at the implications in some detail as part of the church's existence and mission in the world.

An alarming effect of globalization and global markets has to do with the movement of people against their will. Migration, displacement, and corollary challenges also call for theological reflection.

Migration, Displacement, and Slavery

One phenomenon in the contemporary postmodern milieu is the return of the nomadic lifestyle. Displacement, including landlessness, is of course not a new phenomenon. As the Korean *minjung* theologian Byung Mu Ahn reminds us,

222. Meeks, "The Economy of Grace," p. 207.
223. Meeks, "The Economy of Grace," p. 210.

many in NT times who were named *ho ochlos*[224] were migrants and landless. The nature of migrancy now, however, is different from the past in that now all are nomads, just differently.[225] "Never has the urgency of the geographical dimension of human existence been greater."[226] Bauman has famously made a distinction between "tourists" and "vagabonds." Whereas the former travel because they can, the latter are on the move because they don't have a choice. Vagabonds are useless to global markets as they don't make good consumers; they are the outcasts, the marginalized, but they form the majority of the world, and are growing rapidly.[227] This stark opposition makes a sociologist of globalization speak of the "wasted lives"[228] of people of the "liquid times" who are "living in an age of uncertainty."[229] Most recently, this famed social theorist has come to speak even of "collateral damage" in reference to "social inequalities in a global age."[230] Most ironically, "Globalization . . . often seems to replace the old dictatorships of national elites with the new dictatorships of international finance."[231] Intensified migration touches a significant number of people: "one in nine lives in a country where international migrants comprise one-tenth or more of the total population."[232]

In the "new world" where whole masses are "disposable people,"[233] against hopes, slavery has not been eradicated. What is astonishing and horrific about the contemporary forms of slavery is that the price paid is dramatically lower than it used to be. In the past the price to enslave a person was about $40,000 in today's money, but the average now is less than $100![234]

224. The Gospel of Mark is the locus for use of this term, which simply means "the people," in contrast to the technical term. See Ahn, "Jesus and the People (Minjung)."

225. A fine theological study of migration both historical and contemporary is Cruz, "Between Identity and Security."

226. Menn, "Land, Displacement, and Hope," p. 161.

227. Bauman, *Globalization,* chap. 4. Regarding implications for helping vagabonds, see Hugman, Moosa-Mitha, and Moya, "Towards a Borderless Social Work"; N. Cooper, "Tourist or Vagabond."

228. Bauman, *Wasted Lives: Modernity and Its Outcasts.*

229. Bauman, *Liquid Times: Living in an Age of Uncertainty.*

230. Bauman, *Collateral Damage.* See also Luttwak, *Turo-Capitalism.*

231. Siglitz, *Globalization and Its Discontents,* p. 7, cited in Meeks, "The Economy of Grace," p. 199.

232. Heyer, "Reframing Displacement and Membership," p. 188; see further, Terrazas, "Migration and Development."

233. Bales, *Disposable People.*

234. Freetheslaves.net, FAQ's, http://www.freetheslaves.net/Document.Doc?id=37 (10/16/2013).

Particularly disconcerting is the lot of child migrants.[235] Part of the wider slavery problem is the widening labor and sex trafficking, which includes also children and the underaged and a high number of female victims.[236]

The victims of (economically and politically) forced migration and all forms of slavery and trafficking not only lack human value but also lack even minimal living conditions — and almost all of them are landless. For the contemporary Global North mind-set, landlessness may not sound like a problem because even land is made a commodity. However, land is a deeply personal, communal, cultural, and religious issue. It has to do with identity, belonging, self-worth — and God! Brueggemann notes that "land is a central, if not *the central theme of* biblical faith."[237] The OT pays particularly deep and wide attention to the issues of land and placement. Promising is the growing networking and collaboration of adherents of religions in the Alliance of Religions and Conservation, which also includes a number of First Nations people from different locations.[238]

Why should Christian theology be concerned about migration, displacement, trafficking, slavery? Consider this fact alone: one-half of the over 200 million migrants in the world are Christians,[239] and a number of them suffer from other forms of dehumanization. Of course, that is not the only reason, but that alone should suffice. Christian theology's continuing upholding of the dignity and equality of all human beings created in the image of God loses credibility if the most vulnerable and marginalized are not on our radar screen. There is also an opportunity for interfaith collaboration. Although Christian theology has a long way to go, much promise can be found in the emerging ecumenical field of migrant theologies.[240] Along with theological reflection, churches and ecumenical organizations are also making a new effort in "practising hospitality in an era of new forms of migration."[241]

235. See further, "Immigrant Children's Legal Program," on the U.S. Committee for Refugees and Immigrants Web site: http://www.refugees.org/our-work/child-migrants/ (10/16/2013).

236. "Human Trafficking Victims," on the U.S. Committee for Refugees and Immigrants Web site: http://www.refugees.org/our-work/child-migrants/human-trafficking-victims-1.html (10/16/2013).

237. Brueggemann, *The Land*, p. 3, emphasis in original.

238. For work, resources, and links, see the Projects Web pages of the Alliance of Religions and Conservation: http://www.arcworld.org/projects.asp?projectID=369 (10/16/2013).

239. Reported in *Christian Century*, April 4, 2012, pp. 15-16.

240. For the recent state-of-the-art review, see Campese, "Irruption of Migrants."

241. "Practising Hospitality in an Era of New Forms of Migration." For an important work in progress, see "God of Life, Accompany Us on Our Journey towards a Life with Dignity, Peace, and Justice"; useful are also Jacques, *The Stranger within Your Gates;* Kismaric and Shawcross, *Forced Out;* Mayotte, *Disposable People?* and Ferris, *Beyond Borders.*

Epilogue: Continuing a Hospitable Dialogical Conversation in "Global" Theology

Writing theologians typically have their favorite topics and loci of doctrinal theology with which they feel most comfortable — even if in teaching we usually have to cover areas that are more foreign and of which we think we have only superficial knowledge. Ironically, with regard to the topics of this monograph, for many years neither creation nor theological anthropology has been a theme I felt competent to handle, let alone suggest a constructive proposal about. Indeed, I feel much resonance in the admission of a theological giant, none other than Barth:

> In taking up the doctrine of creation I have entered a sphere in which I feel much less confident and sure. If I were not obliged to do so in the course of my general exposition of Church dogmatics, I should probably not have given myself so soon to a detailed treatment of this particular material. I know many others to whom, in view of their greater gifts and interest and qualifications, I would willingly have entrusted this part of the task if only I could have had more confidence in their presuppositions.[1]

I was particularly concerned about my lack of training in the natural sciences since (unlike Barth) I felt that any kind of credible and useful theological account of the created reality has to engage deeply and robustly the insights of the sciences. For a humanistically educated person, learning even the basic concepts, let alone the way of thinking of contemporary natural sci-

1. Barth, *CD* III/1, preface.

ences, is almost an insurmountable challenge. And if one gains some limited expertise in sciences, it is of utmost importance for the theologian to avoid hiding behind technical jargon (let alone mathematical formulae) that only hides the layperson's lack of a grasp of the topics. Although the way a non-scientist theologian writes about cosmology, biology, and, say, physics may sound redundant and elementary to the professionals in the science guild, it is a virtue to the theologian to be able to explain to other humanist colleagues the concepts in a clear and unambiguous way. Whether I have succeeded in that enterprise is of course left for the reader to judge.

Not only the sciences but also living faith traditions belong to the sphere of dialogical partners in the current constructive project. While I have felt much more comfortable in the area of religious studies than in sciences, gaining accurate and reliable knowledge of each faith tradition's specific understandings of cosmology, myths of origins, and nature of nature, including human nature, is another utterly complicated task. For comparative theology to advance the dialogical understanding among different traditions, the scholar should make every effort to avoid generalizations, superficial comparison, and folk psychology assumptions. Just take the obvious example (discussed above) of the relation of Asiatic and Abrahamic traditions to environmental concerns — a topic that in itself is interrelated with a number of corollary themes such as the conception of time and history, the nature of reality at large, and the relationship between One and Many. Only a careful scrutiny of determinative scriptural and theologico-historical teachings in each faith may yield some accurate insight — provided that (alas!) the theologian is competent to choose the "right" texts and "normative" interpretations, as well as negotiate their differences.

The dialogical task, however, does not end with an accurate description of views, as necessary and important as that is in itself. *Comparative* theology also seeks to discern similarities and differences, as well as — notwithstanding the fierce opposition from the Enlightenment-based "first-generation pluralisms"[2] that assume a common essence of all religions and reject their right for true otherness and distinctiveness — to advance the cause of one's own truth understanding. While it is goes without saying that such a project can only happen constructively in a hospitable, mutually honoring spirit, a dialogue is interesting and useful only when there is something to dialogue about! Moltmann insightfully argues that only such partners "merit dialogue" who have "arrived at a firm standpoint in their own religion, and who enter into

2. See *Trinity and Revelation*, chap. 14.

dialogue with the resulting self-confidence." Otherwise one "falls victim to the relativism of the multicultural society . . . [and] does not merit dialogue."[3] Such a truly dialogical way of doing theology is much more challenging than the pluralist tendency to subsume the other under modernity's "universal" world explanation that interrupts true identities. Our own convictions are also being clarified and liabilities exposed. I often remind my students of the programmatic statement of Clooney:

> If we are attentive to the diversity around us, near us, we must deny ourselves the easy confidences that keep the other at a distance. But, as believers, we must also be able to defend the relevance of the faith of our community, deepening our commitments even alongside other faiths that are flourishing nearby. We need to learn from other religious possibilities, without slipping into relativist generalizations. The tension between open-mindedness and faith, diversity and traditional commitment, is a defining feature of our era, and neither secular society nor religious authorities can make simple choices before us.[4]

All this said and done, I wish to join in the acknowledgment and wish of Pannenberg, in his preface to volume 1 of his systematics, which begins with a profound discussion of creation and anthropology: "A systematic comparison between the competing conceptions of the world religions is certainly a task that will more fully occupy systematic theology in the future. Perhaps in this field a particularly important contribution might be made to Christian theology by the Third World churches."[5] Now that almost two-thirds of all Christians reside in the Global South, we who write in Euro-American locations can only wish to be taught, challenged, and corrected by our African, Asian, and Latin American colleagues.

The trinitarian unfolding of a constructive theological vision continues in volume 4 of our series with the focus on the work of the Spirit. Whereas volume 1 was entitled *Christ and Reconciliation,* volume 2, *Trinity and Revelation,* and the current volume *Creation and Humanity,* in volume 4 the Spirit's role in the cosmos, creation, religions, history, sociopolitical arena, and Christian life (salvation and integrity of persons and communities) will be the center. Trini-

---

3. Moltmann, *Experiences in Theology,* pp. 18-19.
4. Clooney, *Comparative Theology,* p. 7.
5. Pannenberg, *ST* 1:xiii.

tarian theology does not mean that one first speaks of, say, the Son, thereafter the Father, and finally the Spirit. Rather, it means that one speaks of the unified yet diverse works of the triune God by highlighting the distinctive features of the work of one particular member of the Trinity. Thus, to speak of Christology (vol. 1) is to speak of pneumatological Christology and christological pneumatology; or, to speak of the Father's creative work (vol. 3) is to speak of Christ's agency that makes "room" for the distinction between God and the world and the Spirit's life-giving and uniting work. And so forth. In the final volume of this five-part series, the work of the triune God in the life and mission of the Christian community — the people of God, body of Christ, temple of the Spirit — is placed in the economy of salvation from creation to reconciliation to final eschatological consummation. The church does not "own" the kingdom, the righteous rule of God, but rather participates in its coming, which also includes hope and final resolution for the whole of creation and each of its creatures. The religious vision of Christianity is both vast and "universal."

Bibliography

Abdalla, Mohamad. "Ibn Khaldūn on the Fate of Islamic Science after the 11th Century." In *ISHCP*, 3:29-38.

Abdulaziz, Daftari. "Mulla Sadra and the Mind-Body Problem: A Critical Assessment of Sadra's Approach to the Dichotomy of Soul and Spirit." Ph.D. diss., Durham University, 2010. http://etheses.dur.ac.uk/506/ (4/11/2013).

Abe, Masao. "Kenotic God and Dynamic Sunyata." In *Divine Emptiness and Historical Fullness: A Buddhist-Jewish-Christian Conversation with Masao Abe,* edited by Christopher Ives, pp. 25-90. Valley Forge, Pa.: Trinity, 1995.

Abram, David. *Becoming Animal: An Earthly Cosmology.* New York: Vintage, 2010.

Acar, Rahim. "Creation: Avicenna's Metaphysical Account." In *CGA,* pp. 77-90.

Adams, Marilyn McCord. "Is the Existence of God a 'Hard' Fact?" *Philosophical Review* 76, no. 4 (1967): 492-503.

Adiswarananda, Swami. "Hinduism." Part 2. Ramakrishna-Vivekananda Center of New York, 1996. http://www.ramakrishna.org/activities/message/message15.htm (2/24/2013).

Afrasiabi, Kaveh L. "Toward an Islamic Ecotheology." In *I&E,* pp. 281-96.

Aggañña Sutta: On Knowledge of Beginnings. In *The Long Discourses of the Buddha: A Translation of Digha Nikaya,* translated by Maurice Walshe. Boston: Wisdom Publications, 1987. http://www.columbia.edu/itc/religion/f2001/edit/docs/aggannasutta.pdf.

Ahn, Byung Mu. "Jesus and the People (Minjung)." In *Asian Faces of Jesus,* edited by R. S. Sugirtharajah, pp. 163-72. Maryknoll, N.Y.: Orbis, 1993.

―――. "Minjung: Suffering in Korea." In *The Lord of Life: Theological Explorations of the Theme "Jesus Christ — the Life of the World,"* edited by William H. Lazareth. Geneva: WCC, 1983.

Al-Attas, S. M. N. *Islam, Secularism, and the Philosophy of the Future.* London: Mansell Publishing, 1985.

Alexander, Richard D. *How Did Humans Evolve? Reflections on the Uniquely Unique Species.* Museum of Zoology, University of Michigan, Special Publications, no. 1. Ann Arbor: University of Michigan Press, 1990.

Alexander, Samuel. *Space, Time, and Deity.* 2 vols. Toronto: Macmillan, 1920.

Alfaro, Juan. *Christian Liberation and Sin.* San Antonio: Mexican American Cultural Center, 1975.

————. "God Protests and Liberates the Poor." In *Option for the Poor: Challenge to the Rich Countries,* edited by Virgil Elizondo and Leonardo Boff. Edinburgh: T. & T. Clark, 1986.

Allen, Prudence. "Integral Sex Complementarity and the Theology of Communion." *Communio* 17, no. 4 (Winter 1990): 523-44.

Allman, J. M., et al. "Intuition and Autism: A Possible Role for Von Economo Neurons." *Trends in Cognitive Sciences* 9, no. 8 (2005): 367-73.

Allport, Gordon W. *The Nature of Prejudice.* Cambridge, Mass.: Addison-Wesley, 1954.

Altekar, A. S. *The Position of Women in Hindu Traditions: From Prehistoric Times to the Present Day.* 2nd ed. Delhi: Motilal Banarsidass, 2005.

Ambrose. *Paradise.* In *The Fathers of the Church: A New Translation,* translated by John J. Savage, vol. 42. New York: Fathers of the Church, 1961. http://archive.org/stream/fathersofthechur027571mbp#page/n5/mode/2up (3/7/2013).

Ames, William L. "Emptiness and Quantum Theory." In *B&S,* pp. 285-302.

Amin, Adnan Z. "Preface to *Islam and Ecology.*" In *I&E,* pp. xxxiii-xxxv.

Ammar, Nawal. "Ecological Justice and Human Rights for Women in Islam." In *I&E,* pp. 377-89.

Anderson, Ray. *On Being Human.* Pasadena, Calif.: Fuller Seminary Press, 1982.

Anderson, V. Elving. "A Genetic View of Human Nature." In *WHS,* pp. 49-72.

Anguttara Nikaya. In *The Book of the Gradual Sayings (Anguttara Nik) or More-Numbered-Suttas,* edited and translated by F. L. Woodward. Oxford: Pali Text Society, 1992.

Anscombe, G. E. M. "Causality and Determination" [1971]. In *Metaphysics and the Philosophy of Mind: The Collected Philosophical Papers of G. E. M. Anscombe,* vol. 2. Minneapolis: University of Minnesota Press, 1981.

Apology of the Augsburg Confession. By Melanchthon. In *The Book of Concord: The Confessions of the Evangelical Lutheran Church,* translated and edited by Theodore G. Tappert. Philadelphia: Fortress, 1959.

Aquinas, Thomas. *Summa contra Gentiles.* Edited by Joseph Kenny, O.P. Various translators. New York: Hanover House, 1955-1957. http://dhspriory.org/thomas/ContraGentiles.htm.

Arbib, Michael A. "Towards a Neuroscience of the Person." In *NP,* pp. 77-100.

Aristotle. *On the Soul.* Translated by J. A. Smith. The Internet Classics Archive. http://classics.mit.edu//Aristotle/soul.html.

Armstrong, D. M. *A Materialist Theory of Mind.* Rev. ed. London: Routledge, 1993 [1968].

Astuti, Rita. "Are We All Natural Dualists? A Cognitive Development Approach; The Malinowski Memorial Lecture 2000." *Journal of the Royal Anthropological Institute* 7, no. 3 (2001): 429-47.

Asvaghosa. *Açvaghosha's Discourse on the Awakening of Faith in the Mahâyâna.* Translated by Teitaro Suzuki (1900). www.sacred-texts.com.

Atran, Scott. *In Gods We Trust: The Evolutionary Landscape of Religion.* New York: Oxford University Press, 2002.

Atran, Scott, and Ara Norenzayan. "Religion's Evolutionary Landscape: Counterintuition, Commitment, Compassion, Communion." *Behavioral and Brain Sciences* 27 (2004): 713-70.

Augsburg Confession. In *The Book of Concord: The Confessions of the Evangelical Lutheran Church,* translated and edited by Theodore G. Tappert. Philadelphia: Fortress, 1959. Latin version.

Augustine. *The Happy Life.* In *The Fathers of the Church,* edited by Ludwig Schopp. New York: CIMA, 1948.

———. *The Literal Meaning of Genesis.* Translated and annotated by John Hammond Taylor, S.J. Edited by Johannes Quasten, Walter J. Burghardt, and Thomas Comerford Lawler. 2 vols. Ancient Christian Writers 41-42. New York: Paulist, 1982.

———. *On Order [De Ordine].* Translated and introduced by Silvano Borruso. South Bend, Ind.: St. Augustine Press, 2007.

———. *On the Free Choice of Will.* Translated by Thomas Williams. Indianapolis: Hackett, 1993.

———. *Retractions.* In *The Fathers of the Church: Saint Augustine; The Retractions,* translated by Sister Mary Inez Bogan. Washington, D.C.: Catholic University of America Press, 1968.

Aurobindo (Ghose), Sri. *The Life Divine.* In *Complete Works of Sri Aurobindo,* vols. 21, 22. Pondicherry, India: Sri Aurobindo Ashram Press, 2005. http://www.aurobindo.ru/workings/sa/18-19/the_life_divine_21-22_e.pdf.

Avalos, Hector. *Fighting Words: The Origins of Religious Violence.* Amherst, N.Y.: Prometheus, 2005.

Avicenna's Psychology [De Anima; The Treatise on the Soul]. Translated and edited by Fazlur Rahman. Oxford: Oxford University Press, 1952.

Aviezer, Nathan. "The Anthropic Principle: What Is It and Why Is It Meaningful to the Believing Jew?" *Jewish Action* (Spring 5759/1999): n.p. http://www.ou.org/publications/ja/5759spring/anthropic.pdf.

Ayala, Francisco J. "Darwin's Devolution: Design without Designer." In *EMB,* pp. 101-16.

———. *Darwin's Gift: To Science and Religion.* Washington, D.C.: Joseph Henry Press, 2007.

———. "The Evolution of Life: An Overview." In *EMB,* pp. 21-57.

———. "Human Nature: One Evolutionist's View." In *WHS,* pp. 31-48.

Ayoub, Mahmoud M. "Creation or Evolution? The Reception of Darwinism in Modern Arab Thought." In *SRPW,* chap. 11.

Badiner, Allan Hunt, ed. *Dharma Gaia: A Harvest of Essays in Buddhism and Ecology.* Berkeley, Calif.: Parallax Press, 1990.

Baharuddin, Azizan. "Guardians of the Environment." In *Humanity: Texts and Contexts; Christian and Muslim Perspectives,* edited by Michael Ipgrave and David Marshal, pp. 41-49. Washington, D.C.: Georgetown University Press, 2011.

————. "The Significance of Ṣūfi-Empirical Principle in the Natural Theology and Discourse on Science in Islam." In *ISHCP,* 1:223-42.

Bakar, Osman. *Tawhid and Science: Essays on the History and Philosophy of Islamic Science.* Kuala Lumpur, Malaysia: Secretariat for Islamic Philosophy and Science, 1991.

Baker, Lynne Rudder. *Persons and Bodies: A Constitution View.* Cambridge: Cambridge University Press, 2000.

Baker, Mark C., and Stewart Goetz. Introduction to *The Soul Hypothesis: Investigations into the Existence of the Soul,* edited by Mark C. Baker and Stewart Goetz, pp. 1-25. New York: Continuum, 2011.

————, eds. *The Soul Hypothesis: Investigations into the Existence of the Soul.* New York: Continuum, 2011.

Baker-Fletcher, Garth Kasimu. *Xodus: An African American Male Journey.* Minneapolis: Fortress, 1996.

Bakhtin, Mikhail. "Author and Hero in Aesthetic Activity." In *Art and Answerability: Early Philosophical Essays,* translated by Kenneth Brostrom. Austin: University of Texas Press, 1990.

————. *Toward a Philosophy of Act.* Translated by Vadim Liapunov. Austin: University of Texas Press, 1993.

Balaguer, M. *Free Will as an Open Scientific Problem.* Cambridge: MIT Press, 2010.

Balaram, P. "Editorial: Creation, Evolution and Intelligent Design." *Current Science* (India) 86, no. 9 (May 10, 2004): 1191-92.

Balasuriya, Tissa. "World Apartheid: Our Greatest Structural Evil." In *Spiritual Questions for the Twenty-First Century: Essays in Honor of Joan D. Chittister,* edited by Mary Hembrow Snyder, chap. 20. Maryknoll, N.Y.: Orbis, 2001.

Bales, Kevin. *Disposable People: New Slavery in the Global Economy.* 2nd ed. Berkeley: University of California Press, 2004.

Balthasar, Hans Urs von. *Mysterium Paschale: The Mystery of Easter.* Translated, with introduction, by Aidan Nichols, O.P. Edinburgh: T. & T. Clark, 1990.

Banerjee, Konika, and Paul Bloom. "Would Tarzan Believe in God? Conditions for the Emergence of Religious Belief." *Trends in Cognitive Sciences* 17, no. 1 (2013): 7-8.

Barbour, Ian. *Nature, Human Nature, and God.* Minneapolis: Fortress, 2002.

————. "Neuroscience, Artificial Intelligence, and Human Nature: Theological and Philosophical Reflections." In *NP,* pp. 249-80.

————. *Religion in the Age of Science.* New York: Harper and Row, 1990.

Barnard, A. "On the Relationship between Technique and Dehumanization." In *Advancing Technology, Caring, and Nursing,* edited by R. C. Locsin, pp. 96-105. Westport, Conn.: Auburn House, 2001.

Barr, Stephen M. *Modern Physics and Ancient Faith.* Notre Dame, Ind.: University of Notre Dame Press, 2003.

Barrett, Justin L. *Born Believers: The Science of Children's Religious Belief.* New York: Free Press, 2011.

————. *Cognitive Science, Religion, and Theology.* Philadelphia: Templeton Press, 2011.

————. "Cognitive Science of Religion: What Is It and Why Is It?" *Religion Compass* 1, no. 6 (2007): 768-86.

————. "Counterfactuality in Counterintuitive Religious Concepts." *Brain and Behavioral Sciences* 27 (2004): 731-32.

————. "Theological Correctness: Cognitive Constraints and the Study of Religion." *Method and Theory in the Study of Religion* 11, no. 4 (1999): 325-39.

————. *Why Would Anyone Believe in God?* Walnut Creek, Calif.: AltaMira Press, 2004.

Barrett, Justin L., and E. T. Lawson. "Ritual Intuitions: Cognitive Contributions to Judgments of Ritual Efficacy." *Journal of Cognition and Culture* 1, no. 2 (2001): 183-201.

Barrett, William. *Death of the Soul: From Descartes to the Computer.* New York: Anchor, 1986.

Barrow, John D. *New Theories of Everything.* Oxford: Oxford University Press, 2007.

Barrow, John D., and Frank J. Tipler. *The Anthropic Cosmological Principle.* Oxford: Oxford University Press, 1986.

Barth, Karl. *The Theology of Schleiermacher.* Translated by Geoffrey W. Bromiley. Grand Rapids: Eerdmans, 1982 [1924].

Barthes, Roland. *Mythologies.* London: Paladin, 1973.

Bartholomew, David J. *God of Chance.* London: SCM, 1984.

Batchelor, Martine, and Kerry Brown, eds. *Buddhism and Ecology.* London: Cassell, 1992.

Bauckham, Richard. *The Bible and Ecology: Rediscovering the Community of Creation.* London: Darton, Longman and Todd; Waco, Tex.: Baylor University Press, 2010.

————. "Jesus and Animals I: What Did He Teach?" In *AOA,* chap. 4.

————. "Jesus and Animals II: What Did He Practise?" In *AOA,* chap. 5.

————. *Living with Other Creatures: Green Exegesis and Theology.* Waco, Tex.: Baylor University Press, 2011.

Bauman, Zygmunt. *Collateral Damage: Social Inequalities in a Global Age.* Cambridge: Polity, 2011.

————. *Globalization: The Human Consequences.* New York: Columbia University Press, 1998.

————. *Liquid Times: Living in an Age of Uncertainty.* Cambridge: Polity, 2007.

————. *Postmodern Ethics.* Oxford: Blackwell, 1993.

————. *Wasted Lives: Modernity and Its Outcasts.* Cambridge: Polity, 2004.

Bayer, Oswald. *Martin Luther's Theology: A Contemporary Interpretation.* Translated by Thomas H. Trapp. Grand Rapids: Eerdmans, 2008.

Bayne, Tim. "Libet and the Case for Free Will Skepticism." In *Free Will and Modern Science,* edited by Richard Swinburne, pp. 25-46. Oxford: Oxford University Press, 2011.

Beauvoir, Simone de. *The Second Sex.* New York: Vintage, 1989.

Beck, Ulrich. *Risk Society: Towards a New Modernity.* Translated by Mark Ritter. London: Sage Publications, 1992.

Beckwith, C. A. "Soul and Spirit, Biblical Conceptions." In *The New Schaff-Herzog Encyclopedia of Religious Knowledge,* edited by Samuel Macauley Jackson, 11:12-14. New York and London: Funk and Wagnalls, 1910.

Bellah, Robert N., Richard Madsen, William M. Sullivan, Ann Swidler, and Steven M. Tipton. *Habits of the Heart: Individualism and Commitment in American Life.* Berkeley: University of California Press, 1985.

Belser, Julia Watts. "Returning to Flesh: A Jewish Reflection on Feminist Disability Theology." *Journal of Feminist Studies in Religion* 26, no. 2 (Fall 2010): 127-32.

Bereshit [*Rabbah* or *Genesis Rabbah*]. In *Midrash Rabbah*, vol. 1, *Genesis in Two Volumes*, translated by Rabbi H. Freedman and Maurice Simon. 3rd impr. London: Soncino Press, 1961 [1939].

Bergmann, Sigurd. *Creation Set Free: The Spirit as Liberator of Nature.* Grand Rapids: Eerdmans, 2005.

Bering, Jesse M. "The Folk Psychology of Souls." *Behavioral and Brain Sciences* 29 (2006): 453-98.

Berkhof, Hendrikus. *The Doctrine of the Holy Spirit.* Atlanta: John Knox, 1964.

Berkouwer, G. C. *Man: The Image of God.* Grand Rapids: Eerdmans, 1962.

Betcher, Sharon V. "Becoming Flesh of My Flesh: Feminist and Disability Theologies on the Edge of Posthumanist Discourse." *Journal of Feminist Studies in Religion* 26, no. 2 (Fall 2010): 107-18.

Bevans, Stephen B., and Roger P. Schroder. *Constants in Context: A Theology for Mission for Today.* Maryknoll, N.Y.: Orbis, 2004.

Bhabha, Homi K. *The Location of Culture.* London and New York: Routledge, 1994.

Bharati, Dayanand. *Understanding Hinduism.* New Delhi: Munshiram Manoharlal Publishers, 2005.

Bhikshu, Subhadra [Friedrich Zimmermann]. *A Buddhist Catechism: An Introduction to the Teaching of the Buddha Gotama.* Translated by C. T. Strauss. Rev. ed. Kandy, Sri Lanka: Buddhist Publication Society, 1980 [orig. 1890]. http://www.bps.lk/olib/wh/wh152.pdf.

Bickerton, Derek. "Did Syntax Trigger the Human Revolution?" In *Rethinking the Human Revolution: New Behavioural and Biological Perspectives on the Origin and Dispersal of Modern Humans,* edited by Paul Mellars, Katie Boyle, Ofer Bar-Yosef, and Chris Stringer, pp. 99-105. Cambridge: Short Run Press, 2007.

————. *Language and Human Behavior.* Seattle: University of Washington Press, 1995.

Bickle, John. "Multiple Realizability." In *The Stanford Encyclopedia of Philosophy.* Spring 2013 edition, edited by Edward N. Zalta. http://plato.stanford.edu/archives/spr2013/entries/multiple-realizability/ (6/10/2013).

Birch, Charles, and John Cobb. *The Liberation of Life: From the Cell to the Community.* Denton, Tex.: Environmental Ethics Books, 1990.

Bird, P. A. "'Male and Female He Created Them': Gen. 1:27b in the Context of the Priestly Account of Creation." *Harvard Theological Review* 74, no. 2 (1981): 129-59.

Bishop, Robert C. "Chaos, Indeterminism, and Free Will." In *OHFW,* pp. 84-100.

Bishop, Robert C., and Harald Atmanspacher. "The Causal Closure of Physics and Free Will." In *OHFW,* pp. 101-11.

Blackmore, Susan. *The Meme Machines.* Oxford: Oxford University Press, 1999.

Blanchard, Tsvi. "Can Judaism Make Environmental Policy? Sacred and Secular Language in Jewish Ecological Discourse." In *J&E,* pp. 423-48.

Bloesch, Donald G. *Jesus Christ: Savior and Lord.* Downers Grove, Ill.: InterVarsity, 1997.

Blond, Phillip. "Perception: From Modern Painting to the Vision in Christ." In *Radical*

Orthodoxy: A New Theology, edited by John Milbank, Catherine Pickstock, and Graham Ward. London: Routledge, 1999.

Bloom, Paul. *Descartes' Baby: How the Science of Child Development Explains What Makes Us Human.* New York: Basic Books, 2004.

———. "Religion Is Natural." *Developmental Science* 10, no. 1 (2007): 147-51.

Bodhi, Ven. Bhikkhu. "Arahants, Bodhisattvas, and Buddhas." *Access to Insight,* August 2010. http://www.accesstoinsight.org/lib/authors/bodhi/arahantsbodhisattvas.html (4/5/2013).

Boersma, Hans. *Violence, Hospitality, and the Cross: Reappropriating the Atonement Tradition.* Grand Rapids: Baker Academic, 2006.

Boff, Leonardo. *Holy Trinity, Perfect Community.* Maryknoll, N.Y.: Orbis, 2000.

———. *Liberating Grace.* Translated by John Drury. Maryknoll, N.Y.: Orbis, 1988.

Boisvert, Kate Grayson. *Religion and the Physical Sciences.* Westport, Conn., and London: Greenwood, 2008.

Bonhoeffer, Dietrich. *Creation and Fall: A Theological Exposition of Genesis 1–3.* Translated by Douglas Stephen Bax. Edited by John W. de Gruchy. Minneapolis: Fortress, 1997 [1937].

———. *Letters and Papers from Prison.* Edited by Eberhard Bethge. Translated by Reginald Fuller and others. Rev. ed. New York: Macmillan, 1967.

Borgmann, Albert. *Power Failure: Christianity in the Culture of Technology.* London: SPCK, 1997.

Børresen, Kari Elisabeth. "God's Image, Man's Image? Patristic Interpretation of Gen. 1,27 and 1 Cor. 11,7." In *The Image of God: Gender Models in Judeo-Christian Tradition,* edited by Kari Elisabeth Børresen, pp. 187-209. Minneapolis: Fortress, 1991.

Botman, H. Russell. "Covenantal Anthropology: Integrating Three Contemporary Discourses of Human Dignity." In *GHD,* pp. 72-86.

Böwering, G. *The Mystical Vision of Existence in Classical Islam.* Berlin and New York: Walter de Gruyter, 1979.

Boyer, Pascal. *Religion Explained: The Evolutionary Origins of Religious Thought.* New York: Basic Books, 2001.

Bratsiotis, N. P. *"Basar."* In *Theological Dictionary of the Old Testament,* edited by G. Johannes Botterweck and Helmer Ringgren, 2:313-32. Grand Rapids: Eerdmans, 1975.

Bremmer, Jan N. *The Early Greek Concept of the Soul.* Princeton: Princeton University Press, 1983.

Brennan, William. *Dehumanizing the Vulnerable: When Word Games Take Lives.* Chicago: Loyola University Press, 1995.

Bretzke, James T., S.J. "Minjung Theology and Inculturation in the Context of the History of Christianity in Korea." *East Asian Pastoral Review* 28 (1991): 108-30. http://www.usfca.edu/fac-staff/bretzkesj/MinjungContext.pdf (3/6/2013).

Broadie, Alexander. "Scotistic Metaphysics and Creation *Ex Nihilo.*" In *CGA,* pp. 53-64.

Brock, Rita Nakashima. "Interstitial Integrity: Reflections Toward an Asian-American Woman's Theology." In *Introduction to Christian Theology: Contemporary North American Perspectives,* edited by Roger A. Badham. Louisville: Westminster John Knox, 1998.

————. *Journeys by Heart: A Christology of Erotic Power.* New York: Crossroad, 1988.

Brothers, Leslie A. *Friday's Footprints: How Society Shapes the Human Mind.* New York: Oxford University Press, 1997.

————. "A Neuroscientific Perspective on Human Sociality." In *NP,* pp. 67-74.

Brown, Dee. *Bury My Heart at Wounded Knee.* New York: Holt, Rinehart and Winston, 1971.

Brown, Kerry, ed. *The Essential Teachings of Hinduism: Daily Readings from the Sacred Text.* London: Rider, 1988.

Brown, Kyle S., Curtis W. Marean, Zenobia Jacobs, Benjamin J. Schoville, et al. "An Early and Enduring Advanced Technology Originating 71,000 Years Ago in South Africa." *Nature* 491 (November 7, 2012): 590-93.

Brown, Warren S. "The Brain, Religion, and Baseball: Comments on the Potential for a Neurology of Religious Experience." In *Where God and Science Meet: How Brain and Evolutionary Studies Alter Our Understanding of Religion,* edited by Patrick McNamara, 2:229-44. Westport, Conn.: Praeger, 2006.

————. "Cognitive Contributions to Soul." In *WHS,* pp. 199-25.

————. "Conclusion: Reconciling Scientific and Biblical Portraits of Human Nature." In *WHS,* pp. 213-28.

————. "Nonreductive Physicalism and Soul: Finding Resonance between Theology and Neuroscience." *American Behavioral Scientist* 45, no. 12 (August 2002): 1812-21.

Browning, Don S. *A Fundamental Practical Theology.* Minneapolis: Fortress, 1991.

————. "Human Dignity, Human Complexity, and Human Goods." In *GHD,* pp. 299-316.

Browning, Bishop George. "Sabbath Reflections 5: Capitalism and Inequity versus a Gospel Mandate." Anglican Communion Environmental Network, 2012. http://acen .anglicancommunion.org/resources/docs/Sabbath%20Study%205.pdf (8/14/2013).

Brueggemann, Walter. *The Land: Place as Gift, Promise, and Challenge in Biblical Faith.* Overtures to Biblical Theology 1. Philadelphia: Fortress, 1977.

————. "The Liturgy of Abundance, the Myth of Scarcity." http://www.religion-online .org/showarticle.asp?title=533 (3/12/2013).

Brunner, Emil. *The Christian Doctrine of Creation and Redemption.* Vol. 2 of *Dogmatics.* Translated by Olive Wyon. Philadelphia: Westminster, 1952.

Bucaille, Maurice. *The Bible, the Qu'ran, and Science: The Holy Scriptures Examined in the Light of Modern Knowledge.* Translated by Alastair D. Pannell. 7th rev. ed. New York: Tahrike Tarsile Qur'an, 2003. http://ia700504.us.archive.org/18/items/ TheBibletheQuranScienceByDr.mauriceBucaille/TheBibletheQuranScienceByDr .mauriceBucaille.pdf.

Buckley, Michael J. *At the Origins of Modern Atheism.* New Haven: Yale University Press, 1987.

Budde, Michael L. *The (Magic) Kingdom of God: Christianity and Global Culture Industries.* Boulder, Colo.: Westview Press, 1997.

Buddhagosa. *Visuddhimagga, The Path of Purification: The Classic Manual of Buddhist Doctrine and Meditation.* Translated by Bikkhu Nanamoli. Kandy, Sri Lanka: Buddhist Publication Society, 2011. http://www.accesstoinsight.org/lib/authors/ nanamoli/PathofPurification2011.pdf.

Bulgakov, Sergius. *The Comforter.* Translated by Boris Jakim. Grand Rapids: Eerdmans, 2004.

Bultmann, Rudolf. "New Testament and Mythology." In *Kerygma and Myth,* edited by Hans Werner Bartsch, translated by Reginald H. Fuller. London: SPCK, 1953.

———. *Theology of the New Testament.* Translated by Kendrick Grobel. Vol. 1. New York: Charles Scribner's Sons, 1951.

Burns, Charlene. "'Soul-Less' Christianity and the Buddhist Empirical Self: Buddhist-Christian Convergence?" *Buddhist-Christian Studies* 23 (2003): 87-100.

Burns, Jeffrey M., and Russell H. Swerdlow. "Right Orbitofrontal Tumor with Pedophilia Symptom and Constructional Apraxia Sign." *Archives of Neurology* 60, no. 3 (2003): 437-40.

Burrell, David B. "Freedom and Creation in the Abrahamic Traditions." *International Philosophical Quarterly* 40 (2000): 161-71.

Butler, Judith. *Gender Trouble: Feminism and the Subversion of Identity.* New York: Routledge, 1990.

Cabezón, José Ignacio. "Buddhism and Science: On the Nature of the Dialogue." In *B&S,* pp. 35-68.

Cahill, Lisa Sowle. *Between the Sexes: Foundations for a Christian Ethics of Sexuality.* Philadelphia: Fortress, 1985.

———. *Sex, Gender, and Christian Ethics.* Cambridge: Cambridge University Press, 1998.

Cairns, David. *The Image of God in Man.* London: SCM, 1953.

Call, Josep, and Michael Tomasello. "Does the Chimpanzee Have a Theory of Mind? 30 Years Later." *Trends in Cognitive Science* 12, no. 5 (2008): 187-92.

Callicott, J. Baird, and Roger T. Ames, eds. *Nature in Asian Traditions of Thought: Essays in Environmental Philosophy.* Albany: State University of New York Press, 1989.

Calvin, John. *Commentaries on the Epistles of Paul to the Galatians and Ephesians.* Translated by William Pringle. www.ccel.org. 2005.

———. *Commentaries on the Epistle of Paul to the Hebrews.* Translated by John Owen. www.ccel.org. 2005.

———. *Commentary on Psalms 93–119.* In *Calvin's Commentaries: Psalms 93–119,* vol. 4, translated by James Anderson. Grand Rapids: Christian Classics Ethereal Library. http://www.ccel.org. n.d.

———. *Commentary on the Epistle of Paul the Apostle to the Romans.* http://www.ccel .org.

Cambridge Companion to the "Origin of Species." Edited by Michael Ruse and Robert J. Richards. Cambridge: Cambridge University Press, 2009.

Campese, Gioacchino, C.S. "The Irruption of Migrants: Theology of Migration in the 21st Century." *Theological Studies* 73 (2012): 3-32.

Cantor, Geoffrey, and Marc Swetlitz, eds. *Jewish Tradition and the Challenge of Darwinism.* Chicago: University of Chicago Press, 2006.

Carman, John B. *Majesty and Meekness: A Comparative Study of Contrast and Harmony in the Concept of God.* Grand Rapids: Eerdmans, 1994.

Carr, Anne E. *Transforming Grace: Christian Tradition and Women's Experience.* San Francisco: Harper and Row, 1988.

Carroll, Sean B. *Endless Forms Most Beautiful: The New Science of Evo-devo and the Making of the Animal Kingdom*. New York: Norton, 2005.

Carroll, William E. "Aquinas on Creation and the Metaphysical Foundations of Science." *Sapientia* 54 (1999): 69-91.

Carruthers, Peter. *The Architecture of the Mind: Massive Modularity and the Flexibility of Thought*. Oxford: Oxford University Press, 2006.

Carter, J. Kameron. *Race: A Theological Account*. Oxford: Oxford University Press, 2008.

Cartmill, Matt, and Fred H. Smith. *The Human Lineage*. Hoboken, N.J.: Wiley-Blackwell, 1989.

Cartwright, N. *The Dappled World: A Study of the Boundaries of Science*. Cambridge: Cambridge University Press, 1999.

———. *How the Laws of Physics Lie*. Oxford: Oxford University Press, 1983.

Cary, Phillip. *Augustine's Invention of the Inner Self: The Legacy of a Christian Platonist*. Oxford: Oxford University Press, 2000.

Cela-Conde, Camilo J. "The Hominid Evolutionary Journey: A Summary." In *EMB*, pp. 59-78.

Celesia, Gastone G. "Visual Perception and Awareness: A Modular System." *Journal of Psychophysiology* 24, no. 2 (2010): 62-67.

Center for Islam and Science. http://www.cis-ca.org/.

Chalmers, David J. *The Conscious Mind: In Search of a Fundamental Theory*. New York: Oxford University Press, 1996.

———. "Facing Up to the Problem of Consciousness." *Journal of Consciousness Studies* 2, no. 3 (1995): 200-219. http://consc.net/papers/facing.html (1/24/2013).

Chandngarm, Saeng. *Arriyasatsee* [*The Four Noble Truths*]. Bangkok: Sangsan Books, 2001.

Chapple, Christopher. "Asceticism and the Environment: Jainism, Buddhism, and Yoga." *Cross Currents* 57, no. 4 (2008): 514-25.

Charter of the United Nations. June 26, 1945. Preamble, http://www.un.org/en/documents/charter/preamble.shtml (5/22/2013).

Chatterjee, Susmita. "Acharya Jagadish Chandra Bose: Looking beyond the Idiom." In *Science, Spirituality, and the Modernization of India*, edited by Makarand Paranjape, chap. 8, pp. 3-14. Anthem South Asian Studies. London: Anthem Press, 2008.

Chela-Flores, Julian. "The Phenomenon of the Eukaryotic Cells." In *EMB*, pp. 79-98.

Chenu, M. D. *Nature, Man, and Society in the Twelfth Century: Essays on New Theological Perspectives in the Latin West*. Chicago: University of Chicago Press, 1968.

Chia, Raymond Y. "Quantum Nonlocalities: Experimental Evidence." In *QM*, pp. 17-39.

Chishti, Saadia Khawar Khan. "*Fitra*: An Islamic Model for Humans and the Environment." In *I&E*, pp. 67-82.

Chittick, William C. "The Anthropocosmic Vision in Islamic Thought." In *GLC*, chap. 5, pp. 125-52.

Choudhury, Masudul Alam. "The 'Tawhidi' Precept in the Sciences." In *ISHCP*, 1:243-67.

"Christian Reconstructionism, Dominionism, Theonomy, Dominion Theology, etc." Ontario Consultants on Tolerance. http://www.religioustolerance.org/reconstr.htm (8/14/2013).

Churchland, Patricia Smith. *Brain-Wise: Studies in Neurophilosophy.* Cambridge: MIT Press, 2002.

———. *Neurophilosophy: Toward a Unified Science of the Mind-Brain.* Cambridge: MIT Press, 1986.

———. "A Perspective on Mind-Brain Research." *Journal of Philosophy* 77, no. 4 (1980): 185-207.

Churchland, Paul M. "Eliminative Materialism and the Propositional Attitudes." *Journal of Philosophy* 78, no. 2 (1981): 67-90.

———. *Engine of Reason, the Seat of the Soul.* Cambridge: MIT Press, 1995.

Cicero, M. Tullius. *De Officiis.* Translated by Walter Miller. Cambridge, Mass., and London: Harvard University Press, 1913. http://www.perseus.tufts.edu.

Clark, Gillian. "The Fathers and the Animals: The Rule of Reason?" In *AOA,* chap. 6.

Clark, Ronald W. *The Survival of Charles Darwin.* New York: Random House, 1984.

Clark, Stephen R. L. *Biology and Christian Ethics.* Cambridge: Cambridge University Press, 2000.

Clarke, L. "The Universe Alive: Nature in the *Masnavī* of al-Din Rumi." In *I&E,* pp. 39-65.

Clarke, Sathianathan, Deenabandhu Manchala, and Philip Vinod Peacock, eds. *Dalit Theology in the Twenty-First Century: Discordant Voices, Discerning Pathways.* Delhi: Oxford University Press, 2010.

Clayton, Philip. *Adventures in the Spirit: God, World, Divine Action.* Edited by Zachary Simpson. Minneapolis: Fortress, 2008.

———. "The Case for Christian Panentheism." *Dialog* 37, no. 3 (Summer 1988): 201-8.

———. "Conceptual Foundations of Emergence Theory." In *Re-emergence of Emergence,* edited by Philip Clayton add Paul Davis, pp. 1-31. Oxford: Oxford University Press, 2006.

———. *Explanation from Physics to Theology: An Essay in Rationality and Religion.* New Haven: Yale University Press, 1989.

———. Foreword to *Science and Religious Anthropology: A Spiritually Evocative Naturalist Interpretation of Human Life,* by Wesley J. Wildman. Surrey, U.K.: Ashgate, 2009.

———. "God and World." In *The Cambridge Companion to Postmodern Theology,* edited by Kevin J. Vanhoozer, pp. 203-18. Cambridge: Cambridge University Press, 2003.

———. "The Impossible Possibility: Divine Causes in the World of Nature." In *GLC,* pp. 249-80.

———. *In Quest of Freedom: The Emergence of the Spirit in the Natural World; Frankfurt Templeton Lectures 2006.* Göttingen: Vandenhoeck & Ruprecht, 2009.

———. *Mind and Emergence: From Quantum to Consciousness.* Oxford: Oxford University Press, 2004.

———. "Neuroscience, the Person, and God: An Emergentist Account." In *NP,* pp. 181-214.

———. "On Divine and Human Agency: Reflections of a Co-Laborer." In Peacocke, *ATI,* pp. 163-75.

———. "Toward a Constructive Christian Theology of Emergence." In *E&E,* pp. 315-44.

———. "Toward a Theory of Divine Action That Has Traction." In *SPDA,* pp. 85-110.

————. "Tracing the Lines: Constraint and Freedom in the Movement from Quantum Physics to Theology." In *QM*, pp. 211-34.

Clayton, Philip, and Steven Knapp. "Divine Action and the 'Argument from Neglect.'" In *PC*, pp. 179-94.

Clayton, Philip, and Paul Davies, eds. *The Re-emergence of Emergence: The Emergentist Hypothesis from Science to Religion*. Oxford: Oxford University Press, 2006.

Cleland, Carol E., and Christopher F. Chyba. "Defining 'Life.'" *Origins of Life and Evolution of the Biosphere* 32 (2002): 387-93. http://spot.colorado.edu/~cleland/articles/Cleland_Chyba.OLEB.pdf.

Clifford, Anne M. "Creation." In *Systematic Theology: Roman Catholic Perspectives*, edited by Francis Schüssler Fiorenza and John P. Galvin, 1:193-248. Minneapolis: Fortress, 1991.

————. "Darwin's Revolution in *The Origin of Species*: A Hermeneutical Study of the Movement from Natural Theology to Natural Selection." In *EMB*, pp. 281-302.

————. "When Being Human Becomes Truly Earthly: An Ecofeminist Proposal for Solidarity." In *EG*, pp. 173-89.

Clifford, Richard J. "The Hebrew Scriptures and the Theology of Creation." *Theological Studies* 46, no. 3 (1985): 507-23.

Clooney, Francis X., S.J. *Comparative Theology: Deep Learning across Religious Borders*. Oxford: Wiley-Blackwell, 2010.

————. *Hindu God, Christian God: How Reason Helps Break Down the Boundaries between Religions*. Oxford: Oxford University Press, 2001.

Clooney, Francis X., S.J., with Hugh R. Nicholson. "To Be Heard and Done, but Never Quite Seen: The Human Condition according to the Vivekacūdāmani." In *The Human Condition: A Volume in the Comparative Ideas Project*, edited by Robert Cummings Neville, pp. 73-99. Albany: State University of New York Press, 2001.

Clough, David L. *On Animals: Volume I; Systematic Theology*. Vol. 1. London and New York: T. & T. Clark, 2012.

Coakley, Sarah. "Introduction: Religion and the Body." In *RB*, pp. 1-12.

————. "Kenosis: Theological Meanings and Gender Connotations." In *The Work of Love: Creation as Kenosis*, edited by John Polkinghorne, pp. 192-210. Grand Rapids: Eerdmans, 2001.

Cobb, John B., Jr., and David Ray Griffin. *Process Theology: An Introductory Exposition*. Philadelphia: Westminster, 1976.

Cohen, E., E. Burdett, N. Knight, and J. Barrett. "Cross-cultural Similarities and Differences in Person-Body Reasoning: Experimental Evidence from the UK and Brazilian Amazon." *Cognitive Science* 35, no. 7 (September-October 2011): 1282-1304.

Cohen, Richard. Introduction to *Humanism of the Other*, by Emmanuel Levinas. Translated by Nidra Poller. Urbana: University of Illinois Press, 2003.

Cohon, Samuel S. *Essays in Jewish Theology*. Cincinnati: Hebrew Union College Press, 1987.

————. *Jewish Theology: A Historical and Systematic Interpretation of Judaism and Its Foundations*. Assen, the Netherlands: Royal Vangorcum, 1971.

Collins, Robin. "Evolution and Original Sin." In *Perspectives on Evolving Creation,* edited by K. B. Miller, pp. 469-501. Grand Rapids: Eerdmans, 2003.

————. "A Scientific Argument for the Existence of God: The Fine-Tuning Design Argument." In *Reason for the Hope Within,* edited by Michael J. Murray, pp. 47-75. Grand Rapids: Eerdmans, 1999.

Collins, Steven. "The Body in Theravada Buddhist Monasticism." In *RB,* chap. 11.

————. *Selfless Persons: Imagery and Thought in Theravada Buddhism.* Cambridge: Cambridge University Press, 1982.

————. "What Are Buddhists *Doing* When They Deny the Self?" In *Religion and Practical Reason: New Essays in the Comparative Philosophy of Religions,* edited by Frank E. Reynolds and David Tracy, pp. 59-86. Albany: SUNY Press, 1994.

Comblin, José. *The Holy Spirit and Liberation.* Translated by Paul Burns. Maryknoll, N.Y.: Orbis, 1989.

Cone, James H. *A Black Theology of Liberation.* 2nd ed. 20th anniversary ed. Maryknoll, N.Y.: Orbis, 1986.

————. *The Spirituals and the Blues: An Interpretation.* New York: Seabury Press, 1972.

Connolly, John R. *John Henry Newman: A View of Catholic Faith for the New Millennium.* Lanham, Md.: Sheed and Ward, 2005.

Cooper, John W. *Body, Soul, and Life Everlasting: Biblical Anthropology and the Monism-Dualism Debate.* 2nd ed. Grand Rapids: Eerdmans, 2000.

Cooper, Niall. "Tourist or Vagabond." *Modern Believing* 42, no. 3 (2001): 7-24.

Cooper, Robin. *The Evolving Mind: Buddhism, Biology, and Consciousness.* Birmingham, U.K.: Windhorse, 1996, 2006.

Copan, Paul, and William Lane Craig. *Creation out of Nothing: A Biblical, Philosophical, and Scientific Exploration.* Grand Rapids: Baker Academic, 2004.

Corcoran, Kevin. "Thy Kingdom Come (on Earth): An Emerging Eschatology." In *Church in the Present Tense: A Candid Look at What's Emerging,* edited by Scot McKnight, Kevin Corcoran, Peter Rollins, and Jason Clark, pp. 59-72. Ēmersion: Emergent Village Resources for Communities of Faith. Grand Rapids: Brazos, 2011.

Cornell, Vincent. "Islam and Human Diversity: Vernacular Religion Confronts the Categories of Race and Culture." In *Humanity: Texts and Contexts; Christian and Muslim Perspectives,* edited by Michael Ipgrave and David Marshall, pp. 33-40. Washington, D.C.: Georgetown University Press, 2001.

Cortez, Marc. "Body, Soul, and (Holy) Spirit: Karl Barth's Theological Framework for Understanding Human Ontology." *International Journal of Systematic Theology* 10, no. 3 (2008): 328-45.

Council of Trent. Session V. "Decree concerning Original Sin." June 17, 1546.

Cox, Harvey G. *The Secular City: Secularization and Urbanization in Theological Perspective.* New York: Macmillan, 1965.

Coyne, George V., S.J. "Evolution and the Human Person: The Pope in Dialogue." In *EMB,* pp. 11-17.

Cragg, Kenneth. *The Privilege of Man: A Theme in Judaism, Islam, and Christianity.* London: Athlone Press, 1968.

Craig, William Lane. "Barrow and Tipler on the Anthropic Principle vs. Divine Design." *British Journal for Philosophy of Science* 38 (1988): 389-95.

———. *Divine Foreknowledge and Human Freedom.* Leiden: Brill, 1991.

———. "The Middle Knowledge View." In *Divine Foreknowledge, Four Views,* edited by James K. Beilby and Paul R. Eddy, pp. 119-43. Downers Grove, Ill.: InterVarsity, 2001.

———. *The Only Wise God.* Eugene, Ore.: Wipf and Stock, 1999.

———. *Time and Eternity: Exploring God's Relationship to Time.* Wheaton, Ill.: Crossway, 2001.

Cremo, Michael A. "The Fine-Tuned Universe." In *Rethinking Darwin: A Vedic Study of Darwinism and Intelligent Design,* edited by Leif A. Jensen, chap. 10. Los Angeles: Bhaktivedanta Book Trust, 2010.

———. *Human Devolution: A Vedic Alternative to Darwin's Theory.* Los Angeles: Bhaktivedanta Book Trust International, 2003.

Crick, Francis. *The Astonishing Hypothesis: The Scientific Search for the Soul.* New York: Simon and Schuster, 1994.

———. *Of Molecules and Men.* Seattle: University of Washington Press, 1966.

Cross, Richard. "Where Angels Fear to Tread: Duns Scotus and Radical Orthodoxy." *Antonianum* 76 (2001): 1-36.

Crutchfield, James P., J. Doyne Farmer, Norman H. Packard, and Robert S. Shaw. "Chaos." In *C&C,* pp. 35-48.

Cruz, Gemma Tulud. "Between Identity and Security: Theological Implications of Migration in the Context of Globalization." *Theological Studies* 69 (2008): 357-75.

Culianu, Ioan P. "Introduction: The Body Reexamined." In *Religious Reflections on the Human Body,* edited by Jane Marie Law, pp. 1-18. Bloomington: Indiana University Press, 1995.

Cunningham, Conor. *Darwin's Pious Idea: Why the Ultra-Darwinists and Creationists Both Get It Wrong.* Grand Rapids: Eerdmans, 2010.

Daecke, Sigurd M. "Profane and Sacramental Views of Nature." In *The Sciences and Theology in the Twentieth Century,* edited by A. R. Peacocke, pp. 127-40. Notre Dame, Ind.: University of Notre Dame Press, 1981.

Dalai Lama, His Holiness, the. *The Universe in a Single Atom: How Science and Spirituality Can Serve Our World.* New York: Morgan Road Books, 2005.

Dallavelle, Nancy. "Neither Idolatry nor Iconoclasm: A Critical Essentialism for Catholic Feminist Theology." *Horizons* 25, no. 1 (1998): 23-42.

Daly, Gabriel. *Creation and Redemption.* Dublin: Gill and Macmillan, 1988.

Daly, Mary. *Beyond God the Father: Toward a Philosophy of Women's Liberation.* Boston: Beacon Press, 1985.

———. *Gyn/Ecology: The Metaphysics of Radical Feminism.* Boston: Beacon Press, 1978.

———. *Pure Lust: Elemental Feminist Theology.* Boston: Beacon Press, 1984.

Damasio, Antonio R. *Descartes' Error: Emotion, Reason, and the Human Brain.* New York: Grosset/Putnam, 1994.

———. *The Feeling of What Happens: Body and Emotion in the Making of Consciousness.* New York: Harcourt Brace, 1999.

Damer, T. Edward. *Attacking Faulty Reasoning: A Practical Guide to Fallacy-Free Arguments.* 7th ed. Boston: Wadsworth, 2005.

Daneel, M. L. "African Independent Church Pneumatology and the Salvation of All Creation." *International Review of Mission* 82, no. 326 (1993): 143-66.

Darwin, Charles. *Descent of Man.* In *Great Books of the Western World,* edited by Robert Maynard Hutchins, vol. 49. Chicago: Encyclopaedia Britannica, 1952. The original edition as well as subsequent English and several other language editions are also available at http://darwin-online.org.uk/EditorialIntroductions/Freeman_TheDescentofMan.html.

———. *Origin of Species.* With additions and corrections from the sixth and last English edition. New York: D. Appleton, 1896. In *Great Books of the Western World,* edited by Robert Maynard Hutchins, vol. 49. Chicago: Encyclopaedia Britannica, 1952.

Darwin, Francis, ed. *Charles Darwin: His Life Told in an Autobiographical Chapter, and in a Selected Series of His Published Letters.* Abridged ed. London: John Murray, 1892. http://darwin-online.org.uk/content/frameset?pageseq=1&itemID=F1461&viewtype=text (5/22/2013).

Dasa, Shukavak N. "Ramanujacarya's *Visistadvaita-vada.*" http://www.bvml.org/FVS/laksmi/visistadvaitavada.html (4/1/2013).

Davidson, Donald. "Mental Events" [1970]. In *Essays on Actions and Events,* by Donald Davidson, 2nd ed., pp. 207-25. Oxford: Clarendon, 2001.

Davies, Paul C. *The Accidental Universe.* New York: Cambridge University Press, 1982.

———. *The Cosmic Blueprint: New Discoveries in Nature's Creative Ability to Order the Universe.* New York: Touchstone, 1988.

———. *God and the New Physics.* New York: Simon and Schuster, 1983.

———. *Other Worlds: A Portrait of Nature in Rebellion — Space, Superspace, and the Quantum Universe.* New York: Simon and Schuster, 1980.

———. "Teleology without Teleology: Purpose through Emergent Complexity." In *EMB,* pp. 151-62.

———. "That Mysterious Flow." *Scientific American,* September 2002, pp. 82-88. http://www.ipod.org.uk/reality/reality_mysterious_flow.asp (11/24/2013).

Davies, Shann. *The Tree of Life: Buddhism and the Protection of Nature.* Bangkok: Buddhist Perception of Nature Project, 1987.

Dawkins, Marian S. *Through Our Eyes Only? The Search for Animal Consciousness.* Oxford: Freeman, 1993.

Dawkins, Richard. *The Blind Watchmaker: Why the Evidence of Evolution Reveals a Universe without Design.* New York: Norton, 1986.

———. *The Selfish Gene.* Oxford: Oxford University Press, 1989.

Deacon, Terrence. *The Symbolic Species: The Co-evolution of Language and the Brain.* New York and London: Norton, 1997.

———. "The Symbolic Threshold." In *The Symbolic Species: The Co-evolution of Language and the Brain,* pp. 79-92. New York and London: Norton, 1997.

Deason, Gary B. "Reformation Theology and the Mechanistic Conception of Nature." In *God and Nature: Historical Essays on the Encounter between Christianity and*

Science, edited by David G. Lindberg and Ronald L. Numbers, pp. 167-91. Berkeley: University of California Press, 1986.

"Decree concerning Original Sin." 5th Session of Council of Trent, 1546. In *The Creeds of Christendom,* ed. Philip Schaff, vol. 2 [1877], pp. 83-88. www.ccel.org.

Dehaene, Stanislas, Michael I. Posner, and Don M. Tucker. "Localization of a Neural System for Error Detection and Compensation." *Psychological Science* 5, no. 5 (1994): 303-5.

Dekker, Eef. *Middle Knowledge.* Leuven: Peeters, 2000.

Dembski, William A. "Schleiermacher's Metaphysical Critique of Miracles." *Scottish Journal of Theology* 49, no. 4 (1996): 443-65.

Dennett, Daniel C. *Consciousness Explained.* Boston: Little, Brown, 1991.

—————. *Darwin's Dangerous Idea: Evolution and the Meaning of Life.* New York: Simon and Schuster, 1995.

—————. *Freedom Evolves.* New York: Vintage, 2003.

—————. "The New Replicators." In *Encyclopedia of Evolution,* edited by Mark Pagel. E-reference ed. Oxford: Oxford University Press, December 10, 2010. http://www.oxford-evolution.com/entry?entry=t169.e9.

—————. "True Believers: The Intentional Strategy and Why It Works." In *Mind Design II: Philosophy, Psychology, and Artificial Intelligence,* edited by John Haugeland, revised and enlarged 3rd ed., pp. 57-80. Cambridge: MIT Press, 2000 [1975].

Denton, Michael. *Evolution: A Theory in Crisis.* London: Burnett, 1985.

—————. *Nature's Destiny: How the Laws of Biology Reveal Purpose in the Universe.* New York: Free Press, 1998.

DeSalle, Rob, and Ian Tattersall. *Human Origins: What Bones and Genomes Tell Us about Ourselves.* College Station: Texas A & M University Press, 2008.

Descartes, René. *Meditations on First Philosophy.* Translated by John Veitch [1901]. Classical Library, 2001. http://www.wright.edu/cola/descartes/mede.html.

—————. *Principles of Philosophy.* Edited by Jonathan F. Bennett. First launched March 2008; last amended January 2012. On Some Texts from Early Modern Philosophy Web site: http://www.earlymoderntexts.com/pdf/descprin.pdf.

Dharmasiri, Gunapala. *A Buddhist Critique of the Christian Concept of God: A Critique of the Concept of God in Contemporary Christian Theology and Philosophy of Religion from the Point of View of Early Buddhism.* Colombo, Sri Lanka: Lake House Investments, 1974.

Díaz, Miguel H. *On Being Human: U.S. Hispanic and Rahnerian Perspectives.* Maryknoll, N.Y.: Orbis, 2001.

Di Vito, Robert A. "Here One Need Not Be One's Self: The Concept of 'Self' in the Old Testament." In *The Whole and Divided Life,* edited by David E. Aune and John McCarthy, pp. 49-88. New York: Crossroad, 1997.

—————. "Old Testament Anthropology and the Construction of Personal Identity." *Catholic Biblical Quarterly* 61, no. 1 (1999): 217-38.

Dobkowski, Michael. "'A Time for War and Time for Peace': Teaching Religion and Violence in the Jewish Tradition." In *TRV,* chap. 2.

Donahoe, Daniel Joseph. *Early Christian Hymns*. Series II: *Translations of the Verses of the Early and Middle Ages*. U.K.: Read Books, 2008 [1911].

Doniger, Wendy. "The Body in Hindu Texts." In *RB,* pp. 167-84.

Donovan, Mary Ann. *One Right Reading? A Guide to Irenaeus*. Collegeville, Minn.: Michael Glazier Books, 1997.

Dorner, I. A. *A System of Christian Doctrine*. Translated by Alfred Cave and J. S. Banks. Vol. 2. Edinburgh: T. & T. Clark, 1891.

Drees, Willem B. "A Case against Temporal Realism? Consequences of Quantum Cosmology for Theology." In *QCLN,* pp. 331-65.

Dretske, Fred. *Explaining Behavior: Reasons in a World of Causes*. Cambridge: MIT Press, 1988.

Dreyer, Elizabeth A. "An Advent of the Spirit: Medieval Mystics and Saints." In *Advents of the Spirit: An Introduction to the Current Study of Pneumatology,* edited by Bradford E. Hinze and D. Lyle Dabney, pp. 123-62. Milwaukee: Marquette University Press, 2001.

Drinnon, Richard. *Facing West: The Metaphysics of Indian-Hating and Empire-Building*. Minneapolis: University of Minnesota Press, 1980.

Du Bois, W. E. B. "The Conservation of Races" [1897]. In *The Conservation of Races and the Negro,* by W. E. B. Du Bois. A Penn State Electronic Classic Series, Pennsylvania State University, 2007, at http://www2.hn.psu.edu/faculty/jmanis/webdubois/duboisnegro-conservationraces6x9.pdf (8/13/2013).

Dulles, Avery, S.J. *Models of Revelation*. Maryknoll, N.Y.: Orbis, 1992 [1983].

Dunfee, Susan Nelson. "The Sin of Hiding: A Feminist Critique of Reinhold Niebuhr's Account of the Sin of Pride." *Soundings* 65 (1982): 316-27.

Dunn, James D. G. *Romans 1–8*. Word Biblical Commentary 38A. Dallas: Word, 1988.

———. *The Theology of Paul the Apostle*. Grand Rapids: Eerdmans, 1998.

Duns Scotus. *Ordinatio*. In *Philosophical Writings: A Selection,* translated, with introduction and notes, by Allan Wolter. Indianapolis: Hackett, 1987.

Dupré, John. *The Disorder of Things: Metaphysical Foundations of the Disunity of Science*. Cambridge: Harvard University Press, 1995.

———. *Human Nature and the Limits of Science*. Oxford: Oxford University Press, 2001.

Dupré, Louis K. *The Other Dimension: A Search for the Meaning of Religious Attitude*. Garden City, N.Y.: Doubleday, 1972.

Dussell, Enrique. *Philosophy of Liberation*. Maryknoll, N.Y.: Orbis, 1985.

Dwivedi, O. P. "Classical India." In *A Companion to Environmental Philosophy,* edited by Dale Jamieson, pp. 37-51. Oxford: Blackwell, 2001.

———. "Dharmic Ecology." In *HE,* pp. 3-22.

Dyrness, William A. *The Earth Is God's: A Theology of American Culture*. Maryknoll, N.Y.: Orbis, 1997.

Dyson, Freeman J. *Disturbing the Universe*. New York: Harper and Row, 1979.

Earth Bible, The. Edited variously by Norman C. Habel, Shirley Wurst, and Vicky Balabanski. Sheffield: Sheffield Academic Press, 2000-2002.

"Ecology and World Religions." Edited by Augustine Thottakara. Theme issue of *Journal of Dharma* 26, no. 1 (2001).

Eccles, J. C., ed. *Brain and Conscious Experience*. Berlin: Springer-Verlag, 1966.

Eckel, Malcolm David. "Is There a Buddhist Philosophy of Nature?" In *B&E*, pp. 327-49.

Eckel, Malcolm David, with John J. Thatamanil. "Beginningless Ignorance: A Buddhist View of the Human Condition." In *The Human Condition: A Volume in the Comparative Ideas Project*, edited by Robert Cummings Neville, pp. 49-72. Albany: State University of New York Press, 2001.

Edelman, Gerald, and Giulio Tononi. *A Universe of Consciousness*. New York: Basic Books, 2000.

Edgar, Blake. "Letter from South Africa: Home of the Modern Mind." *Archeology: The Publication of the Archeological Institute of America* 61, no. 2 (March/April 2008): n.p. http://www.archaeology.org/0803/abstracts/letter.html (5/22/2013).

Edicts of Aśoka, The. Translated by N. A. Nikam and Richard P. McKeon. Chicago: University of Chicago Press, 1959.

Edwards, Denis. "The Discovery of Chaos and the Retrieval of the Trinity." In *C&C*, pp. 157-75.

————. "Original Sin and Saving Grace in Evolutionary Context." In *EMB*, pp. 377-92.

Edwards, Jonathan. "Dissertation I: Concerning the End for Which God Created the World." In *Ethical Writings*, edited by Paul Ramsey, vol. 8 of *The Works of Jonathan Edwards*. New Haven: Yale University Press, 1989.

————. *Freedom of the Will*. Indianapolis: Bobbs-Merrill, 1969 [1754].

————. "Miscellanies," no. 104. In *The Miscellanies*, a-500, edited by Thomas A. Schafer, vol. 13 of *The Works of Jonathan Edwards*. New Haven: Yale University Press, 1994.

Efron, Noah J. *Judaism and Science: A Historical Introduction*. Westport, Conn., and London: Greenwood, 2007. http://www.jinfo.org/.

Eichrodt, Walter. *Theology of the Old Testament*. Translated by J. A. Baker. 2 vols. Philadelphia: Westminster, 1967.

Eiesland, Nancy L. *The Disabled God: Toward a Liberatory Theology of Disability*. Nashville: Abingdon, 1994.

Eigen, Manfred. *Steps towards Life: A Perspective on Evolution*. Translated by Paul Woolley. Oxford: Oxford University Press, 1992.

Eldredge, Niles. "Punctuated Equilibria: An Alternative to Phyletic Gradualism." In *Models in Paleobiology*, edited by Thomas J. M. Schopf. San Francisco: Freeman, Cooper and Co., 1972. Available also online: http://www.somosbacteriasyvirus .com/phyletic.pdf.

————. *Reinventing Darwin: The Great Evolutionary Debate*. London: Phoenix, 1995.

Eliade, Mircea. *Myth and Reality*. New York: Harper and Row, 1963.

Eller, Vernard, ed. *Thy Kingdom Come: A Blumhardt Reader*. Grand Rapids: Eerdmans, 1980.

Ellis, George F. R. "Quantum Theory and the Macroscopic World." In *QM*, pp. 259-91.

————. "Science, Complexity, and the Nature of Existence." In *E&E*, pp. 113-40.

Ellis, Marc H. *Toward a Jewish Theology of Liberation: The Challenge of the 21st Century*. 3rd expanded ed. Waco, Tex.: Baylor University Press, 2004.

Ellul, Jacques. *The Technological Society*. Translated by John Wilkinson. New York: Vintage, 1964.

Engel, Mary Potter. "Evil, Sin, and Violation of the Vulnerable." In *Lift Every Voice: Constructing Christian Theologies from the Underside,* edited by M. P. Engel and Susan Brooks Thistlethwaite, pp. 152-64. San Francisco: HarperSanFrancisco, 1990.

Enns, Peter. *The Evolution of Adam: What the Bible Does and Doesn't Say about Human Origins.* Grand Rapids: Brazos, 2012.

Enuma Elish. In Alexander Heidel, *The Babylonian Genesis: The Story of Creation,* pp. 18-60. Chicago: University of Chicago Press, 1951.

Esch, Emily. "Scientific Evidence for Dualism." Presentation at the Center for Christian Thought, Biola University, November 12, 2012.

Etchegoyen, Aldo. "Theology of Sin and Structures of Oppression." In *Faith Born in the Struggle for Life: A Rereading of Protestant Faith in Latin America Today,* edited by Dow Kirkpatrick, translated by L. McCoy, pp. 156-66. Grand Rapids: Eerdmans, 1988.

Evans, Gillian R. *Augustine on Evil.* Cambridge: Cambridge University Press, 1982.

Evans, James H., Jr. *We Have Been Believers: An African-American Systematic Theology.* Minneapolis: Fortress, 1992.

Evernden, Neil. *The Social Creation of Nature.* Baltimore: Johns Hopkins University Press, 1992.

Fairbanks, Daniel J. *Relics of Eden: The Powerful Evidence of Evolution in Human DNA.* Amherst, N.Y.: Prometheus, 2007.

Farrer, Austin. *The Freedom of the Will.* London: Adam and Charles Black, 1958.

Farrow, Douglas. *Ascension and Ecclesia: On the Significance of the Doctrine of the Ascension for Ecclesiology and Christian Cosmology.* Grand Rapids: Eerdmans, 1999.

———. "St. Irenaeus of Lyons: The Church and the World." *Pro Ecclesia* (1995): 333-55.

Fatoorchi, Pirooz. "Four Conceptions of *Creatio Ex Nihilo* and the Compatibility Question." In *CGA,* chap. 7.

Fatula, Ann, O.P. *The Holy Spirit: Unbounded Gift of Joy.* Collegeville, Minn.: Liturgical Press, 1998.

Faur, José. "The Hebrew Species Concept and the Origin of Evolution: R. Benamozegh's Response to Darwin." *La Ressegna Mensile di Israeli* 63, no. 3 (1997): 42-66.

Ferris, Elizabeth G. *Beyond Borders: Refugees, Migrants, and Human Rights in the Post–Cold War Era.* Geneva: WCC Publications, 1993.

Feuerbach, Ludwig. *The Essence of Christianity.* Translated by George Eliot. New York: Harper and Brothers, 1957.

Feynman, Richard. *The Character of Physical Law.* Cambridge: MIT Press, 1965.

Finger, Thomas N. *A Contemporary Anabaptist Theology: Biblical, Historical, Constructive.* Downers Grove, Ill.: InterVarsity, 2004.

Fiorenza, Elizabeth Schüssler. *In Memory of Her: A Feminist Theological Reconstruction of Christian Origins.* New York: Crossroad, 1983.

———. "The Sophia-God of Jesus and the Discipleship of Women." In *Women's Spirituality, Resources for Christian Development,* edited by Joann Wolski, pp. 261-73. New York: Paulist, 1986.

Firnish, Victor Paul. *II Corinthians: Translated with Introduction, Notes, and Commentary.* Anchor Bible 32A. Garden City, N.Y.: Doubleday, 1984.

Fischer, John Martin. "Putting Molinism in Its Place." *Molinism: The Contemporary Debate*, edited by Kenneth Perszyk, pp. 208-26. New York: Oxford University Press, 2011.

Fish, Stanley. *Doing What Comes Naturally: Change, Rhetoric, and the Practice of Theory in Literary and Legal Studies*. Durham, N.C., and London: Duke University Press, 1989.

Fisher, Christopher L. *Human Significance in Theology and the Natural Sciences: An Ecumenical Perspective with Reference to Pannenberg, Rahner, and Zizioulas*. Princeton Theological Monograph Series 128. Eugene, Ore.: Pickwick, 2010.

Flanagan, Owen. *Consciousness Reconsidered*. Cambridge: MIT Press, 1992.

———. *The Science of the Mind*. 2nd ed. Cambridge: MIT Press, 1991.

———. "Varieties of Naturalism." In *OHRS*, pp. 430-52.

Flint, Thomas P. *Divine Providence: The Molinist Account*. Ithaca, N.Y.: Cornell University Press, 1998.

Fodor, Jerry A. "The Big Idea: Can There Be a Science of the Mind?" *Times Literary Supplement*, July 3, 1992, pp. 5-7.

———. "Is Science Biologically Possible?" In *Naturalism Defeated? Essays on Plantinga's Evolutionary Argument against Naturalism*, edited by James Beilby. Ithaca, N.Y.: Cornell University Press, 2002.

———. "Special Sciences (Or: The Disunity of Science as a Working Hypothesis)." *Synthese* 27 (1974): 97-115.

Foltz, Richard C. "Introduction." In *I&E*, pp. xxxvii-xliii.

———. "Islamic Environmentalism: A Matter of Interpretation." In *I&E*, pp. 249-79.

Ford, David F. "Radical Orthodoxy and the Future of British Theology." *Scottish Journal of Theology* 54, no. 3 (2001): 385-404.

———. "A Response to Catherine Pickstock." *Scottish Journal of Theology* 54, no. 3 (2001): 423-25.

Ford, Lewis S. *The Lure of God: A Biblical Background for Process Theology*. Philadelphia: Fortress, 1978.

Formula of Concord, Solid Declaration. In *The Book of Concord: The Confessions of the Evangelical Lutheran Church*, translated and edited by Theodore G. Tappert. Philadelphia: Fortress, 1959.

Foster, Michael B. "The Christian Doctrine of Creation and the Rise of Modern Natural Science." *Mind* 43 (1934): 446-68; *Mind* 44 (1935): 439-66; *Mind* 45 (1936): 1-27.

Foucault, Michel. *The Order of Things: An Archeology of the Human Sciences*. New York: Vintage, 1970.

Fredrickson, B. L., and T.-A. Roberts. "Objectification Theory: Toward Understanding Women's Lived Experiences and Mental Health Risks." *Psychology of Women Quarterly* 21 (1997): 173-206.

Freyne, Sean. *Galilee, Jesus, and the Gospels: Literary Approaches and Historical Investigations*. Philadelphia: Fortress, 1998.

Friedman, William. *About Time: Inventing the Fourth Dimension*. Cambridge: MIT Press, 1990.

Fulkerson, Mary McClintock. "Sexism as Original Sin: Developing a Theacentric Discourse." *Journal of the American Academy of Religion* 59, no. 4 (1991): 653-75.

Fuller, Steve. "Humanity as an Endangered Species in Science and Religion." In *SRPW*, pp. 3-26.

Gandhi, Mohandas K. *The Bhagavad Gita according to Gandhi*. Blacksburg, Va.: Wilder Publications, 2011.

———. *Non-violent Resistance (Satyagraha)*. New York: Schocken, 1951.

Garcia, Jorge J. E., ed. *Race or Ethnicity? On Black and Latino Identity*. Ithaca, N.Y.: Cornell University Press, 2007.

Garcia-Rivera, Alejandro. *The Garden of God: A Theological Cosmology*. Minneapolis: Fortress, 2009.

Gardner, Howard. *The Mind's New Science: A History of the Cognitive Revolution*. New York: Basic Books, 1987.

Gardner, Martin. "Mathematical Games: The Fantastic Combinations of John Conway's New Solitaire Game 'Life.'" *Scientific American* 223 (October 1970): 120-23. http://ddi.cs.uni-potsdam.de/HyFISCH/Produzieren/lis_projekt/proj_gamelife/ConwayScientificAmerican.htm.

Gay, Volney P. "Neuroscience and Religion: Brain, Mind, Self, and Soul." In *Neuroscience and Religion: Brain, Mind, Self, and Soul,* edited by Volney P. Gay, pp. 1-18. Lanham, Md.: Lexington Books, 2009.

Gazzaniga, Michael. *Who's in Charge? Free Will and the Science of the Brain*. Ecco. Kindle Edition, 2011.

Gehlen, Arnold. *Man: His Nature and Place in the World*. Translated by Clare McMillan and Karl Pillemer. New York: Columbia University Press, 1988 [1950].

al-Ghazali. *The Jewels of the Qur'an: Al-Ghazali's Theory*. A translation, with introduction, of al-Ghazali's *Kitāb Jawāhir al-Qur'ān*. Translated by Muhammad Abdul Quasem. Kuala Lumpur, Malaysia: University of Malaya Press, 1977. http://archive.org/details/JewelsOfTheQuranByAlGhazzali-EnglishTranslationOfJawahirAlQuran.

———. *Tahafut Al-Falasifah: The Incoherence of the Philosophers*. Translated by Sabih Ahmad Kamali. 2nd imprint. Lahore: Pakistan Philosophical Conference, 1963.

Ghazanfar, Asif A., and Drew Rendall. "Evolution of Human Vocal Production." *Current Biology* 18, no. 11 (June 2008): R457-60.

Gibbon, Edward. *History of the Decline and Fall of the Roman Empire*. 4 vols. London: W. W. Gibbins, 1890.

Giddens, Anthony. *The Consequences of Modernity*. Oxford: Blackwell/Polity, 1990. http://pol.atilim.edu.tr/files/kuresellesme/kitaplar/The_Consequences_of_Modernity.pdf (8/14/2013).

———. *Runaway World: How Globalization Is Shaping Our Lives*. New York: Routledge, 2003.

Gilkey, Langdon. "Cosmology, Ontology, and the Travail of Biblical Language." *Journal of Religion* 41 (1961): 194-205.

———. *Maker of Heaven and Earth: The Doctrine of Creation in Light of Modern Knowledge*. Lanham, Md.: University Press of America, 1985 [1959].

———. *Naming the Whirlwind: The Renewal of God-Language.* New York: Seabury Press, 1981.

———. *Nature, Reality, and the Sacred: The Nexus of Science and Religion.* Minneapolis: Fortress, 1993.

———. "Protestant Views of Sin." In *The Human Condition in the Jewish and Christian Traditions,* edited by Fredrik Greenspahn, pp. 147-68. Hoboken, N.J.: KTACV; Denver: Center for Jewish Studies at the University of Denver, 1986.

Gillespie, G. T. "A Christian View of Segregation." Address before the Mississippi Synod of the Presbyterian Church (November 1954).

Gillman, Neil. "Creation in the Bible and in the Liturgy." In *J&E,* pp. 133-54.

"God of Life, Accompany Us: Our Journey towards a Life with Dignity, Peace, and Justice." Global Ecumenical Network on Migration Annual Meeting, November 4-8, 2012. http://www.oikoumene.org/en/folder/documents-pdf/Final_GEM_Report_2012.pdf (12/4/2013).

Goetz, Stewart, and Charles Taliaferro. *Naturalism.* Grand Rapids: Eerdmans, 2008.

Goldsmith, Timothy H. *The Biological Roots of Human Nature: Forging Links between Evolution and Behavior.* New York: Oxford University Press, 1991.

Golshani, Mehdi. "Does Science Offer Evidence of a Transcendent Reality and Purpose?" In *ISHCP,* 2:95-108.

———. *The Holy Qur'an and the Sciences of Nature: A Theological Reflection.* New York: Global Scholarly Publications, 2003.

———. "How to Make Sense of 'Islamic Science.'" *American Journal of Islamic Social Sciences* 17, no. 3 (2000): 1-21. http://i-epistemology.net/attachments/647_V17N3%20FALL%202000%20-%20Golshani%20-%20How%20to%20Make%20Sense%20of%20Islamic%20Science.pdf.

———. "Islam and the Sciences of Nature: Some Fundamental Questions." In *ISHCP,* 1:67-79.

Gontier, Nathalie, "Evolutionary Epistemology." *Internet Encyclopedia of Philosophy: A Peer-Reviewed Academic Resource,* n.p. http://www.iep.utm.edu/evo-epis/ (5/22/2013).

González, Justo L. "The Alienation of Alienation." In *The Other Side of Sin: Woundedness from the Perspective of the Sinned-Against,* edited by Andrew Sung Park and Susan L. Nelson. Albany: State University of New York Press, 2001.

———. *A History of Christian Thought.* Vol. 1, *From the Beginning to the Council of Chalcedon.* Nashville: Abingdon, 1970.

———. *Mañana: Christian Theology from a Hispanic Perspective.* Nashville: Abingdon, 1990.

Gonzalez, Michelle A. *Created in God's Image: An Introduction to Feminist Theological Anthropology.* Maryknoll, N.Y.: Orbis, 2007.

Goodenough, Ursula. *The Sacred Depths of Nature.* New York: Oxford University Press, 1998.

Goodman, Lenn E. "Respect for Nature in the Jewish Tradition." In *J&E,* pp. 227-59.

Goosen, Gideon. *Spacetime and Theology in Dialogue.* Milwaukee: Marquette University Press, 2008.

Gordon, Haim, and Leonard Grob. *Education for Peace: Testimonies from World Religions.* Maryknoll, N.Y.: Orbis, 1987.

Gosling, David L. "Darwin and the Hindu Tradition: 'Does What Goes around Come Around?'" *Zygon: Journal of Religion and Science* 46, no. 2 (June 2011): 345-69.

———. *Religion and Ecology in India and Southeast Asia.* London: Routledge, 2001.

———. *Science and the Indian Tradition: When Einstein Met Tagore.* London and New York: Routledge, 2007.

Gottstein, Alon Goshen. "The Body as Image of God in Rabbinic Literature." *Harvard Theological Review* 87, no. 2 (1994): 171-95.

Goudzwaard, Bob. *Globalization and the Kingdom of God.* Grand Rapids: Baker, 2001.

Gould, Stephen Jay. "Darwin and Paley Meet the Invisible Hand." *Natural History* 99 (November 1990): 8-16.

———. "Nonoverlapping Magisteria." *Natural History* 106 (1997): 16-22.

———. *Rock of Ages: Science and Religion in the Fullness of Life.* London: Jonathan Cape, 2001.

———. *The Structure of Evolutionary Theory.* Cambridge: Harvard University Press, 2002.

———. *Wonderful Life: The Burgess Shale and the Nature of History.* New York: Norton, 1989.

Gousmett, Chris. "Creation Order and Miracle according to Augustine." *Evangelical Quarterly* 60, no. 3 (July 1988): 217-40.

Gozzano, Simone, and Christopher S. Hill, eds. *New Perspectives on Type Identity: The Mental and the Physical.* Cambridge: Cambridge University Press, 2012.

Graham, Elaine. "Liberation or Enslavement." *Genewatch,* n.d. http://www.councilfor responsiblegenetics.org/genewatch/GeneWatchPage.aspx?pageId=227 (8/13/2013).

Grant, Jacquelyn. "Black Theology and the Black Woman." In *Black Theology: A Documentary History, 1966-1979,* edited by Gayraud S. Wilmore and James H. Cone, pp. 418-33. Maryknoll, N.Y.: Orbis, 1979.

Grant, Sara. *Towards an Alternative Theology: Confessions of a Non-dualist Christian.* Introduction by Bradley J. Malkovsky. Notre Dame, Ind.: University of Notre Dame Press, 2002.

Green, Arthur. "A Kabbalah for the Environmental Age." In *J&E,* pp. 3-15.

Green, Joel B. "'Bodies — That Is, Human Lives': A Re-examination of Human Nature in the Bible." In *WHS,* pp. 149-73.

———. *Body, Soul, and Human Life: The Nature of Humanity in the Bible.* Studies in Theological Interpretation. Grand Rapids: Baker Academic; Carlisle: Paternoster, 2008.

———. *Practicing Theological Interpretation: Engaging Biblical Texts for Faith and Formation.* Grand Rapids: Baker, 2011.

———. "Three Exegetical Forays into the Body-Soul Discussion." *Criswell Theological Review,* n.s., 7 (2010): 3-18.

Greene, Brian. *The Elegant Universe: Superstrings, Hidden Dimensions, and the Quest for the Ultimate Theory.* 2nd ed. New York: Vintage, 2000.

Gregersen, Niels Henrik. "Emergence: What Is at Stake for Religious Reflection?" In

Re-emergence of Emergence, edited by Philip Clayton and Paul Davis, pp. 279-302. Oxford: Oxford University Press, 2006.

———. "Reduction and Emergence in Artificial Life: A Theological Appropriation." In *E&E*, pp. 284-314.

———. "Special Divine Action and the Quilt of Laws: Why the Distinction between Special and General Divine Action Cannot be Maintained." In *SPDA*, pp. 179-99.

———. "Three Types of Indeterminacy." In *The Concept of Nature in Science and Theology*, part 1, edited by Niels Henrik Gregersen, Michael W. S. Parsons, and Christoph Wasserman, pp. 165-86. Geneva: Labor et Fides, 1997.

———. "Varieties of Personhood: Mapping the Issues." In *The Human Person in Science and Theology*, edited by Niels Henrik Gregersen, Willem B. Drees, and Ulf Görman, pp. 1-17. Edinburgh: T. & T. Clark, 2000.

Gregorios, Paulos Mar. *Cosmic Man: The Divine Presence; The Theology of St. Gregory of Nyssa*. New York: Paragon House, 1988.

Gregory, Frederick. "The Impact of Darwinian Evolution on Protestant Theology in the Nineteenth Century." In *God and Nature: Historical Essays on the Encounter between Christianity and Science*, edited by David C. Lindberg and Ronald L. Numbers, pp. 369-90. Berkeley: University of California Press, 1986.

Gregory of Nyssa. "On What It Means to Call Oneself a Christian." In *Ascetical Writings*. Fathers of the Church, vol. 58, translated by Virginia Woods Callahan. Washington, D.C.: Catholic University of America Press, 1967.

Grenz, Stanley J. *The Social God and the Relational Self: A Trinitarian Theology of the Imago Dei*. Louisville: Westminster John Knox, 2001.

———. *Theology for the Community of God*. Grand Rapids: Eerdmans, 1994.

Griffin, Susan. *Woman and Nature: The Roaring Inside Her*. New York: Harper and Row, 1978.

Gross, Paul R., Norman Levitt, and Martin W. Lewis, eds. *The Flight from Science and Reason*. New York: New York Academy of Sciences, 1996.

Gruender, Hubert. *Psychology without a Soul: A Criticism*. St. Louis: Herder, 1912.

Guessoum, Nidhal. *Islam's Quantum Question: Reconciling Muslim Tradition and Modern Science*. London and New York: I. B. Tauris, 2011.

———. "The Qur'an, Science, and the (Related) Contemporary Muslim Discourse." *Zygon* 43, no. 2 (2008): 411-31.

Guha, Ramachandra. "Radical Environmentalism: A Third World Critique." *Environmental Ethics* 11, no. 1 (1989): 71-83.

Gulick, Robert Van. "Reduction, Emergence and Other Recent Options on the Mind/Body Problem: A Philosophical Overview." *Journal of Consciousness Studies* 8, no. 1 (2001): 1-34.

Gundry, Robert H. *Sōma in Biblical Theology with Emphasis on Pauline Anthropology*. Cambridge: Cambridge University Press, 1976.

Gunton, Colin E. "The Doctrine of Creation." In *The Cambridge Companion to Christian Doctrine*, edited by Colin E. Gunton. Cambridge: Cambridge University Press, 1997.

———. *Enlightenment and Alienation.* Grand Rapids: Eerdmans; Basingstoke: Marshall, Morgan and Scott, 1985.

———. *The One, the Three, and the Many: God, Creation, and the Culture of Modernity.* Cambridge: Cambridge University Press, 1993.

———. *The Promise of Trinitarian Theology.* Edinburgh: T. & T. Clark, 1991.

———. *The Triune Creator: A Historical and Systematic Study.* Edinburgh Studies in Constructive Theology. Grand Rapids: Eerdmans, 1998.

Gushee, David P. *The Sacredness of Human Life: Why an Ancient Biblical Vision Is Key to the World's Future.* Grand Rapids: Eerdmans, 2013.

Gustafson, James. "Theology Confronts Technology and the Life Sciences." *Commonweal,* June 16, 1978, pp. 386-92.

Gutiérrez, Gustavo. *On Job: God-Talk and the Suffering of the Innocent.* Translated by Matthew J. O'Connell. Maryknoll, N.Y.: Orbis, 1987.

———. *The Power of the Poor in History: Selected Writings.* Translated by Robert B. Barr. Maryknoll, N.Y.: Orbis, 1983.

———. *A Theology of Liberation: History, Politics, and Salvation.* Translated and edited by Sister Caridad Inda and John Eagleson. Maryknoll, N.Y.: Orbis, 1986 [1973]; rev. ed. with a new introduction, 1988.

———. *The Truth Shall Make You Free: Confrontations.* Translated by Matthew J. O'Connell. Maryknoll, N.Y.: Orbis, 1990.

Gutting, Gary. *Religious Belief and Religious Skepticism.* Notre Dame, Ind.: University of Notre Dame Press, 1982.

Habel, Norman C., and Peter Trudinger, eds. *Exploring Ecological Hermeneutics.* Society of Biblical Literature Symposium Series 46. Atlanta: Society of Biblical Literature, 2008.

Habito, Ruben L. F. "Environment or Earth Sangha: Buddhist Perspectives on Our Global Ecological Well-Being." *Contemporary Buddhism* 8, no. 2 (2007): 131-47.

Haeckel, Ernst. *Natürliche Schöpfungsgeschichte* (Natural history of creation). Berlin: Georg Reimer, 1873 [1868]. English translation, *The History of Creation,* 1876.

———. *The Riddle of the Universe at the Close of the Nineteenth Century.* Translated by Joseph McCabe. New York: Harper and Brothers, 1900 [1899].

Haggard, Patrick. "Does Brain Science Change Our View of Free Will?" In *Free Will and Modern Science,* edited by Richard Swinburne, pp. 7-24. Oxford: Oxford University Press, 2011.

Haggard, Patrick, and Benjamin Libet. "Conscious Intention and Brain Activity." *Journal of Consciousness Studies* 8, no. 1 (2001): 47-63.

Hagoort, Peter. "The Uniquely Human Capacity for Language Communication: From *Pope* to [po:p] in Half a Second." In *NP,* pp. 45-56.

Haidt, J. "The Emotional Dog and Its Rational Tail: A Social Intuitionist Approach to Moral Judgment." *Psychological Review* 108, no. 4 (2001): 814-34.

Halberstam, Judith, and Ira Livingstone, eds. *Posthuman Bodies.* Indianapolis: Indiana University Press, 1995.

Haldane, John. *Reasonable Faith.* Abingdon: Routledge, 2010.

Hall, Douglas John. *Imaging God: Dominion as Stewardship.* Grand Rapids: Eerdmans, 1986.

Hamilton, Sue. "From the Buddha to Buddhaghosa: Changing Attitudes towards the Human Body in Theravāda Buddhism." In *Religious Reflections on the Human Body*, edited by Jane Marie Law, pp. 46-63. Bloomington: Indiana University Press, 1995.

Hamilton, Victor P. *The Book of Genesis: Chapters 1–17*. In the *New International Commentary on the Old Testament*, edited by R. K. Harrison. Grand Rapids: Eerdmans, 1990.

Hanh, Thich Nhat. "The Individual, Society, and Nature." In *The Path of Compassion: Writings on Socially Engaged Buddhism*, edited by Fred Eppsteiner, 2nd rev. ed., pp. 40-46. Berkeley, Calif.: Parallax Press, 2008.

———. *Our Appointment with Life: Discourse on Living Happily in the Present Moment.* Translation and commentary on *The Sutra on Knowing the Better Way to Live Alone (Bhaddekaratta Sutta)*. Translated by Annabel Laity. Berkeley, Calif.: Parallax Press, 1990.

———. *Peaceful Action, Open Heart: Lessons from the Lotus Sutra.* Berkeley, Calif.: Parallax Press, 2008.

———. *Zen Keys.* Translated by Albert Low and Jean Low. Garden City, N.Y.: Anchor Books, 1974.

Hanson, N. R. *Patterns of Discovery: An Inquiry into the Conceptual Foundations of Science.* Cambridge: Cambridge University Press, 1961.

Happel, Stephen. "Metaphors and Time Asymmetry: Cosmologies in Physics and Christian Meanings." In *QCLN*, pp. 103-34.

Haq, S. Nomanul. Introduction to *GLC*, pp. xvii-xxii.

Hardwick, Charley D. *Events of Grace: Naturalism, Existentialism, and Theology.* Cambridge: Cambridge University Press, 1996.

Hare, R. M. *The Language of Morals.* Oxford: Oxford University Press, 1991 [1952].

Harris, Elizabeth. "Human Existence in Buddhism and Christianity: A Christian Perspective." In *Buddhism and Christianity in Dialogue*, edited by Perry Schmidt-Leukel, pp. 29-52. London: SCM, 2005.

Harris, Ian. "Getting to Grips with Buddhist Environmentalism: A Provisional Typology." *Journal of Buddhist Ethics* 2 (1995): 173-90.

Harris, Murray J. *Raised Immortal: Resurrection and Immortality in the New Testament.* Grand Rapids: Eerdmans, 1983.

Harris, S. *Free Will.* New York: Free Press, 2012.

Harrison, Nonna Verna. *God's Many Splendored Image: Theological Anthropology for Christian Formation.* Grand Rapids: Baker Academic, 2010.

Harthstone, Charles. "The Compound Individual." In *Philosophical Essays for Alfred North Whitehead*, edited by F. S. C. Northrup. New York: Russell and Russell, 1967.

Harvey, David. *The Condition of Postmodernity: An Enquiry into the Origins of Cultural Change.* Oxford: Blackwell, 1989.

Harvey, Susan Ashbrook. "Feminine Imagery for the Divine: The Holy Spirit, the Odes of Solomon, and Early Syriac Tradition." *Saint Vladimir's Theological Quarterly* 37 (1993): 111-40.

Hasker, William. "Divine Knowledge and Human Freedom." In *OHFW*, pp. 39-54.

————. *The Emergent Self.* Ithaca, N.Y.: Cornell University Press, 1999.

————. "Middle Knowledge: A Refutation Revisited." *Faith and Philosophy* 12, no. 2 (1995): 223-36.

————. "The (Non-)Existence of Molinist Counterfactuals." In *Molinism: The Contemporary Debate,* edited by Kenneth Perszyk, pp. 25-36. New York: Oxford University Press, 2011.

————. *Providence, Evil, and the Openness of God.* New York: Routledge, 2004.

Haslam, Nick. "Dehumanization: An Integrative Review." *Personality and Social Psychology Review* 10, no. 3 (2006): 252-64.

Hassan, Ihab. *The Dismemberment of Orpheus: Toward a Postmodern Literature.* New York: Oxford University Press, 1982.

Hauerwas, Stanley, Nancey Murphy, and Mark Nation, eds. *Theology without Foundations: Religious Practice and the Future of Theological Truth.* Nashville: Abingdon, 1994.

Haught, John F. "Darwin's Gift to Theology." In *EMB,* pp. 393-18.

————. *Is Nature Enough? Meaning and Truth in the Age of Science.* Cambridge and New York: Cambridge University Press, 2006.

————. *Making Sense of Evolution: Darwin, God, and the Drama of Life.* Louisville: Westminster John Knox, 2010.

Havel, Václav. *Open Letters: Selected Prose, 1965-1999.* 11th ed. New York: Vintage, 1992.

Hawking, Stephen. *A Brief History of Time.* Updated and expanded 10th anniversary ed. New York: Bantam Books, 1998 [1988].

————. "Theoretical Advances in General Relativity." In *Some Strangeness in the Proportion,* edited by H. Woolf. Reading, Mass.: Addison-Wesley, 1980.

Healy, J. "Henri de Lubac on Nature and Grace: A Note on Some Recent Contributions to the Debate." *Communio: International Catholic Review* 35 (Winter 2008): 535-64.

Hefner, Philip. "Biocultural Evolution: A Clue to the Meaning of Nature." In *EMB,* pp. 329-56.

————. *The Human Factor: Evolution, Culture, and Religion.* Minneapolis: Augsburg Fortress, 1993.

————. "Imago Dei: The Possibility and Necessity of the Human Person." In *The Human Person in Science and Theology,* edited by Niels Henrik Gregersen, Willem B. Drees, and Ulf Görman, pp. 73-94. Edinburgh: T. & T. Clark, 2000.

————. *Technology and Human Becoming.* Minneapolis: Fortress, 2003.

Hegel, G. W. F. *Hegel's Philosophy of Nature.* Part 2 of the *Encyclopedia of the Philosophical Sciences* [1830]. Translated by A. V. Miller. Oxford: Oxford University Press, 2004.

————. *The Philosophy of History.* Translated by John Sibree. New York: Dover, 1956.

————. *Science of Logic.* Translated and edited by George di Giovanni. Cambridge: Cambridge University Press, 2010. http://www.magonzalezvalerio.com/CL.pdf.

Heidel, Alexander. *The Babylonian Genesis: The Story of Creation.* Chicago: University of Chicago Press, 1942.

Heim, Karl. *The Transformation of the Scientific World View.* London: SCM, 1953.

Heller, Michael. "Adventures of the Concept of Mass and Matter." *Philosophy in Science* 3 (1988): 15-35.

————. "Scientific Rationality and Christian Logos." In *PPT*, pp. 141-50.

————. "Where Physics Meets Metaphysics." In *On Space and Time*, edited by Shahn Majid, chap. 5, pp. 238-77. Cambridge: Cambridge University Press, 2008.

Helm, Paul. *Eternal God: A Study of God without Time*. Oxford: Clarendon, 1988.

Helminiak, Daniel A. "Theistic Psychology and Psychotherapy: A Theological and Scientific Critique." *Zygon: Journal of Religion and Science* 45, no. 1 (2010): 47-74.

Hempel, Carl. "The Logical Analysis of Psychology" [1949]. In *A Historical Introduction to the Philosophy of Mind: Readings with Commentary*, edited by Peter A. Morgan, pp. 164-73. Peterborough, Ont.: Broadview Press, 1997.

Henshilwood, Christopher S. "Fully Symbolic *Sapiens* Behaviour: Innovation in the Middle Stone Age at Blombos Cave, South Africa." In *Rethinking the Human Revolution*, edited by Paul Mellars et al., pp. 123-32. Cambridge: Short Run Press, 2007.

————. "Modern Humans and Symbolic Behavior: Evidence from Blombos Cave, South Africa." In *Origins: The Story of the Emergence of Humans and Humanity in Africa*, edited by Geoffrey Blundell, pp. 78-85. Cape Town: Double Storey Books, 2006.

Henshilwood, Christopher S., Francesco d'Errico, and Ian Watts. "Engraved Ochres from the Middle Stone Age Levels at Blombos Cave, South Africa." *Journal of Human Evolution* 57, no. 1 (July 2009): 27-47.

Heppe, Heinrich. *Reformed Dogmatics: Set Out and Illustrated from the Sources*. Revised and edited by Ernst Bizer. Translated by G. T. Thomson. London: Allen and Unwin, 1950.

Herder, Johann Gottfried. *Outlines of a Philosophy of the History of Man*. Translated by T. Churchill. New York: Bergman, 1800. http://archive.org/details/outlinesaphilosoochurgoog.

Hesse, Mary B. "Physics, Philosophy, and Myth." In *PPT*, pp. 185-202.

Hewlett, Martinez J. "True to Life? Biological Models of Origin and Evolution." In *E&E*, pp. 158-72.

Heyer, Kristin E. "Reframing Displacement and Membership: Ethics of Migration." *Theological Studies* 73 (2012): 188-206.

Hick, John. *Evil and the God of Love*. 2nd reissued ed. Hampshire, U.K.: Palgrave, 2010.

————. *An Interpretation of Religion: Human Responses to the Transcendent*. 2nd ed. New Haven: Yale University Press, 2004.

Hielema, Syd. "Searching for 'Disconnected Wires': Karl Barth's Doctrine of Creation Revisited." *Calvin Theological Journal* 30, no. 1 (April 1995): 75-93.

Higgins, Jean M. "Anastasius Sinaita and the Superiority of Woman." *Journal of Biblical Literature* 97, no. 2 (1978): 253-56.

Hillier, H. Chad. "Ibn Rushd (Averroes) (1126-1198)." In *Internet Encyclopedia of Philosophy: A Peer-Reviewed Academic Resource*. James Fieser, founder and editor; Bradley Dowden, general editor. http://www.iep.utm.edu/ibnrushd/#SH9a.

Hodge, Charles. *Systematic Theology*. Vol. 2. Grand Rapids: Eerdmans, 1952 [1871].

Hodgson, David. "Quantum Physics, Consciousness, and Free Will." In *OHFW*, pp. 57-83.

Hoekema, Anthony. *Created in God's Image*. Grand Rapids: Eerdmans, 1986.

Hofstadter, Richard. *Social Darwinism in American Thought*. Rev. ed. New York: George Braziller, 1969.

Holder, R. D. *God, the Multiverse, and Everything: Modern Cosmology and the Argument from Design.* Aldershot, U.K.: Ashgate, 2004.

Holy Qur'an, The. Translated by Yusuf Ali. Beltsville, Md.: Amana Corp., 1983.

Hoodbhoy, Pervez. *Islam and Science: Religious Orthodoxy and the Battle for Rationality.* London and New Jersey: Zed Books, 1991.

Horgan, Terence E., and James F. Woodward. "Folk Psychology Is Here to Stay." *Philosophical Review* 94, no. (1985): 197-226.

Hornbeck, R., and J. L. Barrett. "Refining and Testing 'Counterintuitiveness' in Virtual Reality: Cross-Cultural Evidence for Recall of Counterintuitive Representations." *International Journal for the Psychology of Religion* 23 (2013): 15-28.

Horton, Michael S. "Image and Office: Human Personhood and the Covenant." In *PITP,* pp. 178-203.

———. "Post-Reformation Reformed Anthropology." In *PITP,* pp. 62-63.

Houghton, David D. *Global Climate Change: Basics, Challenges, and International Impacts* (March 15, 2007), at http://www.rc.swls.org/www.old/talks/climatechange2007.pdf.

Howard, Damian. *Being Human in Islam: The Impact of the Evolutionary Worldview.* Florence, Ky.: Routledge, 2011.

Howell, Nancy R. *A Feminist Cosmology: Ecology, Solidarity, and Metaphysics.* Amherst, N.Y.: Humanity Books, 2000.

Hoyle, Fred. *The Intelligent Universe.* New York: Holt, Rinehart and Winston, 1983.

Hudson, W. Donald. *A Philosophical Approach to Religion.* London: Macmillan, 1974.

Hugman, Richard, Mehmoona Moosa-Mitha, and Otrude Moya. "Towards a Borderless Social Work: Reconsidering Notions of International Social Work." *International Social Work* 53, no. 5 (September 2010): 629-43.

Hume, David. *The Natural History of Religion.* London: A. and H. Bradlaugh Bonner, 1889 [1775]. http://oll.libertyfund.org/index.php?option=com_staticxt&staticfile=show.php%3Ftitle=340&layout=html#chapter_44332 (3/1/2013).

———. *A Treatise of Human Nature.* Edited by L. A. Selby-Bigge. Oxford: Clarendon, 1896 (1739). http://files.libertyfund.org/files/342/0213_Bk.pdf.

Hunt, David. "The Simple-Foreknowledge View." In *Divine Foreknowledge, Four Views,* edited by James K. Beilby and Paul R. Eddy, pp. 65-103. Downers Grove, Ill.: InterVarsity, 2001.

Hurd, James P. "Hominids in the Garden?" In *Perspectives on Evolving Creation,* edited by K. B. Miller, pp. 208-33. Grand Rapids: Eerdmans, 2003.

Hussain, Amir. "Confronting Misoislamia: Teaching Religion and Violence in Courses on Islam." In *TRV,* chap. 5.

Hütterman, Aloys. *The Ecological Message of the Torah: Knowledge, Concepts, and Laws Which Made Survival in a Land of "Milk and Honey" Possible.* Studies in the History of Judaism 199. Atlanta: Scholars Press, 1999.

Hutton, Will, and Anthony Giddens, eds. *On the Edge: Living with Global Capitalism.* London: Jonathan Cape, 2000.

Hvidt, Nils Christian. "Historical Developments of the Problem of Evil." In *PC,* pp. 1-35.

Ibn Taymiyyah Expounds on Islam. Selected Writings of Shaykh al-Islam Taqi ad-Din Ibn

Taymiyyah on Islamic Faith, Life, and Society, compiled and translated by Muhammad 'Abdul-Haqq Ansari. Virginia: Institute of Islamic and Arabic Sciences in America, 2007. http://ahlehadith.files.wordpress.com/2010/07/expounds-on-islam.pdf (4/9/2013).

Ickert, Scott. "Luther and Animals: Subject of Adam's Fall?" In *AOA*, chap. 8.

"Immanuel Kant." In *Misogyny in the Western Philosophical Tradition: A Reader,* edited by Beverly Clack, pp. 144-60. New York: Routledge, 1999.

Ingalls, Daniel H. H. "Sankara on the Question: Whose Is Avidya?" *Philosophy East and West* 3, no. 1 (1953): 69-72.

"Introduction to the Constants for Nonexperts." In NIST [National Institute of Standards and Technology] Reference on Constants, Unit, and Uncertainty. http://physics.nist.gov/cuu/Constants/background.html.

Inwagen, Peter van. *An Essay on Free Will.* Oxford: Clarendon, 1983.

———. *God, Knowledge, and Mystery: Essays in Philosophical Theology.* Ithaca, N.Y.: Cornell University Press, 1995.

———. "What Does an Omniscient Being Know about the Future?" In *Oxford Studies in the Philosophy of Religion,* edited by Jonathan Kvanvig. Oxford: Oxford University Press, 2008.

Iozzio, Mary Jo. "Thinking about Disabilities with Justice, Liberation, and Mercy." *Horizons* 36. no. 1 (Spring 2009): 32-49.

Iqbal, Sir Muhammad. *The Reconstruction of Religious Thought in Islam.* Lahore, Pakistan: Ashraf Press, 1960.

Iqbal, Muzaffar. "In the Beginning: Islamic Perspectives on Cosmological Origins." In *ISHCP,* 2:379-96.

———. "In the Beginning: Islamic Perspectives on Cosmological Origins — II." *Islam and Science* 4, no. 2 (Winter 2006): 93-112.

———. "Islam and Modern Science: Questions at the Interface." In *GLC,* pp. 3-41.

———. *Islam and Science.* Aldershot, U.K.: Ashgate, 2002.

Irenaeus. *Proof of the Apostolic Preaching* 22. Translated by Joseph P. Smith. Vol. 16 of *Ancient Christian Writers,* edited by Johannes Quasten and Joseph C. Plumpe. New York: Newman, 1978.

Isasi-Díaz, Ada María. *Mujerista Theology: A Theology for the Twenty-First Century.* Maryknoll, N.Y.: Orbis, 1996.

Isham, Christopher J., and John C. Polkinghorne. "The Debate over the Block Universe." In *QCLN,* pp. 135-44.

Jackelén, Antje. *Time and Eternity: The Question of Time in Church, Science, and Theology.* Translated by Barbara Harshaw. West Conshohocken, Pa.: Templeton Foundation Press, 2005.

Jacobs, Louis. "The Body in Jewish Worship." In *RB,* pp. 71-89.

———. *A Jewish Theology.* London: Darton, Longman and Todd, 1973.

Jacobs, Mark X. "Jewish Environmentalism: Past Accomplishments and Future Challenges." In *J&E,* pp. 449-80.

Jacques, André. *The Stranger within Your Gates: Uprooted People in the World Today.* Geneva: World Council of Churches, 1986.

Jaeger, Werner Wilhelm. *Humanism and Theology.* Milwaukee: Marquette University Press, 1943.

James, William. "The Moral Equivalent of War." *Popular Science Monthly* 77 (1910): 400-412. http://archive.org/stream/popularsciencemo77newy#page/400/mode/1up (8/13/2013).

Jammer, Max. *Concepts of Space: The History of Theories of Space in Physics.* 3rd enlarged ed. New York: Dover Publications, 1993.

Janicaud, Dominique. *On the Human Condition.* New York: Routledge, 2005.

Jantzen, Grace M. *Foundations of Violence: Death and the Displacement of Beauty.* Vol. 1. London and New York: Routledge Taylor and Francis Group, 2004.

Jātakamālā or Garland of Birth Stories by Āryaśūra. Translated by J. S. Speyer (1895). Electronic version from 2010 available at http://www.buddhanet-de.net/ancient-bud dhist-texts/English-Texts/Garland-of-Birth-Stories/Garland-of-Birth-Stories.pdf.

Jeeves, Malcolm. "Brain, Mind, and Behavior." In *WHS,* pp. 73-93.

Jeeves, Malcolm, and Warren S. Brown. *Neuroscience, Psychology, and Religion: Illusions, Delusions, and Realities about Human Nature.* West Conshohocken, Pa.: Templeton Foundation Press, 2009.

Jeffery, Arthur. *The Foreign Vocabulary of the Qur'ān.* Leiden: Brill, 2007.

Jenson, Robert W. *America's Theologian: A Recommendation of Jonathan Edwards.* New York: Oxford University Press, 1988.

———. "Aspects of a Doctrine of Creation." In *The Doctrine of Creation: Essays in Dogmatics, History, and Philosophy,* edited by Colin Gunton, pp. 17-28. London: T. & T. Clark, 1997.

———. *God after God: The God of the Past and the God of the Future, Seen in the Work of Karl Barth.* Indianapolis and New York: Bobbs-Merrill, 1969.

———. *Systematic Theology.* Vol. 2. New York: Oxford University Press, 1999.

Jewett, Paul King, with Marguerite Shuster. *Who We Are: Our Dignity as Human; A Neo-Evangelical Theology.* Grand Rapids: Eerdmans, 1996.

Jewett, Robert. *Paul's Anthropological Terms: A Study of Their Use in Conflict Settings.* Leiden: Brill, 1971.

Jinpa, Thupten. "Science as an Ally or a Rival Phillosophy? Tibetan Buddhist Thinkers' Engagement with Modern Science." In *B&S,* pp. 71-85.

Johnson, Elizabeth. *She Who Is: The Mystery of God in Feminist Theological Discourse.* New York: Crossroad, 1993.

———. *Women, Earth, and Creator Spirit.* Mahwah, N.J.: Paulist, 1993.

Jones, Ken. *The New Social Face of Buddhism: A Call to Action.* Somerville, Mass.: Wisdom Publications, 2003.

Jones, Serene. *Feminist Theory and Christian Theology: Cartographies of Grace.* Minneapolis: Fortress, 2000.

Jones, William R. *Is God a White Racist? A Preamble to Black Theology.* Garden City, N.Y.: Doubleday, 1973.

Jónsson, Gunnlauguer A. *The Image of God: Genesis 1:26-28 in a Century of Old Testament Research.* Translated by Lorraine Svendsen. Revised by Michael S. Cheney. Stockhom: Almqvist & Wiksell International, 1988.

Jordan, Winthrop D. *The White Man's Burden: Historical Origins of Racism in the United States.* New York: Oxford University Press, 1974.

Joseph, R., ed. *NeuroTheology: Brain, Science, Spirituality, Religious Experience.* 2nd ed. San Jose: University Press, 2003.

Juergensmeyer, Mark. *Terror in the Mind of God: The Global Rise of Religious Violence.* 3rd rev. ed. Berkeley: University of California Press, 2003.

Justus, John R., and Susan R. Fletcher. *Global Climate Change.* Congressional Research Service, Library of Congress (May 12, 2006). http://www.earth-news.org/NLE/CRSreports/06apr/IB89005.pdf (11/26/2013).

Kahane, Guy. "Evolutionary Debunking Arguments." *Noûs* 45, no. 1 (2011): 103-25.

Kalin, Ibrahim. "Three Views of Science in the Islamic World." In *God, Life, and the Cosmos: Christian and Islamic Perspectives,* edited by Ted Peters, Muzaffar Iqbal, and Syed Nomanul Haq, chap. 2, pp. 43-75. Farnham, U.K., and Burlington, Vt.: Ashgate, 2002.

————. "Will, Necessity and Creation as Monistic Theophany in the Islamic Philosophical Tradition." In *CGA,* pp. 107-32.

Kallenberg, Brad. "The Descriptive Problem of Evil." In *PC,* pp. 297-322.

Kamali, Mohammad Hashim. "Islam, Rationality and Science: A Brief Analysis." In *ISHCP,* 1:75-93.

Kane, Robert. Introduction to *OHFW,* pp. 3-35.

————. "Rethinking Free Will: New Perspectives on an Ancient Problem." In *OHFW,* pp. 381-404.

————. *The Significance of Free Will.* Oxford: Oxford University Press, 1996.

Kant, Immanuel. *The Critique of Pure Reason* [1781]. Translated by J. M. D. Meiklejohn. Penn State Electronic Classic Series, 2010. http://www2.hn.psu.edu/faculty/jmanis/kant/Critique-Pure-Reason6x9.pdf.

————. *Fundamental Principles of the Metaphysic of Morals.* Translated by T. Abbott. New York: Prometheus Books, 1987 [1785].

————. "Of the Different Human Races." In *The Idea of Race,* edited by Robert Barnasconi and Tommy L. Lott, pp. 8-22. Indianapolis: Hackett, 2000. http://isites.harvard.edu/fs/docs/icb.topic97823.files/I_/Sept_27/KANT.pdf (2/26/2013).

————. *Religion within the Limits of Reason Alone.* Translated by Theodore M. Greene and Hoyt H. Hudson. Harper Torchbook/The Cloister Library edition. New York: Harper and Row, 1960.

Kaplan, Edward K. "Reverence and Responsibility: Abraham Joshua Heschel on Nature and the Self." In *J&E,* pp. 407-22.

Kapolyo, Joe M. *The Human Condition: Christian Perspectives through African Eyes.* Downers Grove, Ill.: InterVarsity, 2005.

Kärkkäinen, Veli-Matti. *Christ and Reconciliation.* Constructive Christian Theology for the Pluralistic World, vol. 1. Grand Rapids: Eerdmans, 2013.

————. *Trinity and Revelation.* Constructive Christian Theology for the Pluralistic World, vol. 2. Grand Rapids: Eerdmans, 2014.

Katz, Eric. "Faith, God, and Nature: Judaism and Deep Ecology." In *Deep Ecology and World Religions,* edited by David Barnhill and Roger Gottlieb. Albany: State University of New York Press, 2001.

Ke, Yuehai, et al. "African Origin of Modern Humans in East Asia: A Tale of 12,000 Y Chromosomes." *Science* 292 (2001): 1151-53.

Kelemen, D. "Are Children 'Intuitive Theists'? Reasoning about Purpose and Design in Nature." *Psychological Science* 15, no. 5 (2004): 295-301.

Kellenberger, J. "'Seeing-as' in Religion: Discovery and Community." *Religious Studies* 38 (2002): 101-8.

Keller, Catherine. *Face of the Deep: A Theology of Becoming.* London and New York: Routledge, 2003.

Keller, Catherine, Michael Nausner, and Mayra Rivera, eds. *Postcolonial Theologies: Divinity and Empire.* St. Louis: Chalice, 2004.

Kellner, Menachem M. *Dogma in Medieval Judaism from Maimonides to Abravanel.* Oxford: Oxford University Press, for the Littmann Library of Jewish Civilization, 1986.

Kelly, J. N. D. *Early Christian Doctrines.* Rev. ed. San Francisco: Harper, 1978.

Kelsey, David H. *Eccentric Existence: A Theological Anthropology.* 2 vols. Louisville: Westminster John Knox, 2009.

———. "On Human Flourishing: A Theocentric Perspective." Yale Center for Faith and Culture Resources, n.d. http://www.yale.edu/faith/downloads/David%20Kelsey%20%20-%20God%27s%20Power%20and%20Human%20Flourishing%202008 .pdf (1/5/2012).

———. "Personal Bodies: A Theological Anthropological Proposal." In *PITP,* pp. 139-58.

Kelsey, George D. *Racism and the Christian Understanding of Man.* New York: Charles Scribner's Sons, 1965.

Kenny, John P. *The Supernatural: Medieval Theological Concepts to Modern.* Staten Island, N.Y.: Alba House, 1972.

Keown, Damien. "Buddhism and Ecology: A Virtue Ethics Approach." *Contemporary Buddhism* 8, no. 2 (2007): 97-112.

Kerr, Fergus. *Immortal Longings: Versions of Transcending Humanity.* London: SPCK, 1997.

———. "The Modern Philosophy of Self in Recent Theology." In *NP,* pp. 23-40.

———. *Theology after Wittgenstein.* 2nd ed. London: SPCK, 1997.

Keyes, Charles F. "Communist Revolution and the Buddhist Past in Cambodia." In *Asian Visions of Authority: Religion and the Modern States of East and Southeast Asia,* edited by Charles F. Keyes, Laurel Kendall, and Helen Hardacre, pp. 43-73. Honolulu: University of Hawai'i Press, 1994.

———. "Monks, Guns, and Peace: Theravāda Buddhism and Political Violence." In *BB,* pp. 145-63.

Khan, Benjamin. *The Concept of Dharma in Valmiki Ramayana.* 2nd ed. New Delhi: Munshiram Mannoharlal Publishers, 1983.

Khatami, Mahmoud. "On the Transcendental Element of Life: A Recapitulation of Human Spirituality in Islamic Philosophical Psychology." *Journal of Shi'a Islamic Studies* 2, no. 2 (2009): 121-40.

Kierkegaard, Søren. *The Concept of Dread.* Translated by W. Lowrie. Princeton: Princeton University Press, 1957 [1844].

————. *Sickness unto Death: A Christian Psychological Exposition for Upbuilding and Awakening.* Edited and translated by Edna H. Hong and Howard V. Hong. Princeton: Princeton University Press, 1983.

Kim, Grace Ji-Sun. *The Grace of Sophia: A Korean North American Women's Christology.* Cleveland: Pilgrim Press, 2002.

Kim, Jaegwon. "Making Sense of Emergence." *Philosophical Studies* 95 (1999): 3-36.

————. *Mind in a Physical World: An Essay on the Mind-Body Problem and Mental Causation.* Cambridge: MIT Press/Bradford, 2000.

————. "The Myth of Nonreductive Materialism." In *The Mind-Body Problem: A Guide to the Current Debate,* edited by Richard Warner and Tadeusz Szubka, pp. 242-60. Oxford: Blackwell, 1994.

————. "The Non-Reductivist's Troubles with Mental Causation." In *Mental Causation,* edited by John Heil and Alfred Mele, pp. 189-210. Oxford: Oxford University Press, 1995.

————. *Physicalism, or Something Near Enough.* Princeton: Princeton University Press, 2005.

————. *Supervenience and Mind: Selected Philosophical Essays.* Cambridge: Cambridge University Press, 1993.

Kim, Kirsteen. *The Holy Spirit in the World: A Global Conversation.* Maryknoll, N.Y.: Orbis, 2007.

Kim, Peter S., James E. Coxworth, and Kristen Hawkes. "Increased Longevity Evolves from Grandmothering." *Proceedings of the Royal Society B [Biological Sciences]* 279, no. 1749 (December 22, 2012): 4880-84.

Kimball, Charles. *When Religion Becomes Evil.* San Francisco: HarperCollins, 2008.

King, David S. "Preimplantation Genetic Diagnosis and the 'New Eugenics.'" *Journal of Medical Ethics* 25, no. 2 (1999): 176-82. http://www.hgalert.org/topics/genetic Selection/PIDJME.html.

King, Winston L. "No-Self, No-Mind, and Emptiness Revisited." In *Buddhist-Christian Dialogue: Mutual Renewal and Transformation,* edited by Paul O. Ingram and Frederick J. Streng, pp. 155-76. Honolulu: University of Hawai'i Press, 1986.

King, Ynestra. "Making the World Live: Feminism and the Domination of Nature." In *Women's Spirit Bonding,* edited by Janet Kalven and Mary I. Buckley. New York: Pilgrim Press, 1984.

Kismaric, Carole, and William Shawcross. *Forced Out: The Agony of the Refugee in Our Time.* New York: Random House, 1989.

Klein, Richard G. "Behavioral and Biological Origins of Modern Humans." At http://www.american-buddha.com/behav.biol.biology.htm (5/22/2013).

————. *The Human Career: Human Biological and Cultural Origins.* Chicago: University of Chicago Press, 1989.

————. "Suddenly Smarter." *Stanford Alumni Magazine,* July/August 2002, n.p. http://alumni.stanford.edu/get/page/magazine/article/?article_id=38306 (12/26/2013).

Klein, Richard G., and Blake Edgar. *The Dawn of Human Culture: A Bold New Theory on What Sparked the "Big Bang" of Human Consciousness.* New York: Wiley, 2002.

Kloetzli, W. Randolph. *Buddhist Cosmology: Science and Theology in the Images of Motion and Light.* Delhi: Motilal Banarsidass Publishers, 1989.

Klostermaier, Klaus K. *A Survey of Hinduism.* Albany: State University of New York Press, 1964.

Knight, Chris. "Language, Ochre, and the Rule of Law." In *The Cradle of Language,* edited by Rudolf Both and Christ Knight, pp. 281-303. Oxford: Oxford University Press, 2009.

Koch, C. "Finding Free Will." *Scientific American Mind* 23, no. 2 (May/June 2012): 22-27.

Koenigs, M., L. Young, R. Adolphs, D. Tranel, F. Cushman, M. Hauser, and A. Damasio. "Damage to the Prefrontal Cortex Increases Utilitarian Moral Judgments." *Nature* 446 (2007): 908-11.

Koertge, Noretta, ed. *A House Built on Sand: Exposing Postmodernist Myths about Science.* Oxford: Oxford University Press, 1998.

Koonin, Eugene V. "The Biological Big Bang Model for the Major Transitions in Evolution." *Biology Direct* 20 (August 2007). http://www.biology-direct.com/content/2/1/21.

Koons, Robert C., and George Bealer, eds. *The Waning of Materialism.* Oxford: Oxford University Press, 2010.

Korsmeyer, Jerry D. *Evolution and Eden: Balancing Original Sin and Contemporary Science.* New York: Paulist, 1998.

Koyama, Kosuke. *Mount Fuji and Mount Sinai: A Critique of Idols.* Maryknoll, N.Y.: Orbis, 1985.

Kraschl, Dominikus. "Das Leib-Seele-Problem als Ausdruck menschlicher Geschöpflichkeit." *Neue Zeitschrift für Systematische Theologie und Religionsphilosophie* 53, no. 4 (2011): 399-417.

Krzysztof, A. Cyran, and Marek Kimmel. "Alternatives to the Wright-Fisher Model: The Robustness of Mitochondrial Eve Dating." *Theoretical Population Biology* 78, no. 3 (2010): 165-72.

Kümmel. Werner Georg. *Man in the New Testament.* London: Epworth, 1963.

Küng, Hans. *The Beginning of All Things: Science and Religion.* Translated by John Bowden. Grand Rapids: Eerdmans, 2007.

———. *Does God Exist? An Answer for Today.* Translated by Edward Quinn. New York: Doubleday, 1980.

Kupperman, Joel J. *Theories of Human Nature.* Indianapolis and Cambridge: Hackett, 2010.

Küppers, Bernd-Olaf. *Information and the Origin of Life.* Cambridge: MIT Press, 1990.

———. "Understanding Complexity." In *C&C,* pp. 93-105.

Kvam, Kristen E., Linda S. Schearing, and Valerie H. Ziegler, eds. *Eve and Adam: Jewish, Christian, and Muslim Readings on Genesis and Gender.* Bloomington: Indiana University Press, 1999.

Kyung, Chung Hyun. *Struggle to Be the Sun Again: Introducing Asian Women's Theology.* Maryknoll, N.Y.: Orbis, 1990.

LaCugna, Catherine Mowry. *God for Us: The Trinity and Christian Life.* San Francisco: HarperSanFrancisco, 1993.

Laing, John D. "Middle Knowledge." *Internet Encyclopedia of Philosophy: A Peer-Reviewed Academic Resource,* June 27, 2005. http://www.iep.utm.edu/middlekn/ (6/11/2013).

Lal, Vinay. "Too Deep for Deep Ecology: Gandhi and the Ecological Vision of Life." In *HE,* pp. 183-212.

Lamm, Norman. "Ecology in Jewish Law and Theology." In *Faith and Doubt: Studies in Traditional Jewish Thought,* by N. Lamm. New York: Ktav, 1972.

Laplace, Pierre Simon. *A Philosophical Essay on Probabilities.* Translated from the 6th French ed. by Fredrick Wilson Truscott and Frederick Lincoln Emory. London: Chapman and Hall, 1902.

Larson, Edward. *Trial and Error: The American Controversy over Creation and Evolution.* New York: Oxford University Press, 1985.

Larsson, Göran. "Islam and Disability: Perspectives in Theology and Jurisprudence." *Islam and Christian-Muslim Relations* 22, no. 3 (2011): 367-68.

La Shure, Charles. "What Is Liminality?" October 18, 2005 (first version). http://www.liminality.org/about/whatisliminality/ (2/25/2013).

Leaman, Oliver. *Islamic Philosophy: An Introduction.* 2nd ed. Cambridge: Polity, 2009.

Lebech, Mette. *On the Problem of Human Dignity: A Phenomenological and Hermeneutical Investigation.* Würzburg: Verlag Königshausen & Neumann, 2009.

Lecky, William E. H. *The History of European Morals from Augustus to Charlemagne.* Vol. 2. New York: George Braziller, 1955 [1869].

LeDoux, Joseph E. *The Emotional Brain: The Mysterious Underpinnings of Emotional Life.* New York: Simon and Schuster, 1996.

Lee, Jung Young. *The Theology of Change: A Christian Concept of God in an Eastern Perspective.* Maryknoll, N.Y.: Orbis, 1979.

————. *The Trinity in Asian Perspective.* Nashville: Abingdon, 1996.

Lee, Sang Hyun. *From a Liminal Place: An Asian American Theology.* Minneapolis: Fortress, 2010.

————. *The Philosophical Theology of Jonathan Edwards.* Princeton: Princeton University Press, 1988.

Lee, Sukjae. "Occasionalism." In *The Stanford Encyclopedia of Philosophy,* Winter 2008 edition, edited by Edward N. Zalta. http://plato.stanford.edu/archives/win2008/entries/occasionalism/.

Leech, David, and Aku Visala. "The Cognitive Science of Religion: A Modified Theist Response." *Religious Studies* 47, no. 3 (2011): 301-16.

Lefebure, Leo D. *The Buddha and the Christ: Explorations in Buddhist and Christian Dialogue.* Maryknoll, N.Y.: Orbis, 1993.

————. *Revelation, the Religions, and Violence.* Maryknoll, N.Y.: Orbis, 2000.

Leftow, Brian. "Souls Dipped in Dust." In *Soul, Body, and Survival: Essays on the Metaphysics of Human Persons,* edited by Kevin Corcoran, pp. 120-38. Ithaca, N.Y.: Cornell University Press, 2001.

Leslie, John. *Universes.* London: Routledge, 1989.

Levinas, Emmanuel. *Totality and Infinity: An Essay on Exteriority.* Translated by Alphonso Lingis. Pittsburgh: Duquesne University Press, 1969.

Lewin, Roger. *The Origin of Modern Humans*. New York: Scientific American Library, 1993.

Lewis, C. S. *Studies in Words*. 2nd ed. Cambridge: Cambridge University Press, 1967.

Lewis, David. "Truthmaking and Difference-Making." *Noûs* 35, no. 4 (2001): 602-15.

Lewis-Williams, David. *Conceiving God: The Cognitive Origin and Evolution of Religion*. London: Thames and Hudson, 2010.

Lewontin, R. C. *The Doctrine of DNA: Biology as Ideology*. London: Penguin Books, 1993.

Libet, Benjamin. *Mind Time: The Temporal Factor in Consciousness*. Cambridge: Harvard University Press, 2004.

Libet, Benjamin, Antony Freeman, and Keith Sutherland, eds. *The Volitional Brain: Towards a Neuroscience of Free Will*. Exeter, U.K.: Imprint Academic, 1999.

Libet, B., C. Gleason, E. Wright, and D. Pearl. "Time of Conscious Intention to Act in Relation to Onset of Cerebral Activity (Readiness-Potential)." *Brain* 106, no. 3 (1983): 623-42.

Lieberman, Daniel E., and Ofer Bar-Yosef. "Apples and Oranges: Morphological versus Behavioural Transitions in the Pleistocene." In *Interpreting the Past: Essays on Human, Primate, and Mammal Evolution in Honor of David Pilbeam,* edited by Daniel E. Lieberman, Richard J. Smith, and Jay Kelley, pp. 275-96. Boston: Brill, 2005.

Lieberman, Philip. *Uniquely Human: The Evolution of Speech, Thought, and Selfless Behavior*. Cambridge: Harvard University Press, 1991.

Lindblom, Charles E. *The Market System*. New Haven: Yale University Press, 2001.

Linzey, Andrew. *Animal Theology*. London: SCM, 1994.

———. *Christianity and the Rights of Animals*. New York: Crossroad, 1987.

———. "Is Christianity Irredeemably Speciesist?" Introduction to *AOA*, pp. xi-xx.

Lipner, Julius L. *Hindus: Their Religious Beliefs and Practices*. London and New York: Routledge, 1994.

Lloyd, Genevieve. *The Man of Reason: "Male" and "Female" in Western Philosophy*. 2nd ed. Minneapolis: University of Minnesota Press, 1993.

Locke, J. *An Essay concerning Human Understanding*. Edited by P. Nidditch. Clarendon edition of the Works of John Locke. Oxford: Oxford University Press, 1979 [1689]. http://oregonstate.edu/instruct/phl302/philosophers/locke.html.

Loewer, Barry. "Freedom from Physics: Quantum Mechanics and Free Will." *Philosophical Topics* 24, no. 2 (1996): 91-112.

Löfstedt, Torsten. "The Creation and Fall of Adam: A Comparison of the Qur'anic and Biblical Accounts." *Swedish Missiological Themes* 93, no. 4 (2005): 453-77.

Lohse, Bernhard. *Martin Luther's Theology: Its Historical and Systematic Development*. Translated and edited by Roy A. Harrisville. Minneapolis: Fortress, 1999.

Lonergan, Bernard J. F., S.J. *Insight: A Study in Human Understanding*. London: Longmans, 1961.

Long, Stephen. *Divine Economy: Theology and the Market*. London: Routledge, 2000.

Lønning, Peter, ed. *Creation — an Ecumenical Challenge: Reflections Issuing from a Study by the Institute for Ecumenical Research, Strasbourg, France*. Macon, Ga.: Mercer University Press, 1989.

Lopez, Donald S. *Buddhism and Science: A Guide for the Perplexed.* Chicago: University of Chicago Press, 2008.

Lossky, Vladimir. *The Mystical Theology of the Eastern Church.* Cambridge: James Clarke, 1991.

Lubenow, Martin L. "Pre-Adamites, Sin, Death, and the Human Fossils." *Creation Ex Nihilo Technical Journal* 12, no. 2 (1998): 222-32.

Lucas, J. R. *The Future: An Essay on God, Temporality, and Truth.* Oxford: Blackwell, 1989.

Ludwig, Theodore M. *The Sacred Paths: Understanding the Religions of the World.* 4th ed. Upper Saddle River, N.J.: Pearson, 2006.

Luther, Martin. *The Bondage of the Will.* In Erasmus and Martin Luther, *Discourse on Free Will,* translated and edited by Ernst F. Winter. New York: Continuum, 1997.

———. *The Small Catechism.* In *The Book of Concord: The Confessions of the Evangelical Lutheran Church,* edited by Robert Kolb and Timothy J. Wengert. Minneapolis: Fortress, 2000.

Luttwak, Edward. *Turo-Capitalism: Winners and Losers in the Global Economy.* New York: HarperCollins, 1999.

Lyotard, Jean-François. *The Postmodern Condition: A Report on Knowledge.* Translated by Geoff Bennington and Brian Massumi. Theory and History of Literature 10. Minneapolis: University of Minnesota Press, 1984.

MacIntyre, Alasdair. *After Virtue: A Study in Moral Theory.* 3rd ed. Notre Dame, Ind.: University of Notre Dame Press, 2007.

———. *Dependent Rational Animals: Why Human Beings Need the Virtues.* Chicago: Open Court, 1999.

———. *Whose Justice? Which Rationality?* London: Duckworth, 1988.

MacKay, Donald M. *The Clockwork Image.* Downers Grove, Ill.: InterVarsity, 1974.

Macquarrie, John. *Principles of Christian Theology.* 2nd ed. New York: Scribner, 1977.

———. "What Is a Human Being?" Review of *Anthropology in Theological Perspective,* by Wolfhart Pannenberg. *Expository Times* 97, no. 7 (1986): 202-3.

Maguire, Daniel. *The Moral Core of Judaism and Christianity: Reclaiming the Revolution.* Philadelphia: Fortress, 1993.

Maimonides, Moses. *The Eight Chapters of Maimonides on Ethics (Shemonah Perakim).* Translated and edited by Joseph I. Gorfinkle. New York: Columbia University Press, 1912. http://archive.org/stream/eightchaptersofmoomaim#page/n9/mode/2up (6/10/2013).

———. *The Essay on the Resurrection.* In *The Epistles of Maimonides: Crisis and Leadership.* Translation and notes by Abraham Halkin. Philadelphia: Jewish Publication Society of America, 1993.

———. *The Guide for the Perplexed.* Translated by M. Friedländer. sacred-texts.com [1903].

"Maimonides: The 13 Principles and the Resurrection of the Dead." Fordham University Medieval Sourcebook. http://www.fordham.edu/halsall/source/rambam13.asp (3/1/2013).

Majid, Abdul. "The Muslim Responses to Evolution." At http://www.irfi.org/articles/articles_151_200/muslim_responses_to_evolution.htm (11/21/2013).

Makransky, John. "Buddhist Analogues of Sin and Grace: A Dialogue with Augustine." Presentation at 2001 Thagaste Symposium, Merrimack College, 2001. http://www.johnmakransky.org/article_12.html (4/5/2013).

Mann, R. B. "Physics at the Theological Frontiers." *Perspectives on Science and Christian Faith* (draft invitational essay, June 25, 2012), at http://www.csca.ca/wp-content/uploads/2012/06/PhysicsAtTheTheologicalFrontiersMann2012.pdf.

Mann, William E. "Augustine on Original Sin and Evil." In *Cambridge Companion to Augustine,* edited by Eleanor Stump and Norman Kretzmann, pp. 40-48. Cambridge: Cambridge University Press, 2001.

Manual of Abhidhamma (Abhidhammattha Sangaha), A. Translated and edited by Nàrada Mahà Thera. 5th ed. Kuala Lumpur: Buddhist Missionary Society, 1987. http://www.buddhanet.net/pdf_file/abhidhamma.pdf (11/14/2013).

Marean, Curtis W., et al. "Early Human Use of Marine Resources and Pigment in South Africa during the Middle Pleistocene." *Nature* 449 (October 18, 2007): 905-8.

Margulis, Lynn, and Dorion Sagan. *Microcosmos: Four Billion Years of Evolution from Our Microbial Ancestors.* New York: Simon and Schuster, 1991.

Marks, Jonathan. *What It Means to Be 98% Chimpanzee: Apes, People, and Their Genes.* Berkeley: University of California Press, 2002.

Marmorstein, Arthur. *The Old Rabbinic Doctrine of God.* Vol. 2, *Essays in Anthropomorphism.* London: Oxford University Press, 1937.

Martin, Raymond, and John Barresi. *The Rise and Fall of Soul and Self: An Intellectual History of Personal Identity.* New York: Columbia University Press, 2006.

Marty, Martin E. *When Faiths Collide.* Malden, Mass.: Blackwell, 2005.

Matsuoka, Fumitaka. *Out of Silence: Emerging Themes in Asian American Churches.* Cleveland: United Church Press, 1995.

Mavrodes, George I. "Is the Past Unpreventable?" *Faith and Philosophy* 1, no. 2 (1984): 131-46.

Mayotte, Judy A. *Disposable People? The Plight of Refugees.* Maryknoll, N.Y.: Orbis, 1992.

Mbiti, John S. *African Religions and Philosophy.* Garden City, N.Y.: Doubleday, 1970.

———. *Concepts of God in Africa.* 2nd ed. Nairobi: Acton Publishers, 2012 [1970].

McBrearty, Sally, and Allison S. Brooks. "The Revolution That Wasn't: A New Interpretation of the Origin of Modern Human Behavior." *Journal of Human Evolution* 39, no. 5 (2000): 453-63.

McCauley, Robert N. *Why Religion Is Natural and Science Is Not.* Oxford: Oxford University Press, 2011.

McClendon, James Wm., Jr. *Ethics: Systematic Theology.* Vol. 1. Nashville: Abingdon, 1986.

McDaniel, Jay. *Of God and Pelicans: A Theology of Reverence for Life.* Louisville: Westminster John Knox, 1989.

McDermott, Brian O., S.J. "The Theology of Original Sin: Recent Developments." *Theological Studies* 38 (1977): 478-512.

McDonnell, Kilian. "The Determinative Doctrine of the Holy Spirit." *Theology Today* 39, no. 2 (1982): 142-61.

McFadyen, Alistair. *Bound to Sin: Abuse, Holocaust, and the Christian Doctrine of Sin.* Cambridge: Cambridge University Press, 2000.

———. *The Call to Personhood: A Christian Theory of the Individual in Social Relationship*. Cambridge: Cambridge University Press, 1990.

McFague, Sallie. *The Body of God: An Ecological Theology*. Minneapolis: Fortress, 1993.

———. "An Ecological Christology: Does Christianity Have It?" In *Christianity and Ecology*, edited by Dieter Hessel and Rosemary Ruether. Cambridge: Harvard University Press, 2000.

———. *Metaphorical Theology: Models of God in Religious Language*. Philadelphia: Fortress, 1982.

———. *Models of God: Theology for an Ecological, Nuclear Age*. Minneapolis: Fortress, 1987.

———. "Models of God for an Ecological, Evolutionary Era: God as Mother of the Universe." In *PPT*, pp. 249-71.

McGrath, Alister E. *A Fine-Tuned Universe: The Quest for God in Science and Theology*. Louisville: Westminster John Knox, 2009.

———. *The Open Secret: A New Vision for Natural Theology*. Oxford: Blackwell, 2008.

———. *A Scientific Theology*. Vol. 1, *Nature*. Vol. 2, *Reality*. Vol. 3, *Theory*. Grand Rapids: Eerdmans, 2001, 2002, 2006 [2003].

———. *Thomas F. Torrance: An Intellectual Biography*. Edinburgh: T. & T. Clark, 1999.

McIntosh, Peggy. "White Privilege and Male Privilege: A Personal Account of Coming to See Correspondences through Work in Women's Studies." Wellesley Centers for Women Paper no. 189 (1988). http://www.wcwonline.org/index.php?option= com_virtuemart&view=productdetails&virtuemart_product_id=259&virtuemart _category_id=223&Itemid=175.

McLaughlin, Brian P. "Varieties of Supervenience." In *Supervenience: New Essays*, edited by Elias E. Savellos and Ümit D. Yalçin, pp. 16-59. Cambridge: Cambridge University Press, 1995.

McLean, Stuart. *Humanity in the Thought of Karl Barth*. Edinburgh: T. & T. Clark, 1981.

McMahon, Kevin A. "Anselm and the Guilt of Adam." *Saint Anselm Journal* 2, no. 1 (Fall 2004): 81-89.

McMullin, Ernan. "Creation *Ex Nihilo*: Early History." In *CGA*, pp. 11-23.

———. "How Should Cosmology Relate to Theology?" In *The Sciences and Theology in the Twentieth Century*, edited by A. R. Peacocke, pp. 17-57. Notre Dame, Ind.: University of Notre Dame Press, 1981.

———. "Natural Science and Belief in a Creator: Historical Notes." In *PPT*, pp. 49-79.

McNamara, Patrick. *Where God and Science Meet: How Brain and Evolutionary Studies Alter Our Understanding of Religion*. Vol. 1, *Evolution, Genes, and the Religious Experience*. Vol. 2, *The Neurology of Religious Experience*. Vol. 3, *The Psychology of Religious Experience*. Westport, Conn.: Praeger, 2006. (This whole work is available at http://m.friendfeed-media.com/a8cb89b353ba1c5245a32c16d8032aab7bfd0a72.)

McNamara, Patrick, and Wesley Wildman, eds. *Science and the World's Religions*. Vol. 1, *Origins and Destinies*. Vol. 2, *Persons and Groups*. Vol. 3, *Religions and Controversies*. Santa Barbara, Calif.: Praeger, 2012.

McTaggart, John Ellis. "The Unreality of Time." *Mind* 17 (1908): 457-74.

Mead, George Herbert. *Mind, Self, and Society from the Standpoint of a Social Behaviorist.* Edited by C. W. Morris. Chicago: University of Chicago Press, 1934.

Meeks, M. Douglas. "The Economy of Grace: Human Dignity in Market System." In *GHD*, pp. 196-214.

―――. *God the Economist: The Doctrine of God and Political Economy.* Minneapolis: Fortress, 1989.

Melanchthon, Philipp. *Loci Communes.* 1543. Translated by J. A. O. Preus. St. Louis: Concordia, 1992.

Melin, Ander. "Environmental Philosophy in Christianity and Buddhism: Meeting Places for a Dialogue." *Ecotheology* 11, no. 3 (2006): 357-74.

Mellars, Paul, and Chris Stringer, eds. *The Human Revolution: Behavioural and Biological Perspectives on the Origins of Modern Humans.* Princeton: Princeton University Press, 1989.

Menn, Esther Marie. "Land, Displacement, and Hope in Jeremiah and in Today's World." In *GHD*, pp. 161-78.

Menon, Sangeetha. "Hinduism and Science." In *OHRS*, pp. 7-23.

Merricks, Trenton. *Truth and Ontology.* Oxford: Clarendon, 2007.

Metzinger, Thomas. "Introduction: Consciousness Research at the End of the Twentieth Century." In *Neural Correlates of Consciousness: Empirical and Conceptual Questions,* edited by T. Metzinger, pp. 1-12. Cambridge: MIT Press, 2000.

Meyendorff, John. *Byzantine Theology: Historical Trends and Doctrinal Themes.* New York: Fordham University Press, 1974.

Meyerhof, Max, and Joseph Schacht, eds. *The Theologus Autodidactus of Ibn al-Nafis.* Oxford: Oxford University Press, 1968.

Middleton, J. Richard. *The Liberating Image: The Imago Dei in Genesis 1.* Grand Rapids: Brazos, 2005.

Midgley, Mary. "The Soul's Successors: Philosophy and the 'Body.'" In *Religion and the Body,* edited by Sarah Coakley, pp. 53-68. Cambridge: Cambridge University Press, 1997.

Milbank, John. "Materialism and Transcendence." In *Theology and the Political: The New Debate,* edited by Creston Davis, John Milbank, and Slavoj Žižek, pp. 393-426. Durham, N.C.: Duke University Press, 2005.

―――. "'Postmodern Critical Augustinianism': A Short *Summa* in Forty-Two Responses to Unasked Questions." *Modern Theology* 7 (1991): 227-37.

―――. "Radical Orthodoxy: Twenty-Four Theses." In *Radical Orthodoxy? A Catholic Enquiry,* edited by Laurence Paul Hemming, thesis 5, pp. 33-45. Aldershot, U.K.: Ashgate, 2000.

―――. *The Suspended Middle: Henri de Lubac and the Debate concerning the Supernatural.* Grand Rapids: Eerdmans, 2005.

―――. *Theology and Social Theory: Beyond Secular Reason.* Oxford: Blackwell, 1990.

―――. *The Word Made Strange: Theology, Language, Culture.* Oxford: Blackwell, 1997.

Milbank, John, Catherine Pickstock, and Graham Ward, eds. *Radical Orthodoxy: A New Theology.* London: Routledge, 1999.

―――. "Introduction: Suspending the Material; The Turn of Radical Orthodoxy." In

Radical Orthodoxy, edited by John Milbank, Catherine Pickstock, and Graham Ward. London: Routledge, 1999.

Milner, Richard, and Ian Tattersall. "Faces of the Human Past: Science and Art Combine to Create a New Portrait Gallery of Our Hominid Heritage." *Natural History*, February 2007, n.p. http://www.naturalhistorymag.com/htmlsite/master.html?http://www.naturalhistorymag.com/htmlsite/0207/0207_feature.html (6/27/2013).

Mir, Mustansir. "Christian Perspectives on Religion and Science and Their Significance for Modern Muslim Thought." In *GLC*, pp. 99-124.

Mirandola, Pico della. *On the Dignity of Man*. Translated by Charles Glenn Wallis. Indianapolis: Bobbs-Merrill, 1965.

Mishkin, M., and T. Appenzeller. "The Anatomy of Memory." *Scientific American* 256, no. 6 (1987): 80-89.

Misner, C. W., K. S. Thorne, and J. A. Wheeler. *Gravitation*. New York: Freeman and Co., 1973.

Mithen, Steven. *The Singing Neanderthals: The Origins of Music, Language, Mind, and Body*. London: Weidenfeld and Nicolson, 2005.

Mnyandu, M. "Ubuntu as the Basis of Authentic Humanity: An African Christian Perspective." *Journal of Constructive Theology* 3, no. 1 (1997): 77-86.

Mohamed, Yasien. *Fitrah: The Islamic Concept of Human Nature*. London: Ta-Ha Publishers, 1996.

Molina, Luis de. *On Divine Foreknowledge*. Part 4 of the *Concordia*. Translated and introduced by Alfred J. Freddoso. Ithaca, N.Y.: Cornell University Press, 1988.

Moltmann, Jürgen. *Experiences in Theology: Ways and Forms of Christian Theology*. Translated by Margaret Kohl. Minneapolis: Fortress, 2000.

———. *God for a Secular Society: The Public Relevance of Theology*. Translated by Margaret Kohl. Minneapolis: Fortress, 1999.

———. *God in Creation: A New Theology of Creation and the Spirit of God*. Translated by Margaret Kohl. Minneapolis: Fortress, 1993.

———. *The Spirit of Life: A Universal Affirmation*. Translated by Margaret Kohl. Minneapolis: Fortress, 1992.

———. *The Trinity and the Kingdom of God: The Doctrine of God*. Translated by Margaret Kohl. San Francisco: Harper and Row; London: SCM, 1981.

———. *The Way of Jesus Christ: Christology in Messianic Dimensions*. Translated by Margaret Kohl. Minneapolis: Fortress, 1993 [1989].

Monod, Jacques. *Chance and Necessity: An Essay on the Natural Philosophy of Modern Biology*. Translated by Austryn Wainhouse. New York: Vintage, 1972.

Morales, Erwin. "Vector Fields as the Empirical Correlate of the Spirit(s): A Meta-Pannenbergian Approach to Pneumatological Pluralism." In *Interdisciplinary and Religio-Cultural Discourses on a Spirit-Filled World: Loosing the Spirits*, edited by Veli-Matti Kärkkäinen, Kirsteen Kim, and Amos Yong, chap. 16. New York: Palgrave Macmillan, 2013.

Moreland, J. P. *Consciousness and the Existence of God: A Theistic Argument*. Routledge Studies in the Philosophy of Religion. New York and London: Routledge, 2008.

Moreland, J. P., and John Mark Reynolds, eds. Introduction to *Three Views on Creation and Evolution*, pp. 7-38. Grand Rapids: Zondervan, 1999.

Moreland, J. P., and Scott B. Rae. *Body and Soul: Human Nature and the Crisis in Ethics*. Downers Grove, Ill.: InterVarsity, 2000.

Morewedge, Parviz. *The Metaphysics of Mullā Ṣadrā*. New York: Society for the Study of Islamic Philosophy and Science, 1992.

Morowitz, Harold. *The Emergence of Everything: How the World Became Complex*. New York: Oxford University Press, 2002.

Morris, Henry M. *Beginning of the World*. Denver: Accent Books, 1977.

———. *Scientific Creationism*. San Diego: Creation-Life Publishers, 1974.

Morris, Simon Conway. *The Crucible of Creation: The Burgess Shale and the Rise of Animals*. New York: Oxford University Press, 1998.

———. "Evolution and Convergence: Some Wider Considerations." In *The Deep Structure of Biology: Is Convergence Sufficiently Ubiquitous to Give a Directional Signal?* pp. 46-67. West Conshohocken, Pa.: Templeton Foundation Press, 2008.

———. *Life's Solution: Inevitable Humans in a Lonely Universe*. New York: Cambridge University Press, 2003.

———. "We Were Meant to Be . . ." *New Scientist*, no. 2369 (November 16, 2002): 26-29.

Mueller, John Theodore. *Christian Dogmatics*. St. Louis: Concordia, 1934.

Muhtaroglu, Nazif. "An Occasionalist Defence of Free Will." In *Classic Issues in Islamic Philosophy and Theology Today*, edited by Anna-Teresa Tymieniecka and Nazif Muhtaroglu, pp. 45-62. Lexington, Ky.: Springer, 2010.

Muller, Richard A. "Arminius and the Scholastic Tradition." *Calvin Theological Journal* 24, no. 2 (1989): 263-77.

Müller-Fahrenholz, Geiko. *God's Spirit: Transforming a World in Crisis*. New York: Continuum; Geneva: WCC Publications, 1995.

Munday, John C., Jr. "Animal Pain: Beyond the Threshold?" In *Perspectives on Evolving Creation*, edited by K. B. Miller, pp. 435-68. Grand Rapids: Eerdmans, 2003.

Murphy, Nancey. *Anglo-American Postmodernity: Philosophical Perspectives on Science, Religion, and Ethics*. Boulder, Colo.: Westview Press, 1997.

———. *Beyond Liberalism and Fundamentalism: How Modern and Postmodern Philosophy Set the Theological Agenda*. Valley Forge, Pa.: Trinity, 1996.

———. *Bodies and Souls, or Spirited Bodies?* Cambridge: Cambridge University Press, 2006.

———. "Divine Action in the Natural Order: Buridan's Ass and Schrödinger's Cat." In *C&C*, pp. 325-57.

———. "Emergence, Downward Causation, and Divine Action." In *SPDA*, pp. 111-31.

———. "Human Nature: Historical, Scientific, and Religious Issues." In *WHS*, pp. 1-29.

———. "Nonreductive Physicalism: Philosophical Issues." In *WHS*, pp. 127-48.

———. "Reductionism: How Did We Fall into It and Can We Emerge from It?" In *E&E*, pp. 19-39.

———. "Science and the Problem of Evil: Suffering as a By-product of a Finely Tuned Cosmos." In *PC*, pp. 131-51.

Murphy, Nancey, and George F. R. Ellis. *On the Moral Nature of the Universe: Theology, Cosmology, and Ethics.* Minneapolis: Fortress, 1996.

Murray, Michael. *Nature Red in Tooth and Claw: Theism and the Problem of Animal Suffering.* Oxford: Oxford University Press, 2008.

Murray, Michael, and Jeffrey Schloss, eds. *The Believing Primate: Scientific, Philosophical, and Theological Reflections on the Origin of Religion.* New York: Oxford University Press, 2009.

"Muslim Scholars Recast Jihadists' Favourite Fatwa." At "A Common Word" in the News, on the official Web site of A Common Word. http://www.acommonword.com/muslim-scholars-recast-jihadists-favourite-fatwa/ (8/13/2013).

Muthiah, Robert A. *The Priesthood of All Believers in the Twenty-First Century: Living Faithfully as the Whole People of God in a Postmodern Context.* Eugene, Ore.: Pickwick, 2009.

Myers, Ched. *The Biblical Vision of Sabbath Economics.* Massachusetts: Bartimaeus Co-operative Ministries, 2007.

Nagel, Thomas. *Mind and Cosmos: Why the Materialist Neo-Darwinian Conception of Nature Is Almost Certainly False.* Oxford: Oxford University Press, 2012.

———. "What Is It Like to Be a Bat?" In *The Place of Mind,* edited by Brian Cooney, chap. 27, pp. 321-31. Belmont, Calif.: Wadsworth, 2000. Originally in the *Philosophical Review* 83, no. 4 (1974): 435-50.

Nahmias, E., S. Morris, T. Nadelhoffer, J. Turner. "Surveying Freedom: Folk Intuitions about Free Will and Moral Responsibility." *Philosophical Psychology* 18, no. 5 (2005): 561-84.

Nambara, Minoru. "Ultimate Reality in Buddhism and Christianity: A Buddhist Perspective." In *Buddhism and Christianity in Dialogue,* edited by Perry Schmidt-Leukel, pp. 117-37. London: SCM, 2005.

Nanda, Meera. "Vedic Science and Hindu Nationalism: Arguments against a Premature Synthesis of Religion and Science." In *SRPW,* chap. 2.

Näreaho, Leo. "The Cognitive Science of Religion: Philosophical Observations." *Religious Studies* 44, no. 1 (2008): 83-98.

NASA/WMAP [Wilkinson Microwave Anisotropy Probe] Science Team. "Cosmology: The Study of the Universe." http://map.gsfc.nasa.gov/universe/WMAP_Universe.pdf (last modified June 3, 2011).

Nasr, Seyyed Hossein. *An Introduction to Islamic Cosmological Doctrines.* Rev. ed. Albany: State University of New York Press, 1993.

———. "Islam, the Contemporary Islamic World, and the Environmental Crisis." In *I&E,* pp. 85-105.

———. "Islam and Modern Science." Lecture at MIT, November 1991. http://www.muslimphilosophy.com/ip/nasr1.htm (6/3/2013).

———. "Islam and Science." In *OHRS,* pp. 71-86.

———. *Islamic Science: An Illustrated Study.* Chicago: Kazi Publications, 1996.

———. *Man and Nature: The Spiritual Crisis in Modern Man.* Rev. ed. Chicago: Kazi Publications, 1997 [1967].

———. *The Need for a Sacred Science.* Suny Series in Religious Studies. Albany: State University of New York Press, 1993.

———. "The Question of Cosmogenesis: The Cosmos as a Subject of Scientific Study." In *ISHCP,* 1:171-87.

———. *Religion and the Order of Nature.* Oxford: Oxford University Press, 1996.

———. *Traditional Islam in the Modern World.* London: Kegan Paul International, 1987.

"Naturalism." *Encyclopædia Britannica Online.* Encyclopædia Britannica Inc., 2013. Web. October 29, 2013. http://www.britannica.com/EBchecked/topic/406468/naturalism.

Nebelsick, Harold P. "Karl Barth's Understanding of Science." In *Theology beyond Christendom: Essays on the Centenary of the Birth of Karl Barth, May 10, 1886,* edited by John Thompson. Princeton Theological Monograph Series 6. Allison Park, Pa.: Pickwick, 1986.

Nelson, David W. *Judaism, Physics, and God: Searching for Sacred Metaphors in a Post-Einstein World.* Woodstock, Vt.: Jewish Lights Publishing, 2006.

Nelson, Derek R. *What's Wrong with Sin: Sin in Individual and Social Perspective from Schleiermacher to Theologies of Liberation.* London: T. & T. Clark, 2009.

Nelson, Lance E. Introduction to *Purifying the Earthly Body of God: Religion and Ecology in Hindu India,* edited by Lance E. Nelson, pp. 1-10. Albany: State University of New York Press, 1998.

Nelson-Pallmeyer, Jack. *Is Religion Killing Us? Violence in the Bible and the Quran.* Harrisburg, Pa.: Trinity, 2003.

Neuhaeuser, Christian, Elaine Webster, Hannes Kuch, and Paulus Kaufmann, eds. *Humiliation, Degradation, Dehumanization: Human Dignity Violated.* Dordrecht: Springer, 2011.

"The Neuroscientist and the Theologian: Unique Collaboration Draws New Insight into Science and Religion." *BU Today,* January 10, 2011. http://www.bu.edu/today/2011/the-neuroscientist-and-the-theologian/ (11/27/2012).

Newberg, Andrew B. *Principles of Neurotheology.* Farnham, U.K., and Burlington, Vt.: Ashgate, 2010.

Newberg, Andrew B., Eugene G. D'Aquili, and Vince Rause. *Why God Won't Go Away: Brain Science and the Biology of Belief.* New York: Ballantine Books, 2002.

Newbigin, Lesslie. *The Gospel in a Pluralist Society.* Grand Rapids: Eerdmans; Geneva: WCC Publications, 1989.

———. *Proper Confidence: Faith, Doubt, and Certainty in Christian Discipleship.* Grand Rapids: Eerdmans, 1995.

———. "Religious Pluralism and the Uniqueness of Jesus Christ." *International Bulletin of Missionary Research* 13, no. 2 (1989): 50-54.

"Nibbana Sutta: Total Unbinding (1)" (*Udana* 8.1). Translated by T. Bhikkhu. *Access to Insight,* July 8, 2010. http://www.accesstoinsight.org/tipitaka/kn/ud/ud.8.01.than.html.

Nickl, Peter, ed. *Über die Ewigkeit der Welt: Texte von Bonaventura, Thomas von Aquin und Boethius von Dacien.* Frankfurt am Main: Vittorio Klotterman GmbH, 2000.

Niebuhr, Reinhold. *Christianity and Power Politics.* New York: Charles Scribner's Sons, 1940.

———. *Moral Man and Immoral Society.* New York: Charles Scribner's Sons, 1932.

————. *Nature and Destiny of Man: A Christian Interpretation.* 2 vols. New York: Charles Scribner's Sons, 1941.

————. *The Self and the Dramas of History.* New York: Scribner's, 1955.

————. "Sin." In *A Handbook of Christian Theology,* edited by Marvin Halverson and Arthur A. Cohen, p. 349. New York: World Publishing, 1958.

Nielsen, Kai. *Naturalism and Religion.* Almerst, N.Y.: Prometheus, 2001.

————. "Naturalistic Explanations of Theistic Belief." In *A Companion to Philosophy of Religion,* edited by Philip L. Quinn and Charles Taliaferro. Oxford: Blackwell, 1997.

Nietzsche, Friedrich Wilhelm. *On the Genealogy of Morals* [1887]. In *Basic Writings of Nietzsche,* edited and translated by Walter Kaufmann. New York: Modern Library, 1966.

Nikhilananda, Swami. "Trip to America." Section 6 in *Vivekananda: A Biography* (1953). http://www.ramakrishnavivekananda.info/vivekananda_biography/vivekananda _biography.htm (10/16/2013).

Nisbett, Richard. *The Geography of Thought: How Asians and Westerners Think Differently . . . and Why.* New York: Free Press, 2003.

Noegel, Scott B. "Dismemberment, Creation, and Ritual: Images of Divine Violence in the Ancient Near East." In *BB,* pp. 13-27.

Norris, Christopher. *Quantum Theory and the Flight from Realism: Philosophical Responses to Quantum Mechanics.* London: Routledge, 2000.

Numbers, Ronald. "Science without God: Natural Laws and Christian Beliefs." In *When Science and Christianity Meet,* edited by David C. Lindberg and Ronald Numbers, pp. 265-85. Chicago: University of Chicago Press, 2003.

"Nurturing Peace, Overcoming Violence: In the Way of Christ for the Sake of the World." Geneva: World Council of Churches, January 1, 1970. Available at the WCC Web site.

Nussbaum, M. C. *Sex and Social Justice.* Oxford: Oxford University Press, 1999.

Ockham. *Predestination, God's Foreknowledge, and Future Contingents.* Translated by Marilyn McCord Adams and Norman Kretzmann. New York: Appleton-Century-Croft, 1969.

O'Collins, Gerald, S.J. *Jesus Risen: An Historical, Fundamental, and Systematic Examination of Christ's Resurrection.* New York: Paulist, 1987.

O'Connor, Timothy. "Agent-Causal Theories of Freedom." In *OHFW,* pp. 309-28.

————. *Persons and Causes: The Metaphysics of Free Will.* New York: Oxford University Press, 2000.

O'Donnell, John J., S.J. *Trinity and Temporality: The Christian Doctrine of God in Light of Process Theology and Theology of Hope.* Oxford: Oxford University Press, 1983.

Oduyoye, Mercy Amba. *Introducing African Women's Theology.* Sheffield: Sheffield Academic Press, 2001.

O'Hear, Anthony. *Beyond Evolution: Human Nature and the Limits of Evolutionary Explanation.* Oxford: Clarendon, 2002.

Oladipo, Caleb Oluremi. *The Development of the Doctrine of the Holy Spirit in the Yoruba (African) Indigenous Christian Movement.* American University Studies, Series II, Theology and Religion 185. Frankfurt: Peter Lang, 1996.

Olcott, Henry S. *The Buddhist Catechism.* 2nd ed. London and Benares: Theosophical Publishing Society, 1903. www.sacredtexts.com.

Oliver, Simon. "Trinity, Motion and Creation *Ex Nihilo.*" In *CGA,* pp. 133-51.

O'Murchu, Diarmuid. *In the Beginning Was the Spirit: Science, Religion, and Indigenous Spirituality.* Maryknoll, N.Y.: Orbis, 2012.

O'Neill, Mary Aquin. "The Mystery of Being Human Together." In *Freeing Theology: The Essentials of Theology in Feminist Perspective,* edited by Catherine Mowry LaCugna, pp. 139-60. San Francisco: Harper, 1993.

Oppenheimer, Stephen. *Out of Eden: The Peopling of the World.* London: Constable, 2003.

O'Shaughnessy, Thomas J. *Creation and the Teachings of the Quran.* Biblica et orientalia 40. Rome: Biblical Institute Press, 1985.

"Oxford Declaration on Christian Faith and Economics" (January 1990). Published in *Transformation: The Oxford Declaration,* April/June 1990. http://www.ocms.ac.uk/transformation/articles/0702.1_various.pdf (8/14/2013).

Özdemir, Ibrahim. "Towards an Understanding of Environmental Ethics from a Qu'ranic Perspective." In *I&E,* pp. 3-37.

Page, Ruth. *God and the Web of Creation.* London: SCM, 1996.

Pagels, Elaine. *Adam, Eve, and the Serpent: Sex and Politics in Early Christianity.* New York: Vintage, 1988.

Pambrun, James R. "*Creatio Ex Nihilo* and Dual Causality." In *CGA,* chap. 12.

Panksepp, Jaak, and Lucy Biven. *The Archeology of Mind: Neuroevolutionary Origins of Human Emotions.* New York and London: Norton, 2012.

Pannenberg, Wolfhart. "Anthropology and the Question of God." In Pannenberg, *The Idea of God and Human,* translated by R. A. Wilson, pp. 80-98. Philadelphia: Fortress, 1973.

———. *Anthropology in Theological Perspective.* Translated by Matthew O'Connell. Philadelphia: Westminster, 1985.

———. "The Christological Foundation of Christian Anthropology." Translated by David Smith. In *Concilium 6: Humanism and Christianity,* edited by Claude Geffré. New York: Herder and Herder, 1973.

———. "Contingency and Natural Law." In *Towards a Theology of Nature: Essays on Science and Faith,* edited by Ted Peters, pp. 72-122. Louisville: Westminster John Knox, 1993.

———. "Contributions from Systematic Theology." In *OHRS,* pp. 359-71.

———. "The Doctrine of Creation and Modern Science." *Zygon: Journal of Religion and Science* 23 (1988): 9.

———. "Eternity, Time and Space." In *The Historicity of Nature: Essays on Science and Theology,* edited by Niels Henrik Gregersen, pp. 163-74. Philadelphia: Templeton Foundation Press, 2008.

———. "God as Spirit — and Natural Science." *Zygon: Journal of Religion and Science* 36, no. 4 (2001): 783-94.

———. *Introduction to Systematic Theology.* Grand Rapids: Eerdmans, 1991.

———. "Speaking about God in the Face of Atheist Criticism." In Pannenberg, *The Idea of God and Human Freedom,* translated by R. A. Wilson. Philadelphia: Fortress, 1973.

———. *Theology and the Philosophy of Science.* London: Darton, Longman and Todd, 1976.

———. *Toward a Theology of Nature: Essays on Science and Faith.* Edited by Ted Peters. Louisville: Westminster John Knox, 1993.

———. "What Is Truth?" In *Basic Questions in Theology,* translated by George H. Kehm, 2:1-27. Philadelphia: Fortress, 1970.

Paranjape, Makarand. "Science, Spirituality and Modernity in India." In *Science, Spirituality, and the Modernization of India,* edited by Makarand Paranjape, pp. 3-14. Anthem South Asian Studies. London: Anthem Press, 2008.

Parekh, Bhikhu. *Colonialism, Tradition, and Reform.* New Delhi and London: Sage Publications, 1989.

Park, Andrew Sung. *Racial Conflict and Healing: An Asian-American Theological Perspective.* Maryknoll, N.Y.: Orbis, 1996.

———. *The Wounded Heart of God: The Asian Concept of Han and the Christian Doctrine of Sin.* Nashville: Abingdon, 1993.

Park, Chan Ho. "Transcendence and Spatiality of the Triune Creator." Ph.D. diss., School of Theology, Fuller Theological Seminary, 2003.

Parsania, Hamid. "Unseen and Visible." In *ISHCP,* 1:155-69.

Pascal, Blaise. "Of Original Sin." Chapter in *The Thoughts of Blaise Pascal* [1669], translated from the text of M. Auguste Molinier by C. Kegan Paul. London: George Bell and Sons, 1901. http://oll.libertyfund.org/title/2407/227512 (3/8/2013).

Patton, Laurie L. "Nature Romanticism and Sacrifice in Ṛgvedic Interpretation." In *HE,* pp. 39-58.

Paul, Diana Y. *Women in Buddhism: Images of the Feminine in the Mahāynāna Tradition.* 2nd ed. Berkeley and Los Angeles: University of California Press, 1985.

Payne, Richard K. "Buddhism and the Sciences: Historical Background, Contemporary Developments." In *Bridging Science and Religion,* edited by Ted Peters and Gaymon Bennett, chap. 9. Minneapolis: Fortress, 2003.

Payutto, P. A. [Venerable Phra Dammapitaka]. *Dependent Origination: The Buddhist Law of Conditionality.* Translated by Bruce Evans. Bangkok: Buddhadhamma Foundation, 1995. http://www.buddhanet.net/cmdsg/coarise.htm.

———. *Dictionary of Buddhism.* Bangkok: Mahachulalongkornrajavidyala University, 2003.

Peacocke, Arthur. "Chance and Law in Irreversible Thermodynamics, Theoretical Biology, and Theology." In *C&C,* pp. 123-43.

———. *Creation and the World of Science: The Re-shaping of Belief.* 1978 Bampton Lectures. Oxford: Oxford University Press, 1979, 2004.

———. "Emergent Monism." In Peacocke, *ATI,* chap. 2.

———. "God's Interaction with the World: The Implications of Deterministic 'Chaos' and of Interconnected and Interdependent Complexity." In *C&C,* pp. 263-87.

———. Preface to Peacocke, *ATI,* pp. 3-4.

———. "Prologue: Naturalism, Theism, and Religion." In Peacocke, *ATI,* pp. 5-11.

————. "The Sound of Sheer Silence: How Does God Communicate with Humanity." In *NP*, pp. 215-47.

————. "Theology and Science Today." In *Cosmos as Creation: Theology and Science in Consonance,* edited by Ted Peters. Nashville: Abingdon, 1989.

————. *Theology for a Scientific Age: Being and Becoming — Natural, Divine, and Human.* Theology and the Sciences. Enlarged ed. Minneapolis: Fortress, 1993.

————. *Theology in the Context of Science.* New Haven: Yale University Press, 2009.

Pedersen, Olaf. "Christian Belief and the Fascination of Science." In *PPT*, pp. 125-40.

Pelikan, Jaroslav. *The Emergence of the Catholic Tradition (100-600).* Vol. 1 of *The Christian Tradition: A History of the Development of Doctrine.* Chicago: University of Chicago Press, 1971.

Pennington, Brian K. "Striking the Delicate Balance: Teaching Violence and Hinduism." In *TRV*, pp. 19-46.

Penrose, Roger. *The Emperor's New Mind: Concerning Computers, Minds, and the Laws of Physics.* New York: Penguin Books, 1989.

————. "The Modern Physicist's View of Nature." In *The Concept of Nature,* edited by John Torrance, pp. 117-66. Oxford: Oxford University Press, 1992.

Persinger, A. "People Who Report Religious Experiences May Also Display Enhanced Temporal Lobe Signs." *Perceptual and Motor Skills* 58 (1984): 963-75.

Perszyk, Kenneth. "Molinism and Compatibilism." *International Journal for Philosophy of Religion* 48 (2000): 11-33.

————, ed. *Molinism: The Contemporary Debate.* New York: Oxford University Press, 2011.

Peters, Karl E. *Dancing with the Sacred: Evolution, Ecology, and God.* Harrisburg, Pa.: Trinity, 2002.

Peters, Ted. *God — the World's Future: Systematic Theology for a Postmodern Era.* Minneapolis: Fortress, 1992.

————. *God as Trinity: Relationality and Temporality in Divine Life.* Louisville: Westminster John Knox, 1993.

————. "On Creating the Cosmos." In *Physics, Philosophy, and Theology: A Common Quest for Understanding,* edited by Robert J. Russell, William R. Stoeger, S.J., and George V. Coyne, S.J., pp. 273-96. Vatican City: Vatican Observatory Publications, 1988.

————. "Playing with Our Evolutionary Future." In *EMB*, pp. 491-510.

————. "Resurrection of the Very Embodied Soul?" In *NP*, pp. 305-26.

————. "The Trinity in and beyond Time." In *QCLN*, pp. 263-89.

Peterson, Gregory R. "Are We Unique? The *Locus Humanus,* Animal Cognition and the Theology of Nature." Ph.D. diss., University of Denver and Iliff School of Theology, 1996.

Pew Research Center. "Religious Differences on the Question of Evolution." 2008. http://www.pewforum.org/Science-and-Bioethics/Religious-Differences-on-the-Question-of-Evolution.aspx (11/21/2013).

Pfeiffer, John E. *The Creative Explosion: An Inquiry into the Origins of Art and Religion.* New York: Harper and Row, 1982.

Phan, Peter C. "Betwixt and Between: Doing Theology with Memory and Imagination." In *Journeys at the Margin: Toward an Autobiographical Theology in American-Asian Perspective,* edited by Peter Phan and Jung Young Lee, pp. 113-33. Collegeville, Minn.: Liturgical Press, 1999.

Phillips, Craig. "Green Creation: Comparative Ecological Theology in the Bible and Qur'ān." *Journal of Comparative Theology* 2, no. 1 (March 2011): 4-20.

Pickstock, Catherine. *After Writing: On the Liturgical Consummation of Philosophy.* Challenges in Contemporary Theology. Oxford: Blackwell, 1998.

———. "Duns Scotus: His Historical and Contemporary Significance." *Modern Theology* 21, no. 4 (October 2005): 543-74.

———. "Radical Orthodoxy and the Meditations of Time." In *Radical Orthodoxy,* edited by John Milbank, Catherine Pickstock, and Graham Ward. London: Routledge, 1999.

Pinker, Steven. *The Blank Slate: The Modern Denial of Human Nature.* London: Allen Lane, 2002.

Pinnock, Clark H. *Flame of Love: A Theology of the Holy Spirit.* Downers Grove, Ill.: InterVarsity, 1996.

Pinnock, Sarah K. *Beyond Theodicy: Jewish and Christian Continental Thinkers Respond to the Holocaust.* Albany: State University of New York Press, 2002.

Plantinga, Alvin. "On Ockham's Way Out." *Faith and Philosophy* 3, no. 3 (1986): 235-69.

———. "Religion and Science." *The Stanford Encyclopedia of Philosophy (Summer 2010 Edition),* edited by Edward N. Zalta. http://plato.stanford.edu/archives/sum2010/entries/religion-science/.

———. "Reply to Robert M. Adams." In *Alvin Plantinga,* edited by James E. Tomberlin and Peter van Inwagen, p. 374. Dordrecht: Reidel, 1985.

———. *Where the Conflict Really Lies: Science, Religion, and Naturalism.* Oxford: Oxford University Press, 2011.

Plantinga, Cornelius. *Not the Way It's Supposed to Be: A Breviary of Sin.* Grand Rapids: Eerdmans, 1995.

Plaskow, Judith. *Sex, Sin, and Grace: Women's Experience and the Theologies of Reinhold Niebuhr and Paul Tillich.* Lanham, Md.: University Press of America, 1980.

Plotkin, Henry C. *Darwin Machines and the Nature of Knowledge.* Cambridge: Harvard University Press, 1993.

Polanyi, Michael, and Harry Prosch. *Meaning.* Chicago: University of Chicago Press, 1975.

Polkinghorne, John. "The Anthropic Principle and the Science and Religion Debate." *Faraday Paper* 4 (2007): 1-4. http://www.st-edmunds.cam.ac.uk/faraday/resources/Faraday%20Papers/Faraday%20Paper%204%20Polkinghorne_EN.pdf.

———. "Anthropology in an Evolutionary Context." In *GHD,* pp. 89-103.

———. *Belief in God in an Age of Science.* New Haven: Yale University Press, 1998.

———. "Demise of Democritus." In *The Trinity in an Entangled World: Relationality in Physical Science and Theology,* edited by John Polkinghorne, pp. 1-14. Grand Rapids: Eerdmans, 2010.

———. "Eschatology: Some Questions and Some Insights from Science." In *The End of the World and the Ends of God: Science and Theology on Eschatology,* edited by Michael Welker and John Polkinghorne, pp. 29-41. Harrisburg, Pa.: Trinity, 2000.

———. *Exploring Reality: The Intertwining of Science and Religion.* London: SPCK; New Haven: Yale University Press, 2004.

———. *Faith, Science, and Understanding.* New Haven: Yale University Press, 2000.

———. *The Faith of a Physicist.* Princeton: Princeton University Press, 1994.

———. *The God of Hope and the End of the World.* New Haven and London: Yale University Press, 2002.

———. "The Hidden Spirit and the Cosmos." In *The Work of the Spirit: Pneumatology and Pentecostalism,* edited by Michael Welker, pp. 169-82. Grand Rapids: Eerdmans, 2006.

———. "The Laws of Nature and the Laws of Physics." In *QCLN,* pp. 429-40.

———. "The Metaphysics of Divine Action." In *C&C,* pp. 147-56.

———. "The Nature of Time." In *On Space and Time,* edited by Shahn Majid, pp. 278-83. Cambridge: Cambridge University Press, 2008.

———. *Quantum Physics and Theology: An Unexpected Kinship.* New Haven and London: Yale University Press, 2007.

———. *Quantum Theory: A Very Short Introduction.* Oxford: Oxford University Press, 2002.

———. *The Quantum World.* Princeton Science Library. Princeton: Princeton University Press, 1985.

———. "The Quantum World." In *PPT,* pp. 333-42.

———. *Quarks, Chaos, and Christianity: Questions to Science and Religion.* Rev. ed. New York: Crossroad, 2005.

———. *Reason and Reality: The Relationship between Science and Religion.* Philadelphia: Trinity, 1991.

———. *Science and Creation: The Search for Understanding.* Boston: New Science Library, 1989.

———. *Science and Providence: God's Interaction with the World.* Philadelphia and London: Templeton Foundation Press, 2005.

———. *Science and Theology: An Introduction.* London: SPCK; Minneapolis: Fortress, 1998.

———. "Theological Notions of Creation and Divine Causality." In *Science and Theology: Questions at the Interface,* edited by M. Rae, H. Regan, and J. Stenhouse. Grand Rapids: Eerdmans, 1994.

———. *Theology in the Context of Science.* New Haven and London: Yale University Press, 2009.

———. "The Universe in a Trinitarian Perspective: A Theology of Nature." In *Science and Trinity: The Christian Encounter with Reality.* New Haven and London: Yale University Press, 2004.

———. "Wolfhart Pannenberg's Engagement with the Natural Sciences." *Zygon: Journal of Religion and Science* 34, no. 1 (1999): 151-58.

———, ed. *The Trinity and the Entangled World: Relationality in Physical Science and Theology.* Grand Rapids: Eerdmans, 2010.

Polkinghorne, John, and Nicholas Beale. *Questions of Truth: Fifty-One Responses to Questions about God, Science, and Belief.* Louisville: Westminster John Knox, 2009.

Pollard, William G. *Chance and Providence: God's Action in a World Governed by Scientific Laws.* New York: Charles Scribner's Sons, 1958.

Popper, K. "Natural Selection and the Emergence of Mind." *Dialectica* 32 (1978): 339-55.

Posner, Michael I., Steven E. Petersen, Peter T. Fox, and Marcus E. Raichle. "Localisation of Cognitive Operations in the Human Brain." *Science* 240 (June 17, 1988): 1627-31.

Post, Stephen G. "A Moral Case for Nonreductive Physicalism." In *WHS,* pp. 195-212.

Powell, Samuel M. *Participating in God: Creation and Trinity.* Minneapolis: Fortress, 2003.

Prabhupada, A. C. Bhaktivedanta Swami. *Life Comes from Life.* http://www.angelfire.com/ego2/prabhupada/life/life_comes.htm (5/22/2013).

"Practising Hospitality in an Era of New Forms of Migration." WCC, 2005. http://www.oikoumene.org/en/resources/documents/wcc-commissions/international-affairs/human-rights-and-impunity/practising-hospitality-in-an-era-of-new-forms-of-migration.html (8/14/2013)

Prenter, Regin. *Spiritus Creator: Luther's Concept of the Holy Spirit.* Philadelphia: Muhlenberg, 1953.

Price, Daniel. *Karl Barth's Anthropology in Light of Modern Thought.* Grand Rapids: Eerdmans, 2002.

Prigogine, Ilya, and Isabelle Stengers. *Order out of Chaos: Man's New Dialogue with Nature.* Toronto: Bantam Books, 1984.

Proctor, Robert. "Three Roots of Human Recency: Molecular Anthropology, the Refigured Acheulean, and the UNESCO Response to Auschwitz." *Current Anthropology* 44, no. 2 (2003): 213-39.

Pseudo-Dionysius. *Divine Names.* In *Pseudo-Dionysius: The Complete Works.* Edited and translated by Colm Luibheid. Classics of Western Spirituality. Mahwah, N.J.: Paulist, 1987.

Pui-lan, Kwok. "Ecology and Christology." *Feminist Theology* 15 (1997): 113-25.

―――. *Postcolonial Imagination and Feminist Theology.* Louisville: Westminster John Knox, 2005.

Purcell, Brendan. *From Big Bang to Big Mystery: Human Origins in the Light of Creation and Evolution.* Hyde Park, N.Y.: New City Press, 2012.

Putnam, Hilary. "Brains and Behavior" [1965]. In *Readings in Philosophy of Psychology,* edited by Ned Joel Block, 1:24-36. Cambridge: Harvard University Press, 1980.

―――. "The Nature of Mental States" [1967]. In Hilary Putnam, *Mind, Language, and Reality: Philosophical Papers,* 2:429-40. Cambridge: Cambridge University Press, 1975.

―――. "Philosophy and Our Mental Life." In Hilary Putnam, *Mind, Language, and Reality: Philosophical Papers,* 2:291-303. Cambridge: Cambridge University Press, 1975.

Pyysiäinen, Ilkka. *How Religion Works: Towards a New Cognitive Science of Religion.* Leiden: Brill, 2001.

―――. *Supernatural Agents: Why We Believe in Souls, Gods, and Buddhas.* New York: Oxford University Press, 2009.

Qutb, Sayyid. "That Hideous Schizophrenia." In *Christianity through Non-Christian Eyes,* edited by Paul J. Griffiths, pp. 73-81. Maryknoll, N.Y.: Orbis, 1990.

Rabbinical Council of America. "Creation, Evolution, and Intelligent Design." December 7, 2005. http://www.rabbis.org/news/article.cfm?id=100635 (11/21/2013).

"The Race Question." UNESCO, Paris. July 1950. http://unesdoc.unesco.org/images /0012/001282/128291eo.pdf (8/13/2013).

Radnitzky, Gerard, and W. W. Bartley, eds. *Evolutionary Epistemology, Rationality, and the Sociology of Knowledge.* La Salle, Ill.: Open Court, 1974.

Rahman, Fazlur. "Some Key Ethical Concepts of the Qur'an." *Journal of Religious Ethics* 11, no. 2 (1983): 170-85.

Rahner, Karl. "Christology within an Evolutionary View of the World." In *Theological Investigations,* vol. 5, translated by Karl H. Kruger, pp. 157-92. London: Darton, Longman and Todd, 1966.

———. *Foundations of Christian Faith: An Introduction to the Idea of Christianity.* Translated by William V. Dych. New York: Crossroad, 1984.

———. "Further Theology of the Spiritual Life I." In *Theological Investigations,* vol. 7, translated by David Bourke. New York: Herder and Herder, 1971.

———. *Hearers of the Word.* Revised edition by J. B. Metz. Translated by Michael Richards. New York: Herder and Herder, 1969.

———. "Natural Science and Reasonable Faith." In *Theological Investigations,* vol. 21, translated by Hugh M. Riley, pp. 16-55. New York: Crossroad, 1988.

———. *On the Theology of Death.* Translated by Charles H. Henkey. New York: Herder and Herder, 1961.

———. *Theological Investigations: Man in the Church.* Vol. 2. Translated by Karl-H. Kruger, O.F.M. Baltimore: Helicon Press, 1963.

———. *Theological Investigations.* Vol. 5. Translated by Karl-Heinz Kruger. New York: Crossroad, 1983.

———. *Theological Investigations.* Vol. 21. Translated by Hugh M. Riley. Edited by Paul Imhof, S.J. New York: Crossroad, 1988.

———. "Theology and Anthropology." In *The Word in History: The St. Xavier Symposium,* edited by T. Patrick Burke, pp. 1-23. New York: Sheed and Ward, 1966.

Rahula, Walpola. *What the Buddha Taught.* Rev. ed. New York: Grove Press, 1974.

Raju, Raghuram. "Sri Aurobindo and Krishnachandra Bhattacharya on Science and Spirituality." In *Science, Spirituality, and the Modernization of India,* edited by Makarand Paranjape, chap. 5. Anthem South Asian Studies. London: Anthem Press, 2008.

Ramachandran, Vilayanur S. "Mirror Neurons and Imitation Learning as the Driving Force behind 'the Great Leap Forward' in Human Evolution." *Edge,* May 31, 2000. http://edge.org/conversation/mirror-neurons-and-imitation-learning-as-the -driving-force-behind-the-great-leap-forward-in-human-evolution (11/27/2012).

Raman, Varadaraja V. "Traditional Hinduism and Modern Science." In *Bridging Science and Religion,* edited by Ted Peters and Gaymon Bennett. Theology and the Sciences. Minneapolis: Fortress, 2003.

Ramanuja. *Vedanta Sutras.* In *SBE,* vol. 48.

Ramsey, Paul. *Basic Christian Ethics.* New York: Charles Scribner's Sons, 1952.

Rao, K. L. Seshagiri. "The Five Elements *(Pañcamahābhūta):* An Ecological Perspective." In *HE,* pp. 23-38.

Rashed, Rashdi. "The End Matters." In *ISCHP,* 1:37-50.

Ratzinger, Joseph. *In the Beginning . . . : A Catholic Understanding of the Story of Creation and the Fall.* Translated by Boniface Ramsey. Grand Rapids: Eerdmans, 1995.

Rauschenbusch, Walter. *The Social Gospel.* 1917. Reprint, Nashville: Abingdon, 1945.

Ray, Stephen H. *Do No Harm: Social Sin and Christian Responsibility.* Minneapolis: Fortress, 2003.

Rayburn, Carole A., and Lee J. Richmond. "Theobiology: Interfacing Theology and Science." *American Behavioral Scientist* 45, no. 12 (2002): 1793-811.

Reimarus, H. S. *The Goal of Jesus and His Disciples.* Translation and introduction by Beorge W. Buchanan. Leiden: Brill, 1970.

Reinders, Hans S. *Receiving the Gift of Friendship: Profound Disability, Theological Anthropology, and Ethics.* Grand Rapids: Eerdmans, 2008.

Rescher, Nicholas. *Evolution, Cognition, and Realism: Studies in Evolutionary Epistemology.* Lanham, Md.: University Press of America, 1990.

Reynolds, Frank. "The Two Wheels of Dhamma: A Study of Early Buddhism." In *The Two Wheels of Dhamma: Essays on the Theravada Tradition in India and Ceylon,* edited by Bardwell L. Smith. Chambersburg, Pa.: American Academy of Religion, 1972.

Rezazadeh, Reza. "Thomas Aquinas and Mulla Sadrá on the Soul-Body Problem: A Comparative Investigation." *Journal of Shi'a Islamic Studies* 4, no. 4 (Autumn 2011): 415-28.

Rich, Greg. "Boethius on Divine Foreknowledge and Human Free Will." *Thinking about Religion* 5 (2005): n.p. http://organizations.uncfsu.edu/ncrsa/journal/v05/rich_boethius.htm (6/10/2013).

Richard, Lucien. *Living the Hospitality of God.* New York: Paulist, 2000.

Richert, R. A., and P. L. Harris. "The Ghost in My Body: Children's Developing Concept of the Soul." *Journal of Cognition and Culture* 6 (2006): 409-27.

Rickabaugh, Brandon L. "Responding to N. T. Wright's Rejection of the Soul: A Defense of Substance Dualism." An unpublished presentation at the Society of Vineyard Scholars Conference, Minnesota, April 28, 2012. http://www.academia.edu/1966881/Responding_to_N._T._Wrights_Rejection_of_the_Soul_A_Defense_of_Substance_Dualism (6/10/2013).

Ricoeur, Paul. "The Image of God and the Epic of Man." In Ricoeur, *History and Truth,* translated by Charles A. Kelbley, pp. 110-28. Evanston, Ill.: Northwestern University Press, 1965.

———. *The Symbolism of Evil.* Translated by Emerson Buchanan. Boston: Beacon Press, 1969 [1967].

Rist, J. M. "Augustine on Free Will and Predestination." *Journal of Theological Studies* 20, no. 2 (1969): 420-47.

Ritschl, Albrecht. *The Christian Doctrine of Justification and Reconciliation.* Translated by H. R. McIntosh and A. B. Macaulay. Clifton, N.J.: Reference Book Publishers, 1966 [1883].

Ritzer, George. *The McDonaldization of Society.* Revised New Century Edition. Thousand Oaks, Calif.: Pine Forge Press, 2004.

Rivera, Mayra. *The Touch of Transcendence: A Postcolonial Theology of God.* Louisville: Westminster John Knox, 2007.

Robinson, H. Wheeler. *The Christian Doctrine of Man.* Edinburgh: T. & T. Clark, 1911.

Robinson, John A. T. *The Body: A Study in Pauline Theology.* London: SCM, 1952.

Rolston, Holmes, III. *Genes, Genesis, and God: Values and Their Origins in Natural and Human History; The Gifford Lectures, University of Edinburgh, 1997-1998.* Cambridge: Cambridge University Press, 1999.

———. "Naturalizing and Systematizing Evil." In *Is Nature Ever Evil? Religion, Science, and Value,* edited by Willem B. Drees, pp. 67-87. London and New York: Routledge, 2003.

———. *Science and Religion: A Critical Survey.* Philadelphia and London: Templeton Foundation Press, 2006.

Rondet, Henri, S.J. *Original Sin: The Patristic and Theological Background.* Translated by Cajetan Finegan, O.P. Staten Island, N.Y.: Alba House, 1972.

Rosenthal, E. I. J. *Political Thought in Medieval Islam: An Introductory Outline.* Cambridge: Cambridge University Press, 1958.

Rosenzweig, Franz. *The Star of Redemption.* Translated by William W. Hallo. New York: Holt, Rinehart and Winston, 1970. http://esotericonline.net/docs/library/Philosophy/Philosophy%20of%20Religion%20_%20Theology/Judaism/Rosenzweig%20-%20The%20Star%20of%20Redemption.pdf.

Ross, Susan A. "God's Embodiment and Women." In *Freeing Theology: The Essential of Theology in a Feminist Perspective,* edited by Catherine Mowry LaCugna, pp. 185-209. San Francisco: Harper, 1993.

Rousseau, Jean-Jacques. "Discourse on Inequality." In *The Essential Rousseau,* translated by Lowell Bair, edited by Matthew Josephson, pp. 125-201. New York: New American Library, 1974.

Routledge Companion to Theism. Edited by Charles Taliaferro, Victoria S. Harrison, and Stewart Goetz. New York: Routledge, 2013.

Rowe, William. "The Problem of Evil and Some Varieties of Atheism." In *PE,* pp. 126-37.

Rubenstein, Mary-Jane. "Cosmic Singularities: On the Nothing and the Sovereign." *Journal of the American Academy of Religion* 80, no. 2 (June 2012): 485-517.

Rubenstein, Richard L., and John K. Roth. *Approaches to Auschwitz: The Holocaust and Its Legacy.* Atlanta: John Knox, 1987.

Ruether, Rosemary Radford. "Dualism and the Nature of Evil in Feminist Theology." *Studies in Christian Ethics* 5, no. 1 (1992): 26-39.

———. *Gaia and God: An Ecofeminist Theology of Earth Healing.* San Francisco: Harper Collins, 1992.

———. *Introducing Redemption in Christian Feminism.* Sheffield: Sheffield Academic Press, 1998.

Runyan, Jason D. "Anatomy of Will: Philosophy of Action and the Neuroscientific Study of Freewill." Prepublication manuscript, 2012.

———. "Freewill, Mental Events and Embodied Cognition." Unpublished presentation at "Neuroscience and Soul," weekly seminar of Center for Christian Thought, Biola University, La Mirada, Calif., Fall 2012.

Ruse, Michael. "Is Darwinian Metaethics Possible (and If It Is, Is It Well Taken)?" In *Evolutionary Ethics and Contemporary Biology*, edited by Giovanni Boniolo and Gabriele de Anna, pp. 13-26. Cambridge: Cambridge University Press, 2006.

Rushdoony, John. *The Institutes of Biblical Law*. Phillipsburg, N.J.: Presbyterian and Reformed, 1973.

Russell, Bertrand. "The Superior Virtue of the Oppressed." In *Unpopular Essays*, pp. 58-64. New York: Simon and Schuster, 1950.

———. *Why I Am Not a Christian, and Other Essays on Religion and Related Subjects*. London: Allen and Unwin, 1957.

Russell, Robert J. "Challenges and Progress in 'Theology and Science': An Overview of the VO/CTNS Series." In *SPDA*, pp. 3-56.

———. *Cosmology: From Alpha to Omega; The Creative Mutual Interaction of Theology and Science*. Minneapolis: Fortress, 2008.

———. "Physics, Cosmology, and the Challenge to Consequentialist Natural Theodicy." In *PC*, pp. 109-30.

———. "Quantum Physics in Philosophical and Theological Perspective." In *PPT*, pp. 343-74.

———. "Special Providence and Genetic Mutation: A New Defense of Theistic Evolution." In *EMB*, pp. 191-223.

———. *Time in Eternity: Pannenberg, Physics, and Eschatology in Creative Mutual Interaction*. Notre Dame, Ind.: University of Notre Dame Press, 2012.

Ryle, Gilbert. *The Concept of Mind*. London: Hutchinson, 1949.

Sachedina, Abdulaziz. *The Islamic Roots of Democratic Pluralism*. New York: Oxford University Press, 2001.

Sadakata, Akira. *Buddhist Cosmology: Philosophy and Origins*. Translated by Gaynor Sekimori. Tokyo: Kōsei Publishing, 1997.

Ṣaḥiḥ Muslim: Being Traditions of the Sayings and Doings of the Prophet Muhammad as Narrated by His Companions and Compiled under the Title al-Jāmiʻ-uṣ-ṣaḥīḥ. Lahore: Sh. Muhammad Ashraf, [1971-1975].

Said, Abdul Aziz, and Nathan C. Funk. "Peace in Islam: Ecology of the Spirit." In *I&E*, pp. 155-83.

Said, Edward. *Culture and Imperialism*. New York: Knopf, 1993.

Saiving, Valerie. "The Human Situation: A Feminine View." In *Womanspirit Rising: A Feminist Reader in Religion*, edited by Carol P. Christ and Judith Plaskow, pp. 25-42. San Francisco: Harper and Row, 1979.

Samuelson, Norbert M. "Judaism and Science." In *OHRS*, pp. 41-56.

Sandell, Klas, ed. *Buddhist Perspectives on the Ecocrisis*. Kandy, Sri Lanka: Buddhist Publication Society, 1987.

Sanders, John. *The God Who Risks: A Theology of Divine Providence*. Rev. ed. Downers Grove, Ill.: InterVarsity, 2007.

Sankara. *Vedanta-Sutras*. In *SBE*, vols. 34 and 38.

Sardar, Ziauddin. *Explorations in Islamic Science*. London: Mansell, 1989.

———. "Islamic Science: The Way Ahead." In *How Do You Know? Reading Ziauddin*

Sardar on Islam, Science, and Cult, edited and introduced by Ehsan Masood, pp. 161-93. Ann Arbor: Pluto Press, 2006.

Saunders, Nicholas. *Divine Action and Modern Science.* Cambridge: Cambridge University Press, 2002.

Scaruffi, Piero. "The Worst Genocides of the 20th and 21st Centuries." http://www.scaruffi .com/politics/dictat.html (10/16/2013).

Scheffczyk, Leo. *Creation and Providence.* Translated by Richard Strachan. New York: Herder and Herder, 1970.

Scheler, Max. *Man's Place in Nature.* Translated by Hans Meyerhoff. Boston: Beacon Press, 1961. Ger. *Die Stellung des Menschen im Kosmos.* 1928.

Schilbrack, Kevin. "Problems for a Complete Naturalism." *American Journal of Theology and Philosophy* 15 (1994): 269-91.

Schleiermacher, Friedrich. *The Christian Faith.* Edited by H. R. Mackintosh and J. S. Stewart. London: T. & T. Clark, 1999.

———. *On Religion: Speeches to Its Cultured Despisers.* Translated, with introduction, by John Oman. London: K. Paul, Trench, Trubner, 1893.

Schloss, Jeffrey P. "From Evolution to Eschatology." In *Resurrection: Theological and Scientific Assessments,* edited by Ted Peters, Robert J. Russell, and Michael Welker, pp. 65-85. Grand Rapids: Eerdmans, 2002.

Schmid, H. H. "Creation, Righteousness, and Salvation: 'Creation Theology' as the Broad Horizon of Biblical Theology." In *Creation in the Old Testament,* edited by Bernhard W. Anderson, pp. 102-17. Philadelphia: Fortress, 1984.

Schmitz, Kenneth L. *The Gift: Creation.* Milwaukee: Marquette University Press, 1982.

Schnelle, Udo. *The Human Condition: Anthropology in the Teachings of Jesus, Paul, and John.* Minneapolis: Fortress, 1996.

Schofer, Jonathan. "The Image of God: A Study of an Ancient Sensibility." *Journal of the Society for Textual Reasoning* 4, no. 3 (May 2006). http://etext.lib.virginia.edu/ journals/tr/volume4/number3/TR04_03_r02.html (5/22/2013).

Schoonenberg, Piet. "Sin and Guilt." In *Encyclopedia of Theology: The Concise Sacramentum Mundi,* edited by Karl Rahner, pp. 1579-86. New York: Seabury Press, 1975.

———. *The Sin of the World: A Theological View.* Translated by J. Donceel. Notre Dame, Ind.: University of Notre Dame Press, 1965.

Schott, Robin May, ed. *Feminist Interpretations of Immanuel Kant.* University Park: Pennsylvania State University Press, 1997.

Schrag, Calvin O. *The Self after Postmodernity.* New Haven: Yale University Press, 1997.

———. "Transversal Rationality." In *The Question of Hermeneutics: Essays in Honor of Joseph J. Kockelmans,* edited by T. J. Stapleton. Dordrecht: Kluwer, 1994.

Schwartz, Eilon. "Judaism and Nature: Theological and Moral Issues to Consider While Renegotiating a Jewish Relationship to the Natural World." *Judaism* 44, no. 4 (1995): 437-47.

Schwartz, Jeffrey H., and Ian Tattersall. *The Human Fossil Record.* Vol. 4, *Craniodental Morphology of Early Hominids (Genera Australopithecus, Paranthropus, Orrorin), and Overview.* Hoboken, N.J.: Wiley-Liss, 2005.

Schwarz, Hans. *Creation.* Grand Rapids: Eerdmans, 2002.

————. "God's Place in a Space Age." *Zygon: Journal of Religion and Science* 21, no. 3 (September 1986): 353-68.

Schwarzschild, Steven S. "The Unnatural Jew." *Environmental Ethics* 6 (1984): 347-62.

Schweizer, E. "Soma." In *Theological Dictionary of the New Testament Theology,* edited by Gerhard Friedrich, translated and edited by Geoffrey W. Bromiley, 7:1024ff. Grand Rapids: Eerdmans, 1971.

Schwöbel, Christoph. "Recovering Human Dignity." In *God and Human Dignity,* edited by R. Kendall Soulen and Linda Woodhead, pp. 44-58. Grand Rapids: Eerdmans, 2006.

Scudder, Lewis. "The Qur'an's Evaluation of Human Nature: An Inquiry with a View toward Christian-Muslim Dialogue." *Reformed Review: A Journal of the Seminaries of the Reformed Church in America* 61, no. 2 (2008): 71-80.

Searle, John. *The Rediscovery of the Mind.* Cambridge: MIT Press, 1992.

Seeskin, Kenneth. *Maimonides on the Origin of the World.* Cambridge: Cambridge University Press, 2005.

Segundo, Juan Luis, S.J. *Evolution and Guilt.* Translated by John Drury. Maryknoll, N.Y.: Orbis, 1974.

Self, Charlie. *Flourishing Churches and Communities: A Pentecostal Primer on Faith, Work, and Economics for Spirit-Empowered Discipleship.* Grand Rapids: Christian's Library Press, 2013.

Sen, Keshub Chunder. *Epistle to Indian Brethren.* In *Modern Indian Thought,* edited by Alexander Duff. London: Asian Publishing House, 1964.

————. *That Marvellous Mystery, the Trinity.* Edited by M. M. Thomas. London: SCM, 1969.

Seo, Bo-Myung. *A Critique of Western Theological Anthropology: Understanding Human Beings in a Third World Context.* Lewiston, N.Y.: Edwin Mellen Press, 2005.

Setia, 'Adi. "*Tashkir,* Fine-Tuning, Intelligent Design and the Scientific Appreciation of Nature." In *ISHCP,* 1:293-318.

Shakespeare, Steven. *Radical Orthodoxy: A Critical Introduction.* London: SPCK, 2007; Perseus Books Group: Kindle Edition, 2007.

Sharma, Arvind. *Classical Hindu Thought: An Introduction.* Oxford: Oxford University Press, 2000.

Shear, Jonathan, ed. *Explaining Consciousness: The Hard Problem.* Cambridge: MIT Press, a Bradford Book, 1999.

Shubin, Neil. *Your Inner Fish: A Journey into the 3.5 Billion Year History of the Human Body.* New York: Pantheon Books, 2008.

Shults, F. LeRon. *Christology and Science.* Grand Rapids: Eerdmans, 2008.

————. *The Post Foundationalist Task of Theology: Wolfhart Pannenberg and the New Theological Rationality.* Grand Rapids: Eerdmans, 1999.

————. *Reforming the Doctrine of God.* Grand Rapids: Eerdmans, 2005.

Siddiqui, Mona. "Being Human in Islam." In *Humanity: Texts and Context; Christian and Muslim Perspectives,* edited by Michael Ipgrave and David Marshall, pp. 15-21. Washington, D.C.: Georgetown University Press, 2011.

Siegel, Daniel J., et al., eds. *The Healing Power of Emotion: Affective Neuroscience, Development, and Clinical Practice.* New York: Norton, 2009.

Siglitz, Joseph E. *Globalization and Its Discontents.* New York: Norton, 2002.

Sikkema, Arnold E. "A Physicist's Reformed Critique of Nonreductive Physicalism and Emergence." *Pro Rege,* June 2005, pp. 20-32. http://www.dordt.edu/publications/pro_rege/crcpi/119717.pdf (11/18/2012).

Sikṣā-samuccaya: A Compendium of Buddhist Doctrine. Compiled by Śāntideva. Translated by Cecil Bendall and W. H. D. Rouse. Reprint, Delhi: Motilal Banarsidass, 1991.

Silva, Lily de. "The Buddhist Attitude towards Nature." *Access to Insight,* June 5, 2010. http://www.accesstoinsight.org/lib/authors/desilva/attitude.html (4/5/2013).

Sindima, Harvey. "Community of Life: Ecological Theology in African Perspective." In *Liberating Life: Contemporary Approaches in Ecological Theology,* edited by Charles Birch, William Eaken, and Jay B. McDaniel, pp. 137-47. Maryknoll, N.Y.: Orbis, 1990.

Skarda, C., and W. Freeman. "How Brains Make Chaos in Order to Make Sense of the World." *Behavioral and Brain Sciences* 10 (1987): 161-95.

Slifkin, Natan. *The Challenge of Creation: Judaism's Encounter with Science, Cosmology, and Evolution.* Bet Shemesh, Israel: Zoo Torah, 2008.

Smith, Adam. *The Theory of Moral Sentiments.* New York: A. M. Kelley, 1966 [1759].

Smith, Barbara. *The Truth That Never Hurts: Writings on Race, Gender, and Freedom.* New Brunswick, N.J.: Rutgers University Press, 1998.

Smith, Brian K. *Classifying the Universe: The Ancient Indian Varna System and the Origins of Caste.* Oxford: Oxford University Press, 1994.

Smith, David Whitten, and Elizabeth Geraldine Burr. *Understanding World Religions: A Road Map for Justice and Peace.* Lanham, Md.: Rowman and Littlefield, 2007.

Smith, James K. A. *Introducing Radical Orthodoxy: Mapping a Post-secular Theology.* Grand Rapids: Baker Academic, 2004.

Smith, Quentin. "The Uncaused Beginning of the Universe." In *Theism, Atheism, and Big Bang Cosmology,* pp. 108-39. New York: Clarendon, 1993.

Smolin, Lee. *Three Roads to Quantum Gravity.* New York: Basic Books, 2001.

Snyder, Gary. *The Practice of the Wild.* San Francisco: North Point Press, 1990.

Sobrino, Jon. "Spirituality and the Following of Jesus." In *Systematic Theology: Perspectives from Liberation Theology (Readings from Mysterium Liberationis),* edited by Jon Sobrino and Ignacio Ellacuría, pp. 233-56. Maryknoll, N.Y.: Orbis, 1996.

Sokol, Moshe. "What Are the Ethical Implications of Jewish Theological Conceptions of the Natural World?" In *J&E,* pp. 261-82.

Solomon, R. C. *The Passions: Emotions and the Meaning of Life.* 2nd ed. Indianapolis: Hackett, 1993.

Soper, Kate. *What Is Nature? Culture, Politics, and the Non-human.* Oxford: Blackwell, 1995.

Soskice, Janet M. "*Creatio Ex Nihilo:* Its Jewish and Christian Foundations." In *CGA,* chap. 2, pp. 24-39.

———. "Knowledge and Experience in Science and Religion: Can We Be Realists?" In *PPT,* pp. 173-84.

———. *Metaphor and Religious Language.* Oxford: Clarendon, 1985.

———. "Resurrection and the New Jerusalem." In *The Resurrection,* edited by Stephen T. Davis, Daniel Kendall, and Gerald O'Collins, pp. 41-58. Oxford: Oxford University Press, 1997.

"Soul." In *A Dictionary of the Bible,* edited by James Hastings. Edinburgh: T. & T. Clark, 1902.

Soulé, Michael E. "The Social Siege of Nature." In *Reinventing Nature? Responses to Postmodern Deconstruction,* edited by Michael E. Soulé and Gary Lease. Washington, D.C.: Island Press, 1995.

Soulen, R. Kendall. "Cruising toward Bethlehem: Human Dignity and the New Eugenics." In *GHD,* pp. 104-20.

Soulen, R. Kendall, and Linda Woodhead. "Introduction: Contextualizing Human Dignity." In *GHD,* pp. 1-24.

Southgate, Christopher. "God and Evolutionary Evil: Theodicy in the Light of Darwinism." *Zygon: Journal of Religion and Science* 37, no. 4 (2002): 803-21.

Southgate, Christopher, and Andrew Robinson. "Varieties of Theodicy: An Exploration of Responses to the Problem of Evil Based on a Typology of Good-Harm Analyses." In *PC,* pp. 67-90.

Spaemann, Robert. *Philosophische Essays.* Stuttgart: Reclam, 1983.

Spear, Andrew D. "Husserl on Intentionality and Intentional Content." In *Internet Encyclopedia of Philosopy: A Peer-Reviewed Academic Resource,* 2011. http://www.iep.utm.edu/huss-int/ (6/10/2013).

Spence, Sean A. *The Actor's Brain: Exploring the Cognitive Neuroscience of Free Will.* Oxford: Oxford University Press, 2009.

———. "Free Will in Light of Neuropsychiatry." *Philosophy, Psychiatry and Psychology* 3, no. 2 (1996): 75-90.

Spencer, Herbert. *First Principles.* New York: De Witt Revolving Fund, 1958 [1867].

Sperry, Roger W. "Psychology's Mentalist Paradigm and the Religion/Science Tension." *American Psychologist* 43, no. 8 (1988): 607-13.

———. *Science and Moral Priority: Merging Mind, Brain, and Human Values.* New York: Columbia University Press, 1983.

Spinoza, Benedict de. *The Ethics* (Ethica Ordine Geometrico Demonstrata, 1677). Translated by R. H. M. Elwespart. http://www.semantikon.com/philosophy/spinoza Ethics.pdf.

Spitzer, Robert J., S.J. *New Proofs for the Existence of God: Contributions of Contemporary Physics and Philosophy.* Grand Rapids: Eerdmans, 2010.

Sponberg, Alan. "Green Buddhism and the Hierarchy of Compassion." In *B&E,* pp. 351-76.

Staniloae, Dumitru. *The Experience of God: Orthodox Dogmatic Theology.* Vol. 2, *The World: Creation and Deification.* Translated and edited by Ioan Ionita and Robert Barringer. Brookline, Mass.: Holy Cross Orthodox Press, 2000.

Stapp, Henry. *Mind, Matter, and Quantum Mechanics.* Berlin and New York: Springer-Verlag, 1993.

Starhawk. *Dreaming the Dark: Magix, Sex, and Politics.* Boston: Beacon Press, 1982.

———. *The Spiral Dance: A Rebirth of the Ancient Religion of the Great Goddess.* San Francisco: Harper and Row, 1979.

Steenberg, M. C. "Children in Paradise: Adam and Eve as 'Infants' in Irenaeus of Lyons." *Journal of Early Christian Studies* 12, no. 1 (2004): 1-22.

Steinkellner, Ernst. "Buddhismus: Religion oder Philosophie? und Vom Wesen der Buddha." In *Der Buddhismus als Anfrage an christliche Theologie und Philosophie,* edited by Andreas Bsteh, pp. 251-62. Studien zu Religionstheorie 5. Mödling: Verlag St. Gabriel, 2000.

Stenberg, Leif. *The Islamization of Science: Four Muslim Positions Developing an Islamic Modernity.* Lund Studies in History of Religions 6. Lund, Sweden: University of Lund Publications, 1996.

Stendahl, Krister. "The Apostle Paul and the Introspective Conscience of the West." *Harvard Theological Review* 56 (1963): 199-215.

Stenger, Laurie. "Judaism and the Environment: A Comprehensive Bibliography." August 1999. Coalition on the Environment and Jewish Life (New York). http://www.coejl.org/_old/www.coejl.org/resources/bi_compre.pdf.

Stephenson, Paul. "Imperial Christianity and Sacred War in Byzantium." In *BB,* pp. 81-93.

Stewart, Ian. *Life's Other Secret: The New Mathematics of the Living World.* New York: Wiley, 1998.

Stich, Stephen P. *From Folk Psychology to Cognitive Science: The Case against Belief.* Cambridge: MIT Press, 1983.

Stoeger, William R., S.J. "The Big Bang, Quantum Cosmology and *Creatio Ex Nihilo.*" In *CGA,* pp. 152-75.

———. "Conceiving Divine Action in a Dynamic Universe." In *SPDA,* pp. 225-47.

———. "Contemporary Cosmology and Its Implications for the Science-Religion Dialogue." In *PPT,* pp. 219-47.

———. "Contemporary Physics and the Ontological Status of the Laws of Nature." In *QCLN,* pp. 209-34.

———. "Describing God's Action in the World in Light of Scientific Knowledge of Reality." In *C&C,* pp. 239-61.

———. "Entropy, Emergence, and the Physical Roots of Natural Evil." In *PC,* pp. 93-108.

———. "Epistemological and Ontological Issues Arising from Quantum Theory." In *QM,* pp. 81-98.

———. "Faith Reflects on the Evolving Universe: Divine Action, the Trinity and Time." In *Finding God in All Things: Essays in Honor of Michael J. Buckley,* edited by Michael J. Himes and Stephen J. Pope, pp. 162-82. New York: Crossroad, 1996.

———. "The Immanent Directionality of the Evolutionary Process, and Its Relationship to Teleology." In *EMB,* pp. 163-90.

———. "The Mind-Brain Problem, the Laws of Nature, and Constitutive Relationships." In *NP,* pp. 129-46.

———. "Reductionism and Emergence: Implications for the Interaction of Theology with the Natural Sciences." In *E&E,* pp. 229-47.

Stokes, George G. *Natural Theology.* London: Adam and Charles Black, 1891.

Stone, Jerome A. *Religious Naturalism Today: The Rebirth of a Forgotten Alternative.* Albany: State University of New York Press, 2008.

Strawson, P. F. *Individuals: An Essay in Descriptive Metaphysics.* London: Routledge, 1959.

529

Stringer, Chris, and Robin McKie. *African Exodus: The Origins of Modern Humanity.* London: Pimlico, 1997.

Stroud, Barry. "The Charm of Naturalism." In *Naturalism in Question,* edited by Mario De Caro and David Macarthur. Cambridge: Harvard University Press, 2004.

Stroup, Sarah Culpepper. "Making Memory: Ritual, Rhetoric, and Violence in the Roman Triumph." In *BB,* pp. 29-46.

Stubenberg, Leopold. "Neutral Monism." In *The Stanford Encyclopedia of Philosophy* (Spring 2010 edition), edited by Edward N. Zalta. http://plato.stanford.edu/ archives/spr2010/entries/neutral-monism/ (6/10/2013).

Stump, Eleonore. "Non-Cartesian Substance Dualism and Materialism without Reductionism." *Faith and Philosophy* 12, no. 4 (1995): 505-31.

Stump, Eleonore, and Norman Kretzmann. "Eternity." *Journal of Philosophy* 78, no. 8 (1981): 429-58.

Sudarminta, Justin. "Big Bang Cosmology and Creation Theology: Towards a Fruitful Dialogue between Science and Religion." In *SRPW,* pp. 141-51.

Sue, Derald Wing, et al. "Racial Microaggressions and the Asian American Experience." *Cultural Diversity and Ethnic Minority Psychology* 13, no. 1 (January 2007): 72-81.

Sullivan, Lawrence E. Preface to *I&E,* pp. xi-xiv.

Swearer, Donald K. "The Hermeneutics of Buddhist Ecology in Contemporary Thailand: Buddhadāsa and Dhammapitaka." In *B&E,* pp. 21-44.

Swinburne, Richard. *The Evolution of the Soul.* Rev. ed. Oxford: Oxford University Press, 1997.

————. *Revelation: From Analogy to Metaphor.* Oxford: Clarendon, 1992.

Syed, Ibrahim B. "The Nature of Soul: Islamic and Scientific Views." Publication of Islamic Research Foundation International, Inc., at http://www.irfi.org/articles/articles_51 _100/nature_of_soul.htm (6/10/2013).

Taliaferro, Charles. *Consciousness and the Mind of God.* Cambridge: Cambridge University Press, 1994.

Tancredi, Laurence. *Hardwired Behavior: What Neuroscience Reveals about Morality.* Cambridge: Cambridge University Press, 2005.

Tanner, Kathryn. *Economy of Grace.* Minneapolis: Augsburg Fortress, 2005.

————. *God and Creation in Christian Theology.* Minneapolis: Augsburg Fortress, 2004.

Tattersall, Ian. *Becoming Human: Evolution and Human Uniqueness.* New York: Harcourt Brace, 1998.

————. "Language and the Origin of Symbolic Thought." In *Cognitive Archeology and Human Evolution,* edited by Sopie A. de Beaune, Frederick L. Coolidge, and Thomas Wynn, pp. 109-16. New York: Cambridge University Press, 2009.

————. *The Monkey in the Mirror: Essays on the Science of What Makes Us Human.* New York: Harcourt, 2002.

————. *The World from Beginnings to 4000 BCE.* New York: Oxford University Press, 2008.

Tattersall, Ian, and Jeffrey H. Schwartz. *Extinct Humans.* New York: Westview Press, 2000.

Taylor, Charles. *The Sources of the Self: The Making of the Modern Identity.* Cambridge: Cambridge University Press, 1989.

Taylor, John Vincent. *Enough Is Enough.* London: SCM, 1975.

Teevan, Donna. "Challenges to the Role of Theological Anthropology in Feminist Theologies." *Theological Studies* 64, no. 3 (2003): 582-97.

Teilhard de Chardin, Pierre. *The Appearance of Man.* Translated by J. M. Cohen. New York: Harper and Row, 1966.

———. *Christianity and Evolution.* Translated by René Hague. New York: Harcourt Brace Jovanovich, 1971.

———. *The Phenomenon of Man.* New York: Harper and Row, 1961.

Telushkin, Rabbi Joseph. *Jewish Literacy: The Most Important Things to Know about the Jewish Religion, Its People, and Its History.* New York: Morrow, 1991.

Terrazas, Aaron. "Migration and Development: Policy Perspectives from the United States." Migration Policy Institute, 2011. http://www.migrationpolicy.org/pubs/migdevpolicy-2011.pdf (8/14/2013).

TeSelle, Eugene. *Augustine the Theologian.* New York: Herder and Herder, 1970.

Thatamanil, John J. *The Immanent Divine: God, Creation, and the Human Predicament; An East-West Conversation.* Minneapolis: Fortress, 2006.

Theissen, Gerd. *Biblical Faith: An Evolutionary Approach.* Translated by John Bowden. Philadelphia: Fortress, 1984.

"A Theological Challenge to the Persistence of Racism, Caste-Based Discrimination, and Other Exclusionary Practices. Statement from the WCC Conference on Racism Today and the Rationale for Continued Ecumenical Engagement, Cleveland, Ohio, August 26-29, 2010." http://www.overcomingviolence.org/fileadmin/dov/files/iepc/expert_consultations/ClevelandStatementon%2520Racism2010_Final.pdf (8/14/2013).

Thielicke, Helmut. *Being Human . . . Becoming Human: An Essay in Christian Anthropology.* Garden City, N.Y.: Doubleday, 1984.

Thistlethwaite, Susan B. "God and Her Survival in a Nuclear Age." In *Constructive Christian Theology for the Worldwide Church,* edited by William R. Barr, pp. 127-42. Grand Rapids: Eerdmans, 1997.

Thuan, Trinh Xuan. "Science and Buddhism." Essay published by Université Interdisciplinaire de Paris (2010). http://uip.edu/en/articles-en/science-and-buddhism (11/21/2013).

Thurman, Robert. "Nagarjuna's Guidelines for Buddhist Social Action." In *The Path of Compassion: Writings on Socially Engaged Buddhism,* edited by Fred Eppsteiner, revised 2nd ed., pp. 120-44. Berkeley, Calif.: Parallax Press, 1988.

Tiessen, Terrance L. *Providence and Prayer: How Does God Work in the World?* Downers Grove, Ill.: InterVarsity, 2000.

———. "Why Calvinists Should Believe in Divine Middle Knowledge, Although They Reject Molinism." *Westminster Theological Journal* 69 (2007): 345-66.

Tilley, Terrence W. "The Problems of Theodicy: A Background Essay." In *PC,* pp. 35-51.

Tillich, Paul. *The Dynamics of Faith.* New York: Harper and Row, 1957.

———. *The Spiritual Situation in Our Technical Society.* Macon, Ga.: Mercer University Press, 1988.

Tipler, Frank J. *The Physics of Christianity.* New York: Doubleday Religion, 2007.

Tirosh-Samuelson, Hava. "Introduction: Judaism and the Natural World." In *J&E*, pp. xxxiii-lxii.

———. "Judaism." In *The Oxford Handbook of Religion and Ecology,* edited by Roger S. Gottlieb, pp. 25-64. Oxford and New York: Oxford University Press, 2006.

Todorov, Tzvetan. *The Conquest of America: The Question of the Other.* New York: HarperCollins, 1992.

———. *Mikhail Bakhtin: The Dialogical Principle.* Translated by Wlad Godrich. Minneapolis: University of Minnesota Press, 1984.

Torrance, Thomas F. *Calvin's Doctrine of Man.* London: Lutterworth, 1949.

———. *Divine and Contingent Order.* Oxford: Oxford University Press, 1981.

———. *Reality and Evangelical Theology.* Philadelphia: Westminster, 1982.

———. *Reality and Scientific Theology: Theology and Science at the Frontiers of Knowledge.* Edinburgh: Scottish Academic Press, 1985.

———. *Space, Time, and Incarnation.* Edinburgh: T. & T. Clark, 1969.

———. *Space, Time, and Resurrection.* Grand Rapids: Eerdmans, 1998.

———. *Theological Science.* Oxford: Oxford University Press, 1969.

———. "The Transcendental Role of Wisdom in Science." In *Facets of Faith and Science,* vol. 1, *Historiography and Modes of Interaction,* edited by Jitse M. van der Meer, pp. 131-49. Lanham, Md.: University Press of America, 1996.

Tracy, Thomas F. "God and Creatures Acting: The Idea of a Double Agency." In *CGA,* chap. 13.

———. "The Lawfulness of Nature and the Problem of Evil." In *PC,* pp. 153-78.

———. "Particular Providence and the God of the Gaps." In *C&C,* pp. 289-324.

———. "Special Divine Action and the Laws of Nature." In *SPDA,* pp. 249-83.

Trible, P. *God and the Rhetoric of Sexuality.* Philadelphia: Augsburg, 1978.

Trinkaus, Charles. *In Our Image and Likeness: Humanity and Divinity in Italian Humanist Thought.* 2 vols. Ideas of Human Nature Series. Chicago: University of Chicago Press, 1970.

Troll, C. W., H. Reifeld, and C. T. R. Hewer, eds. *We Have Justice in Common: Christian and Muslim Voices from Asia and Africa.* Berlin: Konrad-Adenauer-Siftung, 2010.

Tucker, Mary Evelyn, and John Grim. Series foreword to *I&E,* pp. xv-xxxii.

Turner, Victor. *The Ritual Process: Structure and Anti-Structure.* Ithaca, N.Y.: Cornell University Press, 1969.

"Twelfth Ecumenical Council: Lateran IV 1215." In *Internet Medieval Sourcebook,* edited by Paul Halsall, O.B. http://www.fordham.edu/halsall/basis/lateran4.asp. From H. J. Schroeder, *Disciplinary Decrees of the General Councils: Text, Translation, and Commentary,* pp. 236-296. St. Louis: B. Herder, 1937.

United States Conference of Catholic Bishops. "Human Life and Dignity." http://www.usccb.org/issues-and-action/human-life-and-dignity/ (5/22/2013).

U.S. Department of Energy and the National Institutes of Health, Human Genome Project (ended in 2003). http://www.ornl.gov/sci/techresources/Human_Genome/home.shtml (5/22/2013).

Vainio, Olli-Pekka. *Beyond Fideism: Negotiable Religious Identities.* Surrey, U.K.: Ashgate, 2010.

Van den Brink, Gijsbert. *Almighty God: A Study of the Doctrine of Divine Omnipotence.* Kampen: Kok Pharos, 1993.

Van Huyssteen, Wentzel J. *Alone in the World? Human Uniqueness in Science and Theology.* Grand Rapids: Eerdmans, 2006.

―――. *Duet or Duel? Theology and Science in a Postmodern World.* Harrisburg, Pa.: Trinity, 1998.

Van Til, Kent A. *Less Than Two Dollars a Day: A Christian View of World Poverty and the Free Market.* Grand Rapids: Eerdmans, 2007.

Vatican, The. "Declaration on Human Development and Christian Salvation." In *Liberation Theology: A Documentary History,* edited by A. T. Hennelly, pp. 205-19. Maryknoll, N.Y.: Orbis, 1990.

Vawter, Bruce. *On Genesis: A New Reading.* Garden City, N.Y.: Doubleday, 1977.

Velmans, Max. "Making Sense of Causal Interactions between Consciousness and Brain." *Journal of Consciousness Studies* 9, no. 11 (2002): 69-95.

Verhoeven, Martin J. "Buddhism and Science: Probing the Boundaries of Faith and Reason." *Religion East and West* 1 (June 2001): 77-97. http://online.sfsu.edu/rone/Buddhism/VerhoevenBuddhismScience.htm.

Victoria, Brian Daizen. "Teaching Buddhism and Violence." In *TRC,* pp. 74-93.

―――. *Zen War Stories.* London: Routledge, 2003.

Visala, Aku. *Naturalism, Theism, and the Cognitive Study of Religion: Religion Explained?* Surrey, U.K.: Ashgate, 2011.

Vishnu Purana. Translated by Horace Hayman Wilson. 1840. www.ccel.org.

Vivekananda, Swami. *Complete Works of Swami Vivekananda.* http://www.ramakrishna vivekananda.info/vivekananda/complete_works.htm.

―――. "The East and the West: VII. Progress of Civilization." In *Complete Works of Swami Vivekananda,* vol. 5. http://www.ramakrishnavivekananda.info/vivekananda/complete_works.htm.

―――. "Is Vedanta the Future Religion?" In *Complete Works of Swami Vivekananda,* vol. 8. http://www.ramakrishnavivekananda.info/vivekananda/complete_works.htm.

―――. "On the Vedanta Philosophy." In *Complete Works of Swami Vivekananda,* vol. 5. http://www.ramakrishnavivekananda.info/vivekananda/complete_works.htm.

―――. "Questions and Answers: Discussion at the Graduate Philosophical Society of Harvard University." In *Complete Works of Swami Vivekananda,* vol. 5. http://www.ramakrishnavivekananda.info/vivekananda/complete_works.htm.

―――. "Steps of Hindu Philosophic Thought." In *Complete Works of Swami Vivekananda,* vol. 1. http://www.ramakrishnavivekananda.info/vivekananda/complete_works.htm.

―――. "Vedanta Philosophy." In *Complete Works of Swami Vivekananda,* vol. 1. http://www.ramakrishnavivekananda.info/vivekananda/complete_works.htm.

Volf, Miroslav. *Exclusion and Embrace: A Theological Exploration of Identity, Otherness, and Reconciliation.* Nashville: Abingdon, 1996.

―――. *Work in the Spirit: Toward a Theology of Work.* Eugene, Ore.: Wipf and Stock, 2001.

Vries, Hent de. *Religion and Violence: Philosophical Perspectives from Kant to Derrida.* Baltimore: Johns Hopkins University Press, 2002.

Wade, Richard. "Animal Theology and Ethical Concerns." *Australian eJournal of Theology* 2 (February 2004): 1-12.

Waldron, William S. "Common Ground, Common Cause: Buddhism and Science on the Afflictions of Identity." In *B&S*, pp. 145-91.

Wallace, B. Allan. "Buddhism and Science." In *OHRS*, pp. 24-40.

―――. "Introduction: Buddhism and Science ― Breaking Down the Barriers." In *B&S*, pp. 10-20.

Wallace, Mark I. "Christian Animism, Green Spirit Theology, and the Global Crisis Today." In *Interdisciplinary and Religio-Cultural Discourses on a Spirit-Filled World: Loosing the Spirits,* edited by Veli-Matti Kärkkäinen, Kirsteen Kim, and Amos Yong, pp. 197-212. New York: Palgrave Macmillan, 2013.

―――. "Crum Creek Spirituality: Earth as a Living Sacrament." In *Theology That Matters: Ecology, Economy, and God,* edited by Darby Kathleen Ray, pp. 121-37. Minneapolis: Fortress, 2006.

―――. *Finding God in the Singing River.* Minneapolis: Augsburg Fortress, 2005.

―――. *Fragments of the Spirit: Nature, Violence, and the Renewal of Creation.* New York: Continuum, 1996.

―――. *Green Christianity: Five Ways to a Sustainable Future.* Minneapolis: Fortress, 2010.

―――. "The Green Face of God: Recovering the Spirit in an Ecocidal Era." In *Advents of the Spirit: An Introduction to the Current Study of Pneumatology,* edited by Bradford E. Hinze and D. Lyle Dabney, pp. 444-64. Milwaukee: Marquette University Press, 2001.

Waller, Bruce N. *Critical Thinking: Consider the Verdict.* 3rd ed. Upper Saddle River, N.J.: Prentice-Hall, 1998.

Ward, Graham. *Cities of God.* London: Routledge, 2000.

―――. "In the Economy of the Divine: A Response to James K. A. Smith." *Pneuma* 25 (2003): 115-20.

―――. "Theological Materialism." In *God and Reality: Essays on Christian Non-realism,* edited by Colin Crowder, pp. 144-59. London: Mowbray, 1997.

Ward, Keith. *The Big Questions in Science and Religion.* Philadelphia: Templeton Press, 2008.

―――. *Defending the Soul.* Oxford: Oneworld, 1992. Original: *The Battle for the Soul.* Hodder and Stoughton, 1985. Reissued as *In Defence of the Soul.* Oneworld, 1998.

―――. "Divine Action in an Emergent Cosmos." In *SPDA*, pp. 285-98.

―――. *God, Chance, and Necessity.* Oxford: Oneworld, 1996.

―――. "God as a Principle of Cosmological Explanation." In *QCLN*, pp. 247-62.

―――. *Images of Eternity: Concepts of God in Five Religious Traditions.* London: Darton, Longman and Todd, 1987. Reissued as *Concepts of God: Images of the Divine in Five Religious Traditions.* Oxford: Oneworld, 1998.

―――. *More Than Matter: Is Matter All We Really Are?* Grand Rapids: Eerdmans, 2011.

―――. "Personhood, Spirit, and the Supernatural." In Peacocke, *ATI*, pp. 152-62.

―――. *Religion and Creation.* Oxford: Oxford University Press, 1996.

―――. *Religion and Human Nature.* Oxford: Clarendon, 1998.

―――. *Religion and Revelation: A Theology of Revelation in the World's Religions.* Oxford: Clarendon, 1994.

Warren, Charles E. *Original Sin Explained? Revelations from Human Genetic Science.* Lanham, Md.: University Press of America, 2002.

Waskow, Arthur. "Is the Earth a Jewish Issue?" *Tikkun* 7, no. 5 (1992): 35-37.

Waters, Malcolm. *Globalization.* London: Routledge, 1996.

Watson, Francis. *Text, Church, and World: Biblical Interpretation in Theological Perspective.* Edinburgh: T. & T. Clark, 1994.

Watts, Fraser. "Psychological and Religious Perspectives on Emotion." *Zygon: Journal of Religion and Science* 32, no. 2 (1997): 243-60.

Weber, Otto. *Foundations of Dogmatics.* Translated by D. L. Guder. 2 vols. Grand Rapids: Eerdmans, 1981.

Weiming, Tu. "The Ecological Turn in New Confucian Humanism: Implications for China and the World." *Dædalus: Journal of the American Academy of Arts and Sciences* 130, no. 4 (2001): 243-64.

Weiskrantz, Lawrence. *Blindsight: A Case Study and Implications.* Oxford: Oxford University Press, 1986.

Welker, Michael. *Creation and Reality.* Translated by John F. Hoffmeyer. Minneapolis: Fortress, 1999.

———. "Theological Anthropology versus Anthropological Reductionism." In *GHD*, pp. 317-30.

Wellman, Henry M., and Carl N. Johnson. "Developing Dualism: From Intuitive Understanding to Transcendental Ideas." In *Psycho-Physical Dualism Today: An Interdisciplinary Approach,* edited by Alessandro Antonietti, Antonella Corradini, and E. J. Lowe, pp. 3-36. New York: Lexington Books, 2008.

Wellman, James K., Jr. "Introduction: Religion and Violence; Past, Present, and Future." In *BB*, pp. 1-10.

Wenham, Gordon. *Genesis 1–15.* Edited by David Hubbard, Glenn W. Barker, and John D. Watts. Word Biblical Commentary 1. Waco, Tex.: Word, 1987.

West, Cornel. *Prophesy Deliverance! An African-American Revolutionary Christianity.* Philadelphia: Westminster, 1982.

Westermann, Claus. *Creation.* Translated by John J. Scullion. Philadelphia: Fortress, 1974.

———. *Genesis: An Introduction.* Translated by John J. Scullion. Minneapolis: Fortress, 1992.

———. *Genesis 1–11: A Commentary.* Translated by John J. Scullion. Minneapolis: Augsburg, 1984.

Westfall, Richard S. "The Scientific Revolution of the Seventeenth Century: The Construction of a New World View." In *The Concept of Nature,* edited by John Torrance, pp. 63-93. Oxford: Oxford University Press, 1992.

"What Is the Inflation Theory?" http://map.gsfc.nasa.gov/universe/WMAP_Universe.pdf (11/21/2013).

"When Plants Say 'Ouch.'" February 5, 2002. On Deutsche Welle Web site. Permalink: http://www.dw.de/when-plants-say-ouch/a-510552.

White [Shukla] Yajurveda. In *The Texts of the White Yajurveda.* Translated by Ralph T. H. Griffith [1899]. http://sacred-texts.com.

White, Andrew Dickson. *History of the Warfare of Science with Theology in Christendom.*

1896. 2002 Blackmask Online version. http://aren.org/prison/documents/religion/ Misc/History%20of%20the%20Warfare%20of%20Science%20with%20Theology %20in%20Christendom — Andrew%20Dickson%20White.pdf (11/21/2013).

White, Lynn, Jr. "The Historical Roots of Our Ecological Crisis." *Science* 155, no. 3767 (March 10, 1967): 1203-7. http://www.drexel.edu/~/media/Files/greatworks/pdf _fall09/HistoricalRoots_of_EcologicalCrisis.ashx.

Whitehead, Alfred North. *Process and Reality: An Essay in Cosmology.* Edited by David R. Griffin and Donald W. Sherburn. Corrected ed. New York: Free Press, 1978.

Wicken, Jeffrey S. *Evolution, Thermodynamics, and Information: Extending the Darwinian Program.* Oxford: Oxford University Press, 1987.

Wieman, Henry Nelson. *The Source of Human Good.* Chicago: University of Chicago Press, 1946.

Wiggins, David. "Reflections on Inquiry and Truth Arising from Peirce's Method for the Fixation of Belief." In *The Cambridge Companion to Peirce,* edited by Cheryl Misak. Cambridge: Cambridge University Press, 2004.

Wikler, Daniel. "Can We Learn from Eugenics?" *Journal of Medical Ethics* 25, no. 2 (April 1999): 183-94.

Wildman, Wesley J. "The Divine Action Project, 1988-2003." *Theology and Science* 2, no. 1 (April 2004): 31-75.

————. "Incongruous Goodness, Perilous Beauty, Disconcerting Truth: Ultimate Reality and Suffering in Nature." In *PC,* pp. 267-94.

————. *Science and Religious Anthropology: A Spiritually Evocative Naturalist Interpretation of Human Life.* Ashgate Science and Religion Series. Surrey, U.K.: Ashgate, 2009.

————. "The Use and Meaning of the Word 'Suffering' in Relation to Nature." In *PC,* pp. 53-66.

Wildman, Wesley J., and Robert John Russell. "Chaos: A Mathematic Introduction with Philosophical Reflections." In *C&C,* pp. 49-90.

Wiles, Maurice. "Religious Authority and Divine Action." In *God's Activity in the World: The Contemporary Problem,* edited by Owen C. Thomas, pp. 181-94. Chico, Calif.: Scholars Press, 1983.

Wiley, Tatha. *Original Sin: Origins, Developments, Contemporary Meanings.* New York: Paulist, 2002.

Wilken, Robert Louis. "Biblical Humanism: The Patristic Convictions." In *PITP,* pp. 13-28.

Willard, Huntington F. "Genome Biology: Tales of the Y Chromosome." *Nature* 423 (June 19, 2003): 810-13.

Williams, Delores S. "A Womanist Perspective on Sin." In *Troubling in My Soul: Womanist Perspectives on Evil and Suffering,* edited by Emilie M. Townes, pp. 130-49. Maryknoll, N.Y.: Orbis, 1993.

Williams, Patricia A. *Doing without Adam and Eve: Sociobiology and Original Sin.* Minneapolis: Fortress, 2001.

Williams, Paul. "Some Mahāyāna Buddhist Perspectives on the Body." In *RB,* pp. 205-30.

Williams, Rowan. "On Being Creatures." In *On Theology.* Oxford: Blackwell, 2000.

Williams, Thomas. "The Doctrine of Univocity Is True and Salutary." *Modem Theology* 21, no. 4 (2005): 575-85.

Willoughby, Pamela. *Evolution of Modern Humans in Africa: A Comprehensive Guide.* Lanham, Md.: Altamira Press, 2007.

Wilson, Boyd H. "Vinoba Bhave's Talks on the *Gita*." In *Modern Indian Interpreters of the Bhagavadgita,* edited by Robert N. Minor. Albany: State University of New York, 1986.

Wilson, Edward O. *On Human Nature.* Cambridge: Harvard University Press, 1978.

————. *The Social Conquest of Earth.* New York: Liveright Publishing, 2012.

————. *Sociobiology: The New Synthesis.* Cambridge: Harvard University Press, Belknap Press, 1975.

Winkler, Lewis. *Contemporary Muslim and Christian Responses to Religious Plurality: Wolfhart Pannenberg in Dialogue with Abdulaziz Sachedina.* Eugene, Ore.: Pickwick, 2011.

Witherington, Ben, III. *Conflict and Community in Corinth: A Socio-Rhetorical Commentary on 1 and 2 Corinthians.* Grand Rapids: Eerdmans, 1995.

Witsz, Klaus G. "Vedānta, Nature, and Science." *Religious Studies and Theology* 15, no. 2-3 (1996): 30-39.

Witte, John, Jr. "Between Sanctity and Depravity: Human Dignity in Protestant Perspective." In *In Defense of Human Dignity,* edited by Robert P. Kraynak and Glenn E. Tinder, pp. 119-38. Notre Dame, Ind.: University of Notre Dame Press, 2003.

Wittgenstein, Ludwig. *The Blue and Brown Books: Preliminary Studies for the "Philosophical Investigations."* Oxford: Blackwell, 1958.

————. *Culture and Value.* Edited by G. H. von Wright. Translated by Peter Winch. Oxford: Blackwell, 1980.

————. *Philosophical Grammar.* Edited by R. Rhees. Translated by A. Kenny. Berkeley and Los Angeles: University of California Press, 1974.

————. *Zettel.* Edited by G. E. M. Anscombe and G. H. von Wright. Translated by G. E. M. Anscombe. Berkeley and Los Angeles: University of California Press, 1967.

Wolff, Hans Walter. *Anthropology of the Old Testament.* Translated by Margaret Kohl. Philadelphia: Augsburg/Fortress, 1974.

Wolfson, Henry Austry. "Patristic Arguments against the Eternity of the World." *Harvard Theological Review* 59 (1966): 351-67.

————. *The Philosophy of the Kalam.* Cambridge: Harvard University Press, 1976.

Wolterstorff, Nicholas. *Justice: Rights and Wrongs.* Princeton: Princeton University Press, 2008.

Woodbridge, Frederick J. E. *An Essay on Nature.* New York: Columbia University Press, 1940.

Woodhead, Linda. "Apophatic Anthropology." In *GHD,* pp. 233-46.

Woodley, Randy S. *Shalom and the Community of Creation: An Indigenous Vision.* Grand Rapids: Eerdmans, 2012.

World Council of Churches. *Churches' Compassionate Response to HIV and AIDS.* September 6, 2006. http://www.oikoumene.org/en/resources/documents/wcc-commissions/international-affairs/human-rights-and-impunity/churches-compassionate-response-to-hiv-and-aids.

"World Report on Violence and Health." Edited by Etienne G. Krug, Linda L. Dahlberg, James A. Mercy, Anthony B. Zwi, and Rafael Lozano. WHO, 2002. http://whqlib doc.who.int/publications/2002/9241545615_eng.pdf (8/14/2013).

Worthing, Mark William. "Christian Theism and the Idea of an Oscillating Universe." In *GLC,* chap. 11 (pp. 281-301).

———. *God, Creation, and Contemporary Physics.* Theology and the Sciences. Minneapolis: Fortress, 1996.

Wright, George H. von. *Explanation and Understanding.* Ithaca, N.Y.: Cornell University Press, 1971.

Wright, N. T. "Mind, Spirit, Soul and Body: All for One and One for All; Reflections on Paul's Anthropology in His Complex Contexts." Paper presented at Society of Christian Philosophers Eastern Meeting, March 18, 2011. http://www.ntwrightpage .com/Wright_SCP_MindSpiritSoulBody.htm (11/26/2013).

Wuketits, Franz M. *Evolutionary Epistemology and Its Implications for Humankind.* Albany: SUNY Press, 1990.

Wykstra, Stephen. "The Humean Obstacle to Evidential Arguments from Suffering: On Avoiding the Evils of 'Appearance.'" In *PE,* pp. 138-60.

Wyschogrod, Michael. "The Sanctification of Nature in Judaism." In *Judaism and Environmental Ethics,* edited by Martin D. Yaffe, pp. 289-96. Lanham, Md.: Lexington Books, 2001.

Yamamoto, Dorothy. "Aquinas and Animals: Patrolling the Boundary?" In *AOA,* chap. 7.

Yong, Amos. *The Cosmic Breath: Spirit and Nature in the Christianity-Buddhism-Science Trialogue.* Leiden and Boston: Brill, 2012.

———. *Pneumatology and the Christian-Buddhist Dialogue: Does the Spirit Blow through the Middle Way?* Leiden: Brill Academic, 2012.

———. *Theology and Down Syndrome: Reimagining Disability in Late Modernity.* Waco, Tex.: Baylor University Press, 2007.

———, ed. *The Spirit Renews the Face of the Earth: Pentecostal Forays in Science and Theology of Creation.* Eugene, Ore.: Pickwick, 2009.

Young, G. "Preserving the Role of Conscious Decision Making in the *Initiation* of Intentional Action." *Journal of Consciousness Studies* 13, no. 3 (2006): 51-68.

Yu, Carter. *Being and Relation: A Theological Critique of Western Dualism and Individualism.* Edinburgh: Scottish Academic Press, 1987.

Zaehner, R. C. *Mysticism, Sacred and Profane.* Oxford: Clarendon, 1957.

Zagzebski, Linda. *The Dilemma of Freedom and Foreknowledge.* New York: Oxford University Press, 1991.

Zakai, Avihu. "The Rise of Modern Science and the Decline of Theology as the 'Queen of the Sciences' in the Early Modern Era." *Reformation and Renaissance Review* 9, no. 2 (2007): 125-51.

Ziadat, Adel A. *Western Science in the Arab World: The Impact of Darwinism, 1860-1930.* London: Macmillan; New York: St. Martin's Press, 1986.

Zimmerli, Walther. "Ort und Grenze der Weisheit im Rahmen der altestestamentlichen Theologie." In *Gottes Offenbarung: Gesammelte Aufsätze zum Alten Testament.* Munich: Kaiser, 1963.

Zimmermann, Jens. *Incarnational Humanism: A Philosophy of Culture for the Church in the World.* Downers Grove, Ill.: InterVarsity, 2012.

Zizioulas, John. "The Doctrine of the Holy Trinity: The Significance of the Cappadocian Contribution." In *The Trinity Today,* edited by Christoph Schwöbel. Edinburgh: T. & T. Clark, 1996.

———. "Human Capacity and Human Incapacity: A Theological Exploration of Personhood." *Scottish Journal of Theology* 28, no. 5 (October 1975): 401-47.

———. "Preserving God's Creation: Three Lectures on Theology and Ecology: Lecture One." *King's Theological Review* 12, no. 1 (1989): 1-5.

Index of Authors

Index of Subjects

Adam (and Eve), 55, 154, 233, 236, 303-4, 388-89, 391-93, 396, 400-405, 413-17, 457. *See also* Pre-Adamic species

Adaptation, 254, 262

Adharma, 421-22

Advaita, 95-96, 98, 306, 343, 369, 378-81, 421, 423-24. *See also* Dualism(s); Monism(s)

Aesthetic principle, 197

Ahimsa, 435, 450-51. *See also* Nonviolence; Violence

Altruism, 352

Anattā, 383-84, 418. *See also* Self

Annihilation, 211

Anthropic principle, 140-41, 143, 165. *See also* Biopic principle

Anthropocentrism, 82, 201, 208, 210, 214, 216, 241, 270

Anthropocosmic, 83

Apostles' Creed, 55

Aristotelianism, 68, 119, 121, 146, 182, 271, 311-13, 344, 362, 372, 376

Arminianism, 366

Astrology, 22

Atheism, 280, 288, 326

Atman, 94-95, 98, 378-80, 386, 422, 451

Atomism, 326, 331; social, 460

Atonement theories, 390

Attributes of God: omnipotence, 183, 368; omnipresence, 66, 134, 138, 184, 191, 368; omniscience, 184, 186, 350, 368. *See also* Foreknowledge, divine; Immanence, divine; Immutability, divine; Infinity, divine; Love, divine; Transcendence, divine

Autocatalysis, 147-48

Avataras, 379, 451. *See also* Krishna

Avidya, 89, 422-25, 434. *See also* *Dukkha*

Behaviorism, 321

Bell's theorem, 103

Bhagavad-Gita, 92-93, 379, 435, 450-51. *See also* Upanishads; Vedas

Biblical studies, 3

Bioethics, 438

Biogenetics, 438

Biological constancy principle, 158

Biopic principle, 141-42, 165. *See also* Anthropic principle

Black theology, 59, 443-45. *See also* Theology

Blindsight, 318

Body: in Buddhism, 294-95, 385; in Christianity, 300-301, 309, 312, 336-37, 346-47, 455; in Enlightenment, 299; in

gion and science; Theology; Theology and science

Scientism, 17, 32, 34

Scripture principle, 26

Secularism, 42, 49, 152, 220, 452, 454

Self, 271-74, 280-81, 285, 289, 292, 306, 337, 372, 383, 402. *See also Atman*

Self-networks, 358

Self-organization, 161, 184, 326

Sexism, 410, 431, 445

Sexuality, 298, 301, 396, 455

Shalom, 227, 399

Sharīʾa, 217, 304

Shintoism, 39

Sickness, 428, 438

Signification, 48, 85

Sin, 234, 388-407; in Abrahamic traditions, 412-17; in Buddhism, 418-21; in Hinduism, 421-25; original, 244, 387-99, 401; as personal and structural, 408-11; total depravity, 396. *See also* Misery

Slavery, 457, 463-64

Solidarity, 441

Soteriology, 59, 79, 228, 234, 276, 283, 373, 417, 419, 468

Soul: in Buddhism, 295, 384-86; in Christianity, 234, 272, 275, 293, 307-10, 312, 313-15, 334-36, 345-48, 390; in Greek philosophy, 310-11; in Hinduism, 379-81, 434; in Judaism, 372; immortality of, 284, 309-10, 312, 334, 346-49, 371, 375, 393; in Islam, 374-75; in modernity, 299, 313-14; preexistence of the, 371; science and, 321. *See also* Body

Space, ecological, 139

Space-time continuum, 108, 112, 124, 129, 131-33, 136-39, 173, 205, 257-58. *See also* Time

Special relativity theory, 108, 131

Spirit: of God, 61-69, 75, 80-81, 105, 185, 192, 224-26, 277, 280, 303, 314-15, 341-42, 367, 370, 458, 467; of humans, 65-66, 225, 346-47, 373

Steady state theory, 109, 119, 122, 124

Stoicism, 64, 221, 310, 361

String theories, 129, 344

Suffering and pain, 194-98, 200-201, 205, 207, 428, 434. *See also* Sickness

Sunna, 21

Sunyata, 54, 90-91

Superimposition, 423, 425

Supernaturalism, 187, 267, 393

Superposition principle, 339

Supervenience, 322-24, 327, 329-30, 351

Supranaturalism, 187

Symbols, 13

Tawhid, 86, 218, 303-4

Teleology, 160-61, 165, 197-98, 312, 344

Terrorism, 449-50

Thanatology, 335

Theistic evolution, 149, 151-52, 160. *See also* Evolutionary theory

Theobiology, 320

Theodicy, 14-15, 195-96; Augustinian, 197-98; consequentialist natural, 204-5; cosmic, 202, 205; evolutionary, 197-98; Irenaean, 197-98; natural, 199, 202, 229

Theological anthropology: in Buddhism, 381-85; in Christianity, 148, 195, 233-35, 239, 242-43, 270-71, 278, 290, 302, 308, 314, 335, 381, 393, 461, 465; in Hinduism, 379; in Islam, 374-75; in Judaism, 373; Trinitarian, 240-41, 274, 279, 282-83, 289, 301, 367

Theological correctness, 266

Théologie, nouvelle, 50

Theology: animal, 228-29; communion, 279, 291, 301, 337, 460; comparative, 6, 99-100, 466; confessional, 6; constructive, 1-3, 11-12, 64, 118, 134, 189, 219, 223, 244-45, 270, 273, 284, 286-87, 290-91, 296, 315-16, 344, 388, 400, 410, 429, 431, 440, 447, 465; contextual, 10; creation, 10-11; ecumenical, 11; historical, 3; method in, 1-3, 12; modern, 9, 285-86, 387, 397; neurotheology, 319-20; patristic, 57-58, 75, 147, 241, 276-77, 389-90, 435; Pauline, 333, 335, 389, 403-